D1504989

SHAKESPEARE
for Students

SHAKESPEARE
for Students

**Critical Interpretations of Shakespeare's
Plays and Poetry**

SECOND EDITION: VOLUME 1

Anne Marie Hacht, Editor

Foreword by Cynthia Burnstein

THOMSON

GALE

Detroit • New York • San Francisco • New Haven, Conn. • Waterville, Maine • London

822.33
SHA
v.1

Pacific Grove Public Library

Shakespeare for Students, Second Edition

Project Editor
Anne Marie Hacht

Rights Acquisition and Management
Lisa Kincade, Robbie McCord, Lista Person, Kelly Quin, and Andrew Specht

Manufacturing
Rita Wimberley

Imaging
Lezlie Light

Product Design
Pamela A. E. Galbreath and Jennifer Wahi

Vendor Administration
Civie Green

Product Manager
Meggin Condino

LIBRARY OF CONGRESS CATALOGING-IN-PUBLICATION DATA

Shakespeare for students : critical interpretations of Shakespeare's plays and poetry.–2nd ed. / Anne Marie Hacht, editor ; foreword by Cynthia Burnstein.
    p. cm.
    Includes bibliographical references and index.
    ISBN-13: 978-1-4144-1255-9 (set)
    ISBN-10: 1-4144-1255-X (set)
    ISBN-13: 978-1-4144-1256-6 (v. 1)
    ISBN-10: 1-4144-1256-8 (v. 1)
    [etc.]
    1. Shakespeare, William, 1564-1616–Outlines, syllabi, etc. 2. Shakespeare, William, 1564-1616–Criticism and interpretation. 3. Shakespeare, William, 1564-1616–Examinations–Study guides. I. Hacht, Anne Marie.
    PR2987.S47 2007
    822.3'3–dc22
                                           2007008901

ISBN-13	ISBN-10
978-1-4144-1255-9 (set)	1-1444-1255-X (set)
978-1-4144-1256-6 (vol. 1)	1-4144-1256-8 (vol. 1)
978-1-4144-1258-0 (vol. 2)	1-4144-1258-4 (vol. 2)
978-1-4144-1259-7 (vol. 3)	1-4144-1259-2 (vol. 3)

This title is also available as an e-book.
ISBN-13 978-1-4144-2937-3 (set) ISBN-10 1-4144-2937-1 (set)
Contact your Thomson Gale sales representative for ordering information.
Printed in the United States of America

10 9 8 7 6 5 4 3 2 1

Table of Contents

Foreword

This may be a scene from your experience: You have been assigned to read a play by William Shakespeare in your literature class. The students look a little skeptical as the books are distributed. That evening at home you do your best to understand as you read the play alone, fiercely studying the footnotes and employing a dictionary, but you still have serious doubts that you are correctly grasping the plot. Although the next day's class discussion helps enormously, you are now positive that you will never get all the characters' names straight. Then one day in class a couple of students disagree about the motivation of the main character and press each other to back up their interpretations with evidence from the text. The rest of the class sits forward in their seats. The debate is intense. For some reason, your teacher is smiling. Hours later you find yourself thinking about the play. Finally, you watch a film version of the play, or, if you are really lucky, you see it performed live. Now everyone in the class has a question as well as an opinion, and the discussions that ensue take a tone of authority that is new and exhilarating.

Someone has said that books are like having the smartest, wittiest, most profound and poetic friends in the world, friends who are there to speak to you anytime you wish. Literary criticism, which is what the book you are holding in your hands is primarily concerned with, is valuable for just the same reason. It is a way of having a thought-provoking conversation about a piece of literature with an intelligent friend. As sometimes happens between friends, you may not always agree with or fully grasp his or her point. Other times, a particular interpretation may seem so preposterous that you stomp off, sputtering. But then there are times you listen and say, "I never thought of it *that* way" or better yet, "Wow!"

The purpose of this book, then, is to enable you to continue those discussions. The heart of *Shakespeare for Students* is a collection of essays by Shakespeare scholars that have been carefully selected to be of interest to students at the high school or undergraduate college level. Some essays appear as excerpts for your convenience. If you are still hungry for more discussion after reading each essay, you will find the Further Reading section to be very helpful.

Shakespeare for Students contains a number of other features that will help you as you study Shakespeare's plays and poetry. For each entry there is: an introduction, which provides basic background information about the play or poem; a plot synopsis, which summarizes the action by act or by lines; a character list, which briefly describes the role and personality of each character in the play or poem; a discussion of the work's principal themes, which are the most commonly discussed issues the play or poem explores; information about the style and literary devices used within the play or poem; a conversation about the work's historical context, which is what affects the meaning of the poem or play when one regards the time in which it was written or the time in which it is set; and a critical overview, which is a summary of what some of the critics have had to say about the work through the years.

Here is a scene I am imagining about your future: Scholars from the past and students from the present are speaking to each other intensely. They are discussing the plays and poetry of William Shakespeare. Ideas are everywhere—in the air, careening off of walls, bouncing through space. As I look around the room at the faces that glow with energy, I see one that looks very familiar. It is yours.

Cynthia Burnstein
Burnstein is affiliated with Plymouth-Salem High School in Canton, Michigan.

Introduction

Purpose of the Book

This second edition of *Shakespeare for Students* (SFS) is intended to present the beginning student of William Shakespeare and other interested readers with information on the writer's most popular and frequently taught plays, his sonnets, and his epic (long) poems. A further purpose of SFS is to acquaint the reader with the use and function of literary criticism itself. Selected from the immense and often bewildering body of Shakespearean commentary, the essays and excerpts in this edition offer insights into Shakespeare's plays from a diverse range of commentators representing many different critical viewpoints. Readers do not need a wide background in literary studies to use this book. Students can benefit from using SFS as a basis for class discussion and written assignments, new perspectives on the plays and poems, and noteworthy analyses of Shakespeare's artistry.

Each work is treated with a separate entry. The information covered in each entry includes an introduction to the work; a plot summary, to help readers understand the action and story of the work; a list of characters, including explanation of a given character's role in the work as well as discussion about that character's relationship to other characters in the work; an analysis of important themes addressed in the work; an examination of style elements used by the author; and a section on important historical and cultural events that shaped both the author and the work.

In addition to this material, which helps the reader analyze the work itself, students are also provided with a critical overview that provides information about how the work has been received through the centuries. Accompanying the critical overview are excerpts from previously published critical essays and, in some cases, original critical essays written explicitly for this edition. For further analysis and enjoyment, a list of media adaptations is also included, as well as reading suggestions for works of fiction and nonfiction on similar themes and topics. Classroom aids include topics for discussion, which include ideas for research papers, and lists of critical sources that provide additional material on the work.

Selection Criteria

The titles for *Shakespeare for Students*, Second edition, were selected by surveying numerous sources on teaching Shakespeare and analyzing course curricula for various school districts. Input was also solicited from our advisory board as well as from educators.

How Each Entry Is Organized

Each entry heading includes the title of the work being discussed and the year it was first published or performed. The following sections are included in the discussion of each entry:

Introduction: a brief overview of the work that provides information about its publication, its literary standing, any controversies surrounding the work, and major conflicts or themes within the work.

Plot Summary: a review of the action and story-line divided by act (for the plays), by lines (for the long poems), or by groups of poems (in the sonnets).

Characters: an alphabetical listing that describes the role and personality of each character in the play or poem, as well as that character's importance to the overall plot and theme of the work.

Themes: a detailed discussion of the work's principal themes, which are the most commonly discussed issues the play or poem explores.

Style: an in-depth review of the stylistic and literary devices in each play or poem with comments as to how these devices affect the work's overall meaning.

Historical Context: this section provides information about the historical events and cultural movements that influence the meaning of the poem or play.

Critical Overview: an essay that provides a summary of what some of the critics have had to say about the work through the years.

Criticism: a collection of essays by Shakespeare scholars that have been carefully selected to be of interest to students at the high school or undergraduate college level.

Sources: a list of the sources used to research and compile the entry in question.

Further Reading: an annotated list of sources at the end of each entry is provided for additional study.

Other Features

Throughout the book, various illustrations—including artist's renditions of certain scenes and performance photographs—add a visual dimension, enhancing the reader's understanding of the critical discussion of each play.

An alphabetical index to major themes and characters identifies the principal topics and characters from each play or poem. A glossary defines the literary devices that are vital to the discussion of Shakespeare's work.

Chronology of Shakespeare's Life and Works

1564: William Shakespeare is born in Stratford-upon-Avon. His notice of baptism is entered in the parish register at Holy Trinity Church on April 26. While the actual date of his birth is not known, it is traditionally celebrated on April 23.

1571: Shakespeare probably enters grammar school, seven years being the usual age for admission.

1575: Queen Elizabeth visits Kenilworth Castle, near Stratford. Popular legend holds that the eleven-year-old William Shakespeare witnessed the pageantry attendant on the royal progress and later recreated it in his dramatic works.

1582: Shakespeare marries Anne Hathaway of Shottery. The eighteen-year-old Shakespeare and twenty-six-year-old Hathaway are married on November 27 at Temple Grafton, a village about five miles from Stratford.

1583: Susanna, the first child of William and Anne Shakespeare, is born. Susanna's birth occurs five months after Shakespeare and Hathaway wed. Susanna dies in 1649.

1585(?): Shakespeare leaves Stratford sometime between 1585 and 1592 and joins a company of actors as a performer and playwright.

1585: Twins Hamnet and Judith Shakespeare are born. Hamnet dies in 1596. Judith dies in 1662.

1589-90: Shakespeare probably writes *Henry VI, Part One*. The dates given for the composition of Shakespeare's plays, though based in scholarship, are somewhat conjectural.

1589-94: Shakespeare probably writes *The Comedy of Errors*.

1590-91: Shakespeare probably writes *Henry VI, Part Two* and *Henry VI, Part Three*. The latter is not published until 1595.

1590-94: Shakespeare probably writes *The Taming of the Shrew*.

1592: Shakespeare was known in London as an actor and a playwright by this time, as evidenced by his being mentioned in Robert Greene's pamphlet *A Groats-worth of Wit*. In this pamphlet (published this year), Greene chides Shakespeare as an "upstart crow" on the theater scene. Greene charges that Shakespeare is an unschooled player and writer who "borrows" material from his well-educated betters for his own productions.

1592: London theaters are closed due to plague.

1592-93: Shakespeare probably writes *Venus and Adonis*, *Richard III*, and *The Two Gentlemen of Verona*.

1592-93: Shakespeare probably begins composing his sonnets. He will eventually write 154 sonnets.

1593: Shakespeare's narrative poem *Venus and Adonis* is published.

1593-94: Shakespeare probably writes *Lucrece* and *Titus Andronicus*.

1594: Shakespeare's narrative poem *Lucrece* is published.

1594: Shakespeare performs with the theater troupe the Lord Chamberlain's Men. The group includes leading actor Richard Burbage and noted comic performer Will Kempe.

1594-5: Shakespeare probably writes *Love's Labour's Lost*.

1594-96: Shakespeare probably writes *King John*.

1595: Shakespeare probably writes *Richard II*. The play is first performed the same year.

1595: Shakespeare probably writes *A Midsummer Night's Dream*. The play is probably composed for performance at a wedding.

1595: Shakespeare probably writes *Romeo and Juliet*.

1596: Henry Carey, Lord Hunsdon and patron of the Lord Chamberlain's Men, dies.

1596: Shakespeare's company comes under the patronage of George Carey, second Lord Hunsdon.

1596-7: Shakespeare probably writes *The Merchant of Venice* and *Henry IV, Part One*.

1597: Shakespeare probably writes *The Merry Wives of Windsor*. The play was performed before the Queen during the Christmas revels.

1597: Shakespeare purchases New Place and the grounds surrounding the spacious Stratford home.

1598: Shakespeare appears in a performance of Ben Johnson's *Every Man in His Humour* and is listed as a principal actor in the London performance.

1598: Shakespeare probably writes *Henry IV; Part Two*.

1598-99: Shakespeare probably writes *Much Ado about Nothing*.

1599: Shakespeare probably writes *Julius Caesar*, *Henry V* and *As You Like It*.

1599: The Lord Chamberlain's Men lease land for the Globe Theatre. Nicholas Brend leases the land to leading shareholders in the Lord Chamberlain's Men, including

Shakespeare. Later this year, the Globe Theatre opens.

1599: Earliest known performance of *Julius Caesar*. Thomas Platter, a German traveler, mentions the production at the Globe Theatre on September 21 in his diary.

1599: John Weever publishes the poem "Ad Guglielmum Shakespeare," in which he praises Shakespeare's *Venus and Adonis*, *Lucrece*, *Romeo and Juliet*, and other works.

1599-1602: Shakespeare probably writes *Hamlet*.

1601: Shakespeare probably writes the narrative poem *The Phoenix and Turtle* and *Twelfth Night*.

1601-02: Shakespeare probably writes *Troilus and Cressida*.

1603: Shakespeare probably writes *All's Well That Ends Well*.

1603: *A Midsummer Night's Dream* is performed before the Queen at Hampton Court.

1603: Queen Elizabeth dies. The new king, James I (James VI of Scotland), arrives in London a month later and proves to be a generous patron of the theater and of acting troupes.

1603: King James grants a patent, or license, to Shakespeare's acting troupe, the Lord Chamberlain's Men. The patent is required for the troupe to perform. They take the name the King's Men to honor the new king.

1603: The King's Men enact a play, probably *As You Like It*, before King James at Wilton.

1603: Shakespeare appears in a performance of Ben Johnson's *Sejanus*. This is the last recorded occasion of Shakespeare appearing in a theatrical production.

1603: An epidemic of the Black Death kills at least 33,000 in London. This is the worst outbreak of disease in London until the plague recurs in 1608.

1604: Shakespeare probably writes *Measure for Measure*. The play is staged at court before King James.

1604: Shakespeare probably writes *Othello*. The play is first performed at Whitehall on November 1.

1605: Shakespeare probably writes *King Lear*. It is first performed in 1606.

1605: *The Merchant of Venice* is performed at court. The play is performed twice and is commended by the king.

1606: Shakespeare probably writes *Macbeth.* This play's Scottish background was almost certainly intended to celebrate the new king's ancestry.

1607: Shakespeare probably writes *Antony and Cleopatra.*

1607: *Hamlet* and *Richard III* are performed. The plays are acted aboard the English ship *Dragon* at Sierra Leone.

1607-08: Shakespeare probably writes *Coriolanus, Timon of Athens,* and *Pericles.*

1608: The King's Men lease the Blackfriars Theatre. The Blackfriars was the first permanent enclosed theater in London. Shakespeare, Richard Burbage, Cuthbert Burbage, Thomas Evans, John Hemminges, Henry Condell, and William Sly lease the theatre for a period of twenty-one years. Stage directions indicate that Shakespeare wrote *The Tempest* with specific features of the new playhouse in mind.

1608: London theaters are closed due to plague. This is one of the longest periods of theater closure due to plague. The playhouses are shut from spring 1608 throughout 1609.

1609: Shakespeare's sonnets are published. This publication of Shakespeare's sonnets is unauthorized.

1609-10: Shakespeare probably writes *Cymbeline.*

1610: The King's Men perform *Othello* at Oxford College during the summer touring season. An Oxford don records his impressions of the play in Latin, finding the spectacle of Desdemona's death, in particular, deeply moving.

1610-11: Shakespeare probably writes *The Winter's Tale.*

1611: Shakespeare probably writes *The Tempest.* The play is first performed the same year.

1612-13: Frederick V, the elector platine and future king of Bohemia, arrives in England to marry Elizabeth, King James's daughter. The King's Men perform several plays, including *Othello* and *Julius Caesar.*

1612-13: Shakespeare probably writes *Henry VIII,* most likely collaborating with John Fletcher, another highly reputed dramatist, on this history play.

1612-13: Shakespeare probably writes *Cardenio,* the only play of Shakespeare's that has been completely lost.

1613: Shakespeare probably writes *The Two Noble Kinsmen.* An entry in the Stationer's Register for 1634 indicates that this play was jointly written by Shakespeare and John Fletcher.

1613: The Globe Theatre burns down.

1614: The Globe Theatre reopens on the opposite bank of the Thames.

1616: Shakespeare dies on April 23. His burial is recorded in the register of Stratford's Holy Trinity Church on April 25.

1619: *Hamlet* and several other of Shakespeare's plays are performed at court as part of the Christmas festivities.

1623: Anne Hathaway Shakespeare dies.

1623: Shakespeare's fellow actors, John Hemminges and Henry Condell, compile and publish thirty-six of the dramatist's works. This collection is known as the First Folio.

Acknowledgments

The editors wish to thank the copyright holders of the excerpted criticism included in this volume and the permissions managers of many book and magazine publishing companies for assisting us in securing reproduction rights. We are also grateful to the staffs of the Detroit Public Library, the Library of Congress, the University of Detroit Mercy Library, Wayne State University Purdy/ Kresge Library Complex, and the University of Michigan Libraries for making their resources available to us. Following is a list of the copyright holders who have granted us permission to reproduce material in this volume of SFS. Every effort has been made to trace copyright, but if omissions have been made, please let us know.

COPYRIGHTED EXCERPTS IN *SFS*, *SECOND EDITION*, WERE REPRODUCED FROM THE FOLLOWING PERIODICALS:

American Imago, v. 25, 1968. Copyright © 1968 The Johns Hopkins University Press. Reproduced by permission.—*CLA Journal*, v. xxvi, March, 1983. Copyright © 1983 by The College Language Association. Used by permission of The College Language Association.—*Critical Quarterly*, v. 16, spring, 1974. Copyright © 1974 Basil Blackwell Ltd. Reproduced by permission of Blackwell Publishers.—*Critical Survey*, v. 17, 2005. Republished with permission of Berghahn Books Inc., conveyed through Copyright Clearance Center, Inc.—*Educational Theatre Journal*, v. xix, October, 1967. Copyright © 1967 University and College Theatre Association of the American Theatre Association. Reproduced by permission of The Johns Hopkins University Press.—*The English Review*, v. 12, November, 2001; v. 13, November, 2002; v. 15, September, 2004; v. 15, November, 2004. Copyright © 2001, 2002, 2004 Philip Allan Updates. All reproduced by permission.—*English Studies*, v. 43, October, 1962; v. 45, April, 1964; v. 61, February, 1980; v. 78, July, 1997. Copyright © 1962, 1964, 1980, 1997 by Swets *Essays in Criticism*, v. ii, January, 1952. Reproduced by permission of Oxford University Press, conveyed through Copyright Clearance Center.—*Essays in Literature*, v. xiii, fall, 1986. Copyright © 1986 by Western Illinois University. Reproduced by permission.—*Etudes Anglaises*, v. xvii, October—December, 1964. Reproduced by permission.—*The Explicator*, v. 51, spring, 1993; v. 56, fall, 1997; v. 57, fall, 1998; v. 64, spring, 2006. Copyright © 1993, 1997, 1998, 2006 by Helen Dwight Reid Educational Foundation. All reproduced with permission of the Helen Dwight Reid Educational Foundation, published by Heldref Publications, 1319 18th Street, NW, Washington, DC 20036–1802.—*Journal of Evolutionary Psychology*, v. 27, October, 2005. Copyright © 2005 Institute for Evolutionary Psychology. Reproduced by permission.—*The Listener*, v. 100, December 21-28, 1978 for "As You Like Shakespeare," by Brigid Brophy. Reproduced by permission of the author.—*Modern Language*

Quarterly, v. 35, December, 1974. Copyright © 1974 Duke University Press. All rights reserved. Used by permission of the publisher.—*New Literary History*, v. 9, spring, 1978. Copyright © 1978 The Johns Hopkins University Press. Reproduced by permission.—*Notes and Queries*, v. 44, March, 1997. Copyright © 1997 Oxford University Press. Republished with permission of Oxford University Press, conveyed through Copyright Clearance Center, Inc.—*Philological Quarterly*, v. 65, spring, 1986. Copyright © 1986 University of Iowa. Reproduced by permission.—*Renaissance Papers*, April, 1963. Reproduced by permission.—*Representations*, summer, 1995 for "'The Merry Wives of Windsor': Sharing the Queen's Holiday" by Leslie S. Katz. Copyright © 1995 by The Regents of the University of California. Reproduced by permission of the publisher and the author.—*Shakespeare Jahrbuch*, v. 114, 1978. Reproduced by permission.—*Shakespeare Quarterly*, v. 13, summer, 1962; v. 15, autumn, 1964; v. 38, autumn, 1987. Copyright © 1962, 1964, 1987 The Johns Hopkins University Press. All reproduced by permission.—*Shakespeare Studies*, v. 11, 1978; v. 14, 1981. Copyright © 1978, 1981 by Rosemont Publishing *Shakespeare Survey: An Annual Survey of Shakesperian Study and Production*, v. 13, 1960; v. 19, 1966; v. 32, 1979; v. 35, 1982. Copyright © 1960, 1966, 1979, 1982 Cambridge University Press. All reprinted with the permission of Cambridge University Press.—*Studies in English Literature*, 1500-1900, v. 42, winter, 2002. Copyright © 2002 The Johns Hopkins University Press. Reproduced by permission.—*Texas Studies in Literature and Language*, v. 18, winter, 1977; v. 42, spring, 2000. Copyright © 1977, 2000 by the University of Texas Press. All rights reserved. Both reproduced by permission.—*The Use of English*, v. xvii, spring, 1966. Copyright © 1966 The English Association. Reproduced by permission.

COPYRIGHTED EXCERPTS IN *SFS, SECOND EDITION*, WERE REPRODUCED FROM THE FOLLOWING BOOKS:

Anderson, Linda. From *A Kind of Wild Justice: Revenge in Shakespeare's Comedies*. University of Delaware Press, 1987. Copyright © 1987 by Associated University Presses, Inc. All rights reserved. Reproduced by permission.—Auden, W. H. From *The Dyer's Hand and Other Essays*. Random House, Inc., 1962. Copyright © 1948, 1950, 1952, 1953, 1954, 1956, 1957, 1958, 1960, 1962 by W. H. Auden, renewed 1990 by Edward Mendelsohn (Executor of W.H. Auden). All rights reserved. Used by permission of Random House, Inc. In the U.K. by Faber Bernthal, Craig. From *The Trial of Man: Christianity and Judgment in the World of Shakespeare*. ISI Books, 2003. Copyright © 2003 ISI Books. All rights reserved. Reproduced by permission.—Bloom, Allan. From *Shakespeare on Love and Friendship*. The University of Chicago Press, 2000. Copyright © 1993, 2000 by the Estate of Allan Bloom. All rights reserved. Reproduced by permission.—Calderwood, James L. From *Shakespeare and the Denial of Death*. University of Massachusetts Press, 1987. Copyright © 1987 by The University of Massachusetts Press. All rights reserved. Reproduced by permission.—Charney, Maurice. From *All of Shakespeare*. Columbia University Press, 1993. Copyright © 1993 Columbia University Press, New York. All rights reserved. Republished with permission of the Columbia University Press, 61 W. 62nd St., New York, NY 10023.—Clemen, Wolfgang. From *The Development of Shakespeare's Imagery*. Methuan and Co., 1977. Copyright © 1951, 1977 Wolfgang Clemen. Reproduced by permission of the publisher.—Cohen, Walter. From "'Antony and Cleopatra,'" in *The Norton Shakespeare*. Edited by Stephen Greenblatt. W.W. Norton and Co., 1997. Copyright © 1977 by W. W. Norton Cowhig, Ruth. From *The Black Presence in English Literature*. Manchester University Press, 1985. Reproduced by permission of the author.—Cox, John D., and Eric Rasmussen. From an *Introduction to King Henry VI, Part 3*. Edited by John D. Cox and Eric Rasmussen. Arden Shakespeare, 2001. Editorial material © 2001 John D. Cox and Eric Rasmussen. All rights reserved. Reproduced by permission.—Dash, Irene G. From *Wooing, Wedding, and Power: Women in Shakespeare's Plays*. Columbia University Press, 1981. Copyright © 1981 Columbia University Press, New York. All rights reserved. Republished with permission of the Columbia University Press, 61 W. 62nd St., New York, NY 10023.—Free, Mary. From "'All's Well that Ends Well' as Noncomic Comedy," in *Acting Funny: Comic Theory and Practice in Shakespeare's Plays*. Edited by Frances Teague. Fairleigh Dickinson University Press, 1994. Copyright © 1994 by Associated University Presses, Inc. All rights reserved. Reproduced by permission.—Frye, Northrop.

New York, NY 10023.—Thompson, Ann. From *The Taming of the Shrew*. Cambridge University Press, 1984. Copyright © 1984 Cambridge University Press. Reprinted with the permission of Cambridge University Press.—Traversi, D. A. From *An Approach to Shakespeare*. Doubleday and Company, Inc., 1969. Copyright © 1969 by Doubleday, a division of Random House, Inc. Used by permission of the publisher.—Yates, Frances A. From *The Occult Philosophy in the Elizabethan Age*. Ark Paperbacks, 1983. Reproduced by permission.

Contributors

Bryan Aubrey: Aubrey holds a Ph.D. in English and has published many essays on drama. Entry on *Antony and Cleopatra*. Original essay on *Antony and Cleopatra*.

Jennifer Bussey Bussey holds a master's degree in Interdisciplinary Studies and a bachelor's degree in English Literature. She is an independent writer specializing in literature. Entries on *Macbeth*, *The Taming of the Shrew*, and *Twelfth Night*.

Joyce Hart: Hart is a freelance writer and published author. Entries on *Henry V*, *Henry VI, Part Three*, *Julius Caesar*, *The Merchant of Venice*, *The Merry Wives of Windsor*, *Much Ado about Nothing*, *Othello*, and *Romeo and Juliet*. Original essays on *Henry VI, Part Three* and *The Merry Wives of Windsor*.

Neil Heims: Heims is a writer and teacher living in Paris. Entries on *Coriolanus*, *Hamlet*, *King Lear*, *Measure for Measure*, *The Tempest*, and *The Winter's Tale*. Original essays on *Coriolanus*, *King Lear*, *Measure for Measure*, and *The Tempest*.

Michael Allen Holmes: Holmes is a freelance editor and writer. Entries on *As You Like It*, *The Comedy of Errors*, *Henry IV, Part One*, *Lucrece*, *Richard II*, *Richard III*, *The Sonnets*, and *Venus and Adonis*.

David Kelly: Kelly is an instructor of creative writing and literature at two colleges. Entry on *A Midsummer Night's Dream*. Original essay on *A Midsummer Night's Dream*.

Kathy Wilson Peacock: Wilson Peacock is an author, editor, and contributor to many reference publications specializing in literature. Entry on *All's Well That Ends Well*.

All's Well That Ends Well

1603

All's Well That Ends Well was probably written sometime between 1600 and 1605, and many experts date the work to 1603. Others believe that the play is the lost Shakespearean drama titled *Love's Labour Won*, which was written before 1598. The first written mention of the play under its current title appeared in 1623, when it was licensed to be printed in Shakespeare's Folio. Attempts to date the play have involved a bit of detective work regarding some of its language, particularly Helen's letter to the countess in act 3, which exemplifies Shakespeare's less-sophisticated early style. Conversely, some critics note similarities between the tone and style of the play with that of *Measure for Measure*, which was written in 1604. Some commentators have theorized that the uneven nature of the play suggests that it was written at two different times in Shakespeare's life. This sketchy history indicates that the play did not attract much attention when it was first written and performed, a testament to its status as a lesser work in Shakespeare's canon.

All's Well That Ends Well has often been called one of Shakespeare's problem plays or dark comedies, a category that usually includes *Measure for Measure* and *Troilus and Cressida*. The problem refers to the cynical nature of the plot's resolution, in which Bertram, a rather unbecoming hero who is sought after by a woman who is too good for him, has a last-minute change of heart and vows to love Helena, his wife, forever. This declaration comes on the heels of a

rather devious scheme and is not prompted by a personal revelation deep enough to be convincing to the audience. The problem plays are more similar in tone and theme to Shakespeare's tragedies than they are to his romantic comedies.

Shakespeare's primary inspiration for the plot of *All's Well That Ends Well* was William Painter's collection of stories *The Palace of Pleasures* (1575), which itself was an English translation of "Giletta of Narbonne," a story in Giovanni Boccaccio's collection of folk tales called the *Decameron* (1353). Shakespeare fleshed out the story by adding the characters of Parolles, the Countess of Rossillion, Lavache, and Lafew. The events of the play, in which a low-born woman schemes to marry a count and wins both his ring and his child by switching places with another woman during an illicit rendezvous (a tactic known as the bed-trick), has its roots in folk tales. This may account, some believe, for the play's unbelievable nature and thus its failure as a comedy. Others believe that audiences of the day would have been familiar with such folk tales, as well as with Painter's *The Palace of Pleasures* and Boccaccio's *Decameron*, and thus would have received the play more warmly. That said, nearly all critics have at least some reservations about it.

Early critics of the play focused their attention on the incongruous plot elements and the themes of merit and rank, virtue and honor, and male versus female. More recent critics also address these issues, but they focus more attention on topics such as gender and desire. Helena's bold sexuality and her reversal of gender roles, in which she is the pursuer rather than the pursued, has generated much discussion, especially for how they intertwine with other main conflicts in the play, such as social class, the bed-trick, and marriage. Whether the play does end well, as the title suggests, has also historically been much debated.

The three main characters—Helena, Bertram, and Parolles—have generated a great deal of literary criticism over the years. Some critics brand Helena as conniving and obsessive in her love for Bertram, while others find her virtuous and noble. In general, critics are not fond of the character of Bertram, though some judge him more harshly than others. Some critics find him thoroughly unrepentant and unredeemable at the end of the play, making the ending implausible. Others are more sympathetic toward him, finding him merely immature at the beginning of the play and in need

of life experience, which he obtains while fighting in Florence. Parolles has generated less controversy in terms of the nature of his character (even Parolles himself recognizes his deficiencies and is not ashamed of them), and some critics find the subplot involving Parolles the only thing that saves the play from failure.

There is no record of *All's Well That Ends Well* having been performed in Shakespeare's time (although it probably was), and it remained unpopular for several hundred years. In England, it was performed only a few dozen times in the eighteenth century and only seventeen times in the nineteenth century. The Victorians abhorred the sexual nature of the play. Writing in 1852, critic John Bull (quoted in the New Cambridge edition of the play edited by Russell Fraser) found that such wantonness cannot "be made presentable to an audience of which decent females form a portion." In the United States, the play was not staged until well into the twentieth century. In most cases, when it was performed, many changes were made to the text to make it more contemporary, often highlighting Parolles's part and turning the play into a farce.

PLOT SUMMARY

Act 1, Scene 1

All's Well That Ends Well opens at the palace in Rossillion, a region in France that borders Spain and the Mediterranean Sea. Here, the Countess of Rossillion mourns her recently deceased husband and the imminent departure of her son, Bertram, the Count of Rossillion, who has been summoned to Paris by the king. The countess and her friend, the elderly Lord Lafew, discuss the king's poor health and lament that Gerard de Narbon, a famous court doctor who has just died, is not around to heal him. The doctor's daughter, the beautiful and vivacious Helena, has become the countess's ward.

In a soliloquy, Helena reveals her love for Bertram. Because she is a commoner, there is no hope of them being together, and yet she cannot bear the thought of his departure. Parolles, Bertram's best friend, whom Helena acknowledges is a liar and a coward, enters and engages Helena in a coarse conversation about the pros and cons of her virginity. Helena intends to protect her virginity, but Parolles urges her to give it up. To him it is a wasted virtue, particularly once a woman becomes a certain age. The conversation prompts Helena to take matters into her own hands. Her love for Bertram can be realized only through her own actions, and not by waiting for something to happen: "Our remedies oft in ourselves do lie, / Which we ascribe to heaven," she says.

Act 1, Scene 2

In Paris, the King of France confers with two lords, the Brothers Dumaine, about the dispute between Sienna and Florence; he states that he will allow his soldiers to fight on either side. Bertram, Parolles, and Lafew enter, and the king welcomes them, reminiscing fondly about Bertram's father, and wishing that Gerard de Narbon were still alive to cure his fistula.

Act 1, Scene 3

Back in Rossillion, the countess confers with Lavatch, a morose and ribald clown. The countess calls him a knave (stupid) and urges him to marry the servant woman he has gotten pregnant. She then asks her steward to fetch Helena. The steward tells the countess that he has overhead Helena talking to herself about her love for Bertram. When the lovesick Helena appears, the countess comments sympathetically on the girl's emotional state, for she was once young and in love.

The countess tells Helena that she loves her like a daughter, but Helena objects. If the countess were her mother, then Bertram would be her brother. Initially, Helena states that she cannot be the countess's daughter because she is a servant, and Bertram is a lord; they cannot be equals. The countess urges Helena to admit her real objection—that having feelings for her own brother would be improper—and she does. Helena also admits that she has plans to follow Bertram to Paris in order to try her father's cures on the king. The countess is doubtful; she says that the king's doctors have told him nothing can be done. Helena objects; she bets her life that she can cure the king. The countess relents and sends her off to Paris.

Act 2, Scene 1

In Paris, the king bids farewell to the Brothers Dumaine, who are off to fight for Florence in the war with Sienna. Lafew announces the arrival of Gerard de Narbon's daughter, Helena, who has come to cure the ailing king. Helena explains

An engraving of the Florentine camp with Bertram and Parolles, Act IV, scene iii

(© Shakespeare Collection, Special Collections Library, University of Michigan)

that upon his deathbed, her father passed on his knowledge to her. The king doubts her ability to make him better, but she swears upon her life that he will be healed within a day or two. She offers a wager: If she fails, she will be put to death; if she succeeds, she will be able to choose her own husband from among "the royal blood of France." With little conviction, the king accepts her offer.

Act 2, Scene 2

The countess entrusts Lavatch with the task of traveling to Paris to give Helena a note and check up on Bertram. In a series of bawdy comments that frustrate the countess, Lavatch agrees.

Act 2, Scene 3

Bertram, Parolles, and Lafew are stunned to see the king miraculously cured. The king urges Helena to have a seat and take her pick of husbands from the assembled gathering of lords. Lafew wishes he were younger so Helena might pick him. Helena addresses the lords, claiming to be a simple maid, and all refuse her. Then she decides on Bertram. "This is the man," she says. Bertram argues with the king on account of the fact that she is "a poor physician's daughter." The king responds that "From lowest place, whence virtuous things proceed, / The place is dignified by th'doer's deed." Furthermore, she is pretty and smart, and Bertram should be happy to have her. As for her lack of wealth and the social status, the king states that he is capable of granting them.

Bertram reiterates that he will never love her. Helena briefly recants her decision, but the king will not hear of it. His reputation is at stake, so he forces Bertram to marry her that night.

When the others have departed, Lafew and Parolles talk about what Lafew perceives as Parolles's lack of loyalty to Bertram. Lafew also derides Parolles's pompous personality and gaudy clothes. Parolles dismisses Lafew as an old man with no wisdom to impart. Lafew warns that such foolishness will lead Parolles to ruin. Offstage, Helena and Bertram are married. When Lafew tells Parolles that he has a new mistress (Helena), Parolles responds that he has no mistress and no lord other than God. Lafew responds that the devil is his master and that he should be beaten.

After Lafew leaves, Bertram enters. Bertram says that he will never consummate his marriage to Helena. Instead, he will go off to fight in the Tuscan wars and send Helena back to Rossillion. Parolles agrees to join him.

Act 2, Scene 4
Lavatch arrives in Paris and greets Helena and Parolles, whom he insults by calling him a knave. Parolles does not realize Lavatch has insulted him. Parolles tells Helena to prepare for her wedding night, and she leaves to await Bertram.

Act 2, Scene 5
Lafew tries to convince Bertram that Parolles will not be a trustworthy ally in battle, to no avail. Helena reappears, and Bertram tells her that he will not sleep with her that night because of his prior obligations. He gives her a letter to give to his mother and tells her to return to Rossillion. Helena vows that as his obedient servant she will do what he asks. After she leaves,

Bertram confesses to Parolles that he will never return to her, and they go off to battle.

Act 3, Scene 1
In Florence, the duke addresses his troops, which include the Brothers Dumaine, who are both serving as captains. The duke is perturbed that the king of France has not sided exclusively with him in the war, but the two lords proclaim their allegiance to the duke nonetheless.

Act 3, Scene 2
Lavatch returns to Rossillion and delivers Bertram's letter to the countess. The letter states that Bertram has been forced to marry Helena against his will. He has run away and plans never to return to the palace. The countess is angry that he is dishonoring both the king and Helena, whom she calls "a maid too virtuous / For the contempt of empire."

Helena arrives in Rossillion with the Brothers Dumaine. She realizes that Bertram is gone for good when the two lords tell the countess that Bertram has gone to battle for the Duke of Florence. Helena reads a passage from Bertram's letter, which states that she can only be his wife if she wears his ring (which he has refused to give her) and bears him a child. Furthermore, he says that as long as Helena is alive in France, he shall not return. The countess renounces him as her son.

In a soliloquy, Helena laments her position. She is sad for herself, but also worried that Bertram will be hurt or killed in battle. She decides to leave France so Bertram can return home safely.

Act 3, Scene 3
In a brief scene, the Duke of Florence leads Bertram and others into battle. Bertram bravely heads up the troops, and Parolles, coward that he is, follows in the rear.

Act 3, Scene 4
In Rossillion, the countess receives a letter from Helena stating that she has gone on a pilgrimage to the burial site of Saint Jacques le Grand (St. James the Greater) in hopes that her departure will prompt Bertram to return home. The countess urges her steward to write to Bertram in an effort to extol Helena's virtues and point out how childish he is being in refusing her as his wife. The countess thinks that if Bertram returns

home and Helena hears about it, then she will return as well due to her immense desire to be near him.

Act 3, Scene 5

In the city of Florence, the Widow Capilet and her daughter, Diana, discuss the war. News of the young Count Bertram's heroism on the battlefield has spread fast, and they are aware of his brave deeds. However, Parolles has been seeking a female companion for the count and has spied Diana. Both the Widow and her friend Mariana warn Diana vehemently against becoming involved in an affair. If Diana loses her virginity to the Count of Rossillion, she will be ruined.

Helena arrives at the Widow's house in search of a place to stay on her pilgrimage to Saint Jacques le Grand. The Widow welcomes her and says that the Count of Rossillion, a war hero, is in town. Helena says she does not know him, but finds him handsome. Diana says that the count should not be so mean to his wife, but that Parolles should be poisoned.

Act 3, Scene 6

At the camp, the Brothers Dumaine try to convince Bertram that Parolles is a scoundrel, liar, and coward. Bertram doubts that they can prove such accusations. The lords offer to pose as the enemy, capture and blindfold Parolles, bring him back to the tents, and interrogate him, knowing full well that he will incriminate Bertram to save his own skin. Bertram agrees to the plan. Parolles enters the tent, stating his intent to find a prized regimental drum that was lost in battle. The others tell him to forget about it, but he is adamant, believing he will be deemed a hero for retrieving it. They relent, deciding that it will be the perfect time to capture him. Parolles proclaims he will attempt the dangerous maneuver that night.

Act 3, Scene 7

Helena convinces the Widow that she is the count's wife. She proposes a plan in which Diana's virtue will be spared by switching places with Diana during her scheduled rendezvous with Bertram. Thus, Bertram will be sleeping unknowingly with his wife, not Diana. Ahead of time, Diana will ask that Bertram give her his ring and that neither of them speak for the hour they are together. The Widow agrees to the plan, because it will allow her daughter to retain her chastity. To seal the deal, Helena offers a great deal of money to Diana so that she will have a significant dowry and will be able to find herself a worthy husband afterward.

Act 4, Scene 1

Parolles arrives in a field, ostensibly on his quest to find the drum, but he has no intentions of doing so. Instead, he plans to take a nap, feign some injuries, and return to camp with a story about his brave but unsuccessful exploit. The two lords are hiding in the bushes, and they jump out, throwing a sack over his head. They have an interpreter utter some mumbo jumbo—"Boskos thromuldo boskos"—to make Parolles believe he has been captured by the foreign enemy. Parolles immediately offers to spill the beans about his army's secrets in an effort to spare his life. His "captors" agree to take him to their general, so Parolles can tell him everything.

Act 4, Scene 2

In his effort to plan his conquest, Bertram tries to seduce Diana by comparing her to the Greek goddess Diana and saying that remaining chaste would be a waste of her beauty. Diana reminds him that he is married, but Bertram brushes it off. He says he loves only Diana. Diana is not convinced; she knows that he just wants to sleep with her. She declares that she will believe his declaration of love only if he backs it up with the promise to marry her after his wife dies and if he gives her the family ring he wears on his finger. He protests, but gives in fairly quickly. Diana says she will meet him at midnight in her room. He will stay for only one hour, and neither of them will speak. In return for his ring, she will give him one of her own in return. After Bertram leaves, Diana gives a short soliloquy stating that her mother was right about him. All men are the same; they will promise anything to get a woman into bed.

Act 4, Scene 3

The Brothers Dumaine discuss Bertram. The first lord tells the second lord that Helena is dead, having succumbed to grief on her pilgrimage to Saint Jacques le Grand. Her death was confirmed by the priest of the shrine. Furthermore, Bertram knew this when he made his deal with Diana. The lords are saddened by Helena's death, and they are dismayed (but not surprised) that Bertram is cheered by it and happily announces that he will return to Rossillion shortly.

The two lords tell Bertram that Parolles has been held in the stocks, offering his "captors" a litany of confessions. Bertram still does not believe Parolles would say anything bad about him. To prove him wrong, Parolles is sent in, still blindfolded. Parolles says that the duke's horses are weak, his troops scattered, and his commanders are poor rogues. He further indicts Captain Dumaine as a low-level apprentice who once impregnated a mentally retarded girl. One of the captors retrieves a letter from Parolles's pocket, in which he wrote that Bertram is a fool. He claims to have been warning Diana that the count was "a dangerous and lascivious boy, who is a whale to virginity, and devours up all the fry it finds." He begs for his life and continues to say terrible things about Captain Dumaine, including that "drunkenness is his best virtue." He also condemns the other Captain Dumaine and readily agrees to betray all of them if only he is allowed to live. Bertram is livid at Parolles's betrayal. When Parolles is unmasked, he balks at being fooled but readily apologizes.

Act 4, Scene 4

Following the bed-trick (which takes place offstage), Helena tells the Widow and Diana that they will all return to France in order to make good on her promise. When they get there, Diana will need to do one more thing before their scheme is complete. Diana vows to do whatever Helena desires, such is her gratitude for having her virtue saved by the bed-trick. Helena assures her that "all's well that ends well."

Act 4, Scene 5

In Rossillion, Lafew criticizes Parolles, and the countess wishes she had never known him. She laments Helena's death, stating that she loved her as if she were her own child. Lafew proposes that Bertram marry his daughter, and the countess agrees. Lavatch engages in some off-color banter with Lafew and the countess; they both state that he is morose but harmless. Lavatch announces that Bertram has returned.

Act 5, Scene 1

While traveling to Rossillion as fast as they can, Helena, Diana, and the Widow encounter a gentleman. Helena asks him to take a message to the King of France. The gentleman states that the king is not in Paris but in fact heading for Rossillion. "All's well that ends well yet," Helena

reminds the Widow. Helena promises a reward to the gentleman if he can deliver her letter to the king promptly, and he obliges.

Act 5, Scene 2

Parolles returns to Rossillion and urges Lavatch, who roundly criticizes Parolles's withered clothes and body odor, to give Lafew a letter. But Lafew enters, and Lavatch introduces Parolles as a "poor, decayed . . . foolish, rascally knave." Parolles begs forgiveness from Lafew, who grants it.

Act 5, Scene 3

The king mourns Helena's death, and with Lafew and the countess present, he summons Bertram. The king asks Bertram if he knows Lafew's daughter. The count says he was in love with her, and the king announces their betrothal. Lafew asks Bertram for a ring to give his daughter. He presents the ring he believes Diana gave him during their rendezvous. Lafew instantly recognizes it as Helena's ring, but Bertram objects. He claims it was thrown from a window by a woman who wanted to sleep with him. The king sides with Lafew, saying that Helena promised only to take it off her finger if she consummated her marriage with Bertram. Bertram remains adamant—he did not receive the ring from Helena. The king orders Bertram to be taken away. As Bertram is being led away, he says that if the ring belonged to Helena, then she, in fact, became his wife in Florence, and yet, she was not there, so the ring was not hers and she is not his wife.

Bertram is led away, and the king is perplexed. Meanwhile, the gentleman arrives with a letter to the king from Diana. The letter claims that Bertram promised to marry her upon the death of his wife, but that he fled Florence without making good on that promise. She is on her way to Rossillion to seek justice.

At this turn of events, Lafew recants his daughter's hand in marriage, believing Bertram not worthy of being her husband. The king agrees and starts to believe that Helena met with foul play, possibly at Bertram's hands. Bertram and Diana, along with her mother, are brought to court. The king asks Bertram if he knows either Diana or her mother, and Bertram refuses to answer, but states that Diana is not his wife. Diana insists that Bertram believes he took her virginity. Bertram says she was a whore. Diana presents his ring as proof that she is telling

MEDIA ADAPTATIONS

- *All's Well That Ends Well*, directed by John Barton and Claude Whatham and produced by the Royal Shakespeare Company, was filmed in 1968 by the BBC and released on video. The production stars Lynn Farleigh, Ian Richardson, and Catherine Lacey.

- *All's Well That Ends Well*, a 1981 production directed by Elijah Moshinsky and starring Ian Charleson, Angela Down, and Celia Johnson, was released by BBC Time/Life Series and distributed by Ambrose Video.

- An audiobook of *All's Well That Ends Well*, read by William Hutt and published as part of the CBC Stratford Festival Reading Series, is available on compact disc.

- A two-cassette full-cast recording of *All's Well That Ends Well*, starring Claire Bloom and Lynn Redgrave, was released by Caedmon Audio.

the truth. The countess and the king instantly believe her. Diana says that Parolles can vouch for her story, and he is ordered to appear. Bertram backtracks, saying he slept with Diana and she stole the ring. Diana says that she gave Bertram the ring the king is now wearing.

Bertram finally confesses; Parolles appears and confesses that he was the go-between for Bertram and Diana. The king questions Diana about the ring some more, and she cryptically says she never gave it to Bertram. The king knows full well the ring was Helena's and orders Diana to be sent to jail for refusing to cooperate. She sends her mother to fetch her bail.

Diana enjoys the riddle she has presented, and knowing of Helena's ensuing pregnancy, she tells the king: "Dead though she be, she feels her young one kick. So there's my riddle: one that's dead is quick."

The Widow presents Helena, who quotes Bertram's original letter: "When from my finger you can get this ring, / And are by me with child," proving that she has achieved Bertram's seemingly unattainable criteria. Presented with this evidence, Bertram professes his undying love for Helena and promises to be a faithful husband. The king, delighted at this turnabout, applauds Diana for retaining her chastity while allowing Helena to fulfill her role as Bertram's wife. He offers Diana a dowry and her choice for a husband.

CHARACTERS

Bertram, Count of Rossillion

Bertram is the Count of Rossillion. His father has recently died, and his mother, the Countess of Rossillion, is still in mourning. Bertram is quite young, perhaps no more than twenty, and he is eager to join the king's ranks in Paris and then go off to battle in Florence. Bertram's best friend is Parolles, but he is oblivious to the fact that Parolles is an opportunist and a scoundrel. Bertram balks at marrying Helena because she is a commoner with no wealth or status. He agrees reluctantly only after the king promises to endow Helena with wealth and a title in order to sweeten the deal. This is evidence of Bertram's snobbishness, as Helena's social standing outranks all her other positive qualities in Bertram's eyes. Finding himself trapped in a marriage to Helena, whom he does not love, he flees to Florence to join the wars. While there, he proves himself valiant on the battlefield, and his reputation as a hero spreads quickly throughout the city. He spies Diana in town and sends Parolles to set up a rendezvous. Before their scheduled tryst, he promises the young virgin that he truly loves her and will marry her as soon as his wife dies. That night, he believes he sleeps with her, but he beds his wife, Helena, instead. Thinking he is with Diana, he gives her his family ring as a token of his affection.

Bertram's first change of heart takes place when he witnesses the blindfolded Parolles's exuberant confessions to the Brothers Dumaine. Parolles declares that Bertram is a coward, liar, and promiscuous to boot. Bertram is forced to accept that Parolles has been duplicitous. After the wars are over, Bertram returns to Rossillion. He thinks Helena is dead and that he has slept with Diana; in fact, he is adamant about it when Diana appears before him and the king. When the bed-trick is revealed and Helena appears, ostensibly pregnant with his child and bearing his ring, he happily concedes defeat. She has fulfilled the requirements he stipulated in his letter as being necessary for him to accept her as his wife, and he vows to love her forever.

Commentators are divided over Bertram. Most agree that he is immature and full of short-comings, but some critics find him sincere and repentant by the end of the play and thus worthy of the honorable Helena. Others find this turn-around in his character implausible and false. "No Shakespearean hero is so degraded and so unsparingly presented," wrote Russell Fraser in the New Cambridge edition of the play. One of the harshest summaries of Bertram's charac-ter came from renowned literary critic and phi-losopher Samuel Johnson, who summarized Bertram (as quoted in Fraser) as "a man noble without generosity, and young without truth; who marries Helena as a coward and leaves her as a profligate; when she is dead by his unkind-ness, sneaks home to a second marriage, is accused by a woman whom he has wronged, defends himself by falsehood, and is dismissed to happiness." The outrage, for those who dislike Bertram, is that he is given a happy ending he does not deserve.

Critics who argue that Bertram has truly repented by the end of the play suggest that it is his immaturity and desire for life experience that cause him to initially reject Helena. Elizabethan audiences, they argue, would have found Ber-tram's desire to go to war entirely honorable. Likewise, his blindness to Parolles's true nature is attributed to his inexperience, but once it is demonstrated via the kidnapping episode, Ber-tram becomes wiser. Those scholars who find Bertram entirely despicable and without merit conclude that his acceptance of Helena in the final scene of the play is one calculated to save his neck, as he finds himself backed into a corner with all the evidence (Helena, Diana, and Parol-les all testify against him) stacked against him. A few critics abstain from roundly praising or con-demning Bertram, offering other ways to inter-pret his character.

Brothers Dumaine

The Brothers Dumaine, sometimes called the two French lords, serve as captains for the Duke of Florence in the war with Sienna. They are hono-rable men, fond of Helena, friends with Bertram, and convinced of Parolles's bad nature from the start. They try in vain to convince Bertram that Parolles cannot be trusted. In order to prove their case, the Brothers Dumaine enact a plan to ambush Parolles and reveal his true nature to Bertram. They disguise themselves as enemy sol-diers and kidnap Parolles near Florence when Parolles embarks on a mock-heroic quest to recapture the regiment's drum. The Brothers pre-tend to speak a different language, and while Parolles is blindfolded, he betrays Bertram openly and vociferously.

Countess of Rossillion

The Countess of Rossillion is Bertram's mother, and she is still mourning the recent death of her husband. She has also willingly become Helena's guardian since the young woman's father, a physician of local renown, has also recently passed away. Kind and generous, the countess exemplifies the best of the noble tradition and encourages Helena's love for Bertram, even though she thinks her son is foolish and head-strong for rejecting the talented, vivacious girl. The countess rates honesty and virtue higher than valor in battle or nobility of rank, even when this means that she must side against Bertram. She believes her son is old enough to get married, but too young to go into battle. She mourns Bertram's departure for Paris in the same way she mourns the loss of her husband.

The countess's fondness for Helena is evi-dent when she tells the girl she loves her as if she were her own daughter. But when Helena offers to travel to Paris to heal the king, the countess encourages her to go. Even after Helena pro-fesses her love for the countess's son, the count-ess is understanding and does not discourage Helena's passion. She understands the spell of "love's strong passion," having fallen under it herself when she was younger.

The countess has been widely praised as one of Shakespeare's best female characters. Famed nineteenth-century critic and playwright George Bernard Shaw (as quoted in Fraser) called the countess "the most beautiful old woman's part ever written." One of the most famous actresses to play the role was Academy Award-winner Judi Dench, who played the countess in 2003 at the Swan Theatre in Stratford, England.

Diana

The daughter of the Widow Capilet, Diana is courted by the Count of Rossillion while he is

An engraving of Act V, scene iii, with the King, the Countess of Rossillion, Lafew, Betram, Helena, and Diana (© Shakespeare Collection, Special Collections Library, University of Michigan)

fighting with the king's regiment in Florence. She is a virgin, and she knows Bertram's reputation as a cad, and that he is married. When Helena arrives in Florence as a traveler and agrees to stay at the Widow's inn, Diana tells her about the count's awful wife. At first, Helena pretends to be someone else, but after she confesses to being Bertram's wife, Diana agrees to the bed-trick scheme as a way to preserve her own honor. She is also happy to help Helena achieve the demands of Bertram's letter. After the bed-trick has been carried out successfully, she and her mother accompany Helena back to Paris.

Diana plays a major role in revealing the bed-trick in the play's final act. She delights in this role, presenting a maddening riddle for the king, Bertram, and others to decipher. She insists she never slept with Bertram, even as Bertram insists that she did. When the king threatens to put her in jail for her insolence, she presents her bail in the form of Helena, the answer to the riddle and the person they all

thought was dead. When all is revealed, the king applauds Diana's role in the bed-trick scheme and rewards her by letting her choose a husband from among the men at court. She will thus be spared the hardship and poverty of her life in Florence. For her, the story truly ends well.

Duke of Florence

The Duke of Florence welcomes Bertram and Parolles when they escape Paris to fight the war. He is allied with France in a war against Sienna, another province of what would later become Italy.

Helena

Helena is the daughter of the recently deceased court physician, Gerard de Narbon, from whom she has learned his healing secrets. She has become the ward of the Countess of Rossillion, with whom she has a very maternal relationship, though she has fallen in love with the countess's son, Bertram. She is disturbed by the thought of being considered the countess's daughter, because that would make Bertram her brother and her romantic interest in him would be unseemly. Because of these concerns, she admits her love for Bertram to the countess, who is sympathetic to the girl's predicament. Helena is admired by nearly everyone except Bertram for her charm, beauty, intelligence, and honesty. Her name, as several characters in the play remind her, is equivocal with Helen of Troy, the most beautiful woman of Ancient Greece, over whom the Trojan War was fought.

Helena is tormented by the thought of being separated from Bertram when he departs for Paris. She takes it upon herself, with the countess's blessing, to travel to Paris in order to heal the king, who is suffering from an incurable condition, but also because it will keep her in proximity to Bertram. She miraculously heals the king and thereby earns his loyalty, admiration, and a valuable ring that figures prominently in the story when the bed-trick is revealed.

Bertram rejects Helena because of her low-born status. He is a count, and she is a commoner. No matter how virtuous she may be, it would be improper to marry her. Helena understands this, yet she does not accept it. She takes matters into her own hands and hatches a plan: first, to become Bertram's wife, and second, to fulfill his demands to obtain his ring and bear his child. Even in the face of repeated rejection, she persists in her goals, so strong is her infatuation with Bertram.

Helena has the gift of healing, as did her father, and bets the king her life that she can make him well, another example of her remarkable self-confidence. He accepts the offer, and as a favor in return, Helena asks for Bertram's hand in marriage. The king readily complies.

Helena is considered the central figure in the play, and all of the major themes of the play (gender issues, desire, the bed-trick, marriage, and social class) are influenced by her actions. As the heroine of *All's Well That Ends Well*, Helena is often described by admiring commentators as noble, virtuous, honorable, and regenerative, and by detractors as obsessive and narrow-minded. Her dogged pursuit of Bertram has been both ridiculed (particularly in Victorian times) as unfeminine and commended as being bold, mostly in more recent times. Many wonder why she is attracted to a man who does not like

her at all. Nearly all critics agree that she is a complex character.

Fraser and others find similarities between Helena and the real-life historical figure Christine de Pisan, an educated woman of the early fifteenth century who was renowned for her piety, goodness, intelligence, and a type of proto-feminism in which she attributed a woman's success to her own resourcefulness. Additionally, her father was the well-known doctor and astrologer Thomas of Pisano, who had been called upon in 1365 to heal England's Charles V. Fraser theorizes that Shakespeare added dimension to the character of Helena by making her a knowingly frail character, as evidenced by her pilgrimage to Saint Jacques le Grand. This suggests that though Helena is strong and brave enough to get what she wants (Bertram), she understands her limitations as a person, and possibly her faults (that is, desiring the flawed Bertram is perhaps not the healthiest thing for her). "Shakespeare's Helena is frail in that 'we are all frail,'" Fraser writes, "and it is this generic human frailty that dictates the pilgrimage to Saint Jacques." Irish playwright W. B. Yeats, quoted by Patrick Carnegy in the *Spectator*, called Helena "one of Shakespeare's 'glorious women who select dreadful or empty men.'"

Commentators who unequivocally admire Helena find her guiltless in plotting to wed Bertram and in fulfilling the terms of his letter through the bed-trick. One critic even refers to her as a genius. Scholars who are critical of her character find her obsessed by her sexual passion and an example of noble womanhood degraded, using her abilities as a huntress to realize her plans for a union with Bertram with no thought of their consequences to others (primarily Diana).

Most critics, however, see Helena as a many-sided character. Several critics have noted her regenerative and restorative powers; she saves the king from almost certain death, but how she does it remains a mystery. She is the key to restoring a kingdom whose noble elders are dying and who have no honorable replacements. When Helena heals the king, she restores the kingdom at least for a time, and saves Bertram (and Diana) from making what would have been a mistake of lifelong regret. She is pregnant at the end of the play, symbolically the provider of a new generation of nobility. Other critics have noted her embodiment of both feminine passivity and masculine action. She is the desiring subject (the pursuer of Bertram), yet she longs to be the desired object (pursued by Bertram).

King of France

The King of France represents a dying breed of nobility, one in which honor and virtue are supremely important. When the play opens, he is suffering from a debilitating illness, fistula, in which some of his internal organs have developed abscesses. He is nostalgic for the past and has fond memories of Bertram's father, the former Count of Rossillion. Helena, who has followed Bertram to Paris, offers to heal the king. When she succeeds, the king is grateful and generous, giving her a valuable ring, allowing her to choose a husband from among his noblemen. When Bertram rejects Helena for being common, the king offers her a title and a dowry.

The king forbids Bertram from traveling to Florence to fight in the war, stating that the count is too young. He is protective of his troops and makes sure they are trained sufficiently. He is ambivalent about Florence's war with Sienna and allows his men to choose which side they will fight for. When the bed-trick is revealed at the play's conclusion, the king is pleased that all has worked out, and he allows Diana to choose a husband. This gesture shows that, although he is grateful and gives generous rewards, he has not learned his lesson. He offered Helena the same reward, which led to the chain of events that caused Diana to be there in the first place. However, the king's actions most likely rescue Diana (and her mother) from a life of poverty, proving he is much more forgiving of class differences than Bertram, despite possessing the ultimate title. His actions prove him to be cautious, thoughtful, and ultimately benevolent.

Lafew

Lafew is an elderly lord, a friend and confidant of the countess. He is quick to perceive the true character of Parolles, calls him a knave (an unscrupulous person), ridicules his flashy clothes, and warns Bertram against him. Lafew travels to Paris with Bertram, and he is one of Helena's strongest defenders. When the king allows her to choose a husband, he wishes he were young enough to be considered. Even though Lafew represents the old guard—he would have been close to Bertram's father—and his values are somewhat traditional, he is still a good judge of character and is capable of forgiveness. His sympathy and kindness become apparent at the end of the play when he assures the unmasked and humiliated Parolles that he will not be tossed out of the palace.

Lavatch

Lavatch is a cantankerous, pessimistic clown and servant of the Countess of Rossillion. He provides some comic relief in the play, usually in somewhat lascivious prose that espouses his gloomy world view. He is the lowest character on the totem pole in the play, so unscrupulous that even Parolles calls him a knave. He has an affair with Isabel, a servant, and gets her pregnant. He decides to marry her, but later changes his mind. Lavatch is the one older character in the play who is unwise, proving that age and wisdom do not always go together.

Parolles

Mentor and confidant to Bertram, Parolles is a social climber and a scoundrel. On the other hand, he exhibits more self-awareness than Bertram and speaks several languages. He dresses in flashy clothes that border on the ridiculous and does not put his intelligence to good use. He is a prime example of a *miles gloriosus*, a boastful soldier, which was a stock character type in Shakespeare's day. He also has qualities of a *servus callidus*, a tricky slave, another type of stock character. The first glimpse of his false allegiance to Bertram is when he tells Lafew that Bertram is not his master; he answers only to God. This displays his arrogance and disloyalty; Parolles is in service to the Count of Rossillion, and likewise is expected to remain steadfast, especially so when he follows Bertram into battle. But he betrays Bertram in Florence when he is captured and tricked into believing he is about to be tortured. His boasts and deceit finally bring about his unmasking, at last enlightening Bertram as to his true character. Parolles is quick to realize he has been a fool, suffers humiliation, and assumes a new veneer of humbleness in accepting Lafew's mercy, which will enable him to remain in Rossillion.

Parolles has a long conversation with Helena in the first act. They discuss her virginity in rather flirtatious terms. One wonders why Helena would choose to confide in Parolles, a man whose advice she would almost certainly never take. For his part, Parolles tells Helena that virginity is a handicap. The longer she preserves it, the more danger she is in of becoming damaged goods. That Parolles would give such advice to a young woman so highly regarded by the countess speaks of his contempt for those in authority as well as his lax morals.

Critics praise Shakespeare for his creation of Parolles, a character not found in Boccaccio's version of the tale, whether they like him or not. He appears in thirteen of the play's twenty-three scenes, and some consider the scene of his unmasking (the longest scene in the play) to be the structural center of the play (especially since the critical scene of the bed-trick occurs offstage). Parolles is responsible for most of the laughter (albeit scant) in the play, and although he is generally regarded as a liar, a coward, a fop, and a character lacking in honor and principle, he is essential to the plot.

For many, Parolles is a more interesting character than Bertram. Some directors have created versions of the play that revolve more around Parolles than Helena, and some renowned actors have been attracted to the part, most notably Laurence Olivier in a 1927 production. Some critics debate whether or not Parolles is a bad influence on Bertram, or if they are simply like minds that have found each other. Fraser believes that "Parolles is an extension of Bertram."

Widow Capilet

The Widow Capilet is Diana's mother, and she runs the inn in Florence where Helena stays on her pilgrimage to Saint Jacques le Grand. She tells Helena that Bertram has been trying to seduce Diana. When Helena proposes the bed-trick as a way to fulfill her wifely duties and save Diana's virginity in the process, the Widow reluctantly agrees because she sympathizes with Helena's predicament. Afterward, she accompanies Diana and Helena back to Rossillion at the end of the play. When Diana presents the bed-trick to the king and others, the Widow is excused to fetch Diana's bail, which is revealed to be Helena herself.

THEMES

Gender Roles

Much of the plot of *All's Well That Ends Well* hinges on Helena's willingness to dismiss the constraints of her traditional, feminine gender role. Because Helena subverts her own pre-scribed gender role (mainly, that a woman should be demure and not exhibit unprompted sexual interest in a man) in pursuing her heart's desire, Bertram is also forced against his will into a reversed gender role by becoming the pursued. Her other actions are also quite bold for a woman. She engages in a frank discussion about her virginity with Parolles but is adamant about remaining a virgin, thereby embodying both gender roles of participating in a sexual debate with a man while remaining chaste. She travels alone to Paris, heals the king (traditionally a male job), and thereby is allowed to choose her husband, a complete subversion of normal gender roles. She also leaves Rossillion and travels on a very long pilgrimage all by herself, arranges the bed-trick for her own benefit, and craftily stages her own death in order to get what she wants. However, also implicit in her proactive role is a desire to engage in a more traditional role. She longs to be desired by Bertram and to have his child. In the sense that both of these happen at the end of the play, all does end well for Helena.

This dual nature of Helena's character, in which she exhibits elements of both female passiveness and masculine action, is demonstrated in the scene where she selects Bertram as a husband. She emphasizes her low social status to the king and how unworthy she is. It could be that she is only playing up her feminine side in order to seem more attractive to the assembled suitors. But when Bertram rejects and humiliates her in front of the entire court, she retracts her choice. The marriage proceeds only because the king insists on keeping his word. When Bertram leaves her—their marriage still unconsummated—to go to the wars in Italy, she passively sits at home and then wanders off as a pilgrim so that Bertram can return to Rossillion. In a sense, this is a passive act in that it reveals her sense of defeat. Even when Bertram sends the letter with the conditions of his acceptance of her as his wife, conditions that he believes she could never fulfill, Helena is not angered but takes pity on him instead, noting how she stole rank by marrying him. Finally, once Helena has completed the tasks Bertram required of her and he takes her as his wife, she is satisfied with the role of wife and mother, which will presumably place her permanently back in a more traditional female role.

Several critics note the quest-romance and the knight-errant themes in *All's Well That Ends Well*, only in this case the initiator of action—the hero—is a woman. Helena possesses the knowledge and skill to influence events and other characters and thus is able to secure Bertram as a husband. However, she cannot force him to love her, and his rejection requires her to pursue an alternate plan of action. Some think that Helena's active role, her ability to go out and get what she wants (Bertram), is motivated only by sexual desire. Others excuse her unorthodox means of fulfilling Bertram's conditions because they were created with the intent of being impossible to fulfill. Thus, she had no other recourse after having been publicly humiliated by Bertram than to arrange the bed-trick.

Bed-trick/Marriage

The bed-trick in *All's Well That Ends Well* pervades much of the commentary on the play and intersects with the discussion of marriage. Commentators tend to focus on whether Helena's use of the bed-trick is justified and lawful and whether it provides a means for a satisfactory ending to the play. Critics who believe Helena's switch with Diana is justified argue that as Bertram's wife, Helena had every right to take Diana's place and consummate her marriage, thus saving both Diana and Bertram from dishonor. Helena saves a maiden from what would have been a grave mistake, and she keeps Bertram from committing what would have been an unlawful act of adultery. By thus saving Bertram, and, as a result, securing his ring and carrying his child, Helena is an agent in restoring the dying kingdom. Those who find Helena's actions unlawful note that Helena is actually encouraging Bertram to engage in adultery (even though Helena knows that what she is doing is technically lawful). They note that although Helena satisfactorily fulfills Bertram's requirements in his letter, this does not necessarily dictate a happy ending, since their sexual union was based on deception.

Social Class

Despite the fact that she lives in the palace, Helena is a commoner. Her mother died when she was young, and her father was a doctor. Without property, money, or a title to her name, she has no assets to attract Bertram, who is a member of the noble class. Most marriages in that time were arranged to benefit both families, and Bertram's marriage to Helena would benefit only her. Some view this as a justifiable reason for Bertram to reject Helena. However, we are told early on in the play that Helena possesses true nobility and honor, which cannot be obtained by birth. Bertram, though born with wealth and status, has no nobility or honor to speak of. The noble and honorable older generation, represented by the king, the countess, and Lafew, recognize Helena's virtues and Bertram's lack of them.

A few commentators have noted that wealth and rank actually mean little to either Helena or Bertram. Helena wants Bertram, not his money, and Bertram wants his freedom, not a marriage to a woman everyone considers noble and virtuous. If Bertram were truly in pursuit of great rank, he would have accepted Helena, whom the king has endowed with wealth to make her Bertram's equal (although a few critics note that this is actually unnecessary, for Helena's fine qualities erase the social gap between her and Bertram). Also, if Bertram were truly invested in maintaining his class distinction, he would not have befriended Parolles, a man of notably low birth and, worse, base and vile qualities.

Youth versus Experience

The bittersweet tone of *All's Well That Ends Well* is established by the play's older characters, especially the Countess of Rossillion and Lafew, both of whom have suffered the loss of loved ones and express their patience with those of the younger generation. The countess sympathizes with Helena's passion for Bertram, because she was once young and in love herself. Likewise, Lafew forgives Parolles for being a traitor and gives him a second chance by offering him a position. The King of France offers his sympathy to Bertram on the loss of his father, and tells the count he is too young to fight in the war. Ultimately, the happy ending of the play is in the fact that the elders will take no retribution out on the younger generation for the follies to which they have subjected themselves. A counterpoint to this is Lavatch, the aging clown, who talks dirty, impregnates a chambermaid, and then changes his mind about marrying her. He still acts like a child, and his position as a clown—a person no one takes seriously—underscores that fact. Lavatch exhibits the whims of a young person, even though he is old. He serves as an example of the misery that awaits those who fail to live up to their responsibilities as they enter into adulthood. The older generation understands that youth is a time of trial and error, and they remain hopeful that the younger generation—Bertram and Parolles especially—have learned their lessons as their elders continue to

TOPICS FOR FURTHER STUDY

- Helena is Shakespeare's only female character to address the audience through a soliloquy. Scan her soliloquy in act 1, scene 1, that begins "O, were that all." Do you find any particular meter or rhyme scheme? Do you agree with critics who say that the prose of *All's Well That Ends Well* is sloppy and uninspired? List three reasons why it is so or why it is not so.

- Using a map, trace the path from Rossillion in France to Galicia in Spain, where the Cathedral of Santiago is. Where is Florence in relation to the cathedral? Calculate the distance between Rossillion and Florence. How long do you think it took Helena to get there on foot? Discuss the weather, terrain, and other obstacles (natural or manmade) she may have encountered on her journey.

- Lafew chides Parolles for his flashy clothes, asking, "Pray you, sir, who's his tailor?" and describing him to the countess as that "snipped-taffeta fellow there, whose villainous saffron would have made all the unbaked and doughy youth of a nation in his colour." Research clothing of the Elizabethan period and photocopy or draw three examples of the types of outfits Parolles may have been wearing, befitting his social class and garish taste, that Lafew was making fun of.

- Some critics have noted the discrepancy between the rash behavior of the play's younger characters (namely, Bertram, Parolles, and Helena), and the forgiving nature of the play's older characters (Lafew, the countess, and the king). Using the theory of personality developed by twentieth-century German psychologist Erik Erikson, who described the eight stages of psychosocial development, write a five hundred word essay explaining how the characters' stages of development influence their behavior. Support your reasoning with examples.

take them under their wings and prepare them for the future.

Endings

The abrupt ending of *All's Well That Ends Well* is partly responsible for giving the play its problem status. Does the play end well? If so, for whom? Most modern critics conclude that the ending is unsatisfactory and unconvincing, even though it provides the required comedic resolution whereby the hero and heroine are joined at last. They have a hard time believing that Bertram could enter into a happy marriage with Helena after being confronted with her deception. Early commentators, however, tended to have less trouble accepting the ending and argued that Elizabethan audiences, familiar with the folk tales on which the play was based, would not have found the ending lacking.

Some argue that Shakespeare lost interest in the character of Helena once she succeeded in securing Bertram, and he proceeded to a hasty closing scene. Others sense a difficult future ahead for Helena and Bertram because, even though he now acknowledges Helena as his wife, he has demonstrated no change of heart through his actions. Marjorie Garber, in her book *Shakespeare After All*, approves of the ending because of the careful way it was set up. The ending "is constructed like an elaborate mechanism and goes off with a bang in the powerful final scene." Furthermore, she states, that "whatever our estimation of the callow but promising Bertram and the astonishingly patient Helena, both the genre of fairy tale and the history of noble marriage suggest that ending well—at least onstage—may be the best medicine."

STYLE

New Comedy

In literature, "comedy" refers to a story with a happy ending and a "tragedy" is a story with a sad ending. The earliest comedies date from fifth century B.C.E. Greece, and that style is known as Old Comedy, which was known for lampooning famous people and events of the day. Beginning in 320 B.C.E., the style of comedy changed to reflect stock characters and situations. This style was dubbed New Comedy, and often featured a love story of a young couple as part of the plot. Some other famous New

Comedies include Dante's *Divine Comedy* and Geoffrey Chaucer's *The Canterbury Tales. All's Well That Ends Well* is also a New Comedy. When Bertram is confronted with evidence of his shenanigans and Helena outwits him in ful- filling his impossible demands, he undergoes a complete change of heart. Helena obtains her prize—Bertram. Diana is also saved from a mea- ger existence, the king's life is saved, the countess gains a daughter, and even Parolles repents. Everyone is better off than when the play began, and the solemn tone of mourning has been replaced by wedding bells and the good news of Helena's pregnancy. Parolles exhibits traits of both a *miles gloriosus* (boastful soldier) and a *servus callidus* (tricky slave), which are both stock characters of New Comedy. There are, however, plot elements responsible for the play's reputation as a problem play, which are those that run counter to the idea of comedy. These include the feeling of foreboding caused by Bertram's superficial acceptance of Helena, and the king's offer to Diana to choose a hus- band, which one suspects could create a whole new set of problems.

Double Entendre

A double entendre is a word or phrase that can be construed as having two meanings, due to an intentional ambiguity on the part of the author or speaker. Often, one of those meanings is ris- qué. Much of the humor in Shakespeare's plays comes from double entendres, and in *All's Well That Ends Well* the speech of Lavatch, the clown, and words of Parolles and others can be con- strued as double entendres. For example, when Helena asks Parolles for advice on how to retain her virginity, he replies that it is impossible: "Man, setting down before you, will undermine you and blow you up." To which Helena responds, "Bless our poor virginity from under- miners and blowers-up! Is there no military pol- icy how virgins might blow up men?" The humor in their exchange comes from the double mean- ing of the term "blow you up." Undoubtedly, Helena is clever enough to understand the sig- nificance of what she is saying to Parolles, and it represents her complexity as a character. She is a virtuous maiden, intent on retaining her virtue, yet she is not above engaging in a bit of ribald repartee with a man—one of low morals, at that. In another example, Lavatch tells Lafew the difference between his roles as a fool and a knave. He says he is "a fool, sir, at a woman's

Jamie Glover as Bertram and Judi Dench as The Countess of Rossillion at the Swan Theatre, Stratford-upon-Avon, England, 2003 (© Donald Cooper/Photostage. Reproduced by permission)

service, and a knave at a man's." When Lafew asks what the difference is, Lavatch responds, "I would cozen the man of his wife and do his service." In this case, the term "service" means he would take up the duties of being the wife's husband, including those of a sexual nature.

Aphorism

An aphorism is a concise and memorable phrase that lends itself to being quoted outside of its original context. "All's well that ends well" itself is an aphorism—one that was known to audien- ces at the time Shakespeare wrote his play. Though *All's Well That Ends Well* does not contain as many well-known aphorisms as some of his other plays, such as "To be, or not to be, that is the question" from *Hamlet* or "Out, out, damn spot" from *Macbeth*, it has its moments. In particular is Helena's declaration that "Our remedies oft in ourselves do lie, /

Which we ascribe to heaven." She means that when a person prays for the answer to a problem and it is solved, it is likely that the person solved the problem him or herself. God did not solve it for them. She uses this belief to pursue Bertram after he leaves for Paris; she knows that if she is ever to win his love it will be through her own actions, not simply by wishing or praying. Another aphorism is Parolles's declaration that "a young man married is a man that's marred," when he sympathizes with Bertram's plight of being married to Helena against his will. Diana's friend Mariana warns her against Bertram's advances, stating, "no legacy is so rich as honesty," meaning that the greatest thing she has going for herself is her virtue, and to lose it to Bertram would be tragic. All of these phrases can stand alone in meaning beyond the context of the play.

HISTORICAL CONTEXT

Literature in Shakespeare's Time

Shakespeare based much of *All's Well That Ends Well* on Giovanni Boccaccio's *Decameron*, a collection of one hundred novellas wrapped around a frame story. Boccaccio was a Florentine writer of the fourteenth century who wrote in the Italian vernacular, thereby making the *Decameron* popular among the middle class, as opposed to scholars who shunned anything not written in Latin. The *Decameron*, which means literally "ten days," is ostensibly the tale of ten people (seven women and three men), who are hiding out in the hills above the city of Florence during an outbreak of the Black Plague. Each day, they take turns telling stories in order to pass the time. Many of their stories are retellings of folk tales.

Boccaccio's *Decameron* influenced many writers, beginning with Geoffrey Chaucer, also a fourteenth-century writer, who adopted some of the Italian writer's ideas for *The Canterbury Tales*, which is commonly acknowledged as the first work of poetry written in English. *The Canterbury Tales* adopts a similar frame story; an assembled group of pilgrims takes turns telling each other stories on a sojourn from London to Canterbury.

Even if Shakespeare was not directly influenced by the *Decameron*, he almost certainly was familiar with *The Palace of Pleasure*, a work by

William Painter closely based on the *Decameron*. Painter's thirty-eighth story in the collection is about Giletta di Narbona, the daughter of a physician who cures the King of France. In return, she asks the king if she can marry Beltramo, the Count of Rossiglione. Though the king complies, the count escapes to Florence. Giletta follows him, seduces him against his knowledge, and becomes pregnant with twin boys. When the scheme is revealed, the count promptly apologizes and becomes a willfully faithful husband. In Shakespeare's telling, he added the characters of Parolles, the countess, and Lafew in order to give the story more depth.

Many critics have surmised that Shakespeare based the character of Helena on Christine de Pizan, an early-fifteenth-century writer who was the daughter of the famous Venetian physician and astronomer Tommaso di Benvenuto da Pizzano. De Pizan was the first widely known female writer, well-regarded, who exhibits many of the admirable traits with which Shakespeare endowed Helena. Her *Book of the City of Ladies* is widely regarded as a proto-feminist masterpiece.

Traditions of Marriage

In Shakespeare's time, marriages were usually arranged. A love match was unusual, and even more unusual was a woman choosing her prospective groom. Bertram's objection to marrying Helena is rooted in these traditions. Because he is a count, he would have expected to marry someone of a similar status, not a commoner with neither wealth nor property to her name. A man would base his opinion of his prospective wife on the extent of her dowry, or marriage portion, which would include any land, money, or other goods, such as jewelry, which would become the husband's property upon marriage (as would his wife). Helena had none of these, so Bertram considered her an inappropriate wife, regardless of her talents and personality.

As for the marriage ceremony, the king in *All's Well That Ends Well* dispenses with tradition, which would have necessitated the Crying of the Banns, a public declaration of the couple's intent to marry on three successive Sundays in their respective churches. This procedure allowed people time to voice objections to the marriage, for whatever reason. Exceptions to the Crying of the Banns were rare; ironically, Shakespeare himself was one of these exceptions, due to the fact that his prospective wife, Ann Hathaway, was already pregnant. As in *All's Well That Ends Well*, certainly the king had the power to conduct a wedding ceremony without a prior Crying of the Banns.

Other traditions alluded to in the play include the expectation that the bride be a virgin. The bed-trick did indeed save Diana from ruining her life. Additionally, an exchange of rings was not uncommon, but it was not the norm. When Bertram states that Helena would never wear his ring, this would have been widely understood to mean that his ring on her finger would symbolize his acceptance of their union. Likewise, when Helena tricks Bertram into wearing her ring (the one the king gave her), she has succeeded in claiming him as would a bride who presented her groom with a wedding ring.

Medicine and Healing

In Shakespeare's time, medicine was little more than trial and error mixed with a great deal of superstition. Little was known about proven treatments, and disease and germs were not understood. Sanitation and hygiene, even among the upper classes, was rudimentary at best. Streets were filled with garbage and raw sewage, which spilled over into the rivers and lakes. Rats and vermin abounded, and no one made the connection between these conditions and the sicknesses that killed people. Typhoid, syphilis, influenza, and plague exacted a toll on life expectancy, as did poor nutrition, which led to life-threatening anemia and dysentery. Many upper-class women covered their faces with white make-up, which contained high amounts of lead. The make-up poisoned, and even killed, many of them.

Because these health dangers were not understood, the work of physicians often included astrology. Astrologers and doctors, such as Tommaso de Benvenuto da Pizzano (Shakespeare's possible model for Helena's father, Gerard de Narbon), often resorted to bleeding people when they became ill in an effort to cleanse their bodies from bad humors, or bodily fluids.

Physicians in Shakespeare's day wore unusual outfits, complete with a long black cloak, leather gloves, leather boots, a pointed hood, and a mask with a long, pointed beak, which was filled with bergamot oil. Though the outfit may have been rooted in superstition, it probably did protect doctors, simply because it provided a barrier against the germs and bugs that would have covered their patients. Their odd appearance, however, often inspired dread in townspeople, who came to regard physicians with wariness. Anyway, only the very wealthy—mainly the nobles—would have been able to afford treatment by a doctor. Other segments of the population might be treated by a barber, who, in addition to cutting hair, also pulled teeth and bled patients.

The ailment the King of France suffers from in *All's Well That Ends Well*, fistula, which is an abscess that creates an opening between two organs, would not have been well understood at the time, and it is true that a physician may have told those afflicted with the condition that there was nothing that could be done. How Helena cures the king so quickly and completely is inexplicable, certainly in terms of medical knowledge either then or now, and her healing powers remain one of the story's most implausible folk-tale elements.

Pilgrimages

After she heals the king and is wed to Bertram, Helena is ordered back to Rossillion. Distraught by Bertram's letter stating he will never return home as long as she is there, she departs on a pilgrimage to the burial site of Saint Jacques le Grande. Also known as the Way of St. James, the pilgrimage leads travelers to the Cathedral of Santiago in northwest Spain, the burial site of the Apostle James, St. James the Greater, a follower of Jesus Christ and the brother of the Apostle John. The purpose of the pilgrimage was to have the pilgrim's greatest sins forgiven; the only other two pilgrimages that could do the same thing were to Rome and Jerusalem. There were several popular routes pilgrims could take to the shrine, each passing through other towns and stopping at notable locations along the way. A majority of those who undertook the trip were French, and the Way includes many stops in France before continuing on to Spain. The Cathedral of Santiago is still a popular pilgrimage site in the twenty-first century, and priests hold weekly services to welcome those who have made the trip, often on foot or bicycle.

In Shakespeare's time, this pilgrimage was still popular but considered somewhat dangerous because of the violence resulting from the Protestant Reformation. Audiences would have been familiar with the journey and accepted

COMPARE
&
CONTRAST

- **1600:** Rossillion (Rousillon in French) is a Spanish territory, formerly part of the Kingdom of Majorca. It is conquered by Louis XIII in 1642 and is ceded to France by the Treaty of the Pyrenees in 1659.

  Today: Rousillon is a thriving region in France that produces vast quantities of wine, particularly red *vin ordinaire*. The area and its capital city, Perpignan, is a major tourist region.

- **1600:** Doctors can do little to cure fistula, a medical ailment in which two organs become connected via the abnormal development of an abscess or passageway. Typical treatment may include bleeding with leeches.

  Today: Treatment for fistula includes a surgical procedure known as a fistulotomy, followed by antibiotics. Doctors prevent recurrence of the condition by treating

other conditions that sometimes cause fistula, such as Crohn's disease and colitis.

- **1600:** Christians from around Europe, but particularly from France, undertake the pilgrimage known as the Way of St. James, which leads them to the Cathedral of Santiago in the north of Spain. It is an arduous journey undertaken on foot or by horse, and may take many months. Hostels are located along the way to provide accommodations for the travelers. The pilgrimage was sometimes undertaken as penance for a grave crime.

  Today: Thousands of pilgrims travel on foot or by bike each year to the Cathedral of Santiago along the pilgrimage route, which was named a UNESCO World Heritage Site in 1993. Pilgrims receive an official pass that allows them to stay in hostels at reduced rates along the way.

Helena's reasons for undertaking it. However, given that Helena leaves for the trip from Rossillion, which borders Spain, how she ends up in Florence, which is hundreds of miles in the opposite direction from the shrine, is never explained. The fact that she is traveling alone is also puzzling.

CRITICAL OVERVIEW

Critical interpretation of *All's Well That Ends Well* often hinges on whether the critic believes the play lives up to its title. The widespread belief that it does not has led to its reputation as a problem play, or rather, a comedy with strings attached. Shakespeare, who was by all accounts an astute observer of the human condition, seems not to have invested the lead characters of Bertram and Helena with enough depth to

understand the error of their ways, or permitted them to have meaningful moments of enlightenment that would bring about the necessary changes. For centuries, critics have been vexed by Bertram's about-face in the last scene, when he suddenly realizes his foolishness and agrees to be Helena's faithful husband and the father of their child. At the very least, critics have detected a bit of irony in the title; even Shakespeare had to know that these characters were not about to live happily ever after. As they settled into their marriage, would the very pro-active Helena have been satisfied to revert to the feminine ideal of a passive wife? And would Bertram truly be able to put his days as a scoundrel behind him and love a woman who previously repulsed him? How can their relationship succeed, given that it is based upon the deception of the bed-trick? All of these questions pose problems for critics. Some find ways to reconcile them with Shakespeare's intentions, and others cannot. For them, *All's Well*

That Ends Well is one of Shakespeare's sloppier plays, and therefore unsuccessful. As William Witherle Lawrence writes in *Shakespeare's Problem Comedies*, "critical explanations have nowhere shown wider divergence than in regard to this play, nor have the points at issue ever been more sharply marked."

The play has been praised for several factors, however, including the characterization of the Countess of Rossillion, one of Shakespeare's more well-rounded older females. In fact, most of the older characters in the play exhibit good judgment and work hard at guiding the younger generation into accepting their roles and responsibilities. Russell Fraser, in his introduction to *All's Well That Ends Well*, published in the New Cambridge Shakespeare series, goes so far as to say "*All's Well That Ends Well* is a great play whose time has come round." In support of this idea, he writes that,

> [Shakespeare's] characters may change for the better or worse, and things beginning at the worst may turn upwards in the course of the play. But no character puts off altogether what he was at first, and if the play begins in darkness, the darkness is never altogether dispelled. Characters in *All's Well* are left open to mortality, and in the world they inhabit the best is behind. This feeling, conveyed in the first scene of the play, is borne out in the ending.

In a similar manner, Eileen Z. Cohen, writing in *Philological Quarterly*, defends Shakespeare's use of the bed-trick as a narrative device and disagrees with those who find it unbecoming of Helena. "[Shakespeare] requires us to believe that virtuous maidens can initiate and participate in the bed-trick. He insists that it saves lives and nurtures marriage, that it leads the duped men out of ignorance and toward understanding, and that the women who orchestrate it end with a clearer image of themselves."

Most critics also approve of the way Shakespeare fleshed out Boccaccio's original story, "Giletta of Narbonne," by adding the subplot of Parolles, in which the kidnapping trick serves as a parallel to the bed-trick and exposes his treasonous behavior to Bertram. In addition to fulfilling the New Comedy roles of the *miles gloriosus* and the *servus callidus*, Parolles, in the scene of his unmasking, serves as the fulcrum of the play, since the other main event—the bed-trick itself—takes place off stage. According to R. J. Schork, writing in *Philological Quarterly*, "The several New Comedic roles enacted by Parolles in *All's Well That Ends Well* are proof of Shakespeare's versatility and ingenuity in blending New Comedic motifs into a plot lifted from Boccaccio. All the characters in the play … could be matched to analogous characters in Roman comedy; none of them, however, plays the stock role straight." Others attribute the play's weaknesses to its folk-tale elements, which almost by definition render it immune to criticism based on lack of character development. According to Lawrence, both the Healing of the King and the Fulfillment of the Tasks are well-known folk-tale conventions that turn up in many cultures, including India, Norway, and Turkey, and which would have influenced Boccaccio. Many of these tales also "exalt the cleverness and devotion of the woman," Lawrence writes in *Shakespeare's Problem Comedies*, "the wits of the wife are more than a match for those of the husband, and her purpose is a happy reunion with him."

No matter what the play's virtues, critics eventually return to its problems. Irish poet W. B. Yeats, according to *Spectator* theater critic Patrick Carnegy, "saw Helena as one of Shakespeare's 'glorious women who select dreadful or empty men.'" And Samuel Johnson, says Carnegy, wrote off Bertram "as a bad lot whose fate was, in a devastating phrase, to be 'dismissed to happiness.'" However, Charles Isherwood, reviewing a modern production of the play for the *New York Times*, writes that Bertram is "an adolescent forced before his time into manhood, and is only obeying the impulses of his young blood when he flees the embrace of his wiser new wife." In another *New York Times* review of the play, Alvin Klein notes that "most contemporary directors have transposed into the twentieth century the play's very considerable obstacles, which have nothing to do with time, but with the tediousness, thinness and inherent unpleasantness of a timelessly ineffectual tale." Ultimately, according to Maurice Charney in *All of Shakespeare*, a major problem with the play is the bed-trick itself: "We are not comfortable with the fiction of substituting one woman for another, as if in bed all women were alike." Additionally, in regard to Helena's miracle cure for the king, Charney wonders "if Helena does indeed have magical powers, why does she need to go to so much trouble to fulfill her tasks?"

In the end, Helena's feminist take on creating her own reality in a patriarchal world has proven attractive enough for some to resurrect the play from its near-forgotten status of previous centuries. Modern-day directors have taken pains to show why she would be attracted to Bertram, sometimes successfully and other times less so. The play's other themes—of generational differences, class distinctions—have proven sturdy enough to sustain the play through its more questionable moments. It may remain forever a problem play, but critics have shown that it contains enough nuance, humor, and truth to remain a relevant part of Shakespeare's canon. Poet John Berryman, in his essay "Pathos and Dream" quoted in *Berryman's Shakespeare*, notes that Shakespeare wrote four plays that are deemed "failures": *The Two Gentlemen of Verona, King John, Timon of Athens*, and *All's Well That Ends Well*. "The reasons for his failure in each case were different," Berryman says, "but at least he was always capable of failure, and it is pleasant to know this."

CRITICISM

Mary Free

In this brief excerpt, Free examines how All's Well That Ends Well *is unlike Shakespeare's other comedies through its central coupling (marriage) of Helena and Bertram. The play has only this one pairing, whereas Shakespeare's other comedies have many couples. Helena and Bertram share only five scenes together, during which they do not always engage each other in dialogue. There is no battle of wit and will between them. Helena's role "outside" her social sphere further increases the comic distance, and there is scant "lightness" or "playfulness" in the play.*

... Marriage is a central element in the construct of Renaissance comedy. In the Shakespearean canon, a number of the comedies include marriages, placing them (or implying that they impend) close to or at the plays' ends as a reaffirmation, restoration and promise for the continuation of society. Other comedies deal with married women as in *The Comedy of Errors* and *The Merry Wives of Windsor*; or they move the marriage forward, thus foregrounding it and making it precipitate further action in the main plot as in *The Taming of the Shrew* and *Much Ado about Nothing*. What makes *All's Well That Ends Well*'s foregrounded marriage unique is the undeniable fact that Bertram does not want

> WHAT MAKES *ALL'S WELL THAT ENDS WELL*'S FOREGROUNDED MARRIAGE UNIQUE IS THE UNDENIABLE FACT THAT BERTRAM DOES NOT WANT HELENA REGARDLESS OF HOW MUCH SHE WANTS HIM OR HOW MUCH THE MEMBERS OF THE NOBILITY—MOST NOTABLY THE KING, THE COUNTESS, AND LAFEW— WANT HIM TO WANT HER."

Helena regardless of how much she wants him or how much the members of the nobility—most notably the King, the Countess, and Lafew— want him to want her. Further, in its institution, its mixing of high personages with low, and the alliances between social groups, the foregrounded marriage in *All's Well That Ends Well* subverts the comic by creating discomfiting inversions in the play's social spheres. While the concept of marriage as regenerative force via Helana's pregnancy obtains in principle at the end, when the "broken nuptial" comes together, no wonder we, along with the King in the epilogue, feel little if any delight: things but "seem" well; we have no guarantees. We cannot be certain even there that Bertram truly wants her.

A distinction that contributes to my thesis is that *All's Well That Ends Well* stands apart from the Shakespearean comedic mainstream in that Helena and Bertram, however estranged their relationship, remain the single couple in the play. Elsewhere Shakespeare provides us with sets of couples: twins who marry and woo in *The Comedy of Errors* and *Twelfth Night*, two men in pursuit of one woman in *The Two Gentlemen of Verona* and *A Midsummer Night's Dream*, two married women who plot to outwit one man and teach another a lesson in *The Merry Wives of Windsor*, Rosalind and Celia with their loves in *As You Like It*, and a triad of lovers in *The Merchant of Venice*. Even *Measure for Measure*, the play most often closely linked to *All's Well That Ends Well*, provides us pairings. *All's Well That Ends Well* gives us two windows, a virgin, and a wife in name only. While all these pairings deal with power in

Guy Henry as Parolles and Claudie Blakley as Helena at the Swan Theatre, Stratford-upon-Avon, England, 2003 (© Donald Cooper/Photostage. Reproduced by permission)

relationships, they do not constitute the exact marked hierarchies of power that *All's Well That Ends Well* presents to us.

The foregrounded marriage in *All's Well That Ends Well* differs from those in *The Taming of the Shrew* and *Much Ado about Nothing* in origination and ordination. While Kate in *The Taming of the Shrew* has no more choice than does Bertram about whom each marries (Baptista and Petruchio merely strike a bargain as do the King and Helena), Petruchio and Kate as a pair remain this play's focal point. We observe the battle of wit and will between them, and the entire fourth act centers on them. Whether we grant or disallow the concept of mutuality of consent, whether the production relies on Zefferellian horseplay or a more restrained production concept, *The Taming of the Shrew* provokes laughter—the *sine qua non*

of the comic—because of the physical and verbal interaction between the principal characters. The same holds true for *Much Ado about Nothing*. Like Kate and Petruchio, Beatrice and Benedick command our attention, their wit and wordplay amuse and distract us, and they are more interesting to us than the play's other couple Claudio and Hero. Even in that relationship, the comedy of *Much Ado about Nothing* remains more comic than does *All's Well That Ends Well*. Claudio and Hero agree to marry, an important distinction between their relationship and that of Helena and Bertram. The distasteful circumstances of the broken nuptial notwithstanding, the separation between Claudio and Hero fails to disrupt wholly the play's overall comic spirit for two reasons: first, we know Dogberry and the Watch hold the key to reconciliation; second, as well as more important, the comic Beatrice and Benedick remain our primary focal point.

Helena and Bertram appear on stage together in but five scenes. Their exchanges generally indicate the dynamic of power in their relationship as Helena oozes subservience to her lord and master, while Bertram, until the final scene, plays his superiority, both of class and gender, for all it's worth. In three scenes where they appear together, they speak to or about one another but engage in no dialogue. In 1.1 Bertram in one and a half lines commands that Helena, "Be comfortable to my mother, your mistress, / And make much of her" (76–77). In 2.3 she subserviently offers herself to him in two and a half lines:

> I dare not say I take you, but I give
> Me and my service, ever whilst I live,
> Into your guiding power
> (2.3.102–104)

The remainder of this scene has them each talking to the King, but not to one another. In a third scene (3.5), Helena merely views Bertram from a distance as the army passes and asks about him. Only two scenes have them exchanging dialogue. In 2.5, comprising thirty-five lines, Bertram, without having consummated the marriage and refusing Helena's modest request for a departing kiss, dismisses his bride by sending her back to Rossillion. His language is primarily in the command form, hers acquiescent. She comes "as [she] was commanded from [him]" (2.5.54). She declares herself Bertram's "most obedient servant" in a scene that allows for no possible irony (2.5.72). Even when she musters the courage to hint at a parting kiss, she hesitates and stumbles as a young woman very much in love and unsure of herself. In 5.3, the reconciliation, they exchange two lines each, and arguably Bertram's "If she, my liege, can make me know this clearly / I'll love her dearly, ever, ever dearly" is addressed more to the King than to Helena. These two encounters comprise but thirty-nine lines all told.

All's Well That Ends Well remains a comedy in structure, yet Helena's agency in the enforced marriage, as well as the subsequent separation and ploys, distances us from the comic. Other elements distance us as well. When the Countess learns that Helena loves Bertram, we have the perfect occasion for a traditional blocking figure, but no. The Countess not only enjoys, but also encourages Helena in her aspirations. No witty bantering about sex, love, fidelity in wedlock—that which might create the comic within the matrix of comedy—takes place between Helena and Bertram, the play's only couple. Certainly some comic playfulness occurs within the play. No one will deny its presence in the virginity dialogue between Helena and Parolles, nor in the choosing scene as Helena walks from budding youth to budding youth before "giving" herself to Bertram, nor in Parolles's humiliation. Nevertheless, what lightness exists remains apart from the focal couple. Of added significance is how little of the playfulness associated with earlier comedies takes place among the women. Beyond the Countess' hope for Helena's love, her brief acknowledgement of her own past, and her teasing in the "I say I am your mother" dialogue (1.3), women's dialogue as they assess man's fecklessness has a more brittle edge than do similar assessments given in the earlier comedies.

Helena's actions set her apart from her Shakespearean sisters. Other independently-acting heroines—Viola, Rosalind, Portia—play at their love-games and are, in some cases, willing to leave Time to fadge things out. They also employ masculine disguise to effect the amount of control or empowerment they enjoy. Helena does what she does without disguise. In some respects Helena and Portia are the most closely akin. Portia is willing to comply with her father's will; Helena is willing to submit herself to Bertram's. Both work purposefully to achieve their goals. However close that kinship, differences obtain. Allies from the play's outset, Portia

and Nerissa plot to test true love's faith; Helena, who must create her allies, has yet to gain mere acceptance as wife. To achieve her goals, she acts with what Western culture sees as male prerogatives. As A. P. Riemer has said, she acts with a "male purposefulness" (Riemer 1975–76, 54). In order for her to succeed undisguised, she must perform these actions in a way that the empowering male structure (i.e., the King and Lafew as members of the *ancien régime*) fails to recognize as violating sex or class differences.

In *All's Well That Ends Well* Helena follows Bertram to Paris. There she originates the marriage by striking a bargain with the King and curing him. Unlike the other pairings and marriages in the comedies, however, no tacit nor overt mutuality exists between this nuptial pair. Here the King must ordain an enforced marriage of his ward Bertram to comply with the terms of the bargain. Such ordination violates the usual circumstances that we find in the festive comedies. In those comedies, ordination, directed against a woman, may initiate the flight from authority into the saturnalian world of comic license.

Bertram's response to the King's command is like that of Silvia or Hermia: forced into marriage ordained against his will, a marriage that is originated by a spouse who is not loved, he runs away, as do the heroines. Bertram's running away to Florence offers a different kind of escape from that of the heroines. Not only is his escape to a city but to one associated with sexual licentiousness. The King himself warns his courtiers against "Those girls of Italy." When Helena discovers Bertram in Florence, she entraps him by means of the bed trick, which inverts predicated male-female sex roles just as "girl gets boy" inverts what we would recognize as the clichéd phrasing. Her action substitutes the legal for the licentious. Helena entraps Bertram a second time as well in 5.3 by her further employment of Diana before the King. Even the King becomes confused as Helena employs her skills. What allows everyone to escape prison is Helena's ability to use the language of empowerment without disturbing the status quo. . . .

Source: Mary Free, "*All's Well That Ends Well* as Noncomic Comedy," in *Acting Funny: Comic Theory and Practice in Shakespeare's Plays*, edited by Frances Teague, Fairleigh Dickinson University Press, 1994, pp. 41–45.

Eileen Z. Cohen

In the following excerpt, Cohen examines how Helena and Isabella in, respectively, All's Well That Ends Well *and* Measure for Measure, *use the bed-trick as a disguise, and in doing so, these characters "reverse traditional female behavior, invert stereotypes, and turn apparent lechery into the service of marriage."*

Western literature abounds in characters who have arranged bed-tricks—from Lot's daughters to Iseult, and by the seventeenth century the bed-substitution was a commonplace convention of English drama. Yet it is Shakespeare's use of the device in *All's Well That Ends Well* and *Measure for Measure* that disturbs us, doubtless because of the women who perpetrate it, Helena, a virgin-bride, and Isabella, a would-be nun. We seem unwilling to accept that Shakespeare deliberately intends to disrupt our sensibilities. Scholars have told us that we must accommodate ourselves to conventions or fairy tale traditions that are outmoded, or they call these heroines sluts, or saints and tell us to forget about the bed substitutions.

Shakespeare, however, does none of these. Instead, he requires us to believe that virtuous maidens can initiate and participate in the bed-trick. He insists that it saves lives and nurtures marriage, that it leads the duped men out of ignorance and toward understanding, and that the women who orchestrate it end with a clearer image of themselves. Thus, we have a simple theatrical device that effects complex response in the characters and in us, the audience. The convention "deconventionalizes" and makes the world of each play and the characters therein more real. Paradoxically, a device associated with lust abets love and marriage; it utilizes illusion and deception to bring perception and understanding. In so doing, it strips away stock responses to the women who design the deception. Shakespeare apparently does not associate virtue in women with blindness or passivity—or even predictability. He will not allow the audience to generalize about female virtue. Given popular sixteenth-century attitudes towards women, Helena and Isabella must have been as disturbing to their original audience as they have been to subsequent ones, and the bed-trick, because of its ultimate affirmation of the complexity of virtue, just as jarring.

In the sixteenth and seventeenth centuries, the controversy concerning women was part of

> THE BED-TRICK CAN BE THOUGHT OF AS A KIND OF DISGUISE SINCE THE FEMALE LOVER IS DISGUISED BY DARKNESS AND SILENCE FROM THE MALE LOVER. IN THAT SENSE IT IS NO MORE OR LESS DECEPTIVE THAN DISGUISE."

the literary and social experience of the middle and upper classes of society. It surfaced in the 1540s and again at the beginning of James I's reign, with reprintings of various pieces throughout these decades. What emerges from the debate, whether the writer was a critic or a defender of women, is that he or she rarely considers women except in the most general ways. Devil or angel, she is a stereotype. A flurry of popular pamphlets was precipitated by the publication of *Schole House of Women*, which went through four editions between 1541–1570, and is alluded to in several other pamphlets. Here, women are "loud and sour" (Aiii), gossipy (Aiv), adulterous (Bii), frail, crooked, crabbed, lewd (Cii), and weak and feeble in body (Cii). A female's function, because she is made of man's rib, "in every nede / Shulde be helpe to the man, in word and dede" (Biii). There is a remedy for each of man's afflictions, except gout and marriage ([London: John Kyng, 1560], Biii).

Responses to this attack abound. Readers were assured that woman was not created out of dog bones, but from man—the crown of creation. There have been many good women, a fact to which the Bible, the classics, and their very own Queen attest. Anthony Gibson, in addition to cataloguing great women, ebulliently lists their virtues: Women are beautiful and their voices are soft (20). Since they are by nature inclined to sadness, they are wiser than men (21), and more charitable (30). Philip Stubbes, too, had a good word to say for virtuous women—or rather, a virtuous woman, in a eulogy to his dead wife, *A Christal Glasse for Christian Women* (London: R. Ihones, 1592). He describes her as a perfect pattern for virtue: modest, courteous, gentle, and zealous for truth. (A2). "If she saw her husband merry, then she was merry: if he were sad, she was sad: if he were heavy or passionate, she would endeavor to make him glad: if he were angry, she would quickly please him so wifely she demeaned herselfe towards him" (A3). In both Stubbes and Gibson, the burden of virtue is as heavy as that of vice.

Very few of the writers in this controversy approach women as other than very good or very bad. Perhaps the most aggressive of those who do blur the stereotypic perceptions of both men and women is the author of *Jane Anger Her Protection for Women* (London: Richard Jones, 1589). "She" is less rigid than most of her contemporaries with regard to male and female characteristics. "Jane Anger" lowers the barriers between the sexes in that she does not say that women are necessarily more or less virtuous than men. Rather, she equalizes the sexes by suggesting that women pay men in just coin. "Deceitful men with guile must be repaid ..." (B2). Woman's greatest fault is that she is too credulous (B2). Though "Jane Anger" still deals in stereotypes, she perceives the weaknesses and strengths of men and women in different ways from most of her contemporaries. She condemns men for failing to see women in terms of these strengths, "We being wel formed, are by them fouly deformed" (B3).

Even though many of these pieces are satiric and were probably written because there was a ready market for them, rather than out of sincere beliefs, their popularity indicates an interest in the nature of women and an insistence that their virtues were different from those of men. From these pages and more, there emerges an ideal woman in whom the virtues were chastity, patience, piety, humility, obedience, constancy, temperance, kindness, and fortitude—all passive characteristics. Even her supporters urged her to suppress assertiveness. The ideal male virtues were justice, courtesy, liberality, and courage. For a man the ideal was self-expansion and realization of self; for a woman, self-abnegation and passivity. For a man chastity was unimportant; for a woman it was everything. Her honor and reputation were defined in terms of it. The educator Vives frankly states, "As for a woman [she] hath no charge to se to, but her honestie and chastitie."

Helena and Isabella offer a marked contrast to many of the prevailing presumptions about women that the popular literature manifests, and in some ways a sharp difference from the portrayals of Rosalind and Viola, both in earlier plays. If art does hold a mirror up to nature, then Shakespeare's drama reflects, refracts, and refocuses the ideas of his time. In *Twelfth Night* and *As You Like It*, the remover of affectation from the other characters is a woman, who for much of the play is disguised as a man. Necessarily, disguise was inherent in the role even before the play began since the woman was played by a male actor. But now the deception is double because we have a male actor, dressed as a woman, disguised as a man, and in the case of Rosalind, sometimes pretending to be a woman. Disguise, instead of conveying ambiguity, gives the audience distance from the characters, whose dialogue is now ironic and conveys double meanings. Our response thus becomes intellectual rather than emotional, as perhaps it had been when we were faced with Rosalind's exile and Viola's grief—before they donned male clothing. In these comedies disguise thus clarifies and helps to confirm the point of view of the play.

However, in *All's Well* and *Measure for Measure* Shakespeare alters this presentation of illusion. Rather than wearing male clothing, Helena and Isabella assume another form of disguise, the bed-trick. Isabella perpetuates the disguise because she believes in the legality of Marianna's plight-troth and Helena because she is a married woman. Among Shakespeare's most interesting and courageous characters, they reverse traditional female behavior, invert stereotypes, and turn apparent lechery into the service of marriage. The ultimate irony, or secret hidden behind illusion, is that resourceful, autonomous women shore up marriage. Helena and Isabella show why they force us to redefine virtue, rather than simply lowering our opinion of them. They encourage the audience to reevaluate virtue, chastity, honesty, and honor in the context of character development. Stock responses to these characters, merely to like or dislike them, will not do because their subtlety demands that the audience respond with subtlety as well.

The bed-trick can be thought of as a kind of disguise since the female lover is disguised by darkness and silence from the male lover. In that sense it is no more or less deceptive than disguise. Like Rosalind and Viola, Helena and Isabella know who they are—a wife and novice, respectively; the characters whom they trick do not see them as they see themselves. One might here use the defense of "Jane Anger" that deceitful men should be repaid in kind, that to men for whom all women are the same in the dark, deception is exactly what they deserve. The bed-trick is, however, far more significant and more "theatrical" than that. Disguise is obviously conventional, but the bed-trick is even more unrealistic if we concede that disguise—that is, role playing and putting on uncharacteristic clothing—is the reality of actors and plays. The bed-trick serves, in addition to its obvious plot function, as the inherent symbol of the play, comparable to Hermione's statue coming to life. Life, death, fertility, and renewal cannot easily be portrayed realistically on the stage. Bertram and Angelo do not get what they deserve. In fact, they get far better, and the bed-trick provides the opportunity to effect their union with feeling and harmony. Lust may have driven them to their ignorance of the women with them, but these women in their love both demand recognition.

Ironically, as the disguise device that is embodied in the bed-trick becomes more theatrical, the plays in which the bed-trick appears are more realistic than the earlier comedies in which the disguise is of a more conventional nature. Here, we have sickbeds, barracks, courtrooms, and cities instead of pastoral forests and imaginary seacoasts. The heroines, themselves, are less mannered and witty; instead they have the drive and zeal of conviction. Perhaps Shakespeare is suggesting in these later comedies that the male protagonists, who are also not typical and indeed are very unlikely heroes, make obvious disguise impossible. Their corruption ought to be confronted directly. Male disguise establishes Viola and Rosalind as the friends of Orsino and Orlando, and it momentarily submerges their feminine identity. Bertram and Angelo cannot be treated in the same way. For Isabella and Helena to put on male clothing is to create a visual similarity between them and their antagonists. Such disguise would imply amicable relationships. Perhaps, too, Shakespeare is suggesting that in ethical confrontations such as these, one cannot stare down ruthlessness in someone else's clothes. One must take a stand in one's own person. Isabella and Helena must simultaneously be themselves and more daringly theatrical in order to reinforce the differences between them and the men they confront. The bed-trick affirms the feminine sexuality of these women and, in part, their identities. Helena must be recognized as wife and consummate her marriage, and Isabella must be recognized as virgin

and not consummate the relationship with Angelo. They will also ensure that the men will honor their vows as a result.

With this peculiar merging of the realistic and the theatrical, Shakespeare redefines societal expectations of female virtues. Role playing, identity, and integrity of self are examined through the characters involved in this obviously sexual disguise, in plays that are about life and death, marriage, fertility, and renewal—all of which are tied together by the image of the bed.

Both Helena and Isabella are associated with and ultimately effect recovery and generosity in their respective plays. The outcome of their machination is marriage. Thus the stereotypic female roles—nurturing and insuring generation—are at the heart of the plays. However, the rare, unstereotypic personalities of these women and the use of the bed-trick—a seemingly adulterous theatrical device, establishes them as unconventional. The bed-trick, with its secrecy, silence, and deceit, is the device that strips away illusion and ignorance, and confirms truth and understanding. It uses carnal knowledge to effect compassion and knowledge of the spirit. Thus, the use of the bed-trick to beget marriage and the miracle of loving confirms what is unique in these women.

Both the stereotype of nurturer and the more complex and realistic portrait of a passionate-virtuous woman are established very early in *All's Well*. A litany of family designations begins this plays as the Countess says, "delivering my son from me, I bury a second husband" (1.1.1–2), thus initiating the rhythm of family, generation and death—in short, all of life. In the ensuing exchange between her and Lefew, family designations recur, *father, child, husband*, as they will in act 1, scene 2, when the King greets Bertram, and again in act 1, scene 3, when the Countess and Helena have their exchange between *mother* and *daughter*. Also in act 1, scene 1, Helena and Parolles discuss virginity. Though chaste, Helena does indicate that virgins do fall in love and do passionately feel desire.

The stereotyping and unstereotyping of Helena is further established in her two "miracles." She takes her legacy from her father to the court to heal the King and her love to Bertram's bed to give him the blessings of life. She does not perform a miracle in either case unless the human capacities to cure and to love are miracles. If the healing and loving are wondrous, then the bed-*trick* is a misnomer and is the bed-*miracle*, instead, just as the King's recovery apparently is. Miracle or not, loving sets people apart from the rest of the natural world, and both the King and Bertram benefit from Helena's precipitation of event. Indeed, Helena anticipates the similarities between her two *miracles*, both occurring in bed as they do. She acknowledges her daring in her venture to heal the King and tells him that should she fail she will feel the "Tax of impudence, / A strumpet's boldness, a devulged shame, / Traduc'd by odious ballads; my maiden's name / Sear'd otherwise" (2.1.169–172). In short, her reputation will be destroyed. Like her discussion about virginity with Parolles and her asking for a husband in payment for curing the King, this speech reveals Helena's many facets, not the least of them being her vulnerabilty. She acknowledges the sexuality of love and marriage; indeed, she welcomes it. She also acknowledges that there are risks of failure, suffering, and public disgrace in acts of daring. There are hazards in shaping destiny.

Helena later decides to make her pilgrimage to save her husband from the dangers of war by encouraging him with her absence to come home. This decision, made from love, will lead to resolution of events by the bed-trick. Helena's motive for leaving Rousillion is quite different from Giletta's in *The Palace of Pleasure*, where the latter planned to seek and bed her husband from the outset of her journey. In *All's Well*, as in the variation from the source in *Measure for Measure*, Shakespeare gives greater complexity to his character. Indeed, fate seems to approve of Helena's love and generosity for it introduces her to the Widow and Diana, the means to love Bertram. Had ambition been her motive for marriage, she would not have denied herself the comforts of her new station in life. At Rousillion she has the name of wife without the excess baggage of a petulant boy-husband.

However, she cares about Bertram's well-being and off she goes. She ruefully describes herself to Diana and the Widow as being "too mean / To have her name repeated; all her deserving / Is a reserved honesty, and that / I have not heard examin'd" (3.5.60–63). As with Parolles in act 1, scene 1, her virginity is the topic of discussion, but now the stakes are quite different. Then the question was how a modest maid might pursue the man she loved; now virginity should no longer be the normal condition of her life. As before when she declined modesty in favor of Bertram, she is aware of the ambiguities of what she is about to do. She acknowledges that her plan may be misunderstood and must be defended, "which, if it speed, / Is wicked meaning in a lawful deed, / And lawful meaning in a lawful act / Where both not sin, and yet a sinful fact" (3.7.44–47). With it all, she will save Bertram from adultery and give him love. . . .

The men whom Helena and Isabella confront expect stereotypic replies from them; Bertram and Angelo judge by appearances and are taken in by the bed-trick while it asserts complexity and reality over superficiality and mere appearances. George Bernard Shaw described Bertram as a very ordinary young man with "unimaginative prejudices and selfish conventionality." Bertram certainly seems to embody some of the attitudes toward women that the sixteenth century expressed. He expects that Helena will passively accept the role of virgin-wife which he assigns to her and that his superior intelligence will defeat her. For him women are wives to be rejected, or wenches to be seduced. When Diana defends her honor and equates her chastity with his aristocratic legacy, he is so enmeshed in his lust that he gives away the symbol of that legacy. Want of feeling marks his behavior throughout, culminating in his description of his night's work. He has "buried a wife, mourn'd for her, writ to my lady mother I am returning, entertain'd my convoy, and between these main parcels of dispatch effected many nicer needs; the last was the greatest, but that I have not ended yet" (4.3.85–89). The last is the liaison with Diana-Helena.

Bertram will not accept his good fortune, either in marrying Helena or in the contingent good will of the king. He sees her not as herself, but as his "father's charge / A poor physician's daughter" (2.3.114–115). The King, recognizing her virtues, in gratitude defines honor in terms of deeds, not heritage. "Honours thrive / When rather from our acts we them derive / Than our foregoers" (2.3.135–37). He makes a distinction that the myopic Bertram cannot see, "Virtue and she / Is her own dower; honour and wealth from me" (2.3.143–44). Bertram rejects her and goes off to be a soldier, to be brave, and to wench. Thus, he even makes a stereotype of himself. Parolles delivers his lord's message in conventional courtly love language—serious business has called Bertram away from his "rite of love" (2.4.39). Bertram later smugly declares, "I have wedded her, not bedded her, and sworn to make the 'not' eternal" (3.2.20–1). He is too arrogant to realize that his decision may not be Helena's, and he anticipates that she will do as she is told. Lavatch had sung, "marriage comes by destiny" (1.3.60). Surely the action of this play denies that platitude. It comes to Helena in name and in actuality through her own actions. Bertram will not bed her; so she will bed him.

As the bed-trick is being planned, so is the drum-trick. Both Parolles and Bertram will be in the dark, literally and metaphorically. Neither will know that his "friends" are beside him. One will speak and hear nothing and the other will be blindfolded and hear foreign sounds. By agreeing to the strictures of darkness and silence, Bertram acknowledges his lust. Love seeks and knows the differences between people; lust makes them all the same. Ultimately, each will reveal his worst when caught. It is Parolles who says, "Yet who would have suspected an ambush where I was taken?" (4.3.291–92). Bertram could as well have said the same thing.

When Bertram makes his assignation with Diana, his language is once again that of the highly conventional, literary, courtly tradition. He will do "all rights of service" (4,2.17); Diana is "holy-cruel" (4.2.33); and he suffers from "sick desires" which only her acquiescence will cure (4.2.35–36) He vows "for ever" (4.2.16). The darkness then disguises Helena from Bertram, but he also does not know himself, so caught up is he in the roles of lover and warrior. The bed-trick will open him up to feeling and an understanding of his own vulnerability.

Helena, through her active assertion of first, her role as physician, and then her role as wife, acts as restorative for Bertram and will perhaps enable him to cultivate the kinds of feelings that do heal and comfort, that do express humanity and the complexity of the human experience, "a mingled yarn, good and ill together" (4.3.68). Helena brings intelligence, compassion, and fertility to the world of Bertram and Parolles. Theirs is the world of battle and of superficial friendship based on flattery and self-seeking. . . .

Like the bed-trick, the endings of *All's Well* and *Measure for Measure* are at once conventional and unconventional. They both end with marriage, but "happily ever after" may not rule the day. Equally, the heroines who have effected these endings and revealed the subtleties of a world in which the illusions of the characters

who have expected stereotypic behavior have been removed elude arbitrary classifications.

In *All's Well*, when morning comes, after the bed-trick, Helena anticipates better times, "When briars shall have leaves as sweet as thorns / And be as sweet as sharp" (4.4.32–33). Thus she expresses hope but is also mindful of the "mingled yarns of life" (4.3.74). Even in the final scene when it is full daylight and many voices of propriety and family are heard, the bed-trick seems re-enacted as it had been anticipated by the King's illness, with the exchange of rings, the substituted women, the oaths, the lies—all until the light comes and the truth is revealed. Once more the ambiguities of life are defined. In an ideal world, all would be well. Here all is well only *if* Helena can make the riddle clear to Bertram (5.3.310). *If* she cannot, divorce will follow (5.3.311). The play is a success *if* the suit for applause is won (epilogue, 1–2). Of course, she will prove the consummation, there will be no divorce, and we will applaud when the player asks us to. With the introduction of the *ifs*, however, comes the confirmation that people behave in individual ways. There are mitigating circumstances, and not to recognize them condemns us to a life based on appearances and assumptions. Bertram thought he got an evening's fling; what he got instead was blessing and love. The *ifs* tell us that life can go sour; it can also rise and bake sweet.

Women like Helena are more risky to love than passive, conformable women. They ask for more—that their husbands be as chaste as they for one thing—and give more. They are reckless and dare to assert themselves with the means available in order to give their gifts. The convention of the bed-trick confirms and enriches their specialness. Further, it ties together the past and present, dying and fertility, role playing and disguise, all of it, to deny the ordinary and unimaginative.

The final discovery in *Measure for Measure*, like that in *All's Well*, exposes a man who has misjudged the subtleties and complexities of the personality of the woman who confronts him. Isabella, to expose Angelo's misuse of power, allows her good name and reputation to be tarnished. She publicly denounces him but must say that he has seduced her in order to do so. For her, reputation of chastity is not the same as chastity itself. And virtue means much more than chastity as she risks public disgrace to expose evil. Throughout, however, Angelo remains alienated. He is given love and marriage, neither of which he wants. Because he cannot tolerate public shame, he requests death, which is denied him. Finally, Isabella makes her grandest assertion for life, and once more her sincerity and directness surface. Angelo's death will not revive Claudio; therefore she pleads for his life. As she had participated in the bed-trick to save her brother's life, so she now pleads for Angelo's out of compassion for Marianna.

As in *All's Well*, the ending of *Measure for Measure* is precarious. None of the marriages seems ideal. We do not believe that distress is over and happiness necessarily follows. Instead, there is sense of a beginning, of new opportunities and second chances, rather like life. We have arrived at this realization in part by having had our sensibilities shocked. Chastity typically demands reticence and passivity, but Shakespeare says *no* in these plays. The bed-trick is unseemly to the unimaginative, indecorous to the conventional and undemanding. These plays ask of their heroines that they be virtuous and assertive, chaste and outspoken; that they search for the harmonies of life. These characters and their participation in the bed-trick shock, disorient and ultimately extend a reality—that part of virtue which actively reaches for the elusive commitment to life. In creating plays in which the stereotypes are distorted, Shakespeare via an old and much used convention seeks to define honor, chastity, virtue—not as abstractions but as realities.

Source: Eileen Z. Cohen, "'Virtue Is Bold': The Bed-trick and Characterization in *All's Well That Ends Well* and *Measure for Measure*," in *Philological Quarterly*, Vol. 65, No. 2, Spring, 1986, pp. 171–86.

John M. Love

In this excerpt, Love examines how social rank "debases" Helena and Bertram and determines their fate as well as that of Parolles. He argues that the issue of social rank is pervasive throughout all of the action of the play. Love also points out the differences between All's Well That Ends Well *and Boccaccio's "Giletta of Narbona," particularly in terms of the difference between Helena's and Giletta's stations and how this is directly related to their actions.*

... The alien, ineradicable element of *All's Well that Ends Well* and the source of its darkness is the barrier of class. Class debases the characters of Bertram and Helena throughout the play,

> THROUGHOUT THE THIRD AND FOURTH ACTS, EACH STEP OF THE FRENCH LORD'S PLOT AGAINST PAROLLES IMMEDIATELY PRECEDES THE CORRESPONDING STEP IN HELENA'S WINNING OF BERTRAM."

and in the final scene it determines their fates and that of Parolles, despite the measure of virtue and vice each character possesses. At that point Helena, "a maid too virtuous / For the contempt of empire" (II.ii.30–31), must plead with a pampered husband, Bertram's fellow-prodigal Parolles appears beaten into due submission, and Bertram is, in Johnson's words, "dismissed to happiness." The difference between *All's Well* and the comedies that preceded it lies in its greater darkness, for class pervades the action and influences all the main characters.

Shakespeare's Helena hardly resembles the heroine of William Painter's tale of "Giletta of Narbona," the likeliest source of the play. In the first place, she has been deprived of the wealth and independence that made Giletta her spouse's equal in all respects save those of blood. Giletta, "diligently loked unto by her kinsfolke (because she was riche and fatherlesse)," clearly managed her own affairs. Having "refused manye husbandes, with whom her kinsfolke would have matched her," she journeyed to Paris alone and unaided, and there sealed her bargain with the King. Once married, she "went to Rossiglione, where she was received of all his subjects for their Lady. And perceyving that through the Countes absence, all things were spoiled and out of order: she like a sage Ladye, with great diligence and care, disposed his thinges in order againe, whereof the subjects rejoysed very much, bearing to her their harty love & affection." By contrast, from the moment the Countess presents Helena to Lafew as Gerard de Narbon's "sole child ... bequeath'd to my overlooking" (I.i.35–36), Helena's dependence upon her mistress and adopted mother is apparent. As much "unseason'd" as Bertram, she presumes to travel to Paris only with the Countess's knowledge and approval, "my leave and love, / Means and

Sophie Thompson as Helena and Andree Evans as the Old Widow in Act III, scene vii, at the Swan Theatre, Stratford-upon-Avon, 1992 *(© Donald Cooper/Photostage. Reproduced by permission)*

attendants, and my loving greetings / To those of mine at court" (I.iii.246–48). There, with the aid of Lafew, Helena gains a timid entrance to the King. But she does not in any sense come into her own upon her return to Rossillion as the wife of Bertram.

In those scenes which Painter's narrative suggested, Helena's application to the King in act 2 and her encounters with Diana and the Widow, Helena displays a heroic confidence in the heavenly source of her healing power and in her eventual success. Elsewhere in the play, in keeping with the dependent status that Shakespeare bestowed upon her, she remains mistrustful of others, fearful of earning their contempt by her slightest gesture of self-assertion, and self-effacing before her wayward husband.

Fearfulness leads her first of all to deceive the Countess, ironically her staunchest ally. After the soliloquy she utters upon Bertram's farewell, Parolles's meditation on virginity, and his farewell, "Get thee a good husband, and use him as he uses thee" (I.i.210–11), the soliloquy

with which Helena concludes the first scene clearly outlines a plan to win Bertram by means of the king's disease:

> Our remedies oft in ourselves doe lie,
> Which we ascribe to heaven; the fated sky
> Gives us free scope; only doth backward pull
> Our slow designs when we ourselves are
>   dull....
> The king's disease—my project may deceive
>   me,
> But my intents are fix'd, and will not leave
>   me.
> (I.i.212–25)

Under persistent questioning by the Countess, Helena admits her love, but equivocates, and finally denies any intention of pursuing Bertram, notwithstanding the audience's knowledge to the contrary:

> ... I follow him not
> By any token of presumptuous suit,
> Nor would I have him till I do deserve him;
> Yet never know how that desert should
>   be ...

... O then give pity
To her whose state is such that cannot
    choose
But lend and give where she is sure to lose;
That seeks not to find that her search implies
But riddle-like lives sweetly where she dies!
(I.iii.192–212)

Helena admits only that Bertram's journey reminded her of the king's illness, and when in the scene immediately following her interview with the Countess she demands of the King, "What husband in thy power I will command" (II.i.93), the deception becomes unmistakable. Helena's guardedness in the first scene and her frequent reiteration of courtesy titles and deferential gestures in the presence of the Countess suggest the acute consciousness of an inferior place that might lie behind this unwarranted secrecy.

Helena remains uneasy even after her miraculous cure of the King. In act 2, scene 3, she balks at the mere prospect of choosing a husband from among the assembled courtiers, anticipating a rebuke even though the King has expressly forbidden one:

Please it your majesty, I have done
    already.
The blushes on my cheeks thus whisper me:
"We blush that thou should'st choose, but,
    be refused,
Let the white death sit on thy cheek for ever,
We'll ne'er come there again."
(II.iii.68–72)

The terms of her address to individual lords indicate that Helena fears contempt for her class, not her person or unmaidenly forwardness:

The honour, sir, that flames in your fair
    eyes
Before I speak, too threat'ningly replies.
Love make your fortune twenty times above
Her that so wishes, and her humble love!
    . . . . .
Be not afraid that I your hand should take;
I'll never do you wrong, for your own sake.
    . . . . .
You are too young, too happy, and too good,
To make yourself a son out of my blood.
(II.iii.80–97)

Like the unswerving support of the Countess, the young lords' protestations at being passed over underscore the extent of Helena's misapprehension.

Thereafter, the most poignant moments of the play grow out of Helena's self-effacement in the presence of her renegade husband: her choosing of him, "I dare not say I take you, but I give / Me and my service, ever whilst I live" (II.iii.102–03); their farewell, in which Bertram denies her the courtesy of the kiss that she can barely bring herself to ask; her self-accusing letter to the Countess; her bittersweet recollection of the rendezvous with Bertram, "But, O, strange men! / That can such sweet use make of what they hate" (IV.iv.21–22); and, finally, her dramatic reappearance at Rossillion:

King. Is there no exorcist
Beguiles the truer office of mine eyes?
Is't real that I see?
Hel. No, my good lord;
'Tis but the shadow of a wife you see;
The name and not the thing.
(V.iii.298–302)

Though Shakespeare gave Helena a far greater advantage over Bertram than Giletta held over Beltramo, Painter's heroine confronted her husband far more conscious of her power: "knowing that they were all assembled. . . . shee passed through the people, without chaunge of apparell, with her twoo sonnes in her arms. . . . 'My Lorde, . . . I nowe beseche thee, for the honoure of God, that thou wilt observe the conditions, which the twoo (knightes that I sent unto thee) did commaunde me to doe: for beholde, here in myne armes, not onely one sonne begotten by thee, but twayne, and likewyse thy Ryng. It is nowe time then (if thou kepe promise) that I should be received as thy wyfe.'"

Unlike her mistrust, Helena's humility is a virtue, yet the circumstances under which it appears make her at least potentially a pathetic heroine. Her nature and her circumstances ally her more nearly to the heroines of the later romances than to her predecessors in the festive comedies, but the pathos she evokes finds its closest counterpart in Desdemona. Even though it leads to a reconciliation with Bertram, her manner during the final scene cannot but recall her character and status throughout, as well as the somber emotions she has frequently stirred.

That the unworthy husband presumes upon the class barrier that works against his virtuous wife is one of the pervasive ironies of *All's Well*, and in that sense Bertram's nobility of blood corrupts him by licensing his misdeeds. But Shakespeare's juxtaposition of each stage of Bertram's career and its counterpart in Parolles's creates a second irony, for the two finally emerge as wayward youths, possessed of the same degree and kind of vice, but distinguished by class and thus by fate.

The parallel courses that Bertram and Parolles run begin with their farewells to Helena in the opening scene. The Count, characteristically attentive to the niceties of rank, departs with the charge, "Be comfortable to my mother, your mistress, and make much of her" (I.i.73–74). The farewell between Helena and Parolles that follows parodies Bertram's patronizing air, from the opening gambit:

> *Par.* Save you, fair queen!
> *Hel.* And you, monarch!
> *Par.* No.
> *Hel.* And no.
> (I.i.104–07)

to the valedictory:

> *Par.* Little Helen, farewell. If I can
>   remember thee,
> I will think of
> thee at court.
> *Hel.* Monsieur Parolles, you were born
>   under a charitable star.
> (I.i.184–87)

That in the presence of the despised Parolles Helena relaxes the guard she had earlier maintained, and that his absurd meditation on virginity proves more fruitful advice than the elders' precepts, only increases the apparent distance between Helena and the nobles, a distance that her earlier silence and tears had suggested.

Parolles's fall from grace likewise mirrors Bertram's. In the same scene in which Bertram's presumption earns the King's rebuke, the Captain runs afoul of Lafew for forgetting his proper place:

> *Laf.* Your lord and master did well to
>   make his recantation.
> *Par.* Recantation! My lord! My master!
> *Laf.* Ay. Is it not a language I speak?
> *Par.* A most harsh one, and not to be under-
>   stood without bloody
> succeeding. My master!
> *Laf.* Are you companion to the Count
>   Rossillion?
> *Par.* To any Count; to all Counts; to what is
>   man.
> *Laf.* To what is Count's man.
> (II.iii.186–94)

Lafew objects less to Parolles's outlandish garb and manner than to the pretensions to equality with his social superiors which the manner and garb signify: "Why dost thou garter up thy arms a' this fashion? Dost make hose of thy sleeves? Do other servants so?... You are more saucy with lords and honourable personages than the commission of your birth gives you heraldry" (II.iii.245–58). In this sauciness Parolles copies Bertram, yet reverses the attitude of his fellow-commoner, Helena. In his own humiliation Parolles seconds Bertram's resolve to flee "to those Italian fields / Where noble fellows strike" (II.iii.286–87), strengthening the parallel.

Throughout the third and fourth acts, each step of the French lord's plot against Parolles immediately precedes the corresponding step in Helena's winning of Bertram. In the final two scenes of act 3, the lords unfold their scheme to Bertram and enlist his aid, and Helena does the same with Diana and the Widow. Act 4 begins with the ambush of Parolles, and his vow to reveal "all the secrets of their camp" (IV.i.84), a promise that seals his fate as surely as Bertram's gift of his family ring and promise of a rendezvous seals his in the scene following. In act 4, scene 3, the parallel lines converge. Not only does Bertram report his nocturnal meeting, which the audience knows to be the last stage of Helena's plan, but Parolles's exposure becomes the exposure of both wayward youths. Although they would have Bertram believe that they aim at Parolles only "for the love of laughter" (III.ii.32), among themselves the French lords "would gladly see his company anatomiz'd, that he might take the measure of his own judgements" (IV.iii.30–32). Their disapproval of Bertram's conduct with Helena and Diana, his concern over the Captain's confession, "Nothing of me, has a'?" (IV.iii.109), the pointed warning that "If your lordship be in't, as I believe you are, you must have the patience to hear it" (IV.iii.111–12), the aptness of Parolles's slanderous portrait of the Count as "a foolish idle boy, but for all that very ruttish" (IV.iii.207), and the contrast between Bertram's rage and his companions' amusement at the slanders, all serve to unite the two youths in folly.

Once the time comes for Parolles and Bertram to answer for these equivalent offenses, the parallel abruptly breaks off. In the soliloquy that follows his exposure, Parolles seems beyond chastisement:

> Yet am I thankful. If my heart were
>   great
> 'Twould burst at this. Captain I'll be no
>   more,
> But I will eat and drink and sleep as soft
> As captain shall. Simply the thing I am
> Shall make me live. Who knows himself a
>   braggart,
> Let him fear this; for it shall come to pass
> That every braggart shall be found an ass.
> Rust, sword; cool, blushes; and Parolles live
> Safest in shame; being fool'd, by fool'ry
>   thrive.
> There's place and means for every man alive.
> I'll after them.
> (IV.iii.319–29)

Nevertheless, his offenses earn him the lowest place and the poorest means. When he reappears in the fifth act, he shows respect even to the Clown, whom he had earlier patronized: "Good Master Lavatch, give my Lord Lafew this letter; I have ere now, sir, been better known to you, when I have held familiarity with fresher clothes; but I am now, sir, muddied in Fortune's mood, and smell somewhat strong of her strong displeasure" (V.ii.1–5). In the same scene, he abjectly confesses to Lafew, "O, my good Lord, you were the first that found me" (V.ii.41). He acknowledges Bertram as his master in the trial scene, and that Lafew will see to it that atonement follows conviction of sin and repentance is apparent from the charge he gives his newest servant as they observe the lovers reunited: "Good Tom Drum, lend me a handkercher. So, I thank thee. Wait on me at home, I will make sport with thee. Let thy curtsies alone, they are scurvy ones" (V.iii.315–18).

Bertram sins more than this and suffers less. He arrives at Rossillion unmuddied, spared the "exceeding posting day and night" (V.i.1) that Helena endured, needing no letter to the King, and in the height of fashionable attire. In the trial scene, Parolles suffers the contempt of Diana, Lafew, the King, and even Bertram, while Bertram lies, contemns, slanders, but finally embraces Helena. In the absence of Parolles, one might call the treatment that Bertram receives mercy; the Captain's presence makes it something less attractive than that....

Source: John M. Love, "'Though many of the rich are damn'd': Dark Comedy and Social Class in *All's Well That Ends Well*," in *Texas Studies in Literature and Language*, Vol. XVIII, No. 4, Winter, 1977, pp. 517–27.

SOURCES

Carnegy, Patrick, "Fruitful Follies," in the *Spectator*, Vol. 293, No. 9151, December 27, 2003, p. 42.

Charney, Maurice, "All's Well That Ends Well," in *All of Shakespeare*, Columbia University Press, 1993, pp. 95–103.

Cohen, Eileen Z., "'Virtue Is Bold': The Bed-Trick and Characterization in *All's Well That Ends Well* and *Measure for Measure*," in *Philological Quarterly*, Vol. 65, 1986, pp. 171–86.

Fraser, Russell, ed., "Introduction" to *All's Well That Ends Well*, Cambridge University Press, 1985, pp. 1–37.

Garber, Marjorie, "All's Well That Ends Well," in *Shakespeare After All*, Pantheon, 2004, pp. 617–33.

Haffenden, John, ed., "Pathos and Dream," in *Berryman's Shakespeare: Essays, Letters, and Other Writings by John Berryman*, Farrar, Straus & Giroux, 1999, p. 51.

Isherwood, Charles, "Maybe He's Just Not into You, Helena," in the *New York Times*, February 14, 2006.

Klein, Alvin, "What a Woman Wants (Never Mind Why)," in the *New York Times*, July 26, 1998.

Lawrence, William Witherle, "All's Well That Ends Well," in *Shakespeare's Problem Comedies*, 2nd ed., Frederick Ungar, 1960, pp. 32–77.

Schork, R. J., "The Many Masks of Parolles," in *Philological Quarterly*, Vol. 76, No. 3, Summer 1997, p. 263.

Shakespeare, William, *All's Well That Ends Well*, 2nd Series, edited by G. K. Hunter, Arden Shakespeare, 1968.

FURTHER READING

Beck, Ervin, "Shakespeare's *All's Well That Ends Well*," in *Explicator*, Vol. 55, No. 3, Spring 1997, p. 123.
  Beck writes about the symbolism of Helena's name, particularly as it relates to other characters in classical literature, all of whom were bearers of truth.

Briggs, Julia, "Shakespeare's Bed-Tricks," in *Essays in Criticism*, Vol. 44, No. 4, October 1994, pp. 293–314.
  Briggs discusses the influences on Shakespeare in his use of the bed-trick and how Shakespeare used the bed-trick in his own work. Briggs focuses on *Arcadia*, a work preceding Shakespeare's plays, and Shakespeare's own *Measure for Measure* and *All's Well That Ends Well*.

Bryant, J. A., Jr., "*All's Well That Ends Well* and *Measure for Measure*," in *Shakespeare and the Uses of Comedy*, University Press of Kentucky, 1986, pp. 203–20.

Bryant examines how the two plays, although "traditional" comedies, veer from the usual paths of such tales, arriving "at the prescribed destination with marks of the passage still showing."

Clark, Ira, "The Trappings of *All's Well That Ends Well*," in *Style*, Vol. 39, No. 3, Fall 2005, p. 277.

Clark focuses on the verbal trickery and the plot reversals of the play, arguing that these "traps" are essential style elements and should be analyzed as such.

Friedman, Michael D., "Male Bonds and Marriage in *All's Well and Much Ado*," in *Studies in English Literature*, Vol. 35, No. 2, Spring 1995, pp. 231–49.

Friedman discusses male bonding in *All's Well That Ends Well* and *Much Ado about Nothing*, primarily the relationship between Bertram and Parolles, and Claudio and Benedick, and how it pertains to marriage in the plays.

Haley, David, "Bertram at Court," in *Shakespeare's Courtly Mirror: Reflexivity and Prudence in All's Well That Ends Well*, University of Delaware Press, 1993, pp. 17–51.

Haley's article examines *All's Well That Ends Well* as a courtly play (and Shakespeare's approach to the courtier in general), with specific emphasis on Bertram as a courtier.

———, "Helena's Love," in *Shakespeare's Courtly Mirror: Reflexivity and Prudence in All's Well That Ends Well*, University of Delaware Press, 1993, pp. 87–122.

This essay by Haley examines Helena's character, including her love melancholy, her "prophetic virtue" and "providential mission," and her "erotic motive" to be united with Bertram after he has rejected her (thus abandoning "providence for Eros").

Hodgdon, Barbara, "The Making of Virgins and Mothers: Sexual Signs, Substitute Scenes and Doubled Presences in *All's Well That Ends Well*," in *Philological Quarterly*, Vol. 66, No. 1, Winter 1987, pp. 47–71.

Hodgdon approaches a reading of *All's Well That Ends Well* from Helena's point of view, examining in particular how Shakespeare based his play on Boccaccio's play and what he did differently; how "sexual signs are articulated in character and event"; and how substitute scenes are used, particularly the bed-trick.

Hunt, Maurice, "Words and Deeds in *All's Well That Ends Well*," in *Modern Language Quarterly*, Vol. 48, No. 4, December 1987, pp. 320–38.

Hunt's essay examines the "competition" between words and deeds in *All's Well That Ends Well* primarily through the King of France, who vacillates between valuing word and deed and thus the two cannot be brought into harmony; Helena, through whom Shakespeare implies that "not only that deeds can on occasion speak but also that they can prompt an eventual honesty in words"; and Bertram, who merges word and deed in the final scenes of the play when he embraces Helena.

Jardine, Lisa, "Cultural Confusion and Shakespeare's Learned Heroines: 'These Are Old Paradoxes,'" in *Shakespeare Quarterly*, Vol. 38, No. 1, Spring 1987, pp. 1–18.

Jardine's article discusses how Helena and Portia, in, respectively, *All's Well That Ends Well* and *The Merchant of Venice*, possessed knowledge traditionally associated with the "male sphere." Helena, in particular possessed knowledge as a healer (the community's "wise woman"), in her upbringing (her "education"), and as the "woman who knows" in her deception of Bertram. Jardine discusses the tension between possessing knowledge as a part of female virtue and possessing it in the "male sphere."

Kastan, David Scott, "*All's Well That Ends Well* and the Limits of Comedy," in *ELH*, Vol. 52, No. 3, Autumn 1985, pp. 575–89.

Kastan argues that, although *All's Well That Ends Well* and Shakespeare's other "problem plays" are classified as comedies and not tragedies because "fictive aspirations have been gratified," the reader is not entirely satisfied with these "aspirations" and indeed has been "made suspicious of them," thus making the plays "generic mixtures" or "mutations."

Makaryk, Irene Rima, "The Problem Plays," in her dissertation, *Comic Justice in Shakespeare's Comedies*, 1979.

Makaryk discusses *All's Well That Ends Well* within the context of the two other "problem plays" with which it is usually aligned—*Measure for Measure* and *Troilus and Cressida*.

Maus, Katharine Eisaman, "*All's Well That Ends Well*," in *The Norton Shakespeare*, edited by Stephen Greenblatt, W. W. Norton, 1997, pp. 2175–81.

Maus's essay provides an overview of *All's Well That Ends Well*, touching on such topics as the reversal of gender roles, the lack of "endings" in the play, desire, honor, and social class.

Muir, Kenneth, "*All's Well That Ends Well*," in *Shakespeare's Comic Sequence*, Liverpool University Press, 1979, pp. 124–32.

Muir's article gives a brief overview of *All's Well That Ends Well*, focusing on the actions and motivations of Helena and Bertram.

Richard, Jeremy, "'The Thing I Am': Parolles, the Comedic Villain, and Tragic Consciousness," in *Shakespeare Studies*, Vol. 18, Burt Franklin & Co., Inc., 1986, pp. 145–59.

Richard's article demonstrates how the character of Parolles fits into Shakespeare's development of the metamorphosis of the comedic villain in his work: "Parolles and the manner in which he suggests that all is not well that ends well creates a new Shakespearean drama of the pitfalls of the mental world rather than the pratfalls of the physical."

Roark, Christopher, "Lavatch and Service in *All's Well That Ends Well*," in *Studies in English Literature, 1500–1900*, Vol. 28, No. 2, Spring 1988, pp. 241–58.

    Roark argues that examining the role of Lavatch, the clown, can add an important dimension to understanding the play, especially its more problematic elements, such as the unsatisfying ending.

Schroeder, Lori, "Riddles, Female Space, and Closure in *All's Well That Ends Well*," in *English Language Notes*, Vol. 38, No. 4, June 2001, p. 19.

    Schroeder examines the concept of female sexuality in the play from various angles and comments on the significance of pregnancy in terms of the plot and the play's title.

Simpson, Lynne M., "The Failure to Mourn in *All's Well That Ends Well*," in *Shakespeare Studies*, Vol. 22, 1994, pp. 172–88.

    Simpson examines the Oedipal anxieties in Helena and Bertram as they pertain to the failure of each to mourn the death of her/his father. Helena substitutes Bertram for her dead father, and Bertram substitutes the King of France for his. Simpson takes a psychoanalytic approach with regard to the concepts of guilt, death, forgetting, memory, and forgiveness in the play.

Snyder, Susan, "*All's Well That Ends Well* and Shakespeare's Helens: Text and Subtext, Subject and Object," in *English Literary Renaissance*, Vol. 18, No. 1, Winter 1988, pp. 66–77.

    Snyder examines two aspects of *All's Well That Ends Well* as they relate to Helena. The first concerns the "gaps, disjunctions, and silences" in the play, "where we lack an expected connection or explanation in the speeches or actions" of Helena, primarily as they concern her character's mixture of initiative and passivity. In the second part of the essay, Snyder compares the Helena of *All's Well* with the Helena of *A Midsummer Night's Dream* and with Helen of Troy, demonstrating how *All's Well*'s Helena, even at the end of the play, stands in marked contrast to the other two similarly named heroines as undesired subject rather than desired object.

Styan, J. L., *All's Well That Ends Well*, Shakespeare in Performance Series, Manchester University Press, 1984.

    Styan describes how *All's Well That Ends Well* has been performed primarily on stage but also on television in the twentieth century. The first part addresses issues of performance; the second part takes the play scene by scene; and the appendix contains listings of twentieth-century productions, major productions, and principal casts.

Sullivan, Garrett A., Jr., "'Be This Sweet Helen's Knell, and Now Forget Her': Forgetting, Memory, and Identity in *All's Well That Ends Well*," in *Shakespeare Quarterly*, Spring 1999, p. 51.

    Sullivan explores the theme of lost fathers, unrequited love, and the benefits of repressed memories in the play.

Vaughn, Jack A., "*All's Well That Ends Well*," in *Shakespeare's Comedies*, Frederick Ungar Publishing Co., 1980, pp. 153–59.

    Vaughn provides a very brief overview of *All's Well That Ends Well*, touching on the difficulty critics face in assessing the motives and actions of Helena, Bertram, and Parolles. Also provides a brief stage history.

Wells, Stanley, "Plays of Troy, Vienna, and Roussillon: *Troilus and Cressida, Measure for Measure*, and *All's Well That Ends Well*," in *Shakespeare: A Life in Drama*, W. W. Norton, 1995, pp. 234–44.

    Wells's article follows the relationship of Helena and Bertram in *All's Well That Ends Well* to illuminate the play's "moral self-consciousness."

Yang, Sharon R., "Shakespeare's *All's Well That Ends Well*," in *The Explicator*, Vol. 50, No. 4, Summer 1992, pp. 199–203.

    Yang briefly explores the parallels between the characters of Lavatch and Bertram, particularly how Lavatch's "words and experiences expose the absurdity of Bertram's perspective."

Antony and Cleopatra

1607

Antony and Cleopatra is Shakespeare's presentation of one of the most famous stories the ancient world has to offer: the tempestuous love affair between the great Roman warrior and the infinitely seductive queen of Egypt; the quarrel between Antony and Octavius Caesar; the climactic battle of Actium, and the resulting suicides of the two lovers. The play covers a period of about ten years, from 40 B.C.E., shortly after Antony first met Cleopatra, until 30 B.C.E., the year of their deaths.

Antony and Cleopatra was first listed for publication in 1608, but evidence strongly suggests that the play was written and performed one or two years earlier. No evidence exists to indicate that *Antony and Cleopatra* appeared in print before its inclusion in the First Folio of 1623; therefore, the First Folio version of the play is considered authoritative.

The principal source for *Antony and Cleopatra* is Thomas North's "The Life of Antonius" in his *The Lives of the Noble Grecianes and Romans* (1579), an English translation of a work by Plutarch. Shakespeare followed North's translation of Plutarch closely for his play; this can be seen, for example, by a comparison of Shakespeare's poetic rendition of Enobarbus's description of Cleopatra on her barge and North's own prose translation of the episode. Critics, however, are divided on whether Shakespeare's characterizations of Antony and

Cleopatra are more or less flattering than they are in North's translation of Plutarch.

Scholarly debate over *Antony and Cleopatra* has centered around Antony's "dotage," or decline, and the relative nobility of his character; Cleopatra's contradictory behavior and the significance of her death; the nature of the lovers' passion for each other; and the comparative wisdom or rashness of their actions. Some scholars have focused on the connections between Shakespeare's *Antony and Cleopatra* and John Dryden's seventeenth-century version of the play, *All for Love* (1677). Other issues of interest include the play's language, imagery, structure, and political context, as well as its treatment of the mores and politics of a changing Rome versus those of Egypt. Thematic concerns include the relationship in the play between reason and imagination or passion, the nature of love, the choice between love and empire, and political or social disintegration.

PLOT SUMMARY

Act 1, Scene 1
Antony and Cleopatra begins in Cleopatra's palace in Alexandria. Demetrius and Philo, two of Antony's veteran soldiers, complain that Antony's infatuation with Cleopatra has had a bad effect on his qualities as a general. They see him as a great warrior transformed by his passion into a harlot's slave. Antony enters with Cleopatra and her maids, and a messenger from Rome arrives. Cleopatra taunts Antony, saying that maybe his wife, Fulvia, is angry with him, or perhaps the young Octavius Caesar has some orders for him. But Antony will not even hear the messenger. He appears only to be interested in indulging his love for Cleopatra and seeking out pleasure. He has forgotten his role as a Roman general.

Act 1, Scene 2
Cleopatra's two maids-in-waiting, Charmian and Iras, ask a Soothsayer to tell them their fortunes. When he ominously suggests that they will not live long, the women misinterpret his warnings and instead joke about their good luck. Meanwhile, Antony hears of separate battles being waged against Octavius Caesar—one of which was started by Antony's wife, Fulvia. That war is now over, but another warrior, Labienus, leader of the Parthians, is making

widespread conquests while Antony idles his time away in Egypt, neglecting his duty as one of the three rulers of the Roman Empire.

After another messenger tells him of Fulvia's death, Antony berates himself for being enchanted by Cleopatra and decides to return to his duties in Rome. He tells his man Enobarbus that he regrets ever setting eyes on Cleopatra and informs him of the dire military situation. Sextus Pompeius is in full rebellion against Caesar and has control of the seas. The common people are flocking to him in support, and the empire may be in danger.

Act 1, Scene 3
Cleopatra is hurt and angered by this news. She rails at Antony for betraying her while he tries to explain the dire situation in Rome. When he tells her calmly of Fulvia's death, thinking she will be pleased with this news, she taunts him, saying that his lack of grief at the death of his wife shows her how coldly he will react to her own death, when it comes. Antony insists that even though he is returning to Rome, his heart remains with Cleopatra. Cleopatra, although obviously distressed at the prospect of his imminent departure, relents and affectionately bids him farewell.

Act 1, Scene 4
Back in Rome, Octavius Caesar tells his fellow triumvir, Lepidus, that he is disgusted with Antony's infatuation with Cleopatra and with his dissipation in Egypt. Word comes that Pompey is gathering more and more support in his military campaign against Caesar. A second messenger brings news that two more rebels in alliance with Pompey, Menecrates and Menas, are also having success at sea and are making inroads on Caesar's power in Italy, rebelling against the triumvirate; Octavius once more laments that Antony is wasting his time and his reputation in Egypt. He and Lepidus announce that they will assemble a council and decide on a way to counter Pompey by sea and on land.

Act 1, Scene 5
In her palace in Alexandria, Cleopatra whiles away the time in Antony's absence. She thinks of what he must do doing, and also recalls that in the past, she was the lover of Julius Caesar, and of one of the sons of Pompey the Great. Alexas, a messenger from Antony, arrives with the news that Antony has promised Cleopatra many lands in the east to rule over. Cleopatra is delighted to

Michael Redgrave and Peggy Ashcroft star in a 1953 Stratford-On-Avon theatre production of Anthony and Cleopatra *(Kurt Hutton/Getty Images)*

hear from Antony, and prepares to send him a greeting in return. She resolves to write to him several times a day.

Act 2, Scene 1

In Messina, at Pompey's house, Pompey, Menecrates, and Menas discuss the military situation. Thinking that Antony will remain in Egypt, and having a low opinion of both Caesar and Lepidus, Pompey is confident of success. He is disturbed, however, when Menas informs him that Caesar and Lepidus have assembled a powerful army, and then outright concerned when Varrius brings the news that Antony is expected back in Rome shortly. However, Pompey knows that Antony and Caesar are not on good terms, and he keeps an open mind about whether they will patch up their differences and unite against him.

Act 2, Scene 2

Antony and Caesar meet in Rome at the house of Lepidus. Octavius Caesar complains that Antony's wife and his brother made war on him, and that Antony supported them. Antony denies the charge, saying that he had as much cause to resent the rebellion as Caesar did. But Caesar then accuses him of remaining in Alexandria and breaking his oath to provide Caesar with military support when it was required. Antony responds by blaming Fulvia, his wife, claiming that she made war on Caesar with the purpose of enticing Antony away from Egypt. He seeks pardon from Caesar for this, even though it was none of his doing. Caesar seems unwilling to budge in his distaste for Antony until Agrippa proposes that Antony marry Octavia, Octavius Caesar's sister. This will cement an alliance between Antony and Octavius. Both men agree to the match and are reconciled. After they exit, the followers of Antony and of Octavius chat among themselves, and Enobarbus predicts that despite his marriage to Octavia, Antony will never abandon Cleopatra.

Act 2, Scene 3

In Caesar's house, Antony, who is now married to Octavia, pledges that from now on, he will behave more correctly. The Soothsayer warns Antony that Octavius will eclipse him in greatness as long as he stays with him in Rome. Antony knows this is true, and when he is alone he admits that he has married Octavia only to keep the peace; he is still enamored of Cleopatra and resolves to return to her.

Act 2, Scenes 4–5

As members of the triumvirate make preparations for war against Pompey, Cleopatra in Egypt hears of Antony's marriage to Octavia. She is furious and beats the messenger who brought the news. Then she sends a messenger to Rome to find out whether Octavia is beautiful.

Act 2, Scene 6

Pompey meets with the triumvirate. Antony says they do not fear his formidable naval strength, and points out that on land Pompey's forces are greatly outnumbered. Pompey agrees to accept the offer the triumvars have earlier presented him with. He is allowed to keep Sicily and Sardinia and agrees to rid the sea of pirates. He also agrees to send wheat to Rome.

Act 2, Scene 7

The triumvars and Pompey celebrate their successful negotiations with a feast aboard Pompey's galley. Pompey's ally, the pirate Menas, offers to assassinate the triumvirs while they are celebrating, which would then leave Pompey as the dominant force in the empire. Pompey rejects the idea. The celebrants, especially Lepidus, become increasingly drunk, and Octavius Caesar, who does not enjoy such occasions, suggests that it is time to go home.

Act 3, Scene 1

On a plain in Syria, Ventidius, one of Antony's subordinates, and Silius, a soldier in Ventidius's army, discuss their victory over the Parthians. Ventidius plans to write to Antony informing him of their success, but he does not want to appear to be too successful, because Antony may then regard him as a threat.

Act 3, Scene 2

As Antony and his new wife, Octavia, prepare to leave Rome, Octavius makes it clear to Antony that he still distrusts him. Antony promises that he will give no cause for distrust.

Act 3, Scene 3

Back in Egypt, Cleopatra's messenger returns from Rome with the reassuring news that Octavia is unattractive. Cleopatra convinces herself that Antony will not stay with her for long.

Act 3, Scene 4

Meanwhile, now settled in Athens, Greece, Antony complains to Octavia that her brother has resumed warring with Pompey and has also begun slandering Antony. Octavia, torn with distress at this conflict between her brother and her husband, returns to Rome to mediate between Antony and Octavius. In the meantime, Antony says, he will raise an army that will be more than a match for any forces Octavius can muster.

Act 3, Scene 5

In the same house in Athens, Enobarbus reports to Eros that Octavius and Lepidus defeated Pompey and that thereafter, Octavius rid himself of Lepidus by accusing him of treason and imprisoning him.

Act 3, Scene 6

Back in Rome, Octavius is outraged at news that Antony has abandoned Octavia and returned to Cleopatra. He reports that in a great public ceremony, Antony made Cleopatra absolute queen not only of Egypt but also of Lower Syria, Cyprus, and Lydia. He gave other countries to his sons. Octavius also reports that Antony has accused Octavius of not giving him sufficient spoils from the defeat of Pompey, and of not returning some ships he loaned him. Antony is also unhappy about the deposing of Lepidus. Octavius has already replied to Antony's complaints, offering him a share of some territory he has conquered, but demanding that Antony do the same with regard to the kingdoms he has conquered. Octavius also justifies his conduct in respect of Lepidus, saying that the latter deserved his fate.

Octavia arrives to mediate between her brother and husband. She believes Antony is still in Athens, but Octavius informs her that he is in fact in Egypt with Cleopatra, and is preparing for war against his brother-in-law. Octavius tells his sister that Antony has formed a coalition with many powerful kings in order to defeat Octavius.

Act 3, Scene 7

At Antony's camp near Actium, in Egypt, Cleopatra rejects Enobarbus's protests that her presence on the battlefield will distract Antony rather than help him. She insists she will not stay behind. Antony enters, announcing that Octavius Caesar has challenged him to a sea battle at Actium. Enobarbus warns against it, saying that neither Antony's ships nor his men are a match for Octavius's battle-hardened veterans and nimble ships. When Antony insists, Enobarbus tries to convince him to fight on land, for which he is better prepared. But neither Antony nor Cleopatra will listen. Antony says that if they lose at sea, they can then defeat Octavius on land.

Act 3, Scenes 8–10

The warring fleets engage in battle, and Antony's side gains the upper hand until Cleopatra's ships retreat and Antony's follow hers. His men are ashamed of what has happened, and many of them have deserted Antony and joined Caesar's forces. Enobarbus says he will stick with Antony, although this goes against his better judgment.

Act 3, Scene 11

At Cleopatra's palace in Alexandria, Antony is filled with shame for his retreat. He tells his attendants to desert him and make their peace with Octavius, but they affirm their loyalty to him. When Cleopatra enters, he bitterly reproaches her. She asks him to forgive her, saying that she never expected his ships to follow hers in retreat. He forgives her, even though he knows he is now humiliated, powerless and virtually at the mercy of Octavius.

Act 3, Scene 12

At Caesar's camp, Antony's messenger reports that Antony requests to be allowed to retire to Egypt or, if that not be granted, to live as a private citizen in Athens. Cleopatra requests that her sons be allowed to succeed her. Caesar rejects Antony's proposal and instead sends his ambassador, Thidias, to bribe Cleopatra so that she will betray Antony.

Act 3, Scene 13

Antony sends a message to Octavius, challenging him to single combat. Enobarbus knows Octavius will not accept the challenge and comments that Antony has lost his judgment. Thidias arrives and tries to persuade Cleopatra to leave Antony. Cleopatra tells Thidias to convey to Caesar that she lays her crown at his feet; she then allows Thidias to kiss her hand. When Antony enters and sees this, he becomes enraged; he orders Thidias to be whipped and then berates Cleopatra. His men bring back Thidias, who has been whipped, and Antony sends him back to Octavius with a defiant message. He confesses to Cleopatra, however, that his fall is imminent. Cleopatra reassures him of her love, which encourages him. He resolves to fight again with Octavius's forces on land and at sea. They go off to celebrate before resuming battle. Meanwhile Enobarbus, who has witnessed what has happened, confirms his judgment that Antony has lost his reason and thus makes plans to desert him.

Act 4, Scene 1

Octavius Caesar scoffs at the challenge sent by messenger from Antony to fight with him in a duel. He tells Maecenas that he is ready for battle and is confident of victory; many of Antony's soldiers have already deserted him and are ready to fight on Caesar's side.

Act 4, Scene 2

Antony's camp makes its own preparations with foreboding. Before supper, Antony speaks warmly to his servants, but also remarks that the next day they may find themselves with a new master. The servants all weep with sorrow. Questioned by Enobarbus, Antony says that he was trying to cheer his followers up and hopes to lead them all to victory in the battle.

Act 4, Scene 3

Outside Cleopatra's palace, three of Antony's soldiers discuss their prospects in the upcoming battle. They hear some mysterious music and do not know where it comes from. They decide that it is a sign that the god Hercules is leaving Antony.

Act 4, Scenes 4–6

The next day, Eros brings Antony his armor, and Cleopatra affectionately helps him put it on. At first Antony protests at her interference, but then says that she has done better at it than Eros. His captains and some soldiers enter, and Antony greets them confidently. He kisses Cleopatra goodbye. At Antony's camp, word comes that Enobarbus has deserted to Octavius, and Antony generously forgives his old friend and sends his belongings after him. Meanwhile, Octavius gives word for the battle to begin; his instructions are that Antony be taken alive. Enobarbus regrets his decision to leave Antony, and when he learns of his former leader's generosity, he is heartbroken.

Act 4, Scenes 7–9

The fighting begins; Antony is at first victorious, and he and his men are jubilant. Caesar's forces are in retreat. Antony returns in triumph to Cleopatra's palace, saying that they will finish the job the following morning before dawn. He thanks his soldiers for their efforts, and greets Cleopatra joyfully. Meanwhile, back at Caesar's camp, Enobarbus continues to repent for his betrayal of Antony, and calls out for Antony to forgive him. He falls into a swoon and dies. Two Roman sentries observe this and carry his body away.

Act 4, Scenes 11–12

During another sea battle, Cleopatra's forces yield to Caesar, and Antony's forces are routed. A furious Antony blames Cleopatra for the defeat and vows to be revenged on her. When she enters, he tells her to go away or he will kill her.

Act 4, Scene 13

Fearing Antony's rage, Cleopatra takes refuge in a monument and sends her servant Mardian with a message to Antony that she has killed herself. She asks Mardian to tell her how Antony reacts to this news.

Act 4, Scene 14

A distraught Antony laments to Eros that Cleopatra betrayed him. When Antony, who is already ashamed of his military dishonor, receives word of Cleopatra's apparent suicide, he resolves to end his own life. He reminds Eros of the oath the soldier swore that he would kill Antony when ordered to do so. The devoted Eros protests that he cannot do such an act, and Antony repeatedly tries to cajole him into obeying his command. Finally, Eros, having asked Antony to turn his face away, draws his sword, but instead of killing his master, he plunges the sword into his own body. Even more ashamed than before, Antony responds to Eros's death by falling on his own sword. But he succeeds only in wounding himself. He calls in his guards and begs them to finish him off, but they all refuse. When Diomedes, a messenger from Cleopatra, appears with news that Cleopatra only pretended that she was dead because she feared his rage, the dying Antony asks to be carried to her monument.

Act 4, Scene 15

At Cleopatra's monument, Antony and Cleopatra are lovingly reunited. He tells her to make her peace with Caesar and gain assurances for her safety. He also warns her that out of all of Octavius Caesar's entourage, only Proculeius can be trusted. Antony dies, and the grief-stricken Cleopatra faints. When she revives, she tells Charmian and Iras that after they have buried Antony, they will take their own lives.

Act 5, Scene 1

At Caesar's camp in Alexandria, Antony's man Decretas brings Antony's sword as proof of his leader's death. He tells Caesar that Antony killed himself. Octavius seems genuinely distressed by this news, and he laments the destruction of a great warrior. Octavius sends Proculeius to Egypt to meet with Cleopatra and tell her that Caesar means her no harm. Caesar wants to avoid giving Cleopatra any excuse to take her own life, since he intends, as he clearly informs Proculeius, that she should be brought back alive to Rome as captive.

Act 5, Scene 2

In a room in the monument, Cleopatra has calmly resolved to take her own life. When Proculeius arrives, she asks to be allowed to give Egypt to her son. Proculeius assures her that she has nothing to fear from Caesar. But then Gallus and some other soldiers enter and seize Cleopatra, who quickly draws a dagger. Proculeius prevents the queen from stabbing herself—a move that would have foiled Caesar's plan to parade her in captivity through Rome. Cleopatra resolves to starve herself to death if necessary. After Proculeius exits, Cleopatra tells Dolabella of her vision of Antony's greatness, and Dolabella confirms her fears that Caesar will exhibit her to the crowds in Rome as his conquest.

Octavius himself goes to Egypt to meet with Cleopatra, who kneels to him. He assures her that she will be well treated. He warns her not to take her own life, threatening to kill her children if she does. She gives him a list of all her worldly riches, but when Seleucus, her treasurer enters, it transpires that she has listed only half of what she owns. Caesar is not angry with her, but Cleopatra is furious with Seleucus for betraying her secret. She claims that she has only failed to divulge a few small items, as well as some larger pieces that she intended as gifts for Livia (Caesar's wife) and Octavia. Caesar continues to speak respectfully to her, assuring her of his care and concern for her, but Cleopatra is not fooled. Dolabella enters and informs her Caesar will depart for Syria, and that within three days, she and her children will be sent away, their ultimate destination Rome. Cleopatra has already made arrangements for her own suicide, and now a Clown, or comical rustic, arrives and supplies her with poisonous serpents, or asps, hidden in a basket of figs. The queen's maids, Charmian and Iras, bring Cleopatra her robe, crown and other jewels. Just before she puts the asp to her breast, she says farewell to her maids, and Iras faints and dies. Cleopatra then puts another asp to her arm and dies calling out Antony's name. Charmian follows Cleopatra's example by poisoning herself with an asp bite. Octavius Caesar enters, and when he finds Cleopatra dead, he orders that her body be buried with Antony's.

MEDIA ADAPTATIONS

- There are several versions of the play available on DVD and VHS. Charlton Heston directed a film version of *Antony and Cleopatra* in 1972. Heston plays Antony, Hildegard Neil plays Cleopatra, and Eric Porter plays Enobarbus. The film is available only on VHS.

- Jon Scoffield directed a version of the play in which Richard Johnson played Antony and Janet Suzman played Cleopatra. It was released on DVD in 2004 by Lions Gate.

- *The Plays of William Shakespeare*, Vol. 1, *Antony and Cleopatra* (1981) stars Timothy Dalton and Lynn Redgrave. It was released on DVD in 2001 by Kultur video.

CHARACTERS

Agrippa

Agrippa is a friend and follower of Octavius Caesar. It is Agrippa who suggests that the differences between Antony and Octavius might be resolved through marriage between Antony and Caesar's sister, Octavia. Later, Agrippa leads Octavius Caesar's forces against Antony.

Alexas

Alexas is an attendant to Cleopatra. He jokes with Cleopatra's maids, Charmian and Iras, at the beginning of the play. Late in the play, Alexas is reported to have joined with, and then been executed by, Octavius Caesar.

Antony

Antony is the Roman triumvir, or coleader, and lover of Cleopatra. He spends a great deal of his time in Alexandria with Cleopatra, much to the disgust of his younger fellow triumvir, Octavius. After his first wife, Fulvia, dies while rebelling against Octavius, Antony marries Octavius's sister, Octavia, to achieve reconciliation with the

Roman triumvirate. Antony, however, soon returns to Cleopatra, and Octavius angrily declares war against them both. After losing the battle at Actium, Antony asks to be allowed to retire to Egypt with Cleopatra, but Octavius refuses to grant his request. Antony resumes his war with Octavius, winning one skirmish but badly losing another. In despair over his lost honor and the apparent death of Cleopatra, Antony mortally wounds himself. He goes to Cleopatra's monument and the two lovers are reconciled before he dies.

While there is critical consensus that Antony functions as a tragic hero in the play, there is disagreement concerning exactly when he becomes a tragic figure and what it is that transforms him. Those commentators who describe Antony as torn between his Roman values of duty and valor and his Egyptian obsession with sex and dissipation assert that he achieves tragic status when he reclaims his honor through the Roman death of suicide. Similarly, critics have suggested that, as long as Antony allows himself to be treated in Egypt as "a strumpet's fool" (act 1, scene 1, line 13), he remains a ridiculous figure. After he is defeated at Actium, however, Antony's shame is so intense that his fate becomes tragic. Some critics regard Antony's own "weakness" as the source of his tragedy. In essence, these critics argue that Antony's tragedy is that he sacrifices everything—physical strength, honor, political power, respect—simply to indulge his senses with Cleopatra in Egypt. Finally, some scholars assert that Antony stumbles tragically when he tries to have it all—power and respect in Rome alongside ease and love in Egypt.

An alternative view of Antony's tragic status is that he operates according to a moral code different from the one followed by Octavius. According to this view, the public-oriented Octavius adheres to a standard Roman code of honor that takes into account such issues as political expediency. Antony, on the other hand, defines honor in more personal terms. Loving Cleopatra and enjoying himself in Egypt at the expense of his duties in Rome do not impinge on his sense of honor. However, retreating during the sea battle at Actium is, according to Antony, a cowardly act and is therefore highly dishonorable. In light of this assessment, Antony's role in the play is a tragic one because he is unable to reconcile his private concept of honor with the general one exemplified by the activities of the triumvirs in Rome.

Antony's tragic status has also been discussed in tandem with Cleopatra's role. Commentators who view the lovers as equals argue that, at the beginning of the play, both are self-absorbed despite their love for each other and thus, they are continually in conflict. These critics note that toward the close of the play, Antony and Cleopatra transcend their selfishness as a result of their suffering, and then they learn to recognize each other's worth and together achieve status as tragic heroes.

Canidius

Canidius is lieutenant-general to Antony. Along with Enobarbus, Canidius advises Antony against engaging Octavius Caesar in a sea battle at Actium. After the defeat at Actium, Canidius decides to desert Antony and join Octavius.

Charmian

Charmian is an attendant or maid-in-waiting to Cleopatra. She and Iras are Cleopatra's closest servants. A soothsayer predicts that she will outlive the lady whom she serves, which proves true, if only by a few minutes. Charmian attends Cleopatra in the monument where the queen commits suicide; after mournfully straightening Cleopatra's crown, Charmian follows her example by poisoning herself to death with the bite of an asp, a type of venomous serpent, possibly an Egyptian cobra.

Cleopatra

Cleopatra is the queen of Egypt and lover of Antony. Although she is aging, Cleopatra is celebrated in the play for her beauty and sexual magnetism. She is jealous of Antony's connections with Rome and of his apparent subservience to Octavius Caesar. She and Antony join forces to fight Octavius, but when they are ultimately defeated by him, Antony accuses Cleopatra of betrayal. She responds to Antony's anger by locking herself away in her monument and feigning suicide. Antony himself commits suicide as a result of her apparent death, and Octavius arrives claiming victory over Egypt. Mourning Antony, and afraid of being led in captivity back to Rome, Cleopatra uses asps, to kill herself in her monument.

Critical reaction to Cleopatra has been strong and often negative. Early commentators in particular characterized the Egyptian queen as self-indulgent, self-pitying, capricious, and treacherous. They considered the character Philo's description of her in act 1 as a lustful "strumpet," or whore, to be appropriate. They found her taunting of Antony cruel, and her apparent acceptance of Octavius Caesar's bribe in act 3 reprehensible. They roundly blamed her for Antony's downfall. Today, scholarly evaluations of Cleopatra are more moderate. Increasingly, commentators have come to regard Antony and Cleopatra as mutually responsible for their fates. Several critics have described the earlier assessments of Cleopatra as extreme and sexist; they emphasize the importance of objectivity to any discussion of the Egyptian queen; further, they observe that she deserves no more and no less sympathy than does, for example, a tragic hero like King Lear or Othello.

Those commentators who view Cleopatra in a negative light usually insist that she is too self-absorbed to qualify for tragic status. There are those, however, who regard her selfish ignorance as the very source of her tragedy. A more temperate version of this argument is that Cleopatra acts out of self-interest until she witnesses Antony's death. At that point, some critics assert, she recognizes, too late, Antony's worth and the extent of her love for him; as a result, she achieves tragic status. Cleopatra's tragedy has also been ranked as commensurate with Antony's. Scholars contend that both characters are initially self-interested and untrustworthy in love: Cleopatra is jealous of Antony's preoccupation with Rome; at the same time, Antony tries to satisfy political ambitions through marriage with Octavia. Neither, some commentators assert, achieves tragic status until both reach mutual understanding and love before their deaths at the close of the play.

Some commentators dispense with any discussion of Cleopatra's qualification as a tragic hero and concentrate instead on the lines accorded to her in the play. She is, they observe, the vehicle for some of Shakespeare's most eloquent poetry. Her remembrance in act 1, scene 5, for example, of her youth as her "salad days, / When [she] was green in judgment, cold in blood," (lines 73–74) and her vision of Antony in act 5, scene 2, as someone so remarkable as to

Antony and Cleopatra, with Charmian, Iras, and Eros in Act III, scene xi (© *Shakespeare Collection, Special Collections Library, University of Michigan*)

be "past the size of dreaming" (line 97) are evocative, and justifiably famous.

Clown
The Clown is a comical, rustic character. At Cleopatra's command, the Clown brings her venomous serpents, or asps, hidden in a basket of figs. Thus, the Clown delivers to Cleopatra her means of suicide in act 5.

Demetrius
Demetrius is a friend and follower of Antony who discusses Antony's decline with Philo in the first scene of the play.

Diomedes
Diomedes is an attendant to Cleopatra. He is sent by a worried Cleopatra to tell Antony that she is not really dead. But her message comes too late, and the dying Antony asks Diomedes to deliver the final deathblow with his own sword.

Diomedes refuses and instead helps deliver Antony to Cleopatra in her monument.

Dolabella
Dolabella is a follower of Octavius Caesar. In act 5, Dolabella warns Cleopatra that Octavius Caesar plans to humiliate her by parading her in disgrace back to Rome. Thus Dolabella precipitates Cleopatra's decision to commit suicide.

Domitius Enobarbus
Enobarbus is a friend and follower of Antony. He delivers the famous description of Cleopatra on her barge and accurately predicts that Antony will never be able to leave the Egyptian queen for Octavia. After the sea battle of Actium, Enobarbus decides to desert Antony, whom he thinks is overly influenced by Cleopatra. When Antony learns of his betrayal and generously sends him his belongings, Enobarbus is stricken with guilt and dies of remorse.

Eros

Eros is a servant to Antony. In act 3, Eros announces the resumption of war between Octavius and Pompey as well as Octavius's imprisonment of Lepidus. In act 4, Antony (who is in despair over his losses to Caesar and the apparent suicide of Cleopatra) orders Eros to kill him. The devoted Eros responds to this command by killing himself instead.

Iras

Iras is an attendant or maid-in-waiting to Cleopatra. She and Charmian are the Egyptian queen's closest servants. Along with Charmian, Iras waits upon Cleopatra in the monument. Iras helps to dress Cleopatra, then dies of grief shortly before the queen commits suicide.

Lepidus

Lepidus is the third and weakest member of the Roman triumvirate. Lepidus tries to act as conciliator between the two rival members of the triumvirate—Antony and Octavius. He has a minor role in the peace negotiations with Pompey. Afterward, Lepidus becomes the most drunken participant in the celebration on Pompey's galley. In act 3, it transpires that Lepidus has been accused of treason and imprisoned by Octavius, who intends to have him executed.

Mardian

Mardian is a eunuch in attendance at Cleopatra's court. Mardian entertains Cleopatra with sexually suggestive jokes in act 1. In act 4, the queen sends him to Antony with false news of her death, thus precipitating Antony's own suicide.

Menas

Menas is a pirate and supporter of Pompey. In act 1, it is reported that Menas is having great success at sea and making raids on the coasts of Italy. Menas believes that Pompey is too cautious in his dealings with the triumvirate. After Pompey refuses to follow Menas's advice to assassinate the triumvirs while they are celebrating on his galley, Menas deserts him.

Octavia

Octavia is the sister of Octavius Caesar. Octavia's marriage to Antony is meant to result in reconciliation between the two antagonistic triumvirs. Although devoted to her brother, Octavia is loyal to Antony once she becomes his wife, and thus she tries—unsuccessfully—to mediate between the two men and their disagreements. In personality, Octavia is the opposite of Cleopatra. Whereas Cleopatra is lively and flirtatious, Octavia is worthy, dutiful, and dull. Enobarbus sums up Octavia when he predicts that the newly married Antony will soon leave his wife for Cleopatra: "Octavia is of a holy, cold, and still conversation."

Octavius Caesar

Octavius Caesar is the Roman leader and head of the triumvirate that includes himself, Antony, and Lepidus. Octavius is younger than Antony, and Cleopatra calls attention to his youth in act 1, when she refers to him as "the scarce-bearded Caesar." Octavius is disgusted with Antony's love for Cleopatra and condemns Antony for luxuriating in Alexandria while there are wars to be fought in the empire. Octavius and Antony are briefly reconciled through Antony's marriage to Octavius's sister, Octavia. Octavius imprisons Lepidus—the weakest member of the triumvirate—and declares war on Antony, claiming that he has betrayed Rome by deserting Octavia and returning to Cleopatra. Octavius ultimately defeats Antony and Cleopatra's forces, and becomes sole emperor of the known world. But Octavius is saddened by Antony's suicide, and is prevented from parading Cleopatra in triumph back to Rome by her suicide.

While earlier critics regarded Octavius Caesar primarily as a representative of Imperial Rome, today most commentators look to the play for what it reveals about Octavius as a character. Significantly, it has been noted that this leader of the triumvirs delivers no soliloquies or personality-revealing asides. Octavius is so terse in his remarks that several commentators are in disagreement concerning such details as whether or not he becomes drunk along with the other triumvirs on Pompey's galley in act 2.

Most scholars agree that Caesar is cold and self-restrained. Some argue that he is thus meant to function as a foil to the extravagant lovers, Antony and Cleopatra. Others consider his prudish criticism of Antony as hypocritical in light of the fact that he cruelly betrays the weakest triumvir, Lepidus. There is a general consensus that Octavius carefully calculates each move he makes and that he is a manipulator. Thus he exploits Antony's sensitivity about his honor by challenging his competitor to a sea battle in act 3. Similarly, Octavius sends Thidias to Cleopatra in act 3, hoping to bribe and flatter her away from Antony. After Antony's death, Octavius lies to Cleopatra, telling her she has nothing to fear from him, when he is in fact planning to capture her and exhibit her in Rome.

An alternative perspective on Octavius Caesar is that he lacks imagination and empathy and is therefore vulnerable to faulty judgment. So, for example, he is unable to prevent either Antony or Cleopatra from committing suicide and as a result is robbed of the satisfaction of parading them—and their defeat—through Rome. According to this view, Octavius is less in control than he thinks he is or than he wishes to be.

Philo
Philo is a friend and follower of Antony. As the play opens, Philo tells Demetrius of his disgust with Antony's "dotage" or infatuation with Cleopatra.

Pompey
See Sextus Pompeius.

Sextus Pompeius
Sextus Pompeius, known as Pompey, is a rebel against the triumvirate. Pompey feels secure in the strength of his forces as long as the strongest member of the triumvirate—Antony—is luxuriating in Egypt. Once Pompey hears of Antony's return to Rome, he decides to seek peace with the triumvirate, and the negotiated settlement is celebrated on board Pompey's galley. During the celebration, Pompey rejects Menas's dishonorable offer to assassinate the members of the triumvirate while they are drunk on board his galley. Pompey and the triumvirate are at war again later in the play, and in act 3, we hear that Pompey has been murdered.

Proculeius
Proculeius is a friend and follower of Octavius Caesar. When Antony is dying, he tells Cleopatra that Proculeius is the only follower of Octavius whom she can trust. Proculeius in fact proves unreliable: on orders from Caesar, he lies to Cleopatra and prevents her from committing suicide so that she can be brought back to Rome in humiliation.

Scarus
Scarus is a friend and follower of Antony. In act 3, a distressed Scarus describes Antony's retreat at Actium; unlike Enobarbus and Canidius, Scarus remains faithful to Antony throughout his defeats.

Seleucus
Seleucus is a treasurer to Cleopatra. In act 5, Seleucus contradicts Cleopatra, claiming that she has purposely lied to Caesar regarding the extent of her wealth. An angry Cleopatra berates him and cites his betrayal as an example of her ebb in fortune.

Soothsayer
The Soothsayer is an Egyptian fortune-teller. He predicts that Charmian's fortunes are in decline; her best days are behind her. He says the same about Iras. The Soothsayer travels to Rome with Antony where he declares that Caesar's fortunes will rise higher than Antony's, and that Antony should not stay close to him. Whenever they are close, the Soothsayer says, Caesar has more luck than Antony.

Thidias
Thidias is a follower of Octavius Caesar. After Antony's defeat at Actium, Octavius sends Thidias to bribe Cleopatra to abandon Antony. When Antony catches sight of Thidias kissing Cleopatra's hand, he orders that the man be whipped and returned to Octavius.

Varrius
Varrius is a friend and follower of Pompey. He informs Pompey of Antony's return to Rome, thus setting in motion the peace treaty between Pompey and the triumvirate.

Ventidius
Ventidius is a subordinate of Antony who commands an army that triumphs over the Parthians in Syria.

THEMES

Rome versus Egypt
The play focuses on the personal relationship between Antony and Cleopatra, and in doing so it juxtaposes two value systems, Rome and Egypt. Rome, the West, as embodied in Octavius

Caesar, is a guardian of moral restraint, personal responsibility, social order, reason, and military discipline. Further, Rome places a high value on honor and duty toward one's country. By contrast, Egypt, the east, Cleopatra's realm, is seen as a magnet for decadence, desire, lust, and indolence. Egypt, according to this view, places a high value on physical enjoyment and luxuriant fertility. Egypt is the place to have fun; Rome is the place to work. Egypt equals private life, the sphere of the personal and the individual; Rome equals public life, affairs of state, and politics. Rome is reason; Egypt is emotion. Other pairs of opposites can be applied to this basic duality. The rational world (Rome) and the irrational (Egypt is the realm where dreams and fortune-telling have their place). Masculine self-assertion is opposed by feminine sweetness. Antony, the great Roman warrior who conceives an overwhelming passion for Cleopatra, is torn between these two worlds. He must try to reconcile these two aspects of his own being. As the play opens, he is clearly divided against himself; he has failed to integrate the sensual nature with the martial aspect. When a messenger brings him news from Rome in act 1, he seems to reject it completely, opting instead for passionate personal experience:

> Let Rome in Tiber melt, and the wide
>   arch
> Of the rang'd empire fall! Here is my space,
> Kingdoms are clay: our dungy earth alike
> Feeds beast as man; the nobleness of life
> Is to do thus . . .

He then embraces Cleopatra. In this speech, Antony declares his desire that Rome, the solid, fixed world of clearly defined obligations and boundaries, should melt into the waters of the river Tiber, which represents the fluidity and boundlessness of the emotional life fully and passionately lived. All he wants at this moment is to be alone with Cleopatra. In the next scene, however, Cleopatra reports that Antony was enjoying himself "but on the sudden/A Roman thought hath struck him." He becomes the Roman general again, realizing that he must break "these strong Egyptian fetters" or lose himself "in dotage." Antony is aware that this is a struggle within himself between opposing values, and throughout the play, he vacillates between one or the other, unable to harmonize the two.

This conflict between opposites also suggests the traditional astrological opposition between warlike Mars—in the first speech in the play, Antony in battle is compared to Mars—and loving Venus. In Roman myth, Mars and Venus, Mars's paramour, come together and produce a daughter, Harmony. Many Renaissance paintings depict this harmony between Mars and Venus by showing Venus playing with Mars's armor. Interestingly, in act 2, scene 5, Cleopatra recalls an incident in which she did exactly this. She tells her maid Charmian that one night following drunken revelry, she put Antony to bed and placed her clothes on him, while she wore his sword Philippan, the very sword that Antony wielded in the battle against Brutus and Cassius at Philippi. The difference in the symbolism is that the incident recalled in the play suggests an inappropriate reversal of roles rather than a harmonious interchange between the two. As such, it is typical of the play as a whole. When Antony forgets his Roman role, disaster strikes; similarly, when Cleopatra tries to take on a Roman role—playing a leading part in the battle of Actium, for example—the result is equally disastrous. It appears that the two opposing values are never reconciled. Just as Octavius can never be anything other than the embodiment of all the Roman qualities (including the duplicity of the politician), Cleopatra can never be anything other than the volatile, sensual, bewitching queen, and poor Antony is destroyed because he is inextricably caught between the two.

On the other hand, many critics have argued that analyzing the play in terms of an opposition between the values associated with Rome and Egypt is too simple. They suggest that the elements at work in the play cannot be so neatly grouped into rigid pairs because, just as the political alliances in the play shift, so do the groupings in the play's structure. For example, Antony's dilemma has been described as involving a choice between love and war; between, that is, his life with Cleopatra in Egypt and his profession as a soldier in Rome. In contrast, critics have argued that Antony's dilemma is solved when love and death are paired through his and Cleopatra's suicides. Commentators have observed that, when Octavius commands the burial of the lovers in the same grave in act 5, he acknowledges that death has immortalized the love of "a pair so famous" as Antony and Cleopatra.

Recent criticism has suggested that Rome and Egypt are alike to the degree that they are both in decline, and that the love of Antony and Cleopatra does not reflect the opposition between the two countries or the conflict endured by Antony, but the temporary triumph of imperialism. The love shared by Antony and Cleopatra, some critics argue, is as imperious and undemocratic as the new government in Rome. The lovers themselves describe their feelings in imperial terms; Antony, for instance, claims that his affection is capable of conquering whole worlds and of blotting out geographical formations.

Scholars have also remarked that the decline of Rome and Egypt is the result of changes in both nations: Republican Rome is now Imperial Rome; Egypt is ruled by an unpredictable and aging queen. Rome is prey to shifting alliances and political betrayal by Octavius, who bickers with one triumvir (Antony) and jails another (Lepidus); Egypt is subject to the flooding of the Nile and the unpredictable fortunes of Antony and Cleopatra's love. Both Egypt and Rome, one critic has observed, are pagan nations, which will soon give way to Christianity. Some commentators suggest that ultimately, it is less constructive to view Rome and Egypt as separate entities than as shifting and intermingling locations of waxing and waning power that affect, and are affected by, the two lovers.

Morality and Transcendence

One way of reading the play is to see it as the downfall of a great man through his self-indulgence, his failure to resist temptation and pleasure, and his consequent neglect of his duty. This is certainly how the Roman world viewed the historical Antony, who was contrasted with the "good" Roman, Aeneas, who resisted the temptation to stay with his lover Dido in Carthage and went on to found Rome. (The story of Aeneas is told in Virgil's epic poem the *Aeneid*.) Seen in this light, *Antony and Cleopatra* becomes something of a morality play, in which the two lovers pay a deadly price for their moral transgressions. Antony is weak; Cleopatra selfish; and their deaths are both inevitable and appropriate.

There is plenty of material in the play that would support such a reading. The first thirteen lines, spoken by Antony's disillusioned man Philo, gives the audience, before they have even seen Antony, a devastating picture of the decline

TOPICS FOR FURTHER STUDY

- Research the life of Octavius Caesar, who later became known as Augustus Caesar. Write a paper that describes his principal achievements in building the Roman Empire. Was the peace he brought a fair price for the autocratic form of government he developed?

- Compare *Antony and Cleopatra* to Shakespeare's earlier play about two fated lovers, *Romeo and Juliet*. What do the two plays have in common, and how do they differ? Make a class presentation with your findings.

- Write a paper in which you contrast Antony and Octavius. What qualities does Octavius possess that enable him to triumph over Antony? Which character do you prefer, and why?

- Watch any film version of *Antony and Cleopatra* you can obtain and compare it to the stage play. How faithful is it to Shakespeare's text? What scenes and characters are cut? What does the film emphasize that a stage performance cannot? Make a class presentation, using video clips from the film to illustrate your points.

of the great general, who has now reached his "dotage" (line 1):

> Take but good note, and you shall see in
> him
> The triple pillar of the world transform'd
> Into a strumpet's fool.

To this can be added the appearance of Antony in the next scene, when he struggles to break away from Cleopatra. He is clearly a man in great psychic turmoil, torn between two opposing and apparently irreconcilable worlds. Furthermore, Octavius's harsh words about his fellow triumvar, in act 1, scene 4, add to the picture of a man in a steep decline through lack of self-discipline. According to Octavius, Antony drinks and spends his nights in revelry, and has allowed himself to become feminized by his Egyptian lover: He "is not more manlike / Than Cleopatra; nor the queen of Ptolemy / More womanly than he." Caesar concludes that Antony is "a man who is the abstract of all faults / That all men follow" (lines 8–9).

But in spite of this apparent degeneration of a great hero, audiences and readers often find themselves unwilling to condemn the lovers, even though Antony and Cleopatra's recklessness, their irresponsibility, and their cruelty towards each other is plain for everyone to see. Judgments are suspended because Antony and Cleopatra's love seems to transcend all narrow moral boundaries. They have a vision of each other that makes them seem transfigured. Their love cannot be contained within a mundane sphere but leaps towards a visionary and poetic transcendence. Cleopatra sees Antony as a god-like being, and just before his death, Antony envisions that he and Cleopatra will be together again in Hades, "Where souls do couch on flowers, we'll hand in hand, / And with our sprightly port make the ghosts gaze." At the end of the play, Cleopatra, full of "immortal longings," dons her robe and crown and goes to meet Antony in some spiritual realm of experience that is beyond the ability of the prosaic Roman world to understand.

STYLE

Language and Imagery

Antony and Cleopatra is distinguished among Shakespeare's plays for its lush, evocative language. Some critics have even suggested that it should be classified with Shakespeare's long poems rather than ranked alongside his plays. Scholarly discussion has focused on Enobarbus's vividly detailed depiction of Cleopatra on her barge and on the lovers' continual use of hyperbole, or exaggerated language, to describe each other as well as their affection for one another.

Some critics have argued that the hyperbolic language in *Antony and Cleopatra* makes it a highly problematical play to stage. What actor, for example, is so physically fit that he can portray a character like Antony, whose "legs bestrid the ocean" and whose "rear'd arm / Crested the world"? What actress is charismatic enough to play Cleopatra, who is described as more seductive than Venus, the goddess of love? Other critics have observed that Shakespeare was well aware of this conflict between language and reality and that he makes this clear in act 5 when the defeated Cleopatra imagines that plays written in Rome about the former lovers will feature Antony as a drunk and herself as a "whore" played—as was the custom in Renaissance England—by a "squeaking . . . boy."

Scholars have identified a variety of reasons for the existence of heightened language and vivid imagery in *Antony and Cleopatra*. Some have demonstrated its usefulness in highlighting the changing moods or fortunes of particular characters. Thus Antony's men effectively display their disappointment in their leader and his noticeable transformation when they complain that Antony has been reduced from acting like the god of war to behaving like the mere fawning servant of a lustful woman. Similarly, it has been pointed out that while Antony describes his love for Cleopatra in hyperbolic terms, he does not lose sight of his own importance in the world of politics. For instance, even as he asserts that his love for Cleopatra renders everything else in the world unimportant, he demands that the people of the world take note of his love or else face punishment from him. Thus we are introduced to the conflicting feelings—romantic love versus honorable renown—that plague Antony and that ultimately destroy him.

Several critics have suggested that Antony and Cleopatra's hyperbolic poetry mirrors the paradoxes at work in the play: love versus death, and immortality versus aging, for example. In connection with this, several scholars have noted the frequent use of images that link death, love, and immortality. The preponderance of death imagery intensifies the tragic nature of Antony and Cleopatra's love. Death imagery also emphasizes the fact that both lovers are aging. Aging and death are things that the extraordinary Antony and Cleopatra have in common with ordinary people, all of whom must come to terms with their mortality; therefore, some critics conclude that the imagery and hyperbole in *Antony and Cleopatra* are intended to reinforce the fact that all human beings are by their very nature extraordinary.

Katherine Vance MacMullan is one critic who has closely examined the frequent appearance of death imagery in the play. Noting that the image of death as a bridegroom was commonplace to Renaissance audiences, MacMullan asserts that Shakespeare developed the image beyond this familiar cliché. In *Antony and Cleopatra*, MacMullan contends, death imagery is meant to symbolize Antony's overpowering passion for Cleopatra, his diminishing political powers, and "the weakening of his judgment in the command of practical affairs." MacMullan also demonstrates how Shakespeare connects the image of death with those of sleep, darkness, and light to emphasize the inevitability of the lovers' tragic fate.

HISTORICAL CONTEXT

The Rise of Mark Antony

The Roman general Mark Antony was born in Rome in approximately 83 B.C.E. As a young man he distinguished himself as a cavalry commander in Judea and Egypt. He was a military leader in the Gallic Wars of 58–50 B.C.E. and a staunch supporter of Julius Caesar. During the civil war against Pompey (49–45 B.C.E.), Antony was Caesar's second in command.

Following Caesar's assassination in March 44 B.C.E., the Roman republic had three rivals for power: Antony, Marcus Lepidus, and Caesar's great-nephew Octavian Caesar (historically, he is known as Octavian rather than Octavius as in Shakespeare's play). Antony was defeated in one battle but escaped to Gaul and then marched with Lepidus to Rome, where the eighteen-year-old Octavian had taken power. In 43 B.C.E., the three men called a truce and became a ruling triumvirate. Octavian and Antony then set out for the east in pursuit of Caesar's assassins. Octavian was sick and did not participate in the battle at Philippi in Macedonia in 42 B.C.E., in which Antony triumphed over Cassius and Brutus, both of whom committed suicide. The territories controlled by Rome were then split up amongst the triumvars. Antony received Gaul and the east; Lepidus was given Africa; and Octavian was given Sardinia, Spain, and Sicily.

Antony was not only an effective military leader, he was also extremely popular with his troops. He was warm-hearted and not aloof; he would sit down to eat and drink with his men from the common soldiers' tables. He was also known for his generosity to his friends, and

for his good humor. Resourceful in adversity, Antony was an inspiration to his men. After being defeated at a battle at Modena, for example, Antony and his army encountered famine on their retreat. But Antony, who was used to luxurious living, made no fuss about having to drink foul water and feed on wild fruit, roots, and even the bark of trees. This incident is recorded by the Roman historian Plutarch, in his work *The Lives of the Noble Grecians and Romans*, which is Shakespeare's source for *Antony and Cleopatra*. Antony's stoic acceptance of this difficult situation is mentioned in the play in act 1, scene 4, when Octavius, complaining about Antony's dalliance with Cleopatra, recalls his rival's former greatness.

Plutarch described Antony's physical appearance in this way: "He had also a very good and noble appearance; his beard was well grown, his forehead large, and his nose aquiline, giving him altogether a bold, masculine look that reminded people of the face of Hercules in paintings and sculptures." Although Antony's virtues were many, Plutarch also comments that he was given to folly and extravagance. It appears that Antony was known for his love of luxury and his penchant for self-indulgent amusement when times were easy.

The establishment of the triumvirate did not result in universal peace. In 41–40 B.C.E., Antony's ex-wife, Fulvia, was coleader, with Antony's brother, of a rebellion against Octavian. Fulvia was forced to surrender and was exiled to Sicyon, where she died awaiting Antony's return.

Antony, meanwhile, traveling to the east to subdue rebellions and conquer Parthia, met Cleopatra VII of Egypt in 41 B.C.E. He summoned her to meet him in Cilicia, ready to accuse her of aiding Cassius and Brutus in the war against him. Cleopatra sailed up the river Cydnus adorned as the goddess Aphrodite, and Antony immediately fell under her spell. She quickly became his mistress, and in December 40 B.C.E. bore him twins, Alexander Helios (sun) and Cleopatra Selene (moon).

Not long after this, Octavian was faced with a rebellion by Sextus Pompeius (Pompey). Antony returned to Rome and patched up his uneasy relations with Octavian by marrying Octavian's sister, Octavia. Antony then traveled to Greece with his new wife, intent on continuing his campaign against the Parthians. But Octavian, still dealing with the threat from Pompey, was unable to send him any forces, so in 37 B.C.E., Antony returned to Alexandria, hoping that the wealthy Cleopatra would support his cause. Antony then settled in Alexandria and married Cleopatra (even though he was still married to Octavia). She bore him another son, Ptolemy Philadelphus.

Cleopatra

Cleopatra was born in 69 B.C.E. in Alexandria, the third daughter of the king Ptolemy XII. She became queen in 51 B.C.E., at first sharing the throne with her younger brother, Ptolemy XIII. After a civil war, in which Julius Caesar aided Cleopatra, Ptolemy XIII was drowned and a younger brother, Ptolemy XIV, became coruler.

During his stay in Egypt, from 48 B.C.E. to 47 B.C.E., Caesar took Cleopatra as a lover, and she gave birth to his child, Caesarion. As Cleopatra says in the play of Caesar, "When thou wast here above the ground, I was / A morsel for a monarch." Cleopatra wanted Caesar to name Caesarion as his heir, but Caesar named Octavius instead.

Although she was queen of Egypt, Cleopatra was, in fact, Macedonian. The Romans called her Egyptian as a term of abuse. Cleopatra's language and culture was Greek; she was a highly educated woman who spoke seven languages and was one of the few of the Ptolemies to learn the Egyptian language. Her subjects considered her to be the daughter of the sun god, Re, and some saw her as the future leader of a great uprising of Asia against Rome. Plutarch, while presenting a largely negative view of Cleopatra, did acknowledge her as a fascinating woman: "The attraction of her person, joining with the charm of her conversation, and the character that attended all she said or did, was something bewitching. It was a pleasure merely to hear the sound of her voice."

Struggle between Antony and Octavian

In Rome, Octavian deposed of Lepidus in 36 B.C.E., and after that his relations with Antony steadily deteriorated. Eager to remove his one remaining rival, Octavian systematically defamed Antony's character, saying he was a drunkard who had fallen under the sway of a wicked woman and had forgotten his Roman duties. The Roman senate unleashed an attack on Cleopatra, calling her a sorceress who had bewitched Antony with drugs, sold herself out of a lust for power, and worshipped bestial gods. As Chester G. Starr puts it in *A History of the Ancient World*, "Cleopatra was magnified into a threat to the survival of Roman ways and Roman mastery, and so assumed the image of *femme fatale* which has ever since been her memory."

In 34 B.C.E., in a public ceremony in Alexandria, Antony distributed the kingdoms of the east to his children. Cleopatra was named Queen of Kings and Queen of Egypt, and her son Caesarion was declared the legitimate son and heir of Caesar. Needless to say, this was not well received in Rome, since the claim made for Caesarion was a threat to the legitimacy of Octavian as Caesar's rightful heir.

War between the two sides now became only a matter of time. Antony accused Octavian of usurping power, while Octavian countercharged Antony with treason. In 32 B.C.E., the senate stripped Antony of his powers and declared war on Cleopatra. Both Roman consuls and three hundred of the one thousand Roman senators declared their support for Antony and went to meet him and Cleopatra in Greece. In that year also, Antony divorced Octavia.

Battle of Actium

On September 2, 31 B.C.E., the decisive naval battle of Actium took place near the Roman colony of Actium in Greece, on the Ionian Sea. Octavian's fleet was commanded by Marcus Vipsanius Agrippa. Antony, supported by Cleopatra's fleet, attempted to lead 220 warships out of the gulf to the open seas, where Octavian's fleet attempted to block them. Antony's ships were large but undermanned because of an outbreak of malaria, and morale was low because supply lines had been cut. In contrast, Octavian possessed smaller, nimbler ships that could outmaneuver Antony's, and his men were better trained and in better condition.

When it became clear that Octavian's fleet was gaining the upper hand, Cleopatra's fleet retreated. Antony followed her lead and deserted the battle, while the ships he left behind were either captured or sunk. Antony fled to Egypt, but his military strength was reduced by massive desertions. Octavian pursued him, invading Egypt. Although Antony managed to win a skirmish at Alexandria on July 30, 30 B.C.E., he again suffered from desertions, leaving him with no means of resisting Octavian's advance. Believing

Cleopatra holds a small adder to her exposed breast (Hulton Archive/Getty Images)

that Cleopatra was dead, Antony decided to take his own life. Plutarch records how Antony died in Cleopatra's presence, after the two were reconciled, and Shakespeare closely follows Plutarch's account. Cleopatra attempted to negotiate terms of surrender with Octavian, but then, after learning from Cornelius Dolabella that Octavian intended to take her as a captive to Rome, she committed suicide on August 12, 30 B.C.E. According to Plutarch, Octavian was disappointed by her death, "yet could not but admire the greatness of her spirit, and gave order that her

COMPARE
&
CONTRAST

- **First century B.C.E.:** In 27 B.C.E., Octavian becomes known as Caesar Augustus. He will live until C.E. 14. The era he inaugurates embodies the highest achievements of Roman civilization in arts and letters. Augustus also creates a new, autocratic system of government that leads to several centuries of peace in the Roman Empire.

  Early seventeenth century: The Roman Empire no longer exists. Italy is not an independent nation but a collection of principalities, many of them under foreign domination. Rome forms part of the Papal States which are controlled by the Catholic Church and stretch from the central to the northern parts of what will later become the nation of Italy.

  Today: Italy is an independent, unified nation and is a member of the European Community. The nation is in the forefront of European economic and political unification. There are many ancient Roman structures and artefacts in Italy, and many of these are popular tourist attractions.

- **First century B.C.E.:** The Romans build solid, long-lasting roads throughout the empire. The speed of travel and communications therefore increases. The Romans operate an efficient postal service. The *cursus publicus*, state-sponsored post roads, is founded by Augustus to carry official mail; a relay of horses is able to carry mail quickly, covering about 170 miles in twenty-four hours.

  Early seventeenth century: The efficiency of the Roman *cursus publicus* has not yet been matched in post-Roman Empire Europe. However, a network of private postal services carries mail across the continent. These include the Thurn and Taxis service, which operates a network of postal routes in Spain, Germany, Austria, Italy, Hungary, and the Low Countries from 1512 to 1867.

  Today: Global communication by fax and email is virtually instant. Paper documents are delivered via express airmail to all parts of the world within a few days.

- **First century B.C.E.:** Ancient Rome has a well-established tradition of drama, dating from the comedies of Plautus and Terence, and the tragedies of Accius, in the second century, B.C.E. In 55 B.C.E., Pompey erects the first permanent stone theater in Rome. Roman drama is heavily influenced by the Greek dramatic tradition.

  Early seventeenth century: During the Italian Renaissance there is a movement known as Neoclassicism, which is based on a renewed interest in the classical drama of Rome. Drama follows what are thought to be the rules of classical drama; plays must conform to the three unities of time, place, and action, and must not mix comedy with tragedy.

  Today: The Theatre of Marcellus, completed by Augustus in 11 B.C.E., is the only surviving ancient theater in Rome. It is named after Marcus Marcellus, Augustus's nephew. Originally it could hold eleven thousand spectators. Its surroundings are now used for summer concerts.

- **First century B.C.E.:** The various tribes in prehistoric Britain are in the late stages of what is known as the Iron Age. The population is larger in the south than the north because of a more hospitable climate. Julius Caesar makes two expeditions to Britain in 55 and 54 B.C.E., following his conquest of Gaul. Caesar conquers no territory but coerces many tribes into paying tribute to Rome.

  Early seventeenth century: Queen Elizabeth I dies in 1603 and is succeeded by King James I. The golden age of English drama continues, and Shakespeare's later plays are written during the Jacobean era. England's sailors continue to explore the world and England lays the basis for its rapid rise as a major European and world power.

  Today: The English people treasure Shakespeare as the greatest figure in their literary history. His plays have been translated into almost every language and are performed regularly throughout the world.

body should be buried by Antony with royal splendour and magnificence."

CRITICAL OVERVIEW

Antony and Cleopatra has never been as popular or as frequently performed as the four major tragedies of Shakespeare: *Hamlet, King Lear, Macbeth,* and *Othello.* In the nineteenth century, however, the English Romantic poet Samuel Taylor Coleridge, who was also one of the foremost critics of the age, regarded the play as the "most wonderful" of the history plays and argued that it might be, in its "exhibitions of a giant power in its strength and vigour of maturity, a formidable rival" of the four great tragedies. Coleridge admired the quality of "angelic strength" conveyed in the play.

At the beginning of the twentieth century, one of the most influential of all Shakespearean critics, A. C. Bradley, refuted Coleridge's view. He argued that *Antony and Cleopatra* was not as dramatic as the other four great tragedies, especially in the first three acts, and claimed that the third and fourth acts were "very defective in construction." He noted the number of scenes in these acts and how difficult they are to present on stage. (There are more scenes in *Antony and Cleopatra*—forty-two—than in any other Shakespeare play.) Bradley's verdict that *Antony and Cleopatra*, while a great tragedy, was not the equal of the other four, remained influential throughout the twentieth century. Toward the end of that century, Stanley Wells argued that *Antony and Cleopatra* may be less universal in its appeal because the "central characters invite us not so much to identify with them as to wonder at them; ... they are given virtually no soliloquies in which to reveal themselves to the audience."

Much of the commentary on *Antony and Cleopatra* has been devoted to the play's numerous thematic pairings: Antony and Cleopatra; love and war; Antony and Octavius; self-restraint and luxury; reason and emotion. Scholars customarily argue that all, or at least a large portion of, this dualism flows from one essential pairing—Rome (under the guardianship of the strictly disciplined Octavius Caesar) versus Egypt (under the sway of the flamboyantly unpredictable Cleopatra). Antony is traditionally regarded as the go-between or victim of the Rome/Egypt dualism. As such, commentators have remarked, Antony must deal with his own set of internal conflicts: his Roman honor giving way to dishonor in Egypt; his youthful warrior's physique diminishing with age and dissipation; and his love for Cleopatra undermining his loyalty to Rome.

There has also been much critical debate in recent times about the true nature of Shakespeare's Cleopatra. The traditional view was of Cleopatra as a negative force. Richard C. Harrier, for example, argues that Cleopatra's "selfish and capricious domination of Antony" ruins him. Writing in the 1950s, Austin Wright reflects a view typical of that period. He criticizes Cleopatra for her failure to be supportive of Antony during his time of trouble; he also condemns her lack of virtue and modesty and calls her opportunistic, lubricious, and common. At the same time, Wright concludes that Cleopatra is irresistible to men.

Later scholars, including L. T. Fitz and Ruth Nevo provide more sympathetic portraits of Cleopatra. After asserting that the Egyptian queen is complex enough to elicit a variety of interpretations, Nevo suggests that Cleopatra behaves unpredictably toward Antony because she is afraid of losing him to Rome, to his first wife, Fulvia, and later to Octavia. Fitz argues that the misogynistic views of critics, and not Shakespeare's characterization, are the source of negative attitudes toward Cleopatra. Fitz asserts that male critics are particularly virulent in their dislike of Cleopatra and that they find her behavior in the play incomprehensible. Fitz contends that Cleopatra's actions are no more confusing than those of an equally complex Shakespearean character such as Hamlet, and that in order to judge her fairly, scholars must dispense with their "sexist bias."

Recent scholarship has also discussed the nature of the play's mythological and supernatural elements. Of particular interest to critics today are the patterns of irony and paradox that pervade *Antony and Cleopatra* and that render much of the play's action and many of its themes problematic. There appears to be a growing consensus that Shakespeare intended that this drama of love, politics, aging, and death be both ambivalent and ambiguous.

CRITICISM

Bryan Aubrey
Aubrey holds a Ph.D. in English and has published many essays on drama. In this essay, he emphasizes the transcendental aspects of the love

between Antony and Cleopatra rather than the moralistic view that censures the lovers for foolish and immoral behavior.

At the end of *Antony and Cleopatra* both lovers are dead, and the victorious Octavius, finally respectful of them now they are no longer either a threat or a challenge, gives instructions for a solemn funeral and announces that they will lie next to each other in death. Moralists in the audience (should there be any) will conclude that the downfall and suicide of such a reckless pair was not only inevitable but just. Others may feel unwilling to identify with the triumph of a man as cold and calculating as Octavius, the consummate politician who never wavers in his command of statecraft but who never reveals his heart. Octavius's victory seems to represent the triumph of prudence, reason, and practicality over the unruly world of passion and love. However, few in the audience are likely to embrace such a resolution with much enthusiasm because these two tragic lovers seem, through the imaginative, visionary, poetic language that Shakespeare grants them, to have propelled themselves in death into a transcendental realm of transfigured perception, an eternal sacred marriage that seems to dwarf their earthly incarnations and render them almost god-like. It is this startling metamorphosis of the lovers that most members of the audience will likely be contemplating as they leave the theater after a vibrant performance of this play, rather than an image of two corpses soon to be laid in a tomb.

How does Shakespeare accomplish this astonishing transformation? At the beginning of the play, such an outcome seems unlikely because the lovers are not presented in a very positive light. They seem quarrelsome and possessive, and it is hard to shake the negative portrayals that the Roman world insists on pinning on Antony. His greatness seems all in the past, recalled by others such as Philo or Octavius only to strike a note of regret about the man he has become. However, the very first words Antony speaks in the play, immediately after Philo has encouraged the audience to see "The triple pillar of the world transform'd / Into a strumpet's fool," are certainly not ignoble. After Cleopatra asks him to tell her how much he loves her, he replies, "There's beggary in the love that can be reckon'd". When Cleopatra responds that she will set a boundary to love,

Silver denarius of Cleopatra VII (Erich Lessing/Art Resource, NY)

Antony replies, "Then must thou needs find out new heaven, new earth". If Antony is taken at his word (and why should he not be?), he has dared to conceive a love for this bewilderingly volatile and complex woman that reaches for the infinite. It is an intense, expansive, boundary-breaking love that seems entirely fitting for one whose vitality, generosity and power has raised him to pre-eminence in the competitive world of Roman wars and politics. Antony is not a man who does things by half-measures. Cleopatra is not exactly an easy woman to deal with, yet Antony, still in the first scene of the play, shows his appreciation and understanding of her in a very perceptive manner: "How every passion fully strives / To make itself, in thee, fair and admired". This is a remarkable tribute to Antony's willingness to love qualities in Cleopatra that may not appear on the surface to be lovable. It also hints at the indefinable attractiveness of Cleopatra, in whom the expression of emotions that might be ugly in others— and which she fully demonstrates in this first scene—become simply an expression of the infinite range of her divine womanhood.

Although Antony's feelings are as volatile as Cleopatra's, and there is no denying the force of his outrage when he believes she has betrayed him at the battle of Actium—"triple-turn'd whore" is quite an insult—he nonetheless sees

Cleopatra through transfigured eyes as the "day o' the world", the very light by which he lives. Hyperbole this may be (as many critics point out regarding the language in which the lovers describe themselves and each other), but Antony is completely genuine in his adoration of his beloved, his ability to see in her an infinite treasure more precious to him than, well, the entire Roman Empire.

It is when Antony hears the false news that Cleopatra is dead that the first intimations of immortality and sacred marriage in death are sounded in the play. "I come, my queen," Antony calls out to Cleopatra as he summons his servant Eros to give him a death blow in act 4. Continuing to address Cleopatra, he says, "Where souls do couch on flowers, we'll hand in hand, / And with our sprightly port make the ghosts gaze".

Just as Antony sees Cleopatra through the eyes of love, she too possesses a unique vision of him. To most people, Antony is a man with two selves, the martial, Roman self and the "Egyptian" pleasure-seeking, sensual self, but in Cleopatra's eyes he possesses what might be called a third or transcendental self, a vast cosmic presence that inspires in her nothing less than awe. In the dream vision of Antony that she relates to an uncomprehending Dolabella in act 5, for example, she says of her lover: "His face was as the heavens, and therein stuck / A sun and moon, which kept their course, and lighted / This little O, the earth".

This imagery of the lover as embodying a kind of cosmic light occurs also at Antony's death. For Cleopatra, his fall is associated with the extinguishing of light: "O sun / Burn the great sphere thou mov'st in, darkling stand / The varying shore o' the world". Antony was her light, as she was for him, and now that light is gone: "Our lamp is spent, it's out".

It is this imagery of light and vastness that sets the stage for the translation of the lovers from the earthly to the spiritual realm. Theirs is a love so vast that it cannot be vanquished by death. It is at this point, when the lovers face their own deaths, that the play seems to take flight into the realm of myth; Antony and Cleopatra seem not so much two humans in despair who commit suicide but more like larger-than-life beings in the process of transformation, ready to fulfill their innermost longings for each other in an eternal union not touched by time or change and yet retaining all the delight and ecstasy they knew on the earthly plane of life.

This process of transformation reaches its fulfillment in Cleopatra's final speech. In her determination to join Antony in death and transfiguration she attains a calm strength that has eluded her up to this point in the play. But what is remarkable about this speech is that, even as Cleopatra transcends her fear of death and is fixed in her new resolve, she remains utterly herself; she is still the mercurial, volatile Cleopatra we have known, and she shows herself in all her many guises, from queen and quasi-goddess to sexual temptress and jealous woman. First, as she calls for her royal garments, she stands before us as queen, aspiring to eternity: "Give me my robe, put on my crown, I have / Immortal longings in me". But the lines that follow remind the audience of the sensual life of which Cleopatra has been the embodiment throughout the play: "Now no more / The juice of Egypt's grape shall moist this lip". Next we see her at once visionary and vengeful, sensing Antony's presence and exulting over her defeat of Caesar, a thought that occurs with greater force later in the speech. Now, as she identifies herself explicitly, for the first time in the play, as wife to Antony, she also reveals another side to her nature. No longer the female enchantress, the "triple-turn'd whore" of Antony's invective, it is her masculine qualities which predominate:

> Husband, I come!
> Now to that name, my courage prove my title!
> I am fire, and air; my other elements
> I give to baser life.

But then as Iras falls after being kissed by Cleopatra, the simile that immediately occurs to Cleopatra is a sexual one: "If thou and nature can so gently part, / The stroke of death is as a lover's pinch, / which hurts, and is desir'd. She is once more the lusty Cleopatra we have known, and this is confirmed by her sudden jealousy, even in death, of Iras: "If she first meet the curled Antony, / He'll make demand of her, and spend that kiss / Which is my heaven to have." But as Cleopatra takes the asp to her breast and once more sneers defiantly at Caesar, Charmian interjects the expansive image, "O Eastern star!" (line 308) thus reminding us not only of the hyperbolic language that Antony used of his lover, but also the status accorded to her by her subjects.

WHAT DO I READ NEXT?

- Shakespeare's *Julius Caesar* (first performed in 1599, and available in many modern editions) dramatizes the assassination of the Roman dictator by Brutus and Cassius and shows Antony, in his funeral oration, at the height of his rhetorical powers.

- *The Romance of Tristan and Iseult* (Dover Books on Literature & Drama, 2005) edited by J. Bedier and translated by Hilaire Belloc, is the legendary medieval story of the forbidden love between Tristan, a knight from Cornwall, England, and Iseult, an Irish princess. Tristan was escorting Iseult from Ireland as a bride for his uncle, King Marke, when he and Iseult discovered they were in love with each other. As the story of a fatal, overwhelming love affair, the story of Tristan and Iseult has many elements in common with the story of Antony and Cleopatra.

- *The Reign and Abdication of King Edward VIII* by Michael Block (new edition, 1991) tells the story of Britain's King Edward VIII who, in 1936, abdicated the throne because he wished to marry an American divorcée, Mrs. Wallis Simpson. Mrs. Simpson was not considered a suitable match for the king by the British establishment. Edward insisted that he could not carry out his duties as king without the support of the woman he loved, and he abdicated after less than a year on the throne. Since at the time the British Empire was still in existence, Edward VIII, like Antony, might be considered to have renounced an empire for love.

- *Caesar and Cleopatra* by George Bernard Shaw was first published in 1901 and first produced in 1906. Regarded as Shaw's first great play, it tells the story of Julius Caesar's arrival in Egypt and his relationship with Cleopatra, whom he helps become sole ruler of Egypt. Cleopatra is presented as a spoiled sixteen-year-old girl, while Caesar receives more sympathetic treatment than Shakespeare gives him in *Julius Caesar*. Shaw also uses the opportunity to comment on the politics of his own day. *Caesar and Cleopatra* is available from Penguin Books (reprint edition, 1950).

- *All for Love, or the World Well Lost* (1677), by John Dryden, is a version of the Antony and Cleopatra story by one of the leading Restoration dramatists. It is written in blank verse and, unlike Shakespeare's play, observes the unities of time, place and action. Also, while Shakespeare creates ambiguity about whether Antony and Cleopatra should be condemned for their passion, in Dryden's version the lovers are clearly presented as being in the wrong, even though the dramatist creates a certain sympathy for them in the audience. *All for Love* is available in a modern edition published in 2005 by Dodo Press.

- *The Letters of Abelard and Heloise* by Peter Abelard and Heloise, edited by Michael Clanchy, translated by Betty Radice (Penguin Classics, 2004) tells the story of the tragic love between Peter Abelard (1079–1142), a medieval scholar and teacher, and his young student Heloise. The story has become one of the most famous love stories in Western literature. Their intense, forbidden love resulted in scandal, pregnancy and a secret marriage before the lovers sought refuge from their passion in the church. Abelard became a monk and Heloise a nun. Their letters convey the full range of their romantic and sexual ardor for each other.

And finally, as Cleopatra calmly takes the asp to her breast, she presents herself as tender mother and nurse, a side of her nature that has not been glimpsed up to this point: "Peace, peace! / Dost thou not see my baby at my breast, / That sucks the nurse asleep?"

After her death, the final image of Cleopatra is spoken by Octavius, who remarks on the apparently easeful manner of her death: "she looks like sleep, / As she would catch another Antony / in her strong toil of grace". The word "catch" recalls Cleopatra's earlier comment, in Antony's absence, about going fishing and imagining the fish she caught as "every one an Antony.". "Grace" is perhaps a term that could be applied to Cleopatra only at this point in the play, suggesting that she has attained a final serenity, while "strong toil" evokes the Roman world of masculine effort, work and commitment. Thus the final image of Cleopatra in repose hints that at last those two mighty opposites, Rome and Egypt, have been brought together in an idealized moment of stillness and repose. The "serpent of old Nile" for so, Cleopatra tells Mardian in act 1, Antony calls her, is at one with that formidable figure whose "rear'd arm / Crested the world". In the literal sense, these two lovers may well have been brought down by their own folly, but the language Shakespeare gives them is surely enough to lift them, at least in the imagination of the audience, to an altogether finer plane.

Source: Bryan Aubrey, Critical Essay on *Antony and Cleopatra*, in *Shakespeare For Students*, Second Edition, Thomson Gale, 2007.

Patsy Hall

In this essay, Hall explores the themes of love and war in Antony and Cleopatra. *The critic notes that throughout the play, the character of Antony is associated with Mars, the god of war, while the character of Cleopatra is associated with Venus, the goddess of love. The interplay between love and war finds frequent expression in the relationship between the two title characters, who repeatedly "contend with each other in a battle of words and wills."*

The world presented in *Antony and Cleopatra* is one of friction, division and disagreement. In this world of impending and actual war, even the eponymous lovers frequently contend with each other in a battle of words and wills. Antony came to Alexandria to

> CAESAR'S IS A WORLD OF POLITICS, BUSINESS AND ACTION. ANTONY'S IS A WORLD OF DOMESTICITY, LEISURE AND INACTION. WHILE ANTONY RELIES ON HIS PAST REPUTATION TO DEFINE HIS HONOUR, CAESAR PAYS LIP SERVICE TO HONOUR BUT RATES POLITICAL ACUMEN MORE HIGHLY."

subjugate Cleopatra. Instead, she captivates him. It should be no surprise, then, that images of love and war go hand in hand throughout the play.

From the outset, Antony is associated with Mars, god of War, while Cleopatra in her barge is described as resembling Venus, goddess of Love, surrounded by 'smiling Cupids'. These images of the pair are so potent that the eunuch Mardian, attempting to gratify his queen's yearning for the absent Antony, deliberately sets her thinking 'what Venus did with Mars'.

Venus and Mars are opposites. In classical mythology, Venus is associated with passion, joy, mirth and love of life. Her husband Mars is given to wrath, destruction and death. This attraction of opposites makes for a volatile affair, a union of unlikely bedfellows. Shakespeare's Romans certainly think the same is true of Antony and Cleopatra.

Antony's 'goodly eyes', that once 'glow'd like plated Mars', now turn from war to gaze on the 'tawny front' of Cleopatra. His 'captain's heart', which could 'burst the buckles on his breast', is now 'the bellows and the fan to cool a gypsy's lust'. The martial Antony is spoken of in the past tense. This 'new' Antony is the pleasure-seeking follower of Venus, whose love is considered to be 'lust', and his devotion 'dotage' by his compatriots.

Cleopatra is the queen of 'sport', who turns even serious circumstance into an opportunity for entertainment. When Antony remembers his imperial persona he becomes exasperated by her lack of seriousness: 'But that your royalty/Holds idleness your subject, I should take you / For idleness itself' Cleopatra's idleness, however, is a pretence that masks a deeper purpose. As long

Ancient Egyptian relief of Cleopatra VII
(© Bettmann/Corbis)

as Antony enjoys his Alexandrian revels, he remains distanced—both physically and emotionally—from the serious 'business' of imperial Rome. To detain him, Cleopatra becomes the 'wrangling queen' of 'infinite variety' who laughs him out of patience and into patience, who fascinates and confuses him. By adopting various dispositions, no-one, least of all Antony, is ever quite sure where her allegiance lies.

Cleopatra employs sport, pleasure, play, and levity to entangle Antony in her 'strong toil of grace'. She rejoices when he declares, 'There's not a minute of our lives should stretch /Without some pleasure now'. Such a statement is the antithesis of Caesar's declaration at the drunken banquet: 'our graver business /Frowns at this levity'. In short, Cleopatra knows her man better than he knows himself, and rightly mocks Charmian's advice to give him his own way: 'Thou teachest like a fool: the way to lose him. Antony is a hedonist, a sensualist; rather than lose him, she'd prefer to nourish his vices, emasculate him, and transform him from an 'earthly Mars' into a creature of pleasure-loving Venus.

It is this weakening of Antony which Philo and Demetrius discuss at the beginning of the play. Antony himself acknowledges the change when his good soldiership deserts him at the

Battle of Actium. Savagely, he addresses Mardian, 'O, thy vile lady! / She has robb'd me of my sword'. In metaphorical terms this is precisely what Cleopatra has done, by emotionally castrating the soldier within him. Antony's sword, his prowess, which were once so central to his being, are now merely accessories to their relationship. This is illustrated earlier in the play when Cleopatra triumphantly recalls the night her power transformed Antony from Mars to Venus: 'ere the ninth hour, I drunk him to his bed; / Then put my tires and mantles on him, whilst/I wore his sword Philippan'.

Conquered by her, Antony tries to ignore his Roman critics. But there remains enough of Mars in him to make sparks fly when he and his earthly Venus disagree. The early scenes of the play accentuate the war of wiles and wills which constitutes this explosive relationship. Cleopatra is merciless in her public teasing and testing of Antony's love:

CLEOPATRA: If it be love indeed, tell me how much.

ANTONY: There's beggary in the love that can be reckon'd.

CLEOPATRA: I'll set a bourn how far to be beloved.

ANTONY: Then must thou needs find out new heaven, new earth.

Here, she deliberately appropriates language more suited to the mercantile values of Rome by implying that she can determine love's boundaries. By discussing love in quantitative terms ('tell me how much'), she mocks the Roman pursuit of world domination, just as she ridicules Caesar's commands: 'Do this, or this / Take in that kingdom, and enfranchise that; / Perform't or else we damn thee.'

By his earnest declaration about seeking 'new heaven, new earth', Antony shows how removed he now is from Rome's sphere. Philo's concern is justified. This is no earthly Mars but a man already discounting the value of war. Unlike Caesar, Antony no longer feels the need to conquer the world. The influence of Venus has brought a new reality: 'Kingdoms are clay'. From such a position, Caesar and all he stands for seems transient: 'Let Rome in Tiber melt, and the wide arch/Of the ranged empire fall!' Eternity and immortality are not to be found in all-conquering Rome but in the bliss of 'lips and eyes'. Antony does not see his transformation as 'dotage' but as 'the nobleness of life'. Cleopatra is not 'a gypsy' but his 'space'. By publicly rejecting military Rome, Antony declares allegiance to 'the love of Love and her soft hours'—in other words, the hedonistic Egyptian lifestyle captured in his question, 'What sport tonight?'

Cleopatra recognises that she is in competition with Caesar for Antony's attention. 'Roman thought' is dangerous, but by drawing his anger she may defeat it:

CLEOPATRA: [...] Good now, play one scene/Of excellent dissembling, and let it look / Like perfect honour.

ANTONY: You'll heat my blood: no more.

CLEOPATRA: You can do better yet; but this is meetly.

ANTONY: Now, by my sword,—

CLEOPATRA: And target. Still he mends, / But this is not the best. Look, prithee, Chairman, / How this Herculean Roman does become / The carriage of his chafe.

This merciless harassing of Antony, which he is powerless to check, illustrates how utterly this Venus overwhelms her Mars. Yet beneath the wit and banter lies a dynamic sexual energy which transforms every situation into an opportunity to excite and arouse each other, a private and intimate linguistic foreplay which stimulates the body of their passion. Gentler exchanges seem merely a temporary truce, an opportunity to draw breath before the next offensive.

The conflict at the core of this play may be seen as operating on two principal levels: the personal and the public. At the opening of the play, on the personal level, Antony and Cleopatra (Mars and Venus) engage in a well-matched and mutually satisfying battle of the sexes. In the public arena, however, they are both seen by Rome as creatures of Venus. In Roman terms, Caesar is now perceived as a more powerful and ruthless Mars than the epicurean and dissipated Antony. Thus, as the action unfolds, the contention between Venus and Mars moves inexorably from the personal to the public arena.

Caesar's is a world of politics, business and action. Antony's is a world of domesticity, leisure and inaction. While Antony relies on his past reputation to define his honour, Caesar pays lip service to honour but rates political acumen more highly. The differences between the two ways of viewing the world are illustrated by the conversation between Pompey and Menas on board the galley. When Menas suggests murdering the triumvirate, Pompey replies:

Ah, this thou shouldst have done,
And not have spoke on't! In me, 'tis villainy;
In thee't had been good service.
[...] Being done unknown,
I should have found it afterwards well done
    [...]

To Antony, honour equates with personal integrity: 'If I lose mine honour, I lose myself'. To Pompey—and by association Caesar—it equates with political convenience.

An earthly Mars like Caesar has no room for such a purposeless emotion as human affection. What matter if Octavia becomes a pawn in the power struggle between himself and Antony? The sacrifice of his sister is worth the risk if it results in the elimination of his rival. By contrast, after the defeat at Actium, when Antony has every right to be angry, he comforts Cleopatra: 'Fall not a tear [...] one of them rates / All that is won and lost'.

Caesar is no soldier, but has learned the more devious arts of 'the brave squares of war'. Antony has military superiority, but he is warned by the Soothsayer: 'If thou dost play with him at any game / Thou art sure to lose'. Swayed by Cleopatra's tendency to seize every opportunity for sport, Antony fatally begins to adopt her mind-set. War itself becomes a game to play with Caesar. His decision to fight by sea is quite clearly wrong, undertaken because Caesar 'dares us to't' and to impress Cleopatra.

Enobarbus recognises at once that when a general's judgement is overruled by whim, his fate is sealed. Charisma and bravado are not enough. Antony's conduct at Actium proved that 'The itch of his affection should not [...] Have nick'd his captainship', a fact which Antony himself recognises when he tells Cleopatra:

You did know
How much you were my conqueror, and
    that / My sword, made weak by my
    affection, would / Obey it on all cause.

When Antony challenges Caesar to fight him 'sword against sword, ourselves alone', Enobarbus sees it as a further sign of Antony's diminution and soon decides, 'When valour plays on reason, it eats the sword it fights with'. Antony is living on borrowed time.

It is only Cleopatra's supposed death which persuades Antony to admit to military defeat. As he removes his armour with the words, 'No more a soldier', he finally accepts the inevitable. He belongs henceforth to another sphere, to a 'new heaven, new earth' with his immortal Venus: 'Where souls do couch on flowers, we'll hand in hand, / And with our sprightly port make the ghosts gaze.' His acceptance of death is stoical—he recognises the sport in her latest act of deception and lacks rancour or bitterness. Instead, he feels justified in reclaiming his honour: 'Not Caesar's valour hath o'erthrown Antony, / But Antony's hath triumphed on itself.' In death, Antony's spirit once more mounts to its destiny: 'Noble, courageous, high, unmatchable.'

To Cleopatra, Antony now seems truly 'godlike', and to match him she too must embrace death in 'the high Roman fashion'. Her earthly yearnings for her 'noblest of men' are replaced with 'Immortal longings'. Yet even at the point of death she displays her old levity. Given her sensuality and love of sport, there is a poignant resonance in her assertion that 'The stroke of death is as a lover's pinch /Which hurts and is desired'. By her suicide, Cleopatra defeats Caesar. Venus gains ultimate ascendancy over Mars. There is a triumphant note of celebration in her address to the asp which brings her 'liberty': 'O, couldst thou speak / That I might hear thee call great Caesar ass / Unpolicied'. Caesar may have the Empire, but when the choice is between 'new heaven, new earth' or 'this vile world', Antony and Cleopatra are no longer in dispute: there's simply no contest.

Source: Patsy Hall, "*Antony and Cleopatra*: Venus and Mars in a 'Vile World,'" in *The English Review*, Vol. 12, No. 2, November 2001, pp. 4–8.

Walter Cohen

In this introduction, Cohen places Antony and Cleopatra *within its literary context—with Shakespeare's own* Julius Caesar *as its prequel and the writings of Plutarch as its source. Cohen also remarks on the dualism and eroticism that pervade the play and notes that Shakespeare is asking us to consider whether heroic acts can survive in the "post-heroic world" of Octavius Caesar's Rome or in the "private terrain" of Antony and Cleopatra's love. Finally, Cohen briefly examines Shakespeare's characterizations of Octavius, Antony, and Cleopatra.*

> THROUGHOUT, SHAKESPEARE MAINTAINS A STUDIED AMBIVALENCE: CRITICS DISAGREE ABOUT WHETHER THE PROTAGONISTS' CONCLUDING SUICIDES ARE FRUITLESS OR REDEMPTIVE."

Antony and Cleopatra (1606–07) picks up where *Julius Caesar* leaves off. It presupposes familiarity not only with events dramatized in that play but also with earlier Roman conflicts. During the first century B.C., Rome, the overwhelming military power throughout the Mediterranean and beyond, entered into a protracted civil war that culminated in its transition from a republic (rule by a senatorial aristocracy) to an empire (monarchical power). As *Julius Caesar* opens, Caesar has already defeated his archrival Pompey the Great and governs Rome as dictator. The play recounts the republican assassination of him, led by Brutus and Cassius, and the assassins' subsequent defeat and death at the hands of Mark Antony (Caesar's lieutenant) and Octavius (Caesar's young grandnephew and adoptive son, who took the name of "Caesar" upon Julius Caesar's death and turned it to political use). *Antony and Cleopatra*, which covers the period from 40 to 30 B.CD., completes the narrative of Roman civil war and the final destruction of the republic. Rome and its vast holdings are now ruled by the triumvirate of Lepidus, Octavius Caesar, and Mark Antony, who govern, respectively, the Mediterranean portions of Africa, Europe, and Asia. Yet Shakespeare's tragedy shifts the focus from the struggle over Rome's internal political system to Rome's external imperial domination of the East (the present-day Middle East) and to affairs of the heart. Mark Antony and Octavius Caesar contend for political supremacy, but the love between Antony and Cleopatra occupies center stage.

Much of the play's fascination arises from this intertwining of empire and sexuality. The issue is already present in Thomas North's translation of *Plutarch's Lives of the Noble Grecians and Romanes*—Shakespeare's favorite source, with the exception of Raphael Holinshed's

Chronicles of England, Scotland, and Ireland, and one that he follows closely here. Plutarch and other writers of Greek and Latin antiquity were preoccupied with the opposition between the conquering West, often thought by them to stand for political and moral virtue, and the older civilizations it subjugated in the East, frequently supposed to represent luxury and decadent, feminized sexuality. This particular understanding of empire reemerged in the Renaissance during a new era of Western expansion, as Europe entered the path to genuine global domination armed with an increasingly racialized and still sexualized view of the peoples it sought to subdue. *Antony and Cleopatra* is one response to European expansion, and the play's subsequent fortunes testify to its connection with the imperial enterprise of the West.

Long supplanted onstage by John Dryden's *All for Love* (1677), a rewriting of Shakespeare's story as a tragedy of private life, Shakespeare's version came into its own only after 1800, when England became the world's leading power. During the last two centuries, both Cleopatra and the East with which she is identified have seemed female, dark, colonized, available, animalistic, exotic, and excitingly dangerous. Comments on the text or on its performance have stressed the play's "strange pervasive influence of Oriental luxury and vice," its "effect of Oriental repose," Cleopatra's "corrupt and half-barbarous Oriental court." "Just as Antony's ruin results from his connection with Cleopatra," one critic argued, "so does the fall of the Roman Republic result from the contact of the simple hardihood of the West, with the luxury of the East." Actresses playing Cleopatra recall "an Indian dancer" and "Asiatic undulations of form." They bring to mind a "panther," a "sensuous tigress," "a wicked monkey," and a creature full of "feline cunning."

Not all of these responses chauvinistically assume Western superiority, and *Antony and Cleopatra* itself seems designed to elicit complicated judgments. Rome is contrasted to Egypt, West to East, the conquerors to the conquered; rapid shifts of scene across enormous distances accentuate this division. A sober, masculine military ethos opposes a comically frivolous, pleasure-loving, feminized, emasculated, and sexualized court. Antony must decide between Octavius Caesar and Cleopatra, Octavius's sister Octavia and Cleopatra, the world and the flesh. Political opportunism drives Antony's marriage

to Octavia, love and sexual desire his relationship with Cleopatra; he chooses between fidelity to a chaste, white wife and adultery with a promiscuous, "tawny," "black" seductress (1.1.6, 1.5.28). Where Caesar employs a rational self-interest (he is the "universal landlord," 3.13.72), Antony revels in an impetuous, extravagant generosity and challenges Caesar to one-on-one combat. Young Caesar is a bureaucrat of the future, old Antony a warrior of the past. Caesar's concerns are public and political, Antony's private and personal. Whereas Antony's brother and his previous wife, Fulvia, attack Caesar, Caesar promises that "the time of universal peace is near" (4.6.4). This assertion anticipates the *pax Romana* (Roman peace) instituted by Caesar throughout the empire. It also links the empire to Christianity by evoking the birth of Christ, which occurred in a Roman province during Caesar's long rule.

Through these conflicts, the play investigates the possibility of heroic action in a post-heroic world. It offers an epic view of the political arena, but deprives that arena of heroic significance. In this diminished environment, the protagonists' flaws are writ large. *Antony and Cleopatra* then asks whether heroic meaning can be transplanted to the private terrain of love. Throughout, Shakespeare maintains a studied ambivalence: critics disagree about whether the protagonists' concluding suicides are fruitless or redemptive. Following a series of tragedies— *Hamlet*, *Othello*, *King Lear*, and *Macbeth*—in which the protagonist's psychology is consistently probed, *Antony and Cleopatra* almost completely avoids soliloquy and thus inaugurates a final phase in Shakespeare's career, in which individual tragic intensity is sacrificed in favor of more broadly social representation. As a result, Antony's and Cleopatra's motives remain opaque to audiences and readers, to other characters in the play, to each other, and, arguably, even to themselves. Though we are invited to guess, we never definitively learn why Cleopatra flees at Actium, why she negotiates with Caesar in the last two acts, or why Antony thinks marriage to Octavia will solve his political problems. Instead of self-revelation, the play offers contradictory framing commentary by minor figures. These external perspectives help impart an epic feel, as do the geographical and scenic shifts, which also produce a loose, fragmentary, and capacious structure alien to classically inspired notions of proper dramatic form.

Furthermore, like the other Roman plays based on Plutarch—*Julius Caesar* and *Coriolanus*—*Antony and Cleopatra* relies heavily on blank verse while almost entirely avoiding rhyme: Shakespeare may have been following the Earl of Surrey's sixteenth-century blank verse translation of part of the *Aeneid* (19 B.C.), Virgil's enormously influential epic of the founding of Rome. The Roman Empire would thus seem the obvious stage for heroic performance.

Yet this proves not to be the case, partly because the play's structuring dichotomies are unstable. It is as if *Antony and Cleopatra* created distinctions only to undermine them. For instance, the antitheses between Caesar and Antony and between Rome and Egypt lack political resonance. *Julius Caesar*'s struggle between republic and empire arises only peripherally in *Antony and Cleopatra*, where it is voiced by Pompey:

> what
> Made the all-honoured, honest Roman
> Brutus,
> With the armed rest, courtiers of beauteous
> freedom,
> To drench the Capitol but that they would
> Have one man but a man?
> (2.6.15–19)

Pompey's rebellion is bought off by Caesar, Antony, and Lepidus. Pompey is then attacked by Lepidus and by Caesar (who later disposes of Lepidus) and is subsequently murdered by one of Antony's men, who may or may not have been acting on his master's orders. Although Antony supposedly "wept / When at Philippi he found Brutus slain" (3.2.56–57), he asserts that "'twas I / That the mad Brutus ended" (3.11.37–38). The republic is thus already dead when *Antony and Cleopatra* opens. Caesar astutely conforms to the style of a republic, whereas Antony offends traditional Roman sensibilities by ostentatiously taking on the trappings of monarchy (3.6.1–19). Nonetheless, their political conflict concerns not rival systems of government but simply the desires of two ambitious men, each of whom wants absolute power. The independence of Egypt is at stake, although this occurs to no one except Cleopatra and then only belatedly and perhaps duplicitously. The end of civil war is also important, but it is hard either to celebrate the victory of the ruthless Caesar or to lament the defeat of the incompetent Antony.

Other apparent distinctions between the rivals also conceal basic similarities. Antony boasts of his valor at Philippi, while Caesar "alone / Dealt on lieutenantry" (battled exclusively through his officers; 3.11.38–39). Earlier, however, Antony's "officer" Ventidius, whom Plutarch calls "the only man that ever triumphed of the Parthians until this present day," remarks, "Caesar and Antony have ever won / More in their officer than person" (3.1.16–17). In addition, Caesar's promise of "universal peace" is anticipated in a version of Christ's Last Supper that Antony shares with his followers.

> Tend me tonight.
> Maybe it is the period of your duty.
> Haply you shall not see me more; or if,
> A mangled shadow. Perchance tomorrow
> You'll serve another master.
> (4.2.24–28)

Appropriately, Antony is criticized for moving his friends to tears by Enobarbus, a Judas-figure soon to betray Antony by defecting to Caesar and destined to die shortly thereafter, his heart broken by Antony's generosity.

Even the geographical contrast of the play partly dissolves into parallelisms and connections: Egyptian love is militarized, Roman war eroticized. Shakespeare does give Cleopatra a smaller political role than she has in Plutarch, to accentuate the basic conflict and perhaps also to reduce the threat of a powerful woman. But the external representation of the lovers' relationship, the absence of scenes of them alone, and their pride in exhibiting their affair intensify the feeling that love and war influence each other, that there is no distinction between public and private because nothing is private. Further, love is on both sides of the divide. Antony is preceded in suicide by his aptly named servant Eros (love), a figure from Plutarch. But the play opens with a criticism of "this dotage of our General's" by Philo (also "love"; 1.1.1), a figure invented by Shakespeare.

Antony and Cleopatra also renders problematic the object of desire. Presumably that object is Cleopatra. Loved by Antony, she elicits powerful responses from Enobarbus and Dolabella and had been the lover of "great Pompey" and "broad-fronted Caesar" (1.5.31, 29). Though this list may indicate the power of the Eastern femme fatale, the roll call of Romans in love has no Egyptian equivalent. It is unclear what they literally see in Cleopatra. Enobarbus's description of her initial meeting with Antony at Cydnus (2.2.192–232) elicits enthusiastic responses from Agrippa—"Rare Egyptian!" and "Royal wench!" (224, 232). But when Enobarbus says that "her own person ... beggared all description" (203–04), he draws the logical inference, almost renouncing "all description":

> She did lie
> In her pavilion—cloth of gold, of tissue—
> O'er-picturing that Venus where we see
> The fancy outwork nature.
> (2.2.204–07)

All we know of Cleopatra's appearance is that she was reclining.

This absence of the seductress points in the same direction as the list of Roman lovers—toward the feelings of Roman men and away from any inherent attractiveness of an Egyptian woman. Some of these feelings are directed toward Antony. The Pompey and Caesar of *Antony and Cleopatra* at times act almost as if they were the sons—rather than the younger brother (Pompey) and grandnephew and adopted son (Caesar)—of Cleopatra's former lovers, whose paternal roles Antony has now assumed. In lines whose erotic charge goes beyond the intended objects (Antony and Cleopatra) to include the speaker himself, Pompey expresses pleasure that Antony takes him seriously (2.1.35–38). And Caesar is disgusted by Antony and Cleopatra's theatrical coronation:

> At the feet sat
> Caesarion, whom they call my father's son,
> And all the unlawful issue that their lust
> Since then hath made between them.
> (3.6.5–8)

Here, there is a possible confusion between Antony and the older Caesar and a definite one between Caesarion and the younger Caesar, both of whom are "my father's son." This is not the only intense familial feeling Caesar has for Antony. When he weeps at Antony's death, Maecenas sees a noble narcissism: "When such a spacious mirror's set before him / He needs must see himself" (5.1.34–35). Caesar himself recalls Antony movingly:

> thou, my brother, my competitor
> In top of all design, my mate in empire,
> Friend and companion in the front of war,
> The arm of mine own body, and the heart
> Where mine his thoughts did kindle.
> (5.1.42–46)

This outpouring of emotion, however calculated, leads in contradictory directions. By calling Antony his "mate" and invoking a meeting of "heart" and mind, Caesar on the one hand suggests an intimacy between the two men that recalls Renaissance celebrations of close male friendship but that also borders on the erotic. On the other hand, he neutralizes any filial anxiety he may feel by describing Antony as "my brother" and then as a subordinate, "the arm of mine own body."

Though Caesar betrays various kinds of emotional intensity, that is not what he consciously espouses. His ideal Antony is not the lover who "o'erflows the measure" (1.1.2) but the soldier who exercised heroic self-deprivation (1.4.58–61). He certainly does not emulate the older Caesar, whose sexual and military conquests were completely intertwined (3.13.82–85). Thus Octavius Caesar represents not the preservation but the diminution of traditional Roman values, a constriction of a heroic culture of which Antony is the last survivor. The jaundiced view of political power that emerges could be construed as an implicit critique of the centralizing monarchs of Shakespeare's own time. In any case, the play insists that one can no longer have it both ways, that politics and sex (or any kind of grandeur) are irrevocably sundered.

Antony and Cleopatra must exercise their peculiar brand of paradoxical hyperbole in this new and smaller world. Antony's heart "is become the bellows and the fan / To cool a gipsy's lust": his heart is a fan that cools Cleopatra's lust by satisfying it, but in so doing he rekindles her passion, as if his heart were also a bellows (1.1.9–10). Similarly, when Cleopatra meets Antony, "pretty dimpled boys" (2.2.208) attend her

> With divers-coloured fans whose wind
> did seem
> To glow the delicate cheeks which they did
> cool,
> And what they undid did.
> (2.2.209–11)

And when told that marriage to Octavia will force Antony to abandon Cleopatra, Enobarbus demurs in perhaps the play's most famous lines:

> Never. He will not.
> Age cannot wither her, nor custom stale
> Her infinite variety. Other women cloy

The appetites they feed, but she makes hungry
Where most she satisfies.
(2.2.239–43)

But the protagonists' inexhaustibility and their "infinite variety" do not fare well until the final scene. Though Shakespeare makes Antony and Cleopatra more sympathetic than they are in Plutarch, they remain maddeningly self-absorbed and self-destructive—ignoring urgent business, acting impulsively, bullying underlings, reveling in vulgarity, lying, apparently betraying each other.

Moreover, except for the first Battle of Alexandria, in which the couple briefly synthesize military and amorous arms, the fighting scenes testify to their belatedness, their irrelevance. Shakespeare's uncharacteristic decision to follow the practice of classical theater and keep all fighting offstage leaves only a feeling of being let down, as helpless observers report on the debacle. Thus, Enobarbus laments at Actium:

Naught, naught, all naught! I can behold
    no longer.
Th'*Antoniad*, the Egyptian admiral,
With all their sixty, fly and turn the rudder.
(3.10.1–3)

At the last battle of the play, it is Antony's turn:

All is lost.
This foul Egyptian hath betrayèd me.
My fleet hath yielded to the foe, and yonder
They cast their caps up, and carouse together
Like friends long lost.
(4.13.9–13)

Beginning with Act 4, however, the restlessness of the play diminishes as Antony and Cleopatra's sphere of activity is reduced to Alexandria. The manipulative report of her death that Cleopatra sends Antony, his botched suicide in response, and her refusal to leave her monument to attend him as he lies dying convert Antony's presumably climactic death into a mere false ending and shift the weight of significance to the final scene. Instead, Egypt and Cleopatra are what matter. Both have been associated throughout with the overflowing that Antony is faulted for at the outset. Antony declares his love for Cleopatra by rejecting the state he rules: "Let Rome in Tiber melt, and the wide arch / Of the ranged empire fall" (1.1.35–36). Upon hearing of Antony's marriage to Octavia, Cleopatra prays, "Melt Egypt into Nile, and kindly creatures / Turn all to serpents!" (2.5.78–79). This apocalyptic imagery, which dissolves all distinction, anticipates Antony's loss of self when he thinks Cleopatra has betrayed him. His body seems to him as "indistinct / As water is in water" (4.15.10–11).

The language of liquefaction is also connected to the confusion of gender identity. Antony

is not more manlike
Than Cleopatra, nor the queen of Ptolemy
More womanly than he.
(1.4.5–7)

And Cleopatra reports, "I . . . put my tires and mantles on him whilst / I wore his sword Philippan" (2.5.21–23). Depending on one's perspective, this behavior either dangerously confuses gender roles, thereby leading to Antony's ignominious flight at Actium, or overcomes a destructive opposition. Furthermore, the language of inundation recalls not only the rise of the Nile, which fertilizes the surrounding plain, but Cleopatra herself, who is identified with Egypt throughout the play. The conclusion seeks this regenerative property in her. Shakespeare's probable recourse to Plutarch's *Of Isis and Osiris* apparently inspires the repeated invocation of the goddess Isis, the sister-wife of Osiris, whom she restores after he is pursued to his death by his brother-rival. Typhon. When Caesar complains of Antony's monarchical behavior, he finds Cleopatra's divine impersonation "of the goddess Isis" even more galling (3.6.17).

Cleopatra's suicide makes good on these imagistic patterns, retrospectively justifying Antony's decision to die for her. Unlike the protagonists' deaths in Shakespeare's earlier tragedies, this outcome is desired by readers and audiences. The ending also evokes the synthesis precluded by the play's dichotomies but implied by its more subtle patterns. Cleopatra dies a death that might be associated with a Roman man:

My resolution's placed, and I have nothing
Of woman in me. Now from head to foot
I am marble-constant. Now the fleeting
    moon
No planet is of mine.
(5.2.234–37)

But in rejecting the inconstancy of the moon, of which Isis was goddess, arguably she also dies the death of a faithful Roman wife.

> methinks I hear
> Antony call. I see him rouse himself
> To praise my noble act....
> .....
> ... Husband, I come.
> Now to that name my courage prove my
>   title.
> (5.2.274–79)

And in taking the poisonous asp to her breast, she may become a Roman matron as well:

> Peace, peace.
> Dost thou not see my baby at my breast,
> That sucks the nurse asleep? ...
> As sweet as balm, as soft as air, as gentle.
> O Antony!
> [*She puts another aspic to her arm*]
> Nay, I will take thee too.
> (5.2.299–303)

Since the Folio lacks the stage direction included here, perhaps the final line can mean that she takes Antony to her breast, like a mother comforting her infant son.

But "O Antony" is also a cry of orgasm that looks back to Cleopatra's earlier sexual assertions, "I am again for Cydnus / To meet Mark Antony" and "Husband, I come," and forward to Charmian's orgasmic dying words, which Shakespeare added to his source: "Ah, soldier!" (5.2.224–25, 319). Furthermore, Cleopatra's manner of death is clearly Egyptian. The asp recalls Antony's description of her as "my serpent of old Nile" (1.5.25). Thus Rome and Egypt, Antony and Cleopatra, martial valor and sexual ecstasy, are united in death as they cannot be in life. "Dido and her Aeneas" (4.15.53), in Antony's vision soon to be eclipsed by himself and Cleopatra, wander together through the afterlife of the play. But the two legendary lovers remain bitterly unreconciled in the *Aeneid*, Shakespeare's source for the characters. With full awareness of the complexities and ironies at stake, Virgil narrates Aeneas's abandonment of Dido, who is associated with Eastern sensuality, in the name of a higher cause, Roman civic virtue. *Antony and Cleopatra* thus answers the *Aeneid*, ambivalently distancing itself from Roman and, by extension, Renaissance imperialism. It seems to be saying that you *can* have it both ways. East and West,

conquered and conquerer are affirmed in a final synthesis.

Yet countercurrents trouble even the metaphorical validation of Cleopatra's "immortal longings" (5.2.272). She resolves on suicide not when she learns that Antony killed himself for her but when she becomes certain that Caesar plans to lead her in a humiliating triumph in Rome. This explains her pleasure in imagining that Antony will "mock / The luck of Caesar," that the asp will "call great Caesar ass/ Unpolicied" (5.2.276–77, 298–99). The concluding triumphant rhetoric thus cleans up earlier dubious behavior and puts the best face on defeat. Heroic aristocratic individualism can act in the world only by leaving it. Moreover, the domestic Cleopatra of the conclusion can be seen as the reduction to a conventional gender role of a woman who challenged sexual hierarchy. At her death, Cleopatra "lies / A lass unparalleled" (5.2.305–06), or has the play instead presented "lies alas unparalleled"?

How *Antony and Cleopatra* should be interpreted depends on the relationship one sees between the ending and the partly incompatible material that has preceded it. Most, though not all, critics have found the conclusion affirmative on balance. But the work registers ambivalence to the last. This duality is captured in Cleopatra's account of the response she expects in Rome:

> The quick comedians
> Extemporally will stage us, and present
> Our Alexandrian revels. Antony
> Shall be brought drunken forth, and I shall
>   see
> Some squeaking Cleopatra boy my greatness
> I'th' posture of a whore.
> (5.2.212–17)

Cleopatra shudders at the absurdity of a boy actor badly impersonating her, yet the part of Cleopatra in *Antony and Cleopatra* was originally performed by a boy. This reminder punctures the dramatic illusion just when it would seem most essential. Arguably, we are being asked to recognize that a boy in the role of an extremely seductive woman can establish the same emotional intensity with the men in the audience that sometimes seems to exist between the male characters in that play. These lines certainly look back to Cleopatra's deliberate blurring of gender division. And they emphasize the artifice of Cleopatra herself, a veteran actress in her final performance. Shakespeare is here flaunting the power of his medium. But if it is impossible to "boy" Cleopatra's "greatness," to represent her adequately, perhaps that is merely an invitation to look beyond what can be shown, to take seriously her "immortal longings."

Source: Walter Cohen, "Antony and Cleopatra," in *The Norton Shakespeare*, edited by Stephen Greenblatt, W. W. Norton & Company, 1997, pp. 2619–27.

David Daiches

Daiches demonstrates how Shakespeare uses vivid imagery and point of view to depict the various roles of both Antony and Cleopatra. In the language of his soldiers, for example, Antony is a great general who has been made foolish by love. By contrast, the metaphors exchanged between Antony and Cleopatra depict them as magnificent lovers whose affection for each other surpasses boundaries and inspires our admiration. Daiches remarks further that the contrasting imagery in the play coalesces as each lover commits suicide but that it also leaves us wondering whether the play is about "human frailty or human glory."

Antony and Cleopatra is at once the most magnificent and the most puzzling of Shakespeare's tragedies. Its magnificence resides in the splendour and amplitude of its poetry, in the apparently effortless brilliance with which language is employed in order to search and illuminate the implications of the action; it puzzles because the action itself seems to be of no moral interest yet it compels a kind of wondering attention which would normally be given only to a play with a profoundly challenging moral pattern. Bradley sensed this paradox when he asked, 'Why is it that, although we close the book in a triumph which is more than reconciliation, this is mingled, as we look back on the story, with a sadness so peculiar, almost the sadness of disenchantment?' And he added: 'With all our admiration and sympathy for the lovers we do not wish them to gain the world. It is better for the world's sake, and not less for their own, that they should fail and die.' This is surely to simplify the problem to the point of distortion, for it is not that Anthony and Cleopatra arouse our admiration while doing wrong, so that we thrill to them yet cannot in conscience wish them success. It is rather that in this play Shakespeare seems to be building a moral universe out of non-moral

> ***ANTONY AND CLEOPATRA* IS A PLAY ABOUT WAYS OF CONFRONTING EXPERIENCE, ABOUT VARIETY AND IDENTITY."**

materials. Yet I do not think that we can answer Bradley merely by making a spirited defence of the characters of the hero and heroine, as Dover Wilson does, convincingly enough, if not altogether relevantly.

Shakespeare's play is not, of course, as Dryden's was to be, about 'All for Love, or the World Well Lost', though this is one strand woven into the total fabric. It is—to summarize it crudely—about the different roles that man can play on the various stages which human activity provides for him, and about the relation of these roles to the player's true identity. Shortly before his suicide, when Antony sees events as having cheated him out of his role both of lover and of conqueror, he expresses his sense of the dissolution of identity:

> Sometime we see a cloud that's dragonish,
> A vapour sometime, like a bear, or lion,
> A tower'd citadel, a pendent rock,
> A forked mountain, or blue promontory
> With trees upon 't, that nod unto the world,
> And mock our eyes with air.

He goes on to say that he

> made these wars for Egypt, and the queen,
> Whose heart I thought I had, for she had mine,

and having, as he believes, lost Cleopatra's heart, he no longer has a real identity either as lover or as man or action. The melancholy music of the lines rises up to involve us in this sad sense of loss of self. When however, he is informed by Mardian that Cleopatra has killed herself for love of him, his identity as lover is immediately re-established and he assumes this role again with a new confidence:

> I will o'ertake thee, Cleopatra, and
> Weep for my pardon. So it must be, for now
> All length is torture: since the torch is out,
> Lie down and stray no farther. Now all
> labour

Nicholas Jones as Mark Antony and Frances Barber as Cleopatra at Shakespeare's Globe, Bankside, London, England, 2006 (© Donald Cooper/Photostage. Reproduced by permission)

Mars what it does: yea, very force entangles
Itself with strength: seal then, and all is
    done.
Eros!—I come, my queen:—Eros!—Stay for
    me,
Where souls do couch on flowers, we'll hand
    in hand,
And with our sprightly port make the ghosts
    gaze:
Dido, and her Aeneas, shall want troops,
And all the haunt be ours.

At first it seems that the re-establishment of his identity as lover means the abandonment of his identity as soldier—'No more a soldier', he exclaims; but soon it becomes clear that in his resolution to follow Cleopatra to death he is at last adequately uniting both roles. Cleopatra has now assumed the role of conqueror, and he will imitate her:

I, that with my sword
Quarter'd the world, and o'er green
    Neptune's back
With ships made cities, condemn myself, to
    lack

The courage of a woman, less noble mind
Than she which by her death our Caesar tells
'I am conqueror of myself.'

When he discovers that Cleopatra has not killed herself after all, he does not fall back into his earlier state of disillusion with her; he remains the lover and the loved, ready to act out the last of love's gestures:

I am dying, Egypt, dying; only
I here importune death awhile, until
Of many thousand kisses, the poor last
I lay upon thy lips.

Finally, at the moment of death, he re-assumes the character of conqueror also:

but please your thoughts
In feeding them with those my former
    fortunes
Wherein I liv'd: the greatest prince o' the
    world,
The noblest; and do now not basely die,
Not cowardly put off my helmet to
My countryman: a Roman, by a Roman,
Valiantly vanquish'd.

Cleopatra's great cry of grief at his death is the equivalent from her side of Antony's speech about the changing shapes of the clouds: no identities are now left in the world, no distinction between mighty and trivial; she is overwhelmed in a patternless and so meaningless world in which all roles are interchangeable:

> O, wither'd is the garland of the war,
> The soldier's pole is fall'n: young boys and girls
> Are level now with men: the odds is gone,
> And there is nothing left remarkable
> Beneath the visiting moon.

Her love for Antony, we now realise, had been what gave meaning to reality for her; it had been the top in a hierarchy of facts, and when Antony is gone there is no hierarchy, no order, and so no significance in reality. Her own position as queen equally becomes meaningless: she is

> No more but e'en a woman, and commanded
> By such poor passion as the maid that milks,
> And does the meanest chares.

At the end of the play Cleopatra re-establishes order by the culminating role-taking of her death.

There are many ways in which Shakespeare uses poetic imagery to establish his main patterns of meaning. The opening lines give us with startling immediacy the stern Roman view of Antony's love for Cleopatra, separating at once the Roman from the Egyptian world:

> Nay, but this dotage of our general's
> O'erflows the measure: those his goodly eyes,
> That o'er the files and musters of the war
> Have glow'd like plated Mars, now bend, now turn
> The office and devotion of their view
> Upon a tawny front: his captain's heart,
> Which in the scuffles of great fights hath burst
> The buckles on his breast, reneges all temper,
> And is become the bellows and the fan
> To cool a gipsy's lust.

The word 'dotage' strikes hard in the very first lines—a damning and degrading word. But note that it is 'this dotage of our general's'. Antony is still, to the Roman onlooker, 'our general': there is a shared pride in that word 'our' and a deliberate placing in the hierarchy of command in the word 'general'. The general is

a general, but his observed behaviour is to be described by this viewer as dotage. This *viewer*, because when Philo says '*this* dotage' he is pointing at what he sees, drawing his companion's attention to the visible paradox, a general, yet in his dotage. Antony is seen by Philo as playing two contrary roles at the same time—and this is not in accordance with the proper proportions of things, it 'o'erflows the measure'. It would be proportionate for a general to love, but not for him to *dote*. For a general to dote 'reneges all temper', that is, it renounces all decent self-restraint, it is disproportionate, an improper placing of a particular kind of behaviour in the hierarchy of human activities and emotions.

A general has his proper 'office and devotion', his appropriate service and loyalty. For a general's eyes—'goodly eyes', it is emphasised, that have in the past appropriately and suitably 'glowed like plated Mars'—now to turn

> The office and devotion of their view
> Upon a tawny front

is again outrageous indecorum, wild disproportion. This disproportion is emphasized again and brought to a climax in the lines about 'a gipsy's lust'. What has military glory to do with such domestic objects as a bellows and a fan? The juxtaposition is deliberately outrageous. Similarly, the captain's heart put at the service of a gipsy's lust reiterates the disproportion, the total scrambling of that hierarchy which gives people and objects their proper virtue and the proper meaning. As the spectacle of the two lovers moves across to the middle of the stage to Philo's cry of 'Look, where they come'—the lovers are now before our eyes as well as his—Philo's sense of the disproportion involved becomes agonizing:

> Take but good note, and you shall see in him
> The triple pillar of the world transform'd
> Into a strumpet's fool.

And he invites his companion, in biblical-sounding language, to 'behold and see'.

But it is we, the audience or the reader, who now both see and hear. And what is it that we hear?

> *Cleopatra*: If it be love indeed, tell me how much.
> *Antony*: There's beggary in the love that can be reckon'd.

Cleopatra: I'll set a bourn how far to be belov'd.

Antony: Then must thou needs find out new heaven, new earth.

We move at once from the Roman soldier's view of Antony's behaviour to the view of the lovers themselves. Here, too, is disproportion, but disproportion of a very different kind from that seen by Philo. Antony declares that there is no limit to his love, that to measure it would involve going beyond the confines of both heaven and earth. To part of the audience—Philo and Demetrius, the shocked Roman soldiers—the role represents a monstrous confounding of categories; to the actors themselves, it is a glorious extravagance and subsumes everything else; to us who read or watch the play—well, what is it to us? Whose side are we on? We are jolted from Philo's offensively debasing comments to the sight and sound of the two lovers protesting their love. 'All the world loves a lover', the proverbs goes, and one naturally takes the lovers' side. But with Philo's words ringing in our ears we remain watchful, eager, interested: what is the true identity of this pair?

No pause for speculation is allowed. At once an attendant enters, saying

News, my good lord, from Rome

—from that Rome whose representative has just so devastatingly described Antony's behaviour. The brisk official announcement crashes into the world of amorous extravagance that the lovers' dialogue has been building up. Antony's barked, annoyed response—'Grates me, the sum'—shows him forced suddenly out of one role into another which he is most reluctant to play. At this Cleopatra suddenly changes too, quite unexpectedly yet wholly convincingly, into the playful, teasing mocker of her lover:

Nay, hear them, Antony:
Fulvia perchance is angry; or who knows
If the scarce-bearded Caesar have not sent
His powerful mandate to you, 'do this, or
    this;
Take in that kingdom, and enfranchise that;
Perform't, or else we damn thee.'

This shocks Antony out of his second role—the lover whose love-making is broken into by the claims of business—into yet a third, the surprised and puzzled lover:

How, my love?

With what wonderful economy does Shakespeare capture this third movement of mind and feeling in Antony. He is surprised out of his annoyance with the interrupter, wondering what Cleopatra is up to. She soon shows him, as she goes on:

Perchance? nay, and most like:
You must not stay here longer, your
    dismission
Is come from Caesar, therefore hear it,
    Antony.
Where's Fulvia's process? Caesar's I would
    say. Both?
Call in the messengers. As I am Egypt's
    queen,
Thou blushest, Antony, and that blood of
    thine
Is Caesar's homager: else so thy cheek pays
    shame
When shrill-tongued Fulvia scolds. The
    messengers!

She ends, note, by brusquely telling him to attend to the messengers: but she has made sure that, for the time being at least, he won't. Her mocking references to Fulvia, Antony's deserted wife, sting Antony into rejection of all that Rome means. In his next speech he confirms Philo's view of the monstrous disproportion of his behaviour in a remarkable outburst which gains our sympathy not by any explicit or implicit justification but by its taking in all of human existence by the way and then including and surpassing it:

Let Rome in Tiber melt, and the wide
    arch
Of the rang'd empire fall! Here is my space,
Kingdoms are clay: our dungy earth alike
Feeds beast as man; the noblenesss of life
Is to do thus: when such a mutual pair,
And such a twain can do't, in which I bind,
On pain of punishment, the world to weet
We stand up peerless.

All nobility of action is subsumed in the embrace of 'such a noble pair'. If the two poles between which Antony moves are Rome and Egypt, for the moment the Roman pole is annihilated. But Antony has a long way to go before he can find a role which combines his character of man of action and lover, which *justifies* him (not perhaps in a moral sense but in the sense that it accommodates his full *psyche*): the chain of events which finally drives him to suicide is made, in virtue of the poetic imagery in the play, to be the only way in which his various roles can come together in the same act. At this stage, we see him changing parts, but every change is accompanied by some awareness of what is being given up by not participating in other kinds of human action. How compelling and inclusive is the phrase 'our dungy earth alike / Feeds beasts as man', taking as it does into its purview in one sweep of perception the very basis of human and animal life and their common dependence on the 'dungy earth'. And how that phrase 'dungy earth' stresses the coarse and common, yet rich and life-giving, elements that link the highest with the lowest in any hierarchy. In a sense Antony is not here abandoning everything in the world by his and Cleopatra's mutual love: he is taking it all with him. But only in a sense: as the play moves on Shakespeare develops more and more ways of taking all life with him in presenting the adventures of this couple. Between this speech and the recurrence of the image in a different context in Cleopatra's speech in Act V, scene II, whole worlds of meaning have been established:

My desolation does begin to make
A better life: 'tis paltry to be Caesar:
Not being Fortune, he's but Fortune's
    knave,
A minister of her will: and it is great
To do that thing that ends all other deeds,
Which shackles accidents, and bolts up
    change;
Which sleeps, and never palates more the
    dung,
The beggar's nurse, and Caesar's.

Here the search for a timeless identity, 'which shackles accidents, and bolts up change', is movingly linked to a profound sense of the common necessities of all human existence. And when the dying Cleopatra, with the aspic at her breast, exclaims

Peace, peace!
Dost thou not see my baby at my breast,
That sucks the nurse asleep?

the imagery takes on yet another new dimension, so that not only does Cleopatra establish herself at the end as combining the roles of mistress and wife, of courtesan and queen, of Egyptian and Roman, of live-giver and life-taker, but this final unification of roles is linked—in ways that go far beyond the actual story—to a compassionate awareness of the sad yet satisfying realities of human needs and human experience.

But to return to the dialogue in Act I, scene I. Antony's moment of abandon to his vision of his and Cleopatra's mutual love cannot be sustained, for it cannot at this stage correspond to all the demands of his and Cleopatra's nature. He again repudiates his Roman business and then, by associating love with pleasure and pleasure with mere sport, modulates rapidly from the lover to the mere hedonist:

There's not a minute of our lives should
    stretch
Without some pleasure now. What sport
    tonight?

Cleopatra with continuing provocativeness acts the part of his Roman conscience—'Hear the ambassadors' is her only reply to the speech just quoted—but Antony, who has moved from passion to hedonism to joviality, insists on taking this as simply part of her attractive variety:

Fie, wrangling queen!
Whom everything becomes, to chide, to
    laugh,
To weep: how every passion fully strives
To make itself, in thee, fair and admired!

This topic of Cleopatra's infinite variety is to sound again and again, in many different ways, throughout the play before the hero and the heroine come to rest in the final and fatal gesture that can make variety into true identity. At this stage in the play Shakespeare deftly moves the royal lovers off the stage to let us hear again the two tough Roman soldiers whose comments had opened the action.

I am full sorry
That he approves the common liar, who
Thus speaks of him at Rome,

says Demetrius, giving another shake to the kaleidoscope so that we now see Antony neither as the debauched general nor as the passionate lover but simply as a nasty item in a gossip column.

We move straight from this splendid opening, with its shifting points of view and provocative contrasts between the former and the present Antony and between the Roman and the Egyptian view, to be given what Granville-Barker calls 'a taste of the chattering, shiftless, sensual, credulous Court, with its trulls and wizards and effeminates'. The queen enters, seeking Antony, aware that 'A Roman thought hath struck him', and worried. She prepares her tactics, bidding Enobarbus fetch Antony and then sweeping out as Antony enters. Antony, when he appears, is purely Roman: the blank verse he speaks is brisk and business-like, moving in short sentences. The news from Rome shames him. He is shaken into wishing to hear Cleopatra named 'as she is call'd in Rome' and to see himself through Fulvia's eyes. He has changed roles very thoroughly, and the atmosphere of the Egyptian Court, to which we have just been exposed, helps to make us sympathize. When Cleopatra reappears she has already been diminished, not only by the Court atmosphere and by Antony's Roman speech, but—and most of all—by Enobarbus' sardonic commentary on her behaviour and motives. Her tricks are all in vain, and after trying out a variety of moods and responses she is firmly shut up by Antony's Roman 'Quarrel no more, but be prepared to know / The purposes I bear'. She then tries the pathetic—

> Sir, you and I must part, but that's not it:
> Sir, you and I have lov'd, but there's not
> it;—

and in the end, unable to deflect him from his 'Roman thought', she acts the goddess of Victory and leaves him with the memory of an impressive parting:

> Upon your sword
> Sit laurel victory, and smooth success
> Be strew'd before your feet!

But Antony has already come to see himself as Philo and Demetrius had seen him at the play's opening; we have heard him repeat Philo's very word, 'dotage'—

> These strong Egyptian fetters I must
> break,
> Or lose myself in dotage.

At this point it looks as though the play is to be a tug-of-war comedy, with Antony being pulled now by Egyptian sensuality, now by Roman duty. And indeed, there is an element of this in the play, and some critics have seen this element as its main theme. But any attempt to see the play as merely a balancing of opposites, geographical and psychological, impoverishes it intolerably and also results in the sharpening of the dilemma I described at the beginning. *Antony and Cleopatra* is a play about ways of confronting experience, about variety and identity.

In Act I scene IV we suddenly see Antony in yet another light, when Octavius Caesar refers to

him as 'our great competitor', and this is followed by further images of disproportion applied to Antony—'tumble on the bed of Ptolemy', 'give a kingdom for a mirth', and so on; yet with these words still in our ears we are brought back to Alexandria to hear Cleopatra, seeing Antony's meaning for her more clearly at a distance, describe him as

> The demi-Atlas of this earth, the arm
> And burgonet of men

—a first foretaste of the grand mythological description she gives of him after his death to Dolabella:

> His legs bestrid the ocean, his rear'd
> arm
> Crested the world: his voice was propertied
> As all the tuned speres, and that to friends:
> But when he meant to quail, and shake the
> orb,
> He was as rattling thunder. For his bounty,
> There was no winter in 't: an autumn 'twas
> That grew the more by reaping: his delights
> Were dolphin-like, they show'd his back
> above
> The element they lived in: in his livery
> Walk'd crowns and crownets: realms and
> islands were
> As plates dropp'd from his pocket.

These tremendous images of power, benevolence and sensuality—or of greatness, love and joy—sum up the different aspects of Antony's identity, which are seen together, as co-existing, at last after his death. In life they interfered with each other, and can only be described separately. Nevertheless, the introduction of the figure of 'the demi-Atlas of this earth' so soon after Octavius Caesar's complaints about what Antony has declined to, is deliberate and effective. We should note, too, that even Caesar shows himself fully aware of the heroic Antony, though he sees him as the Antony who was and who may be again, not as the present Antony:

> Antony,
> Leave thy lascivious wassails. When thou
> once
> Was beaten from Modena, where thou
> slew'st
> Hirtius and Pansa, consuls, at thy heel
> Did famine follow, whom thou fought'st
> against,
> Though daintily brought up, with patience
> more
> Than savages could suffer. Thou didst drink

The stale of horses, and the gilded puddle
Which beasts would cough at: thy palate
    then did deign
The roughest berry, on the rudest hedge;
Yea, like the stag, when snow the pasture
    sheets,
The barks of trees thou browsed. On the
    Alps
It is reported thou didst eat strange flesh,
Which some did die to look on: and all
    this—
It wounds thine honour that I speak it
    now—
Was borne so like a soldier, that thy cheek
So much as lank'd not.

This is not only imagery suggestive of almost super-human heroism: it is also violently anti-sensual imagery. The contrast between 'lascivious wassails' and 'thy palate then did deign' / The roughest berry' is absolute. Victory in Egypt is associated with riotous celebration; in Rome, with endurance. Cleopatra at the end of the play combines both these notions in her death, which is both a suffering and a ceremony.

When Caesar and Antony confront each other in Rome, Antony admits the most important charge—that in Egypt he had not sufficiently known himself:

And then when poisoned hours had
    bound me up
From mine own knowledge.

Caesar, cold and passionless, never has any doubt of his own identity; that is one of the advantages of having such a limited character. Lepidus' character consists in wanting to like and be liked by everybody; he has no real identity at all. Not that Shakespeare presents all this schematically. The presentation teems with life at every point, and some of the situations in which Lepidus is involved are richly comic.

Meanwhile, Antony acts out his re-acquired *persona* of the good Roman leader and dutiful family man. He marries Caesar's sister Octavia, and is all courtesy and affection. But Enobarbus has been with the back-room boys satisfying their eager curiosity about Egypt. In replying to their questions, this sardonic realist with no illusions tells the simple truth about Cleopatra's irresistible seductiveness. It is into his mouth that Shakespeare puts the magnificent and well-known description of Antony's first meeting with Cleopatra (from Plutarch, but how transmuted!), thus guaranteeing its truth; it is

Enobarbus too who evokes her quintessential sex appeal with the brief but brilliant account of her captivating breathlessness after hopping 'forty paces through the public street', and above all it is Enobarbus who replies to Maecenas's 'Now Antony must leave her utterly' with

Never; he will not:
Age cannot wither her: nor custom stale
Her infinite variety: other women cloy
The appetites they feed, but she makes
    hungry,
Where most she satisfies. For vilest things
Become themselves in her, that the holy
    priests
Bless her, when she is riggish.

This is not role-taking: it is the considered opinion of a hard-boiled campaigner, and in the light of it we know that Antony has a long way to go before his different *personae* can unite.

If *we* are never allowed to forget Cleopatra, how can Antony? It takes only a casual encounter with an Egyptian soothsayer to turn him to Egypt again:

I will to Egypt;
And though I make this marriage for my
    peace,
I' the east my pleasure lies.

Mere sensuality is drawing him, it appears. Never up to this point has the love theme, as Antony reflects it, seemed so tawdry. It almost seems as though there is an obvious moral pattern emerging, with Rome on the good side and Egypt on the bad. This is further suggested by the following scene in Alexandria showing Cleopatra's reaction to the news of Antony's marriage to Octavia. Yet, after all her tantrums, with her

Pity me, Charmian,
But do not speak to me,

a new note of quiet genuineness emerges in Cleopatra's love for Antony. And if we have come to feel that the political world of Roman efficiency represents the moral good in this conflict between Rome and Egypt, we are soon brought to the scene in Pompey's galley in which power and politics are reduced to their lowest level. Antony fools the drunken Lepidus by talking meaningless nonsense in reply to Lepidus' questions about Egypt; Menas tries to persuade Pompey to slaughter his guests and so secure the sole rule of the world, and Pompey replies that Menas should have done it first and told him about it afterwards; the reluctant Caesar is persuaded to join in the heavy drinking. Lepidus has already been carried off drunk, the man who bears him away carrying, as Enobarbus points out, 'the third part of the world'. And finally Enobarbus persuades Caesar to join in a dance with Antony and Pompey while a boy sings a drinking song. The utter emptiness of this revelry is desolating, and it casts a bleak light on the whole Roman world.

In the light of this dreary and almost enforced celebration we think of Enobarbus' description of Cleopatra's first welcome to Antony or the later presentation (Act IV, scene VIII) of Antony's response to temporary victory and realise that there is another aspect to Egyptian revelry than the dissolute chatter of Act I, scene II. Egyptian celebration has a humanity and a fullness wholly lacking on Pompey's galley.

> Enter the city, clip your wives, your
>   friends,
> Tell them your feats, whilst they with joyful
>   tears
> Wash the congealment from your wounds,
>   and kiss
> The honour'd gashes whole,

exclaims Antony in genial triumph to his men and, to Cleopatra when she enters:

> My nightingale,
> We have beat them to their beds. What, girl,
>   though grey
> Do something mingle with our younger
>   brown, yet ha' we
> A brain that nourishes our nerves, and can
> Get goal for goal of youth. Behold this man,
> Commend unto his lips thy favouring hand:
> Kiss it, my warrior: he hath fought to-day
> As if a god in hate of mankind had
> Destroy'd in such a shape.

And Antony goes on to proclaim a victory celebration:

> Give me thy hand,
> Through Alexandria make a jolly march,
> Bear our hack'd targets like the men that
>   owe them.
> Had our great palace the capacity
> To camp this host, we all would sup
>   together,
> And drink carouses to the next day's fate,
> Which promises royal peril. Trumpeters,
> With brazen din blast you the city's ear,

> Make mingle with our rattling tabourines,
> That heaven and earth may strike their
>   sounds together,
> Applauding our approach.

Kissing, touching and shaking of hands are frequent where Antony is the center of a celebratory scene; it is the human touch, the contact, the insistence on sharing feeling. So against 'I' the east my pleasure lies' we must set on the one hand Roman pleasure as symbolized by the scene in Pompey's galley and on the other the warm human responsiveness to environment which Antony evinces in so many of his Egyptian moods. The latter part of the play is not simply a psychological study of the decline of the sensual man in intellectual and emotional stability as his fortunes decline (as Granville-Barker, brilliant though his study of the play is, seems to imply). If it were that, it would be merely pathetic, and it would be hard to account for the note of triumph that rises more than once as the play moves to its conclusion. The play is in fact both triumph and tragedy; Antony, and more especially Cleopatra, achieve in death what they have been unable to achieve in life: the triumph lies in the achievement, the tragedy in that the price of the achievement is death. In the last analysis the play rises above morality to strike a blow in vindication of the human species. Queen or courtesan or lover or sensualist, or all of these, Cleopatra in her death does not let humankind down.

Antony's emotional vagaries in the long movement of his decline exhibit him as beyond the control of any stablishing self; it is almost as though Shakespeare is making the point that in order to gain one's identity one must lose it. Antony is seen by his friend Scarus, whose military advice he rejects as he rejects everybody's except Cleopatra's, as 'the noble ruin of her (i.e., Cleopatra's) magic', and Shakespeare makes it clear that this is one aspect of the truth. Antony's military judgment is overborne by Cleopatra's reckless desires and intuitions. Even Enobarbus breaks out of his sardonic acquiescence in whatever goes on, to expostulate with Cleopatra herself in a tone of rising anxiety. Soldier and lover are here contradictory roles, which must be acted separately. To attempt to act them out simultaneously is to risk ruining both. Shakespeare spares us nothing—the bickering, the infatuate action, the changes of mood, the melodramatic gesturing. Yet the poetic imagery works in another direction, not so much in its actual verbal suggestions as in its rising energy and human comprehensiveness. And at least Antony acts all his own parts. His chief reason for scorning Octavius Caesar is that he plays simply the role of cunning policy spinner and refuses to prove himself in any other capacity.

The richness of Antony's humanity increases with the instability of his attitudes. His rage with the presumptuous Thidias, who dares to kiss Cleopatra's hand, is of course partly the result of Thidias' being Caesar's messenger and of Cleopatra's looking kindly on him—he himself shortly afterwards gives Cleopatra Scarus's hand to kiss. But more than that, it is a release of something humanly real within him, and his expression of it has a ring of appeal about it, appeal to our understanding of his emotional predicament, of the human-ness of his situation:

> Get thee back to Caesar,
> Tell him thy entertainment: look thou say
> He makes me angry with him. For he seems
> Proud and disdainful, harping on what I am
> Not what he knew I was. He makes me
>   angry,
> And at this time most easy 'tis to do 't:
> When my good stars, that were my former
>   guides,
> Have empty left their orbs, and shot their
>   fires
> Into the abysm of hell.

The phrase 'harping on what I am / Not what he knew I was' has no equivalent in Plutarch. Antony's consciousness of his different selves represents an important part of Shakespeare's intention. At the same time Antony's almost genial acknowledgement of his own weakness has not only an engaging confessional aspect but also draws on its rhythm and movement to achieve a suggestion of human fallibility which increases rather than diminishes Antony's quality as a man:

> He makes me angry,
> And at this time most easy 'tis to do 't:...

When Cleopatra approaches him, hoping that his angry mood has passed, he is still talking to himself:

> Alack, our terrene moon
> Is now eclips'd, and it portends alone
> The fall of Antony!

It is Cleopatra who is the moon—the changeable planet. (We recall Juliet's reproof to Romeo:

> O, swear not by the moon, th' incon-
>   stant moon,
> That monthly changes in her circled orb...)

But while he is lamenting Cleopatra's changeableness, she is awaiting the change in him that will bring him back to a full recognition of her love for him: 'I must stay his time'. He accuses her of flattering Caesar, and she replies simply: 'Not know me yet?' To which in turn he replies with another simple question: 'Cold-hearted toward me?' Her answer to this, beginning with the quietly moving 'Ah, dear, if I be so, ...' brings him round at once. 'I am satisfied', is all he says to conclude the dispute, then proceeds at once to talk about his military plans. Having declared these, he suddenly realises just who Cleopatra is and where he stands in relation to her:

> Where hast thou been, my heart? Dost
>   thou hear, lady?
> If from the field I shall return once more
> To kiss these lips, I will appear in blood,
> I, and my sword, will earn our chronicle:
> There's hope in't yet.

He is both warrior and lover now, and well may Cleopatra exclaim 'That's my brave lord!' This in turn encourages Antony to move to his third role, that of reveller:

> I will be treble-sinew'd, hearted, breath'd,
> And fight maliciously: for when mine hours
> Were nice and lucky, men did ransom lives
> Of me for jests: but now, I'll set my teeth,
> And send to darkness all that stop me.
>   Come,
> Let's have one other gaudy night: call to me
> All my sad captains, fill our bowls once
>   more;
> Let's mock the midnight bell.

More role-taking now takes place on a very simple and moving plane. Cleopatra adjusts herself to Antony's recovered confidence:

> It is my birth-day,
> I had thought t' have held it poor. But since
>   my lord
> Is Antony again, I will be Cleopatra.

Cleopatra's reference to her birthday is almost pathos, but it rises at once to grandeur with 'But since my lord / Is Antony again, I will be Cleopatra'. The question posed by the play is,

What do these two characters finally add up to? When Antony is Antony again and Cleopatra Cleopatra who *are* they? One cannot give any answer less than the total meaning of the play.

Enobarbus, the 'realist', gives his comment on this dialogue. He knows his Antony; his shrewd and knowing mind give its ironic diagnosis:

> Now he'll outstare the lightning; to be furious
> Is to be frighted out of fear, and in that mood
> The dove will peck the estridge; and I see still,
> A diminution in our captain's brain
> Restores his heart; when valour preys on reason,
> It eats the sword it fights with: I will seek
> Some way to leave him.

But it is the realist who does not see the reality, and Enobarbus' death in an agony of remorse for having deserted Antony in the name of *Realpolitik* is Shakespeare's final comment on this interpretation.

The death of Antony leaves a whole act for Cleopatra's duel with Caesar before she finally outwits him and dies in her own way and in her own time. It is an act in which she plays continuously shifting roles, and while these are obviously related to the exigencies of her conflict with Caesar and the fluctuations in her position, they also show her exhibiting varied facets of her character before deciding on the final pose she will adopt before the world and before history. She is not fooled by Caesar but plays a part designed to fool Caesar into thinking that she wants to live and make the best bargain possible for herself, exclaiming contemptuously to her ladies in waiting: 'He words me, girls, he words me'. Caesar is not an accomplished actor—he is not used to role-taking—and he gives himself away. 'Feed and sleep', he tells Cleopatra, thinking that the exhortation will disarm and soothe her. But the words suggest the treatment one gives to a caged beast and give away, what Dolabella is easily charmed by Cleopatra into confirming, that Caesar intends to lead Cleopatra and her children as captives in his triumphal procession. This role, for all her infinite variety, is one Cleopatra will never play. If she does not arrange her last act properly, the Romans will put her in *their* play:

> Nay, 'tis most certain, Iras: saucy lictors
> Will catch at us like strumpets, and scald rhymers
> Ballad us out o' tune. The quick comedians
> Extemporally will stage us, and present
> Our Alexandrian revels: Antony
> Shall be brought drunken forth, and I shall see
> Some squeaking Cleopatra boy my greatness
> I' the posture of a whore.

The pageant of her death which she arranges is a sufficient antidote to this. Preceded as it is by the characteristically enlarging dialogue with the clown who brings the figs—enlarging, that is, the human implications of the action—she goes through death to Antony whom at last she can call by the one name she was never able to call him in life—'Husband, I come'. The splendour and dignity of the final ritual brings together in a great vindication the varied meanings of her histrionic career and temperament:

> Give me my robe, put on my crown, I have
> Immortal longings in me.

It is both a subsuming and a sublimating ritual. Love and loyalty and courage and queenliness are here together at last. And so is sexyness and sensuality, for this is a vindication through *wholeness* not through a choice of the proper and the respectable elements only. Iras dies first and Cleopatra exclaims:

> This proves me base:
> If she first meet the curled Antony,
> He'll make demand of her, and spend that kiss
> Which is my heaven to have.

This almost flippant sensuality has its place in the summing up, which transcends morality. Charmian, who dies last, lingers to set her dead mistress's crown straight:

> Your crown's awry,
> I'll mend it, and then play.

'Play' means play her part in the supreme pageant of ceremonial death and at the same time refers back, with controlled pathos, to Cleopatra's earlier

> And when thou hast done this chare, I'll give thee leave
> To play till doomsday: . . .

When Caesar arrives, the striking and moving spectacle of the dead queen in all her regal splendour flanked by her two dead handmaidens forces even this cold schemer to see her in the great inclusive role she has arranged for herself. Love, which in the Roman view of the matter has hitherto been opposed to history, the enemy of action and dignity and honour, is now at last, and by the very epitome of Roman authority and efficiency, pronounced to be part of history and of honour:

> Take up her bed,
> And bear her women from the monument:
> She shall be buried by her Antony.
> No grave upon the earth shall clip in it
> A pair so famous: high events as these
> Strike those that make them: and their
>   story is
> No less in pity than his glory which
> Brought them to be lamented. Our army
>   shall
> In solemn show attend this funeral,
> And then to Rome. Come, Dolabella, see
> High order, in this great solemnity.

'Famous', 'high', 'glory', 'solemn', 'order', 'solemnity'—these are the terms which Caesar now applies to a love story which earlier he had dismissed as 'lascivious wassails'. Is the play about human frailty or human glory? We are left with the feeling that one depends on the other, an insight too subtly generous for any known morality.

Source: David Daiches, "Imagery and Meaning in *Antony and Cleopatra*," in *English Studies*, Vol. 43, No. 5, October 1962, pp. 343–58.

SOURCES

Bradley, A. C., *Oxford Lectures on Poetry*, Macmillan & Co., Limited, 1909, p. 283.

Coleridge, Samuel Taylor, "Antony and Cleopatra," in *Shakespeare Criticism: A Selection*, with an introduction by D. Nichol Smith, Oxford University Press, 1934, pp. 279–80.

Fitz, L. T., "Egyptian Queens and Male Reviewers: Sexist Attitudes in Antony and Cleopatra Criticism," in *Shakespeare Quarterly*, Vol. 28, No. 3, Summer 1977, pp. 297–316.

Harrier, Richard C., "Cleopatra's End," in *Shakespeare Quarterly*, Vol. 13, No. 1, Winter 1962, pp. 63–5.

MacMullan, Katherine Vance, "Death Imagery in Antony and Cleopatra," in *Shakespeare Quarterly*, Vol. 14, No. 4, Autumn 1963, pp. 399–410.

Nevo, Ruth, "Antony and Cleopatra," in *Tragic Form in Shakespeare*, Princeton University Press, 1972, pp. 306–55.

Plutarch, *The Lives of the Noble Grecians and Romans*, The Dryden Translation, Encyclopaedia Britannica, Inc., 1987, pp. 749, 757, 779.

Shakespeare, William, *Antony and Cleopatra*, edited by M. R. Ridley, Arden Shakespeare, Methuen & Co., Ltd., 1978.

Starr, Chester G., *A History of the Ancient World*, 4th Edition, Oxford University Press, 1991, p. 550.

Wells, Stanley, *Shakespeare: A Life in Drama*, W. W. Norton & Company, 1995, p. 300.

Wright, Austin, "Antony and Cleopatra," in *Shakespeare: Lectures on Five Plays*, Carnegie Series in English, Number Four, by A. Fred Sochatoff et al., Carnegie Institute of Technology, 1958, pp. 37–51.

FURTHER READING

Barroll, J. Leeds, "Cleopatra and the Size of Dreaming," in *Shakespearean Tragedy: Genre, Tradition, and Change in Antony and Cleopatra*, Associated University Presses, 1984, pp. 130–87.

> Barroll analyzes the wide variety of responses to Cleopatra's character. He acknowledges that Cleopatra's lack of self-understanding or of feelings of guilt might disqualify her for tragic status. Barroll locates Cleopatra's tragedy in the destruction of all of her "grandiose" plans—for herself and for Antony—and in her genuine grief at Antony's death.

Bevington, David, "Introduction" in *Antony and Cleopatra*, by William Shakespeare, edited by David Bevington, Cambridge University Press, 1990, pp. 1–70.

> Bevington provides a detailed overview of the play, including date and source material and critical assessments of the characters. Bevington also focuses on the use of irony—in particular, how irony sets the play's dialogue at odds with the play's action. Finally, Bevington evaluates the numerous ways in which *Antony and Cleopatra* has been performed before live audiences and includes a discussion of the difficulties of staging so elaborate a play, with its barges, battles, and monuments.

Cantor, Paul A., "Part Two: *Antony and Cleopatra*," in *Shakespeare's Rome: Republic and Empire*, Cornell University Press, 1976, pp. 127–208.

> Cantor argues first, that the play cannot be divided neatly into private versus public life; second, he asserts that Antony is not "bewitched" away from Rome by Cleopatra, but that he is already aware and disapproving of Rome's faults; third, Cantor argues that the love between Antony and Cleopatra is made possible through its very originality and

tendency toward exaggeration, and that "the guiding principle of [the two lovers] in both public and private life is open hostility to stale custom." Incidentally, Cantor also argues that Antony and Cleopatra achieve marriage through death—thus turning a potentially tragic play into a comedy.

Doran, Madeleine, "'High Events as These': The Language of Hyperbole in *Antony and Cleopatra*," in *Queen's Quarterly*, Vol. 72, No. 1, Spring 1965, pp. 26–51.

Doran interprets the play in the context of the Elizabethan fascination for hyperbolic language, or the expression of things as grandiose, perfect, and ideal. Doran concludes by suggesting that Shakespeare used hyperbole not only to satisfy his audience's tastes but also to demonstrate that the "true wonder" of human beings—of Antony and Cleopatra, for example—exists not in exaggeration but in the story of their lives.

Honigmann, E. A. J., "Antony versus Cleopatra," in *Shakespeare: Seven Tragedies*, Macmillan Press Ltd., 1976, pp. 150–69.

Honigmann discusses the ways in which the relationship between Antony and Cleopatra changes halfway through the play. Honigmann contends that in the first half, Cleopatra dominates the action and Antony is the butt of her jokes; however, in the second half, Antony, newly ashamed by his military losses, achieves moral and theatrical superiority over Cleopatra.

Kuriyama, Constance Brown, "The Mother of the World: A Psychoanalytic Interpretation of Shakespeare's *Antony and Cleopatra*," in *English Literary Renaissance*, Vol. 7, No. 3, Autumn 1977, pp. 324–51.

In this Freudian interpretation, Kuriyama argues that *Antony and Cleopatra* should not be read merely as a moral lesson or for its poetry. Instead, she asserts that critics should acknowledge that the play functions as a sexual fantasy which provides us the pleasure of knowing that when Antony and Cleopatra are at last "united in death," they achieve "honor," "selfhood," and "immortality."

Williamson, Marilyn, "The Political Context in *Antony and Cleopatra*," in *Shakespeare Quarterly*, Vol. 21, No. 3, Summer 1970, pp. 241–51.

Williamson evaluates Antony and Cleopatra as "rulers as well as lovers." Williamson focuses on the play's politics, arguing that much can be learned about Antony and Cleopatra from their treatment of their subordinates, as well as from the manner in which their subordinates view them.

Wolf, William D, "'New Heaven, New Earth': The Escape from Mutability in *Antony and Cleopatra*," in *Shakespeare Quarterly*, Vol. 33, No. 3, Autumn 1982, pp. 328–35.

Wolf acknowledges the opposing forces at work in the play: politics versus love, public versus private, Rome versus Egypt. Wolf then proceeds to point out that despite these differences, the worlds of Rome and Egypt share an important element: both are subject to violent fluctuations. With regard to Rome, Wolf observes, the change is political; with regard to Egypt, it is emotional. In both cases, Wolf asserts, the changes revolve around Antony.

As You Like It

1599 Commentators have described the comedy *As You Like It* as both a celebration of the spirit of pastoral romance and a satire of the pastoral ideal, where the term *pastoral* refers to the simple, innocent life of the countryside. Audiences usually prefer the light-hearted, love-oriented banter and whimsy that dominate the scenes in the Forest of Arden to the sorrowful, battle-filled atmospheres at the home of Oliver and the court of Duke Frederick. The forest is conceivably a reference to both the Arden woodlands near Shakespeare's hometown and the region of Ardennes, in northeast France, where Shakespeare sets the action of the play. In its tranquility the forest enchants the visitors, who, after securing nourishment and shelter, think of little but love during their wanderings. The non-romantic plot threads established in the first act essentially resolve themselves in the final scenes, in large part because the forest seems to also enchant the antagonists as soon as they arrive. The play's naturally magical aspect is made tangible when Hymen, the Greek god of marriage, appears to officiate at the weddings that close the play.

The final three acts, then, give the audience a chance to feel how "Time ambles" (3.2.305) for those with plenty of leisure and no obligations, as is the case with the main characters. Although Rosalind presumably needs to disguise herself to ensure her safety, nothing actually threatens her union with Orlando; the two are mutually

infatuated from their first meeting. Thus, most of the tension in the play, with the original plot threads picked up only during the scene at the duke's palace at the beginning of the third act, stems from the various witty exchanges. Touchstone and Jaques contribute to the play not through love affairs—the former woos Audrey only halfheartedly, while the latter seems incapable of love—but through philosophical reflection, which the solitude of the pastoral setting encourages.

Shakespeare derived the plot of *As You Like It* directly from the novel *Rosalynde, or Euphues' Golden Legacy*, published in 1590 by Thomas Lodge. (Copyright protection did not exist in the Elizabethan era.) Lodge's novel in turn was based on a more action-oriented fourteenth-century poem entitled "The Tale of Gamelyn." While veering little from Lodge's straightforward pastoral tale, Shakespeare did strengthen the character of Rosalind and add his two philosophers, Jaques and Touchstone, providing the opportunity for greater reflection among the cast as a whole.

Although critics remain divided on whether *As You Like It* should be read as a satire or a celebration of the pastoral ideal, readers can take pleasure in the play's festive atmosphere and its various love affairs. *As You Like It* is one of Shakespeare's most popular and best-loved comedies.

PLOT SUMMARY

Act 1, Scene 1

In the opening scene of *As You Like It*, Orlando tells the old family servant Adam of his discontent with his brother Oliver's management of the family fortune and his treatment of him, for he is being allowed no education and thus will have no means to advance in the world. This speech, with Orlando's referring to "the spirit of my father, which I think is within me" (21–2), introduces a filial connection that establishes Orlando as the novel's hero in both a romantic and a moral sense. When Oliver arrives, Orlando bests him first with wit, then with strength, ultimately demanding the share that their deceased father had allotted to him. Oliver placates Orlando, then curses Adam, who reveals his fond remembrance of their father, Sir Rowland de Boys, and effectively allies himself with Orlando.

Left alone, Oliver summons the court wrestler, Charles, who provides an account of the state of the ducal court (largely for the audience, in that he is only delivering "old news" (96–7): the elder Duke Senior has been ousted and banished by his younger brother Frederick. Rosalind, the daughter of the banished Duke Senior, has remained at the court only because she is highly favored by her cousin Celia. Meanwhile, Duke Senior and the lords who joined him in exile have settled in the evidently idyllic Forest of Arden, where they "fleet the time carelessly, as they did in the golden world" (114–15). As Charles will be wrestling a disguised Orlando the following day, Oliver entreats him to do as much harm as possible. Oliver's scene-closing monologue leaves no doubt about his role as a villain: he despises Orlando solely because the youngest of the three brothers is so benevolent and beloved.

Act 1, Scene 2

Upon their first appearance in the play, Rosalind mourns the absence of her father while Celia tries to persuade her to content herself with the friendship they share. Rosalind suggests that falling in love might distract her from her sorrows, and Celia agrees that she could "make sport withal" (25), which she will indeed do, but cautions against loving "in good earnest" (26), which she will also do. After ruminating on the goddesses Fortune and Nature, the two women greet Touchstone, the court fool, who marks his entrance with a trivial display of wit regarding knightly honor. The courtier Monsieur Le Beau then arrives to inform the three of the wrestling match about to take place there.

When Duke Frederick enters—accompanied by a shift from prose to blank verse, which endows the action with greater gravity until the end of the scene—he entreats the ladies to persuade the young challenger to stand down. When they cannot refute Orlando's tragically heroic reasons for fighting—no one would truly regret the loss of his life anyway, and he wishes to test himself—he proceeds to defeat the champion, Charles, to Rosalind's cry of "Hercules be thy speed, young man!" (199). In turn, Frederick expresses disappointment, because he was an enemy of Orlando's father—while Rosalind's father, Duke Senior, had held Sir Rowland de Boys in the highest esteem. The ladies commend Orlando, with Rosalind dramatically giving him a chain from around her neck, before exiting, leaving Orlando dumbfounded by his growing passion for Rosalind.

Le Beau then returns, first warning Orlando that he ought to leave the dukedom, as he has aroused Frederick's displeasure, then informing Orlando about the identities of Rosalind and Celia.

Act 1, Scene 3

Rosalind discusses her adoration for Orlando with Celia, exchanging a fair amount of wit and referring to him as potentially being her "child's father" (11). Duke Frederick, however, interrupts the scene—to the return of blank verse—to banish Rosalind, citing a general mistrust of her intentions; also, just as Oliver dislikes Orlando for his virtue, Frederick takes issue with the fact that "Her very silence, and her patience, / Speak to the people, and they pity her" (76–7). Frederick also tries to convince his daughter that she would be better off without her cousin as a rival. The two women then decide to journey to the Forest of Arden disguised as peasants, with the taller Rosalind posing as a man named Ganymede and Celia posing as a woman named Aliena; gathering the clown Touchstone and their "jewels" and "wealth" (132), they depart.

Act 2, Scene 1

The second act provides a transition from the court to the forest, with the first scene taking place in Arden, the second at court, the third at Oliver's, and each scene thereafter in the forest. The foremost patriarchal figure of the woodlands is introduced, Duke Senior, who is attended by Amiens and a number of lords. After extolling upon the virtues of the forest, Duke Senior regrets his company's need to kill the deer, who are true forest natives, for their meat. One lord mentions how the "melancholy Jaques" (26, 41), who was just seen mourning a mortally wounded deer, is particularly revolted by their intrusions on nature. Interested in some conversation with the philosophizer—if only for amusement—Duke Senior and his lords depart in search of him.

Act 2, Scene 2

At the court, briefly, Duke Frederick is made aware of the disappearance of both his niece and his daughter and also of their expressed affection for Orlando, who may have accompanied them. Frederick then summons Oliver.

Act 2, Scene 3

At Oliver's house, Adam meets Orlando and praises his many virtues, affectionately referring to him as a "memory / of old Sir Rowland" (2–3), then warns him that Oliver is scheming to have him murdered, if not by arson then by some other means. Knowing he would be unable to live life as an amoral thief, Orlando resolves to face his brother—until Adam volunteers his life's savings and his service to help the youngest brother find shelter and provisions somewhere. The two depart together.

Act 2, Scene 4

Rosalind, Celia, and Touchstone appear in the Forest of Arden, incredibly weary from their travels, with the fool regretting having left the court. The woodland shepherds Corin and Silvius then appear, softening the mood of the scene by speaking of love: Silvius expresses his adoration of Phebe and accuses the elder Corin of having never been a true lover himself, as he remembers none of his lover's follies. Rosalind is reminded of her own aching for Orlando, and Touchstone reminisces somewhat soberly upon a love of his youth. The fool then calls out to Corin, and Rosalind inquires about lodgings and food; through Corin, they secure the purchase of a cottage and a flock of sheep.

Act 2, Scene 5

Amiens and Jaques share songs about the peacefulness of the forest, where the only enemies are "winter and rough weather" (7). Jaques again mentions his distaste for men, specifically their general lack of manners, and notes that he has been avoiding Duke Senior because he finds him "too disputable" (31).

Act 2, Scene 6

Adam and Orlando stumble into the Forest of Arden. When Adam collapses, Orlando sets out to seek help for him.

Act 2, Scene 7

Jaques and Duke Senior meet, and Jaques relates his earlier encounter with Touchstone when the fool uttered some witty comments about the passing of the time. Duke Senior scoffs at the soundness of Jaques's judgments given his checkered past. Orlando then arrives, threatening to attack them and rob them of their food, only to be offered the food gladly by the gentlemanly Duke Senior. As Orlando leaves to return to Adam, Duke Senior and Jaques muse on the theatricality of life, with Jaques giving the famous "seven ages" speech, in which he remarks that a single man goes through seven stages, or acts, in the course of his lifetime. ("All the world's a stage / And all the men and women merely players.") Amiens marks the meal with a song, "Blow, blow, thou winter wind," and the duke rejoices in meeting the son of his beloved and deceased friend Sir Rowland de Boys.

Act 3, Scene 1

At his palace, Duke Frederick orders Oliver to bring his brother to the court within a year or be exiled himself. As Oliver grovels, Duke Frederick scorns him as a villain for having never loved his own brother.

Act 3, Scene 2

Orlando hangs love poems to Rosalind on trees throughout the forest, singing her praises as he does so. With the entrance of the fool and a shepherd, the play reverts to prose form; Touchstone demands that the shepherd Corin give an acceptable accounting of why he should spend his life in the countryside rather than at court. The fool manages to phrase his own reasons for favoring the court with enough nuance to stymie the peasant. Rosalind interrupts them as she arrives reading one of the anonymous poems written about her, which Touchstone promptly ridicules as being pedantic and dull, devising his own pithy and mocking rhymes. Celia then arrives reading a somewhat longer poem that Rosalind finds tedious.

The two women send the two men off so they can talk together. Rosalind begins by deriding the author's poetic abilities. Celia then reveals to her cousin that she saw the poet hanging up one of the sheets—and that he wears Rosalind's chain around his neck, at which news Rosalind reddens but seems not to realize that the man is Orlando. Celia first describes him, then reveals his identity, and Rosalind becomes quite agitated by romantic sentiments.

Orlando himself then appears on the scene, chatting with Jaques, and the women hide. Orlando relates his affections for Rosalind and responds to Jaques's probing inquiries with fine wit. When Jaques slinks off, Rosalind disguised as Ganymede approaches, intending to best Orlando in conversation. She ends up carrying on a profound discourse about the passage of time experienced by people who spend their time differently. From the beginning, the conversation is strained by Rosalind's attempts to conceal her person. After remarking on how glad she is not to be a woman, Rosalind belittles Orlando for allowing himself to be infected with love, which she sees evidenced by his poems more than by his person. Rosalind then remarks that she can cure Orlando of his love if he will focus his affection on her (that is to say, Ganymede), and substitute the name *Rosalind* instead. He is skeptical but he agrees, and they head for the women's cottage.

Act 3, Scene 3

In the forest, Touchstone and Audrey are carrying on something of a courtship, while Jaques watches from a concealed location. Audrey reveals her unfamiliarity with the notion of the "poetical" (15), while Touchstone flaunts his wit and makes little secret of his desire simply to have sexual relations with the female goatherd. After mentioning that he has brought along a local vicar to perform a marriage ceremony to legitimate their lovemaking, he speaks at length about animals and men and their horns, sustaining the sexual references. When Sir Oliver Mar-text begins to conduct the wedding, Jaques offers to give away the bride and then convinces Touchstone that such a dull marriage would not befit the gentleman that he is. Jaques at last leads the couple away.

Act 3, Scene 4

At their cottage in the morning, Rosalind anxiously awaits Orlando, fretting to Celia about the color of his hair while admiring his evident chasteness. Celia admits that she doubts the truth of his love, leading Rosalind to inquire further. Rosalind also mentions that she met her father the day before and successfully maintained her disguise. When Corin arrives to lead them to the spectacle of Silvius trying to court Phebe (at which point the text switches to blank verse, the first time that such a change is introduced for a peasant) Rosalind remarks that she may "prove a busy actor in their play" (56).

Act 3, Scene 5

As Silvius begs Phebe to show him but the smallest kindness, Rosalind, Celia, and Corin arrive to observe. Phebe rejects Silvius saying that no man should be truly hurt by emotional disappointment. As Silvius despairs, Rosalind enters

Illustration of Audrey and the Clown Touchstone, Act V, scene iii

loves. After comparing him unfavorably to a snail, which at least has a home and horns on its head, Rosalind then urges Orlando to try and woo her. They banter about kissing and chasteness, then Rosalind echoes Phebe's earlier remarks about no man having ever truly died from love.

When Orlando objects to Rosalind's lamenting tone, she becomes pleasanter, and they engage in a mock wedding ceremony. Nevertheless, she again grows negative, offering a list of ways in which she would disappoint Orlando as a wife. Ultimately she asserts that above all she would not abandon her wit, and if her husband tried to dismiss her, she would simply turn to another man. Orlando then departs to join the duke at dinner, asserting that he will return in two hours, and Rosalind remarks that if he breaks that promise, he will be thoroughly out of favor. Celia then chastises Rosalind for her disparaging remarks about the female sex, to which Rosalind replies only by celebrating the depth of her love for Orlando.

Act 4, Scene 2

Jaques and a few lords are found celebrating their successful deer hunt, although Jaques had earlier mourned the death of a hunted deer. One of the lords offers a song ritualizing the wearing of the deer's horns, horns that are portrayed as almost sacred.

Act 4, Scene 3

As Celia and Rosalind wonder about Orlando's failure to return on time, Silvius appears—accompanied by blank verse—to present Rosalind, still dressed as Ganymede, with a supposedly caustic letter from Phebe. In fact, finding the message to be one of love, Rosalind seizes the opportunity to jest with Silvius: she first claims that some man, certainly he, must have in fact written the "giant-rude" (35) invective therein, then reads the letter aloud to reveal its actual loving contents. Finally, she sends Silvius on his way, although he is hopelessly in love with Phebe.

Oliver then arrives in search of the cottage and the disguised women, bearing a handkerchief stained with blood. He relates how Orlando had happened upon a man sleeping under a tree with a snake wrapped about his neck and a lioness crouching in the bushes nearby. The snake slithered away, leaving Orlando to discover that the man was none other than his elder brother Oliver;

to first make fun of Phebe's appearance and then suggest to Silvius that he would be better off seeking another mate; ultimately she recommends that they form a union, even if it might produce "ill-favored children" (53). However, Phebe takes an instant liking to Ganymede, despite, if not because of, his aggressiveness. When Silvius and Phebe are again left alone, Phebe agrees to love Silvius not romantically but as a neighbor, as well as to employ him. Subsequently, she inquires about Ganymede and expresses how appealing she found his softer qualities. At last recalling Ganymede's bitterness and claiming to be offended by him, Phebe entreats Silvius to bring Ganymede a letter that she will compose.

Act 4, Scene 1

Jaques is engaging in conversation with the disguised Rosalind and Celia, offering justification for his melancholy, which he claims stems in part from his travels; Rosalind says that she prefers the amusement of a fool to the sadness fostered by experience. When Orlando appears, Jaques exits, leaving Rosalind to chide Orlando for being so late to a meeting with one he supposedly after some indecision, Orlando drove off the lioness, saving Oliver's life. Upon reaching the safety of the realm of Duke Senior, Orlando collapsed from a wound he received, then entreated Oliver to bring the handkerchief to Rosalind as a token. At this news, Rosalind herself swoons, leaving Oliver somewhat unconvinced of her masculinity. She hopes that Oliver will tell Orlando that she had only pretended to faint.

Act 5, Scene 1

Audrey and Touchstone are conversing, with Audrey regretting that they had not been married earlier by the adequate priest. Audrey then confirms that William "lays claim to" (7) but has "no interest in" (8) her, and Touchstone prepares to belittle him with wit. After conversing inconsequentially, the fool concludes by threatening the hapless William with death if he should try to maintain relations with Audrey.

Act 5, Scene 2

Oliver discusses his newfound adoration for Celia (as Aliena) with Orlando, also telling his younger brother that he intends to remain in the forest and live the life of a humble shepherd; if he does, Orlando will inherit their father's estate. Upon Rosalind's arrival, Orlando—who refers to the "greater wonders" (27) related to him by his brother and may thus be aware of Rosalind's disguise—rues the fact that his brother gets to enjoy his love in the present. Orlando states that he "can live no longer by thinking," that is, about his absent love (50). Rosalind, as Ganymede, then relates how she has long "conversed with a magician" (60–1) and promises that she will bring the true Rosalind the following day.

Silvius and Phebe then arrive, with Silvius professing his love for her, while she professes her love for Ganymede—and Orlando once more professes his love for Rosalind. Rosalind then promises to resolve all of their conflicts of love the following day, presenting the intended outcome in such a witty way that everyone is content.

Act 5, Scene 3

Touchstone and Audrey look forward to their coming wedding, with two of Duke Senior's pages arriving and singing the company a song about love and springtime. Touchstone concludes their tune with some sardonic remarks about the time he just wasted.

MEDIA ADAPTATIONS

- Among a number of motion picture versions of *As You Like It*, one of the most notable was produced by International Allied in 1936, directed by Paul Czinner. It features the renowned Laurence Olivier as Orlando in his first Shakespeare role on film, as well as Elisabeth Bergner playing Rosalind.

- An educational video entitled *"As You Like It": An Introduction* was produced by BHE Education in 1969, offering performances of key scenes from the comedy, accompanied by brief instructional narratives.

- A television adaptation of *As You Like It* was produced by the British Broadcasting Corporation in 1979, as distributed by Time-Life Video. It was directed by Brian Coleman and stars Helen Mirren as Rosalind.

- Kenneth Branagh directed a film version of *As You Like It* that was released in 2006, as produced by Picturehouse, featuring such renowned stars as Bryce Dallas Howard (Rosalind), Kevin Kline (Jaques), and Alfred Molina (Touchstone).

Act 5, Scene 4

In the closing scene, Duke Senior, Jaques, Orlando, Oliver, Silvius, Phebe, Celia, and Rosalind are gathered, with Rosalind receiving confirmation from everyone that they will agree to the various proposed unions. The two disguised women then leave, with Duke Senior and Orlando commenting upon Ganymede's resemblance to Rosalind.

Touchstone and Audrey then arrive, with Jaques praising the fool's wit. Touchstone frames his acceptance of Audrey as a noble deed, then goes on to relate a quarrel he had, naming all of the retorts and reproofs according to the conventions of rhetoric; Jaques proves interested enough to ask for a recounting of the seven "degrees of the lie" (88–9).

At last, the undisguised Rosalind and Celia arrive, led by Hymen, the Greek god of marriage, who speaks in blank verse with three or four feet per line, as opposed to Shakespeare's usual iambic pentameter, which has five feet. After Duke Senior and Orlando rejoice in Rosalind's appearance, Hymen proceeds to wed each of the four couples: Orlando and Rosalind, Oliver and Celia, Silvius and Phebe, and Touchstone and Audrey. After a "wedlock hymn" (137), Jaques de Boys, the brother between Oliver and Orlando, arrives to announce news: Duke Frederick, having embarked on a military journey into the forest in search of the banished Duke Senior, was converted to goodness by "an old religious man" (160) and bequeathed the crown and all his land back to his brother. Duke Senior implores the company to fully enjoy the "rustic revelry" (177) before returning to courtly life. The philosophizing Jaques then bids farewell to the company, naming the good fortunes that all the men have happened upon, to join the converted Duke Frederick, from whom he expects "there is much matter to be heard and learned" (185). The play closes with dancing.

Epilogue

The character of Rosalind bids farewell to the audience with the hope that women and men alike found enjoyment in the play. Since in Shakespeare's time the actor playing Rosalind was a man, he notes that he would have even kissed some of the men in the audience had he been a woman; instead, he simply asks that they bid him farewell.

CHARACTERS

Adam

Adam is an aged servant of the de Boys household. Adam bolsters Orlando's claim to having the strongest ties to his father by calling Orlando a "memory / Of old sir Rowland" (2.3.3–4) and by accompanying him in exile, going so far as to offer his life's savings to ensure the young man's survival.

Aliena

See Celia

Amiens

Amiens is a courtier attending Duke Senior in exile.

Audrey

Audrey is a country wench who herds goats and who marries Touchstone. Audrey is portrayed as especially ignorant, not even understanding Touchstone's ridicule of her.

Celia

Celia is Duke Frederick's daughter and Rosalind's cousin. Celia shares a powerful bond with Rosalind, voluntarily accompanying her cousin into exile after remarking, "Shall we be sund'red, shall we part, sweet girl? / No, let my father seek another heir" (96–7). While Rosalind is given far more attention, Celia serves as the catalyst for some of her cousin's thoughts and actions. After Orlando's victory, she states, "Gentle cousin, / Let us go thank him and encourage him" (1.2.229–30); when Rosalind is banished, even before she thinks to visit her father, Celia suggests first that they go "to seek my uncle in the forest of Arden" (1.3.105), then that they wear disguises. Celia poses as a peasant woman named Aliena.

Unlike Celia, her cousin Rosalind seems unable to assume the masculine role without disparaging the feminine. After Rosalind speaks of women's ways with Orlando, Celia scolds her for her remarks about women. Thus, Celia may be viewed as a stronger woman than her cousin.

Charles

Charles is Duke Frederick's wrestler, who fights Orlando in act 1, scene 2. Oliver tricks Charles into believing that Orlando is a villain and that Charles should thus do as much damage to Orlando as possible. However, despite this instruction, Charles is defeated by Orlando.

Corin

Corin is an old shepherd who befriends Rosalind, Celia, and Touchstone. While Touchstone abuses him for his simplicity, Corin is stalwart and genuine in his defense of his pastoral life: "I am a true laborer; I earn that I eat, get that I wear, owe no man hate, envy no man's happiness" (73–5).

Jaques de Boys

Jaques is the second son of Sir Rowland de Boys and is Oliver and Orlando's brother. The news of

Duke Frederick's conversion is delivered by Jaques de Boys, who serves as a neutral mediator between the good and evil forces of the play.

Duke Frederick

Frederick is Duke Senior's younger brother and usurper of his throne. He is also Celia's father and Rosalind's uncle. Duke Frederick is a fairly one-dimensional villain through most of the play; his base nature is aptly summed up by Le Beau: "this Duke / Hath ta'en displeasure 'gainst his gentle niece, / Grounded upon no other argument / But that the people praise her for her virtues / And pity her for her good father's sake" (267–71). Reflecting his irrelevant status as a character, he does not even make an appearance after being converted by an "old religious man" (5.4.160) in the forest.

Duke Senior

The exiled elder brother of Duke Frederick and father of Rosalind, Duke Senior serves as the benevolent patriarchal figure of the Forest of Arden. He utters the first lines in the forest as well as the rhyming couplet that closes the play. His introduction to the forest is essential in establishing the setting's superiority—"Are not these woods / More free from peril than the envious court?" (2.1.3–4)—while also addressing its drawbacks: "the icy fang / And churlish chiding of the winter's wind . . . these are counselors / That feelingly persuade me what I am" (2.1.6–11). That is, Duke Senior fairly delights even in the physical sensation of being cold, which makes him feel far more alive than did the "painted pomp" (2.1.3) of the court.

Ganymede

See Rosalind

Hymen

The Greek god of marriage, Hymen appears in the final scene to marry all the couples. The personification of the god gives substance to the forest's otherworldliness.

Jaques

Jaques is a melancholy lord attending Duke Senior in banishment. Jaques is commonly considered Touchstone's foil, as he provides commentary on the play's diverse issues from a completely different perspective. Jaques's misanthropy, or distaste for humanity, initially casts a dark shadow over the events in Arden forest.

Where Duke Senior expresses regret at the killing of the "native burghers of this desert city" (2.1.23)—the deer—"in their own confines" (2.1.24) essentially as an afterthought, Jaques weeps at the sight and sound of a wounded deer pouring forth tears and heaving its last breaths. As reported by a lord, Jaques goes so far as to "most invectively . . . pierceth through / The body of the country, city, court, / Yea, and of this our life, swearing that we / Are mere usurpers, tyrants" (2.1.58–61). Thus, while Duke Senior has already been cast as a virtuous man, in contrast to the usurper Frederick, Jaques characterizes not only the elder duke but also all the men who have invaded the forest as usurpers in turn. The melancholy philosophizer can be seen as something of an environmentalist. Jaques's antihumanism is highlighted when Duke Senior's party is unable to locate him and one lord remarks, "I think he be transformed into a beast, / For I can nowhere find him like a man" (2.7.1–2).

Overall, the audience does not develop a favorable impression of Jaques. While Jaques reveals a certain fondness for Touchstone and professes his own desire to become a fool, so as to better "Cleanse the foul body of th' infected world" (2.7.60), Duke Senior promptly discredits him for having been a "libertine, / As sensual as the brutish sting itself" (2.7.65–6). Indeed, Jaques is something of a parody of an Elizabethan stereotype (and of a number of Shakespeare's contemporary satirists), the traveler who returns from abroad only to become discontented with domestic life. Shakespeare shows no sympathy for Jaques throughout the play: his cynical statements are rebuked time and again by Rosalind, Orlando, Touchstone, and Duke Senior. Even the initial portrayal of Jaques as an environmentalist is negated when he revels later in the killing of a second deer, hailing the successful hunter as a "Roman conqueror" (4.2.3–4); the text gives no evidence that the line would have been delivered ironically.

In the end, Jaques refuses to take part in the wedding celebration even vicariously, noting, "I am for other than for dancing measures" (5.4.193), and many commentators have read this as Shakespeare's ultimate condemnation of Jaques's character: he simply can not take part in life's joys. Yet while most of the protagonists will be returning to the oft-decried courtly life, Jaques intends to join the newly religious Duke

Frederick, remarking, "Out of these convertites / There is much matter to be heard and learned" (5.4.184–85). His final lines, which are somewhat cryptic—"what you would have / I'll stay to know at your abandoned cave" (5.4.195–96)—at the very least indicate that he is devoted to the ideal of the pastoral world, rather than having merely vacationed there out of necessity.

Le Beau

One of Duke Frederick's courtiers, Le Beau serves as an intermediary between Duke Frederick and his daughter and niece, telling the two women of the wrestling match and also of the duke's ill humor after its conclusion.

Sir Oliver Mar-text

Sir Oliver is a vicar whose marriage of Touchstone and Audrey is interrupted by Jaques.

Oliver

Oliver is the eldest son of Sir Rowland de Boys. Oliver is expressly villainous, remarking that he dislikes Orlando largely because the latter is so virtuous and generally well loved by others. This animosity parallels that harbored by Duke Frederick toward the deceased Sir Rowland de Boys, highlighting the degree to which both men are antagonized by the "honorable" (1.2.215). At the end, Orlando's compassion for Oliver inspires the elder brother to bequeath Sir Rowland's estate to the younger; Oliver subsequently marries Celia.

Orlando

The youngest son of Sir Rowland de Boys, Orlando serves as the play's romantic male hero, eventually marrying Rosalind. Orlando's appearances in the first act well establish his moral virtue, as he craves only "such exercises as may become a gentleman" (1.1.69–70), including a good education, while Oliver, the eldest de Boys brother, professes to despise Orlando expressly because the younger is "so much in the heart of the world, and especially of my own people, who best know him, that I am altogether misprized" (1.1.161–63). Orlando proceeds to outwrestle Charles, a Goliath figure, without boast or bravado, and he even proves humbly shy when Rosalind addresses him afterward.

Much attention is given to Orlando's ties to his father, Rowland, whose name is a loose anagram of his youngest son's. Their last name,

meanwhile, comes from *bois*, which means "forest" in French. When Orlando reiterates the claim, "The spirit of my father grows strong in me" (1.1.67–8), the audience understands that Orlando, not Oliver, is the true heir to the virtuous natural world signified by their last name.

In the Forest of Arden, the audience's impression of Orlando shifts somewhat, as Rosalind, posing as Ganymede, appears to control, if not dominate, the interactions between the destined pair. The audience may feel that Orlando's inability to direct their conversations reflects a lack of masculine assertiveness. Yet in fact, one of Orlando's surest virtues may be his ability to reconcile himself to more feminine qualities. Upon reaching the forest realm of Duke Senior, Orlando first adopts an aggressive stance; however, once he realizes he is being kindly received, he remarks, "Let gentleness my strong enforcement be; / In the which hope I blush, and hide my sword" (2.7.118–19). With Duke Senior serving as a surrogate father figure to Orlando, this scene might be viewed from a Freudian perspective as a resolution of the hostility toward the father associated with the Oedipus complex. Signaling that resolution, Orlando taps his nurturing side, noting, "like a doe, I go to find my fawn" (128). In "Sexual Politics and Social Structure," with reference to Orlando's later rescue of Oliver, Peter B. Erickson observes that the youngest brother "achieves a synthesis of attributes traditionally labeled masculine and feminine when he combines compassion and aggression in rescuing his brother from the lioness" (231).

Ultimately, as Erickson relates, Orlando is confirmed as the foremost authority figure in both his relationship with Rosalind and in the play as a whole. The possession of Rosalind in a literal sense passes from Duke Senior to Orlando. When Duke Senior is restored as the head of the dukedom, his possessions will pass not to his daughter but to the husband of his daughter, meaning that Orlando will inherit the entire land. Thus, as Erickson concludes, "Festive celebration is now possible because a dependable, that is, patriarchal, social order is securely in place" (232).

Phebe

Phebe is a shepherdess. She is indifferent toward Silvius, who is courting her, and falls in love with

Ganymede instead. She eventually agrees to marry Silvius.

Rosalind

The exiled Duke Senior's daughter and niece of Duke Frederick, Rosalind is the play's central character, in that she has both the most lines and brings about much of the play's resolution. She is downhearted from the beginning, as her father has been away in exile, and only when her heart is "overthrown" (1.2.244) are her spirits first lifted. Leaving the court in banishment, along with her fleeing cousin, she adopts the disguise of a man, Ganymede, largely so that she and Celia may appear less vulnerable to any would-be assailants. At this point, she endeavors to transform herself outwardly and bear "a swashing and a martial outside" (1.3.118), that is, a swaggering, confrontational demeanor. Nevertheless, she confesses to yet also bearing "hidden woman's fear" (1.3.117), and many of her lines in the forest reflect her attempts to reconcile her maidenly reserve with her intent to pass as a man.

In posing as Ganymede, Rosalind draws upon her ample reserves of wit, which, as a courtly lady in Elizabethan times, she may not have had much opportunity to use otherwise. When she intends to treat Orlando like "a saucy lackey" (3.2.292), she guides the conversation with her witty remarks on the passage of time. She then arranges for Orlando to dote upon her, in her disguise as Ganymede, as if she were Rosalind, ensuring a sustained connection with him. She later lectures Orlando on the appearances and actions of one who is truly love struck.

Though liberated in terms of the attitude she can adopt around Orlando, Rosalind otherwise professes to be constrained by her disguise. As she, Celia, and Touchstone enter the forest, she notes a desire to "disgrace my man's apparel, and to cry like a woman" (2.4.4–5). Similarly, when she faints at the news of Orlando's having suffered a grievous wound, she rises and first utters, "I would I were at home" (4.3.162), then reflexively negates her emotional state, claiming she had counterfeited the swoon. The audience is left to decide whether such denials are positive steps for a woman of that era to take.

Regardless of how much Rosalind revels in her man's disguise, the play's closure is very much a return to a state of female subservience. Indeed, from the outset, Rosalind is understood to be depressed largely because of the absence of any male figure in her life: her father has been exiled, and the fact that she only grows animated upon meeting Orlando sheds light upon her earlier suggestion that they divert themselves by "falling in love" (1.2.24). Before revealing her identity, Rosalind refers to herself in speaking to her father as "your Rosalind" (5.4.6) and requests confirmation that he will "bestow her on Orlando" (5.4.7). Regarding Rosalind's return to her womanhood, Peter B. Erickson notes, "A benevolent patriarchy still requires women to be subordinate, and Rosalind's final performance is her enactment of this subordination" (232). Erickson also notes that the epilogue, in which the male actor playing Rosalind reveals himself as male, presents a "further phasing out of Rosalind" (233).

Silvius

Silvius is a shepherd who remains in love with the shepherdess Phebe despite her constant scorning. He eventually marries her.

Touchstone

A fool in the service of first Oliver, then Rosalind and Celia, Touchstone is all that his name implies: he acts as a touchstone, testing the qualities of the other characters both at Duke Frederick's court and in the forest. He also is an apt persona for conveying bits and piece of philosophy to the audience, whether they be genuine or ironic. Many commentators have noted that Touchstone differs from the fools in Shakespeare's preceding plays largely because the playwright shaped the part to a different actor: Robert Armin. Armin, who himself wrote a work on the varying natures of court fools, was perhaps fit to play a jester of greater sophistication than the man he replaced within the Lord Chamberlain's Men, Will Kempe, who had proven successful playing strictly comic roles. In fact, Armin may have joined the company midway through Shakespeare's writing of *As You Like It*, which would account for the difference in Touchstone's temperament in the first act as compared to the later acts; in "Touchstone in Arcadia," Robert H. Goldsmith notes that this change may also simply reflect the respective degrees of intellectual freedom that Touchstone felt at court and in the forest, as any court fool would have been wise to restrain his wit somewhat in the presence of a usurper.

Touchstone is perhaps more out of place in the Forest of Arden than any other character in the play. While Touchstone marries Audrey at the end, the audience understands that he does so merely to enjoy the associated conjugal rights. Otherwise, throughout much of the play Touchstone remarks not on the merrier aspects of the forest but on what the forest lacks as compared to the court, as in his remarks to Corin about the shepherd's life, where he expresses the negative view: "in respect that it is a shepherd's life, it is naught.... in respect that it is private, it is a very vile life .... in respect it is not in the court, it is tedious.... as there is no more plenty in it, it goes much against my stomach" (3.2.14–21).

In general, Touchstone looks at every situation from an oblique angle and speaks in a caustic voice. He sees Orlando's poetry not as charming but pedantic; he insists that Corin is a sinner for having never learned court manners; and rather than enjoying their song, he condemns the pages as being off time. He even refuses to acknowledge himself as either witty or a fool: to Rosalind he states, "I shall ne'er be ware of mine own wit till I break my shins against it" (2.4.56–7), while Jaques recalls him remarking, "Call me not fool till heaven hath sent me fortune" (2.7.19). Goldsmith sums up Touchstone's role in part by quoting C. S. Lewis, who notes in *The Allegory of Love* that a tale in the mode of *As You Like It* "protects itself against the laughter of the vulgar ... by allowing laughter and cynicism their place *inside* the poem" (199). Goldsmith himself notes, "Touchstone's presence within the pastoral romance is a concession to our sense of comic realism and protects the play from corrosive criticism" (200). Indeed, Touchstone's sarcastic rejoinders quite likely preempted just such unruly commentary from the groundlings at the Globe Theatre.

William

William is a country fellow who loves Audrey and is rudely threatened by Touchstone.

THEMES

Pastoral Life

Numerous oppositions in *As You Like It* reveal Shakespeare's partiality toward the pastoral rustic life of Arden forest to life at court. At Duke Frederick's court, disorder holds sway. The deterioration of political authority is the most obvious form of disorder, for Duke Frederick has unlawfully seized Duke Senior's kingdom. This political degeneration is compounded by a more personal disorder, since the dukes are also brothers at odds with each other. This conflict is also underscored by the antagonistic relationship of two other brothers at the court, Oliver and Orlando. Arden forest offers a sense of pure, spiritual order in contrast to the corrupt condition of Duke Frederick's court. Indeed, Duke Senior, who introduces the audience to the forest, immediately establishes the realm as a haven from the court, which he refers to as a place of "painted pomp" and as "envious"—that is, a place where people covet what others have—in opposition to the virtual absence of both private property and social position in the wild.

Meanwhile, for those fleeing the court, the journey to the forest is long and difficult; when the characters arrive they are physically exhausted and hungry. The harsh experience of returning to nature acts as a stripping process, however, laying bare the characters' virtuous natures calloused by court life. Some characters, like Orlando and Rosalind, need little improvement and find in Arden a liberation from the oppression they have endured at court. Others, such as Oliver and Duke Frederick, approach the forest with malicious intent only to undergo a complete spiritual reformation. Arden is thus a morally pure realm whose special curative powers purge and renew the forest dwellers, granting them a self-awareness that they will ultimately use to restore order at court.

Fortune vs. Nature

Closely allied with the opposition of court life and the Forest of Arden is the dichotomy between fortune and nature. Here, "fortune" represents both material gain—achieved through power, birthright, or possessions—and a force that unpredictably determines events. "Nature," on the other hand, is both the purifying force of Arden and humanity's fundamental condition stripped of the trappings of wealth, power, and material possessions.

The opposition between fortune and nature is highlighted most in the first act, where the audience finds that fortune has benefited the villainous (Frederick and Oliver) over the virtuous

Alexandra Gilbraith as Rosalind and Anthony Nowell as Orlando with Nancy Carroll as Celia at the Royal Shakespeare Theatre, Stratford-upon-Avon, 2000 (© *Donald Cooper/Photostage. Reproduced by permission*)

(Duke Senior, Orlando, and Rosalind). Celia suggests that she and Rosalind "mock the good housewife Fortune from her wheel, that her gifts may henceforth be bestowed equally" (1.2.30–2), referring to the fact that the goddess Fortune was historically depicted as blind, sitting on a spherical throne, with one foot on a ball and one hand upon her wheel that determined the fates of everyone. The goddess Nature, meanwhile, was considered to be in control of people's innate virtues, such as their nobility and wisdom. In this scene, Rosalind and Celia discuss Fortune and Nature at length, musing on the two goddesses' effects on the world.

Duke Senior is presented as a man who has successfully thwarted Fortune; after his speech praising the rustic over the courtly life, Amiens notes, "Happy is your Grace / That can translate the stubbornness of fortune / Into so quiet and so sweet a style" (18–20). Fortune is mentioned again later by Adam, who, upon fleeing with Orlando, notes, in a rhyming couplet closing a scene, "Yet fortune cannot recompense me

better / Than to die well and not my master's debtor" (2.4.75–6). Nature, meanwhile, is invoked most pointedly when Oliver describes his brother's rescue of him: "But kindness, nobler ever than revenge / And nature, stronger than his just occasion, / Made him give battle to the lioness, / Who quickly fell before him" (4.3.129–32). Thus, the play's protagonists by and large manage to overcome the caprices of Fortune by drawing on the assets of Nature.

Time

Time is also contrasted in the court scenes and in the Forest of Arden. At court, time is referred to in specific terms, marked by definite intervals, in most cases in relation to the duke's threats: he orders Rosalind to leave the court within ten days or she will be executed, and he gives Oliver one year to find Orlando or else his land and possessions will be confiscated. In Arden, however, the meaning of time is less precise. In his first meeting with Jaques, Touchstone provides a slightly whimsical rumination on time; he seems to be remarking on his sense that he is simply rotting away in the uneventful forest. Jaques later offers a disheartened perception of how time passes predictably for all men, as his "Seven Ages of Man" speech illustrates the individual's passage through life in predetermined stages, ending with the image of man as a pathetically ineffectual and dependent creature.

When Rosalind, posing as Ganymede, first addresses Orlando, she asks him, "what is 't o'clock?" (3.2.296), and his response is especially meaningful: "You should ask me, what time o' day. There's no clock in the forest" (3.2.297–98). Indeed, time in Arden is measured "in divers paces with divers persons" (3.2.304–05), as Rosalind subsequently instructs Orlando; the lover's constant sighing and groaning, she contends, ought to be as regular as clockwork, while a young maid, a priest, and a thief would all feel time's passage uniquely. Later on, Rosalind lectures Orlando for not being more punctual, because a true lover would not lose a single moment that he could be spending with his beloved. In general, the sense that time is a subjective, not an objective, quality enhances Arden's mythical and romantic aspects.

Sexual Identity

Sexual identity is examined primarily through the character of Rosalind, who disguises herself as a man named Ganymede—a mythological boy whose name was synonymous with beauty and androgyny—to ensure her safe passage to Arden. Though she can discard her male costume when she reaches the forest, Rosalind does not do so until the end of the play. Critics generally agree that she continues to act as Ganymede because the disguise liberates her from the submissive role of a woman. As a man, she is able to take more control of her own life, especially in her courtship with Orlando. In their playacting scenes, Rosalind controls the tactics of courtship in a way that is usually reserved for men, inverting their roles to teach Orlando the meaning of real love rather than love based on his idealized vision of her. An added complexity of Rosalind's sexual identity is evident if we consider that in Shakespeare's age, boys played the roles of women in dramas. The playwright takes advantage of this convention in *As You Like It* to accentuate flexibility in the presentation of gender. As the boy actor who performs as Rosalind must also play Ganymede, who in turn pretends to be Rosalind in the playacting sessions with Orlando, the audience follows the character's various

transformations and can better appreciate the extent to which Rosalind's presentation of herself as masculine or feminine changes the way the other characters interact with her.

Acting and the Stage

References to acting, role-playing, scenes, and the stage are scattered throughout *As You Like It*, most prominently in reference to Rosalind's posing as Ganymede. When first meeting Orlando in the forest, she aims to "play the knave with him" (3.2.293); aside from her own role as a self-confident man, which is overlaid with her role as the fickle "Rosalind," she has much to say to Orlando about his playing the role of the lover, noting that he lacks the proper disheveled attire and that he is not as punctual as a lover ought to be. At one point she even entreats Celia to conduct a pretend marriage ceremony between herself and Orlando.

Such references to acting would be natural, of course, in the context of a play presented on the spare stage of the Globe Theatre, where boys and men played the parts of the women and, generally speaking, the artifice of the production could not be ignored. However, the passage in which Jaques delivers the "Seven Ages of Man" speech accentuates the theatrical aspect beyond what is found in Shakespeare's other works. After the arrival of Orlando, who tells of the exhausted Adam, Duke Senior observes, "This wide and universal theater / Presents more woeful pageants than the scene / Wherein we play in" (2.7.137–39). With these remarks, referring to both tragedy and drama, the duke lends gravity to Jaques's ensuing speech, about which Shakespearean commentators disagree. Some consider that Adam's consequent arrival is a negation of Jaques's speech as serious philosophy, in that the elderly man has just completed a substantial journey; on the other hand, Adam only reaches the realm of the duke because he has been carried by Orlando—as if he is indeed in the throes of the "second childishness" (2.7.165) Jaques has just described.

The central theme of Jaques's speech, that a single man goes through seven stages, or acts, in the course of his lifetime, echoes similar life-stage theories put forth by ancient thinkers, and the opening line, "All the world's a stage" (2.7.139), was said to adorn the Globe Theatre itself. The speech is rich in detail and imagery, as Jaques paints miniature portraits of each of the stages of man's life, and as fits his character, he highlights the ridiculous, helpless, or ineffectual aspects of each stage. The baby is "mewling and puking" (144), while the schoolboy whines as he is forced to attend school against his will. The lover's sentiments are made to seem absurd and extreme, as he sadly sings of "his mistress' eyebrow" (149), of all possible body parts. The soldier seems to live in isolation from society and friendship, "full of strange oaths" (150), as if belonging to a secret guild, and he is guided by negative, aggressive emotions like jealousy and anger; even when faced with the prospect of death, "in the cannon's mouth" (153), he still gives priority to his reputation. The justice's belly is understood to be lined with capon—a castrated rooster, which serves as another symbol of the impotence of living creatures—because judges were often bribed with capons. As a judge, meanwhile, both his physical appearance and his intellectual state—he is "full of wise saws and modern instances" (156), that is, he does not truly think independently—show him to be fulfilling his function in society without much thought or ability. Jaques's closing descriptions of the pantaloon and of the senile old man offer a vivid picture of every man's descent into obscurity: the pantaloon finds his body and his voice alike shrinking, while the final stage "is second childishness and mere oblivion" (165). Thus, in Jaques's view, not only does man pass through a number of predictable stages but also within each stage the depth of his person is no greater than that of a stock character in a play, meriting a psychological description of a few lines at most. Regardless of how Shakespeare meant the "Seven Ages of Man" speech to be interpreted, its insistence that all men are simply following the scripts of their lives—as cowritten by Fortune and Nature—is thought provoking.

The references to acting, roles, and theater in *As You Like It* may best be interpreted in the context of the play as contrasted with the pastoral life. The characters of *As You Like It*, coming from the upper echelons of the court, would have been accustomed to civilization's comforts; while speaking with Corin, Touchstone regrets the absence of certain aspects of that courtly life, namely the abundances of society and food. Other characters function better than Touchstone in the forest milieu in that they are more willing or more able to "play the roles" of forest dwellers. In making frequent reference to the conventions

TOPICS FOR FURTHER STUDY

- In posing as Ganymede, Rosalind takes advantage of her disguise to comfortably interact with Orlando as if she were another man. Imagine the two roles reversed: Orlando has disguised himself as a woman in order to interact more comfortably with Rosalind. Conduct research on Elizabethan gender roles, and write an essay describing the ways in which such a role reversal would differ from the original situation. Then write a short prose piece portraying a meeting between Rosalind and the disguised Orlando.

- Read Thomas Lodge's *Rosalynde* (the source for Shakespeare's *As You Like It*). Write an essay comparing and contrasting the characters of Rosalynde, from Lodge's work, and Rosalind, from Shakespeare's. Also, why do you think Shakespeare altered the character the way he did?

- Research the way religions have affected patterns of marriage in different parts of the world. Relate your findings to the class, making reference to at least two non-Western cultures.

- Time is one of the major themes of *As You Like It*. Write an essay on how you have felt the passage of time at different points in your own life, making reference to various passages in the play that relate to or contrast with your personal experience.

- Shakespeare devotes much attention to the roles of the goddesses Fortune and Nature in Elizabethan life, specifically in the lives of his characters. Write an essay describing how modern life has been shaped by Fortune and Nature, making reference to passages describing the two forces in *As You Like It*, and explaining how the balance between them has shifted over time.

of dramaturgy, Shakespeare assists his urban crowds to lose themselves in the ethereal theater of the Forest of Arden.

STYLE

The Pastoral

Traditionally, a pastoral is a poem focusing on shepherds and rustic life; it first appeared as a literary form in the third century C.E. The term itself is derived from *pastor*, the Latin word for "shepherd." A pastoral may contain artificial or unnatural elements, such as shepherd characters speaking with courtly eloquence or appearing in aristocratic dress. This poetic convention evolved over centuries until many of its features were incorporated into prose and drama. It was in these literary forms that pastoralism influenced English literature from about 1550 to 1750, most often as pastoral romance, a model featuring songs and characters with traditional pastoral aspects. Many of these elements can be seen in the source for Shakespeare's play, Thomas Lodge's popular pastoral novel *Rosalynde*, written in 1590. But by the time Shakespeare adapted Lodge's tale into *As You Like It* nearly a decade later, many pastoral themes were considered trite.

As a result, Shakespeare treated pastoralism ambiguously in the comedy. Without doubt, the audience is meant to be intoxicated by the carefree atmosphere of the forest along with the main characters, who are essentially given the freedom to concern themselves only with romantic love. The image of Orlando dashing from tree to tree hanging up his poems is perhaps the most emblematic of the play as a whole. Also, with the usurper Frederick as the head of the dukedom and the magnanimous Duke Senior overseeing life in the forest, each setting is endowed with the characteristics of its figurehead; the connotations of the forest are almost exclusively positive. In the speech in which Duke Senior introduces Arden, he praises the "tongues in trees, books in the running brooks, / Sermons in stones, and good in everything" (2.1.16–7).

On the other hand, the audience is rarely given respite from Jaques, whose melancholy is not really lessened by the forest, and Touchstone, who incessantly disparages both forest life in Arden and forest dwellers. While some of Touchstone's comments are merely absurd—such as portraying Corin as a sinner for not having been at court—their presence nonetheless prevents a wholly idealistic tone from taking over. Perhaps most tellingly, the comedy's resolution entails the entire company returning to court rather than remaining in the forest. Overall, *As You Like It* can be viewed as either an endorsement or a satire of the literary form of the pastoral—and that duality is nowhere more evident than in the play's title. Take your choice.

Lyrical Interludes

Shakespeare emphasized the romantic, pastoral aspect of *As You Like It* by including a significant number of songs and poems. In all, five different songs are performed, more than in any other comedy, while the audience hears three poems read aloud, two of Orlando's—one of which is then parodied by Touchstone—and one of Phebe's. In addition, Touchstone offers a few pithy lines upon leaving Sir Oliver Mar-Text, and Hymen's lines, which are written in rhyming trimeter instead of Shakespeare's conventional pentameter, have an immediate poetic ring to them. All of these forms of verse are presented in the Forest of Arden, rather than in the court. Meanwhile, more than half of the play is written in prose, aptly contrasting the characters' offhand everyday discourse with their romantic poetic bursts.

The texts of these songs are generally relevant to the scene in which they appear or to the play as a whole. The fifth scene of the second act seems to exist exclusively as a framework for the first tune, sung by Amiens, which mentions "the greenwood tree" (2.5.1), "the sweet bird's throat" (2.5.4), and "winter and rough weather" (2.5.7) and helps establish the woodland setting; Jaques's subsequent partly nonsensical verse, on the other hand, helps establish his nonconformity. The hunters' effusively masculine song, with its possibly sexual reference to "the horn, the horn, the lusty horn" (4.2.18), also essentially merits its own scene, highlighting the camaraderie and sense of self-determination fostered by hunting for food together.

The song sung by Amiens when Duke Senior welcomes Orlando and Adam, "Blow, blow, thou winter wind" (2.7.174–90), merits particular attention. In each verse, Amiens first invokes the severity of nature in wintertime, then offers as a contrast the greater severity of men toward one another. The winter wind is harsh, but it is "not so unkind / As man's ingratitude" (175–76); the breath of that wind is "rude" (179), but at least it fails to bite, as does the tooth of man. The chorus affirms this trust in nature and mistrust of man, glorifying the "green holly" (180) before stating, "Most friendship is faining"—that is, perhaps, both *yearning* and *pretending* ("feigning")—"most loving mere folly" (181). In the second verse, although the freezing sky stings and warps waters, it is preferred to "benefits forgot" (186) and a "friend rememb'red not" (189). Especially given its location in the play as a whole—at the point when the sorrows of courtly life are being discarded, as food and shelter within the forest have been secured—this song may be interpreted as emblematic of the play as a whole, with its depiction of nature's rhythms, even when bitter, as preferable to the strife of men.

Marginalization of Plot

The plot of *As You Like It* is perhaps the least important plot in all of Shakespeare's plays, at least in terms of the consequences of problematic situations and people's actions. Indeed, the most negative critical comments have come from scholars who perceive carelessness or even indifference in Shakespeare's fabrication of the plot. Albert Gilman sums up this dearth in his introduction to the play:

> What is unusual is the extraordinary dispatch with which the plot unfolds. Almost everything that is to happen, happens in the first act . . . . In the ensuing acts Shakespeare scarcely concerns himself with the troubles that were introduced in the first act. Except for three short scenes we are always in Arden, where the dangers we are chiefly aware of are falling in love or being worsted in a discussion.

To close out the play, the two villains are abruptly converted from villainy, and the four couples are very speedily wed—Oliver and Celia before the audience has witnessed one private conversation between them.

At certain points, Shakespeare's offhand treatment of the plot almost escapes attention. When Rosalind, disguised as Ganymede, first chances across Orlando in Arden, she says, "I will speak to him like a saucy lackey, and under that habit play the knave with him. Do you hear, forester?" (3.2.292–94). As the scene moves along, the audience may not even have time to wonder why Rosalind fails to discard her disguise, though nothing is truly preventing her from doing so. Later, when she tries to persuade Orlando to accompany her and be cured of his lovesickness, after expressing mild skepticism that she can do so, he reverses himself and says,

"Now, by the faith of my love, I will" (3.2.418). Thus, despite all her previous questioning about the sincerity of Orlando's love, Rosalind seems to ignore the fact that he follows her for the express purpose of falling out of love with her; if Orlando follows not to fall out of love but because he has already seen through her disguise, the audience is given no indication of that.

Shakespeare's summary treatment of the play's action seems above all to reflect that Shakespeare did not intend the plot of the play to be the essence of the play. In effect, limiting plot development allows for the greater development of the characters through casual, unforced, and thus particularly revealing, dialogue. Gilman, in highlighting the primacy of the dialogue and the characters' relationships in his introduction, playfully asks, "Who has not looked at his watch during the last act of a well-made plot and sighed to think of the knots still to be untied? We had rather be in Arden where the wicked are converted by fiat and lovers marry in half-dozen lots."

Similes

With the setting and atmosphere emphasized over the plot of *As You Like It*, the play depends heavily on imagery, as well as on wordplay introducing that imagery. In her essay "Image Establishes Atmosphere and Background in the Comedies," Caroline F. E. Spurgeon notes that certain types of comparisons are especially prevalent. Topical similes are those referring to scenes or objects that would have been familiar to the London-based Elizabethan audience. Rosalind's declaration to Orlando that she would "weep for nothing, like Diana in the fountain" (4.1.146–47) may be a reference to a fountain in the Cheapside district featuring a depiction of that goddess. Other topical similes in the text refer to the types of painted canvases that were hung on walls, the whipping treatment that madmen received, and the work of tavern employees. Sturgeon notes that the prominence of such references reflects the fact that Shakespeare was writing for "a highly sophisticated town audience, which delights in bouts of sparkling wit, . . . is ever alive to double meanings, and is quick as lightning to seize on and laugh at a local or topical allusion."

Similes mentioning animals are also found frequently in the text, more than in any other Shakespearean comedy, further emphasizing the natural world. Orlando compares himself to a doe seeking her fawn; Jaques likens himself to a weasel and to a rooster; and Rosalind compares herself to a cock-pigeon. Fittingly, the character who seems to be most in touch with his animal instincts invokes the images of a number of creatures in explaining to Jaques his intent to marry: "As the ox hath his bow, sir, the horse his curb, and the falcon her bells, so man hath his desires; and as pigeons bill, so wedlock would be nibbling" (3.3.76–9). Other natural objects and forces are likewise often brought to the spectators' attention. Orlando presents the image of a rotten tree; Touchstone that of fruit ripening and rotting; and Jaques that of rank weeds. Mention of the weather, too, serves to enhance the sense of being outdoors, such as when Hymen utters to Touchstone and Audrey, "You and you are sure together / As the winter to foul weather" (5.4.135–36).

HISTORICAL CONTEXT

Gender Roles

The way Shakespeare addresses gender roles in *As You Like It* reflects the widespread sexism of the Elizabethan era, and thus the topic merits discussion not only in the fictional but also in the historical context. In his *Bedford Companion to Shakespeare*, Russ McDonald offers an assessment of the state of gender relations:

> That women occupied a position subordinate to men in the early modern period is beyond dispute; that this was the 'natural' state of affairs was almost beyond dispute. Although the idea is repugnant to modern sensibilities, most thinkers in the sixteenth century took it as axiomatic that men are superior to women.

Indeed, many gendered notions are presented not simply through the opinions of certain characters but as established facts, illustrating for the modern reader the common beliefs of the era. In the course of the discussion on the goddesses Fortune and Nature, Rosalind states, "the bountiful blind woman doth most mistake in her gifts to women" (1.2.34–5), and Celia agrees, noting that "those that she makes fair, she scarce makes honest, and those that she makes honest, she makes very ill-favoredly" (1.2.36–8). That is, the story's leading women evidently see beauty and chastity, which are deemed typically exclusive, as the only female qualities worth discussing. Other characteristics attributed to women, as reflected in the play's dialogue, include "fear" (1.3.117), which Rosalind hopes to hide under man's apparel, and excessive emotionality; Rosalind feels obliged to suppress her tears when she, Celia, and Touchstone enter the forest in utter exhaustion, and when she faints at the news of Orlando's wound, Oliver exclaims, "You a man! You lack a man's heart" (4.3.164–65).

Rosalind and Celia refer to the marketability of women—not merely objectifying themselves but even suggesting that they have a quantifiable value—twice later on: Celia notes that if they learn news from Le Beau they will be "the more marketable" (1.2.93), while Rosalind, as Ganymede, tells Phebe, "Sell when you can, you are not for all markets" (3.5.60). This most likely reflects the fact that a potential bride customarily offered a dowry to her suitor, consisting of whatever capital and property her family could afford. The existence of the dowry is also important to consider with respect to the romantic context of the play. McDonald notes,

> Marriage was part of a system of inheritance and economics so ingrained and pervasive that the emotional affectations or physical desires of a man and woman diminished in importance. This was especially true among the upper classes ... where marriage was regarded as a convenient instrument for joining or ensuring peace between two powerful families, for consolidating land holdings, or for achieving other familial, financial, or even political ends.

Thus the Forest of Arden is an idealized pastoral setting not only in the immediacy of nature and the absence of the trappings of courtly life but also in the fact that the play's strictly romantic liaisons, especially between Rosalind and Orlando, might have been impossible in the context of the court.

While women of the time were certainly constrained by male perceptions of their femininity, men were perhaps similarly constrained by perceptions of their masculinity. Phebe finds herself falling not for the beseeching, pitiable Silvius but for the coarse, aggressive Ganymede. She states, "'Tis but a peevish boy; yet he talks well" (3.5.110), then adds, "But sure he's proud. And yet his pride becomes him. / He'll make a proper man" (3.5.115). Later, in turn, in that Phebe's letter has "a boisterous and a cruel style" (4.3.32), Rosalind assumes that it must have been "a man's invention, and his hand"

David Rintoul as Duke Frederick, Martin Herdman as Charles, and David Fielder as Touchstone in Act I, scene ii, Shakespeare's Globe, London, 1998 (© Donald Cooper/Photostage. Reproduced by permission)

(4.3.30). Ultimately, however, Shakespeare may have played a significant role in softening the perception of the masculine, if not in hardening the perception of the feminine; Peter B. Erickson offers some enlightening commentary on gender relations of the Elizabethan era as modified by the theater: "The convention of males playing female roles gives men the opportunity to imagine sex-role fluidity and flexibility. Built into the conditions of performance is the potential for male acknowledgment of a 'feminine self' and thus for male transcendence of a narrow masculinity." In that they did not themselves appear on the stage, women were not truly given the same opportunity to test the boundaries of their gender roles.

Rural Life

While the term *urban* would not be coined until 1619, at the beginning of the seventeenth century London was without doubt an essentially urban locale, with a total population of some two hundred thousand. Thus life in the city would have been remarkably different from life in the countryside, with the residents of the respective milieus perhaps perceiving one another as virtual foreigners. Shakespeare drew on these differences heavily in *As You Like It*, juxtaposing aristocrats and philosophers from the upper echelons of the dukedom like Jaques and Touchstone with simplistic woodland folk like William and Audrey. The conversations between the educated and the uneducated are some of the most comical of the play. Overall, the importance of the setting may have been relatively small, as the stage would not have been decorated with any backdrop or props conjuring the feel of the forest; only the actors' words and costumes and the spectators' imaginations would have placed the action in the fictional forest. Further, Shakespeare focuses foremost on the love stories, not on the practicalities of forest life.

The English Satirists

The character of Jaques has been recognized not only as a fairly common Elizabethan literary personage—the traveler who has returned home to be generally discontented with life—but also as a representative of a group of satirists writing during Shakespeare's lifetime. Englishmen who had

COMPARE
&
CONTRAST

- **Elizabethan era:** Marriages are often conducted not for the sake of love but for the sake of money, property, or even reputation. Especially among the upper classes, brides brought substantial dowries to their husbands, and the consolidation of wealth between two families could shape political alliances. By law, firstborn sons always inherited the estate of the father, where in families with no sons, the firstborn daughter inherited the estate—to be passed on to her future husband.

  Modern era: Marriages among most people in most Western countries are conducted for the sake of the romantic interests of the two parties. Personal wills, rather than estate laws, govern the passing of property and capital from the deceased to their descendants, such that a marriage is no guarantee of earning a substantial inheritance. Still, people occasionally marry more for the sake of money than for the sake of love; some notorious modern cases include those in which the very young have married the very old, if not the dying.

- **Elizabethan era:** With portable clocks still large enough to be cumbersome and only accurate to the nearest fifteen minutes, the passage of time cannot be conceived of definitely. People would not carry timepieces on their person—except sundials, such as the one Touchstone pulls from his pocket while speaking with Jaques. A forested area would truly have no clocks about; people familiar with courtly life might have appreciated that absence of timepieces.

  Modern era: Clocks are constructed in all shapes and sizes, analog and digital, and are everywhere. Virtually all activities conducted within the confines of greater civilization revolve around the precise passage of time. In the age of cell phones, digital signals ensure that the time shown on displays is exactly correct. Many people, especially those involved in the business world, carry watches to ensure their awareness of the hour and their ability to arrive at certain places at certain times. Perhaps especially in the wilderness, most people are careful to bring timepieces so as to know the nearness of sunset and not be caught in the dark.

- **Elizabethan era:** In 1599, by royal order some satires were removed from circulation and the future publication of satires was banned outright. Consequently, the demolition of London playhouses was ordered.

  Modern era: While laws against libel and slander prevent fabricated and hurtful accusations against any individuals, honest and biting commentaries are allowed in almost all forms of media. However, in certain media the content conveyed to audiences is regulated outside the legal system by entities other than governmental ones; for example, television programs are largely sponsored by advertisers and if advertising dollars cannot be raised, programs cannot be broadcast, meaning that corporate commercial interests often control the kinds of information and images available to television viewers. In media realms where the audiences pay the bulk of revenues, content is usually tailored to a target audience. The advent of the Internet and the widespread production of personal Web sites has both increased and distilled the dissemination of ideas and information.

---

availed themselves of the satiric format to address the era's social conditions included John Davies, John Harington, Ben Jonson, Thomas Bastard, and John Weaver. An order put forth by the monarchy on June 1, 1599, called for the burning of many satirical works and banned any future production of work of that genre. Shakespearean scholars have assumed that when Celia states, "Since the little wit that fools have was silenced, the little foolery that wise men have makes a great show" (1.2.85–7), the line is meant to refer to the 1599 order.

One characteristic of the English satirists was that they restricted their commentary to impersonal, generic claims, such that they could not be accused of targeting any individuals in particular. In expressing his desire to become a fool so as to safely comment on society's ills, Jaques notes that he would not "tax any private party" (2.7.71) but would speak broadly and allow anyone who has done wrong to suit "his folly to the mettle of my speech" (2.7.82). In his text *Shakespeare's Satire*, Oscar James Campbell offers a succinct description of what the author may have intended to communicate to his audiences through his depiction of Jaques: "Shakespeare's ridicule of Jaques . . . is amused disapproval of the headlong moral ardor which the satirists in both poem and play felt or pretended to feel. Such a temper, Shakespeare says, is ridiculous and utterly destructive to the comic spirit."

CRITICAL OVERVIEW

Critical commentary on *As You Like It* over the centuries has tended to focus on two facts: first, that the plot itself is thin and treated perhaps with excessive haste by its author, and, second, that the essence of the play—ruminations on love, time, and nature—is certainly best conveyed in the context of a play that treats the plot in just such an offhand fashion. Different critics, then, have weighed the importance of these two factors differently.

As quoted in *The Complete Illustrated Shakespeare*, edited by Howard Staunton, the German scholar August von Schlegel perceived the play quite positively, summarily remarking:

> Throughout the whole picture, it seems to be the poet's design to show that to call forth the poetry which has its indwelling in nature and the human mind, nothing is wanted but to throw off all artificial constraint, and restore both to mind and nature their original liberty. In the very progress of the piece, the dreamy carelessness of such an existence is sensibly expressed: it is even alluded to by Shakespeare in the title.

As quoted in the same volume, the English scholar Nathan Drake notes, "Though this play, with the exception of the disguise and self-discovery of Rosalind, may be said to be destitute of plot, it is yet one of the most delightful of the dramas of Shakespeare." He goes on to observe:

> From the forest of Arden, from that wild wood of oaks, . . . from the bosom of sequestered glens and pathless solitudes, has the poet called forth lessons of the most touching and consolatory wisdom . . . . The effect of such scenery, on the lover of nature, is to take full possession of the soul, to absorb its very faculties, and, through the charmed imagination, to convert the workings of the mind into the sweetest sensations of the heart, into the joy of grief, into a thankful endurance of adversity, into the interchange of the tenderest affections.

In his introduction to the play, Albert Gilman notes, "Some critics have complained of inconsistencies in the plotting," as the length of time for which Duke Senior has been banished and the respective heights of Rosalind and Celia are referred to differently in different passages. Also, Shakespeare has perhaps for no good reason given the name of Jaques to both the melancholy philosopher and the brother of Oliver and Orlando. Regarding this fact, Helen Gardner notes:

> It seems possible that the melancholy Jaques began as this middle son and that his melancholy was in origin a scholar's melancholy. If so, the character changed as it developed, and by the time that Shakespeare had fully conceived his cynical spectator he must have realized that he could not be kin to Oliver and Orlando. The born solitary must have no family: Jaques seems the quintessential only child.

Gilman adds, "These bits of carelessness, if that is what they are, are not unusual in Shakespeare and not peculiar to this play." Gilman does note that another cause for critical concern is the lack of psychological complexity: "The motives of the chief characters in *As You Like It* are as simple and abrupt as the action of the play, and they could surely be put in evidence by those who think the play a piece of indifferent craftsmanship."

A somewhat comically negative take on the work can be found in George Bernard Shaw's play entitled *The Dark Lady of the Sonnets*. Gilman quotes a scene in which the character of Will Shakespeare remarks to Queen Elizabeth:

> I have also stole from a book of idle wanton tales two of the most damnable foolishness in

the world, in the one of which a woman goeth in man's attire and maketh impudent love to her swain, who pleaseth the groundlings by overthrowing a wrestler.... I have writ these to save my friends from penury, yet shewing my scorn for such follies and for them that praise them by calling the one As You Like It, meaning that it is not as I like it.

Helen Gardner sums up the appeal of *As You Like It* by calling it "a play to please all tastes." After citing the simple asset of the romantic aspect of the tale, she observes:

For the learned and literary this is one of Shakespeare's most allusive plays, uniting old traditions and playing with them lightly.... *As You Like It* is the most refined and exquisite of the comedies, the one which is most consistently played over by a delighted intelligence. It is Shakespeare's most Mozartian comedy.

CRITICISM

Steven Doloff

Doloff examines the allusions to classical mythology found in As You Like It. *Among these are three references to oak trees that recall classical mythology by linking the character of Orlando to the Greek mythological hero Hercules. The critic points out that oak trees are symbolically associated with the god Jupiter (also called Jove) of Roman mythology.*

Richard Knowles has argued that many of the numerous allusions to classical mythology in Shakespeare's *As You Like It* join together to form thematically suggestive patterns. (1) Incorporated into one such pattern, identified by Knowles as linking the character of Orlando to the mythological figure of Hercules, are two references to oaks, trees symbolically associated with Jove. (2) A third oak reference in the play, however, and one which extends this Orlando/Hercules pattern, seems to have been overlooked by Knowles.

The first of the oak references is in Rosalind's response to Celia's description of Orlando lying "under a tree like a dropped acorn" (3.2.231).(3) Knowles suggests that Rosalind's observation, "It may well be called Jove's tree, when it drops/ such fruit" (3.2.232–3), echoes a more explicit Orlando/Hercules association that she has made earlier (1.2.198) by indirectly alluding here to Hercules' being the son, or metaphorical fruit of the god Jove.(4) Knowles's second Jovian oak

reference lies in Oliver's identification of "...an old oak, whose boughs were moss'd with age / And high top bald with dry antiquity" (4.3.104–5) (5) as the site of Orlando's victory over a snake and a lion. Beneath this arboreal symbol of the father, Jove, Orlando reenacts versions of the first and second famous labors of the son, Hercules, the defeat of the Nemean lion and the snakelike Lernaean Hydra.(6)

The overlooked, third Jovian oak reference precedes the other two and appears to suggest Orlando's symbolic reenactment of Hercules' third famous labor, the capture in Arcadia of Diana's sacred stag.(7) It occurs in the reported observation of Jaques lying:

Under an oak, whose antique root peeps
    out
Upon the brook that brawls along this wood,
To the which place a poor sequester'd stag,
That from the hunter's aim had ta'en a hurt,
Did come to languish
(2.1.31–35)

Although the wounded deer in this passage ostensibly provides Jaques with an occasion to bemoan man's inhumanity to beasts, its specific location, under an "antique" oak, suggests mythological ties with the play's other two conspicuous oak tree references. In this light, the defeated *hart* [sic] may be seen as an allusion to Hercules' victory over Diana's *hart* [sic] and, punningly, Orlando's victory over Rosalind's heart.

This specific punning link between Hercules' third labor and Orlando's effect upon Rosalind may be found in the play elsewhere. Knowles detects it in Rosalind's further comments upon Celia's report of Orlando under the tree. Associated herself with Diana earlier in the same scene (3.2.2–4), Rosalind jests that Orlando's hunter's garb indicates that "he comes to kill my heart!" (3.2.242). It may appear more faintly suggested as well in a syllepsis-like construction used by Rosalind in the scene immediately preceding the one containing the wounded hart [sic] under the oak. Describing her intended masculine disguise as Ganymede, she imagines:

A boar-spear in my hand, and in my
    heart,
Lie there what hidden women's fear there
    will. (1.3.114–15)

It would seem that in a play in which the name of Jove is invoked seven times, and in which specific reference is made to his sacred tree, we would do well to stop before certain "antique" oaks in the forest of Arden and, as Duke Senior advises, consider what they have to say (2.1.16).

Source: Steven Doloff, "Shakespeare's *As You Like It.* (William Shakespeare)," in *The Explicator*, Vol. 51, No. 3, Spring 1993, pp. 143–146.

John A. Hart

Hart maintains that Shakespeare depicts two contrasting worlds in As You Like It: *Duke Frederick's court, which is governed by Fortune, and Arden forest, which is dominated by Nature. Here, Fortune signifies not only power and material wealth, but the greed and envy that results from possessing them. By comparison, Nature reflects a more virtuous order that promotes humanity's higher qualities. According to Hart, the corrupt court gradually becomes absorbed by the more harmonious world of Arden until it disappears from the play altogether. The critic ultimately asserts that those characters who have assimilated the lessons from both worlds—significantly, Rosalind, Orlando, and Duke Senior—emerge from the forest at the end of the play to redeem the degenerate court, replacing it with a more balanced and harmonious order.*

As You Like It presents an ideal world, just as *The Merchant of Venice* did. The Forest of Arden has as much romance, as many delightful lovers, more laughter and joy. Like *A Midsummer Night's Dream* and *The Merchant of Venice*, it is built by means of two worlds: the world ruled by Duke Frederick and the world of the Forest of Arden. The effect is not the "separate but equal" envelope structure of *A Midsummer Night's Dream*, nor the interlocking and necessary alternation of *The Merchant of Venice*; instead, Frederick's world first seems dominant and then dissolves and disappears into the world of Arden. Its life seems to be in the play not so much for itself as to help us understand and read its successor.

We have seen power presented in *A Midsummer Night's Dream* and *The Merchant of Venice*. In the former, Theseus rules according to judgment or reason; in the latter the Duke of Venice rules according to the laws of the city. Frederick's world is like neither of these. Frederick is in complete command of his court.

> **BOTH FORTUNE AND NATURE, THEN, ARE ABBREVIATED TERMS TO EPITOMIZE THE KINDS OF WORLDS REPRESENTED BY FREDERICK'S ON THE ONE HAND AND THE FOREST'S ON THE OTHER."**

He has taken his brother's place as Duke, exiled him with many of his followers, seized their lands for his own, and now rules. His high-handed behavior is illustrated by his usurpation of his brother's dukedom, his immediate displeasure at Orlando, the sudden dismissal of Rosalind, the quick seizure of Oliver's lands. What is most characteristic of his power is that it is arbitrary; neither reason nor law seems to control it.

When we look for his motives, we discover two kinds. His greed for power and possessions is obvious. But personal attitudes are just as strong. He treats Orlando rudely because he is the son of Sir Rowland de Boys, an old enemy of his. He comes to hate Rosalind, giving as his reasons that he does not trust her, that she is her father's daughter, that his own daughter's prestige suffers by comparison; all these are half-hearted rationalizations rooted in jealousy and envy.

Frederick's behavior is echoed if not matched by Oliver's treatment of his brother Orlando and of his servant Adam. Oliver demeans and debases his younger brother; he plots his serious injury and later his death. He acts ignobly toward his faithful household servant Adam. Again, the motivations are mixed. He states explicitly that he wants Orlando's share of their father's bequest. But, beyond that, he wants to get rid of Orlando out of envy, out of fear of comparison made by others:

> ... my soul (yet I know not why) hates nothing more than he. Yet he's gentle, never school'd and yet learned, full of noble device, of all sorts enchantingly belov'd, and indeed so much in the heart of the world, and especially of my own people, who best know him that I am altogether mispris'd. [I. i. 165–71]

Thus, "tyrant Duke" and "tyrant brother" are described in tandem, public and private images of the same behavior. They have the power; they control their world; they do not fear disapproval or reprisal. Charles the wrestler, Lebeau and other lords surrounding Frederick, however many reservations they may have about the morality of their leaders, do not dare to question their authority. They have their own positions to protect.

Those chiefly harmed by the ruthless domination of these men are Orlando and Rosalind. They have committed no fault but they are hated. Their presence too gives definition to Frederick's world. Orlando has virtue, grace, beauty, and strength. Rosalind is beautiful, intelligent, virtuous, honest. Their action, their reputations, the loyalty they command all testify to these wonders. Yet both of them are conscious of what they do not have—their proper place and heritage in this world. Orlando feels deeply his brother's injury in depriving him of his education and his place in the household. Rosalind is sad at her father's banishment and then indignant at her own dismissal. Both are too virtuous to think of revenge; but they are fully aware that they are being wronged. Having all the graces, they are nevertheless dispossessed of their rightful positions.

Yet, these two have their own power. When they leave Frederick's world, they draw after them others, too loyal, too loving to remain behind. Celia, meant to profit from her counsin's departure, follows Rosalind into banishment without question or remorse. She has already promised that what her father took from Rosalind's father by force, "I will render thee again in affection" [I. ii. 20–1]. And when the test occurs soon after, she meets it at once. In her, love triumphs hands down over possession and prestige.

Her example is followed by the Clown. Not only will he "go along o'er the wide world" [I. iii. 132] with Celia out of loyalty to her; he has also, in Frederick's world, lost place just as Rosalind has. There "fools may not speak wisely what wise men do foolishly" [I. ii. 86–7]. Since he has lost his usefulness as a fool, he may as well leave with Celia and Rosalind.

These gifted models of humanity, Rosalind and Orlando, draw out of Frederick's world the loving, the truthful, the loyal. Frederick and Oliver, seeking to control and ultimately to crush their enemies, only succeed in driving away other worthwhile characters with them.

The world of Frederick is simply in structure. The powerful control, but they envy the virtuous; the virtuous attract, but they want to have their rightful place. Those in authority triumph in their own terms, but things happen to them in the process. They turn against each other—Frederick would devour Oliver as he has so many others. Their world, as it grows more violent, diminishes in importance until it disappears altogether. The virtuous are undefeated though displaced.

In contrast to the specific placing of Frederick's world, the Forest reaches beyond the bounds of any particular place, any specific time. Its setting is universalized nature. All seasons exist simultaneously. Duke Senior speaks of "the icy fang And churlish chiding of the winter's wind" [II. i. 6–7]; but Orlando pins verses to "a palm tree," "abuses our young plants with carving," and "hangs odes upon hawthorns, and elegies on brambles" [III. ii. 360–62]; and Rosalind and Celia live at the "tuft of olives." Again, Orlando does not wish to leave Adam "in the bleak air"; but in the next scene Jacques has met a fool who "bask'd him in the sun." The songs continue this mixture: "Here shall he see No enemy But winter and rough weather" [II. v. 6–8] alongside "the greenwood tree" and "the sweet bird's throat" [II. v. 1, 4] both in the same song, or the alternation between the "winter wind" [II. vii. 174] and the "spring time, the only pretty ring time" [V. iii. 19], dominant notes in two other songs. If the Forest is not to be defined in season, neither is it limited to any particular place. The variety of trees already indicates this; the variety of creatures supports it: sheep, deer, a green and gilded snake, a lioness. Meek and domestic creatures live with the untamed and fierce.

Yet the Forest is more than an outdoors universalized, which largely accommodates itself to the mood and attitude of its human inhabitants. It is a setting in which the thoughts and images of those who wander through it expand and reach out to the animate, as if the Forest were alive with spirits taken for granted by everyone. Even so mundane a pair as Touchstone and Audrey, discussing her attributes—unpoetical, honest, foul—assign these gifts to the gods. Orlando, who is able at first meeting Rosalind only to utter "Heavenly Rosalind," is suddenly release to write expansive verses in praise of her, some of which place her in a spiritual context:

... heaven Nature charg'd
That one body should be fill'd
With all graces wide-enlarg'd ...
Thus Rosalind on many parts
By heavenly synod was devis'd ...
[III. ii. 141–43, 149–50]

Phoebe seconds his view by giving Rosalind qualities beyond the human:

Art thou god to shepherd turn'd,
That a maiden's heart hath burn'd? ...
Why, thy godhead laid apart,
Warr'st thou with a woman's heart?
[IV. iii. 40–1, 44–5]

But in addition to mind-expanding qualities, the Forest produces some real evidence of its extraordinary powers. Oliver, upon his first appearance in the Forest, is beset by the green and gilded snake (of envy?) and by the lioness (of power?), but when these two are conquered, his whole behavior changes. And Frederick, intent on destroying his brother, meets an "old religious man" and

After some question with him, was converted
Both from his enterprise and from the world.
[V. iv. 161–62]

And these events harmonize with Rosalind's producing Hymen, the god of weddings, to perform the ceremony and bless the four pairs of lovers. The Forest is a world of all outdoors, of all dimensions of man's better nature, of contact with man's free imagination and magical happenings.

The Forest has still another quality in its setting. It is not timeliness but it reflects the slow pace and the unmeasurable change of the earth. The newcomers notice the difference from the world outside. Orlando comments that "there's no clock in the forest" [III. ii. 300–01]; Rosalind tells us "who Time ambles withal, who Time trots withal, who Time gallops withal, and who he stands still withal" [III. ii. 309–11]. And Touchstone, as reported by Jaques, suggests the uselessness of measuring changes in the Forest by the clock:

'Tis but an hour ago since it was nine,
And after one hour more 'twill be eleven,
And so from hour to hour, we ripe and ripe,
And then from hour to hour, we rot and rot;
And thereby hangs a tale.
[II. vii. 24–8]

But the qualities of the setting are only part of what goes into the definition of the Forest world. The natives to the Forest make their contributions as well. Corin and Silvius and Phoebe, Audrey and William and Sir Oliver Martext all appear, without seeming consequence or particular plot relevance, put there to show off different dimensions of the Forest, to strike their attitudes, to stand in contrast with the characters newly come from another world, and then, like the deer and the sheep and the snake and the lioness, to retire into the Forest again until or unless called upon by their visitors.

In all these natives there is a non-critical quality, an innocence, a lack of competitiveness that suits well with the Forest world and helps to describe it. But Shakespeare gives us still other ways of distinguishing this world from Frederick's. Early in the play Celia and Rosalind engage in idle banter about the two goddesses, Fortune and Nature, who share equally in the lives of men. Fortune "reigns in gifts of the world," Rosalind says, "not in the lineaments of Nature" [I. ii. 41–2]. It is a shorthand way of distinguishing the Forest world from Frederick's. Frederick's world is a world of Fortune, from which the children of Nature are driven. Power, possession, lands, titles, authority over others characterize that world, and men to live there must advance their careers or maintain their positions in spite of everything. The Forest world is completely Nature's. In its natives the idleness, the lack of ambition and combativeness, the carelessness about ownership and possession, the interest in the present moment without plan for the future, all are signs of a Fortune-less world. Instead there is awareness of the gifts inherent from birth in the individual, no matter how untalented or unhandsome (Audrey's response to her foulness or William's self-satisfaction, for instance). These are "the lineaments of Nature," the basic materials of one's being. In the Forest, the natives neither can nor aspire to change them. And the qualities of the setting—universality, gradual rather than specific change, a linkage between the outdoors world and a projected though perhaps imaginary supernatural, these too are compatible with the world of Nature, Fortune having been removed. Both Fortune and Nature, then, are abbreviated terms to epitomize the kinds of worlds represented by Frederick's on the one hand and the Forest's on the other.

One further means of defining the Forest world emerges with the character of Jaques. He has been in the outside world, but he has chosen the Forest and he is its most eloquent spokesman. He is the personification of the speculative man. He will not react when Orlando threatens his life: "And you will not be answer'd with reason, I must die" [II. vii. 100–01]. He will not dance or rejoice in the final scene. He would prevent action in others if he could. He weeps that the Duke's men kill the deer, he would keep Orlando from marring the trees with his poems, he advises Touchstone not to "be married under a bush like a beggar" [III. iii. 84]. He is like the natives of the Forest, ambitionless, fortuneless, directionless.

Duke Senior, like Jaques, has had experience in both worlds. He too is being "philosophical." Their life in the Forest

Finds tongues in trees, books in the running brooks,
Sermons in stones, and good in every thing.
[II. i. 16–17]

He and his men "fleet the time carelessly, as they did in the golden world" [I. i. 118–19]. But for the Duke and his men, it is only play-acting. They appear in one scene as Foresters, in another as outlaws. He himself has lost his name: he is Duke Senior, not specifically named like Frederick. More than that, he has nothing serious to do. While his brother is seizing Oliver's lands and organizing a search for his daughter and seeking to destroy him, he is contemplating a deer hunt or asking for Jaques to dispute with or feasting or asking someone to sing. Duke Senior has no function to perform; he cannot be a Duke except in title. All the philosophical consolations he may offer himself and his men cannot alleviate the loss he feels at being usurped and banished by his brother.

Touchstone's is the outsider's view of the Forest. His responses are the touchstones which set off the Forest natives most clearly. As Jaques is the "official" voice of the Forest, Touchstone is the "official" voice of the world outside.

The Forest is liberating for the newly arrived lovers, too. Oliver is freed from the burden of envy and absorption with power; and as a consequence he and Celia can fall immediately in love. So satisfying is it that Oliver would give up his possessions to Orlando and live a shepherd's life forever. Celia has assumed the name Aliena, left her father's court so completely that she never thinks of him again, and falls utterly in love when she meets the reformed Oliver. She has never been tied to the idea of possession or prestige and so she is easily open to the lures of the Forest.

Whereas Oliver's and Celia's love experience is muted, described rather than dramatized, Orlando's and Rosalind's is the heart of the play. Orlando, idle in the Forest and "love-shak'd," expresses his love for the lost Rosalind by writing passionate verses for her and hanging them on the trees; later he plays the game of wooing the young man Ganymed as if he were his Rosalind. He makes his protestations of love, he makes pretty speeches of admiration, he takes part in the mock-marriage ceremony, he promises to return to his wooing by a certain time. But his playing the game of courtship is as nothing compared to the game of deception and joyful play that Rosalind, safe in her disguise as Ganymed, engages in when she is with him. Her spirits soar and her imagination and wit expatiate freely and delightedly on the subject of men in love, on their looks, on their behavior, on the cure of their disease, and then specifically on Orlando's mad humor of love, on how he could woo, on how he can be cured through the lore she (he) acquired from the "old religious uncle." The Forest gives both of them an opportunity to play parts free of the restraints that might accompany acknowledged wooing.

But though their fanciful indulgence leads them to forget the rest of the world—Rosalind cries out, "But what talk we of fathers, when there is such a man as Orlando?" [III. iv. 38–9]— the play is only play and basically incompatible with their real natures.

Orlando's behavior outside and in the Forest suggests responsibility, suggests need for significant action. To him the Forest is a "desert inaccessible" and those in it. "Lose and neglect the creeping hours of time" [II. vii. 110, 112]; he himself will keep appointments with Duke Senior, he will care for his loyal servant Adam, he will save his brother's endangered life. He has a general distaste for the company of the speculative Jaques, and he finally gives up the wooing game entirely: "I can live no longer by thinking" [V. ii. 50]. He is Nature's child, but he insists on living by Fortune's standards.

And Rosalind is even more emphatic in the attitudes founded in the outside world. Her first act in coming into the Forest is to buy a sheepcote; she uses the imagery of the market place when she is judging others: "Sell when you can, you are not for all markets" [III. v. 60], she says to Phoebe; "I fear you have sold your own lands to see other men's; then to have seen much, and to have nothing, is to have rich eyes and poor hands" [IV. i. 22–5], she says to Jaques. With Silvius and Phoebe, she has small patience. To him she says, "Wilt thou love such a woman? What, to make thee an instrument, and play false strains upon thee?... I see love hath made thee a tame snake" [IV. iii. 67–8, 69–70]. The natives receive short shrift from her, but she herself is in the depths of love for Orlando, and in her playing with Orlando partly mocks her own condition.

Given the characteristics of the Forest world, given the attachments of Duke Senior, Touchstone, Orlando, and Rosalind to the outside world, the resolution of the play can be foreseen. Under the spell of the Forest, pretended marriage takes place between Orlando and Rosalind (as Ganymed) with Celia officiating. Marriage almost takes place between Touchstone and Audrey with Martext officiating. In the last scene, all four couples are married in the only way possible in the Forest, by the appearance of Hymen, god of marriage, to perform the ceremony: "Then is there mirth in heaven, When earthly things made even Atone together" [V. iv. 108–10]. Hymen joins the lovers and reintroduces the Duke to his Daughter: "Good Duke, receive thy daughter, Hymen from heaven brought her..." [V. iv. 111–12]. He thus re-establishes the father-daughter relationship first devised through his means at Rosalind's birth. The hiatus caused by the Duke's exile and by the disguises in the Forest is broken and the societal structure of father and daughter is made clear once again.

With the appearance of Touchstone another relationship is given social standing. When he is introduced to Duke Senior by Jaques, Touchstone immediately resumes his professional position as fool. His comment on the life of the courtier, his long argument on "the quarrel on the seventh cause" is appreciated by the Duke: "I like him very well"; "By my faith, he is very swift and sententious"; "He uses his folly like a stalking-horse, and under the presentation of that he

shoots his wit" [V. iv. 53, 62–3, 106–07]. A rapport is established between them which suggests that Duke will be Duke and master again and Fool will be Fool and servant.

A final relationship is re-established among the sons of Rowland de Boys. Through its magic the Forest has brought Orlando and Oliver together. Now a third brother appears, carrier of the news of Frederick's resignation—"His crown bequeathing to his banish'd brother" [V. iv. 163]—and agent for restoring his own brothers to the outside world. His coming not only reunites all three but makes a necessary link to the outside world for them. It also sounds an echo: Charles the Wrestler sought advancement and distinction by breaking the ribs of three of his victims, all brothers. That was a symbol of the way power broke blood relationships in Frederick's world—Frederick with his niece and daughter, Oliver with his brother. Now separated families are reunited and friends.

But they have not yet left the Forest. Duke Senior's speech assuming his authority shows that he is in command of both the Forest world and his former Dukedom and that each of them is part of his experience and momentarily under his perfect control. Duke Senior's reference to the lands which will be given to the brothers is balanced and ambiguous:

Welcome, young man;
Thou offer'st fairly to thy brothers' wedding:
To one his lands withheld, and to the other
A land itself at large, a potent dukedom.
[V. iv. 166–69]

To Oliver, the lands taken from him by Frederick are returned; to Orlando, his son-in-law, the heritage of his dukedom is given. Yet there is just a suspicion that the gifts might be directed the other way: to Orlando, whose lands have been taken from him by Oliver, will be returned his father's lands; to Oliver, the Forest world where he has determined to remain; for the Forest is without a ruler and without bounds, a place where he who does not have to own or possess anything may feel himself a powerful ruler.

This distinction between the brothers is followed by a statement of the Duke's own intention in regard to the Forest and the world outside it:

First, in this forest let us do those ends
That here were well begun and well begot;
And after, every of this happy number,

That have endur'd shrewd days and nights
with us,
Shall share the good of our returned
fortune,
According to the measure of their states.
[V. iv. 170–75]

By "those ends," presumably, he means the marriages which have been the contribution and the fruit of the Forest world. Then his attention will be turned to the world outside the forest, where they will enjoy their "returned fortune, According to the measure of their states." Place and prestige are implied here, possession a necessary element. Both Forest and his Dukedom are in his mind and paired. And the retention of both worlds continues right to the end when he repeats the words *fall* and *measure* once to apply them to Nature's world and once to apply them to Fortune's:

Mean time, forget this new-fall'n dignity,
And fall into our rustic revelry.
Play, music, and you brides and bride-
grooms all,
With measure heap'd in joy, to th' measures
fall.
[V. iv. 176–79]

"New-fall'n" applies to his returned Dukedom, "fall" applies to the current Forest life. "Measure heap'd in joy" could apply to both worlds, but it recalls for us "the measure of their states" and the assumption of rank and position looked upon as normal in Fortune's world; the final "measures" refers to the dance they will do in the Forest. We are left, after this balanced holding of both worlds at once, with the departure of Jaques and with the dance which is the sign of the harmony of the moment.

The Epilogue is all that marks the return to the workaday world, spoken by the boy who has played Rosalind. He has gone from the heights of role-playing—this boy playing Rosalind playing Ganymed playing Rosalind— step by step back down the ladder of fantasy to speak directly to the men and women in the audience before him. He speaks of attraction between the sexes, of possible kisses, of the need for appreciation and applause. It is not the Forest nor the Duke's realm. It is the theater, the living reality of the image used so extensively in the play.

Source: John A. Hart, "*As You Like It*: The Worlds of Fortune and Nature," in *Dramatic Structure in Shakespeare's Romantic Comedies*, Carnegie-Mellon University Press, 1980, pp. 81–97.

Nancy K. Hayles

In the excerpt below, Hayles discusses Shakespeare's use of sexual disguise in As You Like It. *The critic argues that this device is developed in distinct stages: first, Rosalind assumes layers of disguise for the journey to Arden, then the layers are slowly removed as she gradually renounces the role of Ganymede, and finally they are eliminated altogether when the heroine abandons her disguise to marry Orlando. The layering-on movement, Hayles contends, suggests selfish control and creates conflict in the play, while the removal of layers fosters reconciliation. Moreover, the critic remarks, this unlayering allows Rosalind to convey her true personality to Orlando, which ultimately supplants his idealized notion of her. Hayles also explores how Shakespeare extended the pattern of sexual disguise and unlayering to the play's epilogue.*

As You Like It opens with scenes that emphasize rivalry and competition. Orlando has been mistreated by his brother Oliver, and Oliver in turn feels that Orlando has caused him to be 'altogether misprised' and undervalued by his own people. The rivalry that Duke Frederick still feels with the rightful Duke is also apparent. Moreover, the chief event of the opening scenes, the wrestling match between Charles and Orlando, is a formalized and ritualistic expression of male rivalry. Against the backdrop of male rivalry, the female intimacy between Celia and Rosalind makes a striking contrast. It is an intimacy, however, maintained at some cost. When Duke Frederick peremptorily orders Rosalind into banishment, Celia's protest is countered by her father's attempt to transform intimacy into rivalry between the two girls, too:

Thou art a fool; she robs thee of thy
name,
And thou wilt show more bright and seem
more virtuous
When she is gone. Then open not thy lips.
[I. iii. 80-2]

The opening scenes of the play, then, draw a society where intimacy among women is implicitly contrasted with the rivalry among men. When the scene changes to the forest, several incidents seem designed as signals that the forest

Hymen, Duke Frederick, and the lovers in Act V, scene iv, at the Royal Shakespeare Theatre, Stratford-upon-Avon, 2000 (© Donald Cooper/Photostage. Reproduced by permission)

is a world where co-operation rather than competition prevails. Orlando meets with civility instead of hostility when he seeks meat for the fainting Adam; Rosalind and Celia find the natives to be kind shepherds rather than would-be rapists; and the exiled Duke hails his followers as "Co-mates and brothers". But we soon discover that competition is not altogether absent from the Forest of Arden. Jaques accuses the Duke of himself usurping the forest from its rightful owners, the deer; Touchstone confronts and bests his country rival, William; and Silvius discovers that his beloved Phebe has fallen in love with a courtly newcomer. The situation is thus more complicated than a simple contrast between court competition and pastoral co-operation, or between female intimacy and male rivalry. The sexual disguise of Rosalind mirrors the complexities of these tensions.

We can consider the disguise as proceeding in two separate movements. First, the layers of disguise are added as Rosalind becomes Ganymede,

and then as Ganymede pretends to be Orlando's Rosalind; second, the layers are removed as Ganymede abandons the play-acting of Rosalind, and then as Rosalind herself abandons the disguise of Ganymede. The layering-on movement creates conflict and the layering-off movement fosters reconciliation as the disguise confronts and then resolves the issue of competition versus co-operation.

In the most complex layering, Rosalind-as-Ganymede-as-Orlando's Rosalind, Rosalind presents Orlando with a version of his beloved very different from the one he imagines in his verses. When Rosalind-as-Ganymede insists that Orlando's Rosalind will have her own wit, her own will and her own way, implicit in the portrayal is Rosalind's insistence that Orlando recognize the discrepancy between his idealized version and the real Rosalind. In effect, Rosalind is claiming the right to be herself rather than to be Orlando's idealized version of her, as female reality is playfully set against male

"ORLANDO'S STRUGGLE AND ROSALIND'S SWOON MARK A TURNING POINT. WHEN THEY MEET AGAIN, ROSALIND TRIES AT FIRST TO RE-ESTABLISH THEIR OLD RELATIONSHIP, BUT … SHE QUICKLY CAPITULATES AND RE-ASSUMES CONTROL ONLY IN ORDER TO BE ABLE TO RELINQUISH IT."

fantasy. In playing herself (which she can apparently do only if she first plays someone else) Rosalind is able to state her own needs in a way she could not if she were simply herself. It is because she is disguised as Ganymede that she can be so free in portraying a Rosalind who is a flesh and blood woman instead of a Petrarchan abstraction. Rosalind's three-fold disguise is therefore used to accentuate the disparity between the needs of the heroine and the expectations of the hero.

Even the simpler layering of Rosalind-as-Ganymede accentuates conflict, though this time the couple being affected is Phebe and Silvius. Rosalind's guise as Ganymede causes Phebe to fall in love with her. Rosalind's on-layering, which inadvertently makes her Silvius's rival, causes Phebe's desires to be even more at variance with Silvius's hopes than before. It takes Ganymede's transformation into Rosalind to trick Phebe into accepting her swain, as the off-layering of Rosalind's disguise reconciles these two Petrarchan lovers. The Silvius-Phebe plot thus shows in simplified form the correlation between on-layering and rivalry, and off-layering and co-operation. It also gives us a standard by which we can measure the more complicated situation between Orlando and Rosalind.

Phebe and Silvius are caricatures of courtly love, and through them we are shown female manipulation and male idealization in a way that emphasizes the less pleasant side of the courtly love tradition. But it is important to see that this rustic couple merely exaggerates tendencies also present in Rosalind and Orlando. Rosalind's disguise creates an imbalance in her relationship with Orlando because it allows Rosalind to hear Orlando's love-confession without having to take any comparable risks herself. Rosalind's self-indulgence in demanding Orlando's devoted service without admitting anything in return could become a variation of the perversity that is anatomized for us in the relationship between Phebe and Silvius. Thus the expectations of Rosalind and the desires of Orlando are not only the responses of these two characters, but are also reflections of stereotypical male and female postures, familiar through the long tradition of courtly love. The layering of the disguise has served to accentuate the conflict between men and women; now the unlayering finally resolves that traditional tension between the needs of the female and the desires of the male.

The unlayering begins when Oliver appears to explain why Orlando is late. Oliver's tale reveals, in almost allegorical fashion, the struggle within Orlando when he sees his brother in peril, and the tale has as its point that Orlando put the needs of his brother before his own natural desire for revenge. More subtly, the tale with its depiction of the twin dangers of the snake and lioness hints at a symbolic nexus of male and female threats. The specificity of the imagery suggests that the details are important. The first beast is described as a lioness, not a lion; moreover, she is a lionesss in suck, but now with teats sucked dry, her hunger presumably made more ferocious by her condition. The description thus links a specifically female animal, and a graphically specific female condition, with the threat of being eaten. The details, taken in sum, evoke the possibility of female engulfment. The snake about to enter the sleeping man's mouth, again a very specific image, suggests even to a non-Freudian the threat of phallic invasion. But perhaps most significant is simply the twinning of the threats itself, which suggests the presence of two different but related kinds of danger.

By overcoming the twin threats, Orlando conquers in symbolic form projections of both male and female fears. Rosalind responds to Oliver's account by swooning. Her faint is a literal relinquishing of conscious control; within the conventions of the play, it is also an involuntary revelation of female gender because fainting is a "feminine" response. It is a subtle anticipation of Rosalind's eventual relinquishing of the disguise and the control that goes with it. The action surrounding the relation of the tale parallels its moral: Orlando performs a heroic and selfless act that hints at a triumph over threatening aspects of masculinity and femininity, and Rosalind responds to the dangers that Orlando faces with an unconscious gesture of sympathy that results, for a moment, in the loss of her conscious control over the disguise and with it, the loss of her manipulative control over Orlando. Rosalind's swoon thus provides a feminine counterpart to Orlando's selflessness.

Orlando's struggle and Rosalind's swoon mark a turning point. When they meet again, Rosalind tries at first to re-establish their old relationship, but when Orlando replies, "I can live no longer by thinking" [V. ii. 50], she quickly capitulates and re-assumes control only in order to be able to relinquish it. From this point on, the removal of the disguise signals the consummation of all the relationships as all four couples are married. The play suggests that control is necessary to state the legitimate needs of the self, but also that it must eventually be relinquished to accommodate the needs of another. Consummation is paradoxically achieved through an act of renunciation.

The way that sexual disguise is used reflects the play's overall concern with the tension between rivalry and co-operation. The disguise is first used to crystallize rivalry between the woman's self-image and the man's desires; in this sense it recognizes male-female discord and implicitly validates it. But because the disguise can be removed, it prevents the discord from becoming perpetual frustration. The workings of the disguise suggest that what appears to be a generous surrendering of self-interest can in fact bring consummation both to man and woman, so that rivalry can be transcended as co-operation brings fulfillment. In *As You Like It*, fulfillment of desire, contentment and peace of mind come when the insistence on self-satisfaction ceases. Duke Senior's acceptance of his forest exile and the subsequent unlooked-for restoration of his dukedom; the reconciliation between the sons of Rowland de Boys, in which Oliver resigns his lands to Orlando and finds forgiveness and happiness in love; the miraculous conversion of Duke Frederick by the old hermit and the voluntary abdication of his dukedom—all express the same paradox of consummation through renunciation that is realized in specifically sexual terms by the disguise.

When the boy actor who plays Rosalind's part comes forward to speak the epilogue, the workings of the sexual disguise are linked with the art of the playwright. The epilogue continues the paradox of consummation through renunciation that has governed sexual disguise within the play, as the final unlayering of the disguise coincides with a plea for the audience to consummate the play by applauding [Epilogue, 11–23]... At this moment the playwright relinquishes control of the audience. As with Rosalind and Orlando, his success is marked by a control that finally renounces itself, a control which admonishes only to release as the audience is asked to "like as much ... as please you" [Epilogue, 13–14]. Our applause is a gesture of acceptance which encompasses both the working of sexual disguise within the play, and the art whose operation parallels it as the play ends. At the same time, the boy actor alludes to the fact that he is not after all the woman he plays ("*if* I were a woman" [Epilogue, 18]), and so relinquishes the last level of the sexual disguise. For the last time, the unlayering of the disguise is linked with a reconciliation between the sexes as the boy actor speaking the epilogue appeals separately to the men and women in the audience. Within the play these two perspectives have been reconciled, and the joint applause of the men and women in the audience re-affirms that reconciliation and extends it to the audience.

The sexual disguise in *As You Like It* therefore succeeds in interweaving various motifs. Many of the problems considered in the play (Duke Frederick's tyranny, Oliver's unfair treatment of Orlando, Phebe's exultation over Silvius) stem from excessive control, and the heroine exercises extraordinary control over the disguise. The removal of the disguise signals a renunciation of control on her part, and this in turn is linked with a voluntary renunciation of control by others, so that the unlayering and the resolution of problems neatly correspond. Moreover, the sexual reversal inherent in the disguise, which itself implicitly promises a reconciliation of male and female perspectives, is used to reconcile the men and women in the play. Since the key to reconciliation has been the renunciation of control, the playwright uses his relinquishing of control over the play to signal a final reconciliation between the men and women in the audience. Because of the correspondence between Rosalind as controller of the disguise, and Shakespeare as controller of the disguised boy actor who plays Rosalind's part, Rosalind's control over her disguise is paradigmatic of the playwright's control over the play. Both use their control creatively and constructively, but for both the relinquishing of control corresponds with the consummation of their art.

The means by which resolution is achieved in *As You Like It* says a great deal about the kinds of problems the play considers. By having Rosalind as surrogate playmaker, the playwright must not pose problems that are beyond her power to solve. There are a few hints that Rosalind's control exceeds the merely human; she tells Orlando she possesses magical powers, and Hymen mysteriously appears to officiate at the wedding. The playwright likewise allows himself some hints of supernatural intervention— witness Duke Frederick's miraculous conversion. But positing a human problem-solver almost necessitates limiting the problems to human scale. Moreover, because the disguise is the key to Rosalind's ability to solve problems, the emphasis on male and female perspectives inherent in the sexual disguise places the problems in the context of the social roles of each sex. The disguise thus gives the play artistic unity, but it also imposes limitations on the play's thematic scope. The brilliance of *As You Like It* is that it so perfectly matches what the play attempts to the inherent limitations of its techniques that it makes us unaware there are limitations.

Source: Nancy K. Hayles, "Sexual Disguise in *As You Like It* and *Twelfth Night*," in *Shakespeare Survey: An Annual Survey of Shakesperian Study and Production*, Cambridge University Press, Vol. 32, 1979, pp. 63–72.

Brigid Brophy

Brigid Brophy surveys the elements of pastoralism in As You Like It *(pastoralism is a literary form that presents an ideal and virtuous vision of rustic life). In addition, the critic discusses the comedy in relation to its source, Thomas Lodge's novel* Rosalynde. *Brophy asserts that among the play's most moving aspects are Shakespeare's brilliant dramatization of the romantic love affair between Orlando and Rosalind and the bond of friendly love exhibited by Rosalind and Celia.*

Almost all Shakespeare's plays have sources of some kind, and any school text will tell you that the source for *As You Like It* is a novel called *Rosalynde* by Shakespeare's contemporary, Thomas Lodge.

The novel was first published in 1590 and it evidently had a considerable success—it ran to three editions within the next decade. That,

> THE ENGLISH-SPEAKING THEATRE'S OTHER GRAND MASTER OF DRAMATIC PROSE, BERNARD SHAW, CONSIDERED *AS YOU LIKE IT* A MELODRAMA, ON THE GROUNDS THAT THE HERO AND HEROINE HAVE NO DISAGREEABLE QUALITIES. PRESUMABLY HE MISSED THE DISTINCT TOUCH OF SADISM WHICH I DETECT IN ROSALIND'S PERSONALITY."

presumably, made it worthwhile for someone to cash in on it. It is notable that Shakespeare did not change the name of the heroine. He kept the name 'Rosalind', and it was towards the end of the decade, in 1598 or 1599—no one knows for sure which—that *As You Like It* appeared on the stage.

But, although Shakespeare changed the names of several of the characters, he did not change the characters themselves, or—which is more important—the relationships between them. He cut down the time spanned by the novel, because a novel has more room to sprawl than a play has. But he made fewer changes than a modern writer would if he were adapting a modern novel for the theatre or for television. Having stayed with Lodge in all the big things, relationships, characters, plot, sequence, Shakespeare often chose to stay with him right down to smallish detail.

The novel and the play are both set in France. One thread concerns a king of France who is driven out of his court by his usurping brother. Shakespeare demotes this pair of brothers from kings of France to dukes of an unnamed part of France. The exiled king or duke is eventually followed into exile by his daughter, Rosalind, but not before she has fallen in love with another ill-used brother, who has been driven out of his inheritance by his elder brother, and who also goes into voluntary exile. The place where all these exiles take refuge and where the threads of the story are woven is what Lodge and Shakespeare called the Forest of Arden.

The ups and downs of fortune which have turned these people into exiles give them all the opportunity to reflect on blind fortune, or random chance, as we would probably call it; and this gives the play its fashionable, philosophical tone. The fact that they have all taken refuge in the forest also puts the play slap in the middle of another high fashion of the Renaissance—which remained in fashion deep into the 18th century—the fashion for the pastoral.

Although a pastor is literally a shepherd who puts his sheep out to pasture, I can assure anyone who feels, as I do, that the countryside is highly overrated, that the pastoral fashion has remarkably little to do with real countryside or with real sheep-rearing. When they arrive in the forest, Rosalind and Celia do buy a sheep farm, but even in Lodge, who has more room, they are only moderately serious about working it. In Shakespeare, it obviously is left to run itself. The object of the pastoral was not to draw any morals from nature. It was to recreate the literature of the ancient world, in particular the pastoral poems—dialogues between shepherds, mainly—which Theocritus wrote in Greek in the third century B.C., and Virgil's imitations of them in Latin.

If you bought a pastoral novel or went to see a pastoral play, you knew pretty much what you were going to get, just as nowadays if you go and see a thriller you know pretty much what you are going to get. You were going to get shepherds with Greek or Latinised names like Sylvius, Corin, Lycidas and Damon, and shepherdesses called things like Phoebe and Corinna. The point of the whole thing was going to be that people were going to fall desperately in love. You knew also that you would get large quantities of lyric verse. It may have begun—this idea that shepherds were poets—from the thought that shepherds piped to their flocks, and, perhaps, having piped a tune, they then set words to the tune.

In Shakespeare, only one of the characters, Orlando, has the actual verse-writing mania—no doubt he picks it up from the pastoral setting like an infection when he arrives in the forest. His verses, incidentally, are all bad. But the entire play is punctuated by songs.

The shepherds in Theocritus and Virgil often fall passionately in love with shepherdesses and they also quite often fall passionately in love with shepherds. The same is probably true of the cowboys in the modern Western, which is a diluted descendant of the pastoral.

This tradition of the pastoral made it a particularly apt mode for Lodge, followed by Shakespeare, to set their story in. When the girl cousins and best friends, Rosalind and Celia, run away to the Forest of Arden, Rosalind—and it is Rosalind rather than Celia because, as she explains, she is the taller of the two—dresses up as a boy.

As you would expect, given that the novel is knee-deep in classical allusions and the play is at least ankle-deep, although some have been cut out to make it more easily assimilable in the theatre, the name which Rosalind chooses for herself while she is disguised as a boy is Ganymede, the name of the page whom Zeus, the father of the gods, fell in love with.

Lodge plays with grammar. He calls Rosalind, or Ganymede, 'he' and then 'she' within a single sentence. Shakespeare, of course, had an extra decorative dimension to play with, because women did not appear as actors on the English stage for another generation and therefore all the parts in *As You Like It* were taken by men. Rosalind was that old favourite of the English theatre, a drag act, from the word go, and when she disguises herself as a boy she goes into double drag, and, at the same time, a very delicate and charming air of sexual ambiguity comes over the story.

Phoebe falls in love with Ganymede; but, of course, Ganymede does not really exist. Is she, in fact, really in love with Rosalind? Orlando is in an even greater dilemma. He believes that if he pretends that Ganymede is his Rosalind and he woos him, he will be cured of his love for her, and so he does woo the boy and, in the process, falls deeper and deeper in love with the woman. Or *is* it with the woman? Is it, in fact, with the boy?

If I ask myself what makes *As You Like It* so moving, I locate the answer in two elements that Shakespeare dramatised quite brilliantly from Lodge's novel: the erotic love between Rosalind and Orlando, obviously; and, slightly less obviously, the non-erotic love between Rosalind and Celia. The dialogue that expresses these relationships may not be positively witty, in the sense that you could go through it taking out bits for an anthology of aphorisms, but it is witty in tone, witty in rhythm, and its tone is, of course, the tone of flirtation. Rosalind and Celia are limbering up their flirtatiousness on one another. If I go on to ask myself how Shakespeare achieved this technically, the answer is one that I think is rather surprising—or would be surprising if you knew only his other comedies. He does it in prose.

CELIA: Trow you who hath done this?

ROSALIND: Is it a man?

CELIA: And a chain, that you once wore, about his neck. Change you colour?

ROSALIND: I prithee, who?

CELIA: O Lord, Lord! it is hard matter for friends to meet; but mountains may be remov'd with earthquakes, and so encounter.

ROSALIND: Nay, but who is it?

CELIA: Is it possible?

ROSALIND: Nay, I prithee now, with most petitionary vehemence, tell me who it is.

CELIA: O wonderful, wonderful, and most wonderful wonderful, and yet again wonderful, and after that, out of all whooping!

ROSALIND: Good my complexion! dost thou think, though I am caparison'd like a man, I have a doublet and hose in my disposition? One inch of delay more is a South Sea of discovery. I prithee tell me who is it quickly, and speak apace... I prithee take the cork out of thy mouth that I may drink thy tidings.

CELIA: So you may put a man in your belly.

[III. ii. 179–204]

Even if you discount the superstitions about the innocence and simplicity of life in the country, there is a way in which shepherds can truly be said to be innocent. This does not apply to cowboys, incidentally. Shepherds are innocent of blood-guilt. Human beings do not always choose to do so, but it is possible to live on reasonably fair terms with a flock of sheep. You can deprive the sheep of their wool, which they are quite glad to get rid of, and not deprive them of their lives. One of the changes that Shakespeare did make in dramatising Lodge's novel was to shift the emphasis from sheep-minding to hunting. His exiled courtiers in the forest kill the deer. And in this way he darkens the sunny landscape he found in Lodge.

All the same, though that imperfect windy instrument Jaques, Shakespeare does allow the point of view of the deer to be stated. It is Jaques who has pointed out to his fellow courtiers in exile that wounded deer weep, which is a matter of fact, incidentally, not a matter of folklore as is usually thought. Jaques makes his entrance asking the telling question, 'Which is he that killed the deer?'—a question in which he is the detective hunting down a killer, as well as looking for someone to congratulate on his victory, and the song that follows—though it does congratulate the killer on his victory—also makes a mockery of him.

> What shall he have that kill'd the deer?
> His leather skin and horns to wear.
> Then sing him home.
> (*the rest shall hear this burden*)
> Take thou no scorn to wear the horn;
> It was a crest ere thou wast born.
> Thy father's father wore it;
> And thy father bore it.
> The horn, the horn, the lusty horn,
> Is not a thing to laugh to scorn.
> [IV. ii. 10–18]

The English-speaking theatre's other grand master of dramatic prose, Bernard Shaw, considered *As You Like It* a melodrama, on the grounds that the hero and heroine have no disagreeable qualities. Presumably he missed the distinct touch of sadism which I detect in Rosalind's personality. He considered that *As You Like It* gives unmixed delight, but he thought this was simply a bid for popularity. He said Shakespeare flung Rosalind at the public with a shout of 'As *you* like it'. Of course, it was a bid for popularity—a bid for popularity which Lodge's novel had already established with readers. My guess is that, when Shakespeare had finished making his adaptation, he riffled through the pages of Lodge's novel, casting about for a title, and finally he came back to the beginning and came upon Lodge's preface, which is addressed to the gentlemen readers. 'To be brief, gentlemen,' Lodge says, after relating how he wrote the book on a sea voyage when he was taking part in a military expedition, 'room for a soldier, and a sailor, that gives you the fruits of his labours that he wrought in the ocean, when every line was wet with a surge, and every humorous passion counterchecked with a storm. If you like it, so...' By the time Shakespeare made his adaptation, the gentlemen readers had already proved that they did indeed like Lodge's novel. It was no longer a question of '*if* you like it', but '*as* you like it.'

Source: Brigid Brophy, "As You Like Shakespeare," in *The Listener*, Vol. 100, No. 2591, December 21–28, 1978, pp. 837–38.

Jay L. Halio

Halio describes time's two functions in As You Like It: *first, as a foil whose two extremes— timelessness and time-consciousness—favourably contrast virtuous rustic life in Arden with dissolute court life, and second, as timelessness alone, as a link between life in the present and life in an earlier, less corrupt, generally better time. The critic maintains that Shakespeare perceives the city and court to be ruthless and degenerate, threatening places from which Arden's timeless world is a refuge, a world where past and present merge and people flourish. Surveying the dramatic and thematic juxtapositions of these two worlds, Halio especially focuses on Rosalind's awareness of time; he notes how, unlike Touchstone's fascination with time's power to ripen things and rot them, Rosalind is strongly influenced by time's regenerative power, particularly as it concerns lovers.*

In *As You Like It* Shakespeare exploits timelessness as a convention of the pastoral ideal along with other conventions taken from pastoralism, but unlike his treatment, say, of Silvius and Phebe, his treatment of time is not so thoroughly satirical. Though neither will quite do, timelessness in Arden (on the whole) contrasts favorably to the time-consciousness of court and city life which Touchstone, for example, brings to the forest. In addition, timelessness links life in Arden with the ideal of an older, more gracious way of life that helps regenerate a corrupt present.

Orlando's first speech immediately voices several aspects of the time theme. Speaking to Adam, he recalls his father's will and its provision that Oliver, the eldest son, should educate the younger brothers. This Oliver has failed to do, at least with respect to Sir Rowland's youngest son; but despite his enforced rusticity, Orlando reveals an innate gentility so wonderful that even his tyrannical brother is brought to remark: "Yet he's gentle, never schooled, and yet learned, full of noble device, of all sorts enchantingly beloved ... " [I. i. 166–68]. These innate qualities derive directly from old Sir Rowland, for the identification between Orlando and his father, as we shall see, is repeatedly and pointedly made. Moreover, Orlando twice remarks in this scene that it is his father's spirit within him that prompts him to revolt against his present humiliation—a revelation which has more than ordinary implications later.

Unlike his counterpart Sir John of Bordeaux in Lodge's *Rosalynde*, Sir Rowland de Boys is

> IF ORLANDO, AS WE HAVE SEEN, IS AN AGENT OF REGENERATION, HE APPEARS THROUGH HIS FORGETFULNESS OF TIME TO BE IN SOME DANGER OF NOT REALIZING HIS FUNCTION."

dead before the play opens, but his memory is kept studiously alive. In the opening lines of Lodge's novel we can get some idea of what he stood for:

> There dwelled adjoining to the city of Bordeaux a knight of most honorable parentage, whom fortune had graced with many favors, and nature honored with sundry exquisite qualities, so beautified with the excellence of both, as it was a question whether fortune or nature were more prodigal in deciphering the riches of their bounties. Wise he was, as holding in his head a supreme conceit of policy, reaching with Nestor into the depth of all civil government; and to make his wisdom more gracious, he had that *salem ingenii* and pleasant eloquence that was so highly commended in Ulysses: his valor was no less than his wit, nor the stroke of his lance no less forcible than the sweetness of his tongue was persuasive; for he was for his courage chosen the principal of all the Knights of Malta.

But we need not go outside the play to discover what Sir Rowland represents. Adam, the old retainer of the de Boys household and himself a living remember of the former age, provides some important clues. When Oliver apparently consents to his brother's departure, he throws Adam out, too:

> OLIVER: Get you with him, you old dog.

> ADAM: Is "old dog" my reward? Most true, I have lost teeth in your service. God be with my old master! He would not have spoke such a word.

> [I. i. 81–4]

Later, when Adam warns Orlando to run from Oliver's treachery and even offers his life's savings—and his life—to assist in the escape, Orlando recognizes the gesture for what it is— the product of a gracious ideal:

> O good old man, how well in thee appears

The constant service of the antique world,
When service sweat for duty, not for meed!
Thou art not for the fashion of these times,
Where none will sweat but for promotion,
And having that do choke their service up
Even with the having. It is not so with thee.
[II. iii. 56–62]

The two dukes also furnish evidence of the esteem in which Sir Rowland was universally held: Duke Frederick, villainously, found him an enemy, but Duke Senior (to Rosalind's evident gratification) "loved Sir Rowland as his soul" [I. ii. 235]. Orlando, who functions in the play partly to bear out the spirit of his father, naturally attracts similar feelings. It is not for nothing that he attaches to himself repeatedly the clumsy-naive epithet "old Sir Rowland's youngest son" [I. iii. 28]; besides, his name is both as anagram of Rowland and its Italian translation. The predicament in which the young man eventually discovers himself will test his true mettle and, more importantly, the worth of all that he and his name may symbolize. Adam awakens in him some sense of his plight when Orlando returns home after throwing Charles the wrestler:

O you memory
Of old Sir Rowland! Why, what make you
    here?
Why are you so virtuous? Why do people
    love you?
And wherefore are you gentle, strong, and
    valiant?
Why would you be so fond to overcome
The bonny prizer of the humorous Duke?
Your praise is come too swiftly home before
    you.
Know you not, master, to some kind of men
Their graces serve them but as enemies?
No more do yours. Your virtues, gentle
    master,
Are sanctified and holy traitors to you.
Oh, what a world is this when what is comely
Envenoms him that bears it!
[II. iii. 3–15]

Orlando's world of court and city is a far different world from his father's. It is a perverse world, where brother plots against brother and virtues become "sanctified and holy traitors" [II. iii. 13]. It is a world ruled over by the usurping Frederick (the "new" Duke), who banishes his elder brother (the "old" Duke) and keeps his niece only so long as convenience allows. When

he fears Rosalind as a threat to the fame and popularity of his own daughter, he drives her out also—just as Oliver plans to kill the brother he fears he can no longer suppress. In short, it is a world based on expediency and the lust for power [III. i. 15–18], not a brave new world, but a degenerate new one. With no obligation to tradition—to the past—it is ruthless in its self-assertion. But while this "new" world may banish its principal threats, Rosalind and Orlando, it does not thus destroy them (we are, after all, in the realm of romantic comedy). In the timeless pastoral world of the Forest of Arden, where past and present merge, they find refuge and there flourish.

The first mention of the life led by Duke Senior and his fellows in the Forest of Arden occurs early in the play in the dialogue between Charles and Oliver. Oliver has decided to use the wrestler to rid himself of Orlando (thus perverting the intention of Charles's visit), but first he inquiries into the "new news at the new Court" [I. ii. 96–7]. Charles recounts what Oliver already knows: the new Duke has driven out the old Duke, and a number of lords have voluntarily accompanied him into exile. For no apparent reason, Oliver next inquires into Rosalind's position, and then asks where the old Duke will live. Charles replies:

They say he is already in the Forest of Arden,
and a many merry men with him; and there
they live like the old Robin Hood of England.
They say many young gentlemen flock to him
every day, and fleet their time carelessly as they
did in the golden world.

[I. i. 114–19]

Here Oliver abruptly changes the subject to the next day's wrestling match. Now, merely as dramatic exposition this dialogue is at least ingenuous—if not downright clumsy. Obviously it must serve another function to justify itself; that is, by describing the conflict between the two dukes, it provides a parallel to the decisive quarrel between Orlando and Oliver which has just taken place. The inversion of roles played by the younger and older brothers is merely a superficial variation of the plot; the point is to suggest an alignment between Duke Senior and Sir Rowland de Boys, between the "golden world" and the "antique world," which coalesce in the fabulous Robin Hood life now led by the banished Duke. Should we require any further evidence of this significance, the change in Sir Rowland's name from its source is clear enough.

The anagram *Rowland-Orlando* has already been explained, but the change from *de Bordeaux* is otherwise meaningful: *de Boys* is simply *de Bois*, "of the forest." Elizabethan spelling commonly substitutes *y* for *i*, as everyone knows, but the pronunciation is the same. While older editors, such as Malone and Dyce, modernize the spelling (without comment), more recent ones prefer the spelling of the Folios, a practice which tends to obscure the reference. And Dover Wilson's note [in his New Cambridge edition of the play], recording the fact that the de Boyses were an old Arden family, gives us more light than it perhaps suspects—or intends.

Lest there be any mistake about the kind of forest in which Duke Senior and (later) Orlando, Rosalind, and the others find themselves, we must listen carefully to the Duke's first speech [II. i. 1ff.]. Its theme is "Sweet are the uses of adversity"; only in this way can he and his followers discover "tongues in trees, books in the running brooks / . . . and good in everything." Here, unlike the conventional pastoral, others besides unrequited lovers may feel the shrewdness of the winter wind; shepherds will confess to smelling of sheep dip; and a Sir Oliver Martex is available for weddings as well as Hymen. The forest may be enchanted—the appearance of a god is only the least subtle indication that it is—but the enchantment is of an unusual kind; the forest still admits of other, qualifying realities. For the right apprehension of a natural, humane order of life, which emerges as Shakespeare's standard, takes account of both the ideal (what should or could be) and the actual (what is). By contrast, the standard of life in court and city is unnatural insofar as it stifles the ideal aspirations of the human imagination and sinks to the level of a crude, animal existence. If Duke Senior finally returns along with the others to his dukedom (despite his earlier assertion that he would not change his "life exempt from public haunt"), he returns not only because his dukedom is ready to receive him, but also (we must infer) because he is prepared to resume his proper role. Tempered by adversity, his virtue matures. To provide this temper, or balance, is the true function of the forest, its real "magic." Neither the Duke nor anyone else who comes to Arden emerges the same.

The trip to the forest is itself exhausting and fraught with danger. Rosalind and her little company are quite unable to take another step.

Similarly, Adam is close to expiring when he arrives with Orlando. But on each occasion the forest at once works its charm. Corin and Silvius are at hand to entertain Rosalind and her friends and to provide them with a gentle welcome and a home. At the end of the scene even the fainting Celia quickens to remark, "I like this place, / And willingly could waste my time in it" [III. iv. 94–5]. Orlando, seeking food in what he calls an "uncouth" desert [II. vi. 6], comes upon the banquet of the banished Duke. Showing the valor of his heritage, he opposes single-handed the entire host of the Duke and his men. Under the conventions of this romance, this show of valor is not quixotic—it fits rather with Orlando's defeat of Charles. But, though hardly despised (except by Jaques), it is misdirected; and Orlando is made to recognize the code that here reigns:

> Speak you so gently? Pardon me, I pray
>   you.
> I thought that all things had been savage
>   here,
> And therefore put I on the countenance
> Of stern commandment. But whate'er you
>   are
> That in this desert inaccessible,
> Under the shade of melancholy boughs,
> Lose and neglect the creeping hours of time,
> If ever you have looked on better days,
> If ever been where bells have knolled to
>   church,
> If ever sat at good man's feast,
> If ever from your eyelids wiped a tear
> And know what 'tis to pity and be pitied,
> Let gentleness my strong enforcement be.
> In the which hope I blush, and hide my
>   sword.
> [II. vii. 106–19]

Gentleness joins with gentleness; golden world merges with antique world—at least through their modern representatives. If the parvenu at first mistakes the appearance of his surroundings, he is soon instructed: this is no ordinary forest. At the same time, he reminds us of what civilization *might* be like, or once was. Certainly he perceives another aspect of his new environment accurately, one he will quickly cultivate: the meaninglessness of time in the forest.

For unlike the life of the court and the city, "men fleet the time carelessly" in Arden, as Charles earlier remarked. Here are no power-seekers like Oliver and Duke Frederick, impatient to rid themselves of encumbrances [I. i. 124, I. iii. 52 ff.], but men who love to lie under the greenwood tree seeking—only the food they eat. Appropriately, this casualness is the theme of many of their songs. Touchstone's comment on the last—"I count it but lost time to hear such a foolish song" [V. iii. 39–40]—briefly expresses the opposing attitude brought from court into the forest. The attitude is shared by the malcontent Jaques, his fellow satirist, and in some respects by Rosalind. Touchstone is, in fact, the play's timekeeper, as Harold Jenkins has called him [in his *"As You Like It," Shakespeare Survey* VII (1955): 40–51], and his most extended disquisition on time is fittingly recounted by Jaques:

> . . . he drew a dial from his poke,
> And looking on it with lack-lustre eye,
> Says very wisely, "It is ten o'clock.
> Thus we may see," quoth he, "how the world
>   wags.
> 'Tis but an hour ago since it was nine,
> And after one hour more 'twill be eleven;
> And so, from hour to hour, we ripe and ripe,
> And then, from hour to hour, we rot and rot;
> And thereby hangs a tale."
> [II. vii. 20–8]

Later in the same scene Jaques *in propria persona* also "morals on the time" in his speech on the Seven Ages of Man, calling our attention to the broader divisions of time's progress and pageant. Between these speeches, it should be noted, occur Orlando's entrance and his words, quoted above, on the neglect of time by the Duke and his foresters. Clearly, Shakespeare throughout the play contrasts the timelessness of the forest world with the time-ridden preoccupations of court and city life, but here the juxtaposition is both dramatically and thematically emphasized. For the court and city habitués, time is a measured progress to the grave—or worse! But for the foresters, time is merely "the stream we go a-fishing in" (to borrow the phrase of a later pastoralist [Henry David Thoreau in *Walden*]). Neither attitude, of course, will quite do in this sublunary world; hence, to present a more balanced view of time—as of love, pastoralism, and poetry—Shakespeare uses the dialectic characteristic of this play and centers it upon his hero and heroine.

For Rosalind's awareness of time, however related to the preoccupation imported from the "outside" world, is different from Touchstone's obsession with "riping and rotting." It is, partly, the awareness of a girl in love and impatient for the attentions of her lover, a healthy consciousness that recalls Juliet's except as it is undarkened by tragic fate. But her awareness has further implications. When she and Orlando first meet in the forest, their dialogue, appropriately enough, is itself about time. Rosalind's question, "I pray you, what is't o'clock?" [III. ii. 299], although banal, suits the occasion; for despite her boast that she will speak like a saucy lackey, she is momentarily confused by confronting Orlando and scarcely knows how to begin. What follows in her account of Time's "divers paces" [III. ii. 308–33], however, is something more than a verbal smokescreen to help her collect her wits, detain her lover, and make sure he keeps coming back: it is a development of Jaques' Seven Ages speech with important thematic variations. Jaques' speech describes a man in his time playing many parts and suggests that his speed, or "pace," will vary along with his role; the series of vignettes illustrates the movement of a person *in* time. Rosalind not only adds appreciably to Jaques' gallery, but showing profounder insight, she shifts the emphasis from the movement *of a person*, to the movement *of time* as apprehended, for example, by the young maid "between the contract of her marriage and the day it is solemniz'd. If the interim be but a se'ennight, Time's pace is so hard that it seems the length of seven year" [III. ii. 314–17]. In this way, she more thoroughly accounts for *duration*, or the perception of time, which, unlike Jaques' portrait of our common destiny, is not the same for everyone.

Naturally, Rosalind is most concerned with the perception of time by the lover, and here her behavior is in marked contrast to Orlando's. Quite literally—and like any fiancée, or wife—she is Orlando's timekeeper. When he fails to keep his appointments, she suffers both pain and embarrassment (III.iv) that are relieved only by the greater follies of Silvius and Phebe that immediately follow. When he finally does turn up an hour late—as if to dramatize his belief that "there's no clock in the forest" [III. ii. 300–01]—Rosalind rebukes him severely:

ROSALIND: Why, how now, Orlando? Where have you been all this while? You a lover? An you serve such another trick, never come in my sight more.

ORLANDO: My fair Rosalind, I come within an hour of my promise.

ROSALIND: Break an hour's promise in love? He that will divide a minute into a thousand parts and break but a part of the thousand part of a minute in the affairs of love, it may be said of him that Cupid hath clapp'd him o' th' shoulder, but I'll warrant him heart-whole.

ORLANDO: Pardon me, dear Rosalind.

ROSALIND: Nay, an you be so tardy, come no more in my sight. I had as lief be woo'd of a snail.

[IV. i. 38–52]

Rosalind's time-consciousness goes beyond the mere moment: she knows the history of love—witness her speech on Troilus and Leander [IV. i. 94–108]—and she predicts its future, as she warns Orlando of love's seasons after marriage [IV. i. 143–149]. Her ardent impulse is thus in comic juxtaposition with her realistic insight, just as Orlando's "point-device" attire and time-unconsciousness comically contrast with his rimes and other protestations of love.

In this fashion we arrive at the theme's center, or balance. If Orlando, as we have seen, is an agent of regeneration, he appears through his forgetfulness of time to be in some danger of not realizing his function. He might like Silvius, were it not for Rosalind, linger through an eternity of unconsummated loving; certainly, like the Duke, he feels in the forest no urgency about his heritage—at least not until he comes upon his brother sleeping beneath an ancient oak tree and menaced by a starved lioness (the symbolism is obvious). Oliver's remarkable conversion after his rescue and his still more remarkable engagement to Celia pave the way for Rosalind's resolution of the action, for under the pressure of his brother's happiness, Orlando can play at games in love no longer. And despite the play's arbitrary finale—Duke Frederick's conversion and the end of exile, in all of which she has had no hand—nevertheless, it is again Rosalind who has had an important share in preparing the principals for this chance. Like her less attractive counterpart Helena in *All's Well That Ends Well*, she remains a primary agent for the synthesis of values that underlies regeneration in Shakespeare's comedy. At the very outset we see her, the daughter of Duke Senior at the court of Duke Frederick, as a link between two worlds, not unlike Orlando's representative linking of two generations. In love, she is realistic rather than cynical, but not without a paradoxical—and perfectly human—romantic bias. So, too, with regard to time she moves with Orlando to a proper balance of unharried awareness. For all of these functions—as for others—the timeless world of the forest, with its complement of aliens, serves as a haven; but more importantly, it serves as a school.

Neither the extremes of idealism nor those of materialism, as they are variously represented, emerge as "the good life" in *As You Like It*. That life is seen rather as a mean of natural human sympathy educated—since that is a major theme in the play—by the more acceptable refinements of civilization (II. vii) and the harsh realities of existence ("winter and rough weather" [II. v. 8]). The "antique world" stands for a timeless order of civilization still in touch with natural human sympathy that, under the "new" regime (while it lasted), had been forced underground. To the forest, the repository of natural life devoid of artificial time barriers, the champions of regeneration repair in order to derive new energy for the task before them. There they find refuge, gain strength, learn—and return. (pp. 197–207)

Source: Jay L. Halio, "No Clock in the Forest: Time in *As You Like It*," in *Studies in English Literature, 1500–1900*, William Marsh Rice University, Vol. II, 1962, pp. 197–207.

SOURCES

Brown, John Russell, "'As You Like It,'" in *Shakespeare's Dramatic Style*, Barnes & Noble, 1971, pp. 72–103.

Burgess, Anthony, *Shakespeare*, Knopf, 1970.

Campbell, Oscar James, "*As You Like It*," in *Shakespeare's Satire*, Oxford University Press, 1943.

Craig, Hardin, "*As You Like It*," in *An Interpretation of Shakespeare*, Citadel Press, 1949, pp. 122–24.

Erickson, Peter B., "Sexual Politics and Social Structure in *As You Like It*," by William Shakespeare, edited by Albert Gilman, New American Library, 1986, pp. 222–37.

Fergusson, Francis, "*As You Like It*," in *Shakespeare: The Pattern in His Carpet*, Delacorte Press, 1958, pp. 148–55.

Fink, Z. S., "Jaques and the Malcontent Traveler," in *Philological Quarterly*, Vol. 14, No. 2, April 1935, 237–52.

Gardner, Helen, "'As You Like It,'" in *As You Like It*, by William Shakespeare, New American Library, 1986, pp. 203–21.

Gilman, Albert, "Introduction," in *As You Like It*, by William Shakespeare, New American Library, 1986, pp. xx–xxxiii.

Goldsmith, Robert H., "Shakespeare's Wise Fools," in *Wise Fools in Shakespeare*, Michigan State University Press, 1955, pp. 47–67.

———, "Touchstone in Arcadia," in *As You Like It*, by William Shakespeare, edited by Albert Gilman, New American Library, 1986, pp. 195–202.

Grice, Maureen, "*As You Like It*," in *The Reader's Encyclopedia of Shakespeare*, edited by Oscar James Campbell and Edward G. Quinn, Crowell, 1966, pp. 41–8.

Hunter, G. K. "*As You Like It*," in *The Later Comedies: "A Midsummer Night's Dream," "Much Ado About Nothing," "As You Like It," "Twelfth Night"*, British Council, 1962, pp. 32–43.

Jenkins, Harold, "*As You Like It*," in *Shakespeare Survey*, Vol. 7, 1955, pp. 40–5l.

McDonald, Russ, *The Bedford Companion to Shakespeare*, 2nd ed., Bedford/St. Martin's, 2001.

Palmer, D. J., "*As You Like It* and the Idea of Play," in *Critical Quarterly*, Vol. 13, No. 3, Autumn 1971, pp. 234–45.

Sen Gupta, S. C., "Pastoral Romance and Romantic Comedy: *Rosalynde* and *As You Like It*," in *A Shakespeare Manual*, Oxford University Press, 1977, pp. 69–84.

Shakespeare, William, *As You Like It*, edited by Albert Gilman, New American Library, 1986.

———, *The Complete Illustrated Shakespeare*, edited by Howard Staunton, reprint, Park Lane, 1979.

Shaw, John, "Fortune and Nature in *As You Like It*," in *Shakespeare Quarterly*, Vol. 6, No. 1, 1955, pp. 45–50.

Spurgeon, Caroline F. E., "Imagery Establishes Atmosphere and Background in the Comedies," in *Readings on the Comedies*, edited by Clarice Swisher, Greenhaven Press, 1997, pp. 62–71.

Stauffer, Donald A., "The Garden of Eden," in *Shakespeare's World of Images: The Development of Moral Ideas*, Norton, 1949, pp. 67–109.

Van Doren, Mark, "*As You Like It*," in *Shakespeare*, Holt, 1939, pp. 151–60.

Wain, John, "Laughter and Judgement," in *The Living World of Shakespeare: A Playgoer's Guide*, St. Martin's, 1964, pp. 73–103.

FURTHER READING

Carroll, William C., *The Metamorphoses of Shakespearean Comedy*, Princeton University Press, 1985.
> Carroll provides a comprehensive analysis of the various personal transformations that the characters in Shakespeare's comedies undergo.

Craun, Edwin David, *Lies, Slander and Obscenity in Medieval English Literature: Pastoral Rhetoric and the Deviant Speaker*, Cambridge University Press, 2005.
> In this academic volume, Craun explains how the work of authors writing centuries before Shakespeare was affected by the rising power and influence of Christianity and the medieval clergy. Touchstone's role in *As You Like It* gains considerable weight when read with this study in mind.

Scheese, Don, *Nature Writing: The Pastoral Impulse in America*, Twayne, 1996.
> After surveying the historical development of literary pastoral conventions, Scheese focuses on how attitudes about and references to nature, especially in opposition to industrialization, have shaped the writings of certain Americans.

Young, David, *The Heart's Forest: A Study of Shakespeare's Pastoral Plays*, Yale University Press, 1972.
> Young examines the intersection of romance and nature in all of Shakespeare's plays featuring pastoral conventions.

The Comedy of Errors

1589

The Comedy of Errors is one of Shakespeare's earliest plays, quite possibly his first. It was written sometime between 1589 and 1594, although it was not printed until 1623, when it appeared in the First Folio. *The Comedy of Errors* also happens to be Shakespeare's shortest play; it has some 1,756 lines. All of the remaining plays number at least 2,000 lines.

The primary source of the play is an ancient drama called the *Menaechmi*, by Plautus, a Roman comic playwright. From the *Menaechmi* Shakespeare took his central plot, which revolves around "errors," or mistakes of fortune, involving identical twin brothers. Shakespeare also borrowed from Plautus's *Amphitryon*, particularly for the episode involving Antipholus of Ephesus being locked out of his home. To these basic elements Shakespeare added additional scenes and characters, most notably another set of twins, who are servants to the twin sons of Egeon. The story of Egeon—his separation from his wife and one of the twin sons—is also a departure from the Roman play. Shakespeare gave greater voice to the primary female characters in the play (and thus to issues of gender and the relationships between men and women), especially to Adriana, who is merely a shrewish "Wife" in Plautus's play; Shakespeare also downgraded the role of an unnamed Courtesan. Critics tend to agree that Shakespeare greatly expanded on the generally one-dimensional, stereotypical characters in Plautus's play. Shakespeare's selection of Ephesus for the play's setting has been

noted as a significant alteration, indicating that Shakespeare certainly relied on Paul's epistle to the Ephesians, as found in the Bible, for the development of certain aspects of the plot. In her essay, "Egeon's Debt: Self-Discovery and Self-Redemption in *The Comedy of Errors*," the critic Barbara Freedman observes, "No other source includes such elements as years of wandering, a shipwreck, the Aegean (Egeon?) and Adriatic (Adriana?) seas, Syracuse, Corinth, Ephesus and its demonic magic, revenge taken upon evil exorcists, and a conflict between law and mercy, between bondage and redemption."

There was a scarcity of commentary on *The Comedy of Errors* prior to the nineteenth century. Samuel Taylor Coleridge was the first to discuss the play as a unified work of art, asserting that it was a farce and therefore should not be judged by the standards applied to comedy. Some critics view it as an apprentice work, since it was written so early in Shakespeare's career. Few critics argue that the play displays the full range of Shakespeare's dramatic talent. Many commentators have seen fit to closely examine the play's genre—its "identity" as a tragedy, farce, comedy, or a combination of these—and the way in which it explores the issues of identity, love, and marriage. While some consider *The Comedy of Errors* to have been produced so early in Shakespeare's career as to merit little recognition, the play has many assets—some more obvious than others—and will continue to entertain audiences and readers alike for centuries to come regardless.

Engraving from Galerie des Personnage de Shakespeare, 1844 (© *Shakespeare Collection, Special Collections Library, University of Michigan*)

PLOT SUMMARY

Act 1, Scene 1

The Comedy of Errors begins in Ephesus, where the duke, Solinus, is punishing Egeon for having trespassed on Ephesian soil. Solinus explains that since the Syracusian duke punished Ephesian merchants simply for doing business in Syracuse, Solinus has decided to likewise punish Syracusian merchants for simply appearing in Ephesus. As such, Egeon, a merchant from Syracuse, must either pay a penalty of one thousand marks—which he does not have—or be put to death.

When asked by Solinus why he had come to Ephesus, Egeon explains his woeful tale: some eighteen years ago, in Epidamnum, his wife bore him sons, and, coincidentally, an impoverished woman gave birth to her own twin sons in the same inn at the same hour. Since the poor woman could not care for her children, Egeon purchased them as servants for his own children. Later, when Egeon, his wife, and the four young children were sailing back to Syracuse, they came upon rough waters and had to resort to tying themselves to the ship's masts. As two other vessels were coming upon them, their ship was split apart by a "mighty rock," such that the wife, one son, and one servant were separated from Egeon, the other son, and the other servant. When the son raised by Egeon reached the age of eighteen, he grew curious enough about his long-lost brother and mother to wish to travel in search of them, in the company of his servant. Egeon also left in search of the family members and had ended up in Ephesus after "five summers" of travels elsewhere. The duke, taking pity on Egeon, gives him leave to seek the thousand marks needed to buy his freedom from friends in Ephesus—but Egeon has only that very day to obtain the sum.

Act 1, Scene 2

At the marketplace, the son who has been traveling, known as Antipholus of Syracuse (and referred to as S. Antipholus), is finishing a deal with a Merchant, who warns S. Antipholus that he should deny his Syracusian origins, as just that day a merchant from Syracuse was arrested and will be executed. S. Antipholus sends his servant, Dromio of Syracuse (referred to as S. Dromio), to take the money he has just received to their lodgings, the inn known as the Centaur. When S. Dromio departs, S. Antipholus makes plans to meet the Merchant again later that evening.

Dromio of Ephesus (to be referred to as E. Dromio) then arrives and begins telling S. Antipholus about how late he is for dinner; the audience can immediately understand that this Dromio believes he is talking to Antipholus of Ephesus (to be referred to as E. Antipholus). S. Antipholus, in turn thinking that E. Dromio is S. Dromio, imagines that his servant is jesting and demands to know what he did with the large sum of money—one thousand marks—that he had been entrusted with. E. Dromio, however, denies that he has any more marks than the ones he is given when he is beaten. Angered by what seems a sustained jest, S. Antipholus indeed beats E. Dromio, who flees. S. Antipholus then announces that he will return to the Centaur to find out what has become of his money.

Act 2, Scene 1

At the Phoenix, the home of E. Antipholus, Adriana and Luciana are discussing Adriana's husband's absence. Luciana advises her sister to be patient and obedient in the extreme, noting that among all animals, the males are the masters of the females. Adriana objects, declaring that within a marriage she ought to have a certain degree of control; Adriana notes that Luciana is only able to advise so much obedience because she is not married herself. Still, Luciana insists that when she marries, she will learn obedience and be patient even if she knows her husband to be cheating on her.

E. Dromio then enters to inform his mistress, Adriana, that he has just come from her husband, who denied that he even had a home or a wife there. E. Dromio notes that he was beaten by

Antipholus, who repeatedly demanded to know about his gold, of which E. Dromio knew nothing. Adriana grows upset with E. Dromio, threatening to beat him and demanding that he depart again to find her husband. Adriana then laments at length about her certainty that her husband is cheating on her. She wonders if he looks elsewhere because she has lost her beauty; she also declares that if she has lost her beauty, she has lost it only because her husband is no longer as kind to her as he used to be. Luciana tries to calm her sister, but Adriana is too sorrowful.

Act 2, Scene 2

S. Antipholus, walking through the marketplace, remarks that he has just discovered that S. Dromio has indeed safely stored the gold at the Centaur. S. Dromio then enters, and S. Antipholus demands that he explain the jest from earlier, when Dromio denied all knowledge of the gold. S. Dromio then denies that he ever made any jests, eventually earning a beating from the angered S. Antipholus. S. Antipholus explains to S. Dromio that he should never jest when his master is not in a jesting mood. The two then start speaking of dinner and of the relationship between a man's wit and the amount of hair on his head.

Adriana and Luciana then arrive, with Adriana immediately launching into a plaint toward S. Antipholus, whom she thinks is her husband. She reminisces about the time when he truly cherished her; she notes that like a drop of water from a gulf, she cannot be separated from him; and she points out that if she were to commit adultery, he would be greatly angered and indignant. She concludes by imploring him to be faithful to her. S. Antipholus professes that he has only been in the town of Ephesus for two hours and that he hardly even understands what people are talking about there. Luciana then notes that they had sent Dromio to speak with him about dinner earlier, of which S. Dromio knows nothing. S. Antipholus, then, imagines that S. Dromio must be conspiring against him along with these women, as Dromio— E. Dromio, actually—had indeed spoken to him earlier about coming home for dinner. S. Dromio, however, denies having ever spoken with Adriana—and Adriana then imagines that Antipholus and Dromio are trying to fool her; at this point she tells S. Antipholus that she is like a vine to his elm, such that he is utterly dependent on her. In an aside, S. Antipholus wonders what is going on and supposes that he may as well go along with the "fallacy," that is, that he may as well join Adriana for dinner. After S. Dromio declares that they must be in a "fairy land," and likewise wonders what is happening, Adriana bids Dromio and Antipholus to finally come home. Indeed, S. Antipholus will dine with Adriana at their home, upstairs, while S. Dromio guards the gate.

Act 3, Scene 1

Antipholus of Ephesus is leading E. Dromio, Angelo, and Balthazar to his home, where he intends to gain favor with the two businessmen by entertaining them at dinner. On the way, E. Antipholus mentions that his wife is "shrewish" whenever he is late and that Angelo, the goldsmith, should assert that he was busy buying something for her. He also mentions that E. Dromio could ruin his story, as E. Dromio claimed to have met him in the marketplace earlier. Indeed, E. Dromio confirms that he received a beating at Antipholus's hand.

When they arrive at the home of E. Antipholus, E. Dromio calls out to gain them entry, only to hear S. Dromio respond rudely, turning them away. S. Dromio declares that Dromio is his name and that he is the porter, and E. Dromio asserts that his office has been stolen by a counterfeit who is using his name. Luce, the cook, then appears above and also speaks rudely to E. Dromio, as she believes that everyone belonging to the household is already inside. Adriana appears to speak with Luce and to hear E. Antipholus call her his wife—but she cannot see him and also believes him to be an impostor, as S. Antipholus is inside.

When the women return inside the house, E. Antipholus declares that he will use force, if necessary to gain entry, asking E. Dromio to fetch him a crowbar. However, Balthazar interrupts to suggest that he refrain from resorting to force, as such an act could ruin his reputation; Balthazar notes that his wife certainly has some reason or another for keeping him out, and he should return later to hear her explanation. E. Antipholus concedes and declares that they will go to the Porpentine—and out of spite Antipholus will give the Courtesan there the chain that he had planned to give to his wife. As they exit, Angelo parts from them to get the chain.

Act 3, Scene 2

Luciana is speaking with S. Antipholus, counseling him to be more cunning with regard to his character around Adriana. Specifically, Luciana tells Antipholus that if he is cheating on his wife, he should make more of an effort to deceive her, to at least make her feel as though he still loves only her. S. Antipholus professes that he understands nothing of what she is saying, as Adriana is most definitely not his wife—and that he is in fact enamored of Luciana herself. Luciana protests that he is being ridiculous, as he must love only his wife, but S. Antipholus insists that he is interested in Luciana alone.

When Luciana leaves to get Adriana, S. Dromio appears to lament that he is being claimed by a woman named Nell (who is understood to be Luce, from act 2, scene 2). He is especially upset by this situation because Nell is quite obese, as his exaggerated comments regarding her girth indicate. S. Dromio makes a number of insulting comparisons between nations and parts of her body. When Nell proves able to tell Dromio about the various marks on his body, he begins to think she is some sort of witch. S. Antipholus then suggests to S. Dromio that he go wait by the harbor; if a seaward wind comes along and a ship is sailing out, S. Dromio should find S. Antipholus in the marketplace, and they will leave immediately. When S. Dromio leaves, S. Antipholus declares his own belief that they are among witches—but also that he will regret leaving Luciana.

Angelo then appears and insists upon giving S. Antipholus the chain that E. Antipholus had ordered. S. Antipholus eventually accepts and tries to pay for it then rather than later, so as not to accidentally cheat the man, but Angelo departs without accepting. S. Antipholus notes that only in such a strangely wonderful place would people bestow random gifts upon him.

Act 4, Scene 1

In the marketplace, a Merchant is demanding the repayment of a debt from Angelo, the goldsmith; the Merchant has summoned an Officer to arrest Angelo if he cannot repay the debt. Angelo notes that he simply needs to obtain the money from E. Antipholus, who owes him the cost of the chain. E. Antipholus then arrives, having just left the Courtesan. E. Antipholus orders E. Dromio to fetch him a rope, with which Antipholus plans to physically punish his wife and any other people responsible for locking him out of his house. Angelo then meets E. Antipholus and demands the sum he is owed, but E. Antipholus remarks that he does not have the money with him and that he will not pay, regardless, until he actually receives the chain. Angelo insists that he already gave him the chain (which S. Antipholus received), leaving both men greatly confounded.

As no one is giving him the money that he is owed, the Merchant has the Officer arrest Angelo; in turn, Angelo, whose reputation will be harmed, has the Officer arrest E. Antipholus, who is likewise greatly offended. S. Dromio then arrives to inform Antipholus that he has found passage for them on a ship that is soon to depart. E. Antipholus is confounded by S. Dromio's uttering such nonsense—and also by S. Dromio's failure to bring a rope. Still, as he has been arrested, E. Antipholus promptly sends S. Dromio to fetch money from Adriana.

Act 4, Scene 2

In front of the Phoenix, Luciana is telling Adriana about how S. Antipholus had professed to have fallen in love with her. Upset that her husband should have scorned her so, Adriana insults him at length, then admits to still having feelings for him. S. Dromio then arrives to demand the money on behalf of E. Antipholus. When the ladies inquire about Antipholus, S. Dromio notes that he had been arrested for nonpayment of a debt. Luciana fetches the money, and S. Dromio runs off with it.

Act 4, Scene 3

In the marketplace, S. Antipholus observes how everyone in the town seems to know him somehow. S. Dromio then arrives to hand him the money—but S. Antipholus objects that he had asked him for no money. S. Dromio inquires about the officer and where he might have gone, but S. Antipholus fails to understand. S. Antipholus then asks whether they might soon depart by sea, and S. Dromio points out that he told Antipholus earlier of a ship, but Antipholus had expressed no interest, so they had missed it.

The Courtesan then arrives, greets Antipholus by name, and asks whether the chain he holds is the one that he had promised her earlier. S. Antipholus and S. Dromio alike then both wonder if the Courtesan is perhaps the devil, in the form of a "light wench." S. Antipholus calls

her a sorceress and tells her to leave, but she only demands the ring of hers that Antipholus had worn at dinner. At last certain that the Courtesan is some sort of witch, S. Antipholus and S. Dromio flee. The Courtesan, thinking Antipholus must be insane, resolves to go to his house and tell Adriana that he had stolen her ring, as the Courtesan does not wish to lose it.

Act 4, Scene 4

As E. Antipholus is being led away by the Officer, E. Dromio returns to give him the rope. When E. Antipholus asks about the money he had sent for, E. Dromio declares that he knows nothing about it; E. Antipholus then grows angry and beats E. Dromio. The Officer urges E. Antipholus to calm down, but he continues verbally abusing E. Dromio, who laments that he has long been subject to beatings at the hand of his master.

As Adriana, Luciana, and the Courtesan arrive with a doctor named Pinch, E. Antipholus continues to beat E. Dromio—providing evidence of E. Antipholus's suspected madness. The women declare that he indeed looks ill, and when Pinch tries to take his pulse, E. Antipholus strikes him. Pinch then attempts to exorcise Satan from E. Antipholus; Antipholus dismisses the man, declares that he is sane, and asks his wife to explain why he had been locked out at dinnertime. Adriana insists that he dined at home, leaving E. Antipholus and E. Dromio to insist that they had been locked out as well as taunted by the kitchen maid.

As the women and the doctor begin to wonder if E. Dromio has also been infected with madness, E. Antipholus and Adriana relate their respective roles in the fetching of the money by S. Dromio—which E. Dromio knows nothing about. Pinch insists that both men must be mad, and when E. Antipholus threatens to assault Adriana, several men appear to bind E. Antipholus. E. Antipholus pleads with the Officer, who asserts that E. Antipholus is in his charge and cannot be taken by the others. Adriana then offers to go with the Officer to repay the debt, and E. Antipholus and E. Dromio are taken away by the doctor.

The Officer tells Adriana that the money is owed for a golden chain, which she knows nothing about. The Courtesan then mentions that after E. Antipholus had taken her ring, she met him holding the chain in question. S. Antipholus and S. Dromio suddenly appear with drawn swords, provoking the Officer and the women to flee. S. Antipholus is glad that the witches fear their weapons, and despite S. Dromio's suggestion that they remain in that "gentle nation" after all, S. Antipholus insists that they depart immediately.

Act 5, Scene 1

Angelo is apologizing to the Merchant while assuring him that Antipholus is held in very high regard in Ephesus. S. Antipholus and S. Dromio then arrive, and Angelo sees that the chain is indeed around S. Antipholus's neck. Angelo questions him, and S. Antipholus declares that he never denied having the chain. The Merchant, who earlier heard E. Antipholus deny having the chain, grows angry; he and S. Antipholus argue and eventually draw swords.

Adriana, Luciana, and the Courtesan then arrive with the intention of binding S. Antipholus and S. Dromio, who flee into the Priory. The Abbess then comes out to ask about the commotion; Adriana demands that the Abbess turn over her husband, as she wants to treat her husband. The Abbess asks of the recent trouble and concludes that Antipholus has only been maddened by Adriana's jealous nagging. The Abbess then declares that she will not deny Antipholus sanctuary there and that she will herself use potions and prayers to try to cure him.

Adriana resolves to ask the duke for assistance, and he presently enters with Egeon, who is to be executed. Adriana tells the duke how she had bound her maddened husband and how he had consequently escaped and was being protected by the Abbess. The duke summons the Abbess, but a Messenger then arrives to tell Adriana that E. Antipholus and E. Dromio have escaped their bonds and were harming the doctor. Everyone is confused, as they believe Antipholus and Dromio to be inside the Priory—but E. Antipholus and E. Dromio indeed then appear.

E. Antipholus relates all that he has suffered to the duke, a wartime friend of his. While Adriana and Luciana claim that he had dined at home, E. Antipholus insists that he had been locked out, which E. Dromio and Angelo confirm. E. Antipholus then explains all that had occurred that day from his perspective, speaking of the missing chain, of Dromio's failure to bring the money, and of the doctor's efforts at exorcism. As they all relate what they know about the

MEDIA ADAPTATIONS

- Among the various televised versions of *The Comedy of Errors* is one directed by James Cellan Jones in 1983, which was produced by the British Broadcasting Corporation.

- Lorenz Hart and Richard Rodgers created a musical based on *The Comedy of Errors* entitled *The Boys from Syracuse*. A film version was directed by A. Edward Sutherland in 1940, and was produced by Universal Pictures.

chain, the duke begins to wonder at how extraordinary the situation seems.

Egeon then finally speaks up, as he believes that E. Antipholus must be his son S. Antipholus. However, both E. Dromio and E. Antipholus profess to having never seen Egeon, who imagines that they simply do not recognize him because they have not seen him for seven years. As the duke confirms that E. Antipholus has not been to Syracuse in the last twenty years, the Abbess enters in the company of S. Antipholus and S. Dromio. The Abbess then tells Egeon that she is Emilia, his long lost wife, and that she had been separated from E. Antipholus and E. Dromio soon after the shipwreck, as the two infants were taken by fishermen from Corinth. E. Antipholus then confirms that he had originally been brought to Ephesus from Corinth. Adriana determines that S. Antipholus was the man with whom she dined, and Angelo sees that S. Antipholus is the one who has the chain. E. Antipholus offers to pay the duke to free Egeon, but the duke releases Egeon without accepting the money. E. Antipholus then returns the ring to the Courtesan.

The Abbess announces that they will hold a festive gathering to celebrate the reunion of all the family members. After a last instance of confusion, when S. Dromio mistakenly addresses E. Antipholus, the Antipholus brothers exit, leaving the Dromio brothers to wonder which of them is older and should lead the other; they at last decide that they will walk side by side, "not one before another."

CHARACTERS

Adriana

The wife of Antipholus of Ephesus, Adriana first appears mourning her husband's absence from dinner and wondering whether he has lost his romantic appreciation for her. Luciana counsels her to be patient and allow E. Antipholus as much liberty as he wants, but Adriana insists that she cannot always make her own desires and needs be of secondary importance. When the two sisters find S. Antipholus in the marketplace, Adriana pleads and manages to persuade her husband's twin to "come home" for dinner. Adriana is later told by Luciana that S. Antipholus was professing his love for Luciana. While despairing, Adriana nonetheless sends bail money through S. Dromio to her true husband (which he never receives). After being visited by the Courtesan, Adriana brings Doctor Pinch to cure her husband of his seeming insanity, and when he is taken home, she goes off seeking to pay her husband's debt. After more confusion at the Priory, Adriana is told by the Abbess, Emilia, that she needs to nag her husband less if she wishes to have a harmonious relationship with him.

Although the plot of *The Comedy of Errors* revolves around the actions of the brothers Antipholus, Adriana is perhaps the play's most profound and intriguing persona. Where the emotional affectations of the other characters remain fairly static throughout (S. Antipholus is nearly always confused, E. Antipholus is usually angry, etc.), Adriana vacillates between reminiscing fondly over the love she and her husband used to share, growing sad over his frequent absences, and getting angry at his supposed infidelities. In that she seems to be demanding no more than equality between herself and her husband— indeed, she asks her sister, "Why should their liberty than ours be more?"—Adriana can be viewed as a prototypical feminist. When Luciana counsels her to be patient and obliging toward her husband, Adriana passionately resists, essentially declaring that she refuses to be submissive toward any man, including her husband. In that E. Antipholus not only intentionally seeks out an untruthful explanation for his lateness on this day, but also frequents the Courtesan enough to make his wife jealous, Adriana seems wholly justified in trying to assert herself in the relationship. To some audience members and readers, the

The Antipholus twins being separated as infants, Act I, scene i (© *Shakespeare Collection, Special Collections Library, University of Michigan*)

Abbess's lecture of Adriana in the fifth act may seem unnecessarily reproachful.

Nevertheless, Adriana certainly has minor flaws that contribute at least to her own happiness, if not to her husband's waywardness. While Luciana's general outlook on marriage seems to be oppressively conservative, she also tries to persuade her sister to be more independent: in particular, she denounces Adriana's "self-harming jealousy." And Adriana certainly allows her jealousy to carry her away, to the point of believing that her husband must be cheating on her. The play does not clearly indicate whether the husband has ever been unfaithful, how often he is late for dinner, or how often he wrongs Adriana in other ways; as such, Adriana's despair may seem extreme. In turn, when she believes her husband is in love with Luciana, she thoroughly curses him—then concedes that she was saying things she did not truly think or feel. Thus, the genuineness of her emotional reactions at other times may be called into doubt. Another question left unclear by the play is how often Adriana has such jealous outbursts, particularly in the presence of her husband. Overall, while Adriana certainly reacts strongly to the extreme circumstance brought about by the unknown presence of her husband's twin, the reader cannot necessarily conclude that she behaves this way under ordinary circumstances, and opinions regarding Adriana's larger role in her marriage may justifiably vary widely.

Angelo

Angelo is a goldsmith who is hired by E. Antipholus to make a gold chain for Adriana. When E. Antipholus, Angelo, and Balthazar are refused entry at the home of E. Antipholus, E. Antipholus sends Angelo to finish the chain and bring it to him. However, Angelo ends up bringing the chain to S. Antipholus. When Angelo needs to pay off a debt, he seeks payment from E. Antipholus, who never received the chain and refuses to pay—Angelo is then arrested and has E. Antipholus arrested in turn.

Antipholus of Ephesus

Also known as E. Antipholus, he is the twin brother of Antipholus of Syracuse, son of Egeon and Emilia, husband of Adriana. E. Antipholus is a well-known, well-respected merchant in the city of Ephesus. He understands that his wife wants him to be home for dinner, but he nevertheless prioritizes business, such that she suspects him of cheating on her. When he is locked out of his home, as Adriana is dining with S. Antipholus, he grows angry and goes to dine at the Courtesan's instead. He also asks Angelo to finish the chain he ordered for his wife, so that he can give it to the Courtesan instead. When Angelo seeks payment for the chain, which he gave to S. Antipholus, E. Antipholus refuses to pay for it and gets arrested. As the confusion has left E. Antipholus seeming somewhat maddened, Adriana hires Pinch to cure him of his illness—but E. Antipholus only strikes at Pinch in public, then tortures Pinch after escaping from bondage at his home. When E. Antipholus shows up outside the Priory, within which S. Antipholus is hiding, he explains everything that has happened to him that day, and Egeon mistakes him for his other son. Upon the arrival of S. Antipholus, the confusion is eventually cleared.

E. Antipholus can hardly be described as anything but a negative force in the play. He is demonstrably violent, and with little provocation; when he is truly upset by his confinement by Pinch and the others, the extent of his violent reaction actually does indicate that he may be mentally unstable, and not just as a result of the day's occurrences. (Of course, the fact that *The Comedy of Errors* is so extensively farcical perhaps accounts for the cartoonish hair burning.) E. Antipholus does almost nothing to gain the sympathy of the reader in the course of the play, and only his final long speech, in which he rationally relates the day's many errors, indicates that he has been suffering anything beyond a schoolboyish frustration. An actor may endow E. Antipholus with decent emotions during this final scene, but his dialogue indicates little to no sentiment—he addresses not a single word to his long-lost brother before they exit together. E. Antipholus may perhaps be viewed as the epitome of the businessman, essentially purchasing, of all things, time away from his wife in the form of a gold chain.

Antipholus of Syracuse

Also known as S. Antipholus, he is the twin brother of Antipholus of Ephesus, son of Egeon and Emilia. At the age of eighteen, S. Antipholus goes off to search for his long-lost brother in the company of his servant, Dromio of Syracuse. In Ephesus, S. Antipholus does some business with a Merchant and is then met by E. Dromio, who bids him return "home" to dine with Adriana. S. Antipholus is angered by what seems like a jest carried out by S. Dromio, but he later meets up with his true servant and is reassured. When Adriana finds S. Antipholus in the marketplace, he eventually agrees to dine with her. Later, when Luciana counsels him to be sweeter with Adriana, S. Antipholus finds himself falling in love with Luciana. Nevertheless, the strange goings-on lead him to ask S. Dromio to wait at the harbor and to find him in the marketplace if a ship is leaving. When the Courtesan later addresses him, he becomes convinced that the town is inhabited by witches, and he runs off with S. Dromio. At length, the two seek refuge in the Priory; when they emerge in the company of Emilia, S. Antipholus's mother, the day's confusion is cleared.

While the plot generally revolves around the actions of S. Antipholus—as framed by the plight of his father, Egeon—few commentators would contend that his character merits the most discussion. In general, S. Antipholus simply serves as a vessel of amazement with respect to the strange reception he gets in Ephesus, where everyone knows him by name and has some unexplained concern for him. That is, not counting his initial interaction with a Merchant, S. Antipholus rarely causes any of the play's action himself; rather, things happen to him, or people address him, and he somewhat passively responds to the situation or person in question. The drama surrounding E. Antipholus's being locked out of his house, which serves as the foundation for the remainder of the play's confusion, comes about because S. Antipholus has allowed himself to be swept into the situation by Adriana—and he allows this knowing full well that some "error" has come about. Indeed, S. Antipholus specifically notes that he feels as if he is sleeping and dreaming, suggesting a state of utter passivity and an absence of control.

Beyond the plot in and of itself, and regardless of S. Antipholus's lack of agency, the relationship between his quest for his long-lost brother and his understanding of his identity form the thematic core of the play. This theme is established early on, not only through Egeon's story and the audience's understanding of the bare facts of the situation, but also through S. Antipholus's own words. In his first scene, after he has dismissed S. Dromio and the Merchant exits—leaving S. Antipholus alone on the stage in the first of several such instances—he compares himself, in his search for his brother, to a drop in an ocean in search of another drop. A drop in an ocean, of course, is not truly an individual drop of water. Indeed, in the course of eleven lines in this scene, in reference to his travels, he twice states, "I . . . lose myself." Thus, S. Antipholus can be understood to lack a feeling of wholeness, and he believes he will only find this wholeness in finding his lost twin brother.

Balthazar

A merchant and business associate of Antipholus of Ephesus, Balthazar dines with E. Antipholus at the Courtesan's when they are refused entry at E. Antipholus's home.

Courtesan

The Courtesan is an acquaintance of Antipholus of Ephesus. When E. Antipholus is refused entry at his house, he goes to dine with the Courtesan. E. Antipholus borrows a diamond ring from her and intends to give her the chain made by Angelo. When the Courtesan finds S. Antipholus, who does not have the ring and fails to give her the chain in return, she concludes that he must be out of sorts. In order to get her ring back, the Courtesan goes to Adriana to inform her that her husband is acting strangely, which leads to Adriana fetching Pinch. The Courtesan then accompanies Adriana until her ring is returned to her.

Dromio of Ephesus

The personal servant of Antipholus of Ephesus, and the twin brother of Dromio of Syracuse, E. Dromio tries to persuade S. Antipholus to join Adriana for dinner and receives a brief beating for his trouble. In the course of the play, E. Dromio relates this incident to Adriana he orders S. Dromio to let E. Antipholus into his home, without success, and he fetches a rope for E. Antipholus after their dinner at the Courtesan's. When E. Dromio brings E. Antipholus the rope but no bail money (which S. Dromio had gone to fetch), E. Antipholus likewise beats him, leading E. Dromio to lament his lot in life. E. Dromio is betrothed to Luce, Adriana's kitchen servant, which leads to additional confusion for S. Dromio. Along with his twin brother, E. Dromio largely serves as a means by which the play's action moves along, with his constant running of errands for the brothers Antipholus. Also, E. Dromio functions as a servile, humble foil to E. Antipholus and his masterly arrogance.

Dromio of Syracuse

Also known as S. Dromio, he is the personal servant of Antipholus of Syracuse, and the twin brother of Dromio of Ephesus. S. Dromio takes his master's money to the inn at which they are staying, the Centaur, then gets beaten when S. Antipholus believes that he had pretended to know nothing about the money. Both Syracusians later go to Adriana's for dinner, with S. Dromio refusing entry to E. Antipholus and E. Dromio. When S. Dromio finds that Luce believes him to be betrothed to her, he complains to S. Antipholus, making many insulting remarks about Luce's size. S. Dromio then waits by the harbor for a departing ship; when he returns, he accidentally tells E. Antipholus about their nearing departure, and E. Antipholus sends him to fetch money from Adriana. He fetches the money, then brings it to S. Antipholus. When the two are met by the Courtesan, they grow convinced that the town is inhabited by witches and flee. They later draw their swords against Adriana and company and ultimately take refuge in the Priory. After they exit and resolve the confusion, S. Dromio and E. Dromio share a brotherly moment. Generally speaking, S. Dromio not only pushes the play's action along, as does his twin, but also provides more comical responses to the strange goings-on than does S. Antipholus. This role is highlighted by his long discourse regarding the physical stature of Luce, who mistakes him for her betrothed, and by comments such as those punningly referring to the Courtesan as a "light wench."

Egeon

Egeon is a merchant from Syracuse traveling in Ephesus in search of his long-lost son; he has also been away from the son he raised, S. Antipholus, for some seven years. It is illegal for a Syracusian to travel in Ephesus; he must pay a large penalty or be condemned to death. Egeon tells the Duke of Ephesus his tragic tale of family separation, and the duke, sympathetic to his plight, gives him one day to gather enough money to free himself. Egeon appears again in the final scene and believes that E. Antipholus is actually S. Antipholus. When Emilia, his long-lost wife, appears, along with S. Antipholus and S. Dromio, Egeon and his family are at last reunited.

While Egeon's plight serves as the framework for the rest of the play, his appearances are brief, and his character seems to merit little interpretation; he has a problem, and at the end of the play it is solved. On the other hand, one critic has offered a convincing interpretation of the play wherein the greater plot can be understood not just as an actual reunion of Egeon's family but also as an allegorical resolution to the psychic difficulties that brought about the problem in the first place. This allegory is discussed at length in the Style section.

Emilia

Emilia is the wife of Egeon, and the mother of both S. Antipholus and E. Antipholus. Some thirty-three years earlier, Emilia was separated first from her husband, Egeon, and one son in a shipwreck, then from her other son by the fishermen who rescued them. She becomes an Abbess in Ephesus. She is reunited at the end of the play with her husband, as well as with both of her long-lost sons. Her appearance finally resolves the confusion surrounding everyone's identities. By virtue of her refusal to surrender S. Antipholus and S. Dromio from the refuge of her sanctuary, and by her chastising of Adriana, Emilia amounts to a significant moral force in the play.

First Merchant

The first Merchant appears early in the play doing business with S. Antipholus and warning him to hide his Syracusian origins.

Jailer

Another officer, referred to in a stage direction as a Jailer, tries to prevent Adriana and Pinch from detaining E. Antipholus, his charge. When Adriana offers to accompany him to pay off the debt in question, the Officer lets them take E. Antipholus away.

Luce

Luce is the servant of Adriana who is betrothed to Dromio of Ephesus. Luce supports S. Dromio in refusing E. Antipholus entry at his home. Later, Luce reportedly mistakes S. Dromio for E. Dromio, such that S. Dromio reports back to S. Antipholus with great concern for his livelihood.

Luciana

The unmarried sister of Adriana, Luciana counsels her jealous sister to suppress her negative emotions and have patience with her possibly adulterous husband. When Luciana in turn counsels S. Antipholus to be more loving to Adriana, S. Antipholus falls in love with Luciana herself. Luciana then tells Adriana about S. Antipholus's affection, greatly upsetting her sister. Luciana supports Adriana as she tries to cure E. Antipholus of his madness.

At first glance, Luciana seems to be something of a model of antifeminism: she seems to find truth in the notion that a woman's place is in the home, and that a wife should be generally subservient to her husband. Luciana implores Adriana to harbor no jealousy over her husband's possible relations with other women, even though E. Antipholus's references to the Courtesan seem to indicate that Adriana's jealousy is justifiable. Later, in her conversation with S. Antipholus, whom she understands to be E. Antipholus, Luciana seems to be dismissing any possible infidelity on his behalf as acceptable, as long as he makes an effort to show affection for his wife.

On the other hand, Luciana could simply be understood as attempting to mediate between her sister and her brother-in-law. She eventually decries Adriana's jealousy not as, say, unwomanly or unbecoming of a wife but as "self-harming"; ultimately, then, her interest seems to lie in Adriana's personal well-being. Also, while she allows for the possibility of E. Antipholus committing adultery, she may simply be wise enough to realize that her counsel is not going to prevent E. Antipholus from slighting his wife. He is obviously antagonistic and perhaps regularly abusive, as evidenced by his frequent beatings of E. Dromio and his declared intent to assault and even "disfigure" Adriana for her actions that day. In this sense, she may simply be a realist. Also, in referring to any possible adultery, in the course of just seven lines she pointedly uses the words "false love," "shame," "disloyalty," "vice," "tainted," and "sin," perhaps in a more subtle attempt to prevent just such adultery from occurring. Overall, then, Luciana can perhaps be understood as primarily an advocate and agent of reconciliation.

Officer

One Officer arrests both Angelo and E. Antipholus.

Pinch

A doctor, or conjurer of a sort, Pinch is brought in to cure E. Antipholus of his supposed madness; E. Antipholus manages to strike Pinch in public, then later as reported by a messenger, to mildly torture Pinch.

Second Merchant

The second Merchant appears later in the play, requesting the repayment of a debt by Angelo. When Angelo cannot get the money from E. Antipholus, this Merchant has Angelo arrested. Later, Angelo and the Merchant come across S. Antipholus, who has the chain that E. Antipholus had denied having. Angered, the second Merchant draws swords against S. Antipholus, who flees with S. Dromio.

Solinus, Duke of Ephesus

After informing Egeon of his transgression—that is, appearing in Ephesus as a merchant from Syracuse—the duke listens sympathetically to Egeon's woeful tale. The duke then grants Egeon the remainder of the day to find the sum needed to buy his freedom. At day's end, as Egeon is being led to his execution, the family is reunited, with the duke serving as a mediator while the confusion is cleared up. The duke then releases Egeon without accepting E. Antipholus's money.

THEMES

Identity

The way the various characters in *The Comedy of Errors* view their respective identities is perhaps the play's most prominent theme. The central quest for identity, of course, is that of S. Antipholus, whom the audience understands from early on to be seeking himself, to a great extent, in his twin brother; this understanding comes primarily from the speech in the first act in which he compares himself to a drop of water seeking another drop in an entire ocean. Coppélia Kahn views S. Antipholus's definition of identity here as tantamount to a desire to cease to exist: "He envisions extinction—total merger with an undifferentiated mass—as the result of his search." Kahn proceeds to frame this form of negating self-definition in psychological terms: "The image of that one drop falling into a whole ocean conveys the terror of failing to find identity: irretrievable ego loss." In these terms, S. Antipholus's search for identity can be understood as a possible step in the maturational process, whereby an adolescent might test the boundaries of his or her identity by fiercely identifying with someone such as a sibling—with such an identification between twins being especially strong. Kahn concludes, "The irony . . . is that seeking identity by narcissistic mirroring leads only to the obliteration, not the discovery, of the self." Thus, while S. Antipholus finds his twin, the extent to which he likewise "finds himself" is unclear, as the reunion between the two does not indicate that they share any instinctive connection.

Adriana's conception of her identity is also of great concern and is, in fact, quite similar to that of S. Antipholus, in that she seeks to define herself in relation to another—namely, to her husband. Echoing S. Antipholus's remarks about feeling like a drop in an ocean seeking a particular other drop, Adriana compares herself to a drop of water in a gulf, where the entire gulf is understood to be her husband. A difference between the two conceptions of identity, then, can relate to the extent to which the two characters wish

A street before a priory, Act V, scene i (© *Shakespeare Collection, Special Collections Library, University of Michigan*)

to be merged, in essence, with others: S. Antipholus feels lost in the ocean and seeks to unite himself only with a single other drop, his brother; Adriana, meanwhile, is perhaps perfectly content to be lost in her gulf, her husband, as long as she is never forcibly removed from it. These dual manners of defining the self through others may fairly reflect the play's greater conception of identity, as related by Barry Weller: "The familial embrace with which the community of Ephesus eventually receives and reassembles the scattered members of Egeon's household intimates the priority of corporate identities over the single and limited life of the individual consciousness." That is, the play's conclusion perhaps demonstrates the primary importance of the intersection of identities that is brought about by love.

Love and Marriage

A second theme that is closely linked to the first and that also relates to certain characters' motivations concerns the nature of love and of marriage. This topic is discussed at length by Adriana

and Luciana, who give conflicting views of what it means to be married and to be in love. Adriana harkens back to her husband's courtship of her and laments that he no longer gives her the attention he once did. Peter G. Phialas points out that Adriana feels a need to maintain control of her husband's liberty. In this sense, he asserts, "Adriana's concept of love is the right to possess, to receive and own and be master of." This concept is problematic largely in that it leads to her jealousy, which may or may not be well founded but, regardless, bears no positive effect on the relationship. The Abbess, serving as a guiding moral force, duly chastises Adriana for failing to deal well with the situation. Phialas claims that another aspect of Adriana's conception of love that proves problematic is her evident belief that physical beauty plays a central role in attraction; however, Adriana may have formed this conception based on an accurate understanding of her own husband's inclinations toward women in general. In opposition to her sister, Luciana seems to believe that a woman's role in a marriage is to do everything possible to maintain peace. In her view, the degree of love shared by the couple is not of the utmost importance, as she counsels E. Antipholus not to search within himself to find his love for Adriana but simply to "comfort my sister, cheer her, call her wife," as "the sweet breath of flattery conquers strife." Luciana essentially dismisses the notion that the flattery in question ought to be sincere.

Much different perspectives are presented by the men of the play. E. Antipholus's actions seem to indicate that love is simply not a priority for him; rather, business and his association and friendship with other businessmen, are of the utmost importance. S. Antipholus, meanwhile, demonstrates himself to be afraid to discover how a union with a woman would affect his sense of his identity. In particular, in speaking to Luciana he expresses his desire to avoid drowning in Adriana's tears—offering an interesting inversion of the situation he described earlier with regard to his search for his twin, where he was already a drop of water in the ocean. Perhaps, however, this can simply be understood as S. Antipholus's image of what marriage with Adriana would be like; he shows himself to be perfectly amenable to a union with Luciana. S. Dromio offers the most comically negative perceptions of marriage in conjuring the various overwhelming physical images associated with the rotund Luce. As Kahn notes, S. Dromio's conception of Luce's physical presence is similar to S. Antipholus's conception of union with Adriana, as both express fear and confusion when confronted with the notion of being "engulfed."

Beyond the individual characters' perceptions, issues surrounding love and marriage are extensively presented through the portrayal of Adriana's relationship to her husband. Specifically, Shakespeare asks a question that Dorothea Kehler notes "is both timeless and peculiarly modern: can love survive marriage?" Indeed, the essence of the situation—that a discrepancy in the levels of affection expressed by husband and wife has led to alienation—has certainly been a subject of discussion ever since the notion of wedding was first conceived. In the marriage in *The Comedy of Errors*, the imbalance of love between Adriana and E. Antipholus has left Adriana feeling utterly powerless. Her husband is free to roam around and, if he so chooses, to ignore predetermined mealtimes,

TOPICS FOR FURTHER STUDY

- *The Comedy of Errors* presents a marriage in which the husband seems to prioritize business over his marital relationship, while the wife is relegated to the home. In a report, discuss the extent to which this situation is found in modern times and analyze various other ways that couples arrange their time with respect to both family and business. Use statistics, such as data from the U.S. Census, to illustrate the frequency of different arrangements: make note of how families in your community align with the statistics you find, or how they differ from the statistics.

- Read Paul's epistle to the Ephesians, which is found in the Bible. Write an essay in which you describe any similarities in theme or content between the epistle and Shakespeare's play. If possible, note ways in which abstract ideas present in the epistle are addressed in the play.

- Interestingly, Shakespeare provides almost no dialogue between the brothers Antipholus at the close of the play; the confusion is cleared, and they walk off stage. Write a brief additional scene, in verse, presenting a dialogue between the two brothers in which they discuss whatever you choose to have them discuss.

- Research laws relating to marriage and debt from Elizabethan times. In an essay, describe several Elizabethan laws of particular interest and compare and contrast them with modern American laws. Discuss whether Elizabethan laws or modern laws seem more just.

- Read any of Shakespeare's later comedies and write an essay in which you compare and contrast the play you chose with *The Comedy of Errors*. Make note of certain respects in which the play you chose seems to be superior in artistic construction to *The Comedy of Errors*, which was possibly Shakespeare's first play.

while she is relegated to simply waiting for him to arrive. Nevertheless, Kehler notes that Adriana wants nothing more than "to subjugate herself in marriage. It is her misfortune that, in a male-dominated society, the possession who becomes possessive is regarded as a shrew." Overall, Adriana and E. Antipholus's problematic situation illustrates just two of the psychological states that can be attained by a couple that has found its way into a less loving partnership than once existed.

STYLE

Comedy, from Farce to Romance

The Comedy of Errors has widely been interpreted as not just a comedy but a farce; a comedic work that features satire and a fairly improbable plot can be considered farcical. In the nineteenth century, the British poet and scholar Samuel Taylor Coleridge affirmed that the play was in fact the epitome of the genre: "Shakespeare has in this piece presented us with a legitimate farce in exactest consonance with the philosophical principles and character of farce.... A proper farce is mainly distinguished from comedy by the license allowed, and even required, in the fable, in order to produce strange and laughable situations." Coleridge goes on to note that the farce is, in a sense, enhanced by the addition of the second set of twins, the two Dromios, to the two Antipholuses; such a situation is indeed so improbable as to be virtually impossible.

A variety of other factors contribute to the perception of the play as a farce. A spectator or reader might expect S. Antipholus to deduce exactly what is going on, given that the purpose of his journey is precisely a search for his lost twin, but even when he is recognized on the street, he deduces nothing. Only his inability to understand his situation, of course, allows for the play's many other misunderstandings. Indeed, Harry Levin notes that such an abundance of "errors" can be another sign of a play's genre: "Farce derives its name from a French word for stuffing; literally it welcomes the gags and the knockabout business that fill in its contours *ad libitum* [without limit]." Barbara Freedman relates in her essay "Egeon's Debt" that a certain degree of aggression can be

another factor emblematic of farce: "Farce derives humor from normally unacceptable aggression which is made acceptable through a denial of its cause and effect." In Freedman's allegorical reading of *The Comedy of Errors*, the circumstances of the brothers Antipholus can be attributed to the guilt suffered by the father; as characters within the farce, of course, the twins can only think to inflict their aggressions on other characters—usually the brothers Dromio.

Certain aspects of the play quite distinctly link it with Shakespeare's other comedies or distinguish it from his tragedies. Freedman notes that, as Egeon's condemnation to death constitutes the introductory scene, the play begins with "the harsh world of law, the cruel and problematic reality with which so many of Shakespeare's romantic comedies commence." In turn, at the end of the play, the world of law is re-entered—as marked by the duke's carrying out his official duties—but it has been endowed with a certain degree of mercy as a result of the play's developments; here, the duke grants Egeon his freedom without accepting E. Antipholus's money. Freedman also notes that the setting bears significant resemblances to the settings in other Shakespearean plays such as *As You Like It* and *A Midsummer Night's Dream*: "The main plot's nightmarish Ephesus corresponds to the improbable, fantastic, dreamlike realm of the imagination, familiar to us as a second stage in Shakespearean comedy." A key difference, however, is that Shakespeare's other comedies feature worlds that are actually more like dreams than nightmares; *The Comedy of Errors*, on the other hand, features what Freedman terms "the imagined fulfillment of repressed fears and desires in everyday reality."

Other commentators have pointed out that the extent of character development is often directly related to genre, and *The Comedy of Errors* has in fact been widely criticized for its general absence of character development. In his introduction to the play, Harry Levin notes that serious drama is typically endowed with more emotional impact when the characterization is as comprehensive as possible, while with farce, plot often takes precedence over character. Levin goes on to describe the basis of this play's plot—everyone's repeatedly mistaking one twin for another, with masters and servants alike—as "the very essence of the farcical: two characters sufficiently alike, so that each might fit interchangeably into the other's situation, could not afford to possess distinguishing characteristics." That is, this comedy would perhaps be hobbled by too much character development.

A last aspect of the comedy worth considering is the romantic one. As Peter G. Phialas has pointed out, *The Comedy of Errors* features a number of romantic elements that will be prominent in the playwright's later comedies. Phialas highlights the fact that "Shakespeare introduces the chief structural principle of his romantic comedies: the juxtaposition of attitudes toward love and toward the ideal relationship of man and woman." These notions are explored in the present play through the pairings of Adriana and E. Antipholus and of Luciana and S. Antipholus. Phialas also articulates a more precise view of love that will be seen in more detail in Shakespeare's romantic comedies to come: "He is able here to isolate, obliquely and in the briefest compass, one of the central conceptions of those later plays: that love does not possess, that it gives without needing to receive, for it gives to another self." Thus, overall, *The Comedy of Errors*, with its interweaving of genres as effective as that of any later play, should be recognized as comedy, farce, and romance alike.

The Arrangement of Awarenesses

One aspect of *The Comedy of Errors* that distinguishes it from later Shakespearean comedies is the absence of situational understanding on the part of the play's characters. Bertrand Evans goes as far as to say that this aspect of the play is of primary importance: "With neither character nor language making notable comic contribution, then, the great resource of laughter is the exploitable gulf spread between the participants' understanding and ours." Evans notes that almost from the very beginning, the spectator is aware that the father has been condemned to death in the same city in which both of his sons, coincidentally, are present at the time; throughout the play, however, none of the characters are aware of these facts. Thus, the audience is fully aware of the play's "single great secret," while the inhabitants of the play are ignorant, and this contrast produces the majority of the play's comical interactions.

This arrangement of awarenesses among the audience and the characters, then, could not have been more basic, and Evans confirms that

it is the simplest of all of Shakespeare's plays. He notes, "In later ones our awareness is packed, often even burdened, with multiple, complex, interrelated secrets, and the many circles of individual participants' visions, though they cross and recross one another, do not wholly coincide." Shakespeare would come to use certain dramatic strategies to establish and reestablish levels of understanding among the audience and the play's characters, particularly soliloquies and asides, wherein a single character can discourse on something without revealing any secrets to any other characters. Indeed, soliloquies and asides are the literary equivalent of narrative descriptions of characters' thoughts. Evans notes that the few short soliloquies in *The Comedy of Errors* do not reveal any unknown thoughts; rather, they "exploit the speaker's ignorance of what we already know." Shakespeare would also come to habitually plant what Evans termed "practicers" within his plays; these practicers serve to subvert whatever moral or societal order exists by intentionally deceiving other characters. The characters of Iago, in *Othello*, and Rosalind, in *As You Like It*, are good examples of such practicers. In a different dramatic respect, Evans notes that in *The Comedy of Errors* Shakespeare did not even provide moments where characters come close to fully understanding the greater situation, as the playwright "risks no dialogue that strikes the unsuspected truth." In later plays, on the other hand, moments of conversational foreshadowing are not uncommon. Overall, then, the singular arrangement of awarenesses in this early play is evident in a number of ways.

The Allegory of Egeon

In terms of the direct plot, Egeon's plight seems to serve only as a framework for the rest of the play, with his tragic family story providing a background but bearing little impact on the action. That is, the plot revolves around the mere fact that one twin is in the home city of the second twin and the confusion surrounding their identities; S. Antipholus's search for his brother is mentioned only by S. Antipholus himself in a few passing asides, such that the reason for and the basic existence of the search are almost irrelevant. However, Barbara Freedman, in her essay "Egeon's Debt," has interpreted the plot as presenting an allegorical explanation of the psychic process Egeon necessarily undergoes in seeking reunion with his family.

Freedman begins by noting the various shortcomings Egeon reveals about himself in the introductory scene, when he relates his tragic story to the duke. Egeon allowed himself to be drawn away from his wife for a full six months by overseas business obligations, as his factor, or agent, had died. Evidently with no assistance from her husband, Egeon's wife then traveled to join him. After the birth of their sons, his wife alone wished to return home; Egeon agreed to go but was in fact "unwilling." Once the storm confronted them with the possibility of death, Egeon would "gladly have embraced" that death, perhaps because he was being forced into a strictly domestic situation that he did not care for. Indeed, although he tells his story in a matter-of-fact tone that leaves the reader sympathizing with his misfortune, he is at least guilty of largely neglecting his wife for the sake of his business. With this understanding of Egeon's past, the personal circumstances of the two twins seem to bear greater relevance. Freedman notes, "When the action of the storm separated Egeon from his former life, the Ephesian twin was, literally, that part of Egeon which was lost. The Syracusan twin was the part of Egeon which remained with him to the present time." Thus, in E. Antipholus the audience sees precisely the person Egeon was before the shipwreck: a man rooted in a domestic situation, respected in his community, and, generally speaking, focused more on his commercial activity than on his marital partnership. S. Antipholus, on the contrary, is a wanderer in search of his twin—in a sense, in search of his own self—just as Egeon is now wandering in search of the life he lost when he was separated from his wife.

Freedman proceeds to demonstrate that beyond the essence of the brothers' circumstances, the allegory is manifested in the play's consistent focus on indebtedness. Egeon's fate can be conceived of as featuring both a marital debt, in that he owes his wife the attention and affection that he neglected to give her, and a monetary debt, as he becomes obligated to either pay a fine for appearing in Ephesus or face the death penalty. Both sons, in turn, undergo experiences with both types of debts, in somewhat inverse manners: "Just as the Syracusan twin progresses

from fear of actual monetary debt to payment for a mistaken marital debt, so his brother moves from fear of an actual marital debt to payment for a mistaken monetary debt." Thus, in that one debt is essentially a mirror image of the other, they can together be understood as symbolic of the father's debts, just as the twins are mirror images of each other and, in the context of the allegory, are symbolic of the father. In summing up the importance of this allegory to an understanding of the play as a whole, Freedman declares, "Egeon's story is the missing link which turns an arbitrary plot into a meaningfully directed fantasy."

HISTORICAL CONTEXT

Room and Board

In general, aspects of the historical situation at the time of Shakespeare's writing his play, and the historical period in which the play takes place, bear little relation to the plot. That is, in what was quite possibly his first dramatic effort, Shakespeare seemed to have been executing a sort of exercise in farcical comedy, rather than seeking to make any political or historical statements. Nevertheless, certain aspects of *The Comedy of Errors* do seem to reflect the changing nature of Elizabethan society. One of these aspects is the significance attributed to the home, particularly by Adriana; the crux of her frustration with her husband is that he fails to fully value the home that she keeps for him. A problem for Adriana, as Ann Christensen notes, is that in Elizabethan times, "the modern bourgeois notion of home as safe haven" was not yet established. That is, Adriana was perhaps ahead of her time in seeking to insulate her home life from her husband's business dealings. Christensen eloquently describes the play's overall relevance with respect to contemporary cultural development: "*The Comedy of Errors* registers a historical moment of social transition and dislocation within the not-yet distinct public and private spheres. Forcing oppositions between desire and profit, leisure and work, women and men, Shakespeare explores contemporary anxieties attending the development of the separation of the spheres."

Christensen explicitly ties the rift between Adriana and E. Antipholus to a particular aspect of home life: "The differences between the masculine world of commerce and law and the feminine domestic environment articulate themselves over the contested cultural form of 'dining.'" Indeed, both Adriana and E. Antipholus voice concerns regarding the other's dining habits: she reminisces about the time when he only ate meat that she carved for him, while he specifically suspects that she had "feasted" with other men in his absence. In this light, the fact that E. Antipholus chooses to dine with the Courtesan after being turned away from his home can be considered a significant act of marital defiance. Christensen points to Adriana's speech at the end of act 2, scene 1—in which she speaks of "starving" at home for loving looks from her husband, while he, like a wild animal, has broken loose to "feed" elsewhere—as evidence of the primary importance attributed to the family meal. Christensen writes, "Adriana's lament for her neglect ranges fully through connotations of feeding, and suggests how crucially food-service defined the domestic on the Shakespearean stage and in early modern society."

Urbanization

Directly related to the Elizabethan conception of the home, especially around London, was the extent of England's urbanization. In general, in any society, the context in which the home exists can be understood to bear a substantial impact on the nature of the home itself. The greater the number of people living in a community of a given size, the less space each individual person will be allotted. Thus, one consequence of urbanization could be increased feelings of claustrophobia—perhaps causing some men to feel a greater need to wander around their community, rather than remaining enclosed in their allotted spaces. E. Antipholus's waywardness, then, beyond being a prioritization of business matters over domestic matters, could be interpreted as a demonstration of a masculine response to urbanization.

On the societal level, Gail Kern Paster finds a significant consequence of urbanization to be the institution of laws that, by their fixed nature, cannot discriminate among various instances of criminality. That is, a law is almost always either broken or not broken; when laws are "bent," the perpetrator, not the system of justice, typically

Lithograph of Stuart Robson and William H. Crane as Dromio of Ephesus and Dromio of Syracuse

does the bending. Paster notes that this inherent property of laws is in effect a small argument against the sheer existence of the urban environment. She states that in *The Comedy of Errors* and also in other Shakespearean plays, "The city is confronted with the self-imposed necessity of enforcing a law whose consequences are so clearly inhuman that they can only make mockery of a city's reason for being." In this instance, of course, the inhumanity is Egeon's being sentenced to death simply for being poor and for looking for his son in a town that has, unbeknownst to him, banned his presence there. In Elizabethan times, when whipping, dismemberment, and beheading were in wide and public use, the breaking of laws and the punishment of criminals were of the utmost popular interest. As such, Shakespeare's depiction of crime and unjust punishment in ancient times was perhaps intended to stress negative aspects of the ever-increasing impersonality of cities.

COMPARE
&
CONTRAST

- **200 B.C.E.:** In regions of the ancient Mediterranean Sea, villages and towns are well organized enough to feature marketplaces and bazaars, where commerce is carried out between community members.

  1600: Urbanization in the greater London area, with a population of some 200,000, has led to the rise of more crowded, chaotic marketplaces and wider varieties of businesses.

  Today: London's population has surpassed seven million, and the city dominates the economy of Great Britain.

- **200 B.C.E.:** The marketplace offers a unique union of domestic and business life, with dwellings surrounding the area, making it a central location in which societal interactions occur.

  1600: The constant emphasis of the importance of money has fostered widespread mentalities whereby business can be considered more important than domestic relationships.

  Today: In general, the alienation among peoples and nations brought about by the focus on business, money, and economic development has produced many of the world's most pressing problems, such as global warming.

- **200 B.C.E.:** As with Egeon's situation, laws allow for people to be convicted of crimes that they could not have known they were committing.

  1600: Laws are constructed with considerably more justice, but people are still often tried for crimes under questionable circumstances, such as in cases of heresy against the Church of England.

  Today: In nations such as England and the United States, legal systems are still being refined, with the existence of the death penalty in the United States, for example, being widely debated.

CRITICAL OVERVIEW

The Comedy of Errors, being one of Shakespeare's earliest efforts, is almost universally viewed as inferior to his other plays. Some critics have offered negative reviews of the work not just in relation to his later plays but also in absolute terms—calling, say, the characterization not just worse than in any other Shakespearean drama but simply bad. In the early nineteenth century the literary critic William Hazlitt, in his *Characters of Shakespear's Plays*, reflected a certain degree of annoyance with the work, declaring with respect to its source, "This comedy is taken very much from the *Menaechmi* of Plautus, and is not an improvement on it. Shakespear [sic] appears to have bestowed no great pains on it, and there are but a few passages which bear the decided stamp of his genius."

Hazlitt goes on to express the opinion that the nature of the situation—two twins being mistaken for each other—simply translates poorly into drama, as on the stage the twins will either be impossible to distinguish or so different as to shatter the illusion of their identicalness, while on the written page their characters fail to substantially distinguish themselves from each other. Hazlitt notes that Shakespeare was simply more virtuous as a creator than as an adapter: "We do not think his *forte* would ever have lain in imitating or improving on what others invented, so much as in inventing for himself, and perfecting what he invented."

Many critics have given the play a fair degree of respect. The renowned German Shakespearean scholar August Wilhelm Schlegel remarked, with regard to the comically ambitious inclusion of two sets of twins, "If the spectator is to be entertained by mere perplexities they cannot be too varied." Making reference to both actual and possible reinterpretations of Plautus's drama, Schlegel concluded (in direct opposition to Hazlitt), "This is perhaps the best of all written or possible *Menaechmi;* and if the piece be inferior in worth to other pieces of Shakespeare, it is merely because nothing more could be made of the materials." This view is directly contrary to Hazlitt's opinion of Shakespeare's artisanship, which was that the play was "not an improvement" on *Menaechmi.*

Some critics have gone as far as to bestow *The Comedy of Errors* with admiring praise. C. L. Barber argued that the presence of certain profound thematic elements cannot be ignored: "Shakespeare's sense of comedy as a moment in a larger cycle leads him to go out of his way, even in this early play, to frame farce with action which presents the weight of age and the threat of death, and to make the comic resolution a renewal of life, indeed explicitly a rebirth." T. S. Dorsch, in turn, seems to appreciate the play simply as a source of entertainment: *"The Comedy of Errors* is not only very good theatre, it is also very good reading. It is a finely-balanced mixture of pathos and suspense, illusion and delusion, love turned bitter and love that is sweet, farce and fun." In explicating the allegorical aspects of the plot, as tied to Egeon's plight, Barbara Freedman notes that many critics had reviewed the play negatively owing to their failure to "resolve two major issues central to an understanding of the play as a meaningful unity: first, the purpose of the farcical confusion of the twins' identities in the main plot, and second, its relation to their father's progress in the frame plot from separation to reunion with his family, and from crime and debt to redemption." Indeed, if these issues are not resolved, the play seems little more than a exercise in farce with a few fairly substantial themes; Freedman's explication of what is perceived as the allegorical aspects of the plot, as tied to Egeon's self-redemption, leaves the play looking far more profound.

As did Hazlitt, many critics have offered perspectives on how the presentation of the play in the theater might affect its dramatic power. The French intellectual Etienne Souriau notes that for such a farcical comedy of errors to be swallowed by the audience, the characters who "grope among the shadows and . . . play blindman's buff with their souls" are almost required to bear themselves in a very particular way: "The danger, in the theater, is to show those souls as too lucid and too sure of themselves, of what they are doing, and of their situation, rather than to show them as too wild and uncertain, proceeding by trials and errors."

CRITICISM

Philip C. Kolin

Kolin argues that The Comedy of Errors *is unusual among Shakespeare's plays because of the way in which specific locations in the play are related to the transformations of characters. The critic analyzes settings such as the Centaur Inn or the Phoenix Tavern by comparing them to Antipholus of Syracuse, his twin brother Antipholus of Ephesus, and Adriana.*

Perplexed by the maddening improbabilities in the last act of *The Comedy of Errors,* Duke Solinus pronounces what could be the topic sentence of the play: "I think you all have drunk of Circe's cup"(5.1.271). In Ephesus, Circean transformations reputedly turn men into beasts, resulting in demonic possession, the loss of self, and the breakdown of social order. Everywhere individuals lose their identity. Shakespeare incorporates Circean transformations into a strong sense of place. In fact, *The Comedy of Errors* "is unique among Shakespeare's plays in the way localities are indicated," including being marked by distinctive signs. The names for three of these locations—the Centaur Inn, the Courtesan's Porpentine, and the Phoenix, for Antipholus of Ephesus's house—symbolize the types of transformations that many of the characters undergo. Appropriately, each place is named for a mythic (or fetishistic) animal whose legacy explains a character's unnatural metamorphosis. Previous commentators have contentedly glossed these names only as specific London taverns (the Centaur, the Phoenix) or a brothel (the Porpentine). Yet on the fluid Elizabethan stage, Shakespeare contextualizes his theatrical environment within the larger mythos of metamorphosis.

Xenophobic traveler Antipholus of Syracuse will reside at the Centaur where, with his servant, "we host," and where, he trusts, "the gold I gave Dromio is laid up safe" (2.2.1–2). The name of this inn resonates with portent about Ephesus's reputation for "dark working sorcerers that change the mind / Soul-killing witches that deform the body . . . And many such-like liberties of sin"(1.2.99–102). Half-man, half-horse, the centaur was represented in Greek mythology as being "bound or ridden by Eros," embodying the lawlessness and lust (see *King Lear* 4.6.124) that ran amuck in Ephesus. Fearful of being transformed by a wizard's spell, Antipholus of Syracuse could not have chosen a more ill-advised address. Even more relevant, the history of the mythic beast signals the transformations that Antipholus himself will experience in Ephesus. (The centaurs burst upon Pirithous's marriage ceremony and carried off his bride and ravished her, earning the stigma as the despoilers of marriage.) When he is mistaken for his married twin brother Antipholus of Ephesus, Antipholus of Syracuse threatens the marital harmony between Adriana and her lawful husband, whom she locks out of his own house so that she may entertain the twin. The mythic strain of the centaurs, if not their literal intent, haunts Antipholus of Syracuse. Shakespeare asks an audience to see Antipholus as a bewitched centaur-guest. Like the centaurs, Antipholus cannot, when in Ephesus "but two hours old"(2.2.148) precisely pin down what kind of creature he is—married or single (horse or man). "What, was I married to her in my dream?...What error drives our eyes and ears amiss?"(2.2.182–84) he asks after Adriana treats him like a spouse.

Like the Centaur, the Porpentine (porcupine) is linked in *Errors* to Circean transformations into bestiality. It is to the porpentine sign of the harlot that Antipholus of Ephesus flees after Adriana refuses to admit him. Under an Ephesian spell himself, Antipholus shouts to his servant, "fetch the chain...to the Porpentine, / For there's the house—that chain will I bestow / (Be it for nothing to spite my wife) / Upon mine hostess there"(3.1.115–19). In front of the Porpentine, Antipholus, as the harlot reveals, "rushed into my house and took perforce / My ring away"(4.3.91–92) Soon thereafter, Antipholus is declared mad and summarily restrained. Famous for its barbed quills, signifiers of both tainted sex and violent aggression, the porpentine appropriately becomes the totem animal for Antipholus's transformation from lawful citizen and espoused husband into public threat and enraged cuckold. Antipholus infects his marriage when he gives away his wife's chain (a symbol of their marital bond) and steals another woman's ring, a sign of the conjugal sex act, as Gratiano realizes when at the end of *The Merchant of*

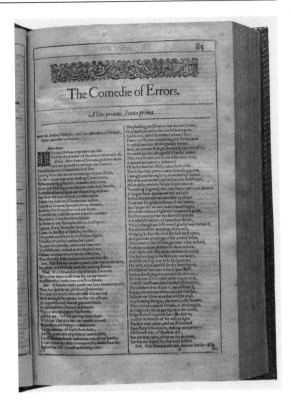

Title page of The Comedy of Errors *from the First Folio, 1623 (By permission of the Folger Shakespeare Library)*

Venice he vows that "while I live I'll fear no other thing, / So sore as keeping safe Nerissa's [his wife's] ring"(5.1.306–07).

The most evocative and sustaining reference to transformation through a symbolic animal occurs at the Phoenix, Antipholus's house, where much of acts 2 and 3 takes place and where many of the errors originate. Shakespeare often invokes the phoenix—the legendary bird that dies in its own funeral pyre, only to rise from the ashes reborn—to represent immortality through love relationships (see, for example, "Sonnet 19" and "The Phoenix and the Turtle"). R. A. Foakes limits the significance of this animal too narrowly, however, in *Errors*: "The image of this mythic bird...is appropriate to the story of Antipholus and Adriana, whose love is finally renewed out of the break-up of their marital relationship." The phoenix also augurs well for the Abbess's other son, Antipholus of Syracuse who, like his twin, at first quarrels with, but then is united with, his (intended) mate, thanks to a phoenixlike experience.

Accusing his servant of madness for claiming that their "house was at the Phoenix" (2.1.11), Antipholus of Syracuse falls in love there with Adriana's sister Luciana, of whom he asks: "Are you a god? Would you create me new / Transform me then, and to your power I'll yield" (3.2.38–40). Although Luciana is at first incredulous that Antipholus of Syracuse, whom she believes is her brother-in-law Antipholus of Ephesus, would try to court her ("What are you mad that you do reason so?" [53]), she does indeed transform him into a new creature by fulfilling his dream of marrying her (5.1.376). Like the self-perpetuating phoenix, Antipholus of Syracuse must die to the old man he was (his brother's twin), to become the new man he is (his brother's twin). This is the paradox of the phoenix myth, as well as the secret to solving the maddening confusions in *The Comedy of Errors*.

Source: Philip C. Kolin, "Shakespeare's *The Comedy of Errors*," in *The Explicator*, Vol. 56, No. 1, Fall 1997, pp. 5–8.

Russ McDonald

In the following excerpt, McDonald first surveys previous criticism on the play regarding its classification as a farce and its position in Shakespeare's canon. He notes that critics have tended to "elevate" the play above the "vulgar" level of farce in explaining its meaning (although its farcical elements are obvious) because it is sometimes perceived as a source of "embarrassment" in the canon. McDonald then examines "how meaning comes about in farce" through the play's "theatrical complexity," concluding that the play should be examined for what it is—a farce and a "source of wonder."

Zeus's sexual lapses notwithstanding, gods are not supposed to be indecorous, and a characteristic of modern Bardolatry has been its insistence on Shakespeare's artistic dignity, particularly his attachment to the approved dramatic forms. The popular image of Shakespeare as the embodiment of high culture, the author of *Hamlet* and certain other tragedies, as well as a very few weighty comedies, is merely a version of a bias that also, if less obviously, afflicts the academy. What I am talking about is a hierarchy of modes, or, to put it another way, genre snobbery. That tragedy is more profound and significant than comedy is a prejudice that manifests itself in and out of the Shakespeare

> THE MOST FAMILIAR AND PERNICIOUS TACTIC OF THOSE WHO WOULD DISSOCIATE SHAKESPEARE FROM THE VULGAR CATEGORY IS TO DISCUSS THE EARLY PLAYS AS PRECURSORS OF THE MATURE STYLE, AS SEEDBEDS, THAT IS, FOR IDEAS AND METHODS THAT WILL FLOWER IN THE LATER COMEDIES AND EVEN IN THE TRAGEDIES."

Establishment: in the impatience of undergraduates who, taking their first class in Shakespeare, regard the comedies and histories as mere appetizers to the main course, the tragedies; in Christopher Sly's equation of "a commonty" with "a Christmas gambol or a tumbling trick"; in the disdain of the tourist at the Barbican box office who, finding *Othello* sold out, refuses a ticket to *The Merry Wives of Windsor*; in the decision of that Athenian student to preserve his notes from Aristotle's lecture on tragedy but not to bother with the one on comedy.

If there is a hierarchy of modes, there is also a hierarchy within modes: *de casibus* tragedy is less exalted than Greek, for example. So it is with the kinds of comedy, and the play to which I shall address myself, *The Comedy of Errors*, rests safely in the lowest rank. Farce is at the bottom of everyone's list of forms, and yet Shakespeare is at the top of everyone's list of authors. Thus, the problem I mean to examine is generated by competing hierarchies. Most literary critics have little occasion to think about farce, and those who concern themselves chiefly with the creator of texts such as *Macbeth* and *Coriolanus* do their best to avoid the form. For many years the earliest comedies were treated unapologetically as farces and Shakespeare was praised, if mildly, for his skill at contriving such brilliant and pleasing trifles. But the need to preserve his association with higher things has led in the last three or four decades to a revision of this opinion. It seems inappropriate that the cultural monument known as Shakespeare should have anything to do with a popular entertainment that we connect with the likes of the Marx brothers (Groucho and Harpo, not Karl and Moritz). Criticism resists a Shakespeare capable of wasting his time on such a trivial form.

My purpose is to suggest that Shakespeare could be "bad," but my definition differs somewhat from those of most of the other contributors to this volume. Rather than re-examine texts that may have been overvalued or seek to locate weaknesses in dramatic technique, I shall argue that Shakespeare's taste was not invariably elevated and that certain plays are less "significant" than others (or at least that they signify different things in different ways). By addressing myself to what is and is not considered "Shakespearean," I claim an interest in one of the fundamental issues of this collection: canonicity. A work like *The Comedy of Errors* must be deformed if it is to conform to that category known as Shakespearean comedy—as a farce it is noncanonical—and such misrepresentation demands a rejoinder.

The first part of this essay surveys the evasions that critics have devised for treating Shakespeare's efforts in farce, with concentration on the dodges applied to *Errors*. The remainder, a straightforward study of that play's theatrical action, proposes to identify the playwright's strategies for the production of meaning in farce. In light of the concerns of this volume, to contend that *Errors* succeeds not as an early version of a romantic comedy or as an allegory of marriage but as an out-and-out farce is risky, for such an argument looks like yet another defense of the artistic experiments of a novice and thus seems to exemplify the very Bardolatry that many of these essays vigorously dispute. In fact, however, my aim is to establish Shakespeare's delight in and commitment to a dramatic form that has become infra dig. To recognize such a bent is to augment our sense of Shakespeare's actual range. We whitewash our subject by refusing to admit his attraction to farce and declining to explore his talent for it.

I

Suspicion of farce has fostered two main critical maneuvers, here summarized by Barbara Freedman: "The first is represented by that group of critics who know that Shakespeare never wrote anything solely to make us laugh and so argue that Shakespeare never wrote farce at all.... The more popular critical approach, however, is to agree that Shakespeare wrote

farce, but to consider *Errors* (as well as Shakespeare's other predominantly farcical plays) to be nonsensical *insofar* as they are farce." To begin with the first group, its members are undaunted by Shakespeare's demonstrable choice of classical or Italian farces for source material: in such cases he may be seen "transcending the farce which a lesser writer might have been satisfied to make," and thus the form is mentioned so that it can be dismissed.

The most familiar and pernicious tactic of those who would dissociate Shakespeare from the vulgar category is to discuss the early plays as precursors of the mature style, as seedbeds, that is, for ideas and methods that will flower in the later comedies and even in the tragedies. (In fact, hothouses would make a better simile, since the ideas and methods are found blooming in the early play itself by the time the critic finishes.) A. C. Hamilton, for example, asserts that *The Comedy of Errors* provides a foundation for the later comedies by revealing "their basis in the idea that life upon the order of nature has been disturbed and must be restored and renewed through the action of the play." Hamilton's reticence to detect inchoate forms of particular dramatic themes from later works is not shared by Peter G. Phialas, who identifies "certain features of structure and theme, and even tone, which anticipate significant elements of Shakespeare's romantic comedies." Specifically, *The Comedy of Errors*, though in the main concerned with the farcical mistakings of identity, touches briefly a theme of far greater significance, the ideal relationship of man and woman." This anticipatory practice amounts to reading the career backward: a play is conditioned by what follows it, and its distinctive qualities may be underrated or deformed. The prophetic approach tends to manifest itself in and to merge with the second defensive strategy.

Put simply, this way of thinking involves deepening the farces, exposing their profundity. It has become the preferred means of protecting Shakespeare against his own immature tastes or the vulgar demands of his audience, and it has attracted some eloquent and powerful advocates. Derek Traversi, for example, unites the two critical defenses, seeing *Errors* as both serious in itself and important in its tonal prefiguration of the later work. He emphasizes "the deliberate seriousness of the story of Aegeon, which gives the entire action a new setting of gravity, a sense of tragic overtones which, elementary though it may be in expression, is yet not without some intimation of later and finer effects." In other words, the play is profound but not too profound.

That the dignifiers succeeded some time ago in making this serious position canonical is apparent in the following passage from R. A. Foakes's Introduction to the New Arden edition, published in 1962:

> These general considerations may help to illustrate the particular quality of *The Comedy of Errors*. The play has farcical comedy, and it has fantasy, but it does more than merely provoke laughter, or release us temporarily from inhibitions and custom into a world free as a child's, affording delight and freshening us up. It also invites compassion, a measure of sympathy, and a deeper response to the disruption of social and family relationships which the action brings about. Our concern for the Antipholus twins, for Adriana and Luciana, and our sense of disorder are deepened in the context of suffering provided by the enveloping action. The comedy proves, after all, to be more than a temporary and hilarious abrogation of normality; it is, at the same time, a process in which the main characters are in some sense purged, before harmony and the responsibility of normal relationships are restored at the end. Adriana learns to overcome her jealousy, and accepts the reproof of the Abbess; her husband is punished for his anger and potential brutality by Doctor Pinch's drastic treatment; and Antipholus of Syracuse is cured of his prejudices about Ephesus. Behind them stands Egeon, a prototype of the noble sufferer or victim in later plays by Shakespeare, of Antonio in *The Merchant of Venice*, and of Pericles, central figure in a play which uses more profoundly the story on which Egeon's adventures are based.

A variation of this argument is found in Harold Brooks's much-cited essay, which associates *Errors* not with a farce such as *Supposes* but with a recognition play such as the *Ion* or *The Confidential Clerk*.

Those who see Shakespeare as "transcending" farce must consent to a divorce between the "serious" issues that they elect to stress and the main business of the play. In other words, the critics analyze delicate sentiments while the characters knock heads. The discovery of gravity requires great emphasis on the frame story of Egeon, or Adriana's matrimonial laments, or the wooing of Luciana. Brooks candidly declares the incongruity between his emphasis

and Shakespeare's: "The *Comedy* appeals first and foremost to laughter, as is obvious at any performance. I have dwelt on its serious themes and strands of romance because it is these that student and producer are prone to discount." One might respond that student and producer would in this case be taking their cue from the author, who was himself prone to discount the serious themes and strands of romance at this stage of his career. We should question critical means that seek to convert the early comedies into something other than they are.

The Comedy of Errors is a superlative example of dramatic farce, a simple form of comedy designed chiefly to make an audience laugh. Freedman points out that farces are almost always characterized by an "insistence on their own meaninglessness, an insistence which by no means should be accepted at face value." In other words, to regard the play as a highly developed form of farce is not to outlaw ideas. Mistaken identity is at the heart of *The Comedy of Errors*, as Antipholus of Syracuse explains in the final moments: "I see we still did meet each other's man, / And I was ta'en for him, and he for me, / And thereupon these errors have arose" (5.1.388–90). This basic formula is the source of pleasure and of meaning in the farcical comedy. My goal is to increase, if only slightly, our sense of how meaning comes about in farce, and my method for doing so is to concentrate on what an audience sees and hears in the main action. It seems reasonable to conclude—and worth pointing out, given the critical history of the text in question—that dramatic significance ought to proceed as much from the essential as from the ancillary features of a text.

II

To err is human, and one way of describing the imperfect condition of our experience is to say that we inhabit a state of division, of disunity, of separation from God, from nature, from one another. Lest this seem too portentous a beginning for a discussion of a farcical comedy, let me hasten to say that splitting (of ships, of families, of other human relations) is one of the most important of the play's patterns of action. In one sense, of course, the plot of *The Comedy of Errors* is founded on the natural division of twinship, for nature has split a single appearance into two persons. In the source play, Plautus exploits the confusion inherent in this division by geographically separating the Menaechmus brothers, and Shakespeare has increased the complexity of the original plot, as everyone knows, by doubling the twins. What is less familiar is his tactic of making the normal avenues of reconciliation into obstacle courses laid with traps and dead ends. Virtually all comedy represents characters' attempts to overcome their isolation through marriage or reconciliation, with farce throwing the emphasis on the amusing difficulties involved in such efforts. Marriage, systems of law, commerce, language—all these are forms of communion or institutions through which people seek or give satisfaction, social instruments and (implicitly) comic means for joining human beings in a happy and fruitful relation.

And yet, for all their value, these means are naturally imperfect and likely to collapse under various pressures, either of accident or human will or their own liability to misinterpretation. When they break down, the confusion that frustrates the characters delights the audience. To a great extent, the comedy of *Errors* arises from the number of barriers Shakespeare has erected and the ingenuity with which he has done so. The greatest obstacles arise in the principal characters' relations with their servants, in the arena of commerce, and in the realm of speech itself. Shakespeare generates amusing conflict by exaggerating the forces that separate people and by weakening the media that connect them.

The presence of four men in two costumes leads first to the attenuation of the normal bonds between servant and master and between husband and wife. From the twin Sosias in Plautus's *Amphitruo*, Shakespeare creates in the Dromios a pair of agents, go-betweens who link husband to wife or customer to merchant. They are extensions of their masters' wills, instruments by which each of the Antipholuses conducts business or gets what he wants. In the farcical world of the play, however, the will is inevitably frustrated as these servants become barriers, sources of confusion, gaps in a chain of communication. For Antipholus of Syracuse, lost in a strange, forbidden seaport, his one sure connection, his "bondman," seems to fail him. This treatment of the twin servants, moreover, is representative of Shakespeare's method with other characters, including Adriana, Luciana, and the Courtesan. Although the females are often said to contribute to the play's Pauline analysis of proper marriage, their primary value is as comic troublemakers. Adriana's eloquence and Luciana's charm make the two women memorable, to be sure, but they

are hardly complex. Adriana's main function is to doubt her husband, to rail against his neglect, to chase him in the streets, to enlist a conjurer to minister to him; Luciana's role is to attract Antipholus of Syracuse and thereby to fuel her sister's rage.

The disintegration of personal bonds is accompanied by the weakening of the multiple commercial connections. Although the thematic importance of debts is familiar enough, it is also relevant that many of the play's amusing confrontations are grounded in thwarted commercial exchanges. Ignoring the maxim that it is best to eliminate the middleman, Shakespeare has added a host of them. Angelo the Goldsmith, Balthazar, and the First and Second Merchants are all Shakespearean inventions—businessmen, literal agents who exist to get in the way. Each functions as an additional barrier separating the twin Antipholuses, as another hedge in the maze at the center of the comedy. The Second Merchant, for instance, appears only twice and exists for no other reason than to make demands and increase the comic pressure: he has been patient since Pentecost and now needs guilders for a journey; he presses Angelo to repay the sum; Angelo must seek payment from Antipholus of Ephesus who, not having received the chain for which the money is demanded, refuses to accommodate him. In short, this importunate stranger is unnecessary: Angelo might have pursued compensation on his own initiative.

In the critical rush to find "meaning" or "tonal variety" in the addition of Luciana, Egeon, and Emilia, the structural value of the lesser auxiliary figures may be overlooked. Their untimely or mistaken demands for payment increase the confusion on the stage and damage the ties that connect them to their fellow citizens. Adriana joins the line of claimants when she tries forcibly to collect the love owed her by her husband, and her vocabulary indicates that Shakespeare has established an analogy between marital responsibilities and the cash nexus.

The setting of the comedy, as the occupations of the secondary figures remind us, is mostly the street, or "the mart," and from the beginning we observe that the business of the street is business. Most of the confrontations between characters and much of the dialogue concern the physical exchange of money or property, and other personal dealings are

Forbes Masson as Dromio of Ephesus and Jonathan Slinger as Dromio of Syracuse at the Novello Theatre, London, 2005 (© *Donald Cooper/Photostage. Reproduced by permission*)

figured in financial terms. Egeon is a Syracusan trader unable to make the necessary financial exchange—a thousand marks for his freedom—and this fine or debt seems to have resulted from a protracted trade war. Many years before, after a period in which his "wealth increas'd / By prosperous voyages," Egeon had found himself separated from his wife by his "factor's death, / And the great care of goods at random left" (1.1.41–42). Now without family or funds, the insolvent businessman leaves the stage, whereupon Antipholus of Syracuse enters with an Ephesian merchant who tells him of the stranger's plight—"not being able to buy out his life"—and warns the young traveler to conceal his identity "lest that your goods too soon be confiscate." The citizen then returns Antipholus's bag of gold and pleads the need to pay a business call: "I am invited, sir, to certain merchants, / Of whom I hope to make much benefit" (1.2.24–25). He leaves Antipholus to his "own content, . . . the thing [he] cannot get."

This endearing soliloquy is usually said to prefigure the theme of self-understanding in the later comedies, but what is less often said is that

Antipholus analyzes his dilemma in terms of self-possession: he fears that in seeking to recover his family he will "lose" himself. At the end of the same scene he frets about the loss of his treasure, worrying that Dromio "is o'er-raught of all [Antipholus's] money" and recalling the city's reputation for "cozenage," "cheaters," and "mountebanks."

The bag of gold that Antipholus gives to Dromio to deliver to the inn is the first in a list of theatrical properties that provoke farcical contention. The initial dispute occurs with the entrance of Dromio of Ephesus, to whom "the money" demanded can only be the "sixpence that I had o'Wednesday last, / To pay the saddler for my mistress' crupper"; the "charge" is not a bag of gold but a command "to fetch you from the mart"; the "thousand marks" are not coins but bruises administered by master and mistress. As Antipholus of Syracuse worries about fraud, Dromio of Ephesus reports the misunderstanding to his mistress in a speech whose opposing clauses suggest the nature of the impasse: "'Tis dinner time,' quoth I; 'my gold,' quoth he." The metal becomes a metaphor at the end of the first scene of act 2, when Adriana speaks of reputation as a piece of enameled gold (2.1.109–15), and thus Shakespeare uses it to link the end of the scene with the beginning of the next: Antipholus of Syracuse enters puzzling over the bag of money, apparently not lost at all, whereupon his own Dromio enters, denies any knowledge of the recent dispute over the gold, and earns a beating. The pattern of confusion thus established with the thousand marks is repeated in squabbles over control of a chain, a ring, a dinner, a house, a spouse, a bag of ducats, a name, a prisoner, and a pair of strangers seeking sanctuary.

The vocabulary of these disputes is almost invariably the parlance of the marketplace: Antipholus of Ephesus and his business cronies politely debate the relative value of a warm welcome and a good meal ("I hold your dainties cheap, sir, and your welcome dear"); Nell "lays claim" to the Syracusan Dromio; to the Courtesan, "forty ducats is too much to lose"; the Officer cannot release Antipholus of Ephesus for fear that "the debt he owes will be required of me"; Antipholus of Ephesus is known to be "of very reverend reputation, . . . / Of credit infinite"; Dromio of Ephesus, declared mad and tied up, describes himself as "entered in bond" for Antipholus; and when the Abbess sees Egeon in act 5, she offers to "loose his bonds, / And gain a husband by his liberty." The great scene before Antipholus's house (3.1) becomes a dispute not just over property but over ownership of names and identity. In their efforts to get paid or to pay others back for wrongs suffered, characters often speak of "answering" each other:

> *Eph. Ant.* I answer you? Why should I answer you?
> *Angelo.* The money that you owe me for the chain.
> (4.1.62–63)

The merchants become enraged when their customers refuse to answer them with payment; Adriana is furious that her husband will not return a favorable answer to her requests that he come home to dinner; Antipholus of Ephesus will make his household answer for the insult of locking him out; and neither Antipholus is able to get a straight answer from either of the Dromios. This financial use of "answer" links cash to language, the most complicated and potentially ambiguous medium of all.

Exploiting the pun as the linguistic equivalent of twinship, Shakespeare creates a series of verbal equivalents for the visual duplications of the action. Initially, it seems to me, his practice is to please the audience with repeated words and images: most obviously, he develops the conflicts by ingeniously employing the language of commerce. The normal give-and-take of business activity and family life is impaired by the mistakings of the action, and when the members of the household take Antipholus of Ephesus for a troublemaker in the street, his Dromio describes him as having been "bought and sold." The "loss" of one's good name or "estimation" is risky in this world of commerce, as Balthazar explains: "For slander lives upon succession, / For ever housed where it gets possession" (3.1.105–6). Adriana's anger at her husband leads Luciana to charge her with possessiveness, and then when Antipholus of Syracuse confesses that Luciana,

> *Possessed* with such a gentle sovereign grace,
> Of such *enchanting* presence and discourse,
> Hath almost made me *traitor* to myself,
> (3.2.158–60; italics mine)

the diction of ownership ("possessions") is cleverly modulated into that of witchcraft and madness ("possession"). This ambiguity pays its most amusing dividends when Doctor Pinch attempts to exorcise the demons from Antipholus of Ephesus:

> I charge thee, Satan, hous'd within this man,
> To yield possession to my holy prayers,
> And to thy state of darkness hie thee straight;
> (4.4.52–54)

The problems of confused identity and the loss of self-control are soon compounded by the question of freedom of action. The Dromios' lives are not their own, as they reiterate in complaining that, as slaves, they are not adequately rewarded for service. These various senses of bondage—to service, to customers, to wives, to the law, to business commitments (the Second Merchant is "bound to Persia"), to a rope—reinforce each other, especially in the last two acts, as the lines of action intersect:

> *Egeon.* Most might duke, vouchsafe me speak a word.
> Haply I see a friend will save my life,
> And pay the sum that may deliver me.

Duke. Speak freely, Syracusian, what thou
  wilt.

Egeon. Is not your name, sir, called
  Antipholus?

And is not that your bondman Dromio?

Eph. Dro. Within this hour I was his bondman, sir;

But he, I thank him, gnawed in two my
  cords.

Now I am Dromio, and his man, unbound.
  (5.1.283–91)

Egeon, expecting to be set at liberty, is mistaken, bound by the limitations of his senses.
And here Dromio, the "freedman," steals from
his master the privilege of response. As mistakes
are exposed and corrected, Shakespeare relies
upon the commercial vocabulary that has served
him from the beginning: Antipholus of Syracuse
wishes "to make good" his promises to Luciana;
when Antipholus of Ephesus offers to pay his
father's line, the Duke pardons Egeon and
restores his freedom and self-control ("It shall
not need; thy father hath his life"); and the
Abbess offers to "make full satisfaction" to the
assembled company in recompense for the confusion of the day.

Words offer a way of resolving the divisions
that the play explores, but at the same time they
entail enormous possibilities for error. Given the
present critical climate, some remarks about the
unreliability of language are to be expected, but
if words are included among the other media of
exchange that Shakespeare has chosen to twist
and complicate, then such a conclusion seems
less fashionable than useful. Shakespeare almost
from the beginning expands the wrangling over
who owns what to include a series of battles over
words and their significance. The two Dromios
again offer the sharpest illustrations of such
cross-purposes, usually in their interchanges
with their masters. In the first meeting of
Antipholus of Syracuse with Dromio of
Ephesus, the shifts in meaning of "charge" and
"marks" I have already cited represent the struggle for control of meaning that underlies the
farcical action. Both servants are adept at shifting from the metaphorical to the literal:

Adr. Say, is your tardy master now at hand?
Eph. Dro. Nay, he's at two hands with me,
  and that my two ears can witness.
  (2.1.44–46)

When Antipholus of Syracuse threatens
Dromio of Syracuse, "I will beat this method in
your sconce," the servant resorts to linguistic
subversion: "Sconce call you it? so you would
leave battering, I had rather have it a head; and
you use these blows long, I must get a sconce for
my head, and insconce it too, or else I shall seek
my wit in my shoulders" (2.2.34–39).

Yet the servants can speak highly figurative
language as well: both describe the arresting
officer in metaphors so elaborate that they baffle
the auditors (4.2.32–40 and 4.3.12–30). Some of
the verbal excursions resemble vaudeville turns,
particularly the banter between the two
Syracusans on baldness, and such jests represent
verbal forms of what happens dramatically in
the main action. In showing that "there is no
time for all things," Dromio of Syracuse jestingly
disproves an indisputable axiom, just as the
errors of the main plot raise a challenge to the
reality that everyone has accepted until now.
This is more than what Brooks deprecatingly
calls "elaborations of comic rhetoric."

The struggle over what words signify quickens as the characters sense that reality is slipping
away from them. The locking-out scene (3.1)
depends for its hilarity on the stichomythic
exchanges between those outside (Dromio and
Antipholus of Ephesus) and those inside
(Dromio of Syracuse and Luce, and later
Adriana). The contestants, particularly those in
the security of the house, manipulate meanings
and even rhyme and other sounds as they taunt
the pair trying to enter, for possession of the
house is apparently an advantage in the battle
of words. The Dromios' attitudes toward language are almost always playful and subversive,
so that even at their masters' most frustrated
moments, the servants take pleasure in twisting
sound and sense, as in Dromio of Ephesus's puns
on "crow" ("crow without a feather?"; "pluck a
crow together"; and "iron crow").

The trickiness of language can cause characters to lose the direction of the dialogue:

Adr. Why, man, what is the matter?
Syr. Dro. I do not know the matter; he is
  'rested on the case.
Adr. What, is he arrested? tell me at whose
  suit?
Syr. Dro. I know not at whose suit he is
  arrested well;
But is in a suit of buff which 'rested him,
  that can I tell.

Will you send him, mistress, redemption,
   the money in his desk?
Adr. Go, fetch it, sister; this I wonder at,
Exit Luciana.
   That he unknown to me should be in debt.
Tell me, was he arrested on a band?
Syr. Dro. Not on a band, but on a stronger
   thing;
A chain, a chain, do you not hear it ring?
Adr. What, the chain?
Syr. Dro. No, no, the bell, 'tis time that I
   were gone,
It was two ere I left him, and now the clock
   strikes one.
   (4.2.41–54)

Rhetorically, the key to this passage is anta-naclasis: Dromio wrests a word from Adriana's meaning into another of its senses, as with "matter" (*trouble* and *substance*), "case" and "suit" (both meaning *case in law* and *suit of clothes*), "band" (*bond* and *ruff*). The ambiguous pronoun reference in "hear it ring" illustrates the power of words to entrap: Adriana and the audience need a moment to adjust as Dromio abruptly shifts the focus from his narrative to the present.

Just as words are apt to slip out of their familiar senses, customers or husbands or servants seem to change from moment to moment. Dialogue and stage action illustrate the limits of human control as characters try to react to these confusing turns of phrase or of event. Antipholus of Syracuse, offered a wife and a dinner, can be flexible: "I'll say as they say" (2.2.214). But words may conflict with other words and realities with other realities, as the Duke discovers in seeking the undivided truth: "You say he dined at home; the goldsmith here / Denies that saying. Sirrah, what say you?" (5.1.274–75). Conflicts of personal identity, of contracts, of words, of stories, all make the truth seem elusive and uncertain.

Shakespeare's strategy of breaking the integuments that bind human beings to one another accounts for much of the mirth in *Errors* and for much of the significance as well. By interfering with familiar and normally reliable systems of relation—master to servant, wife to husband, customer to merchant, speaker to auditor—the dramatist achieves the dislocation felt by the characters and the "spirit of weird fun" enjoyed by the audience. There is, moreover, an additional verbal medium that Shakespeare has twisted to his own use, that of

the play itself. The ironic bond between playwright and spectator, that relation which Shakespeare inherited from Plautus and cultivated throughout the first four acts and by which he assures us that we know more than the characters know, is suddenly abrogated when the Abbess declares her identity at the end of the fifth act: we have thought ourselves superior to the errors and assumptions of the ignorant characters, but we too have been deceived. Emilia's reunion with her husband and sons completes the comic movement of the action. This is farce, so the emphasis throughout is on the delights of disjunction; but this is also comedy, so the drama moves toward a restoration of human ties and the formation of new ones. Sentiment asserts itself in the final moments, of course, but Shakespeare does not overstate it, and the shift from pleasure in chaos to pleasure in order need not jar. The confusion must end somewhere, and it is standard practice for the farceur to relax the comic tension by devising a mellow ending to a period of frenzy.

Shakespeare attempted to write farce in *The Comedy of Errors*, and he succeeded. Certain effects and values are missing from this kind of drama: there is no thorough examination of characters, no great variety of tones, no profound treatment of ideas, no deep emotional engagement. But farce gives us what other dramatic forms may lack: the production of ideas through rowdy action, the pleasures of "non-significant" wordplay, freedom from the limits of credibility, mental exercise induced by the rapid tempo of the action, unrestricted laughter—the satisfactions of various kinds of extravagance. Indeed, farce may be considered the most elemental kind of theater, since the audience is encouraged to lose itself in play. This is bad Shakespeare in the sense that the young dramatist was content with an inherently limited mode; the play is not *Twelfth Night*. Its value is in its theatrical complexity. And yet the boisterous action does generate thematic issues. To admit that Shakespeare willingly devoted himself to farce is to acknowledge a side of his career too often neglected or misrepresented. That the author of *King Lear* was capable of writing *The Comedy of Errors* should be a source of wonder, not embarrassment.

Source: Russ McDonald, "Fear of Farce," in *"Bad" Shakespeare: Revaluations of the Shakespeare Canon*, edited by Maurice Charney, Fairleigh Dickinson University Press, 1988, pp. 77–89.

Robert Ornstein

In this excerpt, Ornstein briefly discusses the characters of Adriana and her sister, Luciana, both of whom he terms "sympathetically drawn intelligent women." He maintains that Adriana's expectations of her husband, Antipholus of Ephesus, are reasonable, and certainly not shrewish. He assesses Luciana as not simply a pious, moralistic woman, but rather one who "knows too much about the world to have any illusions about the way men treat women."

. . . . There is no place in the dramatic world of *Errors* for Plautus's gluttonous Parasite or for the crass Senex, who is replaced as a sounding board for the Wife's complaints by Luciana, Adriana's sister, and later by the Abbess. The presence of these sympathetically drawn intelligent women radically alters the nature of the dramatic action because Ephesus is no longer a man's world in which women exist as household scolds or harlots, but one in which men and women are equally prominent, and the latter are more interesting and fully developed as dramatic personalities. Refusing to see her marriage as simply a domestic arrangement, Adriana regards the bond between husband and wife as intrinsic as that which links father to child. Indeed, when she speaks of her oneness with Antipholus E., it is with the same metaphor that Antipholus S. uses to describe his impossible search for his brother. For her the marriage vow is like a tie of birth and blood in that her sense of self depends on her husband's love and fidelity and she feels defiled by his adultery:

> For it we two be one, and thou play false,
> I do digest the poison of thy flesh,
> Being strumpeted by thy contagion.
> (2.2.142–44)

These lines evoke the noblest Renaissance ideal of love—one soul in body twain—and do not allow us to dismiss Adriana's complaints as shrewish jealousy.

The lack of any scene in which Adriana directly confronts her erring husband is striking because her misery and insistence on the inequity of her situation give *Errors* much of its emotional ballast. First she complains to her sister, then to her husband's twin, and lastly to the Abbess, but her husband is not present to hear any of these speeches. Perhaps Shakespeare feared that any direct confrontation of husband and wife would make the other farcical misunderstandings of the play seem trivial by contrast, and he was not prepared to jettison the farcical supposes that keep his plot moving. And yet he allows Adriana to make a powerful indictment of the double standard that must affect an audience even though her speech is directed to the wrong man—her husband's twin. She protests the conventional attitudes that allow men their casual philandering but condemn an unchaste wife to her husband's pitiless revenges:

> How dearly would it touch thee to the quick,
> Shouldst thou but hear I were licentious,
> And that this body, consecrate to thee,
> By ruffian lust should be contaminate?
> Wouldst thou not spit at me, and spurn at me,
> And hurl the name of husband in my face,
> And tear the stain'd skin off my harlot brow,
> And from my false hand cut the wedding-ring,
> And break it with a deep-divorcing vow?
> (2.2.130–38)

Although some critics have suggested that Adriana alienated her husband by a jealous possessiveness, she is not the eternally suspicious comic shrew that other dramatists portray. Her manner is never strident or undignified; her requests are never unreasonable. Balthazar, a voice of sanity in the play, speaks of her "unviolated honor," of her "wisdom, / Her sober virtue, years, and modesty"—hardly the attributes of a jealous nag. The worst that Antipholus E. can say of her is that she is shrewish if he "keeps not hours"—that is, if he is not home at a reasonable time. Even Luciana, who at first accuses her sister of "self-harming jealousy," stoutly defends her against the Abbess's intimation that her shrewishness caused Antipholus E.'s derangement. Where Plautus's husband is indifferent to his wife's continual complaints, Antipholus E. seems ignorant of his wife's unhappiness and is guilty, so it seems, of insensitivity rather than habitual infidelity. He is obtuse and quick-tempered, ready to engage in a flyting match with his servants or to tear down the gate to his house with a crowbar, but he is not loutish in the manner of his Plautine counterpart. He intended to give the necklace to his wife and presents it to the Courtesan only when he is locked out of his house. Although he is familiar with the Courtesan he does not boast of her sexual favors to

"

ALTHOUGH SOME CRITICS HAVE SUGGESTED THAT ADRIANA ALIENATED HER HUSBAND BY A JEALOUS POSSESSIVENESS, SHE IS NOT THE ETERNALLY SUSPICIOUS COMIC SHREW THAT OTHER DRAMATISTS PORTRAY."

Balthazar. She is, he claims, "a wench of excellent discourse, / Pretty and witty; wild and yet, too, gentle." This circumspect description does not come from the lips of a libertine; Antipholus E. is a successful businessman who uses his wife's mistreatment of him as an excuse for a night on the town. Because he is too coarse-grained and attached to his comforts to spend years in search of a lost brother, one doubts that he would understand Adriana's ideal of marriage even if he heard her pleas.

Antipholus S. is a more interesting character who not only embarks on a hopeless quest for his twin but also demonstrates his romantic temper by falling in love with Luciana at first sight. Like many later romantic heroes he is a rapturous wooer, one who has read many sonnets and knows by heart the literary language of love, the appropriate conceits and hyperboles with which to declare a boundless passion. He protests that Luciana is "our earth's wonder, more than earth divine"; nay, she is a very deity. Like many later heroines Luciana seems wiser than the man who woos her, even though she seems at first priggish in advising her sister to accept her unhappy lot without complaint. A man is master of his liberty, she explains, and his liberty is necessarily greater than a woman's because he is the provider and must be away from the home. To this practical reason, Luciana adds the metaphysical argument that a husband is the rightful bridle of his wife's will because of his superior position in the universe. If Luciana's sermon on order and degree smells a bit of the lamp, it is nevertheless seriously offered, complete with the usual commonplaces about the hierarchy of nature that all animals recognize and obey:

Man, more divine, the master of all these,
Lord of the wide world and wild wat'ry seas,

Indu'd with intellectual sense and souls,
Of more pre-eminence than fish and fowls,
Are masters to their females, and their lords.
(2.1.20–24)

These high sentences are deflated, however, as soon as they are delivered. "This servitude," Adriana dryly responds, "makes you to keep unwed." "Not this," Luciana says, "but troubles of the marriage-bed." "Were you wedded," Adriana suggests, "you would bear some sway." Luciana's lame response is, "Ere I learn to love, I'll practice to obey," a tacit confession that she will have to school herself to the submissiveness that she claims is natural to women. When Luciana says that she would forbear a husband's wanderings, Adriana loses all patience with such pieties:

Patience unmov'd! no marvel though she
   pause [in marrying]—
They can be meek that have no other cause:
A wretched soul, bruis'd with adversity,
We bid be quiet when we hear it cry;
But were we burd'ned with like weight of pain,
As much, or more, we should ourselves
   complain.
(2.1.32–37)

Inevitably Adriana has the last word because here as elsewhere in Shakespeare's plays, platitudinous counsel and painted comforts shatter against the hard reality of suffering and anger. Moreover, Luciana is not simply a spokesman for conventional pieties; she knows too much about the world to have any illusions about the way men treat women. When Antipholus S. woos her, she is not horrified even though she thinks him Adriana's husband. Indignant at his advances, she does not, however, threaten to expose his "adulterous" (indeed, "incestuous") lust to her sister and she does not rebuff him with pious sentences. Instead she pleads with him to be circumspect in his philandering and thereby considerate of his wretched wife. She would have him be prudent if he cannot be faithful:

If you did wed my sister for her wealth,
Then for her wealth's sake use her with more
   kindness:
Or, if you like elsewhere, do it by stealth,
Muffle your false love with some show of
   blindness:
Let not my sister read it in your eye;
Be not thy tongue thy own shame's orator:
Look sweet, speak fair, become disloyalty;
Apparel vice like virtue's harbinger.
(3.2.5–12)

Peter McEnery as Antipholus of Ephesus and Henry Goodman as Dromio of Ephesus with Zoe Wanamaker as Adriana at the Royal Shakespeare Theatre, Stratford-upon-Avon, England

(© Donald Cooper/Photostage. Reproduced by permission)

On other lips this might seem Machiavellian advice, but Luciana's anger shows through her seeming acceptance of the cynical way of the world. She knows too well the emotional dependence of women on men and their willingness to deceive themselves about their marriages if their husbands will give them half a chance:

> ...make us but believe
>
> (Being compact of credit) that you love us;
>
> Though others have the arm, show us the sleeve;
>
> We in your motion turn, and you may move us.
>
> (3.2.21–24)

It is remarkable that the pathos of a woman's subservience in marriage should be made more explicit in *Errors* than any other comedy to follow. The issue is not explicitly resolved in the play, but then Shakespeare never assumes the role of social critic or reformer. On the other hand, the prominence that he allows Adriana, Luciana, and the Abbess in the denouement of *Errors* makes an important if oblique comment on the relations of women and men....

Source: Robert Ornstein, *"The Comedy of Errors,"* in *Shakespeare's Comedies*, University of Delaware Press, 1986, pp. 29–32.

W. Thomas MacCary

In the following excerpt, MacCary examines Antipholus of Syracuse from a Freudian perspective, in terms of his relationships with Adriana, Luciana, Aemilia, and Antipholus of Ephesus. MacCary notes in particular the significance of both Adriana's and Antipholus of Syracuse's use of the phrase "drop of water" in separate conversations.

... If we were to formulate a kind of comedy which would fulfill the demands associated with the pre-oedipal period, it would have many of the aspects which critics find annoying in *The Comedy of Errors*. The family would be more important than anyone outside the family, and the mother would be the most important member of the family. Security and happiness would be

I DO NOT THINK THAT MANY CRITICS TODAY WOULD LABEL *THE COMEDY OF ERRORS* A FARCE AND DISMISS IT AS DESERVING NO MORE SERIOUS ANALYSIS."

sought not in sexual intercourse with a person of the opposite sex but in reunion with or creation of a person like the person the protagonist would like to become, i.e., his alter ego, or, more correctly, his ideal ego. There would be an ambivalent attitude toward women in the play, because the young child (male) depends upon the mother for sustenance but fears being reincorporated by the mother. Such fears of the overwhelming mother might be expressed in terms of locked doors and bondage, but the positive, nurturing mother would occasion concern with feasting and drinking. There might even be ambivalent situations, such as banquets arranged by threatening women, and ambivalent symbols, such as gold rings or chains, which suggest both attraction and restriction.

How much do we want to know about the pre-oedipal period? Can we really believe that certain conceptions of happiness develop in certain stages and all later experience is related back to these? To what extent is our appreciation of comedy based on our ability to identify with its protagonists? If we answer this last question affirmatively, then we must at least consider the implications of the other two. Most of us do not have twin brothers from whom we were separated at birth, so the pattern of action in *The Comedy of Errors* cannot encourage us to identify with Antipholus of Syracuse—clearly the protagonist, as I hope to show below—on the level of superficial actuality. There must be a common denominator, and thus the action of the play must remind us, by way of structural similarity or symbolic form, of something in our own experience. If a play has universal appeal, the experience recalled is more likely to be one of childhood than not, since the earliest experiences are not only the most commonly shared, but also the most formative: what we do and have done to us as children shapes all later experience.

A good comedy "ends happily," which means it follows a pattern of action which convinces us that we can be happy. Happiness is different things at different periods in our lives, and if the argument on development is accepted, the greatest happiness is the satisfaction of our earliest desires. By this I do not mean that comedy should feed us and keep us warm, but rather that it should cause us to recapture, in our adult, intellectualized state, the sensual bliss of warmth and satiety.

I do not think that many critics today would label *The Comedy of Errors* a farce and dismiss it as deserving no more serious analysis. The patterns of farce, like all the patterns of action in drama, are appealing for some good reason. Clearly the comic pattern involving mistaken identity appeals to us because it leads us from confusion about identity—our own, of course, as well as the protagonist's—to security. The most effective version of that pattern would be that which presents to us our own fears and then assuages them, so it must speak to us in language and action which can arouse memory traces of our own actual experience of a search for identity. While it is true that this search goes on throughout the "normal" man's life, it is most intense in the early years. When Antipholus of Syracuse likens himself to a drop of water in danger of being lost in the ocean, he speaks to us in terms which are frighteningly real:

> He that commends me to mine own content
> Commends me to the thing I cannot get.
> I to the world am like a drop of water
> That in the ocean seeks another drop,
> Who, falling there to find his fellow forth,
> Unseen, inquisitive, confounds himself.
> So I, to find a mother and a brother,
> In quest of them, unhappy, lose myself.
> (I. ii. 33–40)

The image is based on a proverbial expression in Plautus' *Menaechmi*: "neque aqua aquae nec lacte lactis, crede me, usquam similius / quam hic tui est, tuque huius autem" ("water is not to water, nor milk to milk, as like as she is to you and you are to her") (1089–90). From a purely physical comparison, Shakespeare has developed a metaphysical conceit which has vast philosophical implications, but its immediate impact is emotional. The plight of the protagonist is felt almost physically, his yearning for his double accepted as natural and inevitable. Water itself is the most frequent dream symbol for birth, and with the mention of the mother and brother, we are set firmly in the child's world. The brother, in our own experience, is not a brother, but another self, the ideal ego which the mother first creates for us and we strive to assimilate. We are reminded of the Narcissus myth, since water can reflect as well as absorb, and Antipholus of Syracuse seeks himself in his mirror image. The water here, as ocean, is the overwhelming aspect of the mother, the mother from whom the child cannot differentiate himself. She projects to us the image of what we shall become; but it is a fragile image, and if we lose it we risk reintegration with her, reabsorption, a reversal of the process of individuation which we suffer from the sixth to the eighteenth month. Only later, when we have developed a sense of alterity, can we distinguish ourselves from the mother, and her image of us from ourselves.

Plautus, of course, does not frame his comedy of twins with a family romance the way Shakespeare does. Neither mother nor father appears; there is not even any serious romantic involvement for either twin. In fact, the negative attitude toward marriage which spreads through Shakespeare's play derives from Plautus', where the local twin lies to his wife and steals from her, and finally deserts her entirely to go home with his brother. As Shakespeare expands the cast and develops themes only implicit in the *Menaechmi*, he provides a complete view of the relation between man and wife and clearly indicates the preparation for this relation in the male child's attitude toward the mother. In Plautus we have only one set of doubles, the twins themselves, but Shakespeare gives us two more sets: the twin slaves Dromio and the sisters Adriana and Luciana. We see these women almost entirely through the eyes of Antipholus of Syracuse, our focus of attention in the play. From his first speech onwards it is from his point of view we see the action, and the occasional scene involving his brother serves only as background to his quest: he is the active one, the seeker. We meet the two sisters before he does, in their debate on jealousy, and then when he encounters them, our original impressions are confirmed. They are the dark woman (Adriana, *atro*) and the fair maid (Luciana, *luce*) we meet with so frequently in literature, comprising the split image of the mother, the one threatening and restrictive, the other yielding and benevolent. The whole atmosphere of the play, with its exotic setting and dreamlike action, prepares us for the epiphany of the good mother in Luciana, the bad mother in Adriana. Antipholus of Syracuse, who seems to have found no time for, or shown no interest in, women previously, is entranced and wonders that Adriana can speak to him so familiarly:

> To me she speaks. She moves me for her
> theme.
> What, was I married to her in my dream?
> Or sleep I now, and think I hear all this?
> What error drives our eyes and ears amiss?
> (II. ii. 183–86)

The extraordinary aspect of his reaction, though quite natural in the context of the play's system of transferences, is that he should take for his dream the strange woman's reality: in other circumstances we might expect him to say that she is dreaming and has never really met him, but he says instead that perhaps he had a dream of her as his wife which was real. She is, then, strange in claiming intimacy with him, but not entirely unknown: she is a dream image, and he goes on to question his present state of consciousness and sanity:

> Am I in earth, in Heaven, or in Hell?
> Sleeping or waking? Mad or well advised?
> Known unto these, and to myself disguised!
> (II. ii. 214–16)

If these women were completely alien to him, had he no prior experience of them in any form, then he could have dismissed them and their claims upon him. As it is, he doubts not their sanity but his own, and wonders whether he dreams or wakes as they persist in their entreaties, suggesting he has dreamed of them before, and not without some agitation.

The exact words of Adriana's address which creates this bewilderment are, of course, very like his own opening remarks. She seems to know his mind exactly, and this makes her even more familiar to him though strange in fact. She takes his comparison of himself to a drop of water and turns it into a definition of married love; this, then, is sufficient to drive him to distraction:

> How comes it now, my Husband, oh, how
> comes it
> That thou art then estrangòd from thyself?
> Thyself I call it. being strange to me,
> That, undividable, incorporate,
> Am better than thy dear self's better part.

Ah, do not tear away thyself from me!
For know, my love, as easy mayst thou fall
A drop of water in the breaking gulf
And take unmingled thence that drop again,
Without addition or diminishing,
As take from me thyself, and not me too.
(II. ii. 121–31)

Most critics would acknowledge the central position of these two passages in the argument of the play, but they do not account for their effectiveness. The impact of the repetition is due to the reversal of the protagonist's expectations. He came seeking his mirror image, like Narcissus, his ideal ego, his mother's image of himself, and finds instead a woman who claims to be part of himself; and she threatens him with that absorption and lack of identity which he had so feared: she is the overwhelming mother who refuses to shape his identity but keeps him as part of herself. In his speech he was the drop of water; in her speech the drop of water is let fall as an analogy, but he becomes again that drop of water and flees from the woman who would quite literally engulf him.

He flees, of course, to the arms of the benign Luciana, she who had warned her sister to restrain her jealousy and possessiveness, to allow her husband some freedom lest she lose him altogether. This unthreatening, undemanding woman attracts Antipholus of Syracuse, and he makes love to her in terms which recall the two drop of water speeches:

> *Luc.* What, are you mad, that you do reason so?
>
> *Ant. S.* Not mad, but mated; how, I do not know.
>
> *Luc.* It is a fault that springeth from your eye.
>
> *Ant. S.* For gazing on your beams, fair sun, being by.
>
> *Luc.* Gaze where you should, and that will clear your sight.
>
> *Ant. S.* As good to wink, sweet love, as look on night.
>
> *Luc.* Why call you me love? Call my sister so.
>
> *Ant. S.* Thy sister's sister.
>
> *Luc.* That's my sister.
>
> *Ant. S.* No,
> It is thyself, my own self's better part,
> Mine eye's clear eye, my dear heart's dearer heart,
> My food, my fortune, and my sweet hope's aim,

My sole earth's Heaven, and my Heaven's claim.
(III. ii. 53–64)

There is as much difference between Adriana and Luciana as between night and day: Adriana is the absence or perversion of all that is good in Luciana. It is not the difference between dark women and fair women we find in the other comedies—Julia and Sylvia in *Two Gentlemen of Verona*, Helena and Hermia in *Midsummer Night's Dream*—but much more like the difference in the *Sonnets* between the dark lady and the fair youth: on the one side we have all that is threatening and corruptive, while on the other there is truth and beauty. Again, all is a dream: Antipholus of Syracuse has seen Luciana before, in dreams, in madness, but then she was indistinguishable from Adriana, the two opposites bound up as one. Now, as if by the dream mechanism of decomposition they are separate, and he can love the one and avoid the other. He has overcome his fear of the overwhelming mother and projects now his image of the benevolent mother upon Luciana.

The relation between these two young women and Aemilia, the actual mother of Antipholus of Syracuse, becomes clear in the climactic scene. He has been given sanctuary in the priory, after having been locked up by Adriana and escaping her; Aemilia emerges, like the vision of some goddess, to settle all confusion. Her attention focuses on Adriana, and she upbraids her son's wife for the mistreatment she has given him. It is a tirade not unlike others in early Shakespearean comedy against the concept of equality and intimacy in marriage. We hear it from Katharina at the end of *The Taming of the Shrew*, and we see Proteus fleeing from such a marriage in *Two Gentlemen of Verona*, as do all the male courtiers in *Love's Labor's Lost*. In the later romances this antagonism between the man who would be free and the woman who would bind him home is equally apparent and more bitterly portrayed; e.g., Portia's possessiveness in *The Merchant of Venice* and Helena's pursuit of Betram in *All's Well*. The identification of the threatening woman with the mother in the man's eyes is developed to varying degrees in these different instances—the maternal aspect of Portia is remarkable, as are Helena's close ties to the Countess—but here it is transparent: Aemilia must instruct her daughter-in-law on the proper treatment of her son, and we see this through the eyes of Antipholus of Syracuse: he has finally been able to conquer his fear of losing his identity in his mother's too close embrace because she herself tells him that this is no way for a woman to treat him:

> The venom clamors of a jealous woman
> Poisons more deadly than a mad dog's tooth.
> It seems his sleeps were hindered by thy railing,
> And thereof comes it that his head is light.
> Thou say'st his meat was sauced with thy
> upbraidings;
> Unquiet meals make ill digestions.
> Thereof the raging fire of fever bred,
> And what's a fever but a fit of madness?
> Thou say'st his sports were hindered by thy
> brawls.
> Sweet recreation barred, what doth ensue
> But moody and dull Melancholy,
> Kinsman to grim and comfortless Despair,
> And at her heels a huge infectious troop
> Of pale distemperatures and foes to life.
> (V. i. 69–82)

This description of madness reminds us of the mythical monsters Harpies, Gorgons, and Furies—all female, like Shakespeare's Melancholy and Despair—bitchlike creatures who hound men to madness. Clearly this entire race is a projection of male fears of female domination, and their blood-sucking, enervating, food-polluting, petrifying attacks are all related to pre-oedipal fantasies of maternal deprivation. By identifying this aspect of the mother in Adriana, he can neutralize it. Antipholus of Syracuse, then, finds simultaneously the two sexual objects Freud tells us we all originally have: his own benevolent and protective mother and the image of himself in his brother he has narcissistically pursued....

Source: W. Thomas MacCary, "*The Comedy of Errors*: A Different Kind of Comedy," in *New Literary History*, Vol. 9, No. 3, Spring, 1978, pp. 528–34.

SOURCES

Arthos, John, "Shakespeare's Transformation of Plautus," in *Comparative Drama*, Vol. 1, No. 4, Winter 1967–68, pp. 239–53.

Baker, Susan, "Status and Space in *The Comedy of Errors*," in *Shakespeare Bulletin*, Vol. 8, No. 2, Spring 1990, pp. 6–8.

Barber, C. L., "Shakespearian Comedy in *The Comedy of Errors*," in *College English*, Vol. 25, April 1964, pp. 493–97.

Barton, Anne, "The Comedy of Errors," in *The Riverside Shakespeare*, edited by J. J. M. Tobin, Herschel Baker, and G. Blakemore Evans, Houghton Mifflin Company, 1997, pp. 79–82.

Berry, Ralph, "'And here we wander in illusions,'" in *Shakespeare's Comedies: Explorations in Form*, Princeton University Press, 1972, pp. 24–39.

Bevington, David, "Introduction," in *The Comedy of Errors*, by William Shakespeare, Bantam Books, 1988, pp. xvii–xxiii.

Brooks, Charles, "Shakespeare's Romantic Shrews," in *Shakespeare Quarterly*, Vol. 11, No. 3, Summer 1960, pp. 351–56.

Bullough, Geoffrey, "Introduction," in *Narrative and Dramatic Sources of Shakespeare*, edited by Geoffrey Bullough, Columbia University Press, 1957, pp. 3–11.

Caroll, William C., "'To Be and Not To Be': *The Comedy of Errors* and *Twelfth Night*," in *The Metamorphoses of Shakespearean Comedy*, Princeton University Press, 1985, pp. 67–79.

Charney, Maurice, "*The Comedy of Errors*," in *All of Shakespeare*, Columbia University Press, 1993, pp. 3–10.

Christensen, Ann C., "'Because their business still lies out a' door': Resisting the Separation of Spheres in Shakespeare's *The Comedy of Errors*," in *Literature and History*, 3rd series, Vol. 5, No. 1, Spring 1996, pp. 19–37.

Coleridge, Samuel Taylor, *Shakespearean Criticism*, 2nd ed., 2 vols., edited by Thomas Middleton Raysor, E. P. Dutton and Company, 1960.

Crewe, Jonathan V., "God or the Good Physician: The Rational Playwright in *The Comedy of Errors*," in *Genre*, Vol. 15, Nos. 1–2, Spring/Summer 1982, pp. 203–23.

Cutts, John P., "*The Comedy of Errors*," in *The Shattered Glass: A Dramatic Pattern in Shakespeare's Early Plays*, Wayne State University Press, 1968, pp. 13–21.

Dorsch, T. S., "Introduction," in *The Comedy of Errors*, by William Shakespeare, Cambridge University Press, 1988, pp. 12–8.

Elliott, G. R., "Weirdness in *The Comedy of Errors*," *University of Toronto Quarterly*, Vol. 9, No. 1, October 1939, pp. 95–106.

Evans, Bertrand, *Shakespeare's Comedies*, Clarendon Press, 1960.

Felheim, Marvin, and Philip Traci, "*The Comedy of Errors*," in *Realism in Shakespeare's Romantic Comedies: "Oh Heavenly Mingle,"* University Press of America, 1980, pp. 13–28.

Foakes, R. A., "Introduction," in *The Comedy of Errors*, by William Shakespeare, Methuen & Co., 1962, pp. xi–lv.

Freedman, Barbara, "Egeon's Debt: Self-Division and Self-Redemption in *The Comedy of Errors*," in *English Literary Renaissance*, Vol. 10, No. 3, Autumn 1980, pp. 360–83.

———, "Errors in Comedy: A Psychoanalytic Theory of Farce," in *Shakespearean Comedy*, edited by Maurice Charney, New York Literary Forum, 1980, pp. 233–43.

———, "Reading Errantly: Misrecognition and the Uncanny in *The Comedy of Errors*," in *Staging the Gaze: Postmodernism, Psychoanalysis, and Shakespearean Comedy*, Cornell University Press, 1991, pp. 78–113.

French, Marilyn, "Marriage: *The Comedy of Errors*," in *Shakespeare's Division of Experience*, Summit Books, 1981, pp. 77–81.

Garton, Charles, "Centaurs, the Sea, and *The Comedy of Errors*," in *Arethusa*, Vol. 12, No. 2, Fall 1979, pp. 233–54.

Girard, René, "Comedies of Errors: Plautus—Shakespeare—Molière," in *American Criticism in the Poststructuralist Age*, edited by Ira Konigsberg, University of Michigan Press, 1981, pp. 66–86.

Greenblatt, Stephen, "*The Comedy of Errors*," in *The Norton Shakespeare*, edited by Stephen Greenblatt, W. W. Norton & Company, 1997, pp. 683–89.

Hamilton, A. C., "The Early Comedies: *The Comedy of Errors*," in *The Early Shakespeare*, The Huntington Library, 1967, pp. 90–108.

Hasler, Jörg, "*The Comedy of Errors*," in *Shakespeare's Theatrical Notation: The Comedies*, A. Francke AG Verlag, 1974, pp. 132–34.

Hazlitt, William, *Characters of Shakespear's Plays*, 2nd ed., Taylor & Hessey, 1818.

Hennings, Thomas P., "The Anglican Doctrine of the Affectionate Marriage in *The Comedy of Errors*," in *Modern Language Quarterly*, Vol. 47, No. 2, June 1986, pp. 91–107.

Huston, J. Dennis, "Playing with Discontinuity: Mistakings and Mistimings in *The Comedy of Errors*," in *Shakespeare's Comedies of Play*, Columbia University Press, 1981, pp. 14–34.

Jardine, Lisa, "'As boys and women are for the most part cattle of this colour': Female Roles and Elizabethan Eroticism," in *Still Harping on Daughters: Women and Drama in the Age of Shakespeare*, Harvester Press, 1983, pp. 44–6.

Kahn, Coppélia, "Identity in *The Comedy of Errors*," in *Man's Estate: Masculine Identity in Shakespeare*, University of California Press, 1981, pp. 199–205.

Kehler, Dorothea, "*The Comedy of Errors* as Problem Comedy," in *Rocky Mountain Review of Language & Literature*, Vol. 41, No. 4, 1987, pp. 230–36.

Lanier, Douglas, "'Stigmatical in Making': The Material Character of *The Comedy of Errors*," in *English Literary Renaissance*, Vol. 23, No. 1, Winter 1993, pp. 81–112.

Levin, Harry, "Introduction," in *The Comedy of Errors*, by William Shakespeare, Signet Classic, 2002, pp. lxiii–lxxvii.

———, "*The Comedy of Errors* on Stage and Screen," in *The Comedy of Errors*, by William Shakespeare, Signet Classic, 2002, pp. 143–59.

———, "Two Comedies of Errors," in *Refractions: Essays in Comparative Literature*, Oxford University Press, 1966, pp. 128–50.

Macdonald, Ronald R., "*The Comedy of Errors*: After So Long Grief, Such Nativity," in *William Shakespeare: The Comedies*, Twayne Publishers, 1992, pp. 1–13.

Maguire, Laurie, "The Girls from Ephesus," in *"The Comedy of Errors": Critical Essays*, edited by Robert Miola, Garland, 1997, pp. 355–91.

Miola, Robert S., "The Play and the Critics," in *"The Comedy of Errors": Critical Essays*, edited by Robert Miola, Garland, 1997, pp. 3–38.

Muir, Kenneth, "*The Comedy of Errors*," in *Shakespeare's Comic Sequence*, Liverpool University Press, 1979, pp. 15–22.

O'Brien, Robert Viking, "The Madness of Syracusan Antipholus," in *Early Modern Literary Studies*, Vol. 2, No. 1, 1996, pp. 1–26.

Parker, Patricia, "Elder and Younger: The Opening Scene of *The Comedy of Errors*," in *Shakespeare Quarterly*, Vol. 34, No. 3, Autumn 1983, pp. 325–27.

Parrott, Thomas Marc, "Apprentice Work: *The Comedy of Errors*," in *Shakespearean Comedy*, Oxford University Press, 1949, pp. 100–08.

Paster, Gail Kern, "The Nature of Our People: Shakespeare's City Comedies," in *The Idea of the City in the Age of Shakespeare*, University of Georgia Press, 1985, pp. 178–219.

Pettet, E. C. "Shakespeare's 'Romantic' Comedies," in *Shakespeare and the Romantic Tradition*, Haskell House Publishers, 1976, pp. 67–100.

Phialas, Peter G. "*The Comedy of Errors*," in *Shakespeare's Romantic Comedies: The Development of Their Form and Meaning*, University of North Carolina Press, 1966, pp. 10–7.

Salgado, Gamini, "'Time's Deformed Hand': Sequence, Consequence, and Inconsequence in *The Comedy of Errors*," in *Shakespeare Survey*, Vol. 25, 1972, pp. 81–91.

Schlegel, August Wilhelm, *Lectures on Dramatic Art and Literature*, translated by John Black, George Bell & Sons, 1889.

Shakespeare, William, *The Comedy of Errors*, Signet Classic, 2002.

Shaw, Catherine M., "The Conscious Art of *The Comedy of Errors*," in *Shakespearean Comedy*, edited by Maurice Charney, New York Literary Forum, 1980, pp. 17–28.

Slights, Camille Wells, "Time's Debt to Season: *The Comedy of Errors*, IV.ii.58," in *English Language Notes*, Vol. 24, No. 1, September 1986, pp. 22–5.

Smidt, Kristian, "Comedy of Errors?" in *Unconformities in Shakespeare's Early Comedies*, Macmillan, 1986, pp. 26–38.

Souriau, Etienne, "From *The Two Hundred Thousand Dramatic Situations*," translated by Harry Levin, in *The Comedy of Errors*, by William Shakespeare, Signet Classic, 2002.

Thompson, Ann, "'Errors' and 'Labors': Feminism and Early Shakespearean Comedy," in *Shakespeare's Sweet Thunder: Essays on the Early Comedies*, edited by Michael J. Collins, University of Delaware Press, 1997, pp. 90–101.

Vaughn, Jack A., "*The Comedy of Errors*," in *Shakespeare's Comedies*, Frederick Ungar Publishing Co., 1980, pp. 12–21.

Von Rosador, K. Tetzeli, "Plotting the Early Comedies: *The Comedy of Errors, Love's Labour's Lost, The Two Gentlemen of Verona*," in *Shakespeare Survey*, Vol. 37, 1984, pp. 13–22.

Weller, Barry, "Identity and Representation in Shakespeare," in *English Literary History*, Vol. 49, No. 2, Summer 1982, pp. 345–46.

Wells, Stanley, "Comedies of Verona, Padua, Ephesus, France, and Athens," in *Shakespeare: A Life in Drama*, W. W. Norton & Company, 1995, pp. 52–7.

Williams, Gwyn, "*The Comedy of Errors* Rescued from Tragedy," in *A Review of English Literature*, Vol. 5, No. 4, October 1964, pp. 63–71.

FURTHER READING

Davis, Jessica Milner, *Farce*, Transaction Publishers, 2002.
    Davis provides a detailed study of the literary genre of the farce, examining characterization, plot, and general themes used in various farces throughout history.

Duckworth, George Eckel, *The Nature of Roman Comedy: A Study in Popular Entertainment*, University of Oklahoma Press, 1994.
    Duckworth provides a comprehensive, academic treatment of the development of drama in ancient Rome, addressing the works of Plautus, including *Menaechmi*, among many other authors.

Short, John, and Yeong Hyun Kim, *Globalization and the City*, Longman, 1999.
    This work examines the impact of widespread urbanization in the modern era, discussing the topic in the context of globalization and the intermixing of cultures.

Wright, Lawrence, *Twins: And What They Tell Us about Who We Are*, Wiley, 1999.
    In this well-researched work, Wright discusses a wide variety of aspects of twinhood, from historical cultural perceptions of twins to modern psychological studies examining the way twins interact and relate to each other.

Coriolanus

1607

There is no record of when *Coriolanus* was first performed. Nor is there solid evidence of its date of composition, but 1607 or 1608 are the dates generally accepted by scholars since there seem to be echoes of some phrases from the play in Ben Jonson's *Epicoene; or, The Silent Woman* (1609). Menenius's parable of the belly is probably derived from a work published in 1605, William Camden's *Remaines of a Greater Work Concerning Britain*. The plebeians' insurrection suggests the English Midland riots of 1607 by the English peasantry against a food shortage and the practice of enclosure, whereby common lands were being removed from common ownership by the aristocracy. The style of *Coriolanus* also suggests a late date in Shakespeare's career. The composition date leads scholars to surmise that the play was also performed around the time it was written, although there are no records, since plays were written so that acting companies could have material to perform.

Coriolanus first appeared in print in the 1623 Folio edition published by John Hemminges and Henry Condell; these two fellows in Shakespeare's acting company published the folio as a memorial tribute to Shakespeare. The text is believed to have been set from Shakespeare's manuscript, with more complete stage directions, supposedly by Shakespeare himself, than most of his plays have. *Coriolanus* seems to be a good text, which is marred, however, by a number of printer's errors.

The primary source for *Coriolanus* is Sir Thomas North's translation of Plutarch's *Lives of the Noble Grecians and Romans*, which was first published in 1579. It is believed that Shakespeare also consulted Livy's *Roman History* in a translation by Philemon Holland published in 1600. While Shakespeare altered, added to, subtracted from, and reshaped Plutarch's tale significantly, there are notable passages in which Shakespeare's language and North's are remarkably similar, as in the following example. Here is a small section of North's translation of Plutarch's account of Volumnia's petition to her son: "Thou shalt see, my son, and trust unto it, thou shalt no sooner march forward to assault thy country, but thy foot shall tread upon thy mother's womb that brought thee first into this world." Here is Shakespeare's adaptation;

> thou shalt no sooner
> March to assault thy country than to tread
> (Trust to 't, thou shalt not) on thy mother's
>   womb
> That brought thee to this world.

As the last of Shakespeare's tragedies, *Coriolanus* is always esteemed but, perhaps because it is a political play, or perhaps because of its protagonist's bristly disposition, or perhaps because of the austerity of its verse, it is not loved as are the great tragedies which preceded it, or the miraculous romances which follow it.

PLOT SUMMARY

Act 1, Scene 1

Coriolanus opens with a revolt of the plebeians in ancient Rome. They are out in the streets shouting for bread and the death of Caius Marcius, whom they blame for being the cause of their suffering. They accuse the patricians, members of the upper class, of hoarding the grain for themselves. The plebeians say that the patricians do nothing and thrive while they, the workers, starve. As they talk among themselves, the plebeians acknowledge that Marcius has fought for Rome and distinguished himself in the wars. But, they add, it was done out of pride and for his mother. As they are about to go to join another contingent of aroused citizens, Menenius encounters them and stops to talk with them. He is a patrician who is pleased to argue with the plebeians and instruct them. In response

to their complaints, he first tells them that the patricians do take care of them and that they ought to rebel against the heavens regarding the scarcity of bread, not against the patricians. Then he tells them a story about the time the other parts of the body rebelled against the belly, complaining that the belly remained idle in the midst of the body, hoarding food, while the other members of the body worked and it did nothing. The belly responded, Menenius tells them, that it was not so, that the belly stored all the food and then distributed it to the other organs of the body through the rivers of the blood stream, keeping only the waste. Menenius explains that his story is a parable. The patricians represent the belly and the people, the parts of the body. He insultingly calls one of the leaders of the group "the great toe of this assembly."

As Menenius is reproaching them for revolting, Marcius enters. His first words are provocations to the citizens. He calls them "dissentious rogues" and "scabs." When one of them observes ironically that they "have ever your good word," he retorts that anyone who speaks well to them is a terrible flatterer. He calls them dogs, neither fit for peace nor war, unreliable and untrustworthy, worthy only of being hated. At the end of his harangue he asks Menenius what they want. Grain at an affordable price, Menenius tells him. Marcius is moved again to fury, belittles the people and concludes by saying he wishes the Roman Senate would give him permission to slaughter them by the thousands. Menenius attempts to calm his rage, noting that he had almost subdued the wrath of the people but Marcius re-enflamed it by his rhetoric. Menenius then asks Marcius what the crowds are doing in other parts of the city. Marcius reports that they have broken up, having won some concessions from the patricians, particularly, the appointment of five tribunes to represent them. The two that Marcius recalls, and the only tribunes who appear in *Coriolanus* are Junius Brutus and Sicinius Velutus. Scornfully, Marcius orders the people to get out of the street and go home.

In the midst of this turmoil a messenger from the Senate enters reporting that the Volsces, enemies of Rome, are in arms and preparing to attack. Marcius is excited and begins to speak of Aufidius, the leader of the Volscians, a rival soldier Marcius admires, with whom he has often fought and with whom he longs to fight again. Marcius compares Aufidius to a lion he is proud to hunt. The Senate then orders Marcius to join the Roman general, Cominius, in the war. The soldiers and the senators exit in martial joy leaving the two tribunes, Sicinius and Brutus alone. They comment on Marcius's pride and call him insolent. They are concerned, moreover, that the present war will bring out even greater superciliousness in Marcius.

Act 1, Scene 2

The scene shifts to Corioles, the capital city of the Volsces, where Aufidius and some senators are discussing intelligence briefings. They have determined that the Romans know that they are ready to attack, that there has been a popular uprising in Rome, and that Marcius and Cominius are leading an army, no doubt, toward Corioli. Aufidius maps out his strategy and shows himself to be just as eager to encounter Marcius in a fight to the death as Marcius has said he was to fight with Aufidius.

Act 1, Scene 3

In Rome, in Marcius's house, Volumnia, Marcius's mother, is urging Virgilia, his wife, not to be gloomy because her husband is away at war but to be cheerful. Volumnia tells Virgilia of the joy she felt the first time Marcius returned from war a hero. Rather than being excited by heroism, Virgilia expresses her anxiety over the possibility of his death. But Volumnia responds that her dead son's good reputation would have replaced her son for her, that she would be proud to have her son die for his country. Valeria is announced. Virgilia asks permission to withdraw rather than entertain a visitor. Volumnia refuses and paints a picture of Marcius in battle, reveling in describing him wounded and bleeding. When Virgilia protests, Volumnia dismisses her as a fool; she glorifies bloody warfare over maternal tenderness and predicts that Marcius will vanquish Aufidius.

When Valeria joins them, the conversation turns to how much like his father Marcius's son is. Valeria describes how she saw him clamp his teeth in rage a few days earlier as he tore apart a butterfly. The women try to persuade Virgilia to lay aside her embroidery and go outside with them, but she refuses any exercise or amusement until her husband returns safely from the war. Valeria cajoles her with news that Marcius and Titus Lartius are camped outside the gates of Corioles and feel sure of victory. Virgilia insists on remaining at home as Volumnia and Valeria depart.

Act 1, Scene 4

Not far outside the gates of Corioles, Marcius, Titus Lartius and the soldiers they command are camped. Marcius bets Titus Lartius that the Roman and Volscian forces have already joined in battle. He loses his horse in the bet when a messenger informs them the armies are in view of each other but the battle has not yet been joined. Volscian troops pour out of the gates of Corioli and beat the Roman soldiers back to their trenches. Enraged, Marcius follows the Volsces back into Corioles and is locked inside with them. As the leaders of the Roman forces grieve over him and speak tribute to his memory, expecting him to have been slaughtered, Marcius appears at the gates, bleeding and being assaulted by the enemy. The Roman forces led by him charge the gates, enter the city, and rout the Volsces.

Act 1, Scene 5

Inside Corioles, Marcius curses the soldiers who are looting the city before the battle is completely won. Marcius, on the other hand sets out to join Cominius's forces and to continue fighting. Lartius tells him to rest since he is bleeding and has fought hard already. Marcius rejects both his advice and the praise implicit in it, saying he has hardly warmed to his work and longs to find Aufidius and battle with him.

Act 1, Scene 6

Cominius is congratulating his troops on having fought well, but warns them that the Volsces will attack them again. A messenger arrives and reports that the Volsces have driven Marcius and Lartius's troops back to their trenches. When Marcius enters bloody but victorious from the last battle, disdaining the poor fighting of the common soldiers, however, Cominius understands that the messenger reported old news. Cominius informs Marcius that his troops are retrenching after an indecisive battle with the Volscians. Marcius requests a division of men to seek Aufidius. By his heroic presence and his rousing words, Marcius inspires a courageous battalion of soldiers to join him, and they go off to battle.

Act 1, Scene 7

Lartius prepares his troops for battle in the field.

Act 1, Scene 8

Marcius and Aufidius encounter each other on the battlefield. They exchange words of hate and fight. During the fight, several Volscians come to the assistance of Aufidius. Alone, Marcius drives them all off, including Aufidius, and then laments that Aufidius has shamed and betrayed him, Marcius, by not fighting man to man.

Act 1, Scene 9

Victorious, the Romans assemble at their camp where Cominius pays tribute to Marcius's valor in battle, insisting on praising him as Marcius shuns the commendations. When Cominius awards him a tenth of all the spoils of war taken from the wealth of defeated Corioles, Marcius refuses it, calling rewards a bribe and flattery. Cominius tells him he is too modest, and, in honor of how he fought at Corioles, confers the additional name of Coriolanus on him. He becomes Caius Marcius Coriolanus. When they are alone, Coriolanus tells Cominius that he must embarrass himself for there is one thing he would request. Of course, Cominius says name it and it is yours. Coriolanus tells them of a poor man in Corioles who gave him hospitality during the battle. Later Coriolanus saw that man was taken prisoner; now he asks that his freedom be granted. Lartius asks for the man's name in order to carry out Coriolanus's request. Coriolanus realizes he has forgotten it and says he is weary, his memory is tired, and he asks for some wine. Cominius sends him to his (Cominius's) tent so that his wounds can be cared for.

Act 1, Scene 10

In the Volsces' camp, Aufidius concedes to his men that Corioles has been taken by the Romans. A soldier reminds him that the Romans will return the city if certain conditions are met. Aufidius is bitter at having to accept terms, but more incensed that he has not beaten Marcius. He vows that he will kill Marcius the next time he encounters him and that he no longer cares if it is with honor in a fair fight.

Act 2, Scene 1

In Rome, Menenius and the people's tribunes, Brutus and Sicinius, are discussing the war and waiting for news. The conversation turns to Marcius, whom the tribunes say loves the people the way wolves love lambs, to devour them. Menenius asks them to name Marcius's faults

and to show one in him that is not more pronounced in themselves. They say he has a host of faults, but pride and boasting are the greatest of them. In response, Menenius tells them that they are known among the patricians for their incompetence and pride, especially for the way they aggrandize themselves when they perform the functions of their office. Marcius, he says, is far superior to them. As he speaks, Menenius sees Volumnia, Virgilia, and Valeria approaching; he leaves the tribunes, and greets them. Volumnia informs him that Marcius has written to her, to his wife, to the senate, and to Menenius that he is returning home. They rejoice. Volumnia even rejoices in the anticipation that Marcius is coming back wounded, numbers his wounds (twenty-seven), describes them, and compares them to wounds he has received in previous battles. The thought of his wounds distresses his wife, Virgilia. They continue to talk of the war, of Marcius's heroism, and of his fight with Aufidius.

As they speak, Cominius and Lartius, with Marcius between them, crowned with a garland of oak leaves, enter. A herald proclaims Marcius's feats of war to the assembled crowd, and he is welcomed by all, but demurs, saying such acclaim offends his heart. Seeing his mother, he kneels before her and she bids him stand, calling him by his newly won name, Coriolanus. Coriolanus then greets Virgilia, whom he gently chides for weeping at his return, telling her that tears are for the widows he has made in Corioles, and for the mothers there he has left without sons. He then greets Menenius. There is great celebration among them. Volumnia expresses her pride and notes there is one honor more she hopes to see bestowed upon her son, to be elected consul. Coriolanus responds that he would prefer to serve Rome in his way than have to ask for the people's votes. As they speak, they move on to the Capitol, leaving the tribunes, Sicinius and Brutus, alone. They acknowledge that Coriolanus is popular with the people for his valor in the war and for saving Rome from conquest. They fear, moreover, should he become consul, that their powers will be severely curbed. They take heart in the belief that Coriolanus has such a temper and a temperament that he will not be able to keep the people's love for long. They note, moreover, that they have heard him swear he would not go through the vote-getting ritual of putting on a simple gown, standing in the marketplace, showing the scars of his wounds to the people and asking, humbly, for their votes, or

Coriolanus being banished from Rome, Act IV, scene i *(© Shakespeare Collection, Special Collections Library, University of Michigan)*

people for their affection. As the patricians, the tribunes, and their attendants arrive, the officers conclude, nevertheless, that Marcius is a worthy man.

Menenius takes the podium and reviews their business. Having decided what terms to impose upon the Voscians, he says, the only thing left to do is confer honor upon Coriolanus. He requests, therefore, that Cominius, who is presently the consul and who was the general of the army, speak about Coriolanus. The senators call upon him to speak and ask the tribunes to report to the people what has been said. In their response, there is already the signal of discord when they say they will report the events, but that it will be easier to make a good report of the proceedings if Coriolanus shows himself more kindly disposed to the people than has been his wont. Menenius reproaches them for inappropriate speech and they rebuke him for his reproach. Cominius mounts the podium to speak on behalf of Coriolanus, and Coriolanus rises to leave the assembly, saying he would "rather have my wounds to heal again / Than hear say how I got them." Brutus, one of the tribunes, suggests that Marcius's attitude towards the people is really the cause of his leaving the assembly. Coriolanus tells him not at all. But he begins, in heat, to add that he does not much value the people because they have shown him nothing worthy of his admiration. Menenius intervenes, telling Coriolanus to stay, but Coriolanus says that he cannot sit and listen to himself praised, "To hear my nothings monstered," he says. And he leaves. Menenius points to this as a sign of Coriolanus's humility.

Cominius begins to speak. It is a typical nominating speech, charting Coriolanus's career and accomplishments. Menenius and the senators cheer him on, and as Cominius finishes his speech, the senate calls for Coriolanus to return. Menenius tells him that the senate is pleased to make him consul and that the only thing that remains to be done is for Coriolanus to speak to the people. Coriolanus thanks them for the honor, accepts it, but begs to forgo the custom of putting on the gown of humility, show his wounds, and solicit the people's approval. Sicinius, the tribune, explains that the people must have their votes heard and that all customary ceremony must be observed. Menenius encourages Coriolanus to go through the traditional formalities. Coriolanus answers that it will

voices. The tribunes hope to take political advantage of that and to remind the people how much Marcius (they continue to call him) has always hated them and treated them with contempt. A messenger enters to report to them that at a rally in the Capitol, it is being suggested that Marcius be named consul. Brutus and Sicinius set off to the Capitol to observe and sharpen their plans for their victory over Marcius.

Act 2, Scene 2

Two officers are preparing the seating for the dignitaries before a rally at the Capitol, where Marcius will be nominated for the office of consul. They discuss his merits and his attitude towards the people. One remarks that the people's love is unsteady. They easily turn from loving a public figure to hating him. Therefore, Marcius is wise not to care about the people's love. True, the other agrees, but Marcius is not indifferent but actively, it seems, seeks their hatred. That, he says, is as bad as flattering the embarrass him to go through that ceremony, for it would make it seem as if he had performed his heroic deeds just to win the people's good opinion, and that the ceremony "might well / Be taken from the people." The tribunes note that statement as a mark against him, arguing that it shows his antipopulist sentiment. Menenius tells Coriolanus not to make an issue of the matter, to just go through it and get it over with, so that he may become consul. Alone, the tribunes agree that Coriolanus will simply use the people, condescendingly, for his purposes. They leave for the marketplace to inform the people of the events that have just transpired.

Act 2, Scene 3

A group of citizens is discussing the upcoming vote and their own power and responsibility. They decide to give Coriolanus their voices, saying that if Coriolanus "would incline to the people, there was never a worthier man." Coriolanus enters wearing the gown of humility. Menenius is by his side, gently scolding him, saying he is wrong to object to performing this ritual, that many worthy men before him have done it. Nevertheless, Coriolanus remains disdainful and sarcastically asks Menenius if he ought to show his wounds saying to the people, look at the wounds I got in my country's service when some of your class fled like cowards from the battle. Exasperated, Menenius tells him to act judiciously or he will ruin everything. Still, as the people approach him, Coriolanus tells Menenius he could treat them a little better if only they would wash and brush their teeth.

The scene in which Coriolanus endures the process of standing for election before the plebeians, who enter in small groups, is composed of a series of dialogues between Coriolanus and the people. These exchanges are punctuated by a short soliloquy Coriolanus speaks between interviews in which he says it would be better to die or starve than endure what this custom enforces. The encounters terminate with his apparent success. They are examples of the people's rather good-spirited and naïve acceptance of Coriolanus and of his condescending, over-polite mockery and even of his downright antipathy towards them. Moreover, he stands in his gown but never lifts it to bare his wounds to their sight; technically he is not fulfilling his obligation.

When Coriolanus departs to change his clothes and go to the Capitol, the tribunes and the people recapitulate the events in the marketplace. The people feel that they have been misled about Coriolanus's sincerity and the tribunes egg them on to rescind their votes; in speeches of deep irony they instruct the people to account for their change of heart by explaining that the tribunes had confused them by their (the tribunes') strong support for Coriolanus's candidacy. It is particularly ironic and fitting that, in attempting to undo Coriolanus, the tribunes give the people a true account of all his virtues, telling them to say that is what they had been told by the tribunals before the election (which is not so) and that is why they were wrongly swayed to consent to make him consul. The people leave for the Capitol and the tribunes go by a shorter way, hoping to get there first. They are confident that when the people voice their intention to rescind their approval, Marcius will erupt in a fit of temper, which the tribunes will be able to use to their own advantage against him.

Act 3, Scene 1

In the Capitol, Coriolanus has begun conducting state business as head of state, discussing the Volsces. Lartius has returned from Corioles, reporting that Aufidius has raised a new army and, consequently, the previous Roman victory has not really made Rome safe from the Voscians. Cominius demurs, arguing that the Volsces are, all the same, worn out, that Rome will not have to confront them in their lifetimes. Coriolanus asks Lartius if he saw Aufidius personally. Under safe conduct, Lartius reports, Aufidius visited him; Aufidius was angered by the poor way the Volsces conducted the war and spoke of his profound hatred for Coriolanus and that he wishes nothing more than to confront him once again in combat. Coriolanus echoes his wish so that he might "oppose his [Aufidius's] hatred fully." As he sees the tribunes approaching, Coriolanus confides to his colleagues that he does "despise" Brutus and Sicinius because they give themselves airs of authority and provoke the patricians. (It is important to notice that he does not despise Aufidius. He *hates* him. To despise is to hold in contempt. Hate indicates a passion which is not tainted with disrespect. Coriolanus values Aufidius and counts him a worthy adversary. That is not his attitude towards the tribunes.)

As Coriolanus and his party are advancing toward the marketplace, the tribunes stop them, forbidding them to go further. Cominius protests, asking if Coriolanus has not been chosen by the nobles and the commons as consul. Brutus answers that he has not been. Astonished, Coriolanus compares the people to irresponsible children. The supercilious prodding by the tribunes as they assert their authority inflames Coriolanus to a fit of temper which causes him to voice his contempt for them, and for the people they represent, even to the point of expressing his opinion that the plebeians must be treated mercilessly, that any concessions to them or their welfare only increases their tendency to assert themselves and flaunt the authority of the nobles. Menenius repeatedly attempts to calm Coriolanus and prevent him from worsening the conflict. The tribunes, of course, do just the opposite and goad him on to greater anger. And when Coriolanus is swirling in the whirlwind of rage and declaring that the people be forcibly suppressed and the tribunes stripped of power, the tribunes summon the *aediles*, officers with police power, to summon the people. Sicinius declares Coriolanus a traitor. Sicinius and Coriolanus scuffle. Menenius tries to keep peace. The people enter. There is a general melee with shouting and grabbing. The plebeians surround Coriolanus. Menenius continues to try to subdue passions, while the tribunes condemn Coriolanus in their attempt to inflame passions, and quickly call for Coriolanus's death. When the tribunes order the *aediles* to seize Coriolanus and bear him to the Tarpeian rock from which they wish to cast him to his death, Coriolanus draws his sword and drives the people and their tribunes to flight.

Menenius advises Coriolanus to go to his home and to wait there, as he and other patricians attempt to mend the situation. Coriolanus answers that there are enough of them to take on and defeat the plebeians. But Menenius and Cominius, despite feeling as he does, urge him to go home rather than make matters even worse. Coriolanus, at last, heeds them. Alone, one of the patricians notes that Coriolanus has "marred his fortune." Menenius answers that, "his nature is too noble for the world." The tribunes return with the plebeians, armed, searching for Coriolanus, and calling him, "this viper." Menenius and the tribunes argue about Coriolanus's merits and his service to Rome. They want to fetch him in order to throw him from the rock. Menenius emphasizes that Coriolanus is a warrior who lacks social grace and a moderate temperament. After much wrangling, the tribunes order the people to lay down their weapons and agree that Menenius will bring Coriolanus to the marketplace, where Coriolanus will face a peaceful trial and answer his accusers rather than endure mob frenzy.

Act 3, Scene 2
Speaking with a member of his own class, Coriolanus insists that no matter with what the plebeians threaten him, he will remain as he is. He wonders, however, why his mother does not support him, she who had always spoken with such contempt for the plebeians. Just as he is speaking of her, she enters and he asks her why "did you wish me milder," rather than being glad he acted like the man he is. She explains to him that it is better to have the power to use before you wear it out. He does not want to hear her. She tells him he would have been more of a man if he had made less of an effort to appear to be one, that he ought to have concealed his views until his adversaries no longer had the power to hinder him from acting on them. "Let them hang," he responds regarding the people. His mother tartly retorts, "Ay, and burn too," meaning the city of Rome, and implicitly reproaching him for a dangerously cavalier attitude. Menenius and a number of senators enter, and everyone advises Coriolanus that he has been too rough in his behavior and that he must, for the common good, apologize for the harsh things he has said. Coriolanus says that he cannot do that. His mother speaks at length to him, cajoling and reprimanding, calling him too stubborn, telling him that it does not dishonor him to say something in order to achieve a desired end, even if he does not mean it. She and all the patricians urge him, then, to dissemble and humble himself before the plebeians for the sake of achieving power over them. Coriolanus struggles against them, arguing that he cannot do it: the dishonor is too great. Volumnia trumps him by pointing out how great the dishonor is to her to have to beg this of him. Coriolanus gives in to her, but she behaves coldly to him. He sets off for the marketplace, repeating to himself that he will answer all accusations with mildness.

Act 3, Scene 3
The tribunes Brutus and Sicinius are discussing the charges they are going to bring against Coriolanus, the strategies they will use to have the crowds affirm with their shouts whatever sentence they (the tribunes) impose upon Coriolanus, and how they can best get Coriolanus into

a rage so that he will speak intemperately and they can impose the most severe punishment. As they speak, Coriolanus enters with Menenius, Cominius, and other patricians. With the encouragement of his friends, Coriolanus is rehearsing the appeasing things he will say. Then the trial begins with Menenius acting as an advocate for Coriolanus, recounting to the crowd the service to the state Coriolanus has done. Coriolanus then asks why, after being granted the honor of being consul, it was rescinded. Sicinius retorts that Coriolanus is not to ask questions but to answer theirs. He accuses Coriolanus of plotting to obtain tyrannical power and states that he is therefore a traitor.

Being called a traitor, despite his attempt at bearing himself mildly, inflames Coriolanus. Menenius's reminder does not keep him calm. Instead Coriolanus lets loose a volley of anger directed at the tribunes. Sicinius takes advantage of his outburst, and inflames the crowd with his condemnation of Coriolanus's wrath. In response, they shout that he should be thrown from the Tarpeian rock. Calm is destroyed. Angry shouting prevails. Coriolanus cannot calm himself and the tribunes sentence him to banishment from Rome, with the addition that should he ever return, he will be cast to his death from the Tarpeian rock. Coriolanus accepts his sentence with rage-filled curses against the tribunes and the people, calling them a "common cry of curs, whose breath / I hate." He ends by saying he turns his back on Rome. "There is a world elsewhere." The people rejoice that their enemy is gone and they follow Coriolanus to the gates of the city.

Act 4, Scene 1
At the gates of Rome, Coriolanus takes his leave of family and friends. While they are angry and mournful at his departure, he is spirited in his courage and optimistic about making a life for himself, telling them that as long as he lives they will always hear from him and that they will never hear anything about him but what is like himself. Refusing to have anyone accompany him in his wanderings, he departs.

Act 4, Scene 2
Once Coriolanus is gone, the tribunes decide it is time to mollify the patricians, who have sided with Coriolanus. They send the people home, saying "their great enemy is gone." As they speak, they see Volumnia, Virgilia, and Menenius

approaching and try to avoid them, but Volumnia sees them and curses them. They call her crazy and leave. She tells her companions that her anger is boundless and self-consuming.

Act 4, Scene 3
A Roman spying for the Volscians and a Volscian spy meet as the Roman is going to Antium to give the Volscians news from Rome. The Roman tells the Volscian that Coriolanus has been banished, and the Volscian lets him know what good news that is: Aufidius and the Voslcians are preparing another attack on Rome.

Act 4, Scene 4
Coriolanus arrives in Antium, poorly dressed and muffled in a cloak. He finds Aufidius's house and determines to present himself to Aufidius, thinking that friends can turn foes and foes can turn friends. He will offer his services to the Volscians, if they will have him, and if they choose instead to kill him, that's only fair, he thinks, considering the number of deaths he has brought to them.

Act 4, Scene 5
Inside Aufidius's house, the serving men are going back and forth bringing wine to guests. Coriolanus enters and is taken for a beggar. He refuses to leave when asked, and when the servants try to remove him bodily he resists. Aufidius is summoned and comes to see what the matter is. Coriolanus opens his cloak to reveal himself but Aufidius does not recognize him. Only when Marcius names himself does Aufidius know him. Rather then calling himself Coriolanus, he says my name is Caius Marcius. Then he narrates the wrongs he has suffered at the hands of the Roman plebeians, explains that he has been banished, and that, for revenge, he wishes to make war against Rome with the Volscians if they will have him. If not, he offers himself to Aufidius, saying he has no desire to live. Aufidius clasps him to his bosom and vows friendship and comradeship with him. He tells him the Volscians are preparing a military campaign against Roman territories, although not the capitol city itself. He offers Coriolanus co-command of his forces and the power to decide if they will assault the city of Rome itself as well as the territories.

When Aufidius takes Coriolanus inside to join the diners, the servants, once so contemptuous of the beggar they had thought he was, now confess to each other how they each sensed there was something special about him. Another servant enters and informs them excitedly that the man they saw is Caius Marcius and that the Volscians are setting off immediately to make new wars against Rome.

Act 4, Scene 6

In Rome, the tribunes, Sicinius and Brutus, are congratulating themselves on how well everything has gone since the departure of Coriolanus. When they meet Menenius they mention that Coriolanus is not missed. Menenius says wistfully he wishes Coriolanus had been more prudent in his speech. None of them has heard any news of Coriolanus. As Roman citizens pass them on the street and offer them their blessings and their thanks, the tribunes become swollen with pride and opine that "Caius Marcius," as they call him, eschewing the honorary "Coriolanus," was a good soldier but had become too proud. As they continue in this vein, an aedile meets them with the news that Rome has captured a Volscian and learned that the Volsces have two armies in the field marching against them. Although Menenius offers the reasonable analysis that when he learned of Coriolanus's banishment, Aufidius undoubtedly had taken to the field against a substantially weakened Rome, the tribunes refuse to believe it and order the man who reported the approach of the Volscian armies whipped for spreading rumors. Menenius advises they question the man before they whip him, lest they fail to get important information about the coming attack. The tribunes dismiss Menenius with haughty contempt.

Another messenger arrives and announces that the senate is convening and that there is bad news. The tribunes in response order the Volscian captive to be publicly whipped to put an end to the panic. But the messenger adds that the report has been confirmed and, even worse news, that Marcius leads one of the Volscian armies against Rome and vows revenge. The tribunes do not believe it, and Menenius himself doubts this part of the news, recalling the fierce enmity between Marcius and Aufidius. But as he is expressing this doubt, another messenger arrives to summon him to the senate with reports that Marcius is indeed leading an army against Rome. Menenius enters, and berates the tribunes

for bringing on such a calamity. Menenius says Rome must ask for mercy. Cominius retorts with the question, Who shall ask for it? and answers, not the tribunes, nor the people, who wronged him, not even his friends, who did not help him but acceded to the tribunes and the people. A group of the people enter, fearful of the punishment they expect Marcius is bringing. They say now that they never really approved of banishing him. The tribunes tell them to go home. They say the reports are patrician propaganda. Alone, the tribunes leave for the capitol to learn more news, still refusing to believe that reports of the attack are true.

Act 4, Scene 7

In a camp outside Rome, Aufidius is talking to his lieutenant about how the soldiers idolize Marcius. Aufidius says he cannot do anything about it before the attack on Rome because it would weaken the army. But after the Volscian victory, Aufidius says, he plans to take his revenge on Marcius and bring him down.

Act 5, Scene 1

Cominius has been to see Marcius, who has arrived at the gates of Rome with his army. Cominius begs Marcius to relent and spare the city, but to no avail. The tribunes plead with Menenius to go to him and see if he can exert his influence more successfully on Marcius. Menenius is reluctant. He declines, arguing that it will be useless, it will only depress him, Menenius, to see himself scorned by the man who had once called him father; finally Menenius agrees to go. Perhaps Marcius will be more tractable after he has eaten, he says. Once he has gone, Cominius assures the tribunes that Menenius will fail, that only if Marcius's mother and wife go to him may he possibly show mercy.

Act 5, Scene 2

Menenius, at the Volscian camp, is stopped by the guards from going further. They say Coriolanus, as they call him, will not see him. Menenius assures them he will, but they mock him. When Coriolanus appears with Aufidius he sees Menenius and spurns his petition, only giving him a letter he had prepared to send him. Coriolanus exits with Aufidius, and the guards further scorn Menenius. Menenius leaves them, broken but stoic, saying he cares not if he dies; his curse to the guards is that they have a long life.

Act 5, Scene 3

Coriolanus is telling Aufidius how dear Menenius has been to him and how, nevertheless, Menenius could not shake him from his purpose, when Volumnia, Virgilia, Valeria (a renowned matron of Rome) and his little son approach. He sees them and confesses that he is moved, but vows to retain the firmness of his objective. He kneels to his mother after embracing his wife, but tells them he will not be swayed. Volumnia then kneels to him and in a long speech expresses the special grief she feels of having to be grieved at seeing him, which is the thing that ought to bring her joy. She assures him that if he marches on Rome he will also tread on his mother's womb, for she will die by her own hand if she fails to persuade him to offer Rome mercy. She argues that he can broker a peace between Rome and the Volscians that will be beneficial to both sides and cause both sides to honor him. When he seems unmoved, she calls him proud and taunts him saying she is not his mother; some woman in Corioles is. At this he takes her hand and surrenders to her. He asks Aufidius if he, too, would not be moved to mercy by such supplication. Aufidius says, indeed, he would. But in an aside, Aufidius notes that he will use Coriolanus's mercifulness to regain his position of dominance over him.

Act 5, Scene 4

Menenius advises the tribune, Sicinius, that there is hardly any hope of Volumnia's succeeding with Coriolanus where he had failed. A messenger enters with news that the people are enraged and have seized the other tribune, Brutus, and threaten to kill him by slow torture if Volumnia and Virgilia do not return with good news. But at his heels, another messenger rushes in with that very unanticipated good news. In the distance, trumpets and other instruments of joy begin to sound as Menenius and Sicinius leave the stage to join the rest of Rome in celebration.

Act 5, Scene 5

This is a scene of only six lines in which the citizens of Rome welcome Volumnia, Virgilia, and Valeria back with shouts of gratitude.

Act 5, Scene 6

Aufidius orders his attendants to summon the people of Corioles to the marketplace, where he will bring accusations of betrayal against Coriolanus, whom he knows intends also to speak there in defense of his capitulation. From his conversation with his henchman, it is clear that Aufidius is plotting to have Coriolanus killed. Their rehearsal of the case they will make against him is interrupted by the shouts of welcome they hear in the distance as the Volscian people welcome Coriolanus with an enthusiasm that Aufidius did not receive. In his jealousy, he is sure that he can rise only if Coriolanus falls.

The lords of the city, unlike the cheering commons who greet Coriolanus, greet only Aufidius warmly, and together they berate Coriolanus for his betrayal of the Volscians. Coriolanus enters and presents the nobles with a report of the spoils of war he has brought back and with the terms of the peace he concluded with Rome, which he characterizes as reflecting "no less honor to the Antiates [the Volscians] / Than shame to th' Romans." Aufidius interrupts and tells the Volscian lords not to read the peace accords; he accuses Coriolanus of treachery and abuse of power. Coriolanus recoils, challenges the accusation, and Aufidius repeats it, addressing Coriolanus only as Marcius. Aufidius condemns Coriolanus's behavior and demeans his manhood, saying he "whined . . . away . . . victory" at the sight of "his nurse's tears," and calls him "boy of tears." Enraged, Coriolanus in a temper of wrath confutes the accusation by reminding his auditors how he brought destruction to Corioles in his battles in the past as a Roman fighter against them and cries out how he would kill Aufidius even now were he six times the man he is. Aufidius's henchmen raise a cry against him and rushing at him, stab Coriolanus, who falls dead.

The Volscian senators are horrified by Aufidius's deed, but Aufidius assures them that he can justify the assassination of Coriolanus when he tells them of the dangers Coriolanus posed to Corioles. The lords agree that Coriolanus's wrath, mitigates Aufidius's act. Aufidius says that now his own rage at Coriolanus is past and he is "struck with sorrow." He orders a ceremonious funeral for

MEDIA ADAPTATIONS

- In 1807, Heinrich Joseph von Collin launched a drama called "Coriolan," based loosely on the story of Coriolanus. Ludwig van Beethoven's "Coriolan Overture opus 62" was written to accompany this play. It is a short piece mixing sharp, staccato heroic chords with the sort of sweet, middle-period melody characteristic of the Eroica Symphony, Opus 55, and the Violin Concerto, Opus 61.

- In 1940, August L. Baeyens (1895–1966) wrote a version of *Coriolanus* as an opera for radio. His version was later made into a stage play which was performed at the Royal Flemish Opera.

- In 1958, Croatian composer Stjepan Sulek adapted Shakespeare's play *Coriolanus* into an opera in Croatian. The world premiere in that same year received significant critical and popular attention.

- *Coriolanus* also ran from 1970–1972 in an opera version written in Czech by the Czechoslovakian composer Jan Cikker.

- A New York Shakespeare Festival production of *Coriolanus* was filmed in 1979. The production starred Morgan Freeman in the title role, with Castulo Guerra, Earle Hyman, CCH Pounder, and Denzel Washington in supporting roles. The production was directed by Wilford Leach and produced by Joseph Papp.

- In 1984, a film version of *Coriolanus* was made as part of *The Complete Dramatic Works of William Shakespeare* series. The film was directed by Elija Moshinsky and starred Alan Howard. It is available on DVD and video as part of the BBC Shakespeare Collection.

Coriolanus, not omitting to add, "though in this city he [Coriolanus] / Hath widowed and unchilded many a one, / Which to this hour bewail the injury."

CHARACTERS

Menenius Agrippa

Menenius is an aged patrician. He opposes the demands of the people for grain or political power. Nevertheless, he attempts to remain a gentleman in his confrontations with them. He is a friend of Coriolanus, but is rebuffed by him when he pleads with him to spare Rome.

Tullus Aufidius

Aufidius is the general of the Volscian army. The Volsces are the enemies of Rome. Aufidius and Coriolanus are personal enemies who have often fought against each other in battles; each longs for the opportunity to kill the other. While Coriolanus admires Aufidius as a rival, Aufidius is jealous of Coriolanus and contrives to destroy him even if he cannot defeat him in combat.

Junius Brutus

Junius Brutus is one of the tribunes of the people. Along with Sicinius, the other tribune, he directs the people's wrath against the patricians and is particularly influential in shaping the defeat of Coriolanus in his bid to obtain the office of consul and in banishing him from Rome. Those opposed to Brutus may see him as a manipulator rather than as a leader.

Cominius

Cominius is the Roman general under whom Coriolanus serves. He has tremendous regard for Coriolanus. It is Cominius who confers upon Marcius the name Coriolanus after his victory at Corioles.

Caius Marcius Coriolanus

Coriolanus is a soldier of the patrician class who is dearly attached to his class and to his mother, who has formed his character. He is proud, stubborn, prone to anger, and detests the people. He sees them as irresponsible and idle. He earns the honorary name Coriolanus by reversing the tide of battle at Corioles and single-handedly leading the Romans to victory after their near defeat. His pride leads him to greatly alienate the Roman plebeians when he seeks the office of consul that they threaten to kill him and in fact banish him. After banishment, he joins forces with Aufidius to avenge himself on Rome, but at the last minute accedes to his mother's pleas for mercy, spares Rome, and is assassinated by Aufidius's henchmen in Antium.

Titus Lartius

Titus Lartius is a Roman general.

Marcius

Young Marcius is Coriolanus's son. He has the same fierce temper and warlike inclination as his father; he appears to Coriolanus and others as the mirror of Coriolanus as a boy.

Nicanor

Nicanor is a Roman spying for the Volscians.

Sicinius Velutus

Sicinius, along with Brutus, is a tribune of the people. He feeds the people's indignation against Coriolanus, engineers his defeat in becoming consul, and is instrumental in banishing him. Brutus is portrayed as manipulative and concerned more with his own power than the people's good.

Valeria

Valeria is a matron of Rome, and a friend of Volumnia, who shares her enthusiasm for war.

Virgilia

Virgilia is Coriolanus's wife. Unlike his mother, she does not celebrate his military prowess but is fearful for his safety. When he is at war, she refuses to leave the house or amuse herself with the other women.

Volumnia

Volumnia is Coriolanus's mother. She has raised him to be a soldier and, in his soldiership, to reflect her glory. She is proud of his heroism, takes pride in his wounds, revels in the sight of him bloodied and values his honor over his life. She is cold and stern. She prods him to seek the consulship when he would rather not, and she persuades him to spare Rome, at the expense of his very life, when no one else could.

THEMES

The Conflict between Honor and Loyalty

The concepts of honor and loyalty usually seem to be interconnected. Loyalty to one's family, to one's country, to one's core values seems to be the mark of honor. It is a mark of dishonor to betray family, country, and core values. In *Coriolanus*, however, rather than being interconnected, loyalty and honor are put at odds with each other. Patriotism, duty to his country, devotion to his mother, and adherence to his code of values, all are fundamental attributes of Coriolanus's character. Yet, Coriolanus endures dishonor in Rome because he remains loyal to his sense of what is honorable. He will not boast about his feats of heroism, nor submit to the values of the tribunes and the plebeians. He steadfastly maintains his integrity. When he joins with the Volscians in their campaign against Rome, he is confronted with the choice of betraying his commitment to the Volscians, by being loyal to his mother and his motherland, and thus dishonoring himself, or dishonoring his mother by being disloyal to her and ignoring her entreaties.

The tribunes, too, are shown to be dishonorable in their loyalty to what they see to be the cause of the people. They are shown manipulating the plebeians, especially when they advise them to rescind their approval of Coriolanus as consul, advising them to say that the tribunes duped them into supporting him by telling them of his virtues. They had not done that before the election. Only afterwards, in order to have the people use that positive information in a negative way do the tribunes recount Coriolanus's worthy deeds.

The Conflict between Nurture and Hunger

Coriolanus begins with the question the plebeians put to each other, "You are all resolved rather to die than to famish?" as they rise up against the patricians in order to have "corn at our own price." Contrasting themselves to the patricians, they point out that just the excess that the patricians eat could feed them. In order to counter their complaints, Menenius tells them the parable of the belly. When Marcius enters, his disdain for the plebeians is marked by expressions of contempt for their hunger. But Marcius himself has been raised by a mother who nurtured him with a steely passion for warfare

The Tent of Coriolanus, Act V, scene iii (© *Shakespeare Collection, Special Collections Library, University of Michigan*)

rather than milk. In her first appearance in the play, Volumnia says, "The breasts of Hecuba, / When she did suckle Hector, looked not lovlier / Then [*sic*] Hector's forehead when it spit forth blood." The tribunes tell Menenius that Coriolanus loves the people the way the wolf loves the lamb, in order to eat them. And Coriolanus says, condemning the people's votes, "Better it is to die, better to starve, / Than crave the hire which first we do deserve." Only in Antium, when Coriolanus allies himself with Aufidius, does he go into dinner with him. And Menenius, worrying that Coriolanus will reject his petition to spare Rome, thinks that he will go to him after Coriolanus has eaten. Thus, throughout *Coriolanus*, there is a constant reference to images of hunger and nurturing as being in conflict with each other and as determining people's actions and attitudes.

Manhood

The insult which overwhelms Coriolanus is being called "boy" by Aufidius at the end of the play after he returns from Rome having yielded to his mother's entreaties to spare the city. He rages in response, and boasts of his power as the soldier who has repeatedly defeated the Volscians in battle. But this outward show of force never achieves for him an inward condition of self-sufficient strength. He is defined by those who oppose him rather than by something in himself. All Coriolanus's acts are designed to assert his manhood, whether through bravery in war or asserting himself against the plebeians. But his very assertion of manhood is dedicated to pleasing his mother. When he asks his mother, after his confrontation with the Roman people and their tribunes, why she would have had him conform himself to the wishes of the plebeians and humiliate himself, he defends himself saying, "I play / The man I am." Her retort contradicts him and suggests that his behavior shows he is not a man. She says, "You might have been enough the man you are, / With striving less to be so."

TOPICS FOR FURTHER STUDY

- Read "The Life of Caius Martius Coriolanus" in Plutarch's *The Lives of the Noble Grecians and Romans* (available in the Signet edition of *Coriolanus*). Then, write an essay of at least five hundred words comparing Plutarch's account and Shakespeare's play, paying particular attention to how Shakespeare used, and altered, Plutarch's account.

- Research a particular historical event that interests you, perhaps an event from the American civil rights movement, like the Montgomery bus boycott or the bombing of the Birmingham Church, or the integration of Little Rock's Central High School. Use the characters, the information and the narratives you find as the basis for a play. This ought to be considered a term-long project.

- In an essay of a least five hundred words, compare and contrast *Coriolanus* and *Julius Caesar*.

- Narrate an incident in your life or, from the life of someone you know, where you or your subject faced a conflict between two forces that exerted equal but opposite pressure and where there was, or seemed to be, no solution that did not involve some unwanted consequence. Describe the problem, its circumstances, and how it was finally resolved.

STYLE

Animal Imagery

Running through *Coriolanus* are images of animals. When Aufidius calls him "boy," Coriolanus responds that he, Aufidius, is a false hound and that he, Coriolanus, has been like an eagle who has attacked the Volscians as if they were doves in a dovecote. The Roman tribunes compare Coriolanus to a wolf and the people to the lambs the wolf loves to devour. The rage that drives Coriolanus is shown in his son as aggression against butterflies. Tigers, wolves, lambs, osprey, fish, horses, dogs, sheep, geese, butterflies, lions, hares, curs, foxes all appear as metaphors for human attributes in the play. The people are called hares rather than lions, geese rather than foxes. Animal imagery suggests an undercurrent of brutality and the dominant pattern of prey and predator subverts the apparent humanity of the characters. In the midst of humanity, the play suggests, bestiality is still at work.

Body Imagery

In a play in which the opposition of brutality and vulnerability is so strong a theme, the recurrent use of body imagery keeps that theme in the forefront of the reader's awareness. References to belly, lungs, arms, tongue, eyes, legs, heart, head, chin, forehead, anus, bloody gashes and blood-covered men, maternal breasts, wounds suffered and wounds healing, teeth set in rage or teeth that want cleaning, big toes, a mother's womb, a fair or blushing face, a soldier's beard, the buttocks, the bowels, the loins, and the knees are all woven into the text. Besides suggesting the material reality and vulnerability, the nobility and filthiness of the individual, body references suggest another thematic element in *Coriolanus*. The political question regarding how closely related the body politic is to the human body is of chief concern in the play and, with it, the problem of where the highest authority in the government of a state ought to reside. The tribunes' model of a state separates the plebeians from the patricians, giving them independent governing rights. Menenius sees the classes as diverse organs united in one body and suggests the patricians must therefore rule over the plebeians.

Crowd Scenes and Military Spectacle

In a play concerned with the conflict between a single figure and great masses of the population, it is appropriate that there be crowd scenes. Most of the pivotal scenes in *Coriolanus*, save for the climactic encounter between Coriolanus and his mother, are crowd scenes pitting Coriolanus against either the Roman plebeians or the Volscian army. Thus the stage is often filled with crowds in domestic or martial conflict with Coriolanus, and the domestic crowd scenes at times take on similarities to battle when scuffles break out between the plebeians and the patricians. Even the scenes of combat or verbal encounter between Coriolanus and his nemesis, Aufidius, which ought to be scenes between two individuals, become crowd scenes, whether in the first battle against the Volscians when Marcius wins the addition Coriolanus or in the last scene, when Aufidius indicts him for treason. In the first instance, Aufidius does not fight alone but with a group of soldiers backing him up. Even so supported, he cannot defeat Marcius. In the second, it is a group of Aufidius's conspirators who rush at Coriolanus and kill him.

HISTORICAL CONTEXT

King James's Attempts to Assert Absolute and Unitary Power

In Shakespeare's time, some members of the nobility believed that King James was attempting to assert his absolute power as governing monarch and was determined to undermine their rights, such as had been won in 1215 through the Magna Carta, in which King John surrendered some of his power to the Barons. They asserted that England was made up of three forces, king, nobles, and commons, and that each had rights, and that Parliament functioned as a defense against tyranny. James was aware of this opposition to his ambition, and believed that it was grounded in admiration for republican Rome. In 1606, he condemned, according to Anne Barton, in "Livy, Machiavelli, and *Coriolanus*, the "tribunes of the people whose mouths could not be stopped." He meant those in parliament who opposed him.

The Midland Riots of 1607 in England

During the famine of 1607, poor peasants, farmers, and laborers in England protested their condition by rioting for food and against the enclosure of common lands by aristocrats, the practice of which removed farm land from the poor. Significantly, the cause of the plebeian revolt in *Coriolanus* is lack of food. In Plutarch, Shakespeare's source, the actual historical cause was the high rate of interest charged the plebeians for their debts.

Roman Government

Until the fifth century before the birth of Christ, Rome was ruled by kings. The last of the kings, Tarquin Superbus, was overthrown and a republic established around 500 B.C.E. The king was replaced by two *praetors* or, as they are called in *Coriolanus*, consuls. The consuls had the same power as the kings except that they did not rule for life but were elected for a term of one year.

Under the old kings, an aristocracy of old families grew up. They were called "patricians," and the elders of the patricians formed an advisory body to the king, with no governing or legislative power, called a senate. (The word for an elder, in Latin is "*senex*.") A socially and economically inferior group of people, immigrants and people captured in wars grew up in the kingdom, too. They were called "plebeians." After the defeat of the kings, which was accomplished by an alliance between patricians and plebeians, and the establishment of the republic, the patricians assumed governing power and the plebeians were granted some of the rights of citizens, with voting power and representatives. Yet they were denied the power and authority that the patricians exercised. Rome was an aristocratic republic, not a democratic republic.

Roman Plebeian Uprising

The patricians were landed, wealthy, and lived within the gates of Rome. The plebeians were poor, lived outside the gates, and eked out a poor living as farmers on land that lay unprotected, especially in times of war when they were off fighting and their farms lay neglected or were ravaged by enemies. Public lands, which in theory belonged to the entire Roman people, in fact were occupied by the patricians. The consequence of economic inequality was that the plebeians were often forced to borrow money, fell into debt, and were subject to usurious interest rates.

Having no legal recourse, in 494 B.C.E., the plebeians refused to fight in the army in the defense of a Rome which exploited rather than supported them; they attempted to secede from Rome and form their own state. Fearing the loss of the army, the patricians capitulated, canceled debts, released prisoners jailed for debt, and created, in 474 B.C.E. a plebeian assembly and the office of tribune of the people. In addition, the patricians granted the plebeians the right to elect two tribunes with veto powers from among

COMPARE
&
CONTRAST

- **Fifth-century B.C.E. Rome:** There is domestic strife. Plebeians revolt against patrician rule. At issue are the availability of grain, which the plebeians assert the patricians are hoarding, and the degree to which the plebeians can participate in government. At issue, too, is the attitude of disdain or contempt, best embodied in Coriolanus, which the plebeians feel in the way the patricians treat them.

  Seventeenth-century England: King James I is intent on consolidating monarchical power and uniting the kingdoms of England and Scotland under his sole rule. He wishes to restrict the power of Parliament and is wary of echoes of the republicanism of ancient Rome, which it seems to him, are guiding those who are trying to limit his power through a stronger Parliament. At the same time, the people, farmers and laborers are revolting against the nobles because of the practice of enclosure. The aristocracy is taking away common land that the people might farm by enclosing, and thus privatizing it. The enclosures combined with the famine of 1607 lead the people to riot in protest.

  Today: In countries like England, the United States, and France, all of which are influenced in their governing structures by republican Rome, various critical conflicts reflecting social division and what some see as unjust division of wealth, social privilege, and responsibility, are causing internal strife. Many members of immigrant populations from eastern cultures in western democracies perceive that they are being ill-treated because of cultural differences. In the suburbs of Paris, immigrant youth find themselves with no employment and face police harassment; in response, they riot sporadically. In the United States, immigrant populations from Latin America, whose members provide a source of cheap labor, stage large demonstrations petitioning for the civil and economic rights of

  citizenship. In Great Britain, immigrant populations from Islamic cultures are torn between integrating into English culture and maintaining their own cultural identities.

- **Fifth-century B.C.E. Rome:** Rome is locked in a hostile competition with the Volscians which often breaks out into actual war. The plebeians make up the bulk of the Roman armed forces, and their farms and families are put at risk during wartime by the men's absence and by enemy raids. As a result of their straightened circumstances, plebeians are forced to borrow money and are required to repay it at very high interest rates.

  Seventeenth-century England: After sixteen years of intermittent war with Spain, dating from the English defeat of a Spanish naval armada in 1588, in 1604, the government of King James I signed the Treaty of London with Spain. The strain on wealth caused by the cost of war affects the people.

  Today: Great Britain, closely allied with the United States, is engaged in a war in Iraq and a war in Afghanistan. Most of the people affected by these wars, those who fight in them and those who are injured and killed in them, are of a class that could be termed plebeian. They come from the middle to lower classes, rather than from the wealthy, governing sectors of society. The cost of the wars drives the countries into unmanageable debt and causes internal domestic needs and programs to be neglected.

- **Fifth-century B.C.E. Rome:** The exigencies of war and domestic strife cause a constitutional crisis. The patricians attempt to consolidate their power by making the senate stronger and focusing authority in a consul. Menenius compares the state to a body, with the patricians serving as the belly, which works in the interest of the entire state, as it controls the distribution of wealth. The plebeians attempt to democratize authority not only by participating in the election of the consul but by electing tribunes, officers of the senate representing them, rather than the interests of the patrician senators.

Seventeenth-century England: King James is intent on showing that the nation of England is like a body of which he is the head, while Parliament is intent on curbing his power. Their conflict continues until parliamentary forces prevail, in the 1640s, when Charles is king. In 1660, the monarchy defeats those parliamentary forces and is restored to power.

Today: In Britain, the conflict between the government and the people over the war in Iraq and the British alliance with the United States causes the Prime Minister to step down and call for early elections. In the United States, many see a constitutional crisis looming because of the increased power of the executive branch, which they see as determined to govern without congressional consent or popular support, violating long-established practices derived from English common law and enshrined in the Constitution. At issue are established rights such as *habeas corpus* (which is a legal protection against unlawful restraint or imprisonment), individuals citizens' right to privacy, and the use of torture during the interrogation of prisoners.

themselves to protect their rights. In *Coriolanus*, these tribunes are Brutus and Sicinius.

Volscians, Antium, and Corioles

At the same time as the domestic strife between the Roman patricians and plebeians was occurring, Rome was under attack by a neighboring people called the Volscians. The Volscians lived in Antium, now called Anzio, a seaport city to the southeast of Rome. In 338 B.C.E., it was conquered by Rome. It became a resort spot for wealthy Romans. The Roman emperors Nero and Caligula were born there. In 1944, it was the scene of an amphibious Allied landing. Corioles was the capitol city of Antium.

CRITICAL OVERVIEW

T. S. Eliot, in his famous contrarian essay "Hamlet and His Problems," argues that *Hamlet* is not the splendid artistic achievement it usually is considered to be. Eliot asserts that while "*Coriolanus* may be not as 'interesting' as *Hamlet* but it is, with *Antony and Cleopatra*, Shakespeare's most assured artistic success." It is the kind of praise that more likely keeps readers away from a work than draws them to it. Harold Bloom, taking another tack, in *Shakespeare: The Invention of the Human*, nevertheless similarly suggests a certain wariness regarding *Coriolanus* when he describes the character, Coriolanus, as lacking the inwardness with which Shakespeare endowed the heroes of the great tragedies like *Hamlet, Othello, King Lear, Macbeth*, and *Antony and Cleopatra*, which immediately preceded it. Derek Traversi's assessment of the play in *Shakespeare: The Roman Plays*, follows Eliot's essay and precedes Bloom's, but expresses, more expansively, a synthesis of both:

> That *Coriolanus* is conceived with admirable dramatic logic is generally recognized; doubt as to the value of the play by the highest standard only seems to arise when we ask ourselves whether it touches the deeper sources of emotion, whether the hero's disaster, so ironic and detached in its presentation, so clearly the result of inadequacies in his own moral make-up, can effect us as truly and universally tragic in its significance.

A. C. Bradley, in his 1912 lecture on *Coriolanus*, had already stated similar doubts about the universality of Coriolanus as a tragic figure. "Coriolanus is angular, granitic, and hence unlovable," Eugene M. Waith wrote in *The Herculean Hero*. Critic after critic, while respecting the craftsmanship *Coriolanus* obviously reflects, seems to be taken up short by the character of the hero himself, while still intrigued by his problem. Rather like the people of Rome, critics have been put off by the man himself.

Perhaps Frank Kermode provides the simplest reason: "Coriolanus," he writes in *Shakespeare's Language*, "is his most political play . . . . It is a study in the relationships between citizens within a body politic; the relationship of crowds to leaders and leaders to led, of rich to poor." Its concerns are "dearth, external enemies, enmity between classes." It is, in fact, just the dynamics that Kermode outlines which might tend to be off-putting to most people, who come to Shakespeare's theater for a penetrating, intellectually arousing experience of emotional depth and complexity. Bertolt Brecht, the communist playwright who invented the alienation effect, deliberately constructed his plays to prevent spectators in the theater from identifying with individual characters so that they might consider the politics of the characters' situations. In his "Study of the First Scene of Shakespeare's *Coriolanus*," framed as a multi-person conversation between Brecht and members of his East Berlin theater, *The Berliner Ensemble*, the focus is precisely on problems of class consciousness, class struggle, and class solidarity. Ann Barton, writing in her essay, "Livy, Machiavelli, and *Coriolanus*," sees the play's strength as a political meditation on the politics of the conflict between King James I and parliament, and considers the play from the perspective of Machiavelli's analysis of governments and leaders. One of the most persuasive readings of *Coriolanus*, however, leaps over the political controversies regarding the play and seems to pierce its "granitic" exterior. Janet Adelman begins her penetrating study "Escaping the Matrix: The Construction of Masculinity in *Coriolanus*" by saying, "*Coriolanus* begins in the landscape of maternal deprivation." After summarizing the political situation in Shakespeare's England and ancient Rome, Adelman discusses the role that lack of maternal nurturing played in forming and undermining Coriolanus's character, thus revealing some of the inwardness that can give the character of Coriolanus life without denying the historical, economic, and social contexts in which that life confronted itself.

CRITICISM

Neil Heims

In the following essay, Heims argues that all the conflicts Coriolanus faces with others stem from a fundamental conflict with his mother that has become internalized as a conflict between parts of himself.

After his candidacy has been approved by the plebeians and he is about to assume the office of Roman consul, when the two tribunes of the people challenge him and rescind the people's vote, Coriolanus, furious that he is being made to bow to what he believes is an illegitimate authority says,

> [M]y soul aches
> To know, when two authorities are up,
> Neither supreme, how soon confusion
> May enter 'twixt the gap of both and take
> The one by th' other.

In this phrase, Coriolanus expresses the theme of the play, the underlying conflict which has shaped his own personality, and the force which will prove his undoing: the conflict between irreconcilable authorities and the clash of irreconcilable values.

The two authorities that are set against each other in *Coriolanus* are first presented and formulated in the context of political or class antagonism. As the play begins, the people of Rome have taken to the streets and are on the verge of rioting for bread, which they say they are being deprived of by the patricians. Their anger has Caius Marcius (who will later acquire the name Coriolanus) as its particular object, for he is vocal in his contempt for the plebeians. The first representative of the patricians whom the audience encounters, however, is not Marcius but Menenius, an older man, a patrician with a refined disposition, but no less bound to the point of view of his class than Marcius.

In his attempt to pacify the plebeians, Menenius tells them the fable of the belly in which he postulates a conflict between all the other parts of the body and the belly. The belly is accused of hoarding all the food the body has taken in through its labor without having earned that nurturance through contributory labor. The belly retorts, correcting the rebellious organs, that it gathers, processes, and distributes the food to all those complaining organs leaving for itself nothing but offal. Menenius proceeds with his tale by declaring it an analogy. The belly is the senate of Rome and the rebelling parts are the plebeians. Fundamental to Menenius's biological model is his formulation of a conflict between parts that actually form an organic unity. So the State is defined in *Coriolanus* as an amalgam of conflicting parts rather than an organic community in which all the parts, that is all its people, are joined together in an interdependent unity.

John Burgess as Sicinius Velutus, Oliver Ford-Davies as Junius Brutus, Alan Howard as Coriolanus, and Graham Crowden as Menenius in Act II, scene ii at the Aldwych Theatre, London, 1979 (© Donald Cooper/Photostage. Reproduced by permission)

When Marcius arrives and confronts the rebellious Roman plebeians, he does not act like the belly of Menenius's parable. Rather he expresses disdain and contempt for them, which must insure division and conflict. His argument is simple. They have not earned the bread they demand; they are a lazy, irresponsible rabble without virtue. The virtue that Marcius represents is military prowess. He is a magnificent soldier whose performance in the wars Rome has fought is unequalled in heroism and prowess. The conflict between the plebeians and the patricians, then, is sharpened into a conflict between the plebeians and Marcius. That conflict is set within the framework of the conflict between Rome and its foreign enemy, the Volscians. The conflict between Rome and the Volscians is sharpened in *Coriolanus* into a conflict between Marcius and Aufidius, the general of the Volsces.

The conflict between Marcius and Aufidius is an external conflict, a foreign conflict. The internal, domestic conflict between Marcius

and the people of Rome takes focus as an antagonism between Marcius and the two leaders of the people, their tribunes, Junius Brutus and Velutus Sicinius. When Marcius returns to Rome after defeating the Volscians in a series of particularly fierce encounters, his conflict, not with the plebeians, but with their tribunes, is greatly intensified when he seeks to become consul, an office in republican Rome with the power of a king, although not accompanied by a king's life-long tenure. His attaining that office, the tribunes, no doubt properly believe, would constitute a serious threat to the scope of their power and authority.

There is an important difference that marks the conflicts between Marcius and his external foe, Aufidius, and his domestic opponents, the two tribunes. Marcius *hates* Aufidius. He *despises* the tribunes. The difference is a difference between respect and contempt. Marcius is eager to confront Aufidius. He measures himself against Aufidius. He esteems and values this enemy highly. He even identifies himself with him; they are both martial men. Marcius is disdainful in his encounters with the tribunes. Contact with them diminishes him. He considers them unworthy opponents with whom contact is debasing. They deny the measure of his prowess.

But all the conflicts which involve Marcius and of which he is aware, whether with the people of Rome, with their tribunes, or with his great foe, Aufidius, seem to be emanations energized by a particular conflict of which he is not aware but which reveals itself as the play proceeds: the conflict within himself with his mother. It is a conflict determined by opposing notions of honor and valor. That conflict with his mother first appears as a relatively insignificant disagreement. It is revealed in passing. After Marcius returns in triumph to Rome, the hero of Corioles, now with the additional, honorary name of Coriolanus, Volumnia, his mother, tells him,

> I have lived
> To see inherited my very wishes,
> And the buildings of my fancy. Only
> There's one thing wanting, which I doubt
> not but
> Our Rome will cast upon thee.

He knows what she is talking about, and so does the audience, for some fifty lines before, as she, Virgilia, Coriolanus's wife, and Menenius await his entrance, Volumnia speaks of the wounds she hopes to see him bearing home on his body, wounds he will have to bare to the people of Rome when he stands for the office of consul. "There will be large cicatrices to show the people, when he stands for his place," she says, overflowing with proud ambition. Is it for him? Or is it for herself, through him? That is the conflict.

His response when she speaks of being on the verge of attaining the "one thing wanting," which she is confident "Rome will cast upon thee," is that he "had rather be their servant in my way / Than sway with them in theirs." "Sway," as Coriolanus uses the word here, means hold power. He wants to be a combat soldier serving the people of Rome, which to him means the patricians, rather than doing the things necessary to obtain governing power, which first means humbling himself to the populace. Volumnia does not respond to his demurral, essentially because it is as if he had not spoken. What he says does not matter to her. It has become so much the case that she wills what

he will be and fashions what he does and he only enacts it.

During her first appearance in the play, Volumnia describes how she fashioned him and, in graphic (and psychologically devastating) terms, conveys how she values him.

> If my son were my husband, I should freelier rejoice in that absence wherein he won honor than in the embracements of his bed where he would show most love. When yet he was but tender-bodied, and the only son of my womb; when youth with comeliness plucked all gaze his way; when, for a day of kings' entreaties, a mother should not sell him an hour from her beholding; I, considering how honor would become such a person—that it was no better than picture-like to hang by th' wall, if renown made it not stir—was pleased to let him seek danger where he was to find fame. To a cruel war I sent him, from whence he returned, his brows bound with oak. I tell thee, daughter, I sprang not more in joy at first hearing he was a man-child than now in first seeing he had proved himself a man.

If this is not enough to show that she values the light he casts upon her over the life that might have burned in him, she concludes by saying that, "had I a dozen sons," she would prefer that they all "die nobly for their country," than that one live at ease.

Thus Marcius is defined by an awful contradiction. He belongs most to himself when he belongs most to his mother. When she wishes him to run for consul, he is put into conflict, not really with himself, since he has no authentic self-driven self, but with the self that she has constructed within him, for him, which she now would see deconstructed and refashioned. No longer is he to be the proud soldier who needs no maternal nurture, who can release his fury at its absence in warfare, feed on the blood of others, and bring back his own spilled blood to feed his mother's pride. He must become a supplicant, humble himself to those whom he abhors and show the wounds to them which properly belong to his mother.

When he is unable to do that, Marcius comes in conflict with the populace and the tribunes of Rome. That encounter enrages him, but it does not undermine him or shake his core identity the way his mother's response threatens to do. When his failure to satisfy the plebeians becomes a failure to satisfy her, and the cause for a second instance of conflict with her, stronger than the first, that is when his world begins to totter. "I muse my mother / Does not approve me further," he says, in act 3, scene 2, after a tempestuous encounter in which he alienates the people with his scornful wrath. His mother, he protests, "was wont / To call them woolen vassals, things created / To buy and sell with groats." He was merely displaying towards the plebeians the very contempt his mother had taught him and approved in him. When Coriolanus asks her, "Why did you wish me milder— Would you have me / False to my nature," he defends himself saying, "I play / The man I am." I am being true to myself, he says, true to the man you have always had me be. This time she does not remain silent as she did when he expressed his reluctance to seek the office of consul but contradicts him with a reproach: "You might have been enough the man you are, / With striving less to be so."

Volumnia is counseling craft, but craft has never been his way. Marcius is open, forthright, and aggressive. It is the mark of his honor not to dissemble. It is the root of his identity to be what he seems and to seem what he is, to play the man and not the politician. She is teaching him a new lesson:

> Lesser had been
> The thwartings of your dispositions, if
> You had not showed them how ye were disposed,
> Ere they lacked power to cross you.

It makes him angry. "Let them hang," he says directing his wrath where it is permissible, not against his mother, where it is truly directed, but against the people. And she returns his anger, with irony. "Ay," she says, "and burn too," warning him of the likely consequences of his forthrightness. But he has never before had to concern himself with the fear of violence directed against himself or Rome. As a soldier, he has confronted and defeated it. As a mother, she had sent "him [to] seek danger where he was like to find fame." Now she reverses herself and tells him that in order to enjoy fame, he must temporize it with danger.

Marcius tries, but he is ill-disposed to remodel himself in the new image his mother presents him with., Fortified by his devotion to his honor and to his integrity, qualities which his mother first shaped in him, he is defeated in his attempt to abruptly change in order to expose himself to the people that he scorns, in order to seek their approval. And so, Coriolanus is banished from Rome, betrayed by motherland and mother. In his loss of self he seeks the only other fitting image of himself that he has ever regarded—Aufidius, whom he has made the mirror of himself—and presents himself to his rival for either extermination at his hand or assimilation into his identity. By this move, without even anticipating the consequences, Coriolanus puts his fundamental conflict, the one that must destroy him, out in the open. He becomes an open enemy of Rome and, just as surely, an enemy of his mother. When Coriolanus goes to battle against his motherland, heart hardened against his adversary as always, his mother's *coup de grâce* is to manage to transfer the conflict between rivals from the outer realm, where it is a matter of self against other, to the inner, where it is the self against the self. His mother turns his conflict with Rome and with her back into the conflict it has always been, a conflict of her making, a conflict with himself, a conflict in which, no matter which side wins, Coriolanus dies.

Source: Neil Heims, Critical Essay on *Coriolanus*, in *Shakespeare For Students*, Second Edition, Thomson Gale, 2007.

Jerald W. Spotswood

In the following excerpt, Spotswood examines Shakespeare's portrayal of mobs and social politics in Coriolanus. *Whereas in earlier plays such as* Julius Caesar, *Shakespeare portrayed crowds as unruly mobs, in* Coriolanus *he depicts the crowd as a potentially legitimate political body in its own right. However, Spotswood argues that in the end, despite the evolution in his portrayal of crowds, Shakespeare "allows no authoritative voice to emerge from the masses."*

For several recent critics, Shakespeare's shift from portraying the crowd as mob in early plays, like *2 Henry VI* and *Julius Caesar*, to portraying the crowd as "political entity" in Coriolanus marks his "most radical position." Shakespeare's presentation of "different political structures" generates tremendous "political risks," according to Thomas Sorge. [in *The Failure of Orthodoxy in Coriolanus*]. For by offering the audience a choice of models—"the rule of one, the rule of the few, the rule of the many"—Coriolanus "potentially challenges authority's representation of monarchy as the only form of rule beneficial for England." While Sorge is correct in asserting that alternative models question the role of the

WHAT DO I READ NEXT?

- "John Brown" is a lesser-known 1963 ballad by Bob Dylan about a mother's pride in her soldier son and the terrible wreck of his life made by war.

- *Julius Caesar* (1599) is an earlier play written by Shakespeare using Roman subject matter and set in ancient Rome. This play has characters that are more accessible than Coriolanus, lacks a pivotal female character like Volumnia, and presents the plebeians more as a rabble than the sometimes thoughtful collection of citizens that Shakespeare shows them to be in *Coriolanus*.

- "Coriolan" (1932), a fragmentary post–World War I work by T. S. Eliot, is a modernist poem combining Roman and early twentieth century elements focusing first on the triumphal march home from war and then on the breakdown of the warrior leader as a civil servant.

- *Germinal* is an epic novel published by Emile Zola in 1885. Zola tells the story of exploited coal miners in mid-nineteenth century France, who rise up against the wealthy families who own the coal mines in an attempt to secure a decent livelihood; ultimately, the mine workers are defeated. The ambivalent relationship of the miners to Jacques Lantier, one of the leaders of the strike who is idealistic and also hot-headed, is woven into the story.

- *Hard Times* is Charles Dickens's 1854 novel. At the center of Dickens's novel about the struggle of exploited nineteenth-century English factory workers to live decently are Mr. Bounderby, the proud factory owner who has broken off his relationship to his mother, and Steven Blackpool, a poor worker who struggles to maintain his honor and integrity despite a corrupt union organizer.

- Sophocles's *Oedipus Rex*, written in 428 B.C.E., is one of the core works of western literature. It tells the story of a proud king who is humbled by a reversal of fortune. When he learns that he has inadvertently killed his father and married his mother, he puts out his eyes and is exiled from Thebes, his homeland.

- *Johnny Tremain* published in 1943 by Esther Forbes, is a historical novel for young adults depicting the social, economic, and political situation in Boston on the eve of the Revolutionary War. Its focus on the young silversmith, Johnny Tremain, engages the reader in problems of pride, responsibility, humbling experiences, and the role of social as well as individual duties in the development of a person's character.

- In *The Weavers* (1892), German playwright Gerhard Hauptman tells the story of an uprising of Silesian weavers in the 1840s.

---

monarch in society, the "rule of the many" (a model of "democracy," as Sorge calls it at one point) is not presented as a viable alternative. Too often in both *Julius Caesar* and *Coriolanus*, the rule of the many is characterized as "Dissentious numbers pest'ring streets" (Cor. 4.6.7).

Contrary to the assertion that Shakespeare endorses majoritarian rule in Coriolanus, I argue that Shakespeare symbolically disarms plebeians by depicting them as a socially indistinct mass: a "beast / With many heads" (Cor. 4.1.1–2) representing "such as cannot rule / Nor ever will be ruled." Shakespeare, of course, does not always fashion commoners quite so monstrously. Bottom, Dogberry, and the first gravedigger in *Hamlet* are all dignified with either names, occupations, or social histories. Bottom, a weaver, is "simply the best wit of any handicraftman in Athens" (MND 4.2.9–10). Dogberry is a "Constable in charge of the Watch" (Ado 1.1), and the first gravedigger has been "sexton here, man and boy, [for] thirty years" (Ham. 5.1.157–58). In placing these characters in positions of authority and in granting them the respect of their peers, Shakespeare sets them apart from

> IN DENYING COMMONERS ANY LEVEL OF STATUS OR ANY MEASURE OF INDIVIDUALITY, WHICH OF COURSE HISTORICALLY THEY DID HOLD, SHAKESPEARE REWRITES INDIVIDUALITY AS A CHARACTERISTIC OF THE ELITE AND DENIGRATES COLLECTIVE ACTION BY ASSOCIATING IT WITH A RABBLE THAT BY DEFINITION HOLDS NO INTEREST IN THE SOCIAL ORDER."

the multitude and lends credence to their social commentary. Yet in *Julius Caesar* and *Coriolanus*—two plays concerned with the form and structure of body politic—Shakespeare allows no authoritative voice to emerge from the masses. In these two "political" plays, Shakespeare persistently marks off distinctions between elite and common culture by invoking a past in which military prowess determines social merit, thus leaving plebeians to appear as "fragments" to the singularity of patricians (Cor. 1.1.221). Like women portrayed in literature, who according to Virginia Woolf [in *A Room of One's Own*] "have served all these centuries as looking-glasses possessing the magic and delicious power of reflecting the figure of man at twice its natural size," commoners in *Julius Caesar* and *Coriolanus* serve to reflect and enlarge the figure of the elite.

In denying commoners any level of status or any measure of individuality, which of course historically they did hold, Shakespeare rewrites individuality as a characteristic of the elite and denigrates collective action by associating it with a rabble that by definition holds no interest in the social order. For in contrast in the self-control and individual accomplishments displayed by aristocrats, collective action carries a taint or dishonor. As Claus Offe and Helmut Wiesenthal observe, [in their essay "Two Logics of Collective Action: Theoretical Notes on Social Class and Organizational Form"] "it is only the relatively powerless who will have reason to act non-individualistically on the basis of a notion of a collective identity that is both generated and presupposed by their association." To speak collectively implies that one lacks voice—and

importance—as an individual. Clearly, collective action is something that a "rabble" does, not individuals... (Cor. 3.1.262).

The actions of plebeians are more restrained in *Coriolanus* as their overwhelming numbers are enough to convince patricians to give them "corn at their own rates" from the "the store-houses crammed with grain" (1.1.187, 78, 79) Although a "company of mutinous Citizens" armed with "staves, clubs, and other weapons" opens the play, they do not "Revenge! About! Seek! Burn! Fire! Kill! Slay!" (JC 3.2.200); instead they remain "prating" (1.1.466) Citing the verbal proficiency of plebeians in *Coriolanus* (always an attribute prized by literary critics), Annabel Patterson suggests [in *Shakespeare and the Popular Voice*] that Shakespeare has acquired an ear for the "popular voice." In *Coriolanus* the people "are allowed to speak for themselves; and in so doing present a critique of precisely those assumptions ... that, in *Julius Caesar* permitted that easy, contemptuous dismissal." "Clearly," adds Sorge, "this is not a mindless, demoralized rabble." Shakespeare's "partial solution" to the problem of the "general will" is to counter "the negative implications of 'multitude'" with "intimations of majoritarianism" and "individualism." Shakespeare speaks the "popular voice," Annabel Patterson claims, when he represents plebeians as individuals rather than members of a collectivity.

Perhaps. But it seems to me that plebeians are powerful in *Coriolanus* when they act collectively, as demonstrated both in the grain uprising opening the play and, later, in banishing Coriolanus from Rome. When they are granted individual voices, as plebeians are in ceremoniously affirming Coriolanus's consulship, their power dissolves. Although every citizen is accorded a "single honour" (2.3.45) allowing them to give their "own voices" with their "own tongues" (2.3.46), the "divide and conquer" strategy of the ceremony ensures that the socially powerful Coriolanus meets the plebeians individually, rather than meeting them "in their ancient strength" as a collective force (4.2.7): they "are not to stay all together, but to come by him where he stands by ones, by twos, and by threes" (2.3.42–44). "[M]ocked," "flouted... downright," and "used ... scornfully" by Coriolanus, the majority still "admit" him consul (2.3.159–). Although plebeians later "revoke" their "judgement" (2.3.218), they do so in their

Ian Hogg as Coriolanus in Act I, scene v, at Royal Shakespeare Theatre, Stratford-upon-Avon, 1972

(© Donald Cooper/Photostage. Reproduced by permission)

strength as a multitude, not in their weakness as powerless individuals. Shakespeare's plebeians are keenly aware of the limitation of their power as individuals, perhaps more keenly aware than a critic like Annabel Patterson who argues that in *Coriolanus* plebeian voices equal "votes." Indeed though plebeians "have power" in themselves to "deny" Coriolanus their "voices" for consul (2.3.1–4), "it is a power" that they "have no power to do" (2.3.5), for their role in the "ceremony" (2.2.142), as the third citizen points out, is not to question or even affirm the validity of Coriolanus's accomplishments, but to show that they are worthy of recognizing his nobility. To dispute the claim that Coriolanus

is worth a "thousand to one good one" is to risk being called ungrateful and monstrous (2.2.79):

> For if he show us his wounds and tell us his deeds, we are to put our tongues into those wounds and speak for them; so if he tell us his noble deeds we must also tell him our noble acceptance of them. Ingratitude is monstrous, and for the multitude to be ingrateful were to make a monster of the multitude, of the which we, being members, should bring ourselves to be monstrous members. (2.3.5–13)

Audible only en masse—not as individuals—plebeians must band together to claim voice, a voice that must only consent to the demands of political ritual.

Plebeians in *Coriolanus* can speak through their "Noble tribunes" (3.1.328), who are granted individuality by Shakespeare. As "Masters o'th' people" (2.2.51), Brutus and Sicinius are set apart from those they represent by their names and official titles. Yet their status are compromised by their association with the masses. Sicinius is mocked by Coriolanus for being no better than a "Triton of the minnows" (3.1.92) "[B]eing the herdsmen of the beastly plebeians" (2.1.93), both Brutus and Sicinius are taunted by Menenius for their inability to act as individuals: "I know you can do very little alone, for your helps are many, or else your actions would grow wondrous single. Your abilities are too infant-like for doing much alone" (2.1.34–37). Yet despite their own compromised status, the tribunes are slow to comprehend the powerlessness of their constituents when acting as individuals. "[L]essoned" and "fore-advised" by the tribunes to pass Coriolanus "unelected" (2.3.177, 191, 199), plebeians still "yield" him their voices (2.3.176). Their "ignorant election" (2.1.175), as Brutus and Sicinius later realize, can be blamed on the plebeians' "childish friendliness" (2.1.175)—their display of deference toward Coriolanus. Thus despite gaining "five tribunes ... Of their own choice" (1.1.213–4), the plebeians' only real claim to political power is the limited power of speaking with "many mouths" as a "din confused" ... (4.6.66, 3.3.20)

Despite the fact that early modern England was pervasively hierarchical—Shakespeare's own acting company included—Shakespeare persistently ignores distinctions below the level of gentleman in both *Julius Caesar* and *Coriolanus*. In doing so, Shakespeare both denigrates traditional modes of collective power and eliminates plebeians from individual rule and responsibility modeled after aristocratic behavior. Portrayed en masse, lacking any individuality, plebeians appear indistinguishable from one another. While plebeians are sometimes identified by their occupations, as the cobbler and the carpenter are in *Julius Caesar* and the host is in *Coriolanus*, Shakespeare gives his audience no sense about where these characters stand in relation to other plebeians. Like the grain hoarded by patricians in *Coriolanus*, individuality and placement within the social hierarchy are "goods" that Shakespeare excludes from plebeians...

In contrast to the outlines he sketches of the multitude, Shakespeare depicts patricians in vivid detail, granting them both individuality and a specific place within the social order. Invoking a past in which military prowess determines social merit, Shakespeare draws clear distinctions between elites and commoners. Being "Most like a soldier," Brutus is remembered as "the noblest Roman of them all." Coriolanus "is simply the rarest man i'th' world," for he "does exceed ... all" plebeians "As far as doth the Capitol exceed / The meanest house in Rome." For Shakespeare's audience, the figure of the warrior would have remained a strong testament of an aristocrat's status and his right to rule in early modern England ...

Military confrontation and its guarantee of winners and losers, of conqueror and conquered, displaces this image of communal tranquillity. Unlike the great warrior Aufidius, who clearly occupies a place in Coriolanus's memory, the poor man represents a function for Coriolanus, not a named and distinct individual. His body, neither notched in scars nor covered in blood, is remembered for the "kindly" service it has performed. Unlike the services of Coriolanus, those of the poor man do not distinguish him or grant him individuality. Not having performed military service, or at least not having been successful at it, the poor man becomes lost in the shuffle of common faces and common deeds, and Coriolanus falters in his attempts to repay his debt of gratitude, remembering not his name but only that a poor man has used him kindly.

In contrast to the poor man's lack of individuality, Coriolanus's name and reputation earn him status and respect even in Antium. "[D]isguised and muffled" in "mean apparel," Coriolanus enters the stage in act 4, scene 4, looking much like a poor commoner, and his "grim appearance" and "torn" clothing momentarily dissolve his "all-noble" status. Three of Aufidius's servingmen attempt to show Coriolanus "to the door," asking him "What have you to do here, fellow?" When Coriolanus identifies himself as a "gentleman," the third servingman replies mockingly, "Pray you, poor gentleman, take up some other station. Here's no place for you. Pray you, avoid. Come." Even Aufidius, who Coriolanus has "ever followed ... with hate," cannot recognize this disguised warrior. Although Aufidius admits that this stranger "show'st a noble vessel" that "Bears a command in't," he cannot identify him, ordering Coriolanus to name himself six times in eleven lines. When Coriolanus finally complies—"My name is Caius Martius, who hath done / To thee particularly, and to all the Volsces, / Great hurt and mischief"—a "strange alteration" occurs. No longer ushered to the door by common servingmen, Coriolanus is "set at [the] upper end o'th' table" where "the senators ... stand bald before him." Even Aufidius, general of the Volscian army, shows Coriolanus respect, turning "up the white o'th' eye to his discourse." As the second servingman reports, Coriolanus's "clothes made a false report of him," for "there was something in him."

Concerned primarily with intra-elite conflict and power struggle—not with the struggle of plebeians—Shakespeare focuses on the turbulent shift from a warrior to a "civilized" society...

In *Coriolanus* the integrity of patricians is threatened by Caius Martius's inability to "temporize" his actions. "[B]red i'th' wars / Since a could draw a sword," and "ill-schooled / In bolted language," Coriolanus cannot accommodate himself to "civilized" society. Coriolanus's actions, as Menenius chides him, "have been too rough, something too rough." Unlike Menenius, whose practiced paternalism earns him the title of "one that hath always loved the people," Coriolanus is tagged as "chief enemy to the people." For despite the twenty-seven "wounds upon him," which elevate Coriolanus to the status of not only the greatest soldier in Rome but also the patricians' prime candidate for council, Coriolanus's inability to mix "Honour and policy" makes him a "disease" within the aristocracy. Refusing to "perform a part," Coriolanus is "banished, / As enemy to the people and his country."

Focusing on intra-elite conflict, Shakespeare largely neglects the concerns of plebeians in both *Julius Caesar* and *Coriolanus*, in part, because he is bound by literary conventions that align tragedy with the most "high and excellent" and that which "is most worthy to be learned." In placing the "individual for the species, the one above the infinite many," tragedy sets our attitudes against the collective actions of commoners, as William Hazlitt argues [in *The Complete Works*]. Even if we do not identify with Coriolanus, the genre demands that we respect his individual accomplishments. Tragedy, [George Wilhelm Friedrich] Hegel insists [in *Hegel on Tragedy*], elicits "fear and pity" only when such emotions are embodied in a "man of nobility and greatness." In the estimation of both patricians and plebeians, Coriolanus is "a worthy man," for the "services he has

done for his country" are achieved "all alone." Plebeians, who according to Menenius "can do very little alone," stand in sharp opposition to the individuality and tragic heroism displayed by Coriolanus. Shakespeare's juxtaposition of the collective suffering of plebeians embellishes Coriolanus's individual accomplishments...

In short, Shakespeare does not "conceive of 'everyman' as tragic." In portraying the elite tragically, that is seriously, Shakespeare isolates the few from the many and, in turn, validates military prowess and "civility" as attributes that privilege the select...

Source: Jerald W. Spotswood, "We Are Undone Already': Disarming the Multitude in *Julius Caesar* and *Coriolanus*," in *Texas Studies in Literature and Language*, Vol. 42, No. 1, Spring 2000, pp. 61–79.

Emmet Wilson

In the following essay (originally published in 1968), Wilson offers a psychoanalytic approach to Coriolanus, *evaluating language and imagery that suggests Freudian conflicts within the play. The critic begins by analyzing the unique bodily imagery of* Coriolanus, *through which sexuality and war are thematically linked. Wilson also notes the psychological resonance of aggression in the play's family relationships. Oedipal, or incestuous, motifs appear as do Coriolanus's anxieties concerning his symbolic castration by his domineering and masculine—or "phallic"—mother, Volumnia. Wilson further explores Coriolanus's hostility toward his mother and his rebellion against her. This revolt, in turn, is characterized by the homoerotic overtones of Coriolanus's relationship with Aufidius—who also becomes a surrogate for Coriolanus's absent father—as the two men join forces to attack Rome, i.e. Volumnia.*

In *Coriolanus*, Shakespeare adapted a plot from North's translation of *Plutarch's Lives* into an intensive exploration of a pathological mother-son relationship. It is the story of a son who attempts to rebel against his mother, to whom he has been inordinately attached. The son is ultimately destroyed when he renounces his rebellion and submits to his mother. In this paper, I wish to examine certain aspects of the play for the unconscious fantasies which may have determined the handling of the narrative material from which Shakespeare worked. In particular, I suggest that an examination of the wedding night references in the play is essential

IN THIS PLAY OF A MOTHER-CHILD RELATIONSHIP, THERE ARE FREQUENT ALLUSIONS TO FOOD, NOURISHMENT, INGESTION, HUNGER, BITING, OR DEVOURING."

for an understanding of the work on a psycho-analytical level.

The play has sometimes been cited as peculiar among Shakespeare's works. Critics discern a "slackness" in Shakespeare's dramatic power. This slackness is supposed to be reflected in the way in which Shakespeare handled his source material. If we compare Shakespeare's adaptation with the original in North's translation, we find at several points an almost slavish closeness to the source. This dependence on North is so extensive that at first reading, the play seems little more than a simple dramatization of the plot from North. Editors have been able to make emendations and fill textual lacunae in the play by referring to North, so faithfully has Shakespeare followed his source. The later acts of the play, especially, show a marked increase in borrowing, and tend to rely almost exclusively on North. Shakespeare might, of course, have been under some merely temporal pressure to complete the play, but this marked change in the processing of the material could also have been due to the conflictual nature of the subject matter. At any rate, Shakespeare seems to have adhered doggedly to his source in order to finish his task.

Yet, the earlier acts and the characters introduced there involve a good deal of revision and reworking of the material. Shakespeare has developed certain characters and added others, and has elaborated on the relationship of Coriolanus to the various individuals who are significant to him. Further, Shakespeare's particular choices of expression in the play are striking. The language has been called harsh. The poetry seems at times to disguise only slightly some rather grotesque ideas. As an example of the grossness of thought, consider Coriolanus' rebuke to the tribunes for their failure to control the mob: "You being their mouths, why rule you not their teeth?" These additions by Shakespeare

to his source material are important for a psychological understanding of the play.

Imagery

The peculiar imagery Shakespeare has chosen tends to support the view that the theme of the play was one to which the playwright was psychologically sensitive. The images tend to fall within a narrow range. Caroline Spurgeon found these to be concerned largely with bodily functions, sickness, and loss of diseased bodily parts. Blood, and things made bloody, are constantly mentioned. Stoller calls attention to the numerous staves, pikes, rakes, swords, and other phallic equivalents. There are many references to wounds and to parts of the body, or simply to parts. Coriolanus shouts angrily to the mob, "Go get you home, you fragments!" (1.1.211).

Combat and sexuality are often linked. Battles are described in sexual images, or talk of battle provides the opportunity for a reference to sexual activity. Cominius, the Roman commander-in-chief, proudly describes some teenage battle exploit of Coriolanus as occurring at an age when he might have acted "the woman in the scene" (2.2.92). Peace is a "great maker of cuckolds" (4.5.225). Coriolanus threatens to beat the Volscians "to their wives" (1.4.41). Volumnia, his mother, says of Coriolanus' impetuous attitude toward the mob,

… I know thou hadst rather
Follow thine enemy in a fiery gulf
Than flatter him in a bower.
(3.2.90–92)

Curiously, while Coriolanus is in battle in Act I, Volumnia and her friend go to visit a lady lying in (1.3.72).

Another significant group of images is oral. In this play of a mother-child relationship, there are frequent allusions to food, nourishment, ingestion, hunger, biting, or devouring. To note one important instance: Some servingmen are speaking of the personal rivalry between Coriolanus and his Volscian opponent, Aufidius. They recall the battle of Corioli:

First Serv. Before Corioli he [Coriolanus] scotched him and notched him like a carbonado [meat cut up for cooking].

Second Serv. And he had been cannibally given, he might have boiled and eaten him too. (4.5.186–89)

In some images, aggressive impulses are characteristically directed towards the interior of the body. Coriolanus' attacks on Rome are said to be "pouring war / Into the bowels of ungrateful Rome" (4.5.129). When Volumnia entreats Coriolanus to cease warring on Rome, he is said to want to tread upon his mother's womb (5.3.124). He is charged with

> Making the mother, wife and child, to
>   see
> The son, the husband and the father, tearing
> His country's bowels out.
> (5.3.101–03)

This juxtaposition of aggression with the family relationships is striking, and provides unambiguous evidence of the symbolic character of the attack on Rome as an attack on those objects whom previously Coriolanus had loved. The repetition of this sort of imagery is impressive, and indicates the extent and strength of certain unconscious fantasies: the fear of being eaten, and the rage against the mother's engulfing body.

The Wedding Night

In the midst of these grotesque images of blood, aggression, and bodily destruction, there is a scene in which Coriolanus rises to intense lyric expression. In the battle at Corioli, he expresses the joy of victory, and greets his general, Cominius with

> O, let me clip ye
> In arms as sound as when I wooed; in heart
> As merry as when our nuptial day was done,
> And tapers burned to bedward!
> (1.6.29–32)

Here, we find an obvious reference to a specific sexual event, and an unconscious reference in the phallic burning tapers. The significance of the image is further heightened by one other reference to a wedding night. When Coriolanus joins Aufidius as an ally against Rome, Aufidius expresses *his* joy by referring to his bride on her first crossing the threshold, and he declares that he is even more rapt by Coriolanus than he was by his bride:

> Know thou first,
> I loved the maid I married: never man
> Sighed truer breath; but that I see thee here,
> Thou noble thing, more dances my rapt
>   heart
> Than when I first my wedded mistress saw
> Bestride my threshold.
> (4.5.112–17)

Commentators have noted these two references to the wedding night. Perhaps the most insightful is Rank's brief discussion. However, the meaning of these two passages in *Coriolanus* has not been sufficiently explored. Further examination of these passages is important, for the wedding night images condense several major themes of the play.

To understand Coriolanus' reference to his wedding night, we need to examine the scene in which the reference occurs. Preceding Coriolanus' lyric recall of this event, there is a series of scenes of the battle before Corioli, in which Coriolanus is especially in danger of being deserted by his men and closed up within the gates of the enemy town. Coriolanus exhorts his soldiers to charge the Volscians when the battle first begins at the gates of Corioli. In particular, he threatens any stragglers with his "edge" (1.4.29). This threat proves insufficient. As Coriolanus follows the Volscians to the gates of their city, he still needs to urge the Roman soldiers to enter the gates with him:

> So, now the gates are ope. Now prove
>   good seconds.
> 'Tis for the followers fortune widens them,
> Not for the fliers. Mark me, and do the like.
> (1.4.43–45)

Yet precisely before the open gates, he is deserted. The Roman response to his exhortation is:

> *First Sol.*: Foolhardiness. Not I.
> *Second Sol.*: Nor I.
> *First Sol.*: See, they have shut him in.
> (1.4.46–47)

In Plutarch, when Coriolanus stormed the gates, others were with him. The complete abandonment is stressed by the soldiers: "He is himself alone, / To answer all the city" (1.4.52–53). They immediately suppose that he is dead, that he is gone "to th' pot" (1.4.48). In view of the recurrent theme of being eaten, it is very likely that those commentators are correct who suppose that the pot here is a cooking pot, and that the line means that Coriolanus has been cut to pieces.

The battle is carried by the Romans as their commander, Cominius, arrives. Coriolanus reappears, covered with blood. He sees Cominius and asks, "Come I too late?" Cominius replies, "Ay, if you come not in the blood of others, / But mantled in your own" (1.6.27–29).

Coriolanus responds to the question whether he is wounded by saying that his arms are as sound as before he married, and then refers to his wedding night in an effusion of joy and enthusiasm. Curiously, Coriolanus does not give a direct answer to Cominius' question until he boasts later to Aufidius: "'Tis not my blood / Wherein thou seest me masked" (1.8.9–10).

In these scenes at Corioli, we have a battle in which the important elements are the opening and penetration of the enemy's defenses with the resulting danger of destruction to the attacker. Following the battle, there is a specific reference to the first sexual union between Coriolanus and his bride. As if to underscore the allusion to defloration, Cominius immediately after the wedding night memory, addresses Coriolanus as "Flower of warriors" (1.6.32). There is, I suggest, a symbolic parallel between the battle at Corioli and unconscious fantasies concerning the experience of the wedding night. The battle is, as it were, a symbolic re-enactment of the anxiety provoking sexual event, defloration. The battle scene at Corioli expresses the unconscious equation of coitus with a violent, damaging assault, an equation which we noted earlier in the imagery of the play. Castration anxieties aroused by coitus are heightened by the actual accompaniment of the sexual act by bleeding and a change in the female's bodily status. In the unconscious, defloration is equated with the castration of the sexual partner, and there is an associated dread of a mutilating retaliation. The feared punishment, castration, is symbolized in the battle by the danger of becoming entrapped within the gates, to be cut up and devoured. In the memory of defloration which follows the battle scenes, Coriolanus may well be attempting to deal with his terrifying discovery that he had created a sexual difference in his bride, by making her into a woman, i.e., a person who had been deprived of the phallus. Ultimately, the punishment that is dreaded for this act is a revenge by his mother on her son for having entertained these notions of assault against her body and, of course, on a deeper level, the woman who is castrated in the sexual act would be the phallic mother, Volumnia.

If I am correct in this analysis of the battle at Corioli, then the award of the name, "Coriolanus," for exploits in that battle may also be of psychological importance. For this, however, we must turn to a passage in North which has not

been transferred to the play, but which may very well have influenced Shakespeare in his conception of the battle scenes. In the play, the hero receives his *agnomen*, "Coriolanus," as an honorary "trophy" for the events of the battle. The unconscious meaning of such a trophy is familiar to us as signifying the castration of the enemy and the sadistic wish to rob him of his penis. But from North's translation of Plutarch's *Life of Coriolanus*, we learn that the name could also have been given to signify, and to compensate for, an injury which the bearer of the name had received. In North, a lengthy discussion occurs on the Roman habit of according such names. In this passage North states:

> Sometimes also [the Romans] give surnames derived of some mark of misfortune of the body. As Sylla, to say, "crooked-nose"; Niger, "black"; Rufus, "red"; Caecus, "blind"; Claudus, "lame." They did wisely in this thing to accustom men to think that neither the loss of sight nor other such misfortunes as may chance to men are any shame or disgrace unto them; but the manner was to answer boldly to such names, as if they were called by their proper names.

In view of this comment from North on the secondary meaning of an *agnomen* as commemorative of mutilation, there is a significant parallel to be noted between the attempt to master the psychological sequellae of mutilation by the award of a compensatory *agnomen*, and the use Shakespeare makes of the scene before Corioli as a repetition in symbolic form of an experience involving an intense fear of bodily mutilation in retaliation for forbidden sexual wishes. The same psychological mechanism would seem to be operative in the *agnomen* and in the repetition of the traumatic scene—the attempt to master a traumatic event by some compensatory maneuver after the fact. Coriolanus was wounded at Corioli, and when he stands for the consulship, Coriolanus must display the scars from the battle at Corioli, scars which mark him as having distinguished himself in the service of Rome just as much as his *agnomen* and other honors do. When Coriolanus rejects the subservient position which he had maintained to Volumnia in the first half of the play, he vehemently rejects his *agnomen* at the same time, and wants to forge another in the "fire of burning Rome" (5.1.14). There are thus some indications of a reversal of the significance of the name received at Corioli to represent Coriolanus' continued subservience to Volumnia, and his acquiescence in the role that she demanded of him.

The wound motif continues and further develops the fantasy which appears in the battle scenes at Corioli. The question of these wounds comes to dominate the scenes subsequent to the battle, and provides us with important information on the relationship between Coriolanus and his mother. The phallic castrating mother rejoices in his wounds for the purpose of going before the people: "O, he is wounded: I thank the gods for't" (2.1.107) because "there will be large cicatrices to show the people when he shall stand for his place" (2.1.132). It was a traditional requirement that all aspirants to the consulship stand before the populace and display battle wounds. Coriolanus, however, finds this custom ignominious and objectionable. The mob has from the first been presented as a cannibalistic threat to Coriolanus (1.1), and it has been suggested that the mob stands for the aggressive and dangerous aspects of the mother. Coriolanus' reluctance to display his wounds to the mob is Shakespeare's modification of his source, for in Plutarch the problem does not arise at all. Moreover, standing for the consulship is Volumnia's idea, and Coriolanus can be prevailed upon to go to the people with his wounds only at his mother's insistent cajoling and threats. Volumnia's wish to see her son as a consul, and her role in forcing him to submit to the people, give evidence of the way in which Shakespeare has adapted the plot to strengthen the dominating influence which Volumnia has over her son. Just as she had rejoiced in his wounds, the mob is to see in these same wounds evidence that Coriolanus loves and will faithfully serve Rome. Volumnia thus forces Coriolanus into a position of pleasing and placating the aggressive aspects of herself which the mob symbolizes. Coriolanus can flatter the mob only if he shows his wounds, i.e., if he shows those symbols of castration which were needed to continue in his mother's favor. The sexual nature of the display of his body to the populace is suggested when Volumnia says that it is to "flatter [his enemy] in a bower" (3.2.92). Menenius excuses Coriolanus' insolence by "He loves your people, / But tie him not to be their bedfellow" (2.2.60–61). But it is clear that this is a sexual submission, not a conquest. At the moment of capitulation to Volumnia's urgings, Coriolanus launches a torrent of petulant language showing that his position is not only ignominious but also a threat to his masculinity. To submit will make his voice "Small as an eunuch ..." (3.2.114). Finally he begins to speak as a little boy:

> Mother, I am going to the market place:
> Chide me no more ... Look, I am going.
> (3.2.131–2, 134)

Rebellion against the Phallic Mother

I have so far explored *Coriolanus* in those sections which express the fantasies associated with the active phase of the Oedipus complex and the expected castration by the phallic mother for entertaining aggressive impulses toward her. I now turn to the episodes in which Coriolanus rebels against the phallic mother and seeks an alternative expression of his oedipal striving. Coriolanus abandons Rome and his mother, and turns traitor to the Romans, joining with their traditional enemies, the Volscians.

Rebellion is introduced in the opening scene, in which the Roman mob is about to turn against established authority. The mob is quieted, by means of a tale of another rebellion, that of the body's members against the belly (1.1). This theme of betrayal is sustained throughout the play. In certain passages, a sexual betrayal is clearly suggested. In the scene immediately preceding Coriolanus' suit to join Aufidius and betray the Romans, a Roman traitor and a Volscian spy meet to exchange information and the following comment is made:

> I have heard it said the fittest time to corrupt a man's wife is when she's fallen out with her husband (4.3.26–28)

These frequent allusions to treachery and betrayal provide a background for the behavior of Coriolanus, who is at first falsely, and later with some justification, labelled a traitor. It is the false charge of treason that provokes Coriolanus and provides him with the excuse to become a traitor in fact by leading an attack on Rome at the head of the Volscian forces. When Coriolanus capitulates to his mother's entreaties in Act V and leaves off his attack on Rome, he is in the awkward position of betraying the Volscian cause which he had joined. Aufidius can justifiably charge him with treason and demand his death.

There are, in addition, some clear indications of Coriolanus' extreme ambivalence toward his libidinal objects. This ambivalence is expressed in a total repudiation and withdrawal when negative feelings have been aroused. In changing allegiance from Rome to the Volscians, Coriolanus plots the total destruction of Rome. When Coriolanus left Rome in Act IV, he was still friendly with his party in Rome, and was ready to acknowledge and express his affection for his mother and his family. In Act V, he rejects all overtures from these friends. In Plutarch, Coriolanus is milder and shrewder. He spares the goods and estates of the nobles in his war on Rome, thereby spreading party dissension in Rome. Revenge on Rome in the form of a humiliating surrender would have been satisfactory for Plutarch's Coriolanus. In Shakespeare, nothing short of the destruction and burning of Rome itself will do. Coriolanus rejects Menenius, his mother Volumnia, and his wife. At the moment that Volumnia's embassy arrives at the Volscian camp, Coriolanus resolves to "stand / As if a man were author of himself / And knew no other kin" (5.3.35–37). He had made the same resolve to Menenius earlier: "Wife, mother, child, I know not. My affairs / Are servanted to others" (5.2.75–76). This insistence on a complete rejection is characteristic of Shakespeare's Coriolanus, who seems unable to tolerate any ambiguity in situations which involve his emotional commitment.

In addition, Coriolanus views any struggle for power with extreme anxiety. He resents the newly established office of tribune. Where, in North's version, Coriolanus' objection is restrained, in Shakespeare, Coriolanus objects to the Tribuneship because

> It makes the consuls base! and my soul aches
> To know, when two authorities are up,
> Neither supreme, how soon confusion
> May enter 'twixt the gap of both and take
> The one by th'other.
> (3.1.108–12)

It is reasonable to suppose that the prototypes in the unconscious of these two warring authorities are to be found in the original family situation, with parental roles presumably confused and conflicting, providing the opportunity to exploit and intensify the difficulties between the parents, and to play one off against the other.

In his soliloquy just before he goes over to the Volscians as an enemy of Rome, Coriolanus also expresses the theme of ambivalence and his concern with the struggle for supremacy:

> O world, thy slippery turns! Friends now fast sworn,

> Whose double bosoms seems to wear one heart,
> Whose hours, whose bed, whose meal and exercise
> Are still together, who twin, as 'twere, in love
> Unseparable, shall within this hour,
> On a dissension of a doit, break out
> To bitterest enmity. So, fellest foes,
> Whose passions and whose plots have broke their sleep
> To take the one the other, by some chance,
> Some trick not worth an egg, shall grow dear friends
> And interjoin their issues. So with me:
> My birthplace hate I, and my love's upon
> This enemy town.
> (4.4.12–24)

Here, Coriolanus anticipates the intensely homoerotic relationship into which he is about to move, when Aufidius will want to "twine" his arms around him (4.5.105). Yet he also anticipates the outcome of the trust he is about to place in Aufidius, for a moment after this extended comment on the transiency of human relationships, we see Coriolanus embraced as a bosom friend, and welcomed with greater joy than the welcome accorded a new bride, by the man who will shortly bring about his death.

Quest for a Surrogate Father

I will now examine the aspects of the play which indicate Coriolanus' attempt to institute a satisfactory expression of the passive phase of the Oedipus complex, in which he aspires to be loved by a powerful father, displacing his mother as his father's primary object.

Coriolanus' biological father remains vague in both North and Shakespeare. Yet two figures in the play serve as psychological representatives of a father to Coriolanus. One of these is the old family friend, Menenius. The other is Aufidius, who becomes an idealized father after the rejection of Volumnia. Menenius is an apt psychological symbol for the weak and conquered father appropriate to Coriolanus' wishes in the active phase of the Oedipus complex in which Volumnia is in the ascendancy as Coriolanus' object. Shakespeare developed the charming and complex character of Menenius almost independently of North, who gives only a few hints concerning a gentle old man who was loved by the people, and was a good choice to carry the

Senate's message to a rebellious populace. But Menenius remains a weak person, especially in comparison with the stalwart Volumnia. He fawns over a letter which Coriolanus had written him, in a fashion virtually indistinguishable from the responses of the women who have also received letters (2.1). Perhaps the most masterly touch in the contrast of Volumnia and Menenius is in their parting exchange after Coriolanus has been accompanied to the gates of Rome as he goes into exile. Menenius' response to this day of emotional trials is to note that he is hungry and to arrange for dinner. Not so for Volumnia:

> *Men*: You'll sup with me?
> *Vol*: Anger's my meat: I sup upon myself
> And so shall starve with feeding.
> (4.2.49–51)

Many passages explicitly refer to Menenius as Coriolanus' father. In his embassy to save Rome, Menenius declares confidently to a guard who is preventing him from seeing Coriolanus, "You shall perceive that a Jack guardant cannot office me from my son Coriolanus" (5.2.59). It is also apparent that the relationship is erotically tinged. Menenius in his frustration shouts at the guard, "I tell thee, fellow, / Thy general is my lover" (5.2.13–14), and Coriolanus, after sending the disappointed old man away, says: "This man, Aufidius, / Was my beloved in Rome" (5.2.85–86). It would seem that Menenius adulated Coriolanus too much to be an ideal substitute for the missing father. Menenius boasts, for example, "I have been / The book of his good acts" (5.2.13–14). Also, Menenius often acts as Volumnia's agent, i.e., as a person who can appeal to Coriolanus and affect his behavior only through Coriolanus' respect and awe for his mother. As Coriolanus' anger against the mob is beginning to get out of control, Menenius attempts to restrain Coriolanus with: "Is this the promise that you made to your mother?" (3.3.87).

In opposition to the quasi-familial situation of the earlier scenes of the play in which a strong mother dominates both Coriolanus and his weak, defeated, and castrated father, there is later the alternative oedipal solution in which Coriolanus repudiates his mother, and all her symbolic representatives, to seek out the strong, masculine father. The awesome figure of Aufidius, a marked contrast to Menenius, provides the second father symbol in the play.

The turn to Aufidius involves an intense and passive homoerotic relationship, for which we have been prepared. Even while Coriolanus and Aufidius are still enemies, Aufidius was admired. Coriolanus tells us in Act I:

> I sin in envying his nobility;
> And were I anything but what I am,
> I would wish me only he.
> (1.1.219–221)

Passive homosexual yearnings which Coriolanus had felt for a strong father now find expression in the renunciation of Volumnia in favor of a loving relationship with the virile Aufidius. The second allusion to a wedding night occurs in Act IV, when Aufidius welcomes Coriolanus as an ally. This time, however, it is Aufidius who thinks of his wedding night. Coriolanus is clearly supplanting Aufidius' previous erotic attachment to a woman. This new and strong father is eager to accept Coriolanus, and he looks on Coriolanus as on a bride crossing the threshold, even preferring his present happiness with Coriolanus to his wedding night.

The sexual character of this turning from Volumnia to Aufidius is also shown in the banter with the servingmen in this scene:

> *Serv*: How, Sir! Do you meddle with my
>   master?
> *Cor*: Ay, 'tis an honester service than to
>   meddle with thy mistress.
> (4.5.45–46)

A servingman later says that Aufidius now loves Coriolanus as a woman: "Our general himself makes a mistress of him ..." (4.5.194).

Earlier, Coriolanus was able to express his memory of defloration anxieties as he embraced Cominius, that is, when he is protected in a homoerotic embrace he can recall the threatening heterosexual experience. Another such embrace occurs between Aufidius and Coriolanus. In both scenes containing the wedding night allusions, the same word is used for this embrace, *viz.*, "clip." Coriolanus had turned to Cominius with the words: "O, let me clip ye / In arms as sound as when I wooed ..." (1.6.29–30). In his welcome to Coriolanus, Aufidius uses this word also:

> *Auf*: Here I clip
> The anvil of my sword, and do contest
> As hotly and as nobly with thy love
> As ever in ambitious strength I did
> Contend against thy valor. Know thou first,

I loved the maid I married. . . .
(4.5.108–113)

In Elizabethan English, "clip" would have meant both "to embrace" and "to cut off." In this repeated word, we thus have an unconscious continuation of the theme of castration which links the two wedding night allusions.

The embrace with Aufidius involves, on the unconscious level, the necessity for undergoing castration as a precondition of the father's love. To gain the love of Aufidius, Coriolanus must reject his city, his family, his mother, he must hate his birthplace, and turn his love onto the man who had previously been his rival. It is precisely the question of what further price must be paid to be loved by Aufidius that leads to difficulties in the new role as Aufidius' minion. Earlier, we saw that Coriolanus had feared castration as a retaliation for what he had wished to do to his mother. Now he expects that he must give up his masculinity in order to be loved by the strong and virile father.

Coriolanus attempts to meet this condition, on a symbolic level. In his soliloquy he had anticipated an eventual rivalry and falling out with Aufidius (4.4.12). Passages in the play indicate Coriolanus' self-destructive tendencies which will cause his own downfall. The tribunes had recognized this self-destructive trait and used it to their advantage. Brutus hoped to make Coriolanus angry because

then he speaks
What's in his heart; and that is there which
    looks
With us to break his neck.
(3.3.28–30)

Aufidius' jealousy is aroused when Coriolanus becomes haughty by the honors bestowed on him by the Volscians. When Volumnia's pleas prevail and the attack against Rome is called off, Coriolanus has in effect given Aufidius sufficient reason for anger. Coriolanus sees his own downfall, although he feels helpless to control or modify the events:

O my mother, mother! O!
You have won a happy victory to Rome;
But, for your son, believe it, O, believe it,
Most dangerously you have with him
    prevailed,
If not most mortal to him. But let it come.
Aufidius. . . .
(5.3.185–90)

He has betrayed the Volscians, and it is with this that Aufidius charges him, and justifies killing him.

The relationship with Aufidius is incomplete until he has made an attack on Coriolanus' body. On a deeper level, Coriolanus' death at the hands of Aufidius is also a love-union with Aufidius, which has been achieved by giving up his masculinity. By the equation of death and castration, Coriolanus has obtained the longed-for union with his father. At the moment of this attack, Coriolanus is denied his *agnomen* and condescendingly called "boy" instead. Almost the last breath Coriolanus takes is expended in his anger at this name of "boy." He boasts of his exploits at Corioli:

'tis there
That, like an eagle in a dovecote, I
Fluttered your Volscians in Corioli
Alone I did it. "Boy!"
(5.6.114–17)

In his anger, Coriolanus recalls his role at Corioli, an episode which symbolized a mutilating attack on the mother's body. This memory occurs precisely at the moment when he is to succumb to a mutilating attack by the strong father to whom he had offered himself as a love object. His identification with his mother is now complete, for he is about to be attacked and loved by his father in her stead, just as he had once desired to love her.

In summary: We may regard the earlier portions of *Coriolanus* as an articulation of the conflict found in those family constellations in which the father abdicates his function as a masculine figure for the son to identify with and to form an ego ideal. Menenius fulfilled this role symbolically in the initial situation. There is a splitting of the unconscious elements, with the defeat and castration of the father pushed into the past as an historical death, while certain aspects of the father are displaced on to Menenius in the present. In the place of a strong father, there is the ineffectual Menenius, whom Coriolanus may disregard as a feared rival for his mother.

However, Coriolanus' incestuous strivings are constantly stimulated and intensified by Volumnia in her erotization of the relationship. Coriolanus fears being engulfed by Volumnia in her ambitious designs to use him for her own goals. He is to function as her penile projection, by winning victories which will make her proud and give her opportunity to extol her blood. She would prefer military exploits to any show of tenderness:

> If my son were my husband, I should freelier rejoice in that absence wherein he won honor than in the embracements of his bed where he would show most love. (1.3.2–4)

The ego boundaries between mother and son are vague and indistinct. Coriolanus feels undifferentiated from his mother who is inimical to his development as an individual distinct from her. Coriolanus' view of his male role is thus markedly disturbed.

The sexualized attachment to Volumnia is uncomfortable because of the awareness of his hostility toward her, and of his aggressive impulses directed toward her body. Coriolanus has to deal not only with his own aggression and hatred, but also with the tendency to project this aggression on to its object in the form of anticipated retaliation for these angry and hostile feelings. Coriolanus is operating on the phallic dichotomy of "having a penis" vs. "being castrated." These were precisely the themes involved in the wedding night reference in Act I, viz., the belief that in intercourse violence is done to the woman's body, and the expectation of castrating punishment for this violence. The symbolic representation of this engulfment and destruction takes place in the battle when Coriolanus is closed off within the enemy gates and supposed dead.

Along with the fears of being castrated by the phallic mother, Coriolanus has feminine, passive wishes to submit to a strong father, even if the price is castration as a precondition for the father's love. The later portions of the play articulate this intense wish for a virile, loving father. Coriolanus joins with Aufidius to war against the mother's body, pouring war into her bowels, and treading upon her womb. Aggression towards Volumnia, which had in the earlier sections of the play been symbolically channeled on to the mob as representative of the mother, is now expressed by the massive rejection of Rome, birthplace, and mother. Aufidius and Coriolanus unite in love for one another and in mutual hatred for Rome and mother. Yet this solution is not completely successful until Aufidius is provoked to attack Coriolanus' own body, and Coriolanus achieves a love-death at the hands of the father for whom he had so ardently yearned.

Source: Emmet Wilson Jr., "Coriolanus: The Anxious Bridegroom," originally published in *American Imago*, Vol. 25, 1968. Reprinted in *'Coriolanus': Critical Essays*, edited by David Wheeler, Garland Publishing, Inc., 1995, pp. 93–110.

Frank Kermode

In his critical introduction to Coriolanus, *Kermode surveys the principal areas of interest in the play. He examines Shakespeare's departure from the primary historical source of the drama, the writings of Plutarch. He comments on the deeply flawed character of Coriolanus, whose "aristocratic loutishness," ferocity, and overdeveloped sense of virtus—the duty of a man—culminate in tragedy. Kermode mentions the relevance of Aristotle's dictum, "a man incapable of living in society is either a god or a beast," as it applies to the figure of Coriolanus. Kermode likewise envisions the theme of the work as the Roman warrior's inability to curb the source of his strength—his brutality on the battlefield—when dealing in the political arena, an area that requires cunning and tact rather than the raw might Coriolanus possesses in abundance. Finally, Kermode considers the subject of language in the play, including the overarching metaphor of the diseased body politic, and describes the "decorous power" of Shakespeare's verse.*

Coriolanus is by no means a favorite among Shakespeare's tragedies. It is harsh in its manner, political in its interests, and has a hero who is not—whatever else may be said of him—presented as a sympathetic character. Wyndham Lewis was not alone in finding Coriolanus the least lovable of tragic heroes; he calls the play "an astonishingly close picture of a particularly cheerless ... snob, such as must have pullulated in the court of Elizabeth"—a schoolboy crazed with notions of privilege, and possessed of a "demented ideal of authority." Lewis uses him to illustrate the theme suggested by his title, *The Lion and the Fox*: Aufidius plays fox to the stupid lion of Coriolanus; what stings the hero to his last fatal outburst of raw anger is a charge of disloyalty, and, significantly, the word "boy." He is an ugly political innocent: "What his breast forges, that his tongue must vent." There is no gap between his crude mind and his violent tongue. And such men are dangerous. Yet the gracelessness of the hero and the harshness of the verse do not in themselves discredit T. S. Eliot's judgment that *Coriolanus* is Shakespeare's finest artistic achievement in tragedy; and when Shaw

> LEADING THE VOLSCIANS AGAINST ROME, CORIOLANUS, IN THE FINAL MOVEMENT OF THE PLAY, CAN AGAIN BEHAVE LIKE A GOD … BUT THE ONLY LOVE OR PIETY HE RECOGNIZES—THAT EXCESSIVE RESPECT FOR HIS MOTHER WHICH USES UP ALL THE LOVE HE NEEDS FOR GOOD GOVERNMENT—FINALLY OVERTHROWS HIM."

Jonathan Cake as Coriolanus and Mo Sesay as Aufidius in Act I, scene viii, at Shakespeare's Globe, London, 2006 (© Donald Cooper/Photostage. *Reproduced by permission*)

called it the best of Shakespeare's comedies he was perhaps making much the same point by means of a paradox: this is a tragedy of ideas, schematic, finely controlled.

The style of *Coriolanus* suggests a late date, and this is confirmed by the scanty external evidence. The simile of the "coal of fire upon the ice" (I.i.173) may have been suggested by fires built on the frozen Thames in January 1608; there had been no comparable frost since 1565. In Jonson's *Epicoene* (1609) there is what looks like another of his gibes at Shakespeare in the line "You have lurch'd your friends of the better half of the garland" (compare II.ii.101). More impressively, the play almost certainly contains allusions to serious riots and disturbances in the Midlands in 1607. In any case, *Coriolanus* could not have been written before the publication of Camden's *Remains* in 1605, since the fable of the belly (I.i.96 ff.), though mainly based on Plutarch, derives something from Camden's version of the same tale. On the whole, 1607–8 seems the most likely date.

The source of the play is North's version of Plutarch's *Life of Coriolanus*, and Shakespeare follows it in his usual way—sometimes very closely, with a liberal use of North's language, sometimes altering emphases, and changing the tone and balance by omission and addition. The events are transcribed almost in Plutarch's order, and the occasional closeness of the rendering of North's text may be gauged by a comparison with the source of the speech in which Coriolanus offers his services to Aufidius (IV.v.65 ff.) and that in which Volumnia pleads with her son to spare Rome (V.iii.94 ff.). Most of the characters are substantially taken from Plutarch, though Shakespeare modifies them in many ways.

Coriolanus himself is in Plutarch "churlish and uncivil, and altogether unfit for any man's conversation"; and although Shakespeare has his own view of the significance of this aristocratic loutishness, one cannot ignore the importance to his theme of Plutarch's prefatory observations on the hero's improper education. He represents this obliquely in the scene of the Roman ladies with their talk of the young Martius (I.iii), which has no source in Plutarch; and many of the alterations he makes are calculated to develop the idea that the education and presumptions of an aristocrat can make him unfit for rule in a complex society. Coriolanus has an imperfectly viable conception of *virtus*, of the duty of a man; it takes no account of social obligations, being based on a narrower concept of military courage and honor (see III.i.318–21).

Thus he is able and honorable above all others in battle; and his modesty and piety in ordinary circumstances are suited to the role of happy warrior. But the spirit of anger, licensed in war, prevents him from dealing sensibly with the plebs, and such dealing is a necessary part of aristocracy, for which prospective leaders require a proper training. Volumnia, herself harshly embracing such narrow ideals of virtue and honor, could not give him this. Coriolanus' subservience to his mother is a mark of immaturity not only in family relationships but also in elementary politics: he is the ungoverned governor, the ill-educated prince.

Shakespeare therefore makes Volumnia more fierce than she is in Plutarch, and emphasizes the powerlessness of Virgilia's pacific spirit and her inability to affect the course of her husband's life, or even her son's. Menenius is much elaborated from the source, being useful as a commentator and as a link with the tribunes; but Shakespeare characterizes him with considerable exactness in such a way as to show that the strife between his class and the common people is not by any means the sole responsibility of Coriolanus, whose friends all share some responsibility for a situation they are anxious to ameliorate by hypocritical displays of compliance.

On the other side of the political dispute, Shakespeare is also at pains to make the behavior of the people and their tribunes somewhat less responsible and more treacherous than it is in the source. In Plutarch, the plebs have real cause for political action; before the Volscian war they are oppressed by usurers, and after it by famine. Shakespeare pays more attention to the characteristic fickleness of the mob, and to their dangerous demands, than to their needs; he does not deny members of the crowd sense and even generosity, but he will not represent their factiousness as the legitimate protest of a starving populace. He also makes them cowards in war, which in Plutarch they are not. As to the tribunes, Plutarch represents them as politicians exploiting new opportunities of power, but in nothing like the same base degree as Shakespeare. For Shakespeare looked at the story not with the sentimental republicanism of Plutarch but with a predisposition to deplore the attribution of power to the people. Given a state without kings (and Coriolanus is set in a Rome which has only recently exiled them), the proper focus of power is in Coriolanus and his friends; but

they are tragically inept in its use, and negligent of the love they owe to inferiors.

The analogy of the body politic with the human body, so prominently stated in the opening scene, is vital to an understanding of the political *données* of the play, and much more important in Shakespeare than in Plutarch, though this does not mean that Shakespeare endorses the actions of his aristocrats or of Coriolanus in his double betrayal of Rome and Corioles. Coriolanus is habitually negligent of his inferiors—Shakespeare reminds us of this when he cancels out the hero's impulse of generosity towards a plebeian benefactor, whose name he can't remember at the important moment. In Plutarch this man is a patrician.

That there is a considerable element of political debate in the play is undoubted. Telling a story of early Republican Rome in the England of James I, Shakespeare not only modified certain Plutarchian details and emphases concerning institutions, but remembered the recent agrarian disturbances in the Midlands. Tudors and Stuarts alike feared mobs, and made propaganda against all forms of levelling; and Shakespeare's mobs, from *Henry VI* on, are dangerous beasts, in which upstart passions have taken control of reason. The risings of 1607 were part of a series of ominous events which had caused foreign observers to prophesy revolution; a royal proclamation of 1607 announced that it was "a thing notorious that many of the meanest sort of our people have presumed lately to assemble themselves riotously in multitudes." Various forms of religious communism gave the genuine grievances of some of these insurgents an ideological coloring. And a few years before *Coriolanus* there had been, in the rebellion of Essex, an aristocratic threat to state security. Essex too was an ungoverned governor; and it was said of him at the time that "great natures prove either excellently good or dangerously wicked: it is spoken by Plato but applied by Plutarch unto Coriolanus, a gallant young, but a discontented Roman, who might make a fit parallel for the late Earl, if you read his life." As in *Julius Caesar*, Shakespeare here adapted Plutarch to fit more urgent interests; he is never merely telling an old tale.

We know Shakespeare as a master of the seminal opening scene, and *Coriolanus* provides a fine example. Here begins a clash of interests and prejudices between members of one body, and the result is disease in the body politic. By the time we reach Act III we can see why Shakespeare has allowed Menenius so deliberate an exposition of his parable. In III.i the imagery of the state as a diseased body becomes dominant. Coriolanus calls the people "measles" that "tetter us" (78–79), speaks of the wars they fear as touching "the navel of the state" (123), and refers to the common people as a "bosom" (stomach) (131), so reversing the allegory of Menenius; they are a "multitudinous tongue" (156) licking up a poison that will kill the state. Meanwhile Coriolanus himself appears to the tribunes as "a disease that must be cut away" (293) and as a gangrened foot (305).

Between the opening scene and this crisis, Shakespeare has proceeded economically, even schematically. At the outset Coriolanus calls the citizens "scabs" (I.i.166); but a war intervenes, and produces a situation in which he is the master-man, and they are weak cowards. As a soldier, Coriolanus is a kind of engine of war—we hear of "the thunder-like percussion" of his sounds (I.iv.59); "before him he carries noise, and behind him he leaves tears" (II.i.158–59). But out of his occupation of war, he feels himself reduced to a mere actor, forced to seek the suffrage of those who left him to enter the gates of Corioles alone; and it is this one-sidedness of Coriolanus that invites not only the vengeful meditation of Aufidius at the end of Act I but the fox-like stratagems of the tribunes in the next part of the play, which concerns Coriolanus in his role of suitor to the electorate.

As we have seen, the idea of the diseased body politic informs this central section, up to the banishment of Coriolanus. Health depends upon his ability to "temp'rately transport his honors" (II.i.224) from the field to the arena of politics; and the tribunes are right in thinking that he cannot—indeed, this is the theme of the tragedy. It has been intelligently suggested that Shakespeare had consciously in mind the saying of Aristotle—which circulated widely at the time—that a man "incapable of living in a society is either a god or a beast." Coriolanus evidently is thus incapable; and it is as a "lonely dragon" that he eventually is cast out from Rome into the void, though he finds again the medium of his narrow nobility in the Volscian service. Throughout the central section, up to his banishment, Coriolanus is repeatedly examined in relation to the concept of "nobility." If it

consists in the licensed rage of war, he is noble enough to be a god; if it is the conduct of a man in civil society, he is a beast. He finds the behavior of the tribunes impossible for a nobleman to bear, and calls the people "foes to nobleness" (III.i.45); Sicinius sneeringly but accurately informs him that he needs "a gentler spirit" to "be so noble as a consul" (55–56). To him the plebs are merely necessary and ignoble "voices"; "his nature is too noble for the world" (254). But by the time Menenius says this, we have heard the words *noble* and *nobility* acquire much irony, and the patrician use of the word sometimes applies best to the behavior of the young Martius as he "mammocks" the butterfly.

The truth about the nobility of Coriolanus is most fully stated in the great speech of Aufidius at the end of the fourth act, where he finds his rival

> not moving
> From th' casque to th' cushion, but commanding peace
> Even with the same austerity and garb
> As he controll'd the war.
> (IV.vii.42–45)

Nobility requires a proper decorum in war and also in peaceful council (the "cushion" of the Senate). In the first, it may display itself as mere "sovereignty of nature"; in the second it calls for arts of dissimulation such as Machiavelli urges upon princes for the good of their people. There is no question that men of Coriolanus' stamp ought to be obeyed; and that is why they must be properly educated to power. This was a preoccupation shared by the Renaissance with Plutarch; and although Coriolanus brings his troubles upon himself through lack of such education, we are left in no doubt that the health of the Roman body politic suffers from his absence. Rome without Coriolanus is at the mercy of its enemies; the momentary calm, the period when the citizens, unprotected by their lion, worked peacefully in their shops, was merely a dangerous illusion. "You have made good work!"

Leading the Volscians against Rome, Coriolanus, in the final movement of the play, can again behave like a god (IV.vi.90); but the only love or piety he recognizes—that excessive respect for his mother which uses up all the love he needs for good government—finally overthrows him. To put it differently, Volumnia forces him to surrender a position in which it is enough for him to be a soldier, and to plunge himself into complexities with which it is impossible for him to deal. There is no moment in the play when one feels more sympathy for him than when he recognizes the implications of this surrender; he sees that it is dangerous, "if not most mortal" (V.iii.189). The final disaster happens because Aufidius has correctly estimated the temper of Coriolanus; with a burst of his old, narrowly military nobility he combats the most dreaded of insults:

> If you have writ your annals true, 'tis there
> That, like an eagle in a dove-cote, I
> Flutter'd your Volscians in Corioles.
> Alone I did it.
> (V.vi.113–16)

At the end, when our minds are charged with many ambiguous senses of the word, Aufidius grants him "a *noble* memory" (V.vi.153).

Coriolanus has been called a debate rather than a tragedy; but this is incautious. It has admittedly proved its durability as political comment (there was a famous Paris performance between the wars at which both Communists and Fascists rioted because they construed the play as propaganda against their respective causes). But it is, as is usual in Shakespeare, much more of a vivid dramatic meditation on certain political themes than a dramatized political debate; and at the heart of it is a hero. Deeply flawed, like Timon and Antony, he is also for the most part unsympathetic, harsh, and graceless; but that he is a great man, that his decision before Rome is crucial and painful—and must (as his mother explains) be in any case wrong—involves us in his fate, exactly as the Rome he "banished" was involved in it. Few plays so completely state their own theme. The skill with which Shakespeare relates the behavior of Coriolanus to his imperfect education is one instance; the brilliant invention of the scene at Aufidius' house is another, when the hero, who in departing from Rome seems to have departed from life, materializes suddenly, presenting himself in an enemy household as an inhabitant of "th' city of kites and crows" (IV.v.42) and, dressed in his poor and worn clothes, asserts his *virtus* not merely over the servants but over Aufidius and the senators of Corioles.

The verse of the play has its own absolutely decorous power. There is more to be said of the late verse of Shakespeare, as to what makes it seem "late," than talk of verse paragraphing, of weak and feminine endings, can yield. Here is verse so far from smooth that it is as if deliberately written in the vein of Hotspur's speech in *I Henry IV*. Hotspur would

> rather hear a brazen canstick turn'd,
> Or a dry wheel grate on the axle-tree,

than have his teeth set on edge by "mincing poetry" (III.i.129–32); and some of the verse of *Coriolanus* has this grating vigor. It has been observed that in this play there is an unusual degree of comment from various characters on the central figure. This is so; but it should also be observed that Shakespeare's turning inward of all the attention upon the hero (before society excludes him altogether) is a movement paralleled by that of the poetry. The verse is whirled about by the anger of Coriolanus; it clanks and thunders and revels in images of physical violence; it denies itself any more gracious aspect. (Virgilia, the tenderest of the characters, is famous for her silence.) Decorum ("which it is the grand masterpiece to observe") was something Shakespeare had continued to learn about. He had known the long, slow pleasures of accurate rhetorical expatiation, and indulged them in *Titus*—even, perhaps, as late as *Richard II*. But with *Coriolanus* we reach an extreme where no indecorous sweetness of language intrudes upon the military violence of the theme. Students come to recognize a certain extraordinary harshness of diction and violence of imagination as characteristics of late Shakespeare. Nowhere is it more exactly reined and controlled than here. The tone is set by the opening words of Coriolanus; then others use it in celebrating his triumph ("[he] struck / Corioles like a planet"). It infects the tribunes, as in Brutus' description of the crowd (II.i.205–21); it is heard finely in the mouth of Aufidius at the end of Act IV. But it is the voice of Coriolanus, the hard tone of nobility understood as military potency. He himself hums like a battery, and so does his play. Against this noise Shakespeare counterpoints the brisk character-writer's patter of Menenius, the elegant conversation of ladies, the lively, unheroic prose of the good fellows in the crowd. But the dominant noise is the exasperated shout of the beast-god Coriolanus. The energy of it is as superb as the control. We never feel that the author allows the hero to come very close to him or to us, but in spite of his keeping Coriolanus at a critical arm's length, Shakespeare can rarely have more fully extended his powers than he does here. There is a sense in which this inhospitable play is one of the supreme tests of a genuine understanding of Shakespeare's achievement.

Source: Frank Kermode, "*Coriolanus*," in *The Riverside Shakespeare*, Houghton Mifflin Company, 1974, pp. 1392–95.

SOURCES

Adelman, Janet, "Escaping the Matrix: The Construction of Masculinity in *Coriolanus*," in *New Casebooks: Shakespeare's Tragedies*, edited by Susan Zimmerman, St. Martin's Press, 1998, p. 23.

Barton, Anne, "Livy, Machiavelli and *Coriolanus*," in *Essays, Mainly Shakespearean*, Cambridge University Press, 1994, pp. 152, 159.

Bloom, Harold, "*Coriolanus*," in *Shakespeare: The Invention of the Human*, Riverhead Books, 1998.

Bradley, A. C., "*Coriolanus*," in *Coriolanus*, by William Shakespeare, edited by Reuben Brower, Signet/New American Library, 1966, pp. 250–51.

Eliot T. S., "Hamlet and His Problems" in *The Sacred Wood: Essays on Poetry and Criticism*, 1922.

Kermode, Frank, "*Coriolanus*," in *Shakespeare's Language*, Farrar, Straus & Giroux, 2000, p. 243.

Shakespeare, William, *The Tragedy of Coriolanus*, edited by Reuben Brower, Signet/New American Library, 1966.

Traversi, Derek, "*Coriolanus*," in *Shakespeare: The Roman Plays*, Hollis & Carter, 1963 p. 207.

Waith, Eugene M., "*Coriolanus*," in *The Herculean Hero in Marlowe, Chapman, Shakespeare and Dryden*, Columbia University Press, 1962, p. 143.

Willet, John, ed., "Study of the First Scene of Shakespeare's *Coriolanus*," in *Brecht on Theater*, Hill and Wang, 1957, pp. 252–65.

FURTHER READING

Cantor, Paul A, *Shakespeare's Rome: Republic and Empire*, Cornell University Press, 1976.

    In a study of *Coriolanus* and *Antony and Cleopatra*, Cantor contrasts the roles of republican and imperial Rome with regard to government, liberty, tyranny, and erotic love.

Garganigo, Alex, "Coriolanus, the Union Controversy, and Access to the Royal Person," in *Studies in English Literature, 1500–1900*, Spring 2002, Vol. 42, No. 2, pp. 335–60.

    Garganigo argues that the concentration on the body, particularly as it is expressed in the fable of the body, which is prevalent in *Coriolanus* implicitly alludes to King James's desire to use the wholeness of the king's body, his own physical body, as an emblem of the body politic in his effort to unite the kingdoms of England and Scotland into one political body.

Pettet, E. C., "*Coriolanus* and the Midlands Insurrection of 1607," in *Shakespeare Survey 3*, 1950, pp. 34–42.

    Pettet discusses the relation of the Midland riots of 1607 to *Coriolanus* and suggests that Shakespeare sided with the patricians against the plebeians in the play.

Spotswood, Jerald W., "'We are undone already': Disarming the Multitude in *Julius Caesar* and *Coriolanus*, in *Texas Studies in Literature and Language*, Spring 2000, Vol. 42, No. 1, pp. 61–79.

    Spotswood argues that, in his Roman plays, Shakespeare presents the members of the mobs without granting them individual identities or distinguishing them from each other, consequently denigrating collective action and, at the same time, portraying members of the aristocracy as individuals capable of being tragic.

Hamlet

Two years passed between *Hamlet*'s being entered in the Stationers' Register, a journal kept by the Stationers' Company of London in which the printing rights to works were recorded, and the play's being printed. In 1602, James Roberts entered "A booke called the Revenge of Hamlett Prince Denmarke as yt was latelie Acted by the Lord Chamberleyne his servantes" in the Stationers' Register; when the quarto text of the play was published in 1604, the title page read as follows:

> The Tragicall Historie of HAMLET, *Prince of Denmarke*. By William Shakespeare. Newly imprinted and enlarged to almost as much againe as it was, according to the true and perfect Coppie. At London, Printed by I.R. [James Roberts] for N.L. [Nicholas Ling] and are to be sold at his shoppe vnder Saint Dunstons Church in Fleetstreet. 1604.

In fact, sometime after Roberts initially registered *Hamlet* but before he printed it, Nicholas Ling published a pirated edition of the play, with the text assembled from memory by actors who had played in touring companies that took *Hamlet* to Oxford and Cambridge. This pirated edition is called the first quarto and is a corrupt text. The 1604 quarto, called the second quarto, seems to be based on Shakespeare's own papers, but it is marred by printer's errors and by corrupt interpolations from the pirated text. A third and a fourth quarto were subsequently printed, both based on the second. In 1623,

seven years after Shakespeare's death, his friends and fellow actors John Heminges and Henry Condell assembled his plays in a single folio-sized volume, called the 1623 Folio. The text of *Hamlet* in the Folio is substantially different from that of the play's second quarto; the Folio text is thought to have come from the prompt book of Shakespeare's acting company, the King's Men, and to be a revision of the second quarto by Shakespeare himself. The later text is shorter than the second quarto by two hundred lines and contains passages not in that quarto.

Scholars are uncertain as to when before 1602 *Hamlet* was written. The best evidence for a date before which *Hamlet* could not have been written is found within the play itself, as Hamlet discusses how the rise of children's acting companies has driven the established adult acting companies out of business. Through Hamlet, Shakespeare is understood to be referring to the "War of the Theaters," which took place during the years 1599 and 1601, setting the date of *Hamlet*'s composition between 1599 and 1602.

Since its first appearance, *Hamlet* has been immensely popular, as evidenced by the number of times it was reprinted in the seventeenth century and by its performance history. Even during the Puritan Interregnum, between 1649 and 1660, when the theaters were closed and performances outlawed, the gravediggers scene from *Hamlet* was performed by actors standing alone, illegally, as a "droll," or a short comic sketch with music and dance. When the theaters were reopened upon the restoration of the monarchy, *Hamlet* was performed frequently. A gentleman named Samuel Pepys noted in his diary that he saw the play performed in 1661, 1663, and 1668. John Downes, the bookkeeper for the acting company of which the popular seventeenth-century actor Thomas Betterton was the principal, noted that between 1662 and 1706, no tragedy "got more Reputation, or Money to the Company than" *Hamlet*. In 1695, two rival acting companies each presented performances of *Hamlet* on the same nights.

For those living in the second half of the seventeenth century, the plot of *Hamlet* could be read to parallel events in England's immediate past—such as the beheading of Charles I, the years of the Commonwealth, and the restoration of the monarchy—as the play tells the story of a usurper who kills the rightful king and is finally overthrown himself. Beyond historical considerations, in 1698, Jeremy Collier, in his *Short View of the Immorality, and Profaneness of the English Stage*, cited *Hamlet* as "lewd" for its depiction of Ophelia in her mad scene. That judgment, however, did not diminish *Hamlet*'s popularity or the esteem it was gaining, particularly because the title role was one that the great actors of the eighteenth century relished, and, in turn, audiences relished their performances. The eighteenth century was also an era of great textual work on Shakespeare. The famous English writers Samuel Johnson and Alexander Pope were both among those who brought out editions of Shakespeare's works, and in 1725 Lewis Theobald notably collated all existing texts of Shakespeare's works in order to produce the most authentic text possible. While *Hamlet* was altered, cut, and adapted over the years, it was never subject to the kinds of radical transformations that plays such as *King Lear* and *The Tempest* were.

In part because of eighteenth-century textual scholarship, in the nineteenth century, *Hamlet*, like the rest of Shakespeare's plays, became something to read as well as to see performed—and in fact, critical opinion largely held that it was better read than seen. The English poet and scholar Samuel Taylor Coleridge affected how audiences and readers would perceive the play ever after with his interpretation of Hamlet as a man averse to action, full of resolve but hesitant and irresolute in action. By the twentieth century, *Hamlet* had achieved the status of being the most famous and most esteemed play in the English language, if not in any language. The character of Hamlet, meanwhile, achieved mythic status, especially after the 1949 publication of the work *Hamlet and Oedipus*, by Ernest Jones, an English Freudian psychoanalyst, who argued that Hamlet's tendency toward inactivity resulted from identification with his uncle, who had accomplished what Hamlet could have only wished for: to kill his father and marry his mother. Hamlet was also given life outside of his play, becoming a subject or an allusion in other works, like James Joyce's *Ulysses* and T. S. Eliot's "The Love Song of J. Alfred Prufrock."

In the Elizabethan era, Shakespeare's focus on Hamlet's intellectual conflicts was a significant departure from contemporary revenge tragedies, like Thomas Kyd's *The Spanish Tragedy* (c. 1584), which tended to dramatize violent acts graphically on stage. Shakespeare largely established dramatic tension in *Hamlet* by focusing on Hamlet's dilemma rather than on the depiction of bloody deeds. To achieve this shift in emphasis, Shakespeare created a character with intellectual depth and emotional complexity that had not yet been present in Elizabethan drama. Shakespeare's genius and his accomplishment are evident in his transformation of *Hamlet*'s literary sources—especially the nearly contemporaneous *Ur-Hamlet*. The *Ur-Hamlet*, or "original Hamlet," is a lost play that scholars believe was written about a decade before Shakespeare's *Hamlet*, providing the basis for the later tragedy. Numerous sixteenth-century records attest to the existence of the *Ur-Hamlet*, with some references linking its composition to Kyd, the author of *The Spanish Tragedy*. The scholar Harold Bloom, on the other hand, drawing on internal and thematic elements in *Hamlet* and also on events in Shakespeare's life, asserts that the *Ur-Hamlet* was actually a first draft of *Hamlet* written by Shakespeare himself in his youth. Other principal sources available to Shakespeare were Saxo Grammaticus's *Gesta Danorum* (c. 1200), which features a popular legend with a plot similar to *Hamlet*, and François de Belleforest's *Histoires tragiques, extraits des oeuvres italiennes de Bandel* (7 vols.; 1559–80), which provides an expanded account of the story recorded in the *Gesta Danorum*. From these sources, Shakespeare created *Hamlet*, a supremely rich and complex literary work that continues to delight and challenge both readers and audiences with the complexity of its themes, the breadth and depth of its portrayal of human nature and consciousness, and the nearly infinite scope of its interpretability.

PLOT SUMMARY

Act 1, Scene 1

Hamlet opens on the battlements of the castle at Elsinore, in Denmark, where the guard is being changed. Bernardo and Marcellus, accompanied by Horatio, come to relieve Francisco. The first words spoken, "Who's there?" a nervous inquiry by Bernardo indicating suspicion and the need to find something out, set the tone for the rest of the play. Francisco reports that his watch has been uneventful. Alone, Bernardo and Marcellus recount to Horatio how a Ghost appeared the night before but would not stay. Now they are waiting to see if it will appear again. If it does, they hope that it will speak to Horatio, who as a scholar may have more success in speaking to the Ghost than they did.

As they wait, the Ghost appears. Horatio's attempt to speak to it fails, however, and the Ghost vanishes. After the men note the Ghost's resemblance to the deceased King Hamlet, the guards ask Horatio why they are keeping the watch and why war preparations are being made in Denmark. Horatio tells them of a feared invasion by Norwegian troops under the command of young Fortinbras. Fortinbras's father, in a war with the old King Hamlet, Prince Hamlet's father, was killed by King Hamlet. Fortinbras is set on avenging his father's death and recapturing the territory lost to King Hamlet. As they speak, the Ghost appears again, then vanishes again. The three decide to inform Hamlet of what they have seen.

Act 1, Scene 2

Inside the castle, the new king, Claudius, is delivering a state address, touching on his ascension to the throne, the old king's death, and his marriage to Gertrude, old King Hamlet's widow and Hamlet's mother. Next on his agenda is the impending war with Norway. He dispatches Cornelius and Voltimand to Norway to negotiate with Fortinbras's uncle, the king of Norway, and prevent a war.

Claudius then turns his attention to Hamlet, who stands among the courtiers, dressed in mourning black. Claudius calls Hamlet "our chiefest courtier, cousin, and our son." Hamlet's first words, an aside, showing his alienation from and disgust with Claudius, are "A little more than kin, and less than kind," acknowledging their kinship but indicating that he thinks of himself as entirely unlike Claudius. When Claudius asks, "How is it that the clouds still hang on you?" Hamlet answers with a pun: "Not so, my Lord. I am too much in the sun." Hamlet is cryptically suggesting that he is too loyal a son for Claudius's treacherous world.

Claudius's apparent solicitude is fraught with purpose. In marrying Gertrude, he has effectively usurped Hamlet's place as successor to the Danish throne. He speaks to Hamlet directly about the prince's grief for his dead father, arguing that to persist in grief for the dead is actually an offense against heaven, since it seems to reflect rebellion against the will of

Kenneth Branagh as Hamlet and Kate Winslet as Ophelia from the 1996 movie Hamlet
(Everett Collection)

seed. Things rank and gross in nature / possess it merely." He himself would prefer to be dead, even by his own hand, if such an act were not against the laws of God. Beyond his father's death, a cause of his despair is his mother's quick and unseemly marriage to Claudius. Hamlet says nothing about his own royal ambitions, presumably not having any. He is powerfully troubled, however, by the differences between his father and his uncle. To him, his father was a god; his uncle is a lecher. Hamlet is most incensed not only at Gertrude's disloyalty to her dead husband but at her apparent hypocrisy, in that she could cling to his father and grieve for him as deeply as she had and nevertheless be so quickly seduced by his uncle. "Frailty," Hamlet generalizes from his mother to the sex as a whole, "thy name is woman."

As Hamlet is finishing his painful meditation, Horatio, Marcellus, and Bernardo enter the chamber and report the night's encounter with the Ghost of his dead father. Hamlet arranges to meet them on the battlements and watch with them that night and vows to talk to the Ghost should it appear.

Act 1, Scene 3
In the third scene, Shakespeare shifts the focus of the play to Polonius and his two children, Ophelia and Laertes. As the scene begins, Laertes, about to embark on his return journey to France, in parting from his sister, advises her to guard herself against Hamlet's advances. She promises that she will and reminds him not to counsel chaste and prudent behavior to her while leading a reckless life himself. Polonius enters to bid Laertes farewell and to give him some precepts that he hopes will guide his behavior in France. Once Laertes has departed, Polonius asks Ophelia what they had been speaking about, and Ophelia reports that her brother had warned her to be wary of Hamlet's courtship. Polonius affirms this warning, telling her that Hamlet is in all likelihood only toying with her and that he wishes her to no longer speak to Hamlet.

Act 1, Scene 4
In the middle of the night, Hamlet, Horatio, Marcellus, and Bernardo wait on the battlements of Elsinore to see if the Ghost will appear. In the meantime they comment on the nightly carousing and revelry at the court of Denmark, which Hamlet acknowledges give Denmark a

heaven. In this address, Claudius also informs Hamlet that he is rejecting the prince's request to return to school in Germany, in Wittenberg, and wishes him to remain at court, especially since Queen Gertrude, his mother, wishes him to remain near her. Claudius's refusal to let Hamlet leave Denmark is particularly pointed because he has just previously granted a similar request by Laertes, the son of his Lord Chamberlain, Polonius, to return to Paris. Hamlet agrees to stay; when his mother asks him why his grief for his dead father seems so strong, he tells her that his grief does not just *seem* strong but actually is strong. Moreover, he tells her that the black mourning clothes he wears and his dejected behavior are outward manifestations of his internal woe.

After the court disperses, Hamlet remains behind and in a soliloquy reveals his internal state. He expresses his disgust with the world, which "is an unweeded garden / That grows to reputation of being a place of drunkenness. Hamlet then philosophizes about human faults, observing that one fault can overwhelm a person who is in all other respects decent. His discourse is interrupted by the appearance of the Ghost, who signals him to follow. Hamlet's companions try to hold him back, fearing that the Ghost may drive him mad or move him to take his own life, but Hamlet resists, drawing his sword, and follows the Ghost. The others follow after.

Act 1, Scene 5

Alone with the Ghost, Hamlet says that he will go no further. The Ghost identifies himself as Hamlet's father's spirit, "doomed for a certain term to walk the night" because he died without having had the opportunity to repent. More significantly, he tells Hamlet that although he is said to have died sleeping in his orchard, the truth is that his brother killed him by pouring a "leperous distillment" in his ear; through this lie, Claudius has abused the ear of Denmark. Hamlet tells the Ghost that he had suspected some foul play by his uncle, and the Ghost tells Hamlet that he is obliged to avenge the murder. Further, the Ghost instructs Hamlet not to hurt his mother but to "leave her to heaven / And to those thorns that in her bosom lodge / To prick and sting her." With the approach of morning, the Ghost vanishes, leaving in Hamlet's ears the words "Remember me." Hamlet believes the Ghost and tells Horatio, Marcellus, and Bernardo that the Ghost is honest, but he refuses to reveal what the Ghost imparted. Hamlet instructs the men to mention nothing of what has just occurred and, if they see Hamlet acting oddly, not to indicate even by the smallest gesture that they know the reason why. He commands them to swear that they will be silent. When they resist, saying that such an oath is not necessary, the Ghost's voice calls out, "Swear," and they do. Hamlet calls the Ghost a perturbed spirit and tells it to rest. He then remarks that "the time is out of joint" and that it is his misfortune that it is his task "to set it right."

Act 2, Scene 1

Polonius is alone with Reynaldo, a courtier whom he is sending to Paris to find out how Laertes is behaving. Polonius instructs Reynaldo in methods of gathering information, emphasizing how he ought to offer demeaning observations about Laertes's character to see if others confirm them or even reciprocate with further accounts

of his faults. Once Reynaldo is dispatched, Ophelia enters and tells her father of a recent, disturbing encounter with Hamlet, who entered her chamber with his clothing in disarray, took hold of her by the wrist, sighed, gazed at her, and left. Polonius interprets the behavior as indicating lovesickness and asks her if she has "given him any hard words of late"; Ophelia tells him that she has not, that she has, as Polonius instructed, returned Hamlet's letters and "denied / His access to me." Polonius determines to tell the king of the episode.

Act 2, Scene 2

Claudius and Gertrude greet Rosencrantz and Guildenstern, old school friends of Hamlet's, thank them for answering their summons, and explain that neither Hamlet's "exterior nor the inward man / Resembles that it was." The king and queen hope that the two might be able to spend time with Hamlet and find out what has caused his "transformation." The two friends then leave to let Hamlet know of their arrival.

Polonius enters and informs Claudius that the ambassadors to Norway, Cornelius and Voltimand, have returned and that he thinks he knows the cause of Hamlet's madness; he advises the king to first hear from the ambassadors. After Polonius leaves to fetch the ambassadors, Claudius tells Gertrude that Polonius thinks he knows the cause of Hamlet's madness. She remarks that she does not doubt that the cause is the combination of his father's death and their "o'erhasty marriage."

Voltimand and Cornelius report that the king of Norway was grieved to learn that Fortinbras was raising an army against Denmark, as he had thought the army was being assembled for an attack against Poland. When he learned the truth, he suppressed Fortinbras's war effort against Denmark but asked for passage through Denmark for the Polish campaign.

With the ambassadors' business concluded, Polonius informs the king and queen with characteristic long-windedness that he believes the cause of Hamlet's apparent madness to be love for Ophelia; he reads a letter from Hamlet to her that expresses love and desperation. The queen finds the hypothesis credible, and the king wishes to know how they might test it. Polonius suggests that he will arrange for Hamlet and Ophelia to meet and converse while the king, queen, and Polonius hide behind an arras, or long heavy curtain, and eavesdrop. Claudius accepts, and Polonius, noticing Hamlet walking toward them, instructs the king and queen to leave while he engages Hamlet in conversation.

Polonius greets Hamlet and, as if talking to a madman, asks Hamlet if he knows him. Hamlet answers that he knows him very well, that he is a fishmonger. Hamlet often speaks in double entendres, expressions that have two meanings, with one of them usually sexually suggestive; a fishmonger is not only a person who sells fish but also a procurer, or pimp. Indeed, Polonius is in a sense using Ophelia ("I'll loose my daughter," he has told Claudius and Gertrude) to snare Hamlet. Hamlet continues to lead Polonius on, teasing him with references to love, sexuality, Ophelia, and death. Polonius takes leave of Hamlet convinced that he is mad and that love for Ophelia is the cause.

As Polonius leaves, Rosencrantz and Guildenstern enter and greet Hamlet, who asks what ill fortune brings them to Denmark, which he calls a prison. They respond that they do not find it to be such, and he tells them that it is one only to him, then, "for there is nothing either good or bad but thinking makes it so." They observe that he must have too much ambition, but Hamlet dissents and, as he had toyed with Polonius, toys with them, telling them he could live happily in a small space but has bad dreams. After they discuss the nature of dreams, Hamlet again asks why they have come to Elsinore, and they answer that it was to visit him. But Hamlet protests that their visit is not voluntary, remarking, "Were you not sent for?...Come, come, deal justly with me." They equivocate, not knowing what to say, and Hamlet tells them that they need not answer; he knows that they were summoned. Still, they do not respond honestly, asking, "To what end?" Hamlet replies, "That you must teach me." Finally, the two admit that they were summoned, and Hamlet says that he will tell them why so that they will not be guilty of revealing their mission.

Hamlet proceeds to inform them that he has lost his ability to take pleasure in being alive and that "man," though a wonderful creature with great capabilities, "delights not me"; when they smile, he suspects they have a bawdy understanding of his words and adds "nor woman neither." Rosencrantz asserts that he was thinking no such thing; rather, he recalled that they encountered traveling players on their way to the court, and if Hamlet takes no pleasure in the ways of men, he will not enjoy the players. Hamlet responds that they will be welcome, especially the one who plays the king. After discussion on the current state of the theater, with reference to the stage in Shakespeare's own London and the rise of children's theater companies, which has forced adult troupes to travel, Polonius enters to inform Hamlet that the players have arrived. Hamlet and Polonius banter about theater and once again about fathers and their daughters. Hamlet refers to the biblical figure of Jephthah, who vowed to God that if he was victorious in battle, he would offer as a sacrifice to God the first thing he saw on his return home. On his return, the first thing Jephtha encountered was his daughter coming out to greet him. "Still on my daughter," Polonius notes, without realizing that Hamlet is suggesting that Polonius is sacrificing his daughter to his own interests. The players enter, and Hamlet greets them and asks one of the players to recite a speech about the fall of Troy to the Greeks in the Trojan War and the suffering of the king and queen of Troy, Priam and Hecuba. Polonius notes that as the player recites the speech, he is filled with emotion. Hamlet then asks the players if they know a play called *The Murder of Gonzago*; they do. Hamlet arranges for them to play it before the court the following night with the addition of some lines Hamlet will write.

Alone, Hamlet compares himself to the player, who was moved to a passion by his own speech, and berates himself in a soliloquy for his lack of determination in real life in his quest for revenge. His meditation leads him to the idea that "guilty creatures" watching a play that mirrors their misdeeds might become so moved as to confess their crimes, if not verbally then by some facial expression or bodily gesture. Thus, Hamlet plans to watch the king's response to *The Murder of Gonzago*, which features a murder similar to King Hamlet's murder. Hamlet remarks in closing, "The play's the thing / Wherein I'll catch the conscience of the King."

Act 3, Scene 1

Rosencrantz and Guildenstern report to the king and queen that they were unable to learn much from Hamlet, who, they say, greeted them like a gentleman but avoided their inquiries with a crafty madness. The two inform the king of the players' arrival and of the performance scheduled for that evening. The king is glad that Hamlet seems to be pursuing pleasure and instructs them to continue trying to lead him to reveal the root of his mad behavior. The king then asks Gertrude to leave them. Gertrude tells Ophelia that she hopes it is for love of her that Hamlet is mad; she would not oppose their marriage. Polonius positions Ophelia with a book to wait for Hamlet; he and the king will watch in hiding when Hamlet arrives.

Hamlet enters and recites perhaps the most famous speech from any play, the soliloquy "To be or not to be," in which he ponders the pain of being alive and the fear of death and of what the afterlife may hold. He concludes that fear of the unknown makes people bear the burdens, injustices, and woes of being alive. He breaks off his meditations when he sees Ophelia, who is reading from a book that Hamlet takes to be a prayer book. In greeting her, he asks her to include him in her prayers. She tells him that she has "remembrances" of his, gifts and letters he has given her that she wishes to return to him. He says that he never gave her anything, but she asserts that he knows he did; when he did, he gave them with sweet words, but now that he is cold to her, the gifts no longer have the richness they once had. He interrupts her to ask if she is honest, suspecting that she is the bait in a trap to catch him. She does not understand his question, and he declares that if she is honest and fair, her honesty would not permit her to be used (as she is being used to lure Hamlet into revealing himself).

In a speech full of words with double meanings, Hamlet tells Ophelia "Get thee to a nunnery," meaning both "sequester yourself in a convent to be away from this sinful, dangerous world" and "go into a brothel, for you are being a prostitute, in being used by Claudius and Polonius." At length, he berates himself and all of mankind. He concludes by asking, "Where's your father?" and she answers with a lie, "At home, my lord." Hamlet then calls her father a fool, tells Ophelia that if she marries she ought to be chaste, and concludes with a condemnation of women who apply makeup and act affectedly, making a mockery of God's creation. He rails against marriage and makes a veiled threat to kill the king. He concludes by once more telling her, "To a nunnery, go."

Alone, Ophelia grieves at Hamlet's apparent madness. The king and Polonius come out of hiding, and the king remarks that Hamlet did not seem to be talking like a disappointed lover, that his words were not really like those of a madman. Furthermore, the king feels that Hamlet is a threat and so resolves to send him to England in an ambassadorial function, to collect some tribute money that England has neglected to pay Denmark. Polonius tells Ophelia that she need not tax herself to relate the conversation as they have overheard everything, thus offering no comfort to the broken-hearted girl. Polonius suggests that after the play, Gertrude ought to talk to Hamlet to see what she can learn; he will hide behind an arras and listen to their conversation. The king agrees and adds that "madness in great ones" must not go unwatched.

Act 3, Scene 2

Before the performance of *The Mousetrap*, Hamlet's adaptation of *The Murder of Gonzago*, Hamlet instructs the players how to act, telling them not to play the scene that evening too broadly and with great gesticulation—not to go for big effects but to perform realistically and to "hold...the mirror up to nature." When the players leave, Horatio enters. Hamlet first tells him how much he loves and admires him for his balanced, stoical disposition, as he is not a flatterer or a slave to the whims of fortune. Hamlet asks Horatio to observe the king's reactions during the play, which will mirror the circumstances of King Hamlet's death as the Ghost has related them.

With ceremonial flourish the king and the court enter. The king greets Hamlet, asking how he "fares," and Hamlet responds with a cryptic pun, since "how do you fare" means "how do you eat?" as well as "how do you do?" Hamlet says that he "eats the air, promise crammed," punning also on "heir," suggesting that Claudius, by marrying Gertrude and becoming king, has usurped Hamlet's rightful place in the royal succession. Claudius says that he does not understand Hamlet's meaning—"these words are not mine"—and Hamlet retorts that now that they have been spoken, the words are not his either. Hamlet then turns to banter with Polonius about his past as an actor. The queen invites Hamlet to sit beside her, but Hamlet indicates that he would prefer to sit by Ophelia and proceeds to make a series of obscene sexual puns and cutting references to his father's death and his mother's remarriage.

The play begins with a "dumb show" or pantomime of the action to come. After a spoken prologue, the Player King and Player Queen enter. They are loving, but the king is not in good health and speaks of the possibility of dying. The queen says that she will never marry again; to do so would be like a second death of her husband. But the king objects; as circumstances change, he asserts, so will she. She protests that she will be constant and then leaves the stage, and the king lies down for a nap. As the scene changes, Hamlet asks his mother what she thinks of the play, and she says that it seems to her that "the lady doth protest too much."

A new character then enters and pours poison into the sleeping king's ear, as Hamlet, like a chorus, narrates what is happening, noting, "You shall see anon how the murderer gets the love of Gonzago's wife." At this point, Claudius rises, Gertrude asks how he fares, Polonius orders the play stopped, and Claudius calls for "some light" and leaves; all the court except Hamlet and Horatio follow. Hamlet is euphoric, and he and Horatio agree that the king's reaction confirms the Ghost's honesty and the king's guilt. As they talk, Rosencrantz and Guildenstern enter and tell Hamlet how disturbed the king and queen are at his behavior and also that the queen wishes to speak with him in her chamber. They apologize for their boldness in speaking somewhat reproachfully to Hamlet, citing the great love they bear him as an excuse. Hamlet takes a flute from one of the players and asks Guildenstern to play it; Guildenstern protests that he lacks the skill to do so. Hamlet remarks on how cheaply, then, Guildenstern must hold Hamlet, in that Guildenstern was trying to "play upon" him. Polonius enters to also announce that the queen wishes to see Hamlet in her chamber. Hamlet then taunts Polonius, too, and the scene ends with Hamlet leaving for Gertrude's chamber, vowing to be severe with her and reprimand her for her remarriage but not to be abusive or violent.

Act 3, Scene 3

Feeling himself to be in danger, Claudius commissions Rosencrantz and Guildenstern to escort Hamlet to England and tells them to arm themselves for the task. They flatter him, telling him how important a king is and how he must protect himself in order to protect all the people of the kingdom who depend on him. As they leave, Polonius enters; he tells the king that Hamlet is going to Gertrude's chamber and that he will hide behind the arras there to listen to their conversation. Polonius adds that a mother is too partial to her son to be trusted in such circumstances.

Alone, Claudius contemplates his crime, admitting to himself how terrible the murder of a brother is. He tries to pray but realizes that his prayer is meaningless as long as he still enjoys the fruits of his crime. Meanwhile, Hamlet passes on his way to Gertrude's chamber and realizes that he might kill the king—but he refrains from doing so because killing Claudius while he is in prayer would send his soul to heaven. That, Hamlet says, would be unfair: "A villain kills my father, and for that / I, his sole son, do this same villain send / To heaven." He leaves Claudius alive. Claudius, alone, ends the scene saying, "My words fly up, my thoughts remain below. / Words without thoughts never to heaven go." Ironically, prayer did, this time, despite his ambivalence, protect him.

Act 3, Scene 4

In Gertrude's chamber, Polonius tells her that Hamlet is coming and that she should scold her son for his "pranks"; meanwhile, Polonius will hide behind the arras. As Hamlet approaches, she tells Polonius not to worry and to hide. Hamlet asks his mother, "What's the matter?" and she answers that he has much offended his father, meaning Claudius, his stepfather. He retorts that she has much offended his father, meaning her first husband, King Hamlet. She tells him that his answer is idle, he tells her that her question is wicked, and they begin to quarrel. She asks if he has forgotten who she is; he says that indeed he has not, that she is her husband's brother's wife and, though he wishes it were not so, his mother. She says that if he will not listen to her, she will have others speak to him, and he takes hold of her and sits her down, saying that he will hold up a mirror for her to see her innermost self. Frightened, she cries out, "What wilt thou do? Thou wilt not murder me? / Help, ho!" Polonius, hearing her cry, calls out "Help!" too, and Hamlet stabs the man behind the curtain without seeing who it is. When his mother asks, "What hast thou done?" he says that he does not know. He asks if the man was the king, but she only says that it was a "bloody deed." Hamlet responds that the act is "almost as bad, good Mother, / as kill a king, and marry with his brother." She responds with the question, "As kill a king?" apparently not knowing what he is referring to. He then lifts the curtain and sees the dead Polonius, to call him a "wretched, rash, intruding fool."

The murder seems to spur them to speak more openly, for Gertrude then asks what she has done to leave him so incensed. Hamlet proceeds to answer, and what he does not say is as interesting as what he does, for he fails to mention his meeting with the Ghost, nor does he explain the expression "as kill a king." Rather, he focuses on the differences he perceives between the two brothers, elevating the old King Hamlet to a divine level and depicting Claudius as a depraved man. He chides his mother for being able to go from a man so fine to a man so base. She breaks down and tells him that he has torn her heart in two. He tells her to throw away the rotten part, the part attached to Claudius. As he speaks, the Ghost enters to remind Hamlet that he has nearly forgotten his mission, to avenge his father's death. Gertrude sees Hamlet talking to the air and grows afraid that he truly is crazy. Hamlet warns her not to think that he is mad rather than realize that she is at fault; he tells her not to go again to Claudius's bed or to be seduced into revealing Hamlet's true condition. She agrees. Hamlet then tells his mother that he is being sent to England, that he suspects a plot against him, that he does not trust Rosencrantz and Guildenstern, and that he will beat them at their own game. He leaves, dragging Polonius's body behind him to deposit it in another room.

Act 4, Scene 1

The king asks Gertrude how the interview with Hamlet went. She asks Rosencrantz and Guildenstern to withdraw and tells Claudius that Hamlet is as mad as the raging sea during a tempest and that he killed Polonius. The king reflects on how he himself might have been killed and on how the people will hold him partly responsible for the killing, as he failed to keep Hamlet in check. He reiterates that he will send Hamlet to England. When Claudius asks Gertrude where Hamlet is now, she reports that he has gone to stow Polonius's body somewhere. The king summons Rosencrantz and Guildenstern back into his presence, tells them of the murder of Polonius, and orders them to find Hamlet and the body.

Act 4, Scene 2

No longer as friends but as agents of the king, Rosencrantz and Guildenstern demand Polonius's body of Hamlet. He does not give them a straight answer, insults them, and runs away as if playing hide-and-seek; they pursue him.

Act 4, Scene 3

The king tells two or three courtiers that he has sent to find Hamlet and the body and that Hamlet is dangerous, though the "multitude," the people, love him. Rosencrantz and Guildenstern enter and tell the king that Hamlet is outside the chamber under guard but will not say where the body is. The king orders Hamlet brought in and asks him where the body is. Hamlet answers cryptically first that Polonius is "at supper," "not where he eats, but where he is eaten," then that perhaps Polonius is in heaven and the king ought to send a messenger there to find him; if he is not there, the king might look in the "other place" himself. Finally, Hamlet says that if the king cannot find him in either place he will soon smell him by a certain staircase. Claudius tells Hamlet that for his own safety he is sending him to England aboard a ship, and Hamlet is removed under guard. In a short soliloquy, the king reveals that he has sent letters to England ordering Hamlet's murder and that he will not know peace until Hamlet is dead.

Act 4, Scene 4

Fortinbras, of Norway, crosses the stage with his troops, passing through Denmark on his way to fight for a barren piece of land in Poland, as a captain tells Hamlet when he inquires. Hamlet is astonished that men should fight and so many should die for the possession of a worthless piece of ground. He concludes that to be great is to "find quarrel in a straw," and reproaches himself for not having accomplished the Ghost's commission yet. He vows that his thoughts will be bloody from then on, thinking that if they are not, they will be worth nothing.

Act 4, Scene 5

In the castle, Gertrude refuses to speak with Ophelia until a courtier tells her that Ophelia is distracted and talks madly in incoherent snatches about her father; Horatio then advises Gertrude to speak with Ophelia lest she bring people to think ill of the king, and Gertrude agrees. Ophelia enters, deranged by grief and singing songs about sexual promiscuity, abandonment, and death. Claudius enters and speaks gently to Ophelia, but she leaves them talking of her father's burial in the cold ground and how her "brother shall know of it." Claudius instructs Horatio to keep an eye on Ophelia, as he is worried that seeing her grief will turn the people against him; Claudius then tells Gertrude that Laertes has secretly returned from France to avenge his father's death, for which he blames the king. As Claudius speaks, there is a commotion, as Laertes has incited a mob looking to overthrow Claudius and make Laertes king. They break down the doors of the castle and enter, and Laertes commands the mob to stand outside and demands to know where his father is. Gertrude unsuccessfully tries to calm Laertes, and Claudius bids her let him go, saying that he is not afraid, for a king is protected by God. The king persuades Laertes to be patient and tries to convince Laertes that they are partners in grief, that he is not responsible for Polonius's death, and that he does not begrudge Laertes his revenge but also does not want Laertes to punish the innocent with the guilty. As Laertes's passion subsides, Ophelia enters again, mad and strewing flowers, rousing that passion again. Once Ophelia has gone, Claudius tells Laertes that he will answer any questions regarding Polonius's death and will satisfy Laertes regarding his own innocence.

Act 4, Scene 6

Sailors bring Horatio a letter from Hamlet, who writes that he is back in Denmark, as pirates boarded their ship at sea, and during the battle Hamlet boarded the pirates' ship. They have dealt fairly with him and for a reward are returning him to Denmark. He requests that Horatio take the sailors to the king and give the king letters from him. Hamlet has much to tell Horatio of Rosencrantz and Guildenstern, who are still traveling to England. Horatio promises the sailors to do as Hamlet requests and asks them to bring him to Hamlet.

Act 4, Scene 7

Explaining what has happened to Polonius, Claudius convinces Laertes of his own innocence regarding Polonius's death and of Hamlet's guilt. When Laertes asks why Hamlet was not punished, Claudius explains that he could not punish him outright because of the love his mother and the people both bear him. Laertes vows to take revenge himself, but the king tells him that more news will soon come to satisfy him. As they speak, a messenger enters with Hamlet's letters, and the king reads that Hamlet has returned to Denmark alone and wishes to see him. Laertes asserts that he must now take revenge, and the king concocts a scheme to make Hamlet's death look accidental. He tells Laertes how much Hamlet admires his skill in fencing and proposes a match between the two. Laertes' sword, however, shall not have a blunt on its tip. Laertes, roused by the king's goading to a passion that would allow him to cut Hamlet's throat in church, agrees. Besides the sword's being naked, the king proposes that its tip be wetted with a deadly poison and that, should Hamlet become thirsty during the duel, the king will offer him a cup of poisoned wine. Gertrude interrupts their conversation to announce that Ophelia has drowned in a brook near the castle, and Laertes is shattered. The king and Gertrude follow him offstage, with the king noting how terrible Ophelia's death is, since he has had so much trouble calming Laertes' rage, and her death has now inflamed it once again.

Act 5, Scene 1

In the graveyard, two clowns are joking and singing as they dig a grave. By their conversation, the audience or reader understands that the grave is Ophelia's and that owing to a dispute over whether her drowning was accidental or suicidal, she will not be given full burial rites. Hamlet and Horatio then enter, and Hamlet is astonished that the First Clown can go about his gravedigging business in such a carefree fashion and engages him in conversation. The First Clown says that he has been employed at his trade for thirty years, since the young Hamlet was born. They speak of mortality, and the clown shows Hamlet a skull, saying that it was the skull of Yorick, the king's jester; Hamlet then meditates on the passing of time.

As they speak, Claudius, Gertrude, Laertes, a Priest, and members of the court enter for Ophelia's burial. When she is laid in the earth, Laertes jumps into the grave after her. Hamlet, seeing everything, his passion aroused, jumps in, too, and there grapples with Laertes, proclaiming his greater love. The king has them parted, and Hamlet protests that Laertes has no cause to be angry with him, that he has always esteemed him. Claudius bids Horatio look after Hamlet, and when he is alone with Laertes, the king asks him to be patient in his desire for revenge, reminding him of the plan they have to murder Hamlet in the dueling contest.

Christopher Eccleston as Hamlet in Act V, scene i, at the West Yorkshire Playhouse, Leeds, 2002
(© Donald Cooper/Photostage. Reproduced by permission)

Act 5, Scene 2

Hamlet tells Horatio how he found the letter that Rosencrantz and Guildenstern were carrying from Claudius to the king of England commissioning Hamlet's immediate execution. He then notes that he substituted another letter that he wrote and sealed with his own royal signet ring, ordering instead the execution of Rosencrantz and Guildenstern, for whose deaths he feels no guilt, so willing were they to go about the king's business. In the course of this discussion, Hamlet reveals a new calmness of temperament founded on his acceptance that things, with time, will be as they are ordained to be.

As they are speaking, Osric, a foppish courtier, enters and tells Hamlet of the fencing wager the king has placed on him against Laertes. Hamlet agrees to the contest and says that he is available immediately. The king, queen, Laertes, and the court then enter, and the contest begins. Hamlet asks Laertes for forgiveness, claiming that his madness, not himself, wronged Laertes, and Laertes, yet planning to kill Hamlet, lies and

says that he forgives him, provisionally. They choose their foils, with Laertes taking the bare, poisoned one and Hamlet accepting the blunted one without checking the other, as the king had said he would. Between rounds, the king offers Hamlet a drink of poisoned wine, but Hamlet declines until later. The queen then begins to take a sip, and the king tries to stop her, but she protests that she will drink; after drinking, she swoons and realizes that she has been poisoned. Hamlet and Laertes then both wound each other with the poisoned sword, for in a scuffle their foils are exchanged. Laertes then has a change of heart and tells Hamlet of the king's plot; Laertes asks Hamlet's forgiveness and dies receiving it. Hamlet then strikes the king with the poisoned sword and forces him to drink some of the wine, and the courtiers call out treason. As Hamlet is dying, Horatio says that he will take the cup and drink as well, thus, like a Roman, following his friend in death. However, Hamlet prevents him, imploring him rather to put off the joys of death for a while and, in the cruel world, to draw his breath in pain and tell Hamlet's

MEDIA ADAPTATIONS

- Laurence Olivier's black-and-white film version of *Hamlet* (1948), for which he won Academy Awards for both acting and directing, cuts Rosencrantz, Guildenstern, and Fortinbras out of the play and emphasizes Hamlet's inability to make up his mind and his oedipal fixation on his mother. The film was released by J. Arthur Rank.

- Elmer Rice's 1958 stage adaptation of *Hamlet*, *Cue for Passion*, transposes Shakespeare's play from Denmark to contemporary California. This play offers the story of a widow who remarries to the only witness to her first husband's apparently accidental death, with her son finding the situation disturbing. The play was first produced by the Playwrights' Company at Henry Miller's Theater in New York.

- For his 1990 film version of *Hamlet*, director Franco Zeffirelli rearranged and cut the text but fully retained the spirit of the original, with Mel Gibson performing admirably as Hamlet. The film was released by Warner Bros. Pictures.

- Kenneth Branagh's four-and-a-half-hour film version of *Hamlet* (1996) is a monumental rendition of the complete play set in the nineteenth century. Branagh adapted the play, directed the movie, and starred as the title character. The film was released by Columbia Pictures.

- As he was filming *Hamlet*, Branagh also filmed *A Midwinter's Tale* (1995), a modest black-and-white film of a group of amateur provincial actors putting together a production of *Hamlet*. *A Midwinter's Tale* includes certain scenes from *Hamlet*, some done as burlesque and some done with an insightful naïveté. The film was released by Sony Pictures.

- *Let the Devil Wear Black* (1999) turns *Hamlet* into a crime thriller set in the boardrooms of Los Angeles. The film was released by Unapix.

- The director Michael Almereyda set his 2000 film version of *Hamlet* in modern Manhattan, with Ethan Hawke starring as the title character. The film was released by Miramax Pictures.

story, for as it stands he dies with a sullied reputation. Hamlet notes that he imagines Fortinbras will be selected king of Denmark, and he approves of that. Fortinbras, indeed, then enters, returning across Denmark from victory in Poland, and has Hamlet placed on a funeral platform and given military rites.

CHARACTERS

Bernardo

Bernardo is a guard at Elsinore. During his watch on the ramparts, along with his partner Marcellus, Bernardo sees the Ghost of Hamlet's father, the old King Hamlet, and reports the event to Hamlet's friend Horatio, who joins the two guards on the night watch.

Claudius

Claudius is the old King Hamlet's brother and Prince Hamlet's uncle. At the play's opening, he has secretly murdered his brother, married his brother's widow, and ascended the throne of Denmark. Claudius soon becomes wary that Hamlet has discovered his crime and is planning to avenge King Hamlet's murder by killing him. Consequently, he arranges for the murder of Hamlet. Although Claudius is unrepentant and unwilling to forfeit the advantages he has gained through his crime, he is plagued by a guilty conscience.

First Clown

As he digs Ophelia's grave, the First Clown sings and makes grim jokes about death. Hamlet encounters him thus and is surprised at his merriness; Hamlet inquires as to whose grave is being dug and contemplates mortality as he holds what the First Clown declares to be the skull of Yorick, Hamlet's father's jester.

Second Clown

The Second Clown essentially plays the role of straight man to the comedic First Clown as they dig a grave for Ophelia.

Fortinbras

Fortinbras is the prince of Norway. His father was killed by King Hamlet in combat years before, and he is determined to go to war against Denmark in order to recapture the territories his father lost in that battle. After Claudius persuades Fortinbras's uncle, the king of Norway, to restrain Fortinbras with respect to Denmark, Claudius, in return, allows Fortinbras to lead his troops through Denmark to conduct war against Poland. At the end of the play, when Hamlet and Claudius are dead, Fortinbras becomes king of Denmark.

Francisco

Francisco appears in the first scene as one of the guards who nightly stand watch on the battlements at Elsinore.

Gertrude

The queen of Denmark, Gertrude is the old King Hamlet's widow and Hamlet's mother. Claudius marries Gertrude two months after her first husband's death. She dies during the fencing match between Hamlet and Laertes when she insists on drinking from a cup intended for Hamlet, not knowing the wine is poisoned.

Ghost

The Ghost is King Hamlet's spirit. King Hamlet is "doomed... to walk the night" for a certain period of time because he died without having the opportunity to repent of his sins, having been murdered in his sleep. He tells his son Hamlet that Claudius, his brother, killed him and commands Hamlet to avenge his murder by killing Claudius. He instructs Hamlet to spare Gertrude, to "leave her to heaven / and to those thorns that in her bosom lodge / To prick and sting her."

Guildenstern

Guildenstern is an old school friend of Hamlet's. Along with his friend Rosencrantz, he is summoned by Claudius to Denmark to spy on Hamlet in order to discover what is troubling him and report back to the king. Hamlet suspects their duplicity. When they are sent by Claudius to escort Hamlet to England, bearing instructions to the English monarch to have Hamlet killed, Hamlet gets hold of the order and substitutes their names for his, and they are later executed.

Hamlet

Hamlet, the prince of Denmark, is King Hamlet's son and Claudius's nephew. After King Hamlet's Ghost tells his son that he was killed by Claudius and that he wishes Hamlet to avenge his murder, Hamlet becomes determined to discover whether he saw an honest ghost or a diabolical spirit summoning him to a sinful act. To accomplish this, he decides to feign madness and also to present a play mirroring his father's murder, called *The Murder of Gonzago*, before Claudius and watch his reaction. In response to his dead father's charge, Hamlet is set on a course of meditation on life, death, responsibility, and fate. Far from being an action hero, Hamlet is a protagonist of reflection and philosophical contemplation. He is mortally wounded during a rigged fencing match with Laertes that Claudius has arranged, but not before he kills Laertes with the poisoned sword surreptitiously prepared for him. He stabs Claudius, as well, with that sword and also forces him to drink from the poisoned cup Claudius had prepared for him. As Hamlet and Laertes are dying, Hamlet forgives Laertes for plotting against him, and Laertes forgives Hamlet for the accidental murder of his father, Polonius. Hamlet then forbids his friend Horatio to commit suicide as a gesture of loyalty and friendship; rather, Hamlet charges Horatio to live and tell the prince's story so that his name will survive in honor after his death.

Horatio

Horatio is a stoic scholar and Hamlet's true and loyal friend. Hamlet notes that Horatio meets good and bad fortune alike with equanimity. When Marcellus and Bernardo invite him to keep the watch with them and the Ghost appears, Horatio tries to speak to it, but without success. He tells Hamlet of the Ghost's appearance and joins him the following night on the battlements; when the Ghost beckons Hamlet to follow, Horatio tries to prevent Hamlet from going off alone with the spirit. He also advises Hamlet not to accept the king's challenge to compete against Laertes in a duel. At his death, Hamlet forbids Horatio to commit suicide, asking his friend to tell his story, explain his erratic behavior, and clear his name.

Laertes

Laertes, Polonius's son, returns from his studies in Paris after Hamlet kills Polonius. Laertes' mission to avenge his father's murder thus mirrors Hamlet's mission to avenge the murder of his own father. Claudius mollifies Laertes, who is angry over both his father's death and his sister Ophelia's madness, and conspires with Laertes, arranging for him to kill Hamlet in a fencing match.

Ophelia

Ophelia is Polonius's daughter and Laertes' sister. When Polonius learns that Hamlet has been courting Ophelia, he warns his daughter that Hamlet may only be toying with her—that, being royalty, his choices in matters like matrimony may not be his own to make. After Ophelia breaks with Hamlet, following her father's instructions, Polonius suggests that the thwarting of Hamlet's love for her is what has maddened him; in effect, Polonius uses Ophelia in order to discover the root of Hamlet's malady. After Hamlet kills Polonius, Ophelia goes mad and eventually drowns. Whether her death is accidental or a suicide is unclear.

Osric

Osric is a courtier who conveys Laertes' challenge to a duel to Hamlet, who mocks Osric without mercy for his affected courtly mannerisms.

Players

The Players are a troupe of traveling actors who visit Elsinore. At Hamlet's request, the principal player recites a speech depicting the fall of Troy and the fate of the king and queen of Troy, Priam and Hecuba. Later, the Players perform *The Mousetrap*, Hamlet's revision of a play called *The Murder of Gonzago*, before Claudius and the entire court. The play presents a situation similar to the murder of King Hamlet and the seduction of his widow. Hamlet hopes to see if Claudius reacts to the play in a way confirming his guilt and the Ghost's assertions—and indeed, Claudius does so.

Polonius

Polonius is Claudius's Lord Chamberlain—one of his closest advisers—and is the father of Laertes and Ophelia. He is verbose and sententious and seems to love to hear himself talk and to make what he considers wise formulations. Hamlet mocks him with contempt. When Polonius is hidden behind a curtain (an arras) in Gertrude's closet, seeking to overhear the interview between Gertrude and Hamlet that he has arranged, Hamlet stabs him, thinking Claudius is hidden there.

Priest

The Priest presides over Ophelia's funeral and defines the limits of the religious rites allowed to her, since her death is considered a suicide.

Reynaldo

Polonius sends Reynaldo to Paris to make inquiries regarding Laertes' behavior.

Rosencrantz

Rosencrantz, along with Guildenstern, is a school friend of Hamlet's whom the king summons to Elsinore to help discover the cause of Hamlet's strange behavior.

First Sailor

When Hamlet is being conveyed to England, the boat he is on is overtaken by pirates who return Hamlet to Denmark. Among others, the First Sailor delivers letters to Horatio and Claudius from him.

Voltimand

Voltimand, along with Cornelius, is an ambassador Claudius sends to Norway to negotiate with the king to prevent Fortinbras's invasion of Denmark.

THEMES

The Active versus the Contemplative Life

As the hero of a revenge tragedy, conventionally, Hamlet ought to be a man of action, not of thought; what thoughts he does have ought to concern carrying out the deed he is dedicated to accomplishing. Shakespeare's hero, however, is

The group of traveling players performing "The Murder of Gonzago," Act III, scene ii

a contemplative man. He thinks about the actions he will take and whether taking them will be morally right. He worries about the authenticity and authority of the Ghost. He contemplates the absurdity of war and the meaning of honor when he sees Fortinbras's army marching to fight in Poland for a tract of land. He meditates on the difficulties and pains of being alive and the fearsomeness of death in his "To be or not to be" soliloquy. When he has the opportunity to slay Claudius when he finds him at prayer, he forbears for fear of sending him to heaven. Still, Hamlet ultimately proves quite active. He kills Polonius; he performs feats of derring-do aboard his ship when it is attacked by pirates; he leaps into Ophelia's grave and grapples with her brother; and he is an excellent fencer, as his final duel with Laertes shows.

Spying

Nearly every character in *Hamlet* spies on another character or at some point conceals something. Polonius sends Reynaldo to spy on Laertes in France and is killed himself when he hides behind the arras to spy on Hamlet as he speaks to Gertrude. He also counsels Claudius to watch with him as Hamlet and Ophelia converse. The king orders Rosencrantz and Guildenstern to spy on Hamlet. Ophelia is used by the king and her father as a bait for their spying. Hamlet himself, in his attempt "to catch the conscience of the king" and authenticate the Ghost's report, devises a complex series of surveillance strategies, including feigning madness and presenting a play during the performance of which he watches the king. Aboard the ship to England, Hamlet engages in espionage that allows him to discover the plot against his life. Horatio, too, at Hamlet's request, becomes a spy during the performance of *The Mousetrap*.

Vengeance

A common type of play performed on the Elizabethan stage was the revenge tragedy. In a revenge tragedy, one act of brutality gives rise to a counteract, which gives rise to another, until all the characters are murdered. Usually, the murders are grim and treacherous. *Hamlet* is a complex example of a revenge tragedy. Hamlet is a man with greater consciousness than the typical heroes of revenge tragedies usually possess, and he struggles with the role of avenger that is cast upon him. After Hamlet's father dies, his father's ghost visits and reveals that he was murdered by his brother, and he calls upon Hamlet to avenge his murder. Parallel revenge plots are also present, as the old

TOPICS FOR FURTHER STUDY

- When Horatio announces, as Hamlet is dying, that he will commit suicide like an ancient Roman, to join his friend in death, Hamlet asks him to instead remain alive and relate his story. Imagine you are Horatio talking to a group of Danish citizens and, either in blank verse or in prose, tell Hamlet's story.

- In an essay, compare and contrast Thomas Kyd's play *The Spanish Tragedy* and *Hamlet*.

- Sources for *Hamlet* include historical chronicles. Choose a period in history that interests you and find one or two narrative accounts of that period and of some particular events and people of that time. Then use what you have studied as the basis for a short imaginative play set in that time period and incorporating some of the events and characters you read about.

- Many filmed versions and adaptations of *Hamlet* have been produced. Choose two, and in a well-organized essay of around one thousand words describe each and compare and contrast them with each other and with the original play by Shakespeare.

- Write an adaptation of a scene from *Hamlet* set in contemporary times, with contemporary characters and dialogue reflecting similar themes and concerns to those found in the original play.

- Write a rap song or a folk song in which the story of *Hamlet* is related.

- Along with Desdemona in *Othello* and Cordelia in *King Lear*, Ophelia is one of Shakespeare's heroines who is in some way sacrificed to the wishes and passions of the lead characters in those plays. Compare and contrast the three women, focusing on their relations to their fathers and to their beloveds.

King Hamlet had defeated Fortinbras, the king of Norway, in a war, and at the beginning of *Hamlet*, the young Fortinbras plans to avenge his father's death by warring on Denmark. After Hamlet kills Polonius, that man's son, Laertes, returns to Denmark in order to avenge his father's death. The king suggests the climactic duel between Laertes and Hamlet as a way of accomplishing that revenge. In the end, Hamlet not only takes vengeance on the king but also avenges himself against Rosencrantz and Guildenstern, who had become the king's agents in his attempts to murder Hamlet.

STYLE

Aside

An aside is the term for a remark uttered out loud but understood by the audience as reflecting a character's thought while not being heard by the other characters on the stage. Hamlet's first words in the play, "A little more than kin, and less than kind," constitute an aside. The words are not directed to the king, who has just addressed him, but reveal Hamlet's own unuttered thoughts. Similarly, when Polonius is trying to sound Hamlet out, in act 2, scene 2, after Hamlet has referred to his daughter, Polonius says to himself, "How say you by that? Still harping on my daughter. Yet he knew me not at first." And then he addresses Hamlet, asking, "What do you read, my lord?"

Blank Verse

Most of *Hamlet*, except for occasional prose passages, is written in unrhymed iambic pentameter, which is called blank verse. *Pentameter* means that there are five poetic feet in each line, where a foot is composed of a certain number of syllables or beats. *Iambic* signifies the rhythm of the feet; in an iambic foot the first syllable is unaccented, the second accented. Thus, the iambic pentameter line "When we have shuffled off this mortal coil," for example, is scanned as follows: "When WE have SHUFFled OFF this MORtal COIL." Spoken English often falls into an iambic pattern.

Punning

Shakespeare is noted for his playing with words—punning—in order to simultaneously suggest multiple meanings in one word or phrase. In *Hamlet*, Shakespeare can be said to have given punning a rhetorical and dramatic relevance that he had not given it since the very

COMPARE & CONTRAST

- **1600s:** The players report to Hamlet that adult actors have been driven off the London stage and been replaced by children's companies, which have become very popular.

  Today: The Broadway theater, which was once the home to plays written by playwrights like Eugene O'Neill, Arthur Miller, Tennessee Wiliams, William Inge, and Clifford Odetts, all writing about complex psychological and political subjects, has become inundated with children's spectacles and juke-box musicals.

- **1600s:** Shakespeare adapted older plays, tales, and historical narratives in the composition of *Hamlet*.

  Today: *Hamlet* continues to serve as the basis for new dramatic, cinematic, and narrative adaptations and reworkings.

- **1600s:** In general, people do not consider it impossible to see a ghost.

  Today: Seeing a ghost would be, by many people, considered a sign of mental or emotional disturbance.

---

early *Comedy of Errors*, when confusion regarding two sets of twins makes many comments have at least two contexts. Hamlet plays with language continuously and puns deliberately in order to tease and confuse those with whom he speaks, and he thereby also reveals the complexity of his personality.

Revenge Tragedy

In the 1590s, when Elizabeth I continued to reign, revenge tragedies were extremely popular. Structurally, these tragedies typically involve an initial crime that engenders waves of retribution for the crime and of counter-retribution for the retribution. These plays are often violent, brutal, and graphic. *Hamlet* follows in the tradition of the revenge tragedy but features a hero who, by virtue of his intellect and philosophical disposition, questions the conventions of his role while undertaking it.

Soliloquy

A soliloquy is a speech a character delivers when alone on stage. It is an address to the audience revealing the character's inner thoughts and feelings. *Hamlet* is famous for its soliloquies, particularly the one that Hamlet relates in act 3, scene 1, beginning "To be, or not to be." Shakespeare gave Hamlet several soliloquies, a feature that emphasizes the character's inward-looking nature and the activity of his mind.

HISTORICAL CONTEXT

Children's Acting Companies

Hamlet speaks about children's acting companies with Rosencrantz and Guildenstern in act 2, scene 2, when they explain to him that the players who are visiting Elsinore have been forced to travel because of the popularity of the newly emerging children's acting companies. In fact, beginning in 1598, after a decade of inactivity, children's acting companies, especially the Children of the Chapel Royal, became so popular on London stages that some established adult companies were forced, from 1599 to 1601, to go on the road in search of audiences. This conflict between boy's and men's acting companies was dubbed the "War of the Theaters."

The Trojan War

One of the players recites for Hamlet the story of the fall of Troy and the grief of Queen Hecuba. The Trojan War was fought between Greece and Troy, ostensibly over the wife of the Greek king Menelaus, Helen, who was seduced and kidnapped by Paris, a Trojan prince. That war was known to Elizabethans through a translation of *The Aeneid* (c. 29–19 B.C.E.), originally written by Virgil, made by the Scotsman Gavin Douglas. That translation appeared in London for the first time in 1553.

CRITICAL OVERVIEW

Hamlet is regarded as being among the greatest plays ever written, if not the greatest, and is as popular as it is critically esteemed. From its first performances, *Hamlet* enjoyed such great success that its first printing was an unauthorized pirated edition, reconstructed from memory by several actors who had been in road company productions at Oxford and Cambridge. It became the most popular work on the Restoration stage when the theaters were reopened in 1661, and it retained its popularity throughout the eighteenth century, in large part because great actors like Thomas Betterton, Colley Cibber, and Edmund Kean were drawn to the role of Hamlet. At the beginning of the nineteenth century, the poet and critic Samuel Taylor Coleridge could write, "Hamlet has been the darling of every country in which the literature of England has been fostered." Undoubtedly, this has been true because of the play's poetry and because of the scope and depth of human character and complexity which it reveals through and in that poetry. A. C. Bradley, in his 1904 classic study *Shakespearean Tragedy*, praises "the dramatic splendour of the whole tragedy" and also states that "the whole story turns upon the peculiar character of the hero." The particular problem that Bradley associates with Hamlet's character is that Hamlet seems to be slow to act after his encounter with the Ghost. This concern extends backward from Bradley to the beginning of the nineteenth century and was also a chief concern in twentieth-century interpretations of *Hamlet*.

In 1818, reviewing his own critical approach to *Hamlet*, Coleridge argued,

> We see a great, an almost enormous, intellectual activity, and a proportionate aversion to real action consequent upon it .... This character Shakspere places in circumstances, under which it is obliged to act on the spur of the moment:—Hamlet is brave and careless of death; but he vacillates from sensibility, and procrastinates from thought, and loses the power of action in the energy of resolve.

In "Hamlet and His Problems," from 1922, T. S. Eliot argues that rather than being a brilliant creation, *Hamlet* is an artistic failure. He asserts, "*Hamlet* the play is the primary problem, and Hamlet the character only secondary." Eliot contends that Shakespeare failed to find an adequate "objective correlative," or "a set of objects, a situation, a chain of events which shall be the formula of that *particular* emotion; such that when the external facts, which must terminate in sensory experience, are given, the emotion is immediately evoked." Eliot argues that in *Hamlet*, the emotional response evoked is greater than the plot can account for. Shakespeare, Eliot asserts, had "intractable" material in Hamlet's character, which defeated Shakespeare because he was dealing with things he did "not understand himself."

James Joyce, in the novel *Ulysses*, offers a biographical interpretation of Hamlet, presenting it as a reflection of the character Stephen Dedalus, who is as much concerned about his relationship to a father as he postulates Hamlet is.

One of the most influential twentieth-century readers of *Hamlet*, and one who was likewise concerned with Hamlet's attitude toward his father and its bearing on his actions, was the British Freudian psychoanalyst Ernest Jones. Jones argued that Hamlet is held back from acting because of his Oedipus complex, which leads him to identify with Claudius because of his unconscious desire to murder his own father and possess his own mother. Jones's thoughts were published in 1946 as *Hamlet and Oedipus* but had been introduced in 1910 in a paper called, "The Oedipus-Complex as an Explanation of Hamlet's Mystery: A Study in Motive." Jones's analysis greatly influenced Laurence Olivier's classic 1948 film version of *Hamlet*.

The majority of critics and interpreters have pursued approaches to the problem of what became known as Hamlet's delay with greater attention to the text itself or to period scholarship, rather than to external theories or systems. Eleanor Prosser, in *Hamlet and Revenge*, attempts to determine the credibility of the Ghost and the morality of its injunction to revenge by determining whether it was a Protestant or a Catholic ghost. If conceived of from a Catholic perspective, the Ghost is a tormented spirit from purgatory, which is a Catholic concept. From a Protestant perspective, the Ghost must be a demon from hell.

(Martin Luther, who sparked the Protestant Reformation, by 1530 had rejected the idea of purgatory, and Protestant teaching does not include belief in purgatory.) Prosser concludes that the spirit is misleading and evil.

What seems to unite all critics throughout the centuries is agreement that Hamlet is a profound study of the human condition with great dramatic excitement, exceptional lengths of the greatest poetry, and penetrating studies of human characters and relationships.

CRITICISM

Ernest Jones

Jones applies Sigmund Freud's techniques of psychoanalysis to Hamlet's character, asserting that the prince is afflicted with an Oedipus Complex. This psychological disorder involves the unconscious desire of a son to kill his father and take his place as the object of the mother's love. According to the critic, Hamlet delays taking revenge on Claudius because he identifies with his uncle and shares his guilt. Thus Hamlet's inaction stems from a "tortured conscience," and his affliction is caused by "repressed" feelings. Furthermore, this theory accounts for Hamlet's speaking to Gertrude like a jealous lover, dwelling on his mother's sexual relations with Claudius, and treating his uncle like a rival. Significantly, the critic also claims that while his father's murder evokes "indignation" in Hamlet, Gertrude's perceived "incest" awakes his "intensest horror." In addition, Jones maintains that the prince suffers from "psychoneurosis," or "a state of mind where the person is unduly, often painfully, driven or thwarted by the 'unconscious' part of his mind." This internal mental conflict reflects Hamlet's condition throughout much of the play.

[The] whole picture presented by Hamlet, his deep depression, the hopeless note in his attitude towards the world and towards the value of life, his dread of death, his repeated reference to bad dreams, his self-accusations, his desperate efforts to get away from the thoughts of his duty, and his vain attempts to find an excuse for his procrastination; all this unequivocally points to a *tortured conscience*, to some hidden ground for shirking his task, a ground which he dare not or cannot avow to himself. We have, therefore, ... to seek for some evidence that may serve to bring to light the hidden counter-motive.

I WOULD SUGGEST THAT IN THIS SHAKESPEARE'S EXTRAORDINARY POWERS OF OBSERVATION AND PENETRATION GRANTED HIM A DEGREE OF INSIGHT THAT IT HAS TAKEN THE WORLD THREE SUBSEQUENT CENTURIES TO REACH. ... IT IS NOW BECOMING MORE AND MORE WIDELY RECOGNIZED THAT MUCH OF MANKIND LIVES IN AN INTERMEDIATE AND UNHAPPY STATE ... OF WHICH HAMLET IS THE SUPREME EXAMPLE IN LITERATURE."

The extensive experience of the psychoanalytic researches carried out by Freud and his school during the past half-century has amply demonstrated that certain kinds of mental process show a greater tendency to be inaccessible to consciousness (put technically, to be "repressed") than others. In other words, it is harder for a person to realize the existence in his mind of some mental trends than it is of others.

Bearing these considerations in mind, let us return to Hamlet ... We ... realize—as his words so often indicate—that the positive striving for vengeance, the pious task laid on him by his father, was to him the moral and social one, the one approved of by his consciousness, and that the "repressed" inhibiting striving against the act of vengeance arose in some hidden source connected with his more personal, natural instincts. The former striving ... indeed is manifest in every speech in which Hamlet debates the matter: the second is, from its nature, more obscure and has next to be investigated.

This is perhaps most easily done by inquiring more intently into Hamlet's precise attitude towards the object of his vengeance, Claudius, and towards the crimes that have to be avenged. These are two: Claudius' incest with the Queen, and his murder of his brother. Now it is of great importance to note the profound difference in Hamlet's attitude towards these two crimes. Intellectually of course he abhors both, but there can be no question as to which arouses in him the deeper loathing. Whereas the murder of his father evokes in him indignation and a plain recognition of his obvious duty to avenge it, his mother's guilty conduct awakes in him the intensest horror.

Now, in trying to define Hamlet's attitude towards his uncle we have to guard against assuming off-hand that this is a simple one of mere execration, for there is a possibility of complexity arising in the following way: The uncle has not merely committed *each* crime, he has committed *both* crimes, a distinction of considerable importance, since the *combination* of crimes allows the admittance of a new factor, produced by the possible inter-relation of the two, which may prevent the result from being simply one of summation. In addition, it has to be borne in mind that the perpetrator of the crimes is a relative, and an exceedingly near relative. The possible inter-relationship of the crimes, and the fact that the author of them is an actual member of the family, give scope for a confusion in their influence on Hamlet's mind which may be the cause of the very obscurity we are seeking to clarify.

Let us first pursue further the effect on Hamlet of his mother's misconduct. Before he even knows with any certitude, however much he may suspect it, that his father has been murdered he is in the deepest depression, and evidently on account of this misconduct.

According to [A. C.] Bradley, [in his *Shakespearean Tragedy*], Hamlet's melancholic disgust at life was the cause of his aversion from "any kind of decided action." His explanation of the whole problem of Hamlet is "the moral shock of the sudden ghastly disclosure of his mother's true nature," and he regards the effect of this shock, as depicted in the play, as fully comprehensible. He says:

> Is it possible to conceive an experience more desolating to a man such as we have seen Hamlet to be; and is its result anything but perfectly natural? It brings bewildered horror, then loathing, then despair of human nature. His whole mind is poisoned...A nature morally blunter would have felt even so dreadful a revelation less keenly. A slower and more limited and positive mind might not have extended so widely through the world the disgust and disbelief that have entered it.

But we can rest satisfied with this seemingly adequate explanation of Hamlet's weariness of life only if we accept unquestioningly the conventional standards of the causes of deep emotion. Many years ago [John] Connolly, a well-known psychiatrist, pointed out [in his *A Study of Hamlet*] the disproportion here existing between cause and effect, and gave as his opinion that Hamlet's reaction to his mother's marriage indicated in itself a mental instability, "a predisposition to actual unsoundness"; he writes: "The circumstances are not such as would at once turn a healthy mind to the contemplation of suicide, the last resource of those whose reason has been overwhelmed by calamity and despair." In T. S. Eliot's opinion, also, Hamlet's emotion is in excess of the facts as they appear, and he specially contrasts it with Gertrude's negative and insignificant personality [in his *The Sacred Wood*]...We have unveiled only the exciting cause, not the predisposing cause. The very fact that Hamlet is apparently content with the explanation arouses our misgiving, for, as will presently be expounded, from the very nature of the emotion he cannot be aware of the true cause of it. If we ask, not what ought to produce such soul-paralysing grief and distaste for life, but what in actual fact does produce it, we are compelled to go beyond this explanation and seek for some deeper cause. In real life speedy second marriages occur commonly enough without leading to any such result as is here depicted, and when we see them followed by this result we invariably find, if the opportunity for an analysis of the subject's mind presents itself, that there is some other and more hidden reason why the event is followed by this inordinately great effect. The reason always is that the event has awakened to increased activity mental processes that have been "repressed" from the subject's consciousness. His mind has been specially prepared for the catastrophe by previous mental processes with which those directly resulting from the event have entered into association... In short, the special nature of the reaction presupposes some special feature in the mental predisposition. Bradley himself has to qualify his hypothesis by inserting the words "to a man such as we have seen Hamlet to be."

We come at this point to the vexed question of Hamlet's sanity, about which so many controversies have raged. Dover Wilson authoritatively writes [in his *What Happens in Hamlet*]: "I agree with Loening, Bradley and others that Shakespeare meant us to imagine Hamlet as suffering from some kind of mental disorder throughout the play." The question is what kind of mental disorder and what is its significance dramatically and psychologically. The matter is complicated by Hamlet's frequently displaying simulation (the Antic Disposition), and it has been asked whether this is to conceal his real mental disturbance or cunningly to conceal his purposes in coping with the practical problems of this task?

What we are essentially concerned with is the psychological understanding of the dramatic effect produced by Hamlet's personality and behaviour. That effect would be quite other were the central figure in the play to represent merely a "case of insanity." When that happens, as with Ophelia, such a person passes beyond our ken, is in a sense no more human, whereas Hamlet successfully claims our interest and sympathy to the very end. Shakespeare certainly never intended us to regard Hamlet as insane, so that the "mind o'erthrown" must have some other meaning than its literal one. Robert Bridges has described the matter with exquisite delicacy [in his *The Testament of Beauty*, I]:

> Hamlet himself would never have been
>   aught to us, or we
> To Hamlet, wer't not for the artful balance
>   whereby
> Shakespeare so gingerly put his sanity in
>   doubt
> Without the while confounding his Reason.

I would suggest that in this Shakespeare's extraordinary powers of observation and penetration granted him a degree of insight that it has taken the world three subsequent centuries to reach. Until our generation (and even now in the juristic sphere) a dividing line separated the sane and responsible from the irresponsible insane. It is now becoming more and more widely recognized that much of mankind lives in an intermediate and unhappy state charged with what Dover Wilson well calls "that sense of frustration, futility and human inadequacy which is the burden of the whole symphony" and of which Hamlet is the supreme example in literature. This intermediate plight, in the toils of which perhaps the greater part of mankind struggles and suffers, is given the name of psychoneurosis, and long ago the genius of Shakespeare depicted it for us with faultless insight.

Extensive studies of the past half century, inspired by Freud, have taught us that a psychoneurosis means a state of mind where the person is unduly, and often painfully, driven or thwarted by the "unconscious" part of his mind, that buried part that was once the infant's mind and still lives on side by side with the adult mentality that has developed out of it and should have taken its place. It signifies *internal* mental conflict. We have here the reason why it is impossible to discuss intelligently the state of mind of anyone suffering from a psychoneurosis, whether the description is of a living person or an imagined one, without correlating the manifestations with what must have operated in his infancy and is *still operating*. That is what I propose to attempt here.

For some deep-seated reason, which is to him unacceptable, Hamlet is plunged into anguish at the thought of his father being replaced in his mother's affections by someone else. It is as if his devotion to his mother had made him so jealous for her affection that he had found it hard enough to share this even with his father and could not endure to share it with still another man. Against this thought, however, suggestive as it is, may be urged three objections. First, if it were in itself a full statement of the matter, Hamlet would have been aware of the jealousy, whereas we have concluded that the mental process we are seeking is hidden from him. Secondly, we see in it no evidence of the arousing of an old and forgotten memory. And, thirdly, Hamlet is being deprived by Claudius of no greater share in the Queen's affection than he had been by his own father, for the two brothers made exactly similar claims in this respect—namely, those of a loved husband. The last-named objection, however, leads us to the heart of the situation. How if, in fact, Hamlet had in years gone by, as a child, bitterly resented having had to share his mother's affection even with his own father, had regarded him as a rival, and had secretly wished him out of the way so that he might enjoy undisputed and undisturbed the monopoly of that affection? If such thoughts had been present in his mind in childhood days they evidently would have been "repressed," and all traces of them obliterated, by filial piety and other educative influences. The actual realization of his early wish in the death of his father at the hands of a jealous rival would then have stimulated into activity these "repressed" memories, which would have produced, in the form of depression and other suffering, an obscure aftermath of his childhood's conflict. This is at all events the mechanism that is actually found in the real Hamlets who are investigated psychologically.

The explanation, therefore, of the delay and self-frustration exhibited in the endeavour to fulfil his father's demand for vengeance is that to Hamlet the thought of incest and parricide combined is too intolerable to be borne. One part of him tries to carry out the task, the other flinches inexorably from the thought of it. How fain would he blot it out in that "bestial oblivion" which unfortunately for him his conscience contemns. He is torn and tortured in an insoluble inner conflict.

Source: Ernest Jones, "The Psycho-Analytical Solution," in *Hamlet and Oedipus* Doubleday & Company, 1954, pp. 51–79.

Kenneth Muir

Muir discusses imagery and symbolism in Hamlet, *beginning with an examination of what he considers the most apparent image pattern in the play—disease. The critic suggests that images of disease are not associated with Hamlet himself, but a sense of infection surrounds both Claudius's crime and guilt and Gertrude's sin. Muir attributes Hamlet's disorder to his melancholic grief over his father's death and his mother's frailty. In addition, the critic includes images of decay, flowers, and prostitution with those of disease in the larger patterns of corruption and appearance versus reality. Finally, Muir explores war imagery in* Hamlet, *noting that it frequently recurs in the text and that its dramatic function is to underscore the fact that Hamlet and Claudius are engaged in a duel to the death.*

A good many of the sickness images are merely designed to lend atmosphere [in *Hamlet*], as when Francisco on the battlements remarks that he is "sick at heart" [I. i. 9] or when Hamlet speaks of the way the courtier's chilblain is galled by the peasant's. Other images . . . are connected with the murder of Hamlet's father or with the corresponding murder of Gonzago. Several of the images refer to the sickness of the state, which some think to be due to the threat of war, but which the audience soon comes to realize is caused by Claudius' unpunished crime. Horatio believes that the appearance of the Ghost "bodes some strange eruption to our state" [I. i. 69] and Marcellus concludes that

> Something is rotten in the state of
> Denmark.
> [I. iv. 90]

Hamlet himself uses disease imagery again and again in reference to the King's guilt. He

thinks of himself as a surgeon probing a wound: "I'll tent him to the quick" [II. ii. 597]. He tells Guildenstern that Claudius should have sent for a physician rather than himself, and when he refrains from assassinating him he remarks:

> This physic but prolongs thy sickly
> days.
> [III. iii. 96]

He compares Claudius to "a mildewed ear Blasting his wholesome brother" [III. iv. 64–5] and in the last scene of the play he compares him to a cancer:

> Is't not to be damn'd
> To let this canker of our nature come
> In further evil.
> [V. ii. 68–70]

It is true that Claudius reciprocates by using disease images in reference to Hamlet. He compares his leniency to his nephew to the behaviour of one suffering from a foul disease who conceals it and lets it feed "Even on the pith of life" [IV. i. 23]. He supports his stratagem of sending Hamlet to England with the proverbial maxim:

> Diseases desperate grown
> By desperate appliance are reliev'd,
> Or not at all.
> [IV. iii. 9–11]

In hatching his plot with Laertes, he calls Hamlet's return "the quick of th'ulcer" [IV. vii. 123]. It is surely obvious that these images cannot be used to reflect on Hamlet's character: they exhibit rather the King's guilty fear of his nephew.

Some of the disease images are used by Hamlet in reference to the Queen's adultery at which, he tells her, "Heaven's face . . . Is thought-sick" [III. iv. 48–51]. He urges her not to lay to her soul the "flattering unction" that he is mad:

> It will but skin and film the ulcerous
> place,
> Whiles rank corruption, mining all within,
> Infects unseen.
> [III. iv. 147–49]

Gertrude herself, suffering from pangs of remorse, speaks of her "sick soul."

Laertes uses three disease images, two in his warnings to Ophelia not to allow herself to be seduced by Hamlet since in youth

> Contagious blastments are most imminent.
> [I. iii. 42]

Richard Easton as the Ghost and Roger Rees as Hamlet in Act I, scene iv, Royal Shakespeare Theatre, Stratford-upon-Avon, 1984 (© Donald Cooper/Photostage. Reproduced by permission)

In the third he tells Claudius that the prospect of avenging himself "warms the very sickness" [IV. vii. 55] in his heart.

Hamlet uses one image to describe the cause of the war between Norway and Poland—

> the imposthume of much wealth and
>   peace
> That inward breaks, and shows no cause
>   without
> Why the man dies.
> [IV. iv. 27–9]

We have now examined nearly all the disease imagery without finding any evidence to support the view that Hamlet himself is diseased—the thing that is rotten in the state of Denmark. It is rather Claudius' crime and his guilty fears of Hamlet, and Gertrude's sin to which the imagery mainly refers; and in so far as it relates to the state of Denmark it emphasizes that what is wrong with the country is the unpunished fratricide committed by its ruler. But four disease images remain to be considered.

While Hamlet is waiting for his interview with his father's ghost he meditates on the drunkenness of the Court and of the way a single small defect in a man's character destroys his reputation and nullifies his virtues in the eyes of the world—"the general censure" [I. iv. 35]. The dram of evil,—some bad habit, an inherited characteristic, or "some vicious mole of nature"—

> Doth all the noble substance of a doubt.
> [I. iv. 24–5]

The line is textually corrupt, but the general meaning of the passage is plain. Some critics, and Sir Laurence Olivier in his film of the play, have assumed that Hamlet, consciously or unconsciously, was thinking of the tragic flaw in his own character. But there is no reason to think that at this point in the play Hamlet suffers from some vicious mole of nature—he has not yet been tested. In any case he is not arguing that a single defect outweighs infinite virtues, but merely that it spoils a man's reputation. The lines cannot properly be applied to Hamlet himself.

"HAMLET SHOWS THAT THINKING ABOUT THE POSSIBLE RESULTS OF ACTION IS APT TO INHIBIT IT."

Two more disease images occur in the speech in which Claudius is trying to persuade Laertes to murder Hamlet. He tells him that love is apt to fade,

> For goodness, growing to a plurisy
> Dies in his own too much : that we would do
> We should do when we would
> [IV. vii. 117–19]

If we put it off,

> this 'should' is like a spendthrift's sigh
> That hurts by easing.
> [IV. vii. 122–23]

The speech is designed to persuade Laertes to avenge his father's death without delay. But as Hamlet and Laertes are characters placed in a similar position, and as by this time Hamlet's vengeance has suffered abatements and delays, many critics have suggested that Shakespeare is commenting through the mouth of Claudius on Hamlet's failure to carry out his duty. It is not inherently impossible; but we should surely apply these lines to Hamlet's case only if we find by the use of more direct evidence that Shakespeare so conceived Hamlet's failure to carry out his duty.

Only one sickness image remains to be discussed, but this is the most famous one. In his soliloquy in Act III scene 1 (which begins "To be or not to be" [III. i. 55ff.]) Hamlet shows that thinking about the possible results of action is apt to inhibit it. People refrain from committing suicide (in spite of the miseries of this life) because they fear that death will be worse than life. They may, for example, be punished in hell for violating the canon against self-slaughter. Hamlet continues:

> Thus conscience does make cowards of
>   us all,
> And thus the native hue of resolution
> Is sicklied o'er with the pale cast of thought,
> And enterprises of great pitch and moment
> With this regard their currents turn awry
> And lose the name of action.
> [III. i. 82–7]

Obviously these lines are an important clue to the interpretation of the play. I used to think that conscience meant both "thinking too precisely on the event" and also the "craven scruple" of which Hamlet speaks in his last soliloquy—*conscience* as well as conscience, in fact. I now think the word is used (as in the words "the conscience of the King" [II. ii. 605]) only in its modern sense. Since Hamlet foresees that in taking vengeance on Claudius he may himself be killed, he hesitates—not because he is afraid of dying, but because he is afraid of being punished for his sins in hell or purgatory. But, as G. R. Elliott has pointed out [in his *Scourge and Minister*], Hamlet is speaking not merely of himself but of every man:

> Thus conscience does make cowards of
>   us all.
> [III. i. 82]

It is apparent from this analysis of the sickness imagery in the play that it throws light on Elsinore rather than on Hamlet himself. He is not the diseased figure depicted by a long line of critics—or, at least, the imagery cannot justifiably be used in support of such an interpretation. On the other hand, the parallels which have been pointed out with Timothy Bright's *Treatise of Melancholy* do suggest that Shakespeare conceived his hero as suffering from melancholy. As depicted in the course of the play, he is not the paragon described by Ophelia, the observer of all observers, the glass of fashion,

> The expectancy and rose of the fair state. [III. i. 152]

But it is necessary to emphasize that his melancholy has objective causes in the frailty of his mother and the death of his father.

Closely connected with the sickness imagery is what may loosely be called symbolism concerned with the odour of corruption... Hamlet, like Webster in Eliot's poem, is much possessed by death. He speaks of the way the sun breeds maggots in a dead dog, he refers to the corpse of Polonius as "the guts"; he tells Claudius that the dead man is at supper at the diet of worms and he proceeds to show how a king may go a progress through the guts of a beggar. The Graveyard scene is designed not merely to provide a last expression of Hamlet's love for Ophelia, and an opportunity for screwing up Laertes' hatred of Hamlet to the sticking-point. This could have been done without the conversation between the gravediggers, and that between the gravedigger and Hamlet. The scene is clearly used to underline the death-theme. Hamlet's meditation on the various skulls serves as a *memento mori* [a reminder of mortality]. We are reminded of Cain, who did the first murder, of Lady Worms, "chapless and knocked about the mazard with a sexton's spade" [V. i. 89–90], of Yorick's stinking skull, and of the noble dust of Alexander which may be stopping a bung-hole. Hamlet is thinking of the base uses to which we may return; but his meditations in the graveyard, though somewhat morbid, are calmer and less bitter than his thoughts earlier in the play.

All through the play there are words and images which reinforce the idea of corruption. Hamlet, feeling himself to be contaminated by the frailty of his mother wishes that his sullied flesh would melt. He suspects "foul play" when he hears of the appearance of the ghost. The intemperance of the Danes makes foreigners *soil* their addition with swinish phrase. Denmark's ear is "rankly abused" by the false account of the death of Hamlet's father; and later Claudius, at his prayers confesses that his "offence is rank" [III. iii. 36]. The Ghost tells Hamlet that Lust

Will sate itself in a celestial bed
And prey on garbage.
[I. v. 56–7]

Polonius speaks of his son's youthful vices as "the taints of liberty" [II. i. 32]. The air seems to Hamlet "a foul and pestilent congregation of vapours" [II. ii. 302–03] and he declares that if his uncle's guilt is not revealed, his

imaginations are as foul
As Vulcan's stithy.
[III. ii. 83–4]

In the scene with his mother, Hamlet speaks of "the rank sweat of an enseamed bed"; he urges her not to "spread the compost on the weeds To make them ranker"; and he speaks of "rank corruption mining all within". The smell of sin blends with the odour of corruption. [III. iv. 92, 151–52, 148]

The only alleviation to this atmosphere is provided by the flowers associated with the "rose of May" [IV. v. 158], Ophelia. Laertes compares Hamlet's love for her to a violet; Ophelia warns her brother not to tread "the primrose path of dalliance" [I. ii. 50], and later she laments that the perfume of Hamlet's love is lost. In her madness she distributes flowers and

the last picture we have of her alive is wearing "fantastic garlands". Laertes prays that violets may spring from her unpolluted flesh and the Queen scatters flowers in the grave with the words "Sweets to the sweet" [V. i. 243]. Hamlet, probably referring to his love for Ophelia, tells Gertrude that her adultery

takes off the rose
From the fair forehead of an innocent love
And sets a blister there.
[III. iv. 42–4]

The rose colour again reminds us of the flower. But the flowers and perfumes associated with Ophelia do not seriously counterbalance the odour of corruption.

I have left to the end what by my reckoning is the largest group of images. This is derived not from sickness, but from war. Many of these war images may have been suggested by the elder Hamlet's campaigns and by the activities of Fortinbras; but we should remember that Prince Hamlet himself is not without martial qualities, and this fact is underlined by the rites of war ordered for his obsequies and by Fortinbras' final tribute. But the dramatic function of the imagery is no doubt to emphasise that Claudius and Hamlet are engaged in a duel to the death, a duel which does ultimately lead to both their deaths.

Hamlet speaks of himself and his uncle as mighty opposites, between whose "pass and fell incensed points" [V. ii. 61] Rosencrantz and Guildenstern had come. All through the play the war imagery reminds us of the struggle. Bernardo proposes to "assail" Horatio's ears which are "fortified against" his story. Claudius in his first speech tells of discretion fighting with nature and of the defeated joy of his wedding. Later in the scene he complains that Hamlet has a heart unfortified. Laertes urges his sister to "keep in the rear" of her affection,

Out of the shot and danger of desire [I. iii. 34–5]

and he speaks of the "calumnious strokes" sustained by virtue and of the danger of youth's rebellion. Ophelia promises to take Laertes' advice as a "watchman" to her heart. Polonius in the same scene carries on the same imagery: he urges her to set her "entreatments at a higher rate Than a command to parley" [I. iii. 122–23]. In the next scene Hamlet speaks of the way "the o'ergrowth of some complexion" breaks down "the pales and forts of reason" [I. iv. 27–8].

Polonius compares the temptations of the flesh to a "general assault," The noise of Ilium's fall "takes prisoner Pyrrhus ear" [II. ii. 477], and Pyrrhus' sword is "rebellious to his arm" [II. ii. 470]. Hamlet thinks the actor would "cleave the general ear with horrid speech," and says that "the clown shall make those laugh whose lungs are tickle o'th'sere" (*i.e.* easily set off) [II. ii. 563, 323–24]. He speaks of "the slings and arrows of outrageous fortune" and derides the King for being "frighted with false fire" [III. i. 57; III. ii. 266]. Rosencrantz talks of the "armour of the mind" [III. iii. 12] and Claudius admits that his "guilt defeats" his "strong intent" [III. iii. 40].

Hamlet fears that Gertrude's heart is so brazed by custom that it is "proof and bulwark against sense", and he speaks of the way "compulsive ardour" (sexual appetite) "gives the charge" [III. iv. 86]. He tells his mother that he will outwit Rosencrantz and Guildenstern:

For 'tis the sport to have the engineer
Hoist with his own petar; and it shall go hard
But I will delve one yard below their mines
And blow them at the moon.
[III. iv. 206–09]

The Ghost speaks of Gertrude's 'fighting soul'. Claudius says that slander's whisper

As level as the cannon to his blank
Transports his pois'ned shot.
[IV. i. 42–3]

He tells Gertrude that when sorrows come,

They come not single spies
But in battalions!
[IV. v. 78–9]

and that Laertes' rebellion,

Like to a murd'ring piece, in many places
Gives me superfluous death.
[IV. v. 95–6]

In explaining to Laertes why he could not openly proceed against Hamlet because of his popularity with the people, he says that his arrows,

Too slightly timber'd for so loud a wind,
Would have reverted to my bow again,
But not where I have aim'd them.
[IV. vii. 22–4]

Hamlet, in apologising to Laertes, says that his killing of Polonius was accidental:

I have shot my arrow o'er the house
And hurt my brother.
[V. ii. 243–44]

(These last two images are presumably taken from archery rather than from battle.) Gertrude compares Hamlet's hairs to "sleeping soldiers in the alarm."

Six of the images are taken from naval warfare. Polonius tells Ophelia he thought Hamlet meant to *wreck* her [II. i. 110] and he advises Laertes to *grapple* his friends to his 'heart with hoops of steel' [I. iii. 63] and, in a later scene, he proposes to *board* the Prince [II. ii. 170]. Hamlet, quibbling on "crafts," tells his mother:

O, 'tis most sweet
When in one line two crafts directly meet.
[III. iv. 209–10]

In the same scene he speaks of hell that *mutines* in a matron's bones; and, in describing his voyage to England, he tells Horatio:

Methought I lay
Worse than the mutines in the bilboes.
[V. ii. 5–6]

In addition to the war images there are a large number of others that suggest violence. There are four images about knives, as when the Ghost tells Hamlet that his visitation is "to whet" his "almost blunted purpose" [III. iv. 111].

The images of war and violence should have the effect of counteracting some interpretations of the play, in which the psychology of the hero is regarded as the centre of interest. Equally important is the struggle between Hamlet and his uncle. Hamlet has to prove that the Ghost is not a devil in disguise, luring him to damnation, by obtaining objective evidence of Claudius' guilt. Claudius, for his part, is trying to pierce the secret of Hamlet's madness, using Rosencrantz and Guildenstern, Ophelia, and finally Gertrude as his instruments. Hamlet succeeds in his purpose, but in the very moment of success he enables Claudius to pierce the secret of his madness. Realising that his own secret murder has come to light, Claudius is bound to arrange for Hamlet's murder; and Hamlet, knowing that the truth of his antic disposition is now revealed to his enemy, realises that if he does not kill Claudius, Claudius will certainly kill him.

We have considered most of the patterns of imagery in the play—there are a few others which do not seem to throw much light on the meaning of the play—and I think it will be agreed that... the various image-patterns we have traced in *Hamlet* show that to concentrate on the sickness imagery, especially if it is divorced from its context, unduly simplifies the play. I do not pretend that a study of all the imagery will necessarily provide us with one—and only one—interpretation; but it will at least prevent us from assuming that the play is wholly concerned with the psychology of the hero. And that, I hope you will agree, is a step in the right direction. It may also prevent us from adopting the view of several modern critics—Wilson Knight, Rebecca West, Madariaga, L. C. Knights—who all seem to me to debase Hamlet's character to the extent of depriving him of the status of a tragic hero. It may also prevent us from assuming that the complexities of the play are due to Shakespeare's failure to transform the melodrama he inherited, and to the survival of primitive traits in his otherwise sophisticated hero.

Source: Kenneth Muir, "Imagery and Symbolism in *Hamlet*," in *Etudes Anglaises*, Vol. XVII, No. 4, October–December 1964, pp. 352–63.

George Detmold

Detmold addresses the question of why Hamlet delays taking revenge on Claudius by assessing his status as a tragic hero. According to the critic, a tragic hero has three prominent characteristics: (1) a will-power that surpasses that of average people, (2) an exceptionally intense power of feeling, and (3) and unusually high level of intelligence. From this definition of a tragic hero, Detmold especially focuses on Hamlet's unorthodox demonstration of will-power in the play, arguing that the protagonist's preoccupation with moral integrity is what ultimately delays him from killing Claudius. Further, the critic asserts that Hamlet *is distinct from other tragedies in that its action commences in the soliloquy of Act I, scene ii where most other tragedies end: "with the discovery by the tragic hero that his supreme good is forever lost to him." Perhaps the most significant reason why Hamlet hesitates, the critic concludes, is that although he is tempted by love, kingship, and even revenge, he is long past the point where he desires to do anything about them. None of these objectives gives him a new incentive for living.*

Hamlet is surely the most perplexing character in English drama. Who has not sympathized with the Court of Denmark in their bewilderment at his mercurial conduct? Theatre-

> **HAMLET, THEN, HAS THE HEROIC TRAITS OF LEAR, OTHELLO, TAMBURLAINE, MACBETH, AND OEDIPUS: HIGH INTELLIGENCE, DEEP SENSITIVITY, AND STRONG WILL."**

goers, to be sure, are seldom baffled by him; perhaps the spectacle and melodrama of his undoing are powerful enough to stifle any mere doubts about his motives. But the more dispassionate audience of scholars and critics—if one may judge from the quantity of their published remarks—are often baffled. Seeking an intellectual satisfaction which will correspond to the pleasant purging of pity and terror in the spectator, they are only perplexed by Hamlet's behavior. They fail to understand his motives. How can a man so dilatory, who misses every opportunity to achieve what apparently he desires, who requires nearly three months to accomplish a simple and well-justified killing—how can such a man be classed a tragic hero? Is he not merely weak and contemptible? How can he be ranked with such forceful men as Lear, Macbeth, Othello, or even Romeo? And yet he is a great tragic hero, as the playgoers will testify. The spectacle of his doings and undoing is profoundly stirring; it rouses the most intense emotions of awe and admiration; it never moves us to scorn or contempt.

In order to understand Hamlet, we must be able to answer the old question about him: "Why does he delay?" Granting—as he does—that he has sufficient "cause, and will, and strength, and means" [IV. iv. 45] to avenge his father, why should he require approximately three months to do so, and then succeed almost purely by accident or afterthought? There is only one possible reason why a strong, vigorous, intelligent man does not kill another when he feels no revulsion against the deed, when his duty requires that he do it, when he is not afraid, when the man to be killed is not invulnerable, and when the consequences of the act are either inconsiderable or are not considered at all. Hamlet delays to kill his uncle only because he has little interest in doing so. His thoughts are

Marianne Faithfull as Ophelia in Act IV, scene V, at the Round House, London, 1969 (© Donald Cooper/Photostage. Reproduced by permission)

is one of aversion. We worship strength and health and power, and will identify ourselves with the hero who displays these qualities. We may even identify ourselves with a Lear during his temporary insanity, but only because we have known him sane and can appreciate the magnitude of his disaster. For the Fool who is his companion we can feel only a detached and tender compassion. Hamlet rouses stronger emotions than these, and only because we can recognize ourselves in him, because he is in the finest sense a universal man: Homo sapiens, man thinking—and man feeling, man acting. The proper habitat of the freak is the side-show or museum, not the stage.

But within this humanity and universality we may distinguish three characteristics which are usually found in the tragic hero. The first of these is a willpower surpassing in its intensity anything displayed by average men; the hero admits of no obstacle and accepts no compromise; he drives forward with all his strength to his desired goal. The second is a power of feeling likewise more intense than that possessed by average men; he rises to heights of happiness forever unattainable to the majority of us, and correspondingly sinks to depths of misery. The third is an unusually high intelligence, displayed in his actions and in his power of language. Aristotle sums up these characteristics in the term *hamartia*: the tragic flaw, the failure of judgment, the refusal to compromise. Passionately pursuing the thing he desires, the hero is incapable of compromise, of the calm exercise of judgment.

It will be seen that Hamlet possesses these three characteristics. His power of feeling surpasses that of all other characters in the play, expresses itself in the impassioned poetic diction peculiar to great tragedy. His intelligence is subtle and all-embracing, displaying itself not only in his behavior but also in word-plays beyond the comprehension of the others in the drama, and in metaphors beyond their attainment. But what can be said of his will-power, the one pre-eminently heroic characteristic? He is apparently a model of hesitation, indecision, procrastination; we seem to be witnessing an examination of the failure of his will. And yet demonstrably it has not failed, and does at odd moments stir itself violently. In no other way can we account for the timidity of his enemies, the respect of his friends, and his own frank

elsewhere. Most of the time he forgets about it, as we forget about a letter that should be answered—and only occasionally does he remember it and ponder his reluctance to perform this simple duty. Rightly or wrongly, he is preoccupied with other things.

Yet revenge, especially when it entails murder, is a tremendously important affair; how can any man overlook it? What kind of man can consider what kind of thing more important? Is Hamlet in any way unique, beyond or above or apart from our experience of human nature? Let us examine him as a man and—more important—as a tragic hero.

We must realize that there is nothing curious or abnormal about him. He is recognizably human; he is not diseased or insane. If this were not so he would rouse no admiration in an audience, for it will never accord to a sick or crazy man the allegiance it usually gives to the tragic hero. The normal attitude toward abnormality acknowledgement that he has "cause, and will, and strength, and means" to avenge his father. And though he is a long time in killing Claudius, he does kill him at last, and he is capable of other actions which argue the rash and impulsive nature of a man with strong will. He will "make a ghost" [I. iv. 85] of any man who tries to prevent him from following his father's spirit. He murders Polonius. He engineers the murder of Rosencrantz and Guildenstern. He boards the pirate ship single-handed. He takes so long to kill Claudius only because he has little interest in revenge—not because he lacks will, but because it is inactive. Will-power does not spread itself in a circle around the possessor, but lies in a straight line toward the thing he desires.

Hamlet, then, has the heroic traits of Lear, Othello, Tamburlaine, Macbeth, and Oedipus: high intelligence, deep sensitivity, and strong will. There is another characteristic of the tragic hero without which the former ones would never be perceived: his delusion that there is some one thing in the world supremely good or desirable, the possession of which will make him supremely happy. And to the acquisition of the thing he desires he devotes all his will, all his intelligence, all his power of feeling. Thus Romeo dedicates himself to the pursuit of love, Macbeth to power, Lear to filial gratitude—and Hamlet to moral beauty.

It is clear that, at some point before the opening of the play, Hamlet has been completely disillusioned. He has failed to discover moral beauty in the world; indeed, by the intensity of his search he has roused instead his supreme evil: moral ugliness. The majority of us, the non-heroes, might disapprove of the sudden remarriage of a mother after the death of her husband—but we would probably not be nauseated. Hamlet, supremely sensitive to the godliness and beastliness in men, was overwhelmed by what he could interpret as nothing but lust. To be sure, the marriage of his mother and uncle was technically incestuous. But his objection to it lies much deeper than surface technicalities. He has worshipped his father, adored his mother (his love for her is everywhere apparent beneath his bitterness). Gertrude has mourned at the funeral "like Niobe, all tears" [I. ii. 149]. And then within a month she has married his uncle—a vulgar, contemptible, scheming drunkard—exposing without shame her essentially shallow, thoughtless, amoral, animal nature.

The blow has been too much for Hamlet, sensitive as he is to moral beauty.

> O, most wicked speed, to post
> With such dexterity to incestuous sheets!
> It is not, nor it cannot come to good.
> [I. ii. 156–58]

That is, it cannot come to his conception of the good, whatever may be said for Gertrude's. He is unable to offer her understanding or sympathy, since to do so would mean compromising with his ideal of her. He fails to realize that no amount of scolding will ever improve her. Instead of accepting her conduct as inevitable or even endurable, he fights it, exaggerates it into a disgusting and an intolerable sin against everything he holds dear. And because the sin may not be undone, and since it has destroyed his pleasure and purpose in living, he wishes to die. The only thing that restrains him from suicide is the moral injunction against it:

> O that this too too sullied flesh would
>   melt,
> Thaw and resolve itself into a dew,
> Or that the Everlasting had not fix'd
> His canon 'gainst self-slaughter.
> [I. ii. 129–32]

The longing for death, once the supreme good has been destroyed, is entirely normal and usual in the tragic hero. Romeo, hearing that Juliet is dead, goes immediately to her tomb in order to kill himself:

> O, here
> Will I set up my everlasting rest
> And shake the yoke of inauspicious stars
> From this world-wearied flesh...
> Thou desperate pilot, now at once run on
> The dashing rocks thy sea-sick weary bark.
> [*Romeo and Juliet*, V. iii. 110–14]

Othello, when he realizes that in seeking to preserve his honor he has ruined it, prepares to die in much the same state of mind:

> Here is my journey's end, here is my
>   butt
> And very sea-mark of my utmost sail.
> [*Othello*, V. ii. 267–68]

Macbeth, discovering at last that his frantic efforts to maintain and increase his power have only destroyed it, finds life a tale told by an idiot—and he too longs for death:

> I 'gin to be a-weary of the sun,
> And wish the estate of the world were now
>   undone.

Ring the alarum bell. Blow wind, come
wrack,
At least we'll die with harness on our back.
[*Macbeth*, V. v. 48–51]

Lear, instead of dying, is driven mad. His
counterpart, Gloucester, who also has lived for
the love of his children, tries to throw himself
from the cliff at Dover. Oedipus [in Sophocles's
Oedipus Rex], too, when he discovers that he has
ruined the city he tried to save, finds life worthless—blinds himself, and begs to be cast out of
Thebes. As a general rule, whenever the tragic
hero discovers that in his efforts to attain his
supreme good he has only aroused his supreme
evil, he kills himself, or goes mad, or otherwise
sinks into a state that is death compared to his
former state. Once he has lost all hope of gaining
what he desires, he quite naturally finds no reason for continuing to live. Life in itself is always
meaningless to him; he lives only for the good
that he can find in it.

The curious thing about *Hamlet* is that it
begins at the point where most other tragedies
end: with the discovery by the tragic hero that his
supreme good is forever lost to him. The play is
surely unique among great tragedies. Elizabethan
drama usually presents a double reversal of fortune—the rise and fall in the hero's prosperity
and happiness—or sometimes, as in *King Lear*,
the fall and rise. Greek tragedy, limited to a
single curtainless stage and thus to a late point
of attack in the plot, could show only a single
reversal—usually the fall in fortune from prosperity to misery, as is observed by Aristotle. But
certainly nowhere else is there a tragedy like
Hamlet, with no reversal at all, which begins
after the rise and fall of the hero have taken
place, in which the action does not coincide
with his pursuit of the good, and which presents
him throughout in despair and in bad fortune.
We never see Hamlet striving for or possessing
his good. Rather, he knows only the evil which is
its counterpart; and in this unhappy condition he
find nothing further desirable except death.

We are now in a position to understand why
Hamlet takes so long to effect his revenge.
Everyone in the play, including himself, recognizes that he is potentially dangerous, that he has
the necessary courage and will to accomplish
anything he desires. But the demand upon these
qualities has come at a time when he has forever
lost interest in exercising them. Upholding the
divinity of man, he is betrayed by the one he

thought most divine, exposed to her rank shameless adultery, bitterly disillusioned in all mankind, and desperate of any further good in
existence. The revelation by the Ghost that murder has cleared a way for the new husband
shocks Hamlet to the base of his nature, but it
gives him no new incentive for living; it merely
adds to his misfortune and confirms him in his
despair. The further information that his mother
has committed adultery provides a final shock.
All evidence establishes him immovably in his
disillusion. The Ghost's appeal to him for
revenge is, remotely, an appeal to his good: if
he may not reestablish the moral beauty of the
world he may at least punish those who have
violated it. But it is a distant appeal. The damage
already done is irreparable. After giving passionate promises to "remember" his father, he regrets
them:

The time is out of joint; O cursed spite,
That ever I was born to set it right.
[I. v. 188–89]

Within ten minutes after his first meeting
with the Ghost he has succumbed again to his
anguish, which is now so intense after the discovery of his mother's adultery and the murder
of his father that his mind threatens to crack
under the strain. His conversation with his
friends is so strange that Horatio comments
upon it:

These are but wild and whirling words, my
lord.
[I. v. 133]

A few minutes later Hamlet announces his
intention to feign madness, to assume an "antic
disposition"—presumably as a means of reliev-
ing his surcharged feelings and possibly forestal-
ling true madness, but certainly not as a means of
deceiving Claudius and thus accomplishing his
revenge. At the moment there is no point in
deceiving Claudius, who knows of no witnesses
to the murder and who is more vulnerable to
attack now than he will be at any point later in
the play.

Two months later the antic disposition has
succeeded only in arousing the King's suspicions. Hamlet has not effected his revenge;
there is no sign that he has even thought about
it. All we know is that he is badly upset—as
Ophelia reports to her father:

My lord, as I was sewing in my closet,
Lord Hamlet, with his doublet all unbrac'd,

No hat upon his head, his stockings foul'd,
Ungartered and down-gyved to his ancle,
Pale as his shirt, his knees knocking each
    other,
And with a look so piteous in purport
As if he had been loosed out of hell
To speak of horrors, he comes before me,
[II. i. 74–81]

It is doubtful that he wishes to deceive the court into thinking that he is mad with unrequited love—only the fool Polonius is so deceived. Most probably he goes to Ophelia because he loves her as he loves his mother, and fears to discover in her the same corruption that has poisoned his mind towards Gertrude. He suspects that her love for him is insincere; his suspicions are later reinforced when he catches her acting as the decoy of Claudius and Polonius. But the one significant thing here is that his mind is still upon his old sorrow and not upon his father.

He does not recall his father until the First Player, in reciting the woes of Troy, speaks of the "mobled queen" who

... saw Pyrrhus make malicious sport
In mincing with his sword her husband's
    limbs.
[II. ii. 513–14]

Shortly afterwards Hamlet asks him to "play the Murder of Gonzago" and to "study a speech of some dozen lines, which I would set down and insert in 't" [II. ii. 541–42]. This, as we learn in the following soliloquy, is to be a trap for the conscience of Claudius. And why is a trap necessary? Because perhaps the Ghost was not a true ghost, but a devil trying to lure him to damnation. Most likely Hamlet is here rationalizing, trying to find an excuse for his dilatoriness, for forgetting the injunction of his father—yet the excuse is a poor one, for never before has he questioned the authenticity of the Ghost. Furthermore, he does not wait for the trap to be sprung; throughout the performance of "The Mousetrap" he seems convinced of the guilt of Claudius, he taunts him with it. But for a while he has stilled his own conscience and found a refuge from the flood of self-incrimination.

Before "The Murder of Gonzago" is enacted we see Hamlet alone once more. What is on his mind? His uncle? His father? Revenge? Not at all. "To be, or not to be, that is the question" [III. i. 55ff.]. He is back where he started, and where he has been all along, with

The heart-ache, and the thousand natural
    shocks
That flesh is heir to.
[III. i. 61–2]

He is still preoccupied with death.

"The Mousetrap" convicts Claudius beyond any doubt; he bolts from the room, unable to endure for a second time the poisoning of a sleeping king. And yet Hamlet, fifteen minutes later, with an admirable opportunity to kill his uncle, fails to do so—for reasons that are evidently obscure even to himself. He wishes, he says, not only to kill the man, but to damn his soul as well, and thus will wait to kill him unconfessed. At this, apparently, the Ghost itself loses patience, for it returns once more to Hamlet in the next scene and exhorts him:

Do not forget: this visitation
Is but to whet thy almost blunted purpose.
[III. iv. 110–11]

The exhortation is wasted. On the same night, Hamlet allows the King to send him to England. Possibly he has no recourse but obedience; probably he knows what is in store for him; quite likely he does not care, may even welcome a legitimate form of dying; certainly he cannot, in England, arrange to kill his uncle. The next day, on his way to exile and death, he meets the army of Fortinbras, whose courage and purposefulness stimulate him to reflect upon his own conduct:

How all occasions do inform against
    me,
And spur my dull revenge!
[IV. iv. 32–3]

He considers how low he has sunk in his despair:

What is a man,
If his chief good and market of his time
Be but to sleep and feed? A beast, no more.
[IV. iv. 33–4]

When he returns he is unchanged, still preoccupied with death. He haunts the graveyard with Horatio, reflects upon the democratizing influence of corruption. Overcome with disgust at the "rant" at Ophelia's funeral (he has seen too much insincerity at funerals), he wrestles with Laertes. He acquaints Horatio with the crimes of Claudius and resolves to revenge himself—and then accepts the invitation to the fencing match, aware that it is probably a trap, but resigned to whatever fate is in store for him.

And with the discovery of his uncle's final perfidy, he stabs him with the envenomed foil and forces the poisoned wine down his throat. But there is still no thought of his father or of the accomplishment of an old purpose. He is stirred to action principally by anger at his mother's death:

> Here, thou incestuous, murderous, damned
>   Dane,
> Drink off this potion: is thy union here?
> Follow my mother.
> [V. ii. 325–27]

The murder of Claudius is simply accomplished. We see how easily it could have been managed at any time in the past by a man like Hamlet, with whatever tools might have come to his hand. Even though the King is fully awake to his peril he is powerless to avert it. The only thing necessary is that Hamlet should at some time choose to kill him.

That Hamlet finally does so choose is the result of accident and afterthought. The envenomed foil, the poisoned wine, Laertes and Gertrude and himself betrayed to their deaths—these things finally arouse him and he strikes out at the King. But he has no sense of achievement at the end, no final triumph over unimaginable obstacles. His uncle, alive or dead, is a side-issue. His dying thoughts are of the blessedness of death and of the sanctity of his reputation—he would clear it of any suggestion of moral evil but realizes that he has no time left to do so himself. Accordingly he charges Horatio to stay alive a little while longer:

> Absent thee from felicity a while,
> And in this harsh world draw thy breath in
>   pain,
> To tell my story.
> [V. ii. 347–49]

Then, after willing the kingdom to Fortinbras, he sinks into the oblivion which he has courted so long, and which now comes to him honorably and gives him rest.

Source: George Detmold, "Hamlet's 'All but Blunted Purpose,'" in *The Shakespeare Association Bulletin*, Vol. XXIV, No. 1, January 1949, pp. 23–36.

SOURCES

Bevington, David, "Canon, Dates, and Early Texts: Appendix 1," in *The Complete Works of Shakespeare*, edited by David Bevington, Scott, Foresman and Co., 1980, pp. 1622–23.

Bloom, Harold, "*Hamlet*," in *Shakespeare: The Invention of the Human*, Riverhead Books, 1998, pp. 383–431.

Bradley, A. C., "Shakespeare's Tragic Period—*Hamlet*," in *Shakespearean Tragedy*, 1904, reprinted by Fawcett Publications, 1992, p. 79.

Coleridge, Samuel Taylor, "*Hamlet*," in *Lectures and Notes on Shakspere and Other English Poets*, George Bell and Sons, 1904, pp. 342–68, available online at http://shakespearean.org.uk/ham1-col.htm, edited by Thomas Larque, 2001.

Eliot, T. S., "Hamlet and His Problems," in *The Sacred Wood: Essays on Poetry and Criticism*, Methuen & Co., 1920, available online at http://www.bartleby.com/200/sw9.html.

———, "The Love Song of J. Alfred Prufrock," in *The Complete Poems and Plays: 1909–1950*, Harcourt, Brace and Co., 1952.

Jones, Ernest, *Hamlet and Oedipus*, Norton, 1976.

———, "The Oedipus-Complex as an Explanation of Hamlet's Mystery: A Study in Motive," in *American Journal of Psychology*, Vol. 21, No. 1, January 1910, pp. 72–113.

Joyce, James, *Ulysses*, Modern Library, 1961, pp.187–89.

Kyd, Thomas, *The Spanish Tragedy* (c. 1590), edited by Philip Edwards, Methuen & Co., 1969.

Prosser, Eleanor, *Hamlet and Revenge*, 2nd ed., Stanford University Press, 1971.

Shakespeare, William, *The Comedy of Errors*, edited by Harry Levin, New American Library, 1965.

———, *Hamlet*, edited by Edward Hubler, New American Library, 1963.

Taylor, Gary, *Reinventing Shakespeare: A Cultural History, from the Restoration to the Present*, Weidenfeld & Nicolson, 1989, pp. 46, 50.

FURTHER READING

Bowers, Fredson, "The Moment of Final Suspense in *Hamlet*: 'We Defy Augury,'" in *Shakespeare, 1564–1964: A Collection of Modern Essays by Various Hands*, edited by Edward A. Bloom, Brown University Press, 1964, pp. 50–5.

> Bowers argues that Hamlet accepts the authority of Christian providence and ignores his sense of the ominous in the duel with Laertes, and consequently he achieves salvation rather than damnation because he resigns his attempt to seek revenge and leaves the disposition of the matter to heaven.

Gana, Nouri, "Remembering Forbidding Mourning: Repetition, Indifference, Melanxiety, Hamlet," in *Mosaic: A*

Journal for the Interdisciplinary Study of Literature, Vol. 37, No. 2, June 2004, pp. 59–78.

> Gana invokes *Hamlet* in a discussion of the dangers involved in the process of remembering during psychoanalytic treatment and cites Hamlet as an example of a character beset by the twin afflictions of brooding melancholy and anxious dread of not being.

Hinten, Marvin D., "Shakespeare's *Hamlet*," in *Explicator*, Vol. 62, No. 2, Winter 2004, pp. 68–70.

> Hintern contradicts the argument that Hamlet knew that Polonius, not the king, was hiding behind the arras in Gertrude's closet when he killed him.

Knowles, Ronald, "Hamlet and Counter-Humanism," in *Renaissance Quarterly*, Vol. 52, No. 4, Winter 1999, pp. 1046–69.

> Knowles sees *Hamlet* as a framework in which occurs a debate between the medieval view that life is full of misery and the Renaissance idea that existence is something to celebrate.

Levy, Eric, "The Problematic Relation between Reason and Emotion in *Hamlet*," in *Renascence: Essays on Values in Literature*, Vol. 53, No. 2, Winter 2001, pp. 83–95.

> Levy considers Hamlet's struggle to resolve the conflict between thinking and feeling, especially in relation to Thomas Aquinas's writing regarding that conflict.

McCormick, Frank J., "Eliot's 'The Love Song of J. Alfred Prufrock' and Shakespeare's *Hamlet*," in *Explicator*, Vol. 63, No. 1, Fall 2004, pp. 43–7.

> McCormick traces the similarities between Eliot's Prufrock and not only Hamlet but also Polonius and Ophelia, with whom he argues Prufrock most identifies.

McFarland, Thomas, "*Hamlet* and the Dimension of Possible Existence," in *Tragic Meanings in Shakespeare*, Random House, 1966, pp. 1–59.

> McFarland puzzles over the problem of determining exactly what constitutes the "thine own self" to which Polonius advises one be true.

Sloboda, Noel, "Visions and Revisions of Laurence Olivier in the *Hamlet* Films of Franco Zeffirelli and Kenneth Branagh," in *Studies in the Humanities*, Vol. 27, No. 2, December 2000, pp. 140–57.

> Sloboda discusses the ways in which Zeffirelli and Branagh both attempted to overcome the influence of Laurence Olivier's interpretation of *Hamlet* in their respective film versions of the play.

Smith, Kay H., "'*Hamlet*, Part Eight, the Revenge'; or, Sampling Shakespeare in a Postmodern World," in *College Literature*, Vol. 31, No. 4, Fall 2004, pp. 135–49.

> Smith examines the use of *Hamlet* as the basis for and as a significant reference in a number of recent popular movies.

Tiffany, Grace, "Hamlet, Reconciliation, and the Just State," in *Renascence: Essays on Values in Literature*, Vol. 58, No. 2, Winter 2005, pp. 111–33.

> Tiffany argues that by fulfilling the Ghost's commission, Hamlet purges a wound given to the state of Denmark through the murder of the rightful king and shortens the days of the Ghost's penitential wanderings.

Wormald, Mark, "Hopkins, *Hamlet*, and the Victorians: Carrion Comfort?" in *Victorian Poetry*, Vol. 40, No. 4, Winter 2002, pp. 409–31.

> Wormald examines the influence of *Hamlet* on a sonnet by the late nineteenth-century poet Gerard Manley Hopkins.

Henry IV, Part One

1596

Henry IV, Part One continues the story Shakespeare began telling in *Richard II*. To fully understand the events of the later play, readers must know that in the earlier one, Henry IV, who was then known as Bolingbroke, returns from exile, has King Richard II imprisoned, and declares himself king. In *Henry IV, Part One*, Henry's former supporters, those who helped put him in power, join forces against him. Henry and his son, Hal, fight together against the rebels. The story continues in *Henry IV, Part Two*, with civil war still threatening the nation. At length, Henry IV dies and Hal becomes King Henry V. Finally, in *Henry V*, the last of the group of plays known as the Lancastrian Tetralogy (Lancaster refers to the family, or house, from which Henry IV and Henry V were descended), Henry V conquers France, establishes peace, and marries Katherine, the French princess. Thus, the Lancastrian Tetralogy consists of *Richard II*, *Henry IV, Part One*, *Henry IV, Part Two*, and *Henry V*.

Scholars estimate that *Henry IV, Part One* was written and performed in late 1596 or early 1597. The play was first published in 1598 and in fact saw the publication of more quarto editions—seven before 1623's First Folio and two after—than any other Shakespearean drama. For the historical plot of the play, Shakespeare drew from several sources of English history that were written during Elizabethan times. His primary source was Raphael Holinshed's *Chronicles of England, Scotland, and Ireland* (2nd edition,

1586–87). Shakespeare also consulted Samuel Daniel's *The First Four Books of the Civil Wars* (1594), Edward Hall's *Union of the Two Noble and Illustre Families of Lancaster and York* (1542), and several other historical works. Finally, Shakespeare seems to have drawn heavily from an anonymous play, *The Famous Victories of Henry the Fifth* (1594?), for information on Hal's youthful escapades.

Regarding the reception of *Henry IV, Part One*, the character of Falstaff, at least, was being popularly quoted and referred to as early as 1598. That character's renown may have had something to do with the controversy that surrounded his name, as Shakespeare is understood to have been persuaded to revise the original performance name of Oldcastle. Scholars have determined that this change likely took place because descendants of the real-life Sir John Oldcastle, a religious figure from the early fifteenth century, bore relation to certain men who were sponsors of Shakespeare's troupe. Reflections on and comparisons between the real-life Oldcastle and the fictional Falstaff have been prominent in criticism of the play.

One of the major interpersonal conflicts in the play stems from Hal's strained relationship with his father. Henry IV is concerned that Hal is tarnishing his princely reputation with his association with the corrupt Falstaff and other common criminals. Falstaff is consistently associated with the idea of disorder, and his friendship with Hal appears to threaten the prince's ability to mature into a responsible ruler. Critics have argued over whether Hal, who after a confrontation with his father suddenly transforms himself into the prince his father wants him to be, was actually only using Falstaff to heighten the impact of his transformation. Hal's demonstrated affection for Falstaff has also been regarded as wholly sincere.

The main action of the play revolves around a rebellion against the Crown and one of its chief instigators, Hotspur. Hotspur's valor is admired by many, especially by Henry himself, who suggests to Hal that Hotspur would have perhaps been a more deserving heir to the throne. Given the complex characterizations of Hal and Hotspur, spectators and readers of the play are justified in wondering which of the two—if not another character entirely—should be viewed as the chief protagonist. As such, Hal's ultimate slaying of Hotspur may be seen as a heroic victory or as a tragic defeat. Regardless, the rise of Hal and the fall of Hotspur has been interpreted as symbolic of the evolution of English society from medieval times to the age of the Renaissance. In that respect, *Henry IV, Part One* may be the most monumental of all of Shakespeare's history plays.

PLOT SUMMARY

Act 1, Scene 1

At the beginning of *King Henry IV*, the king expresses his hope that a Crusade to the Holy Land will serve to preempt the civil strife that has been plaguing the English nation. However, the Earl of Westmorland announces that Sir Edmund Mortimer—who, in the context of the play, would have been heir to the throne had Henry IV not overthrown Richard II—has been taken in battle by Owen Glendower, a Welsh lord who has been wreaking havoc at the English border. Meanwhile, in fighting in the north, Sir Harry Percy, known as Hotspur, has taken as captives the Scottish lord Archibald Douglas and others—which confounds rather than delights Henry, as Hotspur's successes only remind him of his own eldest son's lack of accomplishments. Also, perhaps as influenced by his uncle, the Earl of Worcester, Hotspur intends to hold most of the captives for himself, rather than turn them over to the king. Henry sets aside his intent to commence a Crusade.

Act 1, Scene 2

In a tavern, Prince Henry, often called Hal, and Sir John Falstaff are exchanging remarks on the moon, the fortunes of thieves, and what Hal will do when he is king. Ned Poins then arrives to inform them of a chance for a robbery at Gad's Hill, near Rochester. Although he had just asked Falstaff about where they might "take a purse," Hal subsequently asserts that he is no thief and will not join them; Falstaff departs, leaving Poins to try and persuade Hal to go along. In fact, Poins proposes that they play a joke on their thieving comrades: after Falstaff and others commit the robbery, the disguised Poins and Hal will rob them in turn, specifically so that they can enjoy the excuses and lies that Falstaff will certainly provide afterward. Hal agrees to go along.

Upon Poins's departure, Prince Henry offers a soliloquy that is one of the most significant passages in the play. Comparing himself to the sun as obscured by clouds, he declares that he will soon expose and reform himself "by breaking through the foul and ugly mists." In that he remarks, "I'll so offend, to make offence a skill," he seems to be asserting that his associating with criminals is only part of a calculated plan to make himself appear all the more virtuous after his "reformation."

Act 1, Scene 3

King Henry is holding an audience with Sir Walter Blunt; the Earl of Northumberland; the earl's son, Hotspur; and the earl's brother, Worcester. After Henry scorns the offenses of the latter three, Worcester refers to the king's greatness as "portly" and as a "scourge," provoking Henry to dismiss him. Hotspur asserts that he had not explicitly and stubbornly refused to pass the prisoners along; rather, upon the close of the fighting at Holmedon, when he was physically and emotionally exhausted, a neatly dressed lord appeared, fresh, clean shaven, and perfumed, to demand the prisoners on King Henry's behalf. Thus, pained by his wounds and grieving over the killed soldiers, Hotspur immediately lost patience and could recall only that he responded "indirectly."

Blunt puts forth his belief that under the circumstances Hotspur's comments ought not be held against him, but Henry remains angered that Hotspur will not turn over the prisoners until the king offers a ransom for Mortimer, whose sister is married to Hotspur. The king then professes his belief that Mortimer had "wilfully betrayed" the men that he had led to death in battle—he notes as evidence that Mortimer married the daughter of Glendower, his supposed enemy—such that he should be considered a traitor and in no way deserved to be ransomed and brought home. Hotspur then cites reports of the extended battle fought by Mortimer and of the multiple wounds he received, but Henry simply refuses to believe these reports and again demands the unconditional delivery of the prisoners.

Left alone, Hotspur and Northumberland inform the returning Worcester of what has just taken place; Hotspur notes how the "ingrate and cankered Bolingbroke"—he uses the king's non-royal name to express his discontent—trembled at the name of Mortimer, whom Richard had indeed named as heir to the throne. Hotspur

King Henry IV of England, after the portrait at Hampton Court, circa 1400 (Hulton Archive/Getty Images)

then expresses anger over the fact that his father, who in assisting Henry in attaining the kingship was essentially an accomplice to Richard's murder, should then be subject to "a world of curses" by the king. While his father and uncle try to reason with him, Hotspur speaks of revenge and gets carried away by his emotions. Eventually, Hotspur calms down and Worcester declares that they should free the prisoners, thus allying themselves with Scotland, and consult the Archbishop of York, who will wish to avenge his own brother's death at Henry's orders. Joining forces also with Mortimer and Glendower, then, they can all plot against Henry.

Act 2, Scene 1

At an inn yard in Rochester, two early-rising carriers are discussing their preparations for departure and the laxity of the ostler, or horse keeper, when Gadshill shows up to ask whether he might borrow a lantern. Suspicious, knowing the prominence of thieves in the area, the carriers refuse to give Gadshill even the correct time of day. When the carriers depart, Gadshill converses with the inn's chamberlain, who assists thieves by providing information about wealthy travelers—in this instance, about a company including a well-off landowner and an auditor. After asserting his honor as a thief, Gadshill assures the chamberlain that he will receive his share of the booty.

Act 2, Scene 2

On the road near Gad's Hill, Poins has hidden Falstaff's horse to provide the company of thieves with amusement. Indeed, Falstaff rails against Poins and declares his inability to walk anywhere at all in any comfort. Hal is ineffectually trying to calm Falstaff when Bardolph, Peto, Poins, and Gadshill arrive, with the latter informing the others of the travelers coming their way. Hal declares that he and Poins—who finally informs Falstaff of his horse's whereabouts—will seal off the escape route farther along the road, and they depart just before the travelers arrive. Falstaff and the others proceed to rob the travelers, only to be robbed in turn by the disguised Hal and Poins.

Act 2, Scene 3

At the home of the Percys, in Warkworth Castle, in Northumberland, Hotspur reads a letter from an anonymous lord who declines to take part in the Percys' proposed rebellion, citing the uncertainty of the effort. After affirming to himself the trustworthiness of the rebellion's major players, Hotspur dismisses the lord as "a frosty-spirited rogue" and "a pagan rascal"; he also first expresses, then negates concern that the lord will inform King Henry of their plot. Lady Percy, his wife, then arrives to chastise him for being so uncommunicative and solitary a husband and for focusing so much of his energy on warfare. Ignoring her inquiries as to why he has been especially preoccupied as of late, Hotspur asks a servant about preparations for his departure; growing enraged at Hotspur's stonewalling her, Lady Percy announces her suspicion that he and her brother Mortimer are engaged in some plot against King Henry. Hotspur then asserts that he does not even love his wife, as love is far less important than the political intrigue underway—though he momentarily adds that he will later "swear / I love thee infinitely" but that he

simply will not inform her of the plot, even though she will be joining him wherever he goes.

Act 2, Scene 4

At a tavern, presumably the Boar's Head, in London's Eastcheap district, Hal and Poins emerge from hiding to share in their amusement at their successful robbing of their companions. After boisterously discussing how he has just learned to drink with the peasant servers in the basement, Hal proposes a jest of his own: he will engage the server Francis in conversation while Poins summons him from the other room, such that they can provoke Francis to repeatedly utter "anon." Indeed, while Hal inquires about Francis's age and the price of sugar, among other ramblings, Poins repeatedly calls for service, and Francis parrots away as expected. When the vintner announces that Falstaff and the other thieves are waiting outside, Hal expresses his delight in participating in such playful activity while mocking the ever-industrious, Scot-killing Hotspur.

Upon entering the tavern, Falstaff rants and raves about nothing in particular, repeatedly declaring, "A plague of all cowards." As Prince Henry insists that Falstaff explain his consternation, Falstaff begins his tall tale about how he and the others were overtaken by a hundred adversaries after committing the robbery. Falstaff notes how he received various minor wounds (mostly to his clothing), in fending off these men, their number ever changing as Falstaff's tale continues; he pointedly mentions "two rogues in buckram suits," as Hal and Poins had been dressed in disguise. At length, Hal accuses Falstaff of lying, and the two comically insult each other; Hal then informs the company that he and Poins were actually the two men who had robbed them—at which revelation Falstaff asserts that he had known all along and had simply seen fit to leave the prince unharmed.

When the hostess enters to inform the prince that a nobleman has arrived to speak with him, Falstaff departs to send him away. Meanwhile, Peto informs Hal that Falstaff had compelled them all to hack their swords with their daggers and smear blood on their clothes in hopes of convincing Hal and Poins that they truly had fought valiantly before being robbed of their booty. When Falstaff returns, he relates the news he has learned: that Hotspur, Glendower, Mortimer, Northumberland, Douglas, and Worcester are plotting against the king, and that Hal will need to return to the court in the morning. In spite of the obvious peril, Hal insists that he is not afraid

Falstaff, in turn, insists that Hal practices interacting with his father, whom Falstaff will impersonate, with a cushion as his crown, to the hostess's amusement. As Henry, Falstaff castigates Hal for his engaging in thievery and keeping such base company—excluding a "goodly portly man" whom he holds to be "virtuous." After Falstaff praises himself at length, Hal insists that they switch roles: the prince will play his father, and Falstaff will play the prince. As Henry, Hal seizes the opportunity to thoroughly ridicule the "fat old man" whose company he keeps—and Falstaff pretends not to know the person about whom Hal speaks. When Hal utters his name, Falstaff offers a comical defense of himself; nevertheless, Hal, as king, insists that he will still see fit to "banish plump Jack."

The tavern is thrown into commotion upon the arrival of the sheriff and "a most monstrous watch." After entreating Hal not to turn him over for his thievery, for which he would surely be hanged, Falstaff hides behind a curtain. Hal assures the sheriff that he will send the "gross fat man" to him the following day, and the sheriff departs. Falstaff is then found to have fallen asleep in his hiding place, and Peto extracts from his pocket a number of papers, one of which is a receipt showing that Falstaff had purchased a good deal of wine and a very small amount of bread. Letting his friend sleep, Hal declares that the stolen money will be repaid and that he will procure for Falstaff a position of command in the king's military force. Everyone then retires.

Act 3, Scene 1

Hotspur, Worcester, Mortimer, and Glendower are meeting to discuss specifics regarding their intended rebellion. When Glendower asserts that grand natural events occurred at the time of his birth, Hotspur iterates the Elizabethan belief regarding earthquakes: that they are caused by winds pent up within the earth escaping in an eruption. Glendower insists that his magical powers are unequaled on the isle of Britain—and further that he could teach them to Hotspur, who then insists that Glendower summon the devil.

Glendower eventually turns their attention to the map and their intended division of the country: with the Trent and Severn rivers serving as borders, the archdeacon has allotted the southeastern portion of the nation to Mortimer, the region of Wales to Glendower, and the northernmost region to Hotspur—who remarks that his share seems too small; likewise, Mortimer feels slightly cheated; as such, Worcester helps them agree to divert the river's course—but Glendower is opposed. Hotspur and Glendower resume arguing, now about the Welsh language, before Glendower finally concedes and departs. After Hotspur disparages Glendower and Mortimer defends him, Worcester chides Hotspur for his brashness.

Glendower and the wives of Hotspur and Mortimer then arrive, and Mortimer laments his inability to communicate with his Welsh-speaking mate and declares that he loves her and will soon learn to speak with her. Lady Mortimer then offers her husband a song, which she sings while Hotspur continues speaking coarsely to his wife, who tries to hush him. Hotspur goes so far as to chide Lady Percy for swearing such mild oaths before they all depart.

Act 3, Scene 2

Dismissing some attending lords, King Henry engages in a private discussion with his son, lamenting that his son had thus far so disappointed him with respect to the way he was living his life. The prince seeks pardon for his behavior, and the king goes on to point out the advantages a leader can reap by not allowing the common people to know him too well, pointing out how much Richard had lowered opinions of himself by consorting and even arguing with the masses. The king then invokes Hotspur, his son's peer, as a far better model of a princely warrior, as evidenced by his successes in battle; Henry even mentions his suspicion that his eldest son might rebel against him. The prince then declares that he will soon win his father's respect and his own honor by slaying Percy. When Sir Walter Blunt arrives to announce that Douglas, the Scot, had held counsel with the English rebels, the king notes that Westmorland and his son, John of Lancaster, have already departed for Bridgnorth, where they will engage the rebels in battle. Prince Henry, called Harry by his father, will travel there by a different route so as to collect more men.

Act 3, Scene 3

Back in the tavern, Falstaff asks Bardolph whether or not he appears to have lost some weight and claims that he will reform his ways. Bardolph mocks him, and so Falstaff in turn mocks his friend's red nose at length. When the hostess comes, Falstaff asks whether the person who picked his pocket has been identified; as the hostess responds negatively, Falstaff demands that he be reimbursed for valuables that had supposedly been in his pocket—until Prince Henry marches in to confirm that Falstaff had borne nothing valuable. Falstaff then begins subtly insulting the hostess, Mistress Quickly, who does not comprehend him, and Hal at last admits to having picked Falstaff's pocket. Hal then notes that he paid back the money that had been robbed and informs Falstaff of his commission at the head of a body of foot soldiers. Finally, the men all depart to soon meet the rebels in battle.

Act 4, Scene 1

At the rebels' camp, near Shrewsbury, Hotspur and Douglas are praising each other's qualities as soldiers when a messenger arrives to inform them that Northumberland is bed ridden with sickness and will not be able to join them; in addition, men who had been loyal to Northumberland could not be persuaded to go in his absence, severely reducing the rebels' numbers. Hotspur tries to rally their courage, but Worcester points out that even those rebels who have already joined them may be confused and disheartened by the untimely absence of one of their purported leaders. Nevertheless, Hotspur and Douglas express optimism. Yet Sir Richard Vernon then arrives to inform them that the king's forces are indeed on their way, in great numbers—with Prince Henry appearing especially daunting. Hotspur still declares his excitement over the coming battle with the royal forces and especially with the prince; however, Vernon also notes that Glendower will not be able to reach them in time for that battle, and Hotspur is left declaring, "Doomsday is near; die all, die merrily."

Act 4, Scene 2

Outside of Coventry, Falstaff sends Bardolph to fetch some wine. Falstaff then confesses in a prose soliloquy that he has been abusing his position as the head of a regiment by taking bribes, such that his collection of men was fairly pathetic and hardly battle worthy. Hal and Westmorland arrive to check in, with the prince

calling Falstaff's men "pitiful rascals," then leave again to prepare for the coming battle.

Act 4, Scene 3

Back at the rebel camp, Hotspur thinks they should attack immediately, while Douglas, Worcester, and Vernon think that they should wait until they have secured supplies and their horses have all arrived and rested. Sir Walter Blunt shows up, representing the king, to inform them of his offer of full pardons and attention to their grievances if they will cease their rebellion. Hotspur recalls how his father had helped the king return to England from his exile, and how the king had gained the favor of the masses before executing supporters of the absent King Richard; at length, Hotspur details the ways in which the king had betrayed the very lords who had helped him attain his power. Still, Hotspur tells Blunt that Worcester will visit them in the morning in the interest of negotiating peace, with Westmorland to be held at the rebel camp to ensure Worcester's safe return.

Act 4, Scene 4

At his house, the Archbishop of York is dispatching Sir Michael to the rebel forces with urgent messages. The archbishop expresses to Sir Michael his fear that without Northumberland, Glendower, and Mortimer, the rebel forces will be soundly defeated—leaving the archbishop himself, a rebel supporter, in grave danger as well.

Act 5, Scene 1

At the king's camp, near Shrewsbury, the king and Prince Henry are greeting the day when Worcester and Vernon arrive from the rebel camp. After the king exhorts them to abandon their rebellion, Worcester insists that they had only fallen out of line because they had been so severely disrespected by the king himself. As Hotspur did before, Worcester details how the rebels had helped Henry obtain the kingship and how he had come to oppress them afterward. The king denounces their complaints as hardly worth rebelling over, and Prince Henry offers to fight Hotspur man to man so as to resolve the conflict without mass bloodshed—but the king withdraws his son's offer and asks Worcester to simply bring his offer of pardons back to his comrades. Prince Henry expects that the offer will be refused by the confident Douglas and Hotspur, and everyone prepares for battle—Falstaff by explaining to himself the worthlessness of honor.

Act 5, Scene 2

Returning to the rebel camp, Worcester tells Vernon that he will not relay the king's offer to Hotspur and the others, as he believes that even if they receive the king's pardons, he will not truly forgive them and sometime in the future will intrigue against them. Indeed, Worcester tells Hotspur that the king has called them to battle, with no offer of mercy, and Douglas sends Westmorland back to the king with words of "brave defiance." Worcester then tells Hotspur of Prince Henry's gentlemanly challenge, and Hotspur again expresses his desire to meet the prince in battle. A messenger then arrives to tell them that the king's forces are on the way, and the rebels rally to fight.

Act 5, Scene 3

With the battle raging, Douglas happens upon Blunt, who is impersonating the king. Douglas tells of having already killed one of the king's doubles, Lord Stafford, and proceeds to kill Blunt as well. Hotspur arrives to tell Douglas that the man he has killed is not the king after all, and the two return to the fray. Falstaff appears, comments on the slain Blunt, and notes that he has led all but three of his men to their deaths. Prince Henry appears seeking to make use of Falstaff's sword or pistol, but Falstaff has only a bottle of wine to give him.

Act 5, Scene 4

The king implores Prince Henry, who is wounded, to return to their tents, but the prince refuses to leave the battle, as does his young brother John, who in returning to battle earns praise from Prince Henry. Douglas then comes upon the king and doubts his authenticity; the two fight, and Douglas gains the upper hand—but Prince Henry then storms in and fights Douglas until he flees, saving his father's life. When the king sets off, Hotspur arrives, and he and Prince Henry exchange words before engaging each other. While watching, Falstaff is set upon by Douglas; when Falstaff falls as if dead, Douglas immediately departs. Then, Hotspur, too, falls to the ground, mortally wounded, and laments his defeat before dying. Prince Henry praises the fallen warrior and shows his respect by hiding Hotspur's mangled face with a small piece of his battle gear.

Prince Henry then discovers Falstaff and laments his passing—but as soon as the prince departs, Falstaff rises and expresses how glad he

MEDIA ADAPTATIONS

- A television production of *Henry IV, Part I*, was directed by David Giles for the British Broadcasting Corporation in 1979 as part of "The Shakespeare Plays" series. A DVD collection of the entire series is available for purchase on the B.B.C. website.

is to have counterfeit his death so as to remain alive. Fearing that Hotspur, too, may still live, he stabs him in the thigh before hefting the body onto his back. When the two princes return, they express amazement at Falstaff's being alive, as Prince Henry had seen him dead. Falstaff then insists that Hotspur, too, had risen, and that they had fought for an hour before Falstaff killed him. Prince Henry expresses his indifference toward receiving the credit for Hotspur's death, and in departing Falstaff once again speaks of reforming himself.

Act 5, Scene 5

With the battle over, and the royal forces having proven victorious, the king scorns the captured Worcester for having failed to deliver the offer of pardon to the other rebels. The king then announces that Worcester and Vernon will be executed, while Prince Henry declares that the captured Douglas should be freed. To close the play, the king dispatches John and Westmorland to meet Northumberland, while he and Prince Henry will travel to Wales to strike at Glendower, so that the rebellion might be fully quashed.

CHARACTERS

Archibald, Earl of Douglas

Leader of the Scottish army, Douglas forms an alliance with the Percys, his former enemies, to rebel against King Henry IV; the Scot's interactions with Hotspur largely reflect their similar warrior-like characters. In the closing act,

Douglas slays Sir Walter Blunt and nearly kills King Henry IV, but Prince Henry drives him off. Perhaps in that Douglas declines to interfere in Hal's battle with Hotspur, Hal suggests that the captured nobleman be freed.

Bardolph

One of Falstaff's thieving companions, Bardolph is depicted as even more of a coward and drunkard than the unruly Falstaff.

Sir Walter Blunt

Blunt is a nobleman who, with the Earl of Westmorland, leads King Henry IV's army. While the real-life Blunt was given little attention in historical records, Shakespeare molded him into an embodiment of honor: during the battle at Shrewsbury, when he is disguised as King Henry, he fails to inform Douglas that he is not the true king even when his death is at hand.

Earl of Westmorland

The Earl of Westmorland is a nobleman who, with Sir Walter Blunt, leads King Henry IV's army.

Sir John Falstaff

An irresponsible, merry, and often drunk companion of Prince Hal, Falstaff tempts Hal into a variety of mischievous deeds, but eventually loses his influence over the prince, as Hal accepts his responsibilities as heir to the throne. Falstaff is often called a tempter or a corrupting force; upon his first appearance, after he has uttered no more than "Now, Hal, what time of day is it, lad?" the prince launches into an invective against his gluttony, drunkenness, and general debauchery, leaving little doubt as to his character. Falstaff proves himself a coward on more than one occasion, such as when Hal and Poins beset his band of thieves after their robbery at Gad's Hill and when Falstaff leads his regiment to death at Shrewsbury but somehow escapes death himself. Falstaff never really denies his cowardice; rather, he frames it as the simple valuing of life over death, which any reasonable human being should choose.

Falstaff may justifiably be seen as the central character in *Henry IV, Part One*, as an aspect of almost every major theme is illustrated through his personality, and in particular ways he rests in distinct opposition to King Henry, Prince Henry, and Hotspur. In fact, Falstaff

has more lines than any other character, with 585 lines, as followed by Hotspur (545) and Hal (535). In almost every scene in which Falstaff appears, he is literally and figuratively the center of attention, as demonstrated by conversational patterns and topics, and by the innumerable references to his girth.

With respect to the king, Falstaff serves as an alternative role model for Hal. Hal's private audience with his father features a series of longer speeches produced first by the king, then by the prince; that is, the king is essentially relating his perceptions to Hal, who respectfully receives them. Falstaff, on the other hand, is ever conversationally parrying with Hal, allowing the prince to actively develop and refine his own thoughts (even if they are merely comical ones), rather than leaving him passively absorbing information. The scholar Valerie Traub, for one, has posited that Falstaff in fact serves as more of a mother figure than a father figure in that he embodies certain qualities that Shakespeare denotes as feminine—such as cowardice.

With respect to Hal, then, Falstaff is effectively attempting to draw him fully out of the world of the court and join him in the world of thievery. In his introduction to the play, David Bevington characterizes the world Falstaff dangles in Hal's face as one of eternal immaturity:

> "Falstaff offers Hal a child's world in which he need never grow up, in which even King Henry's most serious worries can be parodied in the comic language of euphuistic bombast. Falstaff's plea is for the companionship of eternal youth: sport with me, he says in effect to Hal, and let those who covet the world's rewards suffer the attendant risks."

Hal, of course, declines to lose himself in Falstaff's world of irrelevance, largely out of a sense of moral obligation to his father, to his country, and perhaps most prominently to himself.

Finally, with respect to Hotspur, Falstaff offers the extreme opposite of Hotspur's glorification of honor; Falstaff in fact utterly devalues honor through question-and-answer rhetoric, dismissing the notion as little more than a word. The sight of the slain Blunt leads Falstaff to remark, "There's honor for you." In general, then, Falstaff lies in opposition to what other characters hold as virtues; as such, Shakespeare's genius may be evident in the fact that Falstaff is portrayed not as a deplorable monster but as a lovable teddy bear, often placing the other characters' moral high ground in doubt.

Francis

Francis is a tapster, or server of wine, at the tavern. With the help of Poins, Hal subjects Francis to a prolonged jest, provoking him to repeatedly utter, "Anon, anon." Commentators have noted that Francis's dilemma, being caught between two opposing forces (that is, customers), loosely mirrors Hal's dilemma, as he is caught between the two opposing worlds of court and tavern.

Gadshill

Gadshill is the "setter" among Falstaff's company of thieves, meaning that he obtains information about travelers from inns and relays that information to his companions on the road.

Owen Glendower

A Welsh soldier and ally of the Percys, he is reputed to have magical powers. He and Hotspur bicker during the rebels' division of what they hope to be the conquered English nation, as Hotspur denounces Glendower's powers as worthless superstition and empty claims. If Hotspur, with his undying devotion to soldierly honor, represents the medieval era, Glendower and his purported magic may be seen as representing the dark ages. Indeed, Glendower's Wales, where the women commit "shameless transformation" on the bodies of the defeated English soldiers, and where the language is ridiculed as savage by Hotspur, is depicted as less civilized than England.

King Henry IV

Formerly known as Bolingbroke, Henry, who won the crown through rebellion, faces the same threat of usurpation that he once posed. In the first scene of the play, Henry decides not to embark on a Crusade to the Holy Land due to the civil unrest in his kingdom. He had originally decided to undertake the journey at the end of *Richard II*, when he vowed to atone for the guilt he felt when Richard was murdered by Sir Pierce of Exton. Sir Pierce, an associate of Henry's, acted upon Henry's comment that the death of Richard would ease his fears.

King Henry is fearful that the Percys will succeed in deposing him, perhaps so as to install as king the lord Edmund Mortimer, whom Richard II had named as his heir. Henry refuses to give in to Hotspur's demand that the captive Mortimer be ransomed, citing the belief that Mortimer had purposely led his soldiers to their deaths at the hands of the Welsh despite Hotspur's insistence that he had fought honorably. This is one of several instances when the spectator may not be sure whether the king truly believes something or is simply demonstrating that he believes it for political purposes. In this case, Hotspur then tells his father and uncle—with no evidence of willful deceit—that he observed the king "trembling" at the mention of Mortimer's name; as such, spectators likely believe that the king indeed fears the potential popularity of Mortimer.

As word spread of the Percys' intended rebellion, Henry summons his son, whom he entreats to leave behind his life of misdeeds. The king in fact speaks at length about the political benefits he reaped by not allowing the common people to grow too familiar with him. This profession of personal belief helps explain why even the play's spectators will not be privileged enough to see the king's most profound depths. Later, in the course of the battle, spectators may be left with the impression that the king is somewhat cowardly, in that he has dressed several men in royal garb to confuse the rebels. Interestingly, Shakespeare gives no indication as to how valiantly the king fought, while in *Shakespeare's Kings*, John Julius Norwich writes, "There can, however, be no doubt that the King—who, it must be remembered, was still only thirty-six—fought with exemplary courage throughout." Shakespeare perhaps wished to shine the spotlight most pointedly on Prince Henry rather than on the king.

Overall, Henry's character ever remains mysterious, as he leaves much unsaid or only hinted at; also, the spectator does not gain insight into Henry through a soliloquy at any point. Different actors might easily play Henry's character with varying tones of sincerity, such as during his heart-to-heart talk with his son, when his words and sentiments could be presented as utterly honest or as calculated toward bringing about Prince Henry's reformation. Henry's voicing the suspicion that his son might even fight against him along with the Percys seems to force Prince Henry's hand, as at that point the son has little choice but to offer assurance that he will become the man his father needs him to become. From the play in print, Shakespeare's indirect characterization of Henry forces the spectator to understand the king based on what others say about him and on his actions. Through this indirect characterization, Henry generally comes

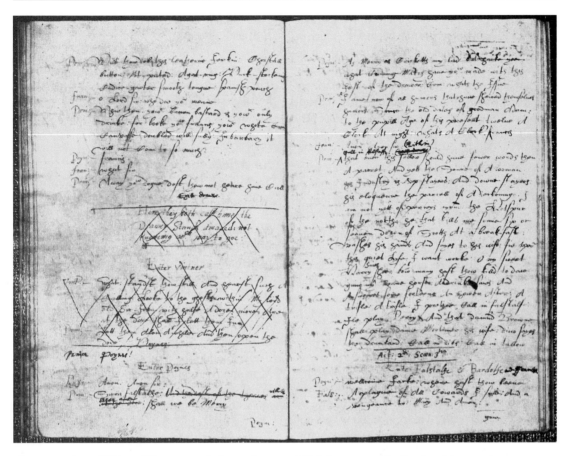

A manuscript of Henry IV, prepared about the year 1611, known as the Dering Manuscript

across as a Machiavellian character, using whatever means he deems appropriate, whether straightforward or manipulative, to achieve his political goals.

Henry, Prince of Wales

Known as Prince Hal and called Harry by his father, King Henry IV, Hal is a high-spirited youth who provokes his father's anger and disapproval by associating with common criminals, most notably with Falstaff. Hal regains his father's trust when he vows to change his ways, and he fully gains his father's favor when he both saves his father's life and bests his rival, Hotspur, in battle.

Hal's motivation to behave the way he does—first irresponsibly participating in illegal activities and tarnishing his reputation as a nobleman and prince, then later undergoing a radical transformation that proves so impressive that Henry allows him to command troops in warfare—is a subject of much debate. Many critics have argued that Hal's motives are

Machiavellian: that his political ambitions are such that he can coldly use Falstaff, for whom he has no true affection, to make his transformation from careless youth to responsible prince seem dramatic, deeply impressive, and well timed. Other critics agree about Hal's calculations but argue that he establishes a true friendship with Falstaff for the purpose of gaining knowledge about the people he will one day rule. Still other critics believe that Hal was genuinely enamored of Falstaff from the beginning, in that the latter served as a favorable alternative to his own father, and that the prince's transformation is not staged but quite sincere. Finally, some believe that Hal has to deal with two conflicting natures within himself—the carefree youth and the ambitious prince. His ambition is strong and he understands his responsibilities as heir, such that he manages to suppress his easy-going nature in order to assume those responsibilities.

The reader can perhaps deduce some of Shakespeare's intentions regarding Hal's character by examining the ways in which he did not strictly follow the historical record. To begin with, much of the prince's boisterous youth was passed on as legend, not as fact, and the account of Hal's early life that Shakespeare used, *The Famous Victories of Henry V*, was a dramatic account that did not claim to be accurate itself. That anonymous play actually featured a more sudden, unexpected conversion of the prince than Shakespeare presents. Thus, Shakespeare endows his Hal with a greater degree of self-reflection than his unknown predecessor. On the other hand, in real life, the prince had fought in several military engagements over the few years before the battle at Shrewsbury; at one point he even advanced into Wales alongside Hotspur, and he was occupied in Wales, not in the Boar's Head tavern, when word reached him of the Percy's rebellion. Overall, then, Shakespeare develops a Prince Henry whose conversion is more dramatic than history would indicate, but is not exaggerated.

With respect to the battle at Shrewsbury itself, the real-life prince was not known to have offered to fight Hotspur one on one so as to avoid a full battle. The prince likely did not personally save his father from imminent death, with Norwich noting, "Holinshed goes no further than to say that the prince 'holpe his father like a lustie yoong gentleman.'" Also, Holinshed only indirectly suggests that Hal himself killed Hotspur. In adding these three aspects to his plot, Shakespeare endows the prince with inflated degrees of courtesy and heroic valor. One last passage that perhaps reveals much about Shakespeare's intention is the one in which Vernon describes the prince to Hotspur as "gallantly armed," as rising "like feathered Mercury," and as "an angel" riding atop "a fiery Pegasus." In his essay entitled "The Protean Prince Hal," Matthew Wikander notes, "The taming of Pegasus was considered in Renaissance iconography to be an allegory of self-mastery, triumph over the appetites, and statesmanship." Thus, in sum, the reader may justifiably conclude that the prince should be viewed in a favorable light—if he is calculating or cunning, he is at least also benevolent, honest, and courageous.

John of Lancaster

The younger brother of Prince Henry, John, who in real life was only thirteen during the battle at Shrewsbury, fights valiantly there and earns his brother's esteem.

Richard le Scroop, Archbishop of York

The archbishop is a supporter of the Percy rebellion against King Henry IV. The archbishop's brother, a supporter of King Richard II, was executed at the behest of Henry.

Sir Michael

Sir Michael is a follower of the Archbishop of York.

Edmund Mortimer, Earl of March

Edmund Mortimer is Lady Percy's brother, and rightful heir of the deceased Richard II. (For this character, Shakespeare in fact conflated two real-life Edmund Mortimers, one of whom was captured by Glendower, the other of whom was the nephew of the first and was Richard's heir.) Mortimer marries Glendower's daughter, effectively allying the Welshman with the Percys. Mortimer's inability to communicate with his Welsh-speaking wife serves to highlight the distances between men and women in the play.

Lady Mortimer

Glendower's daughter and Mortimer's wife, she speaks and understands only Welsh, while her husband comprehends only English. Her portrayal as relatively exotic serves to heighten the perceived psychological distance between the men and the women of the play.

Henry Percy, Earl of Northumberland

Hotspur's father, Northumberland was one of the original supporters of Henry IV, assisting in allowing the exiled Bolingbroke to return to England. Northumberland and his family rebel against the king because they believe he has turned his back on those who helped him gain power. Northumberland fails to assist in the rebel cause, however, in that he falls ill before the battle at Shrewsbury.

Sir Henry Percy

Known as Hotspur and also as Harry, Hotspur is a passionate, hot-headed youth who regards honor, chivalry, and bravery in battle above all else. With his father and uncle, Hotspur plots a rebellion against King Henry IV. While the real-life Henry Percy, at around forty years of age during the battle at Shrewsbury, was in fact older even than Henry IV himself, Shakespeare made him a younger man, such that Hotspur and Hal are agemates and their rivalry is intensified.

While Hotspur's sense of honor is generally seen as admirable, his obsession with it may also be seen as foolish and deadly; even when the odds have fully turned against the rebels, he announces, "Doomsday is near; die all, die merrily," but he does not consider avoiding the military engagement so as to save his men's lives. Shakespeare seems to tie Hotspur's obsession with honor to an exaggerated, if not absolute, masculinity, as evidenced by his conversations with his wife. In the first, when Hotspur has just read the letter from an anonymous lord and the impending rebellion is foremost in his mind, Lady Percy proves utterly unable to draw out his softer sentiments. She notes that even in his sleep he thinks (and speaks) only of courage and war; when she attempts to turn his thoughts to his love for her, he momentarily denies that he loves her at all rather than concede the argument. Only when he is on horseback, geared toward battle by his activity, will he allow himself to admit his affection. In their second conversation, Lady Percy quite accurately characterizes him as being wholly "governed by humors." When he disparages the Welshwoman's singing and she tells him to "be still," he remarks that he will not do so because stillness is "a woman's fault." Indeed, Hotspur seems compelled to always remain in motion.

In his dealings with other men, then, Hotspur conversely comes across as childishly unable to control his passions in several scenes. When he, his father, and his uncle are discussing the best course of action after meeting with the king, he repeatedly digresses into angry tirades, and when the rebels are discussing the potential division of the nation he cannot help but express his doubts regarding Glendower's magical powers. Indeed, he largely fails to mature or evolve over the course of the play, and in certain respects this leads to his extinction.

Lady Percy

Hotspur's witty and affectionate wife, Lady Percy proves her worth as the temperamental Hotspur's mate; she chides him for being emotionally withdrawn and even threatens to break one of his fingers if he fails to communicate with her.

Thomas Percy, Earl of Worcester

Worcester is Hotspur's uncle. Like his brother, Northumberland, Worcester questions King Henry IV's treatment of his former supporters. Worcester is held to be largely responsible for the uprising, as Westmorland refers to him as "malevolent to [the King] in all aspects." Indeed, Worcester declines to communicate Henry's final offer of pardons to the rebels, as he believes that Henry will never again trust them and will certainly attempt to dispose of them sometime in the future.

Peto

Peto is one of Falstaff's thieving companions.

Edward Poins

Poins is a companion of Hal's and Falstaff's; he is referred to simply as Ned. Poins draws Hal into the Gad's Hill jest, leading to Falstaff's comical tall tale about the robbing of the thieves. In that Poins and Hal together mock Falstaff, Poins serves to illuminate the distinctions between the prince and the paunchy old soldier.

Mistress Quickly

The hostess of the Boar's Head Tavern, she is portrayed as fairly slow witted, understanding few of Falstaff's lewd comments and sexual references.

Sir Richard Vernon

Vernon is a nobleman and rebel.

THEMES

Honor

In *Henry IV, Part One*, different characters signify various distinct versions of honor. Hotspur's honor is achieved through warfare, and is marked by chivalrous action, family loyalty, and patriotism; to a certain extent, Hotspur's aggressive pursuit of honor shows his disregard for human life. Hotspur's conception of honor is partly portrayed as an outdated one, losing its relevance as early as the action of the play, at the turn of the fifteenth century. As such, Hal's view accords more with what Shakespeare's audiences would have been familiar with and approving of. Indeed, scholars have cited certain Elizabethan sources as containing references to the type of honor represented by Hal, which might also be labeled "courtesy." Hal's honor is demonstrated largely by his loyalty to his father, to his country, and to his fellow man. Hal's sense of honor is more humane than Hotspur's in that Hal does not seek warfare but fights when necessary; with the battle at Shrewsbury imminent, Hal even seeks to avert the thousands of deaths to come at the possible expense of his own life, offering to engage in one-on-one combat with the pre-eminent Hotspur.

A virtual negation of the importance of honor is presented by Falstaff, as he comments on the futility of possessing honor and fully demonstrates that he has no interest in honestly attaining it. Perhaps even more than Hal, Falstaff recognizes the human cost of honor, and he refuses to let that cost prove to be his own life. The short soliloquy Falstaff offers before the Shrewsbury battle demonstrates his ambivalence to the prideful concept of honor: "Who hath it? He that died o' Wednesday. Doth he feel it? No. Doth he hear it? No. 'Tis insensible, then? Yea, to the dead. But will it not live with the living? No. Why? Detraction will not suffer it. Therefore I'll none of it. Honor is a mere scutcheon." That is, since the disparagement of others is enough to destroy it—since the attainment of honor depends on the opinions of others—he has no interest in it; as such, he can retain the utmost control of his own life. Thus, while Falstaff will gain no favor with the community through honorable acts, he provides for himself a maximum degree of self-determination.

Fathers and Sons

The father-son relationship is loosely configured in three different ways in *Henry IV, Part One*: as between King Henry and Hal, between King Henry and Hotspur, and between Falstaff and Hal. Through the play's earlier acts, Henry expresses more than once his admiration for Hotspur, especially in contrast to his disappointment with Hal. Henry goes so far as to call Hotspur "the theme of honor's tongue"—thus aligning Hotspur's and Henry's high regard for honor—and to declare that "riot and dishonor stain the brow" of his own son. He even wishes that "some night-tripping fairy" had switched the two men at birth, such that Hotspur would in fact have been his son.

Still, the king does not personally treat Hotspur with any particular respect, such as in

the discussion about Hotspur's prisoners; the spectator might expect as much from so practiced a politician. King Henry instead focuses his fatherly energy on his own son, desperately hoping that his instruction will bring about the youth's reformation. The interview between the two in the third act is perhaps indicative of why Hal had felt a need to stray from his father in the first place: the king primarily wishes to mold his son to be a good king, allowing little room for the kind of self-exploration that Hal demonstrates a need for.

Thus, in accord with his desire for a degree of self-determination, Hal ends up turning to Falstaff, who explicitly teaches Hal very little. Rather, Falstaff is constantly providing Hal with entertainment and, perhaps most importantly, with friendship and love. Valerie Traub argues that in this capacity, Falstaff is in fact filling a maternal role, not a paternal one. She observes that Falstaff is presented as effeminate in that he lacks the masculine inclination toward the pursuit of honor and the personal test of battle. (She notes that his name can be regarded as "false-staff," suggesting a negation of a phallic symbol.) In psychological terms, then, Traub views Hal's outgrowing his attachment to Falstaff and turning toward his father as parallel to the process whereby any son must outgrow his exclusive attachment to his mother.

Role Playing

Closely linked to the multiple father-son relationships in *Henry IV, Part One* is the theme of role playing. This link is most evident in the scene where Falstaff assists Hal in preparing to speak with his father by impersonating King Henry. In this scene, after Falstaff presents a speech similar to the one the king will indeed produce, he and Hal exchange a number of comical comments with respect to Hal's association with Falstaff. The dialogue features two very significant moments: First, Hal "deposes" Falstaff, switching roles with him, foreshadowing Hal's actual transferring of his filial feelings away from Falstaff. Second, in portraying his father—thus anticipating the time when he will indeed be king—he confirms that he will indeed "banish plump Jack" even if it means banishing "all the world." (In *Henry IV, Part Two*, Hal becomes King Henry V and indeed informs Falstaff that he will no longer associate with him.)

TOPICS FOR FURTHER STUDY

- The failures and successes of political and revolutionary movements often depend upon the qualities of their leaders. Research the rebellion depicted in *Henry IV, Part One* and one other rebellion from English history. Then, write an essay comparing and contrasting the personalities of Hotspur and of the leader of the rebellion you chose to research. Make reference to Shakespeare's portrayal of Hotspur in the course of your discussion.

- Characters in Shakespeare's play make frequent reference to lions and to hares. Research the symbolism that would have been associated with these two animals in Elizabethan times and write an essay on the significance of these references.

- The pursuit of honor is a major theme in this play. Think of times in your own life when you have made decisions based on the pursuit of honor. Present a report to the class in which you discuss one situation where you made a decision that you believe was honorable and one situation where you made a decision that you believe was dishonorable. Where appropriate, compare your actions to the actions of characters from *Henry IV, Part One*.

- King Henry IV is given no soliloquies in this play, despite the fact that his name constitutes the title. Write a soliloquy for King Henry IV, in which he reveals what you believe his innermost thoughts might be. As the king always speaks in verse, your soliloquy should likewise be in verse. Indicate where in the play your soliloquy would be placed.

- While rulership was almost strictly hereditary in England in medieval times, it is almost never so in the United States of America. Nevertheless, George W. Bush went on to become president eight years after his father, George H. W. Bush, was president. Write an essay examining the lives of the two Bush presidents alongside the lives of Henry IV and Henry V. Include within your essay passages from Shakespeare's play that bear relevance to the two Bush presidents.

- Read a play published before 1600 that could be classified as a morality play. In a report, discuss the various ways in which *Henry IV, Part One* is similar to, and is different from, the morality play you chose to read.

Such role playing is perhaps the only way Hal could have communicated to Falstaff what he knew the future would hold for them, because, as David Bevington observes, Falstaff is inextricably immersed in the world of role playing: "Play-acting to him is more than a means of captivating Hal. It is the essence of the temptation he lays before Hal." Bevington adds, "This kind of all-consuming play world offers an invaluable critique and means of testing reality, but as an end in itself it becomes an escape." Thus, while Hal has learned much about himself by sharing in the type of role playing that Falstaff encourages, he understands that he must eventually cease trivial role playing so as to inhabit the real-life roles of prince and, later, of king.

In a more symbolic strain, commentators have noted how Hal's ability to play different roles at will is characteristic of the evolution of English society from the Medieval period into the Renaissance. R. A. Martin takes care in phrasing the course of this societal change: "Men come to be seen as actors rather than as mere performers—men *play* roles rather than *embody* them." That is, rather than simply exhibiting himself before a crowd as a juggler or circus performer does, a man of the new era must be able to inhabit different personae, like an actor, as appropriate to different circumstances. Hotspur, Martin notes, meets with much difficulty in developing genuine relationships and in stepping back from his hyper masculine pursuit of honor: "He only feels comfortable with his role as a warrior, not his role as a husband. In the end he forsakes single combat with his wife in favor of single combat with Prince Hal." In that Hal emerges from this combat victorious, the spectator can understand that he is the better adapted to the role-playing demanded by the changing times.

Heavenly Bodies

Shakespeare makes extensive reference to heavenly bodies throughout *Henry IV, Part One*, in two contexts in particular. The first context highlights the opposition between sun and moon, or between day and night. In the first tavern scene, Falstaff refers to thieves as "Diana's foresters" and "minions of the moon," in that they carry out their thievery at night. Hal replies to these comments by noting that in being governed by the moon, "the fortune of us, that are the moon's men, doth ebb and flow like the sea"; that is, the moon is associated with secrecy and inconstancy. At the end of this scene, Hal informs the spectator that he intends to soon "imitate the sun" by emerging from behind the "base contagious clouds" that have been obscuring his true self from the world. Thus, in maturing, Hal, the king's son, will prove himself as permanent as the sun in the sky.

A second context is revealed most prominently in the passage where King Henry is beseeching Prince Henry to reform himself. The king repeatedly invokes images of heavenly bodies: soon after his return from exile, when he was gaining a good reputation he was wondered at "like a comet"; in time, he "stole all courtesy from heaven"; and ultimately, he refers to the "sun-like majesty" he certainly believes he possesses. His speaking in such grand terms reflects not only the obvious gravity of the situation—success or defeat in civil war may hinge on the prince's actions—but also the king's conception of how life in England truly does revolve around him, as the world was believed to revolve around the sun. The kingship had indeed been historically perceived as a divine position, such that the concepts of God, heaven, sun, and king were all very closely linked. While

an Elizabethan viewer may have taken such royal and astronomical associations for granted, the modern reader may find them instructive about the perceptions of the era.

STYLE

Prose vs. Verse

Shakespeare's alternate uses of prose and verse are more pronounced in *Henry IV, Part One* than in many of his other plays. In the world of the tavern, Falstaff's world, prose is spoken, and in the world of the court, also identified as the historical world, verse is spoken. Hal, at ease in both worlds, uses the appropriate language when in the tavern or at court, except for his tavern soliloquy in the first act, which he delivers in verse. Also, when Hal leaves Eastcheap for the last time, at the end of the third act, he finishes his speech with a rhyming couplet, and Falstaff responds likewise. Aside from this couplet, Falstaff speaks only in prose, demonstrating his complete opposition to the courtly world. Hotspur, who embodies honor and a certain historical courtliness, perhaps speaks the best verse in the play, with his speeches especially well metered and ornamented with elaborate phrasings. *Richard II*, the preceding play in the Lancaster tetralogy, bears not a single line of prose, such that the fairly even split between prose and verse in *Henry IV, Part One* is especially apparent to a modern reader comparing the two plays. Bevington observes that this marked difference characterizes "the shift in language from the medieval and ceremonial speech of *Richard II* to the Renaissance and practical speech of *[Part] I, Henry IV* ."

Oaths

The extensive use of oaths throughout the play can be seen as reflective of the means by which Henry IV originally obtained the kingship. Speaking to the king before the battle at Shrewsbury, Worcester reminds him, "And you did swear that oath at Doncaster, / That you did nothing purpose 'gainst the state." Worcester goes on to note how the king later dismissed that oath in gaining the favor of the people and ultimately usurping the crown. With respect to these events, Bevington states, "King Henry, having instigated the idea that a king's word lacks sacred ranking, must suffer the consequences: for him, the oath as a locutionary act can no longer be binding." Indeed, oaths are produced and contradicted repeatedly by many of the play's characters, especially Falstaff. By highlighting these instances of dishonesty, Shakespeare highlights the way Henry ushered into history a new era of political ambiguity.

The Morality Play
In devising the plot of *Henry IV, Part One*, Shakespeare drew to a fair extent on the established tradition of the morality play, as David Bevington discusses at length. Morality plays were typically far less subtle than Shakespeare's works, with characters bearing names such as Idleness and Gluttony, and with plots often featuring sudden conversions rather than complex characterizations. In *The Famous Victories of Henry V*, the anonymous author attributes just such a conversion to Hal. Tavern scenes were also common in morality plays, as they provided fitting locales in which the darker, more irresponsible sides of characters could be revealed. The morality play is most pointedly evoked when Hal describes Falstaff as "that reverend Vice, that grey iniquity, that father ruffian, that vanity in years." Indeed, the Vice was a common morality play character, ever intentionally tempting protagonists to adopt sinful ways. Bevington notes that while Falstaff is not presented as explicitly evil, as the Vice was typically portrayed, the two share "a double image of witty *bonhomie* and incorrigibility, thereby giving rise to an inextricable mixture of farce and high moral seriousness."

Aside from the tavern setting and the Vice-like character of Falstaff, the overall framework of *Henry IV, Part One* also largely reflects the worlds of virtuous and dissipated alternatives presented in moral drama. Shakespeare constantly shifts his scenes from the world of the king and the various lords to the world of thieves and common people, highlighting for spectators the contrasting natures of those two worlds. Bevington notes that the tableau presented when Hal stands over the two apparently dead bodies of Hotspur and Falstaff is a fitting symbolic end to Hal's evolution: both of his possible extreme choices—that of obsession with honor and that of utter indifference to it—have perished, and he has successfully chosen a moderate path between those two choices. Also, Falstaff's rising to bear the dead Hotspur on his back is reminiscent of morality play scenes in which the devil carries a man of the world off to hell.

Overall, Bevington concludes, "the legacy of moral choice expressed concretely through the pairing and contrasting of characters is central to *[Part] I Henry IV*'s dramatic structure."

HISTORICAL CONTEXT

The Middle Ages vs. the Renaissance
Many critics have noted that *Henry IV, Part One* symbolically documents the evolution of English society from the Middle Ages, also referred to as medieval times, into the Renaissance. The Middle Ages are generally seen as having ended sometime in the fifteenth century throughout the world, with the English Renaissance beginning around the 1520s. Thus, Shakespeare was writing of medieval times from well within the Renaissance period (also called the early modern period), and an awareness of that cultural shift permeates the play, especially as it is viewed in the context of the Lancastrian tetralogy. That tetralogy, also known as Shakespeare's second tetralogy and as the Henriad, includes the preceding *Richard II*, and the ensuing *Henry IV, Part Two*, and *Henry V*.

This monumental cultural shift from medieval to modern world is demonstrated in *Henry IV, Part One* in a wide variety of ways. Bevington notes that changing religious and theological views played a substantial role in the shift, as provoked in part by the Reformation. The Reformation began in Europe around 1517, when Martin Luther's objections to the absolutist authority of the Roman Catholic Church led to the rise of Protestantism. In general, then, Europeans began to place less emphasis on divine command—traditionally, the English monarchs claimed that authority was vested in them by God himself—and more on the acts of individual men. This did not entail disbelief in God but simply a greater admission of human impact on the world. Bevington writes, "Renaissance humanism ... reconciled a belief in God as the ordainer of a rational and good design with an increased awareness of secondary causes in history attributable to behaviour of men." In *Henry IV, Part One*, Henry negated the popular perception that English royalty derived their power from God because he himself was not a descendant of previous kings; he was a usurper. Nevertheless, Shakespeare does not offer an unqualified endorsement of either King Henry

Michael Maloney as Henry, Prince of Wales and Owen Teale as Henry Percy in Act V, scene iv at the Royal Shakespeare Theatre, Stratford-upon-Avon, 1991 (© *Donald Cooper/Photostage. Reproduced by permission*)

and his supporters, or of the rebels, as he might have done if he himself had believed that, say, God must have been supporting the ultimate victors. Rather, as Bevington declares, Shakespeare "gives us a whole range of possible answer to questions of rebellion and loyalty in a kind of empirical openness that is characteristic of the best political theorists of the age."

Some critics have seen the inception of Renaissance ideals as especially evident with regard to gendered constructs within and between characters; this notion is closely linked with the theme of role playing. R. A. Martin begins his discussion in "Metatheater, Gender, and Subjectivity in *Richard II* and *Henry IV, Part I*," by describing the cultural shift in question as "a movement from a static, ceremonial view of human life to a dramatic and historical one." With respect to the dramatic aspect, women in particular are keen to demonstrate their individuality and devise roles for themselves within the Renaissance world. Martin notes that in *Richard II*, "Women are thoroughly assimilated to the existing values and hierarchies

of a monolithic patriarchal state even when they might appear to be criticizing them." In *Henry IV, Part One*, on the other hand, as demonstrated by the willful, aggressive Lady Percy, "Women are no longer benign extensions of the patriarchal social order: they are autonomous, self-motivated, and problematic." In that women are portrayed as thus asserting themselves, men must come to terms with the broadened emphasis on "personal relationships and life as opposed to honor and heroic death." This shift in emphasis proves most difficult for Hotspur to deal with. Martin concludes with regard to the ultimate demise of the chivalric, honor-seeking Hotspur, "He does not solve the problems posed by a heterogenous and sexually differentiated world ... and he illustrates the extent to which masculine subjectivity is being restructured."

David Bevington appropriately sums up the cultural shift Shakespeare demonstrates in this play: "The ideal world of what ought to be gives way to the unselected, chaotic flow of history, to contingency and temporality." He further speaks

COMPARE
&
CONTRAST

- **1400s:** Political leaders do not necessarily act with the intent of shaping public opinion about themselves. As asserted by the character of King Henry in *Henry IV, Part One*, Richard II, his predecessor, fully engaged himself with the common people, frequently appearing before them and responding to their inquiries and accusations alike. Henry IV, on the other hand, limited public access to him under the belief that the less people understood of him, the more he would retain an aura of elevated majesty.

  1600s: Queen Elizabeth, nearing the end of her reign, has proven a master at shaping the public's perception of her. Among other image-defining acts, in 1588 she gave a speech before English troops at Tilbury while dressed in a coat of armor and riding on horseback. Russ McDonald notes in his *Bedford Companion to Shakespeare*, "Leaving ministers and lackeys to censure, to punish, to refuse, she dwelt on the affirmative themes of unity, forgiveness, and affection for her people, and doing so with graciousness and majesty, she thereby won their hearts."

  Today: The political consideration and manipulation of public opinion is ubiquitous. In England and America alike, politicians nearly always employ image consultants or, at the very least, assistants who pay particular attention to the public perception of their image and how that perception can be shaped. Politicians often prove unsuccessful because they fail to project a likable and genuine personality; that is, politicians who are not also decent actors may have difficulty getting elected.

- **1400s:** The kingship is seen as directly connected to divine authority, with Roman Catholicism being the official state religion. Thus, treason, or rebellion against the state, and heresy, or rebellion against the church, are often equated. Bevington discusses how Shakespeare's portrayal of the characters in *Henry IV, Part One* reflect an awareness of this connection: "Lancastrian supporters of Bolingbroke and his son reflect the Lancastrian myth that Providence overthrew Richard II and favoured his successor; Yorkist supporters ... reflect the Yorkist myth branding the Henrys as usurpers and regicides who deserve providential punishment in the form of civil rebellion."

  1600s: Elizabeth I, following in the footsteps of Henry VIII, makes England a Protestant nation rather than a Catholic nation; in 1570, Elizabeth herself is officially excommunicated by the Pope. In that Protestantism features a rejection of papal authority, a natural consequence is that divine authority is also farther removed from the English monarch. Thus, while religion continued to play a significant role in the actions of heads of state, humans were seen as possessing greater degrees of control and authority.

  Today: While England retains a state-sponsored church and incorporates church teachings and authority into schooling and political bodies in certain respects, political leaders such as the prime minister are not also considered religious leaders. Meanwhile, religion and politics are fully separated by law in America, with intersections such as those between prayer and schools, between the Ten Commandments and federal law, and between religious and secular views of contraception provoking widespread debate.

- **1400s:** The future Henry V reportedly spends much of his youth fraternizing with thieves and scoundrels; however, public awareness of his activities is limited, and since he will bear himself regally, his past will not affect his rule as king.

  1600s: James I has been king of Scotland since he was a year old and as such has led a highly supervised life; nevertheless, his manner is crude, and he will prove less respected than his predecessor, Elizabeth.

  Today: Members of the British royal family still sometimes come under intense public criticism for poor behavior.

of "the destruction of a divinely sanctioned culture only to be replaced by cunning and political expediency." Matthew H. Wikander goes on to note that Shakespeare had a number of models of such political intelligence in Elizabethan times—most notably, Queen Elizabeth herself, as well as the Earl of Essex, who was long rumored to be a potential mate for the queen.

The Character of Sir John Falstaff

The way Shakespeare formulated the character of Falstaff, who is widely understood to have been based on the real-life personage of one Sir John Oldcastle, reveals much about religious and political currents of the era. The true Oldcastle was a devout Protestant who heralded the doctrines of the fourteenth-century theologian John Wycliffe, a critic of the excesses of the Catholic Church. Oldcastle was indeed at one time a friend of the man who became Henry V, but he was nevertheless ultimately burned to death as a heretic, or one who contradicts church doctrine. Both Oldcastle and Wycliffe, then, emphasized personal salvation, especially as obtained through close reading of the Bible, over the institutionalized salvation of the church.

As Tom McAlindon describes him in "Perfect Answers: Religious Inquisition, Falstaffian Wit," Oldcastle was "a reformed sinner who publicly confessed that in his youth he offended grievously in pride, wrath, gluttony, covetousness, and lechery." Oldcastle went on, however, to thoroughly familiarize himself with the verses and teachings of the Bible. When he went on trial, for both treason and heresy, he responded intelligently, even wittily, to the various accusations put forth by the team of theologians that interviewed him. That is, while his religious conceptions were ridiculed and condemned by those in power, he was without doubt a learned, respectable man in his own right with a thoroughly moral conception of God. What McAlindon finds most interesting about Shakespeare's portrayal is that he did not simply "caricature Oldcastle's biblical babbling" and create a wholly despicable character; rather, Shakespeare's parody "metamorphosed the object of its mockery into something beguilingly attractive and even admirable." Falstaff is generally perceived as both whimsically and genuinely witty in his responses to accusations regarding his character and in his discourses regarding concepts such as honor and courage. Thus, this partly belittling, partly respectful

depiction of Falstaff perhaps reflects not only Shakespeare's personal open-mindedness but also the increasing respect for subjective interpretations that was one aspect of the Renaissance era.

CRITICAL OVERVIEW

Henry IV, Part One is considered to be one of the more controversial and popular of Shakespeare's histories, due to its political and moral implications as well as to the fascinating nature of the characters struggling for power in the play. Increasingly, criticism on *Henry IV, Part One* has shifted from an emphasis on character studies and the historical sources which Shakespeare drew on to define his characters and plot to an emphasis on the language, structure, and deeper psychological truths evident in the play. The debate over the exact relationship between the two parts of Henry IV intensified during the twentieth century, although an understanding of the conjectures on this topic is not necessary to understand and enjoy either play.

Samuel Johnson, the renowned eighteenth-century Shakespearean scholar, discussed both the first and second parts of Shakespeare's plays revolving around King Henry IV. As quoted by Howard Staunton in *The Complete Illustrated Shakespeare*, he noted, "Perhaps no author has ever in two plays afforded so much delight." Regarding Shakespeare's craftsmanship, he wrote, "The incidents are multiplied with wonderful fertility of invention, and the characters diversified with the utmost nicety of discernment, and the profoundest skill in the nature of man." Johnson had the most to say about the "unimitated, unimitable Falstaff," eventually concluding, "The moral to be drawn from this representation is, that no man is more dangerous than he that, with a will to corrupt, hath the power to please; and that neither wit nor honesty ought to think themselves safe with such a companion, when they see Henry seduced by Falstaff."

David Bevington similarly connotes a positive perception of the play: "The greatness of *Henry IV, Part I* is witnessed by its undiminished popularity in both performance and reading, and by an equally undiminished critical debate about its structure, themes, language, and characterization." He goes on to cite the wide array of topics over which critics have met with disagreement, such as the actual virtuousness of Hal, the extent to which Falstaff presents himself genuinely, and whether Shakespeare was supportive of one side of the rebellion or the other. Bevington asserts, "These issues are illuminated by striking motifs and images, including those of vocation and recreation, the redeeming of time, bodily illness and wounding, commercial exchange and thievery, sun and moon, lion and hare, Scriptural iteration and parody." Indeed, the play is so rich with various modes of metaphorical imagery that few critical treatments have even attempted to discuss them comprehensively.

Over the years, of course, critical treatments of Shakespeare's plays have delved ever deeper into the abstract notions exemplified therein. In the course of her own highly complex critical essay entitled "Prince Hal's Falstaff: Positioning Psychoanalysis and the Female Reproductive Body," Valerie Traub summarily notes, "Psychoanalytic criticism of the Henriad has tended to perceive Prince Hal's developmental problem as a choice between two fathers: a biological father, King Henry IV, standing for conviction, duty, and control, yet burdened by his guilty acquisition of the crown; and a father substitute, Falstaff, whose hedonism, lawlessness, and wit provide an attractive, if temporary, alternative." Traub herself alters this paradigm somewhat in presenting Falstaff as essentially maternal, rather than paternal.

CRITICISM

Marjorie Garber

Garber offers a detailed analysis of the character of Falstaff. The critic notes that the character embodies Vice, as such symbolizing corruption and decadence. In addition, Falstaff represents the so-called Lord of Misrule, a custom popular during the time of Henry VIII in which a man of low station was temporarily raised to high position to preside over holiday gatherings at a noble's estate. Garber further discusses other negative aspects of Falstaff's character, while averring that he serves as an antidote to "unrealistic idealism" in the play as well as offering comic relief in the play.

... For Falstaff time is only a dimension of pleasure. His use of it is an aspect of disorder. Timelessness, as we will see, is a capacity of

> TO FALSTAFF, HONOR IS JUST THE EMPTY SIGN OF SOMETHING, NOT A COMMODITY, AN AGENT, OR ANYTHING ACTUALLY PALPABLE OR USEFUL."

comedy, but history—and history plays—will demand a consciousness of time. We have already noted that beneath the exterior of this supple and lifelike play is the vestige of an older allegorical structure, the battle between vice and virtue for the soul of a prince—a familiar topic for the old moralities. In Falstaff we encounter the early modern equivalent of one of the most popular morality play characters, the Vice—the personified figure of depravity or corruption. In the mumming scene in the tavern in act 2, when Hal and Falstaff take turns playing the parts of "Prince" and "King," Hal, in the role of his father, King Henry, admonishes his "son" to avoid the "old fat man" whom he characterizes as "that reverend Vice, that grey Iniquity, that father Ruffian, that Vanity in years." Like the Vice figure, Falstaff is established as the contrary of everything virtuous and orderly. He himself speaks at one point of hitting the Prince with a dagger of lath (2.5.124), the light wooden sword that was the usual stage prop of the medieval Vice. In other words, the play deliberately points in the direction of this medieval heritage, which forms a kind of moral scaffolding for it.

But if Falstaff is a Vice, he is also a Lord of Misrule, a figure popular in, and after, the time of Henry VIII. An ordinary man temporarily raised to high estate, the Lord of Misrule was a personage chosen to preside over Christmas games and revels in a great man's house, as a kind of anti-lord or anti-king. Part of the topsy-turvy world of carnival, the Lord of Misrule reigned chiefly at night, promoting wild singing and dancing as well as drinking, and his "misrule" provided a temporary safety valve for pent-up social, sexual, and political energies. Such festivals predate the Christian era (one such was the Roman Saturnalia), but they are also closely associated with Christian holidays. Thus, for example, Mardi Gras precedes Lent, and Halloween precedes All Saints' Day. (The word "carnival," from *carnevale*, "farewell to meat," gives a sense of the stakes: first there is a defined period of social anarchy—much eating of meat and drinking of wine—then a return to a more repressive or regulatory order of abstinence and law.) As rebellious subjects, analogous to the political rebels led by Hotspur, Falstaff and the Gads Hill robbers mark this carnival instinct in society, and it is characteristic of Hal's role as both rebel and lawgiver that he pays back the money Poins and Falstaff have stolen from the travelers, turning their theft into play. Yet Falstaff himself literally embodies carnival, misrule, and vice, as he cheerfully admits in the tavern at Eastcheap. His language incorporates both rule and misrule, as can be seen in the speech below, which resembles the comically disordered prologues of the plays-within-the-play in *Love's Labour's Lost* and *A Midsummer Night's Dream*, with the important exception that Falstaff's linguistic undoing is deliberate rather than inadvertent:

> Come, sing me a bawdy song, make me merry. I was as virtuously given as a gentleman need to be: virtuous enough; swore little; diced not—above seven times a week; went to a bawdy house not—above once in a quarter—of an hour; paid money that I borrowed—three or four times; lived well, and in good compass. And now I live out of all order, out of all compass. *3.3.11–17*

Falstaff's huge fat body is a visual metaphor similar to that of Nell, the kitchen wench in *The Comedy of Errors*: he *is* out of all compass, the grotesque physical opposite of the enclosed and classical body of a Hotspur or a Hal. As early as the play's second act both Falstaff and Hal have made the most obvious comparison of all, between Hal's deceased grandfather, John of Gaunt, and the companion the Prince calls "Sir John Paunch" (2.2.58). It is as such a living metaphor that Falstaff lumbers across the stage, constantly wishing to be anything but afoot. Once again Shakespeare makes the balance and dramatic elegance of his play clear, for just as Hotspur is almost unimaginable when not astride a horse ("That roan shall be my throne"), so Falstaff roams the stage, and the play, calling for a horse almost as insistently as Richard III. (Falstaff: "Give me my horse, you rogues, give me my horse, and be hanged!" [2.2.27–87]). When war is declared against the rebels, the Prince finds a commission for Sir John, and of course it is an infantry regiment, a "charge of foot." "I would it had been of horse" is Falstaff's

response. Standard pronunciation in Shakespeare's time would have made this a manifestly bawdy homonym, "horse"/"whores." Just as Falstaff walks afoot and wants a horse, is old and pretends to be young—"They hate us youth," he shouts lustily during the Gads Hill robbery (2.2.76)—so he is Hotspur's complementary opposite when it comes to the question of honor. Falstaff, it turns out, is a materialist of sorts, and in the lively internal dialogue he calls his "catechism" he finds that honor has neither sense nor substance:

> [H]onour pricks me on. Yea, but how if honour prick me off when I come on? How then? Can honour set-to a leg? No. Or an arm? No. Or take away the grief of a wound? No. Honour hath no skill in surgery, then? No. What is honour? A word. What is in that word "honour"? What is that "honour"? Air. A trim reckoning! Who hath it? He that died o'Wednesday. Doth he feel it? Doth he hear it? No. 'Tis insensible then? Yea, to the dead. But will it not live with the living? No. Why? Detraction will not suffer it. Therefore I'll none of it. Honour is a mere scutcheon. And so ends my catechism. *5.1.129–139*

A catechism is a summary in question-and-answer format, especially one designed for elementary instruction in the Christian religion. A "scutcheon," or escutcheon, was an armorial shield bearing a coat of arms, and thus a badge of family honor. To Falstaff, honor is just the empty sign of something, not a commodity, an agent, or anything actually palpable or useful. Hotspur had sworn to pluck bright honor from the pale-faced moon; Falstaff will have none of it. Again, it should be no surprise that Falstaff lives, while Hotspur dies.

Yet the play takes an evenhanded view of Falstaff's qualities. While he is not the sublime antihero sometimes claimed by his uncritical admirers and adherents ("They hate us youth"), he is an excellent antidote to unrealistic idealism, as well as (in this play, at least) a diverting and amusing stage presence. For all of his flaws, he speaks, upon occasion, a crucial and even a painful truth, as when, for example, he acknowledges that he lives in a fallen world: "Thou knowest that in the state of innocency Adam fell, and what should poor Jack Falstaff do in the days of villainy?" (3.3.151–153). Not only do human beings eat and drink and make love, they also die, and where Hotspur had faced the possibility of death in battle with a kind of ecstatic joy ("die all, die merrily"), Falstaff, predictably,

Timothy Dalton as Henry Percy, Simon Templeman as Edmund Mortimer, John Franklyn-Robbins as Thomas Percy, and Bernard Lloyd as Owen Glendower in Act III, scene i, at the Barbican Theatre, London, 1982 (© Donald Cooper/Photostage. Reproduced by permission)

takes the opposite approach, and recruits for his unit the most ragged fragments of humanity he can find, first drafting young husbands and men about to be married, allowing them to buy their way out of army service, and then, taking his profit, filling his ranks with ragamuffins. "I never did see such pitiful rascals," says the Prince, and Falstaff replies,

> Tut, tut, good enough to toss, food for powder, food for powder. They'll fill a pit as well as better. Tush, man, mortal men, mortal men. *4.2.58–60*

This, too, is a truth about war, a fact that Hotspur has all but forgotten, and that Hal, as King Henry, will do well to remember. In the same way, one of Falstaff's companions, preparing to set out to rob the travelers at Gads Hill, asks casually how many there are, and is told there are perhaps nine or ten. "Zounds," says Falstaff in alarm, "will they not rob *us*?" (2.2.57; emphasis added). Winners can also be losers, victors can also be victims. King Henry IV, who was the thief and usurper of the kingdom, is himself on the brink of being robbed of his crown ("Zounds, will they not rob *us*?"). In many ways Falstaff provides a necessary antidote to the excessive idealism that is Hotspur, and he does so by reminding his fellows, and the audience, of the nature of "mortal men." Yet there is also danger and risk in Falstaff's character. He is not a misunderstood roly-poly Everyman. Rule cannot finally be guided by Misrule, or history and order by appetite and desire.

> Falstaff: Why, Hal, thou knowest as thou art but man I dare, but as thou art prince, I fear thee as I fear the roaring of the lion's whelp.
>
> Prince Harry: And why not as the lion?
>
> Falstaff: The King himself is to be feared as the lion. Dost thou think I'll fear thee as I fear thy father? Nay ... *3.3.134–139*

That Falstaff does not fear Hal, when he becomes King, as he feared his father, will ultimately be Falstaff's undoing. Between these two poles, the Hotspur world and the Falstaff world, Hal must find his own position, his own identity.

It is a measure of Shakespeare's tremendous power as a dramatist that these two worlds come so vividly to life in this play, and that they offer the audience, as they do the Prince, a choice—as the poet Wallace Stevens remarked in another connection—"not between, but of . . . "

Source: Marjorie Garber, "*Henry IV Part I*," in *Shakespeare After All*, Pantheon Books, 2004, pp. 325–28.

Moody E. Prior

Prior examines the place of honor in the disorderly world of Henry IV, Part One. *On the surface, argues Prior, honor appears to serve only in the context of chivalry and warfare. Prior shows how a closer examination reveals that Hotspur, Hal, and Henry have a deeper understanding of the concept of honor. Prior also illuminates the limitations of honor. He first focuses on how little attention is paid in the play to the broken promises and rebellion related to Henry's road to kingship. Next, Prior notes that Falstaff denies "the reality of honor" by seeing honor only as an intangible, valueless result of bravery in battle. Prior contrasts Hotspur's extravagant desire for honor with Falstaff's rejection of honor, commenting that Falstaff overlooks those aspects of honor that are unrelated to warfare and that could therefore be useful to him. Finally, Prior discusses Hal's conception of honor, showing it to be demonstrated by Hal's loyalty to the King and to the nation.*

The word "honor" occurs frequently in Part 1, and its presence has raised some troublesome questions. What place can honor have in a world in which subjects rebel against a usurper whom they placed in office, the prince plays at robbery with a dissolute knight, and the contending parties in government seem guided by "policy" rather than principle? Superficially, the answer appears to be that honor has little to do with the conduct of most of the characters, and where it is invoked the concept often seems narrow. At first glance honor seems to mean no more than a reputation for prowess and skill in arms gained in battle by noblemen and knights. That is the implication when the word first appears in the opening scene, in which the king contrasts the victorious Hotspur, "the theme of honor's tongue," with his son, who was not at the battle and whose brow is stained with "riot and dishonor," (1.1.80, 84), and also when, later in the play, the king upbraids the prince, comparing his son's dissoluteness and negligence with the

> THE DISHONOR THAT THE KING ATTRIBUTES TO HIS SON IS NOT SIMPLY THAT HE FAILED TO DISTINGUISH HIMSELF IN BATTLE, BUT THAT BY INDULGING IN RIOT AND BAD COMPANY AT A TIME WHEN THE KING'S INTEREST WAS IN DANGER HE FAILED IN A PRINCIPAL OBLIGATION OF A PRINCE."

boldness of young Hotspur leading his rebellious followers "to bloody battles and to bruising arms" and to the "never-dying honor" which he gained against Douglas. It is also the prince's meaning when he promises to redeem his bad reputation against the "child of honor and renown" and exchange his own shames "for every honor sitting on his helm." (3.2.139, 142). Hotspur glorifies the honor to be gained in battle against worthy foes, and the more hazardous the enterprise the greater the chance of gaining honor. The extravagance of his speech about plucking "bright honor from the pale-faced moon" and "drowned honor by the locks" is inspired by Worcester's warning that the matter he is about to reveal is "deep and dangerous." (1.3.188).

Even in this narrow military context, however, honor demands from these warriors something more than bravery and success in battle. This is a society in which the nobility constitutes and elite expected to bear arms, and honor stands for the special virtues which distinguish this class in the exercise of its vocation—gallantry in combat with a worthy foe, adherence to the accepted code of arms, and individual loyalty to friends, family, and comrades in arms. These qualities are taken seriously and have currency in *I Henry IV*, even though men accuse each other of breaking their solemn word, rebellions are plotted, and warriors fight for something less than the highest moral principles and national glory. It says something for the world of *I Henry IV* that such distinctions can be made . . . The battle of Shrewsbury is a deadly serious affair, yet the prince can call Hotspur "a valiant rebel of that name" before engaging him in fair fight to the death.

There are further shades of meaning which extend the idea of honor in *I Henry IV* beyond the demands of chivalry and war. Even for Hotspur honor can mean something more than meeting dangers and triumphing over great warriors in battle. His first use of the word is, in fact, not in connection with warfare at all. He upbraids his father and uncle for having dishonored themselves by putting down Richard, setting the crown on Bolingbroke, and having to endure the humiliation of being discarded by him now that he is Henry IV. From these shames, he urges,

> time serves wherein you may redeem
> Your banished honors and restore yourselves
> Into the good thoughts of the world again.

The dishonor that the king attributes to his son is not simply that he failed to distinguish himself in battle, but that by indulging in riot and bad company at a time when the king's interest was in danger he failed in a principal obligation of a prince. The king rejoices when his son joins him, not only because Hal has promised to use Hotspur's glory to redeem his own, but because he has returned to his proper princely role. "A hundred thousands rebels die in this," Henry exclaims. (3.2.160). Honor, then, goes beyond chivalry and military fame.

Nevertheless, at its broadest it is a concept with serious limitations. Henry's perjury is a case in point. It is charged against him by his former supporters that in taking the crown from Richard II he had broken an oath which he made to them on returning from exile, that he had come only to claim his inheritance; but, in spite of the gravity of this charge, little enough is made of it, because the oath was taken for expedient reasons and broken with the connivance of his then allies, now his enemies. And yet for most of the characters, including the king, honor is a serious matter. Judgment of conduct is referred to it, and it is invoked to bind men to a cause and to inspire the exercise of such private virtues as are demanded by one's public obligations. Its prominence is thus a mark of the secular atmosphere of *I Henry IV*, in which the characters do not normally look beyond the immediate present to a cosmic scheme of justice or expect the wrath of God for neglecting a solemn obligation. In a world of politics and civil war it functions as a substitute for moral principle. It is not a static or a univocal concept, however; in the changing patterns of the play its merits are revealed, its limitations exposed, and in due course even the reality of honor is questioned.

The most direct, and indeed the only, denial of the reality of honor comes from Falstaff. His soliloquy on honor is a virtuoso performance of clever negation. It comes just after the king has ended his interview with the rebel leaders and the royal party awaits the almost certain sign for battle. Falstaff, the realist, says apprehensively, "I would 'twere bedtime, Hal, and all well." The prince's casual reply, "Why, thou owest God a death," provides the cue to the opening line of Falstaff's reflections, "'Tis not due yet, I would be loath to pay him before his day." (5.1.125–28). Restricting honor to its limited sense of the intangible rewards for valor in battle, Falstaff rejects it as empty and valueless, incapable of repairing wounds or surviving detraction after death. The sight of Sir Walter Blunt dead on the field of battle confirms him in his views— "There's honor for you" (5.3.32–33)—and it leads him to this final word on the subject: "I like not such grinning honor as Sir Walter hath. Give me life, which if I can save, so; if not, honor comes unlooked for, and there's an end." (5.3.58–61). "'Tis not due yet," "Give me life"— these phrases sum up Falstaff's determination to hold on to life as the final good, even if it is only a precarious hold defiantly maintained against the decay of youth and the coming of age, the loss of moral virtue and of the world's esteem. The direct opposite of this is summed up in Hotspur's remarks shortly before the battle. A messenger comes with letters and Hotspur dismisses them—"I cannot read them now"; and as though this incident has suddenly brought home to him the realization that nothing matters now until the dangerous business is over, he continues,

> O gentlemen, the time of life is short!
> To spend that shortness basely were too
>   long
> If life did ride upon a dial's point,
> Still ending at the arrival of an hour.

There are things which are more important to Hotspur than life. Though addressing his men, Hotspur seems in these lines almost to be speaking to himself, surprised by the circumstances into a moment of self-revelation which suggests something of the depth of feeling that underlies his earlier extravagant sentiments about honor or the apparent flippancy of his comment when he learns of the big odds against them in the battle, "Doomsday is near; die all, die merrily." (4.1.134).

Shakespeare has made both of these spokesmen for opposing attitudes attractive, each in his own extraordinary way. They have, moreover, some basic traits in common. Both conduct their lives and make their choices in accordance with a settle principle. Both have a distaste for the reserve and calculation of official public life. Their loyalties are narrow. Falstaff's loyalty is to himself and his cronies when they are useful, and Hotspur's is personal and clannish. Both reveal a lively extravagance at times when they feel challenged or aroused, and both display a trace of desperation in seeking to extract the full measure of gratification out of life. Both men have a zest for life, though Falstaff's inclinations carry him to dissoluteness and even degeneracy, and Hotspur's valor and sense of personal integrity express themselves in discourtesy, eccentricity, and foolhardiness. It is in the aberration of qualities which can enhance life that the danger lies in these two men Hotspur's sense of honor which makes him despise Henry as a "vile politician" and a "king of smiles" also makes him the victim of politicians who need his virtues to glamorize a rebellion, and his wholly personal coveting of honor "without corrival" inspires him to seek out occasions to exercise his youth and virtues in the destructive enterprise of war. Falstaff's ridicule of honor is a corollary of his guiding principle, "give me life," as he understands it; honor at Shrewsbury involves the danger of self-sacrifice, and so he will not seek it. If we see his position as a reply to the extravagances of Hotspur, we may be inclined to agree with him that honor is an empty illusion—Falstaff would not have ordered the charge of the Light Brigade. But by strictly limiting the scope of the term, Falstaff excludes its usefulness in defining a secular idea of loyalty and of dedication to the best demands of a serious calling, and thus as a means of maintaining one's self-esteem. Oddly enough, Falstaff has not completely lost the need for some modicum of that last quality. When they decide to do a play extempore and the prince proposes, "the argument shall be thy running away," Falstaff replies, "Ah, no more of that, Hal, and thou lovest me." (2.4.277–78). But Falstaff's chief use for the respectable world is to exploit it for his own purposes. He welcomes the rebellion as an opportunity to replenish his purse: "Well, God be thanked for these rebels, they offend none but the virtuous;

I laud them, I praise them." (3.3.189–91). Lacking a sense of honor, he is capable of leading his wretched recruits to the thick of the battle where most of them will be killed so that he can keep their pay for himself . . .

The prince, early in the play, shows a distaste for the questing after military victory that is the bad side of Hotspur's love of honor:

> I am not yet of Percy's mind, the Hotspur of the North, he that kills me some six or seven dozen of Scots at a breakfast, washes his hands, and says to his wife, "Fie upon this quiet life, I want work." "O my sweet Harry," says she, "how many hast thou killed today?" "Give my roan horse a drench," says he, and answers, "Some fourteen," an hour after, "a trifle, a trifle."

Just before this he had described a drinking bout with a group of tapsters at the inn, and tells Poins, "I tell thee, Ned, thou hast lost much honor that thou wert not with me in this action." (2.4.19–21). This fleering use of "honor" may represent an indirect attempt to justify his present truancy, but the use of the military term "this action" to describe the heavy drinking and the "honor" gained by staying with it may also express some impatience with the cant of the warrior class. In comparison with Hotspur, Hal's attitude toward honor may be likened to Starbuck's attitude toward courage in *Moby Dick*—"one of the great staple outfits of the ship in their hazardous work of whaling, thought Starbuck, and, like her beer and bread, not to be wasted." The prince accepts the idea of honor as a mark of the warrior when he promises to exchange his shames for Hotspur's honors, but it is not an exact exchange. There are certain features of Hotspur's code which Hal does not take on. He does not have an excessive craving for military exploits or gloat publicly over his success—he is willing, for the sake of a joke, to allow Falstaff to claim credit for killing Hotspur; and his sense of loyalty is not as clannish as Hotspur's nor as provincial ("this Northern youth," (3.2.145) he calls him)—it is to this father as king and therefore to the nation. It is an idea of honor more befitting a London courtier than a northern earl, and more useful to a national king than to a feudal lord. Hal appreciates Hotspur's gallantry—he honors the dead Hotspur by placing his "favors" on the body of this adversary; and in this connection Falstaff shows up to disadvantage, for we see him dishonoring Hotspur's corpse with a coarse comic bravado that is as unpleasant as it is funny.

This view of the significance of the scheme of multiple comparisons is in keeping with the way the conflicts are resolved at the end. The victory of the king's party seems the only acceptable conclusion—not merely the one imposed by history—and even the most unsympathetic critics do not express offense at the defeat of the rebels at Shrewsbury as they do, for instance, at the sophistry of Prince John at Gaultree or the rejection of Falstaff in Part 2. Nevertheless, it is questionable whether Shakespeare ever fully redresses the balance in favor of Henry and his son in *I Henry IV*, for the rebels are not pictured in a wholly reprehensible light. Once the rebellion gets under way, Hotspur's leadership lends it an air of gallantry and glamor. Aside from Worcester, who seems incapable of controlling the enterprise of which he was the political engineer, the others all have an almost amateurish quality which contributes to their undoing. This comes out in the one scene in which they all assemble to map out their strategy; (3.1); they quarrel and show themselves more eager to divide the spoils of a hoped-for victory than to resolve the divisions within the kingdom, and hence appear as a worse choice politically than the king. Nevertheless, the conclusion which Shakespeare contrives for this episode comes as a surprising close to a scene of rebellious plotting. Glendower ushers in their wives, and there follows an engaging exchange of sentiments between Mortimer and his Welsh wife, with Glendower acting as interpreter, the contrasting affectionate sparring of Hotspur and his Kate, and finally the ethereal music invoked by Glendower which accompanies the Welsh song sung by Mortimer's wife. And these are the men who are threatening the center of order in the kingdom! There is nothing in the whole play that associates the king or the prince with as much charm and genial humanity . . .

Source: Moody E. Prior, "Ideas of History: *Richard II*, 1 and 2 *Henry IV, Henry V*," in *The Drama of Power: Studies in Shakespeare's History Plays*, Northwestern University Press, 1973, pp. 199–218.

Robert B. Pierce

Pierce maintains that in Henry IV, Part One, *personal, familial order is presented as a way of understanding the larger, political structure in the play. He shows how the basic conflicts in the play—the struggle of Henry, and the nation, to create harmony from civil war, the struggle of Prince Hal to mature from a careless youth into an independent*

> IN THE PARABLE THE PRODIGAL SON RESTORED TO HIS FATHER IS MAN RESTORED TO GOD, AND IN THE ELIZABETH SYSTEM OF CORRESPONDENCES THE KING IS TO HIS KINGDOM AS GOD IS TO THE UNIVERSE. HAL'S RECONCILIATION WITH HIS FATHER SYMBOLIZES A LARGER COMMITMENT TO ALL THAT IS GOOD AND ORDERLY IN THE WORLD."

king—illuminate the larger conflict—the struggle to create order from disorder—being examined. Pierce shows how the play is essentially divided between the public story of rebellion and the private story of Hal's adventures with Falstaff and how the additional plot of Hal's estrangement from Henry links the play's public and private worlds.

Shakespeare's Henry IV plays explore the theme of political order with a new depth and subtlety. Not only does the state pass through civil war to harmony, but Prince Hal develops into a king fit to lead his newly united state in war against France. Although political order is central to the plays, Shakespeare uses a more personal order, that of the family, to illuminate his theme. In the early history plays harmony and strife in family relationships become symbols of order and disorder in the kingdom. This device expresses political ideas by analogy with another realm of experience. But in the two Henry IV plays the symbol merges with its referent; Shakespeare displays the quest for political order as fundamentally like the quest for personal order within the family. The values are the same, the problems the same; only the scale is different.

In Hal and his father the historical given of Shakespeare's plot combines the two levels: prince and king, son and father. While Henry IV struggles to keep his throne and the rebels to replace him, England is hungry for renewed order. Though he is in many ways a good ruler, he cannot be the hero-king who compels loyalty as well as submission. Prince Hal is to be such a king, but before he can assume his destined role, he must attain personal maturity. He must find a viable order for his own life, one centered on his duty to become England's king. Only thus will he be saved from self-destruction or personal insignificance, and only thus will England be saved (for a time) from civil war.

Finding in his sources the legend of Hal the wild prince, Shakespeare turns it into an expression of this theme. Like any young man reaching maturity, Hal must emulate his father's role, but at the same time he must escape his father in order to establish his autonomy. Even in the ideal family this task is difficult. In *1 Henry VI* young Talbot must defy his father's command to flee the battlefield so that he may be like his father and hence show a family loyalty deeper than explicit obedience. But Hal's father is a guilty man, one whose piety is tainted by Richard II's blood on his hands. In his personal inheritance from his father, Hal faces the same problem as the realm, how to generate an ordered future out of a disordered present. He must transcend his inheritance without denying it. It is part of the extraordinary scope of the Henry IV plays to study this spiritual process. An abstractly conceived Providence can bring peace to the England of *Richard III* because the process is external to Richard, but only a newly personal and psychological drama can show Hal's development into the king who will lead England to unity and glory.

The portrayal of Hal's growth follows a popular motif in Elizabethan drama, the Prodigal Son story. Hal leaves his responsibilities and his father for a life of tavern brawls, behavior typical of the prodigal, though Hal avoids contamination with the worst evils around him, reckless gambling, wenching, and such. Falstaff, "that villainous abominable misleader of youth" (II.iv.456), parallels a Vice-figure [a stock character in the morality play who, as a tempter, has both evil and comic qualities] ... Henry IV has much in common with the typical father, noble and sententious but somewhat ineffectual toward his son ... Appropriately enough, the parable of the Prodigal Son occurs among Falstaff's frequent allusions to scripture. This theme extends through both plays, since Hal is not completely reconciled to his father until the end of *2 Henry IV.*

In one sense Shakespeare is burlesquing an old dramatic form ... After all, it is the prodigal who mischievously denounces his tempter as "that reverend vice, that grey iniquity, that father ruffian, that vanity in years" (*1 Henry*

IV, II.iv.447–49). And Falstaff himself delights in acting the prodigal, corrupted by his evil companions: "Before I knew thee, Hal, I knew nothing, and now am I, if a man should speak truly, little better than one of the wicked" (*1 Henry IV*, I.ii.90–92). This lightheartedness suggests even more clearly than Hal's soliloquy at the end of I.ii that he will not be significantly corrupted. Yet at the same time Falstaff is a serious threat to Hal's maturity, and the reconciliation with his father is a necessary step in his growth.

... For all Shakespeare's modifications to burlesque the pattern and to make it psychologically plausible, he uses the religious theme embodied in it. In the parable the Prodigal Son restored to his father is man restored to God, and in the Elizabeth system of correspondences the king is to his kingdom as God is to the universe. Hal's reconciliation with his father symbolizes a larger commitment to all that is good and orderly in the world.

The first of the two plays has an obvious division into two levels, the public story of the rebellion of the Percies and the private story of Hal's dissipations [self. indulgent activities] with Falstaff. Part of what raises this play above the typical Elizabethan two-plot drama is the ingenuity with which the two are interwoven, so that the Falstaff scenes parody many of the episodes and characters of the serious scenes. However, there is a third plot, less extended than the other two, that helps to mediate between them. It is the story of Hal's estrangement from his father and their reconciliation. Only in this plot is Hal clearly the central figure, though all three contribute to the most important theme of this and the next play, Hal's preparation for kingship over a united England. The rebellion of the Percies provides the battlefield on which he can prove his chivalric merit; and Hotspur, the dominant figure of the Percy camp, gives a dramatic contrast that illuminates Hal's growth. The scenes with Falstaff show Hal avoiding his duty, but they also help to educate him in the whole order (and disorder) of his future kingdom. Although Shakespeare allows us to glimpse the domestic life of the Percies, they live primarily in a public world, a world of treaties and defiances and battles, of blank verse. Although Falstaff appears, ludicrously out of place, at Shrewsbury, his is essentially a private world without clocks, a world of sack and tavern jests and highway robbery, of prose.

Prince Henry, Falstaff, and others at the Boars-Head Tavern, Act II, scene iv (© *Shakespeare Collection, Special Collections Library, University of Michigan*)

What gives the relationship of Henry IV and Hal special complexity is that in it the public and private worlds merge. As king and prince they embody all the political ideas implied in that relationship throughout the history plays. Hal must inherit the heroic and regal virtues of his father so that he may be a king worthy of his Lancastrian forebears. To teach Hal this lesson, Henry points to the ominous example of Richard II, who betrayed the heritage of the Black Prince with a frivolity that Henry sees in Hal too. Also the public theme of inherited guilt is an important one. Henry fears that his crime in deposing Richard will infect the kingdom even after his death (and Hal in *Henry V* shares that fear). As a public figure Henry IV has a double significance. He is the king, the center of order and virtue in the realm and hence the prime object of Hal's duty. But at the same time he is guilty; all the conscious piety of his life cannot entirely justify him, even to himself.

If Henry were simply a public figure, an emblem like John of Gaunt in *Richard II*, this ambiguity of meaning would destroy him as a dramatic character. What saves him is that he is given a private identity, an individual nature that expresses itself apart from his public stance. A public symbol cannot be ambiguous, but a man can be so various as to evoke two different symbolisms. In the same way Hal can both laugh at and be the Prodigal Son because he has a private identity that transcends both burlesque and symbolism. Henry IV and Hal are not only king and prince; they are also a very concrete father and son, going through all the painful misunderstanding that fathers and sons have always faced.

Henry appears first of all as king. As John Dover Wilson points out [in *The First Part of the History of Henry IV*, 1946, in a note at I. i. 1], he speaks for himself and the kingdom in his opening words:

So shaken as we are, so wan with care,
Find we a time for frighted peace to pant,
And breathe short-winded accents of new
    broils
To be commenc'd in stronds afar remote:
No more the thirsty entrance of this soil
Shall daub her lips with her own children's
    blood.
(I.i.1–6)

The sense of powers declining under strain, the desperate longing for peace, and the vague hope for glory in foreign wars—all these Henry shares with his land. It is a sign of his worthiness as a king that he expresses so accurately the spirit of his realm. The stark family image of lines 5–6, with its biblical echo, is typical of the severe formality of the speech. Henry's language shows the tightly linked world of Elizabethan correspondences, in which the state is a family and civil war opposes those "of one substance bred," so that they war "Against acquaintance, kindred, and allies"(11, 16).

Since most of the audience must have known that this was to be a play about civil war, they would notice the self-deception in Henry's prediction of peace; and it soon emerges that he is willfully deceiving himself, because he knows that England is still wracked with strife and even that the Percies show ominous signs of disloyalty. Henry represents a generation of Englishmen who have fought each other and will go on fighting until they can hardly remember the purpose of the battles and can only say:

We are all diseas'd,
And with our surfeiting, and wanton hours,
Have brought ourselves into a burning
    fever,
And we must bleed for it.
(*2 Henry IV*, IV.i. 54–57)

After his description of civil war in terms of violence within the family, there is irony in Henry's turning to speak with pain of his son's degeneracy. At the moment he seems unconscious of any connection between public and familial disorder. It may seem like a heartless repudiation of family bonds when he wishes:

O that it could be prov'd
That some night-tripping fairy had exchang'd
In cradle-clothes our children where they
    lay,
And call'd mine Percy, his Plantagenet!

But the suffering is clear enough behind the petulant rejection. It is "my young Harry"(85) whose dishonor he feels; the repeated "mine" of the passage shows the grief of an estranged father, not unfeeling repudiation. If the audience perceived the irony of his wish to go to the Holy Land, they must also have seen the happier irony of his despair at the character of the future hero-king, the legendary example of wildness reformed. This speech establishes a contrast between the two young men that runs through the play and reaches its climax in their confrontation at Shrewsbury.

If in the first scene Henry IV seems like an old man, tired and sick from the strains of rule, it soon becomes apparent that he has not lost the strength of will and imposing presence that won him the crown. He sends for the Percies to explain their holding back the Scottish prisoners, and when Worcester shows signs of more pride than is fitting in a subject, Henry abruptly banishes him from the court. Questionable though his accession is, he is a royal king, and Hal can learn only from him the dignity that a king must have. The curious episode of the men in Henry's coats whom Douglas slays at Shrewsbury raises the issue of who is really king when Douglas challenges Henry:

What art thou
That counterfeit'st the person of a king?
(V.iv.26–27)

But Douglas himself gives a worthy answer:

I fear thou art another counterfeit,
And yet, in faith, thou bearest thee like a
    king.
(34–35)

By a great act of will Henry is able to bear himself like a king. If the effort gradually saps his strength, there is little external evidence of his decline until his sickness in *2 Henry IV*. Only in one scene of this play does he fully reveal the private man behind the king, when he is alone with his son in III.ii. The sense of tension, of a will kept forcibly taut in his public appearances, suggests the terrible penalty of being king.

In contrast with his father in the opening scene, Hal in the second appears young, full of vitality, and gaily irresponsible. While his father wrestles with the problems of state, Falstaff and Hal can jest about how he will behave as king. "I prithee sweet wag, when thou art king, as God save thy Grace—Majesty I should say, for grace thou wilt have none" (I.ii.16–18). The fact that the major theme of Hal's development toward the ideal king can be suggested in a pun shows the characteristic tone of the scene. When he comes to this world where time is irrelevant and chivalry no more than the code of the highwayman, he is escaping from the court, from his father, and from his own place as heir apparent.

One can take too solemnly his assertion of virtue in the much-discussed soliloquy that closes the scene. The speech may seem priggish, as though Hal were condescending to sport with Falstaff even while maintaining a severe inner virtue. He says, "I know you all" (I.ii.190), implying that Falstaff's sinfulness is no threat to his self-confident virtue. However, direct exposition of one's moral state is characteristic of Elizabethan soliloquies. It is dangerous to read too much self-consciousness into Hal's proclamation of his own worth. Many critics note that this soliloquy is primarily a device to assure the audience of Hal's final reformation, an assurance especially needed just after he has agreed to join in a highway robbery. And his treatment of Falstaff is not really condescending; he too obviously rejoices in the battle of wits that keeps them on equal terms.

On the other hand, the fact that the soliloquy is a conventional device need not compel one to take it as absolutely true. Only someone determined to believe in Hal's spotless virtue (or his priggishness) could accept at face value the argument that a king gains his people's loyalty from having been a youthful sinner. No doubt Hal plans to reform, but he has not undertaken his sins in order to abandon them with a spectacular public gesture. There is an undertone to his argument that suggests his main reason for avoiding the court:

> If all the year were playing holidays,
> To sport would be as tedious as to work;
> But when they seldom come, they wish'd-for come,
> And nothing pleaseth but rare accidents.
> (199–202)

Explicitly he is arguing that the contrast between a dissolute youth and a reformed king heightens the latter, just as the contrast with working days makes holidays pleasant. Yet at the same time he half-admits to snatching a few last bits of pleasure before assuming the heavy duties of kingship . . .

Hal's sport with Falstaff is not only a young man's escape from responsibility, however. The public world of the play is one of disorder and treachery. Hotspur is caught in the political schemes of his father and uncle and manipulated by them. Henry IV is a nobler man than his former allies (except for Hotspur), but even he is trapped by his dubious past into suspicion and cold scheming. His projected crusade to the Holy Land is never more than a dream of expiation. Thus Hal escapes a tainted atmosphere by leaving the court. The evils of the tavern to which he turns are "like their father that begets them, gross as a mountain, open, palpable" (II.iv.220–21). Even though Falstaff's company sometimes parodies the public world, it is not corrupted by the pervasive disorder of the kingdom. "A plague upon it when thieves cannot be true one to another!" (II.ii.27–28). Falstaff's complaint foreshadows the disintegration among the rebels, but in fact the disloyalty in his band of "thieves" is harmless and even illusory.

In general the vices of Falstaff's group are timeless; the characters themselves are an anachronism brought into the play from Elizabethan life. This habit is not unusual among low-comedy scenes in Tudor drama, but here it is significant in that it provides an escape from the political disorder of the public scenes. In the three parts of *Henry VI* disorder spreads out from the court to infect the whole kingdom, but in *1 Henry IV* the life of England goes on in spite of treachery and rebellion among the governors. Hostlers worry about the price of oats, and Falstaff about the purity of sack. Leaving the court, Hal finds England with all its vices and jests, but also its abiding strength. What Faulconbridge brings to the court of King John, Hal reaches by going out into London.

Yet if Hal can gain strength from contact with English life, there is also the threat of forgetting his special role as England's future king. Just as he must escape from the court and his father to grow beyond them, so he must escape the unreasonable claims on him of his London companions. "O for a fine thief of the age of two and twenty or thereabouts: I am heinously unprovided," says Falstaff (III.iii.187–89). He is unprovided because Hal has kept himself a king's son on a lark. His characteristic defense against Falstaff is his irony, an amused detachment from whatever he is doing. Curiously enough, it is the same quality that allows him to show no concern for the deed when he proves his chivalric merit by killing Hotspur, the key symbolic act of the play. His nature is not "subdued / To what it works in" ("Sonnet 111"), whether he rubs elbows with Falstaff or fights against Hotspur.

Critics find this ironic detachment offensive in Hal ... when it rebuffs Falstaff's claims to intimacy. There is unconscious humor in the fugitive and cloistered vice of literary scholars who condemn Hal for repudiating the free life of a tavern roisterer and highway robber; one explanation of such a view is the absence in our day of much feeling for the importance of calling. Hal is called to be the next king of England, and so he cannot be an ordinary man. He is not denying his humanity in accepting his duty to prepare for royalty, because a man's vocation is the center of his manhood. In this play his calling is defined by his rivalry with Hotspur. He must demonstrate to his father and all the land that he is the true prince, not only in title but in worth. Thus he can turn from the boyish jest of giving Falstaff a company of foot soldiers to a vigorous assertion of his family's destiny:

> The land is burning, Percy stands on
>   high,
> And either we or they must lower lie.

(III.iii.202–3)

Henry IV and his son come together for the first time at III.ii. Ironically, Shakespeare has just shown the charming domesticity of the rebel camp when he turns to the estrangement of the king and crown prince. Henry's speeches to his son are curiously poised between his typical stiff formality and a father's anxious sincerity. His opening words are full of the traditional doctrines of the family. Thus for the first time he acknowledges that Hal's wildness may be punishment for "my mistreadings"(11). He measures Hal against the ideal of aristocratic inheritance, asking how he can reconcile "the greatness of thy blood"(16) with such low pursuits. He misunderstands his son, since he assumes that Hal is "match'd withal, and grafted to" these pleasures (15), the imagery suggesting that their corruption has entered the fibers of his being. But this speech is so formal that it suggests only abstract parenthood, and Hal's reply is in the same vein. They have expressed their abstract relationship, but little of the personal feeling in it.

Up to this point Henry has hidden the intensity of his emotions behind a mask of formality, but in his next speech his grief precariously warps the formality. After an affectionate "Harry" in line 29, he quickly pulls back into the commonplaces of aristocratic inheritance. He again charges Hal with betraying the tradition of his ancestors and losing the affection of his kinsmen. The king's hurt ego swings around to brood on his own past successes as he compares Hal with Richard II. He asserts that Hal has repudiated the moral heritage of the Lancastrians for Richard's corrupted "line"(85). (Primarily the word means "category" here, but it suggests the whole idea of a station in life established by birth.) His emotion gradually rises during the speech until he suddenly finds himself weeping as he complains of his son's neglect in what is no longer a king's reproof but the complaint of a lonely father.

Hal's reply to this display of emotion is embarrassed and terse, though it may reveal a deeper contrition than did his first speech. But the tide of Henry's grief cannot stop, and so he returns to comparing Hal with Richard. Now he raises the most irritating comparison, that with Hotspur. He contrasts Hal's dynastic inheritance with Hotspur's supposed moral superiority:

> Now by my sceptre, and my soul to boot,
> He hath more worthy interest to the state
> Than thou the shadow of succession.
> (97–99)

This pragmatic king has learned that even a title as unstained as Richard II's is only a shadow without *virtù*, the quality that he thinks he sees in Hotspur. The way that he associates Hotspur with himself hints that he wishes Hotspur were his heir. But that wish is no more than a desperate evasion of his parental grief, as the petulance of his next few lines indicates. He even charges that Hal will fight under Percy against his own family.

This final turn allows Hal to feel a cleansing anger. His characteristic irony overcome by hurt love and pride, he makes his most complete and open declaration of aims. The abrupt, almost non-metrical beginning suggests his anger: "Do not think so, you shall not find it so"(129). And the next few lines illuminate its cause; if Hotspur is the barrier between Hal and Henry's love, then Hotspur must die. By Henry's own standard the warrior ideal is the measure of moral worth, and Hal means to establish himself before his father and the kingdom. Already the duel of Act V is foreshadowed and weighted with public and private meaning. Conquering Hotspur will cleanse Hal's name and make him a hero worthy of royalty, but at the same time it will complete the reconciliation of this father and son. Hence the angry reproach of Hal's contrast between "This gallant Hotspur, this all-praised knight, / And your unthought-of Harry" (140–41).

Like most fathers Henry is only too eager to be reconciled. Delighted by his son's heroic zeal and by the affection implied in Hal's hurt feelings, he regains his kingly dignity and his confidence together:

> A hundred thousand rebels die in this—
> Thou shalt have charge and sovereign trust
>   herein.
> (160–61)

Now that he knows the cleavage in his own house to be healed, he can face the challenge of the Percy rebellion with poise. When Blunt reports the gathering of the enemy, Henry gives orders with brisk efficiency and assigns Hal an important place in the plans. This father and son standing together are a symbol of unity in the realm, just as in *1 Henry VI* Talbot and his son fighting together stand for the unity that will die with them. But because Shakespeare has shown their reconciliation in an intensely personal scene, Henry and Hal are more than just symbols of order. Above all, the scene is a step in Hal's growth toward full readiness for kingship, but it also reveals Henry's human struggle to endure the weight of kingly office. The symbol of unity is there, but it is surrounded by a richness of meanings such as the early Shakespeare never achieved.

The king and Hal appear together again at Shrewsbury, now in perfect harmony. Henry is so full of confidence that he can laugh at the ill omen of a gloomy morning. Throughout the day Hal is the picture of a true prince, extorting praise even from his enemies. With becoming humility in his words, he challenges Hotspur to single combat. Henry forbids that, perhaps because of still-continuing doubts in his son, but mainly because it would be foolish to give up the advantage of superior numbers. In the battle Hal shows brotherly pride at Prince John's valor, and afterward he allows his brother the honor of giving Douglas his freedom. When Hal saves his father's life from Douglas, the king recalls the charges that Hal has sought his death. The sincerity of Hal's indignation is supported by his deeds, and in fact only the king's remark makes him point out the significance of his act. Finally Hotspur, Hal's rival, dies under his

sword, and the last picture of the prince is with his family on the battlefield won by their united valor. If the expression of this newly firm tie between the king and his son is almost entirely public and formal at Shrewsbury, those qualities make the last scenes complementary to the personal reconciliation of III.ii. Shrewsbury establishes the forces of order as dominant in the kingdom, and its final moment is this public symbol of unity, a king and his crown prince, reconciled and victorious.

The path of Hal's growth is a great arc. He must move away from his father and the court so that he may find his personal autonomy. He must revitalize the Lancastrian line by renewed contact with the source of all political power, the commonwealth itself. Yet there is peril in this journey. If he plunges too deeply into the world of Falstaff and his companions, he will lose contact with his own heritage, with the birth that calls him to prepare himself for England's throne. And so the arc turns back. Hal must return to his father and prove his worthiness to be the Lancastrian heir. Now he must act for himself, yet to defend the primacy of the House of Lancaster. Only half-understanding what has happened to his son, Henry IV senses the ardor and enthusiasm that Hal has brought with him. The returned prodigal is the new hope of the forces of order, and especially of the king his father. "For this my son was dead, and is alive again: he was lost and is found." Hal, and with him the Lancastrian line, are renewed.

Source: Robert B. Pierce, "The *Henry IV* Plays," in *Shakespeare's History Plays: The Family and the State,* Ohio State University Press, 1971, pp. 171–224.

Maynard Mack

Mack provides basic information about the play, discussing the dates it was written, performed, and published. In identifying the historical sources Shakespeare used to write Henry IV, Part One, *Mack points out some of the historical facts that Shakespeare alters. The critic explains why topics covered in the play, such as the succession of English monarchs, were of interest to Elizabethan audiences.*

The *First Part of Henry IV* was published in 1598; it was probably written and acted in 1596–97. There are some topical allusions in the play to these years, notably the Second Carrier's reference to the high cost of oats that killed Robin Ostler (II.i.12). Topical in a more important sense, during the whole of the 1590's, was the play's general subject matter. Though contemporary concern about succession to the throne need not (though it may) have influenced Shakespeare's choice of materials for his English histories, it inevitably gave them an extra dimension. Elizabeth was now in her sixties, and there was no assured heir, only a multiplicity of candidates, including her sometimes favorite, the Earl of Essex. Many recalled anxiously the chaos in times past when the center of power in the monarchical system had ceased to be sharply defined and clearly visible. This had occurred to an extent after Henry VIII's death, and earlier after Henry V's, and still earlier after the murder of Richard II.

If Shakespeare was at all influenced by these anxieties, his rendering of them is on the whole buoyant and optimistic in his second English tetralogy and especially so in *1 Henry IV*. True, the England seen in this play and its immediate successor is far from reassuring. It has even been described as

> ... an England, on the one side, of bawdy house and thieves'-kitchen, of waylaid merchants, badgered and bewildered Justices, and a peasantry wretched, betrayed, and recruited for the wars; an England, on the other side, of the chivalrous wolf pack of Hotspur and Douglas, and of state-sponsored treachery in the person of Prince John—the whole presided over by a sick King, hagridden by conscience, dreaming of a Crusade to the Holy Land as M. Remorse [i.e., Falstaff] thinks of slimming and repentance [Danby, J.F., *Shakespeare's Doctrine of Nature: A Study of King Lear*, 1949].

But this is only half the picture. Beside it, for the first Henry IV play, we must place the warmth, wit, and high spirits of the tavern scenes, the impetuous charm of Hotspur, the amusing domesticities of Kate and Glendower's daughter, the touching loyalty of Francis, the affections that (along with sponging) bind Falstaff to Hal, and Hal's own magnanimity and self-command. For both the first and second plays, we must weigh heavily into the account the character of the story told. This, the greatest of monarchical success stories in English popular history, traces the evolution of an engaging scapegrace [rascal] into one of the most admired of English kings. Chicanery [trickery] and appetite in the first play, apathy and corruption in the second, form an effective theatrical background against which the oncoming sunbright majesty of the future Henry V may shine more brightly—

"

HAL'S TRIUMPHANT JOURNEY FROM TIPPLING IN TAVERNS TO GLORY ON THE FIELD OF BATTLE DERIVES FROM ... THE MORALITY PLAYS—THAT IS, THE STRUGGLE OF VIRTUES AND VICES FOR POSSESSION OF A MAN'S SOUL, A THEME ACTED AGAIN AND AGAIN IN THE PLAYS OF THE EARLY SIXTEENTH CENTURY, WHICH THE DRAMA OF MARLOWE AND SHAKESPEARE SUPERSEDED."

as we are assured precisely that it will do on our first meeting with him (I.ii).

When Shakespeare turned to this subject in 1596–97, he found in his historical sources, mainly Holinshed's *Chronicles*, two dominant motifs. One was the moral and theological interpretation of the troubles attending Henry IV's reign in consequence of his usurpation ...

The other was the legend of the madcap youth of Henry's son and heir—a legend already exploited in an anonymous play of which we have today only a debased and possibly abbreviated text: *The Famous Victories of Henry the Fifth*. The *Famous Victories* contributes to *1 Henry IV* the germ of the robbery incident (though the Prince's involvement in a thieving episode is found in the chronicles as well); the germ of the tavern high jinks and parodying of authority; the germ of the expectation of Hal's reign as a golden age of rascals; and the germ of the reconciliation scene between the Prince and his father. The extent to which these hints are fleshed out and transfigured by Shakespeare's imagination may be seen in the character of Mistress Quickly. Her entire original in the *Famous Victories* is a sentence spoken by the Prince, favoring a rendezvous at "the old tavern in Eastcheap" because "there is a pretty wench that can talk well."

From the *Famous Victories* come also the names Gad's Hill (for the arranger of the robbery), Ned (our Ned Poins), and Jockey Oldcastle. The last was Shakespeare's name for Falstaff when the play was first performed, as references throughout the early seventeenth century show; Hal's addressing him as "my old lad of the castle" in the play as we have it (I.ii.43–44) is a survival from this. By the time the play was printed, the name had been altered to Falstaff for reasons that can now only be guessed at. Possibly there had been a protest by Oldcastle's descendants, one of whom was Lord Chamberlain during part of 1596–97. How the historical Oldcastle (d.1417), a man of character who was made High Sheriff of Herefordshire and eventually Lord Cobham, came to be metamorphosed into the roisterer of the *Famous Victories* is also an unsolved mystery, though no more mysterious than the dramatic imagination that exalted this dull stage roisterer, lacking eloquence, wit, mendacity, thirst, and fat, into the Falstaff we know.

On Holinshed and minor sources like Samuel Daniel's epic *The First Four Books of the Civil Wars between the Two Houses of Lancaster and York* [1595], Shakespeare based his treatment of the Percy rebellion, recasting the materials to give them an inner coherence. The Hotspur of history, for example, was twenty-three years older than Hal and two years older than the King himself, who at the date of the battle of Shrewsbury was only thirty-seven, his eldest son being then sixteen, and Prince John thirteen. Shakespeare followed the lead of Daniel and made Hotspur a youth, in order to establish dramatic rivalry between him and Hal. He then aged Henry rapidly so that by the time of the battle the King can speak of crushing his "old limbs in ungentle steel" and be the more appropriately rescued (this episode is also derived from Daniel) by his vigorous heir. For the same dramatic purpose, he assigned to Hal the triumph over Hotspur—though the inspiration for this may have come from misreading an ambiguous sentence in Holinshed. The reconciliation of Prince and King, touched on in the chronicles and dramatized briefly in the *Famous Victories* as occurring in Henry's latter years, he moved forward to a position before Shrewsbury, in order to enhance the human drama of father and son and further sharpen our anticipation of Hal's meeting with Hotspur. Hotspur's blunt uncourtly humor, the conception of Glendower as scholar and poet fired by a Celtic imagination, the entertaining clash of temperament and mood that this makes possible at Glendower's house, not only between Welshman and Englishman, but between romantic lovers and seasoned man and wife—all this again is Shakespeare's invention. His transformation of

Holinshed, like his transformation of the *Famous Victories*, may best be indicated by a specific example. All of Hotspur's deliciously impetuous speech about the popinjay lord who came to Holmedon to demand his prisoners, not to mention the wonderfully ebullient scene in which it occurs, has behind it in Holinshed only seventeen words: "the King demanded of the Earl and his son such Scottish prisoners as were taken at Homeldon..."

Hal's triumphant journey from tippling in taverns to glory on the field of battle derives from one other "source," more influential than any yet mentioned here. This is the *psychomachia* of the morality plays—that is, the struggle of virtues and vices for possession of a man's soul, a theme acted again and again in the plays of the early sixteenth century, which the drama of Marlowe and Shakespeare superseded. In these plays, youthful virtue is beset by temptations and misleaders but customarily sees the true light at last and is saved. In the same general manner, Prince Hal "has to choose, Morality-fashion, between Sloth or Vanity, to which he is drawn by his bad companions, and Chivalry, to which he is drawn by his father and brothers. And he chooses Chivalry" [Tillyard, E. M. *W. Shakespeare's History Plays*, 1944].

Source: Maynard Mack, "Introduction," in *The History of Henry IV, Part One*, New American Library, 1965, p. xxiii–xxxvi.

Milton Crane

Crane examines the use of prose and verse in the play and shows how the two modes of speech differentiate between the two worlds of the play—the world of the court and Falstaff's world. Crane demonstrates how Falstaff mimics the play's serious action through his use of prose. Falstaff's world, argues Crane, is in complete opposition to the world of the court; therefore it is appropriate that he never speaks in verse, the language of the court. Crane also shows how Hal moves easily from one world to the other, speaking prose in the tavern and verse in court. Crane analyzes Hotspur's speech as well, arguing that he speaks the best verse in the play.

Nowhere in Shakespeare are the boundaries of two worlds so clearly delimited by the use of prose and verse as in the *Henry IV* plays (1597, 1598). The scenes relating to the historical matter are in verse, the scenes of Falstaff and his followers in prose. There are tri-fling exceptions:

the conventional usages, as in Hotspur's letter (II, iii); Hotspur's short comic dialogue with his lady (III, i), with its startling shifts between prose and verse; and the mock verse of Pistol. [All references to Shakespeare's text are to George Lyman Kittredge's *The Complete Works of Shakespeare,* 1936.] One can hardly say of plays which fall so neatly into two actions and two spheres of influence that the form of either action is basic and the form of the other is the exception. Between the two worlds lies a huge and fundamental opposition, but each is autonomous within itself; Pistol's verse in the Boar's Head tavern is burlesque, not a sadly distorted recollection that the "serious business" of the play is going on elsewhere in verse.

Falstaff is Shakespeare's most brilliant speaker of comic prose, as Hamlet is his most gifted speaker of a prose which defies categories. But why does Falstaff speak prose? This may seem an idle question: Falstaff is a clown, although a nobleman, and must therefore speak prose; he must, furthermore, represent "the whole world" that Hal has to banish before he can become England's Harry, and Falstaff must therefore be opposed in every conceivable way to the world of high action and noble verse in which Hal is destined to move. But beyond all this, Falstaff speaks prose because it is inconceivable that he should speak anything else . . .

Burlesque [a form of comedy, typically mockery or ridiculous exaggeration] lies near the heart of Shakespearean comedy, from *The Comedy of Errors* to *As You Like It.* In the two *Henry IV* plays, the Falstaff-plot offers the broadest conceivable burlesque on the serious action. Falstaff derides the chivalric ideal, the forms of noble behavior, the law itself; he robs the travelers, suffers himself to be robbed in turn without fighting, and at last lies grossly and complacently about the whole affair and is totally unabashed at being found out. He is an unrepentant sinner, and, notwithstanding, is handsomely rewarded for his evil life until the moment of his banishment. He is a particularly noisome stench in the nostrils of the godly. His burlesque of their world is conducted on every plane: he robs them, flouts their ideals, and corrupts their prince. And, because he is in such constant opposition to their world, it is only fitting that he should never really speak its language. The powerful contrast is expressed on the

THE *DRAMATIC* POINT OF THE SCENE IS WELL MADE AND THE MAIN ACTION IS APPRECIABLY ADVANCED. BUT AT THE SIDE, AND ATTEMPTING ALWAYS TO INTRUDE, IS FALSTAFF, AND WHEN THE REST HAVE LEFT, HE HAS THE STAGE ENTIRELY TO HIMSELF."

level of speech as on every other, and thus Falstaff speaks prose because of what he represents as well as what he is.

Most of the characters can be assigned easily enough to one group or the other—Hal's position remaining always ambiguous—but Hotspur's case is somewhat odd. He accepts the code completely; he is honor's fool, and is killed for it. But he is a very downright man, whose hard and realistic common sense makes him impatient with both poetry and milk-and-water oaths; language must speak clearly, directly, and forcefully, or he will have none of it. It is therefore inevitable that he should speak the very best of language, and that especially in verse. His verse is so hard, colloquial, and simple that he really has no need for prose. George Rylands [in *Words and Poetry*, 1928] says that Hotspur's speech marks an important stage in the development of Shakespeare's verse style, a stage at which Shakespeare incorporated into his verse many of the qualities of his prose. And yet one feels that Shakespeare must have known what he was about when he made Hotspur speak much more verse than prose. Hotspur belongs, after all, to the world of the knights, and he must speak their idiom even if only to mock them in it. Occasionally he uses prose, and very well, as in the prose letter in II, iii—a furious stream of prose: letter, comment, and vituperation, all well jumbled together. But as soon as Lady Percy enters, we have verse dialogue. The prose of this first long monologue should perhaps be put down to a combination of conventional epistolary prose and the dramatic necessity for continuing the letter scene in prose, even after the reading of the letter is finished.

In III, i, where Hotspur taunts and enrages the fiery Glendower, he begins in broken verse:

Lord Mortimer, and cousin Glendower,
Will you sit down?
And uncle Worcester. A plague upon it!
I have forgot the map.
(III, i, 3–5)

Glendower's reply has been rearranged as most irregular verse by Pope from the prose of the Quartos. Hotspur's next speech is in prose, whereas Glendower at once breaks into the pompous, inflated verse so characteristic of him. Hotspur then varies between prose and verse; the length of the individual speech appears to be the only determinant. Thus he says at first:

Why, so it would have done at the same
    season, if your mother's cat
had but kitten'd, though yourself had never
    been born.
(18–20).

But, a moment later, he goes on:

And I say the earth was not of my mind,
If you suppose as fearing you it shook.

...

O, then the earth shook to see the heav-
    ens on fire,
And not in fear of your nativity.
Diseased nature oftentimes breaks forth
In strange eruptions; oft the teeming earth
Is with a kind of colic pinch'd and vex'd
By the imprisoning of unruly wind
Within her womb, which, for enlargement
    striving,
Shakes the old beldame earth and topples
    down
Steeples and mossgrown towers. At your
    birth
Our grandam earth, having this distemp'-
    rature,
In passion shook.
(22–23, 25–34)

After Glendower's reply, Hotspur returns to prose for a two-line retort, and, a little later, speaks verse again. Hotspur's prose in this scene appears to be restricted to short gibes, whereas he speaks verse when he becomes aroused.

He uses prose again, briefly, toward the end of the scene, when he jokes with his wife and reproaches her for her genteel swearing. It is difficult to assign any specifc reason for this prose, largely because of the general uncertainty of media in this passage. (227–265) Hotspur speaks prose, then verse, then prose again; after the Welsh lady's song, Hotspur's protest against

his lady's "in good sooth" begins in prose and drops suddenly into verse. His last speech is again in prose...

The Prince, in general, takes his cue from his company, speaking prose in the tavern and verse in the court with equal facility. His one violation of this division is, consequently, all the more striking. He enters in V, iii, to find Falstaff moralizing over the corpse of Sir Walter Blunt. Hal is now no longer the boon companion, but the variant knight, and reproves Falstaff in straightforward verse. Falstaff replies with a jest in prose, and the rest of the scene—a matter of a half-dozen speeches—is wound up in prose. But Falstaff himself has brought his prose into a verse scene, one of noble words and deeds, and he has used Sir Walter's "grinning honour" as a telling proof of his conclusions in his own catechism of honor. The scene thus contains a double contrast between prose and verse, and the old use of prose and verse characters within a single scene is here given a new and effective turn.

In V, i, Falstaff is for the first time brought into the world of the court, and at once sets about his favorite task of deriding it. Worcester pleads his innocence, and to the King's ironic question about the rebellion, "You have not sought it! How comes it then?" (V, i, 27), Falstaff interjects a reply: "Rebellion lay in his way, and he found it." Only Hal's injunction to remain quiet keeps Falstaff from making further comments on the action of the scene. He must needs hold his peace until the nobles have left, but immediately thereafter rediscovers his vein. Hal is short with him, for he is keenly aware of the seriousness of the situation. And so Falstaff must wait for even Hal to leave before he can make his most devastating comment on the ideals of a world he so ambiguously serves.

Shakespeare was too keen a dramatist not to have understood that the most powerful impression a scene creates in the mind of an audience is the final one. The first scene of Act V begins with King Henry, Worcester and the rest; but it ends with Falstaff. The *dramatic* point of the scene is well made and the main action is appreciably advanced. But at the side, and attempting always to intrude, is Falstaff, and when the rest have left, he has the stage entirely to himself. The net effect is produced not by the heroics of the nobles, but by the cynical realism of Falstaff. This is not to say that Falstaff dominates the play as he dominates this scene; as Professor Van Doren has well expressed it [in *Shakespeare*, 1939]: "History is enlarged here to make room for taverns and trollops and potations of sack, and the heroic drama is modified by gigantic mockery, by the roared voice of truth; but the result is more rather than less reality, just as a cathedral, instead of being demolished by merriment among its aisles, stands more august."

Hal must, as he says, "imitate the sun," and Falstaff's charm must be made so great as to convince the spectator that Hal's enjoyment of low life is not caused by a natural preference for the stew or the alehouse. But so charming (to use the word strictly) is Falstaff that Hal's necessary renunciation of him cannot be anything but priggish . . .

Source: Milton Crane, "Shakespeare: The Comedies," in *Shakespeare's Prose*, University of Chicago Press, 1951, pp. 66–127.

SOURCES

Bennett, Robert B., "Hal's Crisis of Timing," in *Cahiers Elisabethans*, No. 13, April 1978, pp. 15–23.

Bevington, David, "Introduction," in *Henry IV, Part 1*, by William Shakespeare, Oxford University Press, 1987, pp. 1–122.

Bueler, Lois, "Falstaff in the Eye of the Beholder," in *Essays in Literature*, Vol. 1, No. 1, January 1973, pp. 1–12.

Callahan, E. F., "Lyric Origins of the Unity of *1 Henry IV*," *Costerus*, Vol. 3, 1972, pp. 9–22.

Cohen, Derek, "The Rite of Violence in *1 Henry IV*," *Shakespeare Survey*, Vol. 38, 1985, pp. 77–84.

Cox, Gerard H. "'Like a Prince Indeed': Hal's Triumph of Honor in *1 Henry IV*," in *Pageantry in the Shakespearean Theater*, edited by David M. Bergeron, University of Georgia Press, 1985, pp. 130–49.

Cruttwell, Patrick, *The Shakespearean Moment and Its Place in the Poetry of the Seventeenth Century*, Chatto & Windus, 1954, pp. 27–8.

Dickinson, Hugh, "The Reformation of Prince Hal," in *Shakespeare Quarterly*, Vol. 12, No. 1, Winter 1961, pp. 33–46.

Goddard, Harold C., "Henry IV," in *The Meaning of Shakespeare*, University of Chicago Press, 1951, pp. 161–214.

Gross, Alan Gerald, "The Justification of Prince Hal," in *Texas Studies in Literature and Language*, Vol. 10, No. 1, Spring 1978, pp. 27–35.

Humphreys, A. R. "Shakespeare's Political Justice in *Richard II* and *Henry IV*," in *Stratford Papers on Shakespeare*, edited by B. W. Jackson, Gage, 1965, pp. 30–50.

Lawlor, John, "Appearance and Reality," in *Tragic Sense in Shakespeare*, Chatto & Windus, 1960, pp. 17–44.

Martin, R. A., "Metatheater, Gender, and Subjectivity in *Richard II* and *Henry IV*, Part I," in *Comparative Drama*, Vol. 23, No. 3, Fall 1989, pp. 255–64.

McAlindon, Tom, "Perfect Answers: Religious Inquisition, Falstaffian Wit," in *Shakespeare Survey*, Vol. 54, 2001, pp. 100–07.

McDonald, Russ, "The Monarchs," in *The Bedford Companion to Shakespeare*, 2nd ed., Bedford/St. Martin's, 2001, p. 313.

Morgann, Maurice, "An Essay on the Dramatic Character of Sir John Falstaff," in *Shakespearian Criticism*, edited by Daniel A. Fineman, Clarendon Press, 1972, p. 444.

Norwich, John Julius, *Shakespeare's Kings*, Scribner, 1999.

Reno, Raymond, "Hotspur: The Integration of Character and Theme," in *Renaissance Papers*, April 1962, pp. 17–26.

Rogers, Carmen, "The Renaissance Code of Honor in Shakespeare's *Henry IV, Part I*," in *The Shakespeare Newsletter*, Vol. 4, No. 1, February 1954, p. 8.

Rowse, A. L., "The First Part of King Henry IV," in *Prefaces to Shakespeare's Plays*, Orbis, 1984, pp. 49–53.

Shakespeare, William, *The Complete Illustrated Shakespeare*, edited by Howard Staunton, 1858, reprint, Park Lane, 1979.

———, *Henry IV, Part 1*, edited by David Bevington, Oxford University Press, 1987.

Siegel, Paul N., "Shakespeare and the Neo-Chivalric Cult of Honor," in *Centennial Review*, Vol. 8, 1964, pp. 39–70.

Sjoberg, Elisa, "From Madcap Prince to King: The Evolution of Prince Hal," in *Shakespeare Quarterly*, Vol. 20, No. 1, Winter 1969, pp. 11–6.

Traub, Valerie, "Prince Hal's Falstaff: Positioning Psychoanalysis and the Female Reproductive Body," in *Shakespeare Quarterly*, Vol. 40, No. 4, Winter 1989, pp. 456–74.

Vickers, Brian, *The Artistry of Shakespeare's Prose*, Methuen, 1968, pp. 1–51, 89–141.

Wikander, Matthew H., "The Protean Prince Hal," in *Comparative Drama*, Vol. 26, No. 4, Winter 1992–1993, pp. 295–311.

Wilson, John Dover, "The Political Background of Shakespeare's Richard II and Henry IV," in *Shakespeare Jahrbuch*, Vol. 75, 1939, pp. 36–51.

———, *The Fortunes of Falstaff*, Cambridge University Press, 1964, p. 143.

Zeeveld, Gordon, "'Food for Powder'—'Food for Worms?'" in *Shakespeare Quarterly*, Vol. 3, 1952, pp. 249–53.

FURTHER READING

Bevan, Bryan, *Henry IV*, Palgrave Macmillan, 1994.
Bevan provides a book-length treatment of the life of King Henry IV, addressing his virtues as well as his faults.

Cooper, Terry D., *Sin, Pride & Self-Acceptance: The Problem of Identity in Theology and Psychology*, InterVarsity Press, 2003.
In a work that bears relevance to the various psychological states Hal may have experienced over the course of his life, Cooper addresses the notion of how pride can lead a person to imagine an idealized self that can be difficult to develop in actuality.

Forrest, Ian, *The Detection of Heresy in Late Medieval England*, Oxford University Press, 2005.
Addressing the case of John Oldcastle among many others, Forrest examines the notion of heresy in England in the fourteenth and fifteenth centuries and the way it was addressed by church and state authorities.

Valente, Claire, *The Theory and Practice of Revolt in Medieval England*, Ashgate Publishing, 2003.
In this text, Valente explores the various rebellions that occurred in England from the thirteenth through the fifteenth centuries, including the one by which Henry IV rose to power as well as the one he faced from the Percys and their supporters.

Henry V

1599 As a tribute to the king who won back the throne of France for England, William Shakespeare's *Henry V* may be narrow in scope, but it is great in majesty. This epic play was probably written sometime between March and early September in 1599. However, there is no record of a performance of *Henry V* before January 7, 1605, when it was presented at court by the King's Majesty's Players.

The play is often referred to as a vehicle for inspiring patriotism, which well might have been the case in Shakespeare's time. Even in 1944, during the Second World War, the British actor Laurence Olivier directed a fresh version of *Henry V*, adapting the play to film to encourage British troops. In the drama, audiences watch the fictionalized character of King Henry V lead his troops across the English Channel to face a French army that is better equipped and at least five times larger in number. The battle at Agincourt is the central action of the play, and the results are astonishing.

Most modern critics maintain that there is strong evidence that Shakespeare consulted both Raphael Holinshed's *Chronicles of England, Scotlande, and Irelande* (1577; 1587) and Edward Hall's *The Union of the Two Noble and Illustre Famelies of Lancastre and York* (2d ed., 1548) as sources for *Henry V*. Commentators note that such passages as Canterbury's speech explaining Salic law in act 1, scene 2 is a paraphrase in verse of Holinshed's narrative of this episode, with only slight variations from the original. On the other

hand, Shakespeare makes no reference to many events that appear in Holinshed's and Hall's accounts of the reign of Henry V. In addition, the dramatist implies only a short passage of time between the battle at Agincourt and the achievement of a treaty with France, when in fact the two were separated by a period of nearly four years. A lost and anonymous play from the 1580s, *The Famous Victories of Henry the Fifth*, survives only in a corrupt edition of 1598, so that it has proved difficult to determine the degree of Shakespeare's familiarity with this work. However, several critics have noticed parallels between Shakespeare's *Henry V* and *The Famous Victories*, including similarities in structure, the prominence in each of the Dauphin's gift of tennis balls to Henry, and the inclusion in both works of a wooing scene between Henry and Katherine.

Henry V has been praised by many scholars as an energetic portrayal of one of England's most popular national heroes. While the central issue for critics has been the character of the king and whether he represents Shakespeare's ideal ruler, modern commentary has increasingly explored both Henry's positive and negative attributes. Although the personality of the king has attracted a significant amount of discussion, commentators have also shown renewed interest in Shakespeare's attitude toward patriotism and war, his use of language and imagery, the absence of Falstaff, a lovable rascal who played an important part in Shakespeare's *Henry IV*, and the play's epic elements, particularly Shakespeare's use of the Chorus.

PLOT SUMMARY

Act 1, Prologue
Shakespeare opens his play *Henry V* with a Chorus (in most productions a single person), who announces that this grand play, with its wars and open fields, powerful characters and armies of men, is unfortunately confined to a small wooden stage. In order to capture the magnitude of the actions and circumstances surrounding the great figure of Henry V, the Chorus asks that the audience generously use its imagination to fill in the missing elements.

Act 1, Scene 1
The first scene opens in England, in the king's court. The first characters to appear are the Archbishop of Canterbury and the Bishop of Ely, announcing, through their dialogue, that King Henry is planning on passing a bill that will take much of the church's wealth away. The king wants to use the excess money that the church enjoyed to finance a war and feed the poor. The powerful clergymen have hatched a plan that they hope will go over well with the king. They will offer to finance Henry's war with France. This will obviously cost them a lot less money; and the war will distract the king, they hope, from going forward with his plan to limit the wealth of the church.

Act 1, Scene 2
The king is in his throne room with his advisers. He calls for the Archbishop of Canterbury, who enters the room. Before the archbishop begins to talk, Henry reminds him of the huge responsibility that hangs over his head. Henry wants to hear the argument that the archbishop has come up with that gives Henry the right to claim the throne of France. If the archbishop can make an educated and rational argument to support that right, Henry is willing to go to war with France to claim the crown and the territory.

In a very complicated explanation, the archbishop describes the lineage of the French throne, which, according to what the French call the Salic law (*Salic* refers to an ancient Frankish tribe), cannot be passed down through the mother. This is why the French deny that Henry is the rightful heir to the French throne, since he is claiming it through his great-great grandmother. This is the French view.

The English do not honor such a law. The archbishop gives the council a brief account of the long history of the kings and queens of the French court and concludes that even the French do not fully apply the Salic law to the royal lineage, and therefore Henry's claim is as good as the current French king's, Charles VI. But the only way Henry can claim the throne is through battle. Although the church is offering to pay for the war, Henry is concerned that if he and his army leave England, rebels in Scotland, who want to take the English throne away from Henry, will invade the country. Therefore the archbishop suggests that Henry take only a small portion of his army to France and leave the larger portion to guard the homeland. The council agrees.

Henry V, King of England

Then Henry calls for the delegation that has come from France. Representatives of the king of France and his son, called the Dauphin, come into the room. They have brought a symbolic gift from the Dauphin. It turns out to be a small chest of tennis balls, a symbol of Henry's so-called reckless youth. The Dauphin's message is that Henry is too immature to be successful in his attempt to claim the throne.

This outrages Henry, who tells the messengers that the Dauphin has made a grave mistake in underestimating and mocking him. He says to tell the Dauphin that the Dauphin's wit will not be enough to make his own people laugh when Henry's army ravages France's villages.

After the messengers leave, Henry makes the final decision to invade France.

Act 2, Prologue
The Chorus announces that all the men of England are afire with their zest to go to war.

Soldiers are selling their land to buy horses. But there is also a warning. The French have found three men, whom they have paid, to kill King Henry. The three men are Richard, Earl of Cambridge, Henry, Lord Scroop of Masham, and Sir Thomas Grey, knight of Northumberland.

Act 2, Scene 1
In a poor section of London, Bardolph and Nym, men who used to hang out with Sir John Falstaff and young Henry, before Henry became king, are sitting in the Boar's Head Tavern. Mistress Quickly, who is referred to as Hostess because she runs the tavern, and Pistol enter. Nym pulls out his sword. He is angry that Mistress Quickly has married Pistol, for Nym had once asked Quickly to marry him. Bardolph breaks up the fight. The men talk about going to war. Then Falstaff's servant boy comes to call them to Falstaff's room. The boy says Falstaff is dying. Quickly says the king has broken Falstaff's heart. Once Henry became king, he cut off his friendship with these men.

Act 2, Scene 2
In Southampton, Henry and his troops are about to set sail for France. Bedford, Exeter, and Westmorland discuss the fact that the king knows about the three traitors. The king enters with Scroop, Cambridge, and Grey (the traitors) and asks the three of them for their advice about another man who was heard talking against the king. Henry, setting them up, says he thinks this man should be excused because he was drunk at the time. But the three traitors tell the king that the man must be punished. Then, leading the traitors to believe that he is praising them, Henry gives each one a letter, saying that he is well aware of their worth. The men open the letters, discovering that the king knows of their plot to kill him. Henry asks what kind of punishment they think they deserve. Then he tells them that they will pay with their lives. After the men are taken away, Henry says that having found them out before they could kill him is a sign that fortune is on England's side.

Act 2, Scene 3
This is a brief scene that takes place back in London. Hostess announces that Falstaff is dead. Nym, Bardolph, and Pistol all mourn him. Then Pistol kisses his wife good-bye, and the men, including Falstaff's boy, go off to join the rest of the army.

Act 2, Scene 4

In France, King Charles VI, his son, the Dauphin, and the king's advisers discuss the impending confrontation with England. The Dauphin thinks King Henry is a fool, coming to France. He wants to fight the English forces, believing that France will take them down easily. King Charles and the Constable of France, however, disagree. They have heard that Henry's armies are strong and that Henry himself is greatly changed, no longer the irresponsible youth that the Dauphin still believes Henry to be. King Charles reminds his son that Henry is the descendant of King Edward, the Black Prince of Wales, who once ravaged France.

King Henry is now in France and sends one of his noblemen, Exeter, to deliver a message to King Charles. Exeter tells King Charles to abdicate the throne and crown in favor of Henry. King Charles asks what will happen if he does not. Exeter tells him that his country will fall in ruins.

Act 3, Prologue

The Chorus describes how swiftly England's forces sailed to France and landed at Harfleur on the French coast. King Charles sends a message that he will not give Henry the throne, but he will turn over some dukedoms to Henry and will give him his daughter, Katherine, as a wife. Henry refuses the offer.

Act 3, Scene 1

King Henry delivers a long speech to his men, arousing them to take the city of Harfleur. He explains that in peacetime men act with humility but when the horns of warfare blow, they must rise to the occasion and become wild and fierce creatures. They must rid themselves of their fair natures and fill themselves with rage. Then he sends them forth to battle.

Act 3, Scene 2

Nym, Pistol, and Bardolph, after hearing King Henry's speech, wish they were back in England. Fluellen, a Welsh captain, enters and reprimands the men, pushing them forward with his sword into the battle. Only Falstaff's boy is left behind. He talks to the audience, saying that he does not want to grow up to be like Nym, Pistol, or Bardolph, who have tried to teach him to steal.

Fluellen returns with Captain Gower. The soldiers discuss the mines, or the tunnels, that the English have dug to gain access to Harfleur. There is a discussion of the different cultures of the Irish, the Scots, and the English. Fluellen criticizes Captain Macmorris, a Scot, who is, according to Fluellen, building the tunnels incorrectly. Fluellen prefers Jamy, an Irishman. Macmorris appears with Jamy. All the men discuss their different military tactics and their philosophies. The discussion becomes heated, but the men quickly come back to their senses. They have an actual war to fight.

Act 3, Scene 3

Before the gates of Harfleur, horns are sounded, signaling a wish for a cease-fire from the local French leaders of Harfleur. Henry calls out to the mayor of the town, telling him to surrender. If the mayor allows the English soldiers entry to the town, the people will live, Henry tells him. If the mayor insists that the English continue fighting, the old people's heads will be bashed, the wives will be raped, the babies will be impaled. The mayor, telling Henry that the Dauphin has sent word that he cannot get a French army to Harfleur, reluctantly surrenders.

King Henry tells Exeter to secure the town. Henry will allow his men to rest, then they will march to Calais, and English-held territory.

Act 3, Scene 4

At the French palace, Katherine, the daughter of King Charles, is having a conversation with her lady-in-waiting, Alice. The curious thing about this scene is that it is mostly spoken in French. Katherine is asking Alice to tell her how to say certain words in English, such as *hand*, *fingers*, *nails*, *neck*, and *chin*. This is a playful scene and the audience's first glimpse of Katherine, the daughter the king had earlier used as a ploy to talk King Henry out of attacking villages in France. This scene contrasts with the previous battle scene and the bloody fight that waits ahead.

Act 3, Scene 5

The scene moves to a council room in the French palace. King Charles, the Dauphin, the Constable, and the Duke of Bourbon are discussing King Henry's advance into France. They define themselves as being more refined than the English, referring to the English as barbarous and savage. But they also wonder where the English army gets its strength. The Dauphin comments that the French women are laughing at the

French lords, saying that they have lost their valor and gallantry and that the women will breed with the English soldiers to bring strength back into the French population.

King Charles, who has been reluctant to fully engage in war, changes his mind. He calls on all the lords of France to gather their men and prepare to meet the English on the battlefield. However, the French underestimate the power of Henry. The Constable states he feels sorry for King Henry and his men, who are tired and unprepared for the punishment that France is about to bestow on them. As the men leave, the French king, for some reason, tells the Dauphin to remain behind, to stay with him, telling him to be patient.

Act 3, Scene 6

The English forces have camped at Picardy. They have captured a significant bridge and are thankful. Fluellen and Gower are talking. Gower is telling Fluellen that one of the men, Pistol, wants to talk to him. Pistol comes in and asks Fluellen to forgive a crime that has been committed. Bardolph has been caught stealing from one of the local churches. Fluellen will have nothing to do with the pardon. It is the rule of the king. Fluellen believes Bardolph needs to be used as an example.

King Henry appears and talks with Fluellen, asking how many casualties the army has suffered. Fluellen says only one, the man who is about to be hanged for thievery.

Montjoy appears, a messenger from the French king. Montjoy tells King Henry that King Charles is ready to go to war. The French king, through Montjoy, explains that he has lost all patience and is ready to punish the English army for all the harm it has done. Henry, the French king states, should consider his ransom to the French court. This means that the French are asking Henry to turn himself in as a prisoner. At the end of Montjoy's message is a statement that, in essence, King Henry has condemned his men to death.

King Henry, although he knows his men are tired and weak and that the French army will outnumber them greatly, does not give in. Instead, he sends Montjoy back to the French court with a defiant message. First Henry says that in every English soldier there is the strength of three of the French. Then Henry apologizes for bragging. He decides to use another tactic.

He tells Montjoy how broken and beaten his men are; and yet the army will move forward. Henry says he is not seeking a battle but if it comes, he and his men will face it. After Montjoy leaves, Gloucester tells Henry that he hopes the French army will not come. Henry tells him that they are in God's hands, not in the hands of the French.

Act 3, Scene 7

In this scene, the audience sees the French army camped at Agincourt. The Constable, the Dauphin, Lord Rambures, and the Duke of Orleans are there. They are discussing how solid their armor is, how strong their horses are. Then they brag about how many English soldiers they will kill the next day. After the Dauphin leaves, the Constable says that he thinks the Dauphin is weak. The Dauphin had talked about how many English he would kill, but the Constable thinks the Dauphin will kill no one. Then the French soldiers insult the English, insisting that if King Henry really understood his fate, he would run away with his men that night.

The French are so confident that they make jokes about the battle which will begin in the morning. The French army is so much bigger than the English, the sheer numbers alone make the battle look like it will be a disaster for the English.

Act 4, Prologue

The Chorus provides an overview of the two different camps—the overly confident French nobility as opposed to the English army, which is mostly common men who expect this may well be their last night of life. The Chorus also mentions how King Henry walks through the camp, talking to each soldier as if he were a brother, cheering his men, inspiring them to face the next day bravely.

Act 4, Scene 1

In the English camp, Henry greets Bedford and Gloucester, reminding them that since the odds are against them in this battle, they need to rouse all their courage. Henry then goes about the camp, not allowing anyone to see his face, talking to his men to find out what they are thinking on the night before the great battle. He first runs into Pistol. Despite the fact that just a little earlier, Henry condemned Bardolph to death, Pistol remains true to the king. Later, Henry speaks to other men about who is responsible for the casualties of a war. The men say the responsibility lies with the king, as do the casualties. Henry disagrees. He says the war is the king's responsibility, but each soldier is responsible for his life. In the end, the men agree. But they hold onto the belief that the king will allow himself to be ransomed, thus saving his own life. The soldiers will not be as fortunate, they say. Henry disagrees, saying that he believes the king will never ransom himself. Henry then prays that his men be instilled with courage.

Act 4, Scene 2

This is a brief scene at the French camp as the sun rises and the noblemen prepare for battle. They are still very arrogant, believing themselves so strong they merely have to blow on the English troops to be rid of them. The Dauphin even offers to send the English army food and new suits before the French fight them.

Act 4, Scene 3

The English have viewed the field and know they are outnumbered by five to one. Henry enters and turns this to their favor by stating that if they win, being so outnumbered, the greater the glory will be. Henry delivers a long, uplifting speech about how, if they outlive this day, the battle will mark them as heroes for the rest of their lives. Montjoy appears once more, offering Henry another chance to turn himself over for ransom. Henry sends Montjoy away.

Act 4, Scene 4

The battle has begun. Pistol fights with a French soldier, who begs for his life and promises Pistol some money. Pistol agrees. Falstaff's boy is there and sees what Pistol has just done. He claims that Bardolph and Nym were much braver and more valiant than Pistol.

Act 4, Scene 5

This is a scene of the battle from the French point of view, with the French nobles announcing that they have been shamed by the English army.

Act 4, Scene 6

King Henry and Exeter discuss the death of two of their men. When Henry sees the French soldiers regrouping, he orders that all the French prisoners be killed.

Act 4, Scene 7

Some of the English soldiers discover the slaughtered bodies of all the young English boy servants. Henry enters, enraged by the death of the boys. As Henry is ordering that more French throats be cut, Montjoy appears announcing that the battle has been won by the English.

Act 4, Scene 8

The English count the dead and those imprisoned. Exeter says that there are at least 1500 prisoners. A messenger tells Henry that there are ten thousand dead French soldiers. The messenger names the English nobles who are dead. There are four. Among the common men, there are only twenty-five that have been lost. God, Henry claims, as do his men, was on their side.

Act 5, Scene Prologue

The Chorus fills in the missing scenes between the end of the battle and the next scene at the French palace. Henry returns to England after the battle at Agincourt. He is welcomed as a hero but disallows a parade to celebrate the victory, playing down his role as warrior king. Time passes, and Henry returns to France.

Act 5, Scene 1

Fluellen and Pistol argue and throw insults at one another. When Pistol is left alone, he mentions that he has heard that the Hostess, his wife, is dead. He bemoans his bad fate.

Act 5, Scene 2

At the French palace, King Henry and King Charles meet. They sign an agreement that will ensure peace between the two countries. King Henry allows King Charles to retain the throne, but demands Katherine as his wife. In this way, their child will inherit the thrones of both countries. Henry and Katherine struggle through the language barriers as Henry tries to get Katherine to agree to marry him. She finally does so.

Act 5, Epilogue

The Chorus tells of the birth of a son to Katherine and Henry. He will become Henry VI, and he will lose France and put England at war again.

MEDIA ADAPTATIONS

- *Henry V* was adapted to film and starred famed British actor Laurence Olivier, who also directed this classic piece in a very innovative manner, giving its audience a sense of what the play might have looked like, in part, in the sixteenth century. It is available from Paramount and produced in 1944 but is well ahead of its time.

- *Henry V* was produced by the British Broadcasting Corporation (BBC) in 1979 as part of the "Shakespeare Plays" series. It is available from Ambrose Video Publishing.

- Kenneth Branagh, who has starred in many of Shakespeare's dramas, plays the lead role in a 1989 production of *Henry V* distributed by CBS/Fox Video. Branagh also directed this adaptation.

CHARACTERS

Alice

Alice is the lady-in-waiting, attending Katherine. Because she has been to England and has some familiarity with the language, Alice serves as Katherine's instructor and interpreter. Her only spoken lines occur in act 3, scene 4, a light-hearted scene, which is mostly spoken in French.

Archbishop of Canterbury

In order to keep the church's land and fortunes, the archbishop conceives a plan. He interprets the Salic law in such a way that it proves that King Henry has a rightful claim to the French throne. The archbishop tells Henry that the church will pay for the war against France, thus taking Henry's mind off a bill he was considering that would have diminished the church's fortunes. The king, in turn, warns the archbishop to be very sure of his interpretation, as many lives may be lost based on his words. Although Henry tells the archbishop that he

will be responsible, at Agincourt, the king tells one of his soldiers that the king is not responsible for lives, exposing a contradiction in Shakespeare's work or in the character of Henry.

Bardolph

Bardolph, a commoner, is a character taken from *Henry IV*, a friend of Falstaff's and therefore part of the group that Prince Hal (King Henry in his youth) used to hang out with. In *Henry V*, Bardolph continues to befriend Nym and Pistol and is present when Falstaff dies. Bardolph goes to France with King Henry, but is hung for stealing from a French church. His death represents a definitive sign that King Henry has turned away from the rabble-rousers of his past and has matured into his role as king. Bardolph explicitly broke one of the king's rules, and Henry would not save him from hanging.

John Bates

Bates is a common soldier in the English army. He is one of the men who talks with Henry the night before the battle at Agincourt, as the king wanders throughout the camp disguised.

Bishop of Ely

The role of the bishop is not developed in this play. He is present, mostly just to give the archbishop someone to talk to. The bishop asks questions of the archbishop so as to provide more detailed information for the audience.

King Charles VI

Though it is not indicated in this play, Shakespeare's audience knew that King Charles VI of France was called the mad king. His feebleness might have been one of the reasons that King Henry decides to invade France, that and the incompetence of King Charles's son, the Dauphin. King Charles is also the father of Katherine, whom King Henry marries. King Charles is reluctant to do battle with the English forces until they near Agincourt. When he does give the order, the constable salutes the king with the phrase, "This becomes the great." This makes clear that the French nobles are anxious to do battle and are glad that the king finally commits to it.

Chorus

The Chorus presents either a preview, summation, or conclusion of the dramatic action in the play. The Chorus's lines are written in blank

The Duke of Alencon crouching in defeat to Henry V at the Battle of Agincourt (Mansell/Mansell/Time and Life Pictures/Getty Images)

verse and begin each of the acts, filling in information or setting the scene when the staged presentations are limited. Whereas the action of the play takes a realistic approach to the characters and their actions, the Chorus is more idealistic, possibly representing what the English audience wants to believe, while the dramatic action is Shakespeare's interpretation of what actually happened. Some critics have called the Chorus some of Shakespeare's worst writing, filled with common phrases, or platitudes, rather than Shakespeare's normally high standard of poetry.

Alexander Court
Court is a common soldier in the English army. Court has only one line in the play, pointing out the rising sun. This one line, however, signals the tension the English are experiencing on the morning of the battle.

Charles Delabreth, Constable of France
The constable is probably the most effective of the French noblemen surrounding the king of France. He is level-headed and attempts to calm down the Dauphin who is overly emotional and often blinded as to King Henry's power. The constable is killed at the battle of Agincourt.

Duke of Bedford
The Duke of Bedford is a minor character who makes brief appearances in the beginning of the play. He is one of Henry's brothers.

Duke of Berry
The Duke of Berry is one of the dukes that the French king sends to meet King Henry's men at Harfleur.

Duke of Bourbon
Bourbon is one of the leaders of the French army at the Battle of Agincourt.

Duke of Britain
The Duke of Britain is ordered by the French king to stop King Henry's soldiers.

Duke of Burgundy

The Duke of Burgundy is French, but he helps Henry V establish power in France by acknowledging Henry's right to the French throne at the end of the play.

Duke of Clarence

Clarence is another of Henry's brothers. He plays a minor role.

Duke of Exeter

Exeter is Henry's uncle and the half-brother of Henry IV. Throughout the play, Exeter is at Henry's side, advising him, supporting him, following him throughout the play. It is Exeter that Henry sends to meet with the French king when the English land in France.

Duke of Gloucester

Gloucester is another of Henry's brothers. He appears at the Battle of Agincourt and worries about the French. It is to Gloucester that Henry says the results of the battle are in God's hands, not in the hands of the French.

Duke of Orleans

Orleans is a leader of the French army at the Battle of Agincourt. Orleans is one of the characters that demonstrate the arrogance of the French on the night before the battle.

Duke of York

The Duke of York is one of Henry's men. He appears in act 4 and asks to lead one section of Henry's army.

Earl of Grandpré

The Earl of Grandpré is with the French army as it prepares to fight at Agincourt. He is impatient with the constable and wants to begin the battle immediately.

Earl of Huntingdon

The Earl of Huntingdon is a British nobleman who helps to command the battle at Agincourt.

Earl of Salisbury

The Earl of Salisbury appears in act 5 with Henry V's men as they fight the French army.

Earl of Warwick

The Earl of Warwick is a British nobleman who is one of Henry's advisers.

Earl of Westmorland

The Earl of Westmorland is an adviser of Henry's who encourages the king to fight for the crown of France.

Sir Thomas Erpingham

Erpingham is an English officer in Henry's army. When he and the king are preparing to go to bed in the camp before the Agincourt Battle, Erpingham says it is one of the few times that he can say that he goes to bed like a king.

Captain Fluellen

Fluellen is a Welsh captain in the English army. Fluellen helps overtake the French city of Harfleur and helps the king keep discipline among the men. It is to Fluellen that Pistol appeals for Bardolph's life when Bardolph is caught stealing from a church in France.

Governor of Harfleur

After failing to receive help from the Dauphin, the governor yields his city to the English, who occupy it and defend it against the French.

Captain Gower

Gower is an English officer in Henry's army. He is often seen with Fluellen in the battle camp scenes in France.

Sir Thomas Grey

Grey is one of the three English traitors, along with Cambridge and Scroop. He has conspired with the French against the life of Henry V. Grey is sentenced to death.

King Henry V

King Henry is known as Prince Hal in *Henry IV*. But in this play, Henry has matured and has recently acquired the title of king. He is concerned about gaining his subjects' loyalty and decides to wage war on France in order to claim the throne in France and to quiet rebellion at home.

Shakespeare demonstrates that Henry is a complex creature who has many facets to his personality. He can forgive a threat to his life and yet threaten to kill babies. He humbles himself to God and yet massacres French prisoners. He leads a small army to battle against a large, well-equipped French army and then softly woos Katherine. As usual, Shakespeare leaves it up to the audience to decide just who Henry might have been.

However, Henry is a complicated character whom many audiences cannot figure out. But most agree, after seeing this play, that Shakespeare shows him to be a great military leader who delivers many speeches that have been praised as some of the best in all of Shakespeare's plays.

Henry, Lord Scroop of Masham

Henry is one of the three English traitors, along with Cambridge and Grey. Scroop was at one time close to the king, which makes Henry especially disgusted with him. In the scene in which the traitors are caught and sentenced to death, Henry calls Scroop an inhuman savage.

Queen Isabel

The Queen of France is King Charles's wife and the Dauphin's and Katherine's mother.

Captain Jamy

Jamy is a Scottish captain in the English army. Jamy, Fluellen, and Macmorris are instrumental in the capture of the city of Harfleur.

Princess Katherine

Katherine is the daughter of King Charles and Queen Isabel. She appears only twice. She is seen with her lady-in-waiting as she tries to learn English and then again at the end of the play when she meets with King Henry. Eventually Katherine marries Henry to restore peace to France and unite the two countries. Although it does not occur in the play, the Chorus does announce that Katherine gives birth to a son (who eventually becomes King Henry VI). Shakespeare creates her character as a witty and intelligent woman who is shy in front of the king, mostly because of their language barriers and their different customs, such as when Henry wants to kiss her and she must refuse. Her role is very small in this play, possibly reflecting the fact that she and Henry were not married very long before Henry's death and he was gone at war most of that time. There were also rumors that Katherine had an affair with another man in Henry's absence, so Shakespeare may have decided that their love was not strong enough to warrant dramatic scenes inspired by it.

Monsieur le Fer

Monsieur le Fer, a French soldier, appears in act 4 with Pistol. The French soldier gives money to Pistol in order to save his own life.

Louis, The Dauphin

The Dauphin (also referred to as the Dolphin) is the eldest son of King Charles and Queen Isabel. The Dauphin constantly overestimates himself and underestimates Henry V and the English army, with disastrous consequences for the French. He is arrogant and frivolous. He claims, right before the Battle at Agincourt, that he will kill many English soldiers. However, the French nobles around him know that the Dauphin is a coward and probably will not kill anyone.

Captain Macmorris

Macmorris is an Irish captain in the English army. Macmorris bravely contributes to the victory at Harfleur.

Montjoy

Montjoy is a French herald. He brings messages to Henry from Charles first demanding Henry's surrender, then later acknowledging Henry's victory. In his first speeches, Montjoy delivers his messages in a defiant tone; but as he grows to know Henry, there is a sense of respect in his voice.

Nell Hostess

Formerly Mistress Nell Quickly, in *Henry IV* and *The Merry Wives of Windsor*, Hostess is now the wife of Pistol and the manager of the inn. Hostess tells Pistol, Nym, and Bardolph of Falstaff's death. After the battle at Agincourt, Pistol informs the audience that Hostess, his wife, has died.

Nym

Nym, like Bardolph and Pistol, is one of the friends who are associated with Falstaff. When he first appears on stage, he is angry with Pistol for having married Quickly (Hostess). Nym had wanted to marry her. After Falstaff dies, Nym joins the English army and goes to France.

Pistol

Pistol is one of Bardolph's and Nym's friends. He is married to Quickly (Hostess). Pistol pleads for Bardolph's life after Bardolph is sentenced to be hung for stealing from a church in France. During the Agincourt battle, Pistol makes a deal with a French soldier, who gives Pistol money so he will not kill him. After the battle at Agincourt, Pistol lets the audience know that Quickly has died.

Mistress Quickly
See *Nell Hostess.*

Richard, Earl of Cambridge
Cambridge is one of the three English traitors, along with Scroop and Grey, who conspire with the French against the life of Henry V. Along with the other two traitors, Cambridge is sentenced to death.

Michael Williams
Williams is a common soldier in the English army. He talks with Henry the night before Agincourt as the king wanders through the camp disguised. Williams is the soldier who argues with Henry over the king's responsibility for his men. Williams gives his glove to Henry, challenging him in a bet that the king will ransom himself to the French if the English lose the battle.

THEMES

Kingship
The theme of kingship, or how Shakespeare perceived the role of a king, is demonstrated in his play *Henry V.* Shakespeare's characterization of King Henry V establishes Henry's right to kingship by illustrating the qualities required of a true king in several different ways. Henry focuses on both securing his right to the English crown and capturing the French throne. He follows the advice given to him by his father at the end of Shakespeare's earlier play *Henry IV, Part Two*, to keep the minds of his subjects busy by diverting attention to foreign quarrels. Henry V accomplishes this task by waging war on France and asserting his claim to the French throne. The throne was denied his great-great-grandmother because of the Salic law, which made succession through the female line illegal. The war against France establishes both Henry's legal and moral right to the throne. By discrediting the Salic law and defeating the French army, Henry captures the crown; and by accepting responsibility and showing concern for his subjects, he earns the ethical right to kingship as well.

Henry's moral growth and acceptance of his role as king is seen throughout the play. Some of the characteristics of kingship include the king's relationship to his counselors, his divinity, his valid succession, and the burden of kingship.

As king, Henry serves as the link between personal order and political unity and is required to show complete dedication to his office. He cannot allow selfishness or weakness to interfere with his duties as king.

Most critics agree that although Henry struggles to achieve a balance between the demands of the crown and his own personal desires, by the end of the play he has accepted his role and learned to integrate his humanity with the office of king.

Patriotism and War
Many modern critics have explored the pervasive presence of war and patriotism in *Henry V.* Some commentators contend that the play is primarily concerned with the price of patriotism, arguing that Henry finally becomes controlled by the role he has assumed, despite the costs. The interaction between structure and theme can be seen throughout the three central movements of the plot: the preparation for war, the combat itself, and the concluding of peace. In addition, scholars have praised Shakespeare's accurate portrayal of Renaissance warfare through his use of specific details such as the slaughter of the prisoners and threats of plundering, sacking, and burning.

Sense of History and Nationalism
The idea of nations in the time of Henry V, or even in Shakespeare's time, was not as defined as it is in the twenty-first century, especially in England and France. Kings and queens were often related to one another, whether they lived in England or France. The English owned land in France because most of the early English monarchs had been born in France and had therefore inherited the lands. Thus, the boundaries between the two countries were relatively blurred.

However, the concept of nations was emerging and growing stronger in Shakespeare's time. Also the Renaissance had arrived in England during Shakespeare's life, which influenced the portrayal of historical events and the details of how England and France had become what they were up to that point. The sense of history is reflected in this play, which is actually the last in a series of three of Shakespeare's plays, which includes *Richard II* and *Henry IV.* The series is called a tetralogy. The three plays follow the development of France and England through the actions of the English monarchs and their relationships, both political and biological, with the monarchy of France. With the battle at Agincourt, King Henry finally wins the right to the throne, though he never actually sits on throne, because he will die two months prior to that opportunity.

Divine Intervention

There are several references in this play to God's intervention on behalf of, or God's blessing of, the English army in its bid to win the French throne. Although this was not a religious war, Shakespeare has Henry acknowledge the idea that God is on his side. The first time this happens is when the three traitors are discovered before Henry leaves England. He takes the fact that the attempt to assassinate him was thwarted as a sign from God that he is doing the right thing, that in fact the English might even win the war. In act 2, scene 2, Henry says: "Since God so graciously hath brought to light / This dangerous treason, lurking in our way / To hinder our beginnings. We doubt not now / But every rub is smoothed on our way." The hand of God, in other words, has smoothed the path to France for the English army.

Henry invokes the power of God again in act 3, scene 7, on the night before the battle at Agincourt. Gloucester hopes that the French might not attack; but Henry says: "We are in God's hand, brother, not in theirs." Then again in act 4, scene 3, in his speech to the troops before the big battle, Henry tries to cheer his men up. They all know by now that the French outnumber them overwhelmingly, and yet Henry tells them "The fewer men, the greater share of honor. / God's will! I pray thee wish not one man more." With this statement, Henry is telling his men that the fact that the numbers are stacked against them is God's will. With the French army so big and the English army so small, the English victory will be that much more significant. Henry is also warning his men not to pray for something that God has already ordained. If God means for them to go against a bigger army, then so be it.

Arrogance Leading to Misconception

Shakespeare's French characters are arrogant in many different ways. The first demonstration of this arrogance is the Dauphin's so-called gift of tennis balls, signifying that the Dauphin takes Henry's threat to his French crown as insignificant as a game of tennis. Later, the Dauphin plays down the danger involved in Henry's crossing the English Channel and landing on

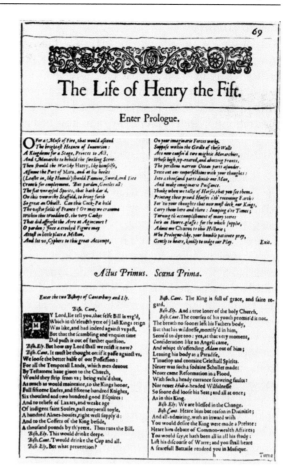

Title page of Henry V *from the First Folio (1623)* (© Bettmann/Corbis)

French soil. His arrogance appears to infect some of the other nobles, even up to the point of the night before the battle at Agincourt, after Henry has ravaged Harfleur. The arrogance of the French makes them blind to their own disadvantages, or weaknesses. They boast about their horses and weaponry and make jokes about the English, instead of investigating the battlefield or spying on them. They do question where the English get their strength, but their attitude is so saturated with arrogance that they cannot perceive that the English might hurt them, let alone completely defeat them.

In contrast, Shakespeare has the English appear as humble commoners, men who believe they might see another day. Instead of arrogance, they are filled with the passion to capture what is rightfully theirs. The king bows to a higher source, putting his life and the lives of his men in God's hands.

Responsibility

Responsibility is another theme that runs through this play. It begins with the first act, when King Henry warns the archbishop to carefully weigh his decision as to whether or not England has a right to the French throne. In essence, Henry is telling the archbishop that what he says and how he has interpreted the law could cost lives and bring hardships, as well as change the course of history.

Later, in act 2, scene 2, when Henry confronts the three traitors, he somewhat contradicts himself in terms of responsibility. Henry excuses the man who "railed against our person," as Henry states it, forgiving the man's irresponsible behavior because the man was drunk. However, when it comes to Scroop, Grey, and Cambridge, the traitors, Henry tells them that they will lose their lives. As Henry makes clear, they have not acted responsibly, for by assassinating the king, they would have put so many others at risk. Further, Scroop, Grey, and Cambridge received money from the enemy French to execute the plot. The consequences of their actions, Henry says, would have been enormous. It was their responsibility as nobles to have thought the assassination through. Whereas the drunken man might have only muttered a vagrant, impulsive thought, the king holds the nobles to a higher standard because they had a better sense of the consequences.

In act 4, scene 1, the idea of responsibility appears for a third time. Henry disguises himself on the night before the battle at Agincourt. He then has conversations with some of his men. Two of those soldiers, Bates and Williams, question the king concerning the battle they are about to fight and whose responsibility it is. The men say that it is the king's. Henry, however, only takes part of that responsibility. He says the king is responsible for the war, but each man must take responsibility for his own life. Every subject's duty is to the king, but every subject's soul is his own. If, in other words, a soldier believes that what the king tells him to do is wrong, then it is on the soldier's conscience if he does the thing he believes is wrong. If the king knows it is wrong but the soldier carries out whatever act the king requests, then the wrong is on the king's conscience.

Cultural Stereotypes

As in many of Shakespeare's other plays, there is a discussion about cultural differences. Whether it is the difference between the Italians and the Moors in Shakespeare's *Othello* or the Italians and the Jews in *The Merchant of Venice*, some characters clash because they come from dissimilar countries. In *Henry V* this occurs between the French and English, as well as between the Scots, the Irish, and the English.

The French make references to the English, such as in act 3, scene 5, when the Constable refers to the English as being cold and pale because their climate is "foggy, raw, and dull." In comparison, the Constable claims, the French are enlivened with "quick blood, spirited with wine." And then before the big battle at Agincourt, the French noble Orleans refers to the English soldiers as King Henry's "fat-brained followers." Even when the French Rambures tries to find something good to say about the English, he is put down by his peers. Rambures thinks that the English are valiant. He points to the brave mastiffs (a large breed of dog) that the English raise. But Orleans points out that though the mastiffs are brave, they are also stupid, rushing a large bear only to have their heads chomped off.

It is not just the French who point out cultural stereotypes, though. Some of Henry's men do the same among themselves. Although their conversation is not as blatantly warped in stereotypes, there is a strain in relationships between Fluellen, who is Welsh, and Macmorris, who is Irish. They are both fighting at the command of an English king for a united cause, but Fluellen seems determined to prove that Macmorris knows nothing of Roman war tactics, which Fluellen, obviously holds in high esteem. At one point in their discussion in act 3, scene 2, Fluellen calls to Macmorris by saying "there is not many of your nation—" and is then interrupted by Macmorris, who has taken offense. "Of my nation? What ish [sic] my nation?" It can be assumed that Fluellen was about to make a broad, generalized statement about the Irish. Macmorris would not let Fluellen finish what he was saying because he sensed the stereotypical statement coming.

Shakespeare often writes his parts for Irish, French, Welsh, and Scottish characters in broken English. In some plays, he also has some of his English characters make fun of the accents. There were political tensions between these countries, and such tensions can lead to stereotyping. Whether Shakespeare was just reflecting these stereotypes so that his audience could analyze them or think about them, or whether Shakespeare used the

TOPICS FOR FURTHER STUDY

- Research the battle at Agincourt. Bring to class a display of the details you have uncovered. The display can be in the form of a chart, a series of photographs, a PowerPoint demonstration, or any other presentation of your choice. The idea is to try to mimic the battle at Agincourt with as much detail as possible. What were the strategies of the French? Of the English? What types of weapons did each side use? How many soldiers were involved? How many horses on each side? What were the jobs of the young boys? Provide as much information as you can gather.

- Find as many portraits of King Henry V as you can, then create a likeness of the monarch. You can use any medium you choose: oil paint, charcoal, water color, pen and ink. You can also make a three-dimensional bust out of clay or other material. By some historical accounts, Henry was called an ugly king. What do you think? Ask your classmates to vote on Henry's looks.

- Imagine that you lived in the Middle Ages in England. Your cousin lived in France. How would your lives differ? How would they be the same? After doing your research for this topic, write two letters: one from you as a teenager in England and a response from your French cousin. In the letters talk about the activities, the challenges, the entertainment, and details of your family life that you might have experienced in the course of one week. Read your letters to your class.

- Find out about the medical practices at the time of the Battle at Agincourt. How were the wounds of soldiers treated? Were there any antiseptics? Were there pain killers? How did medics fix broken bones? How did they sew wounds closed? How did they treat dysentery? Were there any other typical diseases that the soldiers were vulnerable to, especially on a long march, such as the English soldiers had to endure? Share your research with your class.

- Map out the journey that King Henry took from London to Agincourt. How did the army travel? How many miles did some soldiers have to walk? How long did it take them to cross the English Channel? Show all your details on a map and present your findings to your class.

---

stereotypical statements to make his audiences laugh, or whether he used them because he himself was caught up in the stereotypes is not certain.

STYLE

Shakespearian Language Specific to Henry V

While analysis of the language in *Henry V* has yielded different critical interpretations, most scholars agree that the rhetoric used in this play makes a significant contribution to the drama's theme, tone, and meaning. For example, some critics point out that the language requires strenuous effort from its actors to perform, as well as requiring effort from audiences to grasp. These critics point out that this effort relates to the atmosphere of activity in the play as the king decides to go to war and then must prepare his men for the arduous journey and grueling battles that must be fought. Other critics focus on how the language changes as it parallels the preparations for war, the battles, and then the peaceful conclusion. The mode of speech changes from beginning to end, starting with a tone of agreement (the choric appeal to English nationalism, the request for cooperation between the performer and the audience, and the first scenes showing the church and state working together), then moving to a tone of dispute during the war, and concluding with a return to a softer tone as Henry woos Katherine.

Critics also have often debated whether the language of *Henry V* equals that found in the first two plays of Shakespeare's second tetralogy, which includes *Richard II* and *Henry IV*. A number of scholars contend that the language is flatter and less powerful in *Henry V* than in the previous plays. *Richard II* and *Henry IV* contain speeches and passages that are more poetic, they say. However, other critics maintain that the prose in *Henry V* is more natural and deceptively close to common speech, making the depth and artistry of the language more subtle and equally as artful as in the more prominent speeches in Shakespeare's other plays.

Epic Elements

Shakespeare's use of epic elements in *Henry V* has elicited much critical attention. By far the most panoramic of his plays, *Henry V* dramatizes an epic theme and celebrates a legendary hero. According to several scholars, the play therefore fulfills most of the formal requirements of classical epic, in that its hero is of national significance; it emphasizes destiny and the will of God; its action is impressive in scale and centers upon war; and it includes a narrator (the Chorus), an invocation to the Muse, a large number of warriors, battle taunts and challenges, and other traditional epic devices. Most commentators agree that Shakespeare's use of epic elements contributes significantly to the success of the play, stating that an epic drama is the only fitting way to celebrate the noble deeds of Henry V.

Scholars repeatedly focus on the role of the Chorus in exposing the limitations of the Elizabethan stage. Many critics remark that the function of the Chorus is to apologize for the unsuitability of the stage to the grandeur of an epic. However, other commentators point out that Shakespeare's audience would never have expected the kind of cinematic realism that modern theatergoers have come to expect. Though the Chorus fulfills several functions as narrator—creating atmosphere, explaining lapses of time and shifts in locale, apologizing for the limitations of the theater—its most important function is to evoke an epic mood. The Chorus also creates structural unity in the play by building narrative bridges between the five acts.

Dramatic Soliloquy

A soliloquy is a speech given as if the actor were talking to him- or herself, exposing thoughts and emotions but supposedly doing so without anyone (but the audience) hearing what is being said. It is like an interior monologue that one might have with oneself. Through the soliloquy, the actor not only offers the audience a glimpse into his or her inner thoughts but also into his or her personality or character. In *Henry V*, on the night before the battle at Agincourt, Henry considers his role as king through a soliloquy. One of his men has engaged Henry in a discussion of responsibility. Henry reflects on the topic when he is alone. His thoughts are private. It can be assumed that he does not want his men to know how he feels. It is an important reflection, one that Shakespeare wanted the audience to hear and to remember. The soliloquy is written in iambic pentameter, ten stressed and unstressed syllables to each line, providing a regulated rhythm. The form is blank verse, so it flows like poetry but there is no rhyme.

Dramatic Monologue

Henry V has many monologues, which are speeches of several lines in length delivered in a drama by one individual to one or more person without expectations of anyone responding. The monologues stand out from the normal dialogue because they are long, for one thing, but also because they too, like soliloquies, are written in blank verse. All of the Prologues that open every act are written as monologues, as are many of the English king's speeches to his troops. Some of the more powerful monologues of the king include Henry's rebuttal to the Dauphin after having sent the tennis balls (in act 1, scene 2), that begins, "We are glad the Dauphin is so pleasant with us," which sets in motion England going to war with France. Another powerful monologue is the one the king delivers to Scroop in act 2, scene 2, which begins, "God quit you in his mercy! Hear your sentence." This monologue depicts the heavy consequences that the traitors would have inflicted on their country had they killed Henry. Finally, to arouse his men before the battle at Agincourt, King Henry delivers his monologue about the Feast of Crispian. The monologue is found in act 4, scene 3, and begins "What's he that wishes so?" As these monologues demonstrate, this form of writing makes certain parts of the play stand out. Through the monologues, particular passages are etched in the minds of audiences, so they take home the more important messages of the play.

HISTORICAL CONTEXT

Henry V

Henry was born in Wales, in 1387, the oldest son of Henry of Bolingbroke (later to become King Henry IV) and Mary Bohun. In 1398, Henry's father was exiled by the reigning monarch, Richard II, who kept Henry's son and raised him in court. Henry's father snuck back into England the following year, while Richard II was at war in Ireland. He gathered forces and won claim to land throughout the country and was eventually named king. Richard II was imprisoned and later died. The line of inheritance then switched to Henry, which caused much jealousy in the line of Richard II's heirs, Henry's cousins.

Henry was quite an accomplished soldier, having seen battle at the early age of fourteen. Two years later, at the age of sixteen, Henry commanded his father's troops at the battle of Shrewsbury. It was at this battle that Henry received a severe wound, an arrow striking him in the face. Until 1408, Henry was often involved in squelching uprisings in Wales.

Shortly after his coronation, Henry V fought down an uprising by Lollards (members of a religious and political movement led by the theologian John Wyclif) outside of London and put an end to an assassination plot by some of his nobles who were still seeking to restore the monarchy to the descendants of Richard II.

As his reign became somewhat settled at home, King Henry V turned his attention to France. Although Shakespeare puts forward the theory that church officials instigated the move, others have speculated that the feebleness of Charles VI of France, who was said to have a mental illness, and the ineptness of his son might also have concerned Henry, who would have benefited from a more stable France. And so he decided to claim the throne. He asked for the French king's daughter's hand prior to leaving England, but the French king refused. Henry had no other choice than to invade France and take the throne by force.

After wining the battle at Agincourt, Henry later went on to capture Normandy and Rouen. He was beating a path toward Paris. In 1419, the French gave in to Henry. A year later, Henry signed the Treaty of Troyes and married King Charles VI's daughter, Katherine. As stated in the treaty, King Charles VI of France would by- pass his own son as heir to the French throne, thus giving it to Henry.

In 1421, Katherine was crowned Henry's queen and gave birth to a son, who became Henry VI upon his father's death. Henry died of dysentery in 1422 while engaged in battle in France. Had Henry lived two months longer, he would have been crowned king of both England and France. Henry V reigned over England from 1413 until his death in 1422.

Charles VI

Charles VI of France was known by two sub-titles: Charles the Beloved and Charles the Mad. Charles was born in 1368 and ruled France from 1380 until 1422, making him only forty-seven years old at the time of the battle at Agincourt. Although he was not that old, he was infirm by then with what might today be diagnosed as schizophrenia or possibly bipolar disorder. He was known for attacking some of his own men on their way to battle, running naked through the palace, and at times believing he was made of glass. Some believe that the king's daughter, Katherine, passed the king's mental illness onto her son, the future king of England, Henry VI. The king's mental illness also led many people in France to believe that the Treaty of Troyes, which would have made Henry V king of France, was invalid.

English Pastimes during Henry V's Reign

Although war, the plague, and famine were all too familiar in fifteenth-century England, there were ways in which people also celebrated or otherwise enjoyed themselves. There were competitions, such as in archery, a popular sport. Given the military uses of the bow and arrow, archery could be very competitive. But competition could also be seen in an early version of English football (soccer). A game called camp ball, in which teams of men and women engaged, was played with a ball made of a pig's bladder filled with dried beans. Hunting and fishing were two other sports that not only provided food for the table but were also considered good training for young boys who would more than likely end up serving in the military. The young nobles often rode horses and followed a pack of dogs that either killed the animals or held them at bay, waiting for the young men to arrive with their bows and arrows.

Tournaments, testing the skill and courage of knights, lords, and other combatants, were often held throughout the country. Lances were most often used by two men who rode at full charge toward one another. Sometimes a wooden barrier would be placed between the two sides of the track to keep the men's horses from running into one another. Although these tournaments were also looked at as training for military maneuvers, sometimes the two opponents were settling a personal grudge.

But not every entertainment related to warfare. There were also parlor games such as cards, dice, and board games, like early versions of backgammon and chess. Card games offered the players a chance to gamble. The cards that were used were often made of wood and painted by hand. There were also sports such as wrestling, horse racing, and cockfighting to while away the time.

In the arts, mystery plays, derived from stories in the Bible, were very popular. Morality plays, which were meant to teach a specific lesson, were also common fare. These plays were often acted on stages on the backs of wagons that rolled from one town to the next.

Fifteenth-Century English Longbow

One of the reasons the English enjoyed many victories over Ireland, Wales, and France was because of the soldiers' proficiency with longbows. Rather than the normal bow of about three feet in length, longbows were at least five to six feet long, as tall or taller than the men that used them. The weapons were light to carry, cheap to own, blasted an arrow a long distance, and were easy to master. Arrows shot from longbows were also devastatingly powerful, creating deep and wide wounds. The arrows could fly, by some estimates, two hundred or more yards. Longbows were easily reloaded and a master archer could shoot from ten to twenty arrows a minute, some records state. Even after the introduction of the first firearms, bowmen using longbows could shoot several arrows before the newfangled guns could fire one bullet.

It is believed that a typical longbow was made from a single sapling from an English yew. It took several years of curing and shaping for a bow to be fit to use. The string of the bow was made of flax or hemp. Arrows were about twenty-seven inches long, with four-inch arrowheads equipped with barbs that made them difficult to extract.

The War Campaign to France and the Battle at Agincourt

King Henry V needed money to finance programs. He also needed to strengthen his image, which was contaminated by his flamboyant youth. Claiming the throne of France and committing himself and his troops to take it by force would serve those two causes, if he were victorious.

King Henry and his ships landed at Harfleur on the northern coast of France on August 13, 1415. The English met with no resistance upon landing and soon marched to the town, which was well fortified with a thick wall more than two miles in diameter with numerous towers. The English had several cannons and catapults. Their troops numbered over ten thousand, with roughly eight thousand archers and two thousand mounted soldiers. The French were said to have about four hundred fighting men. The town had a large cache of food and supplies, however, so there was no hope of starving them into an early surrender.

The English battered the walls around Harfleur and dug tunnels under them, crumbling the city's best defense. The conflict lasted until September 22. Although successful in the battle at Harfleur, the English suffered many casualties, possibly as many as one-third of the men. Most were lost to illness. The battle was fought in the heat of summer; and the makeshift camp had no proper sanitation. Dysentery soon swept through the camp, the same illness that would kill the young king seven years later. After the battle at Harfleur, the town became an English seaport.

From Harfleur, Henry drove his troops toward Calais, an English stronghold, hoping to spend the winter there, giving him time to re-equip his army. Unfortunately for King Henry and his troops, the French, under Constable d'Albret, had gathered between Calais and Harfleur and forced the English into battle. The English army had marched over two hundred miles, were running out of food, and many were still sick. They were in no condition to fight a rested, well-armored enemy. The English followed the coastline to the Somme River, then they turned east, looking for a safe place to ford the river. The fall had been a very rainy one; and the river was very full and dangerous. The French troops stationed themselves at a place of safe crossing, forcing Henry and his army to travel farther east, away from Calais, before they could cross the river. This added miles as well as days to their march, depleting the food supplies

COMPARE
&
CONTRAST

- **1400s:** The English forces under King Henry V's leadership defeat the French heavily armored army, which outnumbered them five to one, by employing longbows and fast-loading arrows.

  Today: Terrorists wreak havoc on well-equipped United States and British troops in Iraq, employing guerrilla war tactics such as suicide bombings.

- **1400s:** King Henry V leads his troops in battle in an attempt to claim the English right to the French throne.

  Today: Queen Elizabeth II visits French president Jacques Chirac to celebrate the one-hundredth anniversary of the signing of the Franco-British Accords, a pact to join forces in military defense of their countries.

- **1400s:** King Henry V marries the daughter of King Charles VI of France, strengthening the royal bond between France and England. The marriage is well received in London.

Today: Heir to the British throne, Prince Charles marries Camilla Parker Bowles, duchess of Cornwall. Camilla, who has a right to be called queen once her husband is crowned, will defer the title, because of public resentment toward her. The public disapproved of Camilla and Prince Charles's adulterous affair while Charles was still married to Princess Diana.

- **1400s:** The town of Harfleur is a bustling fishing port and a center of the cloth trade with an emphasis on weaving and dyeing. It sits at the mouth of Seine River on the English Channel.

  Today: Harfleur is a town of industries and is most often considered a suburb of Le Havre. Population is estimated at less than 10,000. Due to heavy silting of the estuary of the Seine, Harfleur is no longer a major port on the English Channel.

---

further and exhausting the men. On the other side of the river, the French army was waiting at Agincourt, in between Henry and Calais. Henry did not want to fight; but he would not back down. He wanted the throne and would not stop at anything less.

It had been raining for many days. The field at Agincourt had been recently plowed and was now swampy. This would work to the English army's advantage. The French were heavy with armor, both the men and their horses. Once they fell down, many became stuck in the mud, which in some places was waist deep. At least one French duke was said to have drowned. The English troops, many in bare feet and bare legs, had less trouble moving on the muddy field. Another advantage was the passion of King Henry as the leader of the English troops. The frail French king did not lead his men, and the French army suffered greatly from disorganization. Most of the nobles

led the first line of the French troops. When they fell, the ranks to the rear of the French army fled.

France lost ten thousand men, many from the French nobility, including Constable d'Albret. The French military would go on, in future decades, to learn from this experience, taking back the land the English once claimed. But on this day, Saint Crispin's Day, October 25, the English were victorious.

The Hundred Years' War

The battle at Agincourt was just one of the many bloody conflicts between England and France. A fight for land and kingship had been going on for many decades before King Henry V and would continue for a few decades after his death. England and France fought one another almost continually between 1337 and 1453. This long battle is referred to as the Hundred Years' War.

The claim of English royalty to the French crown has a long and complicated history. It all began before the structured nations that are known today had created sturdy foundations. At one time, for instance, the Normans came into the northern part of France in the tenth century and claimed the territory. The Normans then, under the leadership of William the Conqueror, moved across the channel and claimed England in the century that followed. As descendants of William the Conqueror, English kings claimed the right to Normandy and other lands in what is today French territory. As time went by, England, through a series of battles, lost more and more of that French land; and the Hundred Years' War marks England's concerted effort to finally reclaim it and the authority to rule the people who lived there.

King Edward III, angered by the continual erosion of his control over the lands in France, claimed he was the rightful king of both England and France and went to war to force the French to surrender to him. Edward eventually captured Calais, the English stronghold that Henry V was trying to reach after his battle in Harfleur. Another war ended in 1373, this time with the French winning. That set the scene for Henry V, who regained the right to the French throne. By 1429, England again controlled a lot of French territory. This would be the high point of English control in France. By 1451, almost all land had been restored to France, except that of Calais. England became distracted by its own wars at home after that and stopped pursuing its claim of authority over France.

CRITICAL OVERVIEW

In her Introduction to the 1999 Penguin Books published texts of *Henry V*, Claire McEachern writes that *Henry V* is both "the capstone and the keystone of Shakespeare's engagement with the English history play." This play, McEachern continues, "portrays a high, and perhaps unique, moment in English national history, when it represents a country both internally unified and internationally victorious." Structurally, McEachern points out, "Shakespeare signals" a "contrast between ideal and real perspectives on political community." He does so through the use of a Chorus before every act. It is through the Chorus, McEachern writes, that Shakespeare sets up the ideal, "relentlessly optimistic and positive in presenting future events." This contrasts with the scenes that follow, which often conflict with that positive attitude, such as depicting treason and battles that must be fought. "But if Shakespeare refuses to let the ideal vision of warfare and national unity stand unmolested, at the same time he insists, in an inspiring and rousing rhetoric, on the ennobling capacities of participation in a myth of unity and union." McEachern emphasizes the power of the dramatic monologue that King Henry delivers at Agincourt right before the battle. "Henry produces what is undoubtedly among the most spine-tingling of calls to battle in Shakespeare or anywhere else."

In concluding her critique of the play, McEachern writes, "The idealizing pressures of *Henry V* may at times cloy and coerce; but we ultimately forgive the play its glorifications, not only because we too crave a world where the underdog is the victor, few of the good guys die, and the hero gets the girl, but because we also know ... that such things are all too rare and fleeting."

Harold C. Goddard, in his book *The Meaning of Shakespeare*, begins his analysis of *Henry V* by summing up other critics' comments. "There is near-unanimity among critics that *Henry V* is not a marked success as a play," Goddard begins. Some critics, Goddard goes on, have written that Shakespeare's play "contains much that is splendid and picturesque, these merits cannot atone for [the play's] intellectual and dramatic poverty." This is not, however, Goddard's opinion. Goddard writes: "Before accepting these judgments as final, it is worth noting the presumptive unlikelihood that Shakespeare would have produced a poor play, or even a second-rate one." Goddard is of the opinion that critics who have written against this play might have overlooked Shakespeare's intentions, because *Henry V* was the "culminating play of his great historical series." The critics who relegate this play to such a low position, at this time of Shakespeare's writing career, Goddard continues, seem to believe that "Shakespeare more or less goes to pieces as a playwright and substitutes pageantry and patriotism for his proper business, drama." Goddard dispels this thought. He states that telling a story about a hero-king is a difficult task. "To tell it and to keep the piece in which you tell it popular calls for more than courage. Shakespeare did as life does. Life places both its facts and its intoxicants before us and bids us make out of the resulting clash what we can and will."

Goddard continues, "God does not indicate what we shall think of his world or of the men and women he has created. He puts them before us. But he does not compel us to see them as they are. Neither does Shakespeare."

S. Schoenbaum, writing in his book *Shakespeare, His Life, His Language, His Theater*, points to some of the criticism of this play, too. Schoenbaum, unlike some other critics, found the contradictions between the Chorus that glorified Henry and the actions of the king in the play to be inviting.

> In such contraries does criticism rejoice, and by admitting subversive countercurrents, Shakespeare invites liberty of interpretation. Each reader and viewer must decide for himself [sic] whether the hero is an exemplary Christian prince or a self-righteous imperialist, or some combination of both, and his play a sublime testimonial to national purpose or an exercise in wonderfully eloquent but essentially meretricious jingoism—or any of the innumerable gradations between these polarities.

Maurice Charney, writing in his *All of Shakespeare*, states that "the emphasis in this final play of the Major Tetralogy is on the heroic celebration of Henry as the ideal English king." Charney found much to enjoy in this play; but one particular part was the soliloquy that Henry delivers in act 4, scene 1, on kingship. "There is no speech on kingship in Shakespeare more glorious than this one," Charney writes.

CRITICISM

Anne Crow

In this essay, Crow examines how Shakespeare uses language to illuminate the title character in Henry V. *In scenes when he is acting in an official capacity, the King uses blank verse; when talking informally to his soldiers or trying to woo Katherine, in contrast, he speaks in conventional prose. Through the alternating use of these different forms of language, the critic contends, Shakespeare offers a full-blooded portrait of a man beset by doubts but rising above them to do his duty as monarch.*

Blank verse is a very versatile medium. It can sound majestic and formal, or spontaneous and colloquial. The speed can be varied by judicious choice of words and the introduction of pauses, and the basic rhythm is just asking to be tampered with to make it more interesting. Regular

> SHAKESPEARE HAS PRESENTED US WITH A KING WHO IS A CONSUMMATE ACTOR AND STAGE MANAGER, A MASTER OF THE SPIN DOCTOR'S ART."

blank verse moves at a steady walking pace, alternating stressed and unstressed syllables. There are five iambic feet to a line, and this means it starts, usually, with an unstressed syllable:

—/—/—/—/—/
Now all the youth of England are on fire

Because the movement of the verse is so simple and easy, Shakespeare can introduce any number of variations to suggest the state of mind of the speaker.

In [*Henry V*], Shakespeare uses a Chorus to introduce each act and close the play. The effect is that of a storyteller delivering an epic poem about a home-grown hero, a king who confounds early expectations to restore England's fortunes and lead a miraculous victory against the French. The style of the Chorus's poetry is elevated, as befits his lofty theme.

The Chorus actually opens the play with a lingering stress on 'O' to invoke excitement and anticipation in the audience: 'O for a muse of fire'. His lines often start with a stressed syllable as he encourages us to use our imaginations, as in the speech opening Act III where he describes the English fleet setting sail for France. Several lines start with urgent commands, 'Play', 'Hear', 'Grapple', 'Work', as he tries to compensate for the inadequacies of the theatre. The Chorus projects a heroic and majestic image of Henry at all times, comparing him with the Roman god of war, Mars, and the military hero, Caesar. Nevertheless, he sometimes refers to him as 'Harry', because an important aspect of Henry's image is that he is the people's king, loved by them for his willingness to put ceremony aside and fight alongside them, to mingle with them before the battle and to share a joke with them.

In between each Chorus, Shakespeare gives his audience glimpses of the man behind the myth, and it is significant that when Henry is cultivating his image as a soldier, one of a 'band

Patricia Routledge as Mistress Quickly in Henry
V *at the Royal Shakespeare Theatre, Stratford-
upon-Avon, England, 1984* (© *Donald Cooper/Photostage.
Reproduced by permission)*

of brothers', Shakespeare makes him speak in
prose, like the ordinary characters in the play.
A prose style forms part of his disguise when, in
disguise, he mingles with his men the night
before the Battle of Agincourt, and when he
chats easily to Llewellyn after the battle, setting
up his practical joke with Williams's glove. He
also very quickly drops into prose as he tries to
woo Katherine, adopting the pose of a gauche
soldier, laughing at himself, embarrassed and
lost for words. It seems to be a more intimate
way of speaking than the poetry which is appropriate when he is on his dignity as a king rather
than a man.

His one soliloquy (IV.i.227–81) is a particularly appropriate speech to show how the structure of the poetry helps the actor to portray
Henry's real fears and doubts, which he keeps
masked whenever there is anyone with him, and

which the Chorus never mentions. Near the
beginning of this speech he asks eight questions,
all beginning with 'What'. Several lines are
shorter than the usual ten syllables, making the
actor pause, as if to think about the answers to
the questions which are all asking what advantage he has as king over his subjects, what the
'ceremony' is really worth. When he answers his
long list, ten negatives help to build up the tension as he concludes that none of the symbols
that represent royalty can enable the king to sleep
as soundly as the most wretched of his subjects.
He then summarises his argument so far with
more emphatic negatives, 'No, not all these,
thrice gorgeous ceremony, / Not all these …'.
As he moves on from lamenting the insubstantial
nature of a king's advantages to expressing envy
of 'the wretched slave', his subject, Shakespeare
gives Henry one long, complex sentence with no
repetition, in which to describe in positive terms
the apparently idyllic life of the peasant. So
caught up is Henry in his self-pity that he fails
to see the irony in his words at the end of the
speech, describing 'what watch the king keeps to
maintain the peace', when, in fact, he has led his
people into war and put his army in a position
where it must fight a battle heavily outnumbered,
five to one.

This speech most clearly reveals the conflict
in a king's role, what the Elizabethans called the
king's two bodies: he is both a public figure and a
private man. A good king will suppress his private feelings in front of others, acting out whatever role he needs to play. Here, however,
Shakespeare shows us a man under stress, and
this is very important to the way Henry is presented; the audience can see for themselves that,
as he tells the soldiers, 'I think the king is but a
man as I am' (IV.i.102). He chooses an interesting image to illustrate his essential humanity:
'The violet smells to him as it doth to me'. A
violet is a shy, secretive flower, hiding under its
leaves in dark, wooded places, not at all like the
showy rose, which is the usual emblem of kings.
However, it is in the prayer which follows the
soliloquy that we learn how vulnerable he feels,
begging God not to remember how his father
usurped the throne from his cousin, Richard:
'Not today, O Lord, / O not today, think not
upon the fault …'. The repetition and the multiple breaks in the line help to reveal his troubled
conscience, as he lists everything he has done to
try to atone for this crime and promises to do
more, though a note of despair creeps in at the

end, as he acknowledges that it is too late, because the sin has been committed and all he can do is implore pardon (IV.i.286–302).

When he rejoins his army, however, all doubts and fears are masked behind the persona of a calmly confident monarch. There is no hint of the bitterness and panic of the previous night, as he evokes a golden future for the survivors of the battle, who will be honoured as heroes for the rest of their lives. In a magnanimous confidence trick, he declares:

/——/—/——/—/
Rather proclaim it, Westmoreland, through my host

that anyone who does not want to fight will be given more money and allowed to leave (this may sound like a generous offer, but they are in the middle of enemy territory). By placing 'Rather' at the beginning of the line so that it alters the expected stress pattern, Shakespeare subtly heightens the contrast of the confidence of Henry's gesture with the fear which prompted Westmoreland's wish for more soldiers.

In this speech Henry glosses over the brutality of war, because he does not want to frighten his men before the battle. The only mention of wounds is a brief reference to the scars on his arm that a theoretical soldier will show his friends in future years. This is in sharp contrast to the violent and bloody speech in Act III Scene iv with which he frightens the men of Harfleur into surrendering. There, because his men were tired, sick and unwilling to fight, he had to pretend that they were brutal killers. This is a carefully prepared speech, composed in regular iambic pentameters, which suggests control or even lack of emotion. Shakespeare seems to suggest that Henry is not enjoying the prospect of 'naked infants spitted upon pikes' or 'heads dashed to the walls', but nor is he disturbed by it. This impression is reinforced by the calm composure he shows as the governor submits, and the English army wins its first battle on French soil. There is no gloating, no triumph, just the realisation that 'winter is coming' and 'sickness growing upon our soldiers', and the gentle command 'use mercy to them all' in the town. Shakespeare presents Henry as a king who can be whatever is needed in any situation, threatening or merciful, whichever is appropriate.

There are times, however, when his private feelings seem to break through his composure. His answer to the Dauphin's insulting gift of tennis balls in Act I Scene ii is polite and witty.

His first reaction to the 'tun of treasure' is expressed using the royal 'we'. His threat is at first disguised in an elaborate metaphor comparing the coming war with a game of tennis. Tongue firmly in cheek, he thanks the ambassador for the gift and seems to take pleasure in turning the insult back on the Dauphin, revealing a quick wit but with very sinister undertones, 'We will in France, by God's grace, play a set / Shall strike his father's crown into the hazard'. He says that he understands why the Dauphin underestimates him because of the 'wilder days' of his youth, but warns that he is 'not measuring what use we made of them'—a reminder to the audience that even while he seemed to be profligate in his youth, a soliloquy at the beginning of Henry IV, Part I reveals that he was already calculating the effect of his actions.

Shakespeare now presents Henry as beginning to lose control of his temper and show how much the Dauphin's gibe has upset him as he stops using the formal plural pronoun 'we' and lapses into the personal 'I will keep my state'. He effectively uses imagery to project a mighty show of strength, declaring that he will 'show my sail of greatness / When I do rouse in my throne of France'. The sails of his ships crossing the channel, and his army's flags and banners will announce his right to the kingdom of France, and significantly this is the first time that Henry has explicitly stated to the French that total domination of France is the aim, rather than just claiming back dukedoms that had previously belonged to England. Once again he compares himself to the sun, but, whereas in Henry IV, Part I he intended to appear brighter because of the contrast with his misspent youth (the clouds), here he turns the image into a threat: as he rises in France, the Dauphin will be struck 'blind to look on us'. He reverts to the royal 'we' as he gets his anger back under control to build up to a climactic rhyming couplet in which he warns of the consequences of 'the Dauphin's scorn'. He implies that it is the latter which has persuaded him to go to war and turns the blame for the invasion, which had in fact already been planned, onto the Dauphin: 'his soul / Shall stand sore-charged for the wasteful vengeance'. Shakespeare's choice of words allows the actor to spit out his challenge and contempt with extra stressed syllables and the plosive final consonant of the four times repeated 'mock'.

Nevertheless, we cannot be sure that Shakespeare intended this scene to give insight into Henry's vulnerability. Since he has an audience, it may be a clever piece of play-acting. He may pretend to be hurt and offended so that he can shift the blame for his invasion of France onto the Dauphin. Because of his father's usurpation of the throne, Henry feels insecure, and so Shakespeare shows him shifting the blame from his own shoulders onto others at every opportunity.

The Chorus persuasively narrates the myth of Henry as 'the mirror of all Christian kings', the 'conquering Caesar' who modestly attributes his apparently miraculous achievement to God, the caring leader who boosted the morale of his troops with 'A little touch of Harry in the night'. However, the scenes in between the Chorus's eulogies raise doubts. Instead of spreading 'A largess universal like the sun', Shakespeare shows Henry in disguise, spying on his soldiers because he lacks confidence in their loyalty. When he abandons his former friends, breaking Falstaff's heart and sending Bardolph and Scroop to be executed, the audience is left with a feeling that, although his actions are politically expedient, a hint of private grief and remorse would have made him a more likeable hero. Shakespeare has presented us with a king who is a consummate actor and stage manager, a master of the spin doctor's art. However, as with all spin doctors, while we may admire the skill and rhetoric, we rarely sympathise with him; kingship is a lonely office.

Source: Anne Crow, "Henry V Man and Myth: Anne Crow Shows How Shakespeare's Use of Poetry in *Henry V* Can Illuminate Our Understanding of the Character of the King," in *The English Review*, Vol. 13, No. 2, November 2002, pp. 31–34.

D. A. Traversi

In the following excerpt from an essay first published in 1956, Traversi observes Henry's moral and political conflict between self-control and passion. He contends that as king, Henry must possess a complete devotion to his position and cannot allow selfishness to affect his decisions. Traversi argues that Henry V *provides the link between political unity and personal order in England. He also traces Henry's struggle throughout the play with personal control and order.*

The political success aimed at by Henry IV is finally achieved, in the last play of the series, by his son. The general theme of *Henry V* is the

> THE PROBLEM OF POLITICAL UNITY AND THAT OF PERSONAL ORDER HAVE BEEN BROUGHT IN THE COURSE OF THESE HISTORICAL STUDIES INTO THE CLOSEST RELATIONSHIP."

establishment in England of an order based on consecrated authority and crowned by action against France. The conditions of this order are, again in accordance with the main conception, moral as well as political. The crime of regicide which had stood between Bolingbroke and the attainment of peace no longer hangs over Henry V—unless as a disturbing memory—and the crusading purpose which had run as an unfulfilled aspiration through the father's life is replaced by the reality, at once brilliant and ruthless, of the son's victorious campaign.

This, as critics have not always realized, is less a conclusion than a point of departure for the understanding of *Henry V*. It was the conditions of kingship, at least as much as its results, that interested Shakespeare in these plays: and these conditions are viewed, by the time the last of them came to be conceived, in a light definitely akin to the tragic. The problem of political unity and that of personal order have been brought in the course of these historical studies into the closest relationship. The former has been achieved, in the preceding plays, by the development of a political capacity that recalls, in various of its aspects, the Machiavellian conception of the Prince; but success of this kind increasingly poses for Shakespeare, whose thought was at once more traditional and less limited to the political than that of the great Florentine, wider problems more definitely moral, even religious, in kind. Just as the state, already in *Henry IV*-Part II, is regarded in its divisions as a diseased body ravaged by a consuming fever, so is the individual seen increasingly as torn between the violence of his passions and the direction of reason; and just as the remedy to political anarchy lies in unquestioned allegiance to an authority divinely constituted, so does personal coherence depend upon the submission to reason of our uncontrolled desires. The link between the two states, political and personal, is provided in these plays by concentration upon the figure of the king. The problem of the state becomes that of the individual at its head. The king, who properly demands unquestioning allegiance from his subjects, is first called upon to show, through the perfection of his dedication, a complete and selfless devotion to his office. The personal implications, as well as the patriotic triumphs, which that devotion brings with it are considered in *Henry V.*

It demands, in the first place, an absolute measure of self-domination. Called upon to exercise justice and shape policies for the common good, the king can allow no trace of selfishness or frailty to affect his decisions. He must continually examine his motives, confirm them in the light of reason; and this means that he is engaged in a continual struggle against his share of human weakness. As the play proceeds, we become increasingly aware that there is in Henry an uneasy balance between violent passion, in certain of its forms, and firm self-control. The control is, indeed, an essential part of his political capacity and of his personal stature. Without it, Henry would not be a true king at all; but, precisely because he is a man and not a crowned puppet, there are times when an unmistakable sense of constraint makes itself felt, as for instance in his greeting to the French ambassador:

> We are no tyrant, but a Christian king;
> Unto whose grace our passion is as subject
> As are our wretches fettered in our prisons.
> (I.ii)

The harshness of the comparison is, to say the least, remarkable. Such control, though admirable, and doubly so in a king, is necessarily precarious. The passions, "fettered," treated with a disdain similar to that which, as Prince Hal, he has already displayed to the considerations of normal feeling when the fulfillment of his vocation imposed the renunciation of his past, may be expected to break out in forms not immediately attractive.

Almost at once, in fact, they do so. The French envoys, in fulfilling their mission by presenting him with the Dauphin's tennis balls, touch upon a raw spot in Henry's sensibility; they expose him to ridicule and, worst of all, they refer—by the observation that "You cannot revel into dukedoms here"—to the abjured but not forgotten past. Henry's reaction, in spite of the opening affirmation of self-control, takes the form of one of those outbursts which are habitual with him whenever his will is crossed. As when France was to be "bent" or "broken," his rhetoric, measured and even cold on the surface, is full of accumulated passion:

> When we have match'd our rackets to
>   these balls,
> We will, in France, by God's grace, play a
>   set
> Shall strike his father's crown into the
>   hazard.
> (I.ii)

The reference to "God's grace," rarely omitted from Henry's official utterances, clearly befits a Christian king, and we need not deny its propriety; but from the personal point of view, which the play is also concerned to stress, the note of resentment which rises through the speech is equally significant. It rankles at this point until the real motive, or an important part of it, becomes at last explicit:

> we understand him well,
> How he comes o'er us with our wilder days,
> Not measuring what use we made of them.
> (I.ii)

The personal offense once mentioned, the considerations of conscience are swept aside, at least for so long as the new emotion is in command. The horrors of war, the slaughter and misery attendant upon it, are once again mentioned, but only that he may disclaim responsibility for them. The tone for his words, following the swell of emotion, rises to one of ruthless and triumphant egoism:

> But *I* will rise there with so full a glory
> That *I* will dazzle all the eyes of France,
> Yea, strike the Dauphin blind to look on us.
> And tell the pleasant prince this mock of his
> Hath turn'd his balls to gun-stones; and his
>   soul
> Shall stand sore charged for the wasteful
>   vengeance
> That shall fly with them: for many a thou-
>   sand widows
> Shall this his mock mock out of their dear
>   husbands;
> Mock mothers from their sons, mock castles
>   down;
> And some are yet ungotten and unborn
> That shall have cause to curse the Dauphin's
>   scorn.
> (I.ii)

Kenneth Branagh and Emma Thompson in a scene from the 1989 film of Henry V *(Reproduced by permission of The Picture Desk, Inc.)*

"*I* will rise there"; "*I* will dazzle all the eyes of France." The Dauphin's gibe has set free Henry's "fettered" passion and these express themselves in a cumulative vision of destruction. The tone of the utterance—the impact of "strike," the harsh reference to the balls which have been turned to "gun-*stones*," the sense of irresistible, ruinous force behind "mock castles down"—reflects the new feeling and anticipates the later, more masterly picture of Coriolanus in action. This is not to say that we are to regard Henry as a monster at this point, or to deny that a proper sense of royal responsibility underlies his words. He is uttering a warning, condemning the real irresponsibility of others; but the speech has, beyond this, an intimate content which is also part of the complete effect. The sense of power, inhuman and destructive beneath the surface of righteous anger, has been unleashed in the king. The responsibility for coming events, already assumed by the Archbishop of Canterbury earlier in the same scene, has now been further fastened upon the Dauphin, and Henry is in a position to announce his coming descent upon France with a phrase that incorporates into his new vehemence the convenient certainty of righteousness:

> But all this lies within the will of God,
> To whom I do appeal.

No doubt the conviction is sincere; but the fact remains that the will of God and the will of Henry, now fused in the passion released by the Dauphin's jest, have become identical.

It is not until the opening of the French campaign that Henry's utterances are translated into action. The poetry of war in this play deserves careful attention. Much of it, corresponding to the spirit of the patriotic chronicle, is full of life and vigor; such is the elaborate description in the Prologue to this same act of the "fleet majestical" which bears the English forces to Harfleur. The king "embarks his royalty" on a "brave fleet," adorned and lighted by the dawn:

> behold the threaden sails,
> Borne with the invisible and creeping wind,
> Draw the huge bottoms through the furrow'd sea,
> Breasting the lofty surge: O, do but think

You stand upon the rivage and behold
A city on the inconstant billows dancing;
For so appears this fleet majestical.
(III. Prologue)

Such imagery, splendidly and consciously laden for its effect, is a contribution to the spirit of the play. It may be that some of its deeper notes are not included in it, but the effect of a pageant, of the confident display of might in beauty, is undoubtedly part of Shakespeare's debt to his theme which, whilst balancing it against other elements, it was no part of his intention to forgo. If, in much of this play, he qualifies the note of majesty with more somber and reflective tones, the effect of these tones is in part gained by the contrast with the appeal of majesty itself.

Yet when, immediately after, Henry himself appears, much of his first utterance, as he incites his followers to battle, has about it a strong flavor of artificiality and strain:

Then imitate the action of the tiger;
Stiffen the sinews, summon up the blood,
Disguise fair nature with hard-favour'd
    rage;
Then lend the eye a terrible aspect;
Let it pry through the portage of the head
Like the brass cannon; let the brow
    o'erwhelm it
As fearfully as doth a galled rock
O'erhang and jutty his confounded base,
Swill'd with the wild and wasteful ocean.
Now set the teeth and stretch the nostril
    wide,
Hold hard the breath and bend up every
    spirit
To his full height.
(III.i)

There is about this incitation something forced, incongruous, even (if we may risk taking the point a little too far) slightly absurd. The action of the warrior is an imitation, and an imitation of a wild beast at that, carried out by a deliberate exclusion of "fair nature." The blood is to be summoned up, the sinews stiffened to the necessary degree of artificial savagery, while the involved rhetorical comparisons which follow the references to the "brass cannon" and the "galled rock" strengthen the impression of something very like unreality. In stressing this note of inhumanity, the speech does not intend to deny the poetry of war, which, as we have just seen, Shakespeare expresses most fully in certain passages from the various prologues of this play; but, as later in *Coriolanus,* he balances the conception of the warrior in his triumphant energy as "a greyhound straining at the leash" against that, not less forcible, of a ruthless and inhuman engine of destruction. Both ruthlessness and splendor are inseparable aspects of the complete picture.

Henry's treatment of the governor and citizens of Harfleur relates this conception of the warrior to tensions already apparent in his own character. Not for the first time, two scenes are placed together to point a contrast. The way in which he presents his ultimatum is full of that sense of conflict between control and passion that was so prominent in his early utterances. The grotesque inhumanity implicit in his words is balanced by a suggestion of tragic destiny. Beneath his callousness is a sense that the horrors of war, once unleashed, freed from the sternest control, are irresistible. His soldiers, he warns the governor, are still held uneasily in check. "The cool and temperate wind of grace," whose control over passion is the mark of a Christian soldier, still exercises its authority; but "licentious wickedness" and "the filthy and contagious clouds" of "*heady* murder" threaten to break out at any moment. In his catalogue of the horrors of war stress is laid upon rape and the crimes of "blood." The "fresh-fair" virgins of Harfleur will become the victims of the soldiery, whose destructive atrocities are significantly referred to in terms of "liberty":

What rein can hold licentious wickedness
When down the hill he holds his fierce
    career?
(III.iii)

The process of evil, once unleashed, follows courses fatally determined; but Henry, having described them in words which emphasize his awareness of their horror, ends by disclaiming all responsibility for them, just as he had once disclaimed all responsibility for the outbreak of the war. The whole matter, thus taken out of his hands, becomes indifferent to him:

What is't to me, *when you yourselves are
    cause,*
If your pure maidens fall into the hand
Of hot and forcing violation?
(III.iii)

Yet this very assertion of indifference carries with it, at bottom, a sense of the tragedy of the royal position. Only this denial of responsibility, it would seem, only the exclusion of humanity and the acceptance of a complete dualism between controlling "grace" and the promptings of irresponsible passion, make possible that success in war which is, for the purposes of this play, the crown of kingship.

For it would certainly be wrong to suppose that Shakespeare, in portraying Henry, intends to stress a note of hypocrisy. Rather, his purpose is to bring out the burden of royalty, to point to certain contradictions, human and moral, which seems to be inherent in the notion of a successful king. As the play proceeds, Henry seems at times to be, at least in a moral sense, almost the victim of his position. The treasonable activities of Cambridge, Grey, and Scroop are indications of the duplicity with which monarchs are fated by their position to deal. Somewhere at the heart of this court there is a fundamental flaw which must constantly be allowed for by a successful ruler. It appears to Henry, in his dealings with the conspirators, as something deep-rooted enough to be associated with the original fall of man:

> seem they religious?
> Why, so didst thou: or are they spare in diet,
> Free from gross passion or of mirth or
>   anger,
> Constant in spirit, not swerving with the
>   blood,
> Garnish'd and deck'd in modest complement,
> Not working with the eye without the ear,
> And but in purged judgement trusting
>   neither?
> Such and so finely bolted didst thou seem:
> And thus thy fall hath left a kind of blot,
> To mark the full-fraught man and best
>   indued
> With some suspicion. I will weep for thee;
> For this revolt of thine, methinks, is like
> Another fall of man.
>   (II.ii)

It is remarkable that Henry, in meditating upon this betrayal, should return once more to that theme of control, or freedom from passion, which is so prominent in his own nature. By concentrating on the functioning of the body, and on the sense of mutual divergence between eye, ear, and judgment in the difficult balance of the personality, the speech sets spiritual control in contrast with a sense of anarchy that proceeds, most typically, from the contemplation of physical

processes. "*Gross* passion"—the adjective is significant—is associated with the irrational "swerving of the blood," and the judgment which controls it needs to be "purged" by fasting ("spare in diet") before it can attain a scarcely human freedom from "mirth or anger." By thus emphasizing the difficult and even unnatural nature of such control, the speech casts a shadow, at least by implication, over that of Henry himself; but it is also seen to be necessary, inseparable from his office. The administration of justice, upon which depends order within the kingdom and success in its foreign wars, demands in the monarch a detachment which borders on the inhuman. The state must be purged of "treason lurking in its way" before it can be led, with that single-mindedness of purpose which is both Henry's strength and, perhaps, in the long run, his limitation, to the victorious enterprise in france.

It is clear, indeed, that *Henry V* represents, however tentatively, a step in the realization of themes fully developed in the tragedies. Inheriting from his sources the conception of a victorious king, perfectly aware of his responsibilities and religiously devoted to the idea of duty, Shakespeare seems, in the most individual scenes of his play, to emphasize the difficulties of the conception, the obstacles, both personal and political, which lie between it and fulfillment. These difficulties, however, never amount to a questioning of the royal judgment. Even in the disguised Henry's debate with Williams and Bates on the morning of Agincourt (IV.i), where the implications of his power are most searchingly discussed, the king's right to command obedience is never in question. For Bates the duty of a subject lies in loyal execution of the royal will, and the responsibility for wrong action rests beyond the simple soldier with the king: "we know enough, if we know we are the king's subjects." Nor does Williams, though more skeptical in his attitude, question the postulate that the subject is bound to obey; for to disobey, as he puts it, "were against all property of subjection," and the emphasis is still upon the "proportion" to be observed between king and subject, directing head and executing body, and upon the proper submission which the successful prosecution of the military effort requires.

Henry, of course, accepts this view of his position; but although the questionings of his followers do not—and cannot—lead him to doubt his own authority, they do force him to reflect deeply upon the weaknesses which even kings cannot overcome. "The king is but a man as I am; the violet smells to him as it doth to me; ... all his senses have but human conditions; his ceremonies laid by, in his nakedness he appears but a man; and though his affections are higher mounted than ours, yet when they stoop they stoop with the like wing." There is about the argument a universality which transcends the royal situation. Men, differentiated by vain "ceremony," are united in their common "nakedness," and the most notable feature of human behavior seems to the speaker to be its domination by impulse, its helplessness before the stooping of the affections. In this respect the king is one with his men; and just because he is so like them, because his senses too "have but human conditions" and are constantly liable to break through the guard of rigid self-control imposed upon him by his vocation, there is something precarious, potentially disproportionate in his absolute claim upon the allegiance of his followers.

The royal isolation is further underlined by Williams when he points out the spiritual consequences of a conflict for which the king has accepted full responsibility: "For how can they [Henry's soldiers] charitably dispose of anything when blood is their argument? Now, if these men do not die well, it will be a black matter for the king that led them to it" (IV. i). These words repeat once more, but with a greater urgency, a preoccupation with the horrors of war which Henry has already expressed, even if he succeeded in shaking off responsibility for them, to the French envoys and the governor of Harfleur. They imply, beyond the sense of responsibility which derives from the traditional conception of monarchy, a contrast—already familiar—between the Christian law of "charity" and the impulse to destruction that threatens it in the necessary acts of war with the consequences of unlimited brutality. The connection between this conflict of flesh and spirit and the tendency of human societies, states and families alike, to dissolve by the questioning of "degree" into anarchy is not established in this play as it is in the tragedies which followed. But Hamlet himself might have reflected like Henry on the precarious basis of human pretentions, and Angelo defined in similar terms the catastrophic realization of it brought about by his encounter with Isabella. Had Henry once followed his line of speculation far enough to doubt the validity of

his motives for action, or—on the other hand— had he given free play to the sinister impulses dimly recognized in himself, he would of course have been the protagonist of another and quite different play; but the possibilities are there as a premonition, a first indication of issues brought fully to light in later actions.

For the moment, Henry counters the implications of this argument by pointing out that soldiers "purpose not their death, when they purpose their services." Williams' somber reflections, however, impose themselves upon him, attach themselves to his own meditations, and are profoundly echoed in his own words. Connecting war with sin, he repeats the tone of earlier statements: "Besides, there is no king, be his cause never so spotless, if it come to the arbitrement of swords, can try it out with all unspotted soldiers: some peradventure have on them the guilt of premeditated and contrived murder; some, of beguiling virgins with the broken seal of perjury" (IV. i). The result is, in part, a fresh emphasis on meticulous self-examination as a means of conserving spiritual health— "Therefore should every soldier in the wars do as every sick man in his bed, wash every mote out of his conscience"—and, in the verse soliloquy which closes the scene, one of those outbursts of nostalgic craving for release which have appeared already, in his father's mouth, in *Henry IV*—Part II, and which will be reflected with a new, more *physical* apprehension of existence in Hamlet's soliloquies and in the Dukes's incitations to Claudio in *Measure for Measure:*

what infinite heart's ease
Must kings neglect, that private men enjoy!
(IV.i)

The craving for "heart's ease" in this long speech is still, generally speaking, what it is in *Henry IV*: a desire to be freed from the burden of an office in which human purposes seem fatally divorced from human achievement. The development of the verse in still painstaking, leisurely in the expansion of it long periods, and a little rhetorical; but there are moments which foreshadow the association in *Hamlet* of this nostalgia with a desire to be free from the encumbrances, the "fardels," the "things rank and gross in nature" by which the flesh persistently seems to obstruct the workings of the spirit. "Greatness" is a "fiery fever" which consumes its royal victim like a bodily disease, and the contrasted peace of the humble subject is described with a curious ambiguity of tone:

> Not all these, laid in bed majestical,
> Can sleep so soundly as the wretched slave,
> Who with a body fill'd and vacant mind
> Gets him to rest, cramm'd with distressful
>   bread.
> (IV.i)

In the association of peace with bodily fullness and vacancy of mind, in the impression, harshly and directly physical, behind "fill'd" and "cramm'd," there is a distinct suggestion of certain descriptions of satiated, idle contentment in plays as far apart as *Troilus and Cressida* and *Coriolanus*. Here already such imagery represents a kind of residue, intractable and irreducible, in direct contrast to the king's increasing emphasis on the need for spiritual discipline. It is no more than a suggestion, unabsorbed as yet into the main imaginative design of a play conceived on different, simpler lines; but, tentative as it is, it stands in a certain relationship to the clash of flesh and spirit—"passion" and "grace"—which exacts continual vigilance from Henry and which is slowly moving through these developments of imagery to more open realization.

A similar potential cleavage can be detected in the treatment of the two sides drawn up for battle at Agincourt. Shakespeare differentiates between the French and English forces in a way which sometimes seems to foreshadow the balance held in *Troilus and Cressida* between Greeks and Trojans, though it is true that the unfavorable estimate of the English, which is scarcely compatible with the spirit of the play, is expressed only in the words of their enemies. The English are morally worthy of their victory, but the French account does go a little way to anticipate the possibility of criticism. The French, combining a touch of the unsubstantial chivalry of Troilus with a more than Trojan emptiness, are, like the trojans, and more justly, defeated; the English, whom they represent as gross and dull-witted, are as undeniably successful as the Greeks. Shakespeare's handling of the battle carries on this conception. The French, trusting in a thin and rhetorical belief in their own aristocracy, rush hastily and incompetently to their deaths; the English, deriving their spirit from their king, win the day by their perseverance and self-control. Self-control, however, which is—as in Henry himself—not without some suggestion of harshness and inhumanity.

Henry's righteousness does not prevent him from inflicting merciless reprisals on his prisoners, and, though these matters need to be looked at in the spirit of the times, and the play is careful to emphasize the base act of treachery which rouses Henry to righteous anger, there is something finally sardonic about Gower's comment that "the king, *most worthily*, hath caused every soldier to cut his prisoner's throat. O, 'tis *a gallant king*" (IV. vii). By such excellence, Shakespeare would seem to say, must even the most just and patriotic of wars be won ...

Source: D. A. Traversi, "*Henry IV—Parts I and II*, and *Henry V*," in *An Approach to Shakespeare*, Doubleday and Company, Inc., 1969, pp. 191–258.

Mark Van Doren

In the following excerpt, Van Doren criticizes the lack of unity in Henry V, *stating that the spectacle of the play does not compensate for the inadequate dramatic matter. He condemns Shakespeare's use of the chorus, the inflated style, the sentimental appeal to patriotism, and the weak humor in the play. Van Doren also asserts that Shakespeare fails to establish a relation between Henry's actions and his experiences.*

Shakespeare in *Henry IV* had still been able to pour all of his thought and feeling into the heroic drama without demolishing its form. His respect for English history as a subject, his tendency to conceive kings in tragic terms, his interest in exalted dialogue as a medium through which important actions could be advanced—these, corrected by comedy which flooded the whole with the wisdom of a warm and proper light, may have reached their natural limit, but that limit was not transgressed. *Henry IV*, in other words, both was and is a successful play; it answers the questions it raises, it satisfies every instinct of the spectator, it is remembered as fabulously rich and at the same time simply ordered. *Henry V* is no such play. It has its splendors and its secondary attractions, but the forces in it are not unified. The reason probably is that for Shakespeare they had ceased to be genuine forces. He marshals for his task a host of substitute powers, but the effect is often hollow. The style strains itself to bursting, the hero is stretched until he struts on tiptoe and is still strutting at the last insignificant exit, and war is emptied of its tragic content. The form of the historical drama had been the tragic form; its dress is borrowed here, but only borrowed. The

> THE FIGURE WHOM HE [SHAKESPEARE] HAS
> GROOMED TO BE THE IDEAL ENGLISH KING, ALL
> PLUMES AND SMILES AND DECORATED COURAGE,
> COLLAPSES HERE INTO A MERE GOOD FELLOW, A
> HEARTY UNDERGRADUATE WITH ENORMOUS INITIALS
> ON HIS CHEST."

heroic idea splinters into a thousand starry fragments, fine as fragments but lighted from no
single source.

Everywhere efforts are made to be striking,
and they succeed. But the success is local. *Henry
V* does not succeed as a whole because its author
lacks adequate dramatic matter; or because,
veering so suddenly away from tragedy, he is
unable to free himself from the accidents of its
form; or because, with *Julius Caesar* and *Hamlet*
on his horizon, he finds himself less interested
than before in heroes who are men of action and
yet is not at the moment provided with a dramatic language for saying so. Whatever the
cause, we discover that we are being entertained
from the top of his mind. There is much there to
glitter and please us, but what pleases us has less
body than what once did so and soon will do so
with still greater abundance again.

The prologues are the first sign of
Shakespeare's imperfect dramatic faith. Their
verse is wonderful but it has to be, for it is
doing the work which the play ought to be
doing, it is a substitute for scene and action. "O
for a Muse of fire," the poet's apology begins.
The prologues are everywhere apologetic; they
are saying that no stage, this one or any other, is
big enough or wealthy enough to present the
"huge and proper life" of Henry's wars; this
cockpit cannot hold the vasty fields of France,
there will be no veritable horses in any scene, the
ship-boys on the masts and the camp-fires at
Agincourt will simply have to be imagined.
Which it is the business of the play to make
them be, as Shakespeare has known and will
know again. The author of *Romeo and Juliet*
had not been sorry because his stage was a
piece of London rather than the whole of

Verona, and the storm in *King Lear* will begin
without benefit of description. The description
here is always very fine, as for example at the
opening of the fourth act:

> Now entertain conjecture of a time
> When creeping murmur and the poring dark
> Fills the wide vessel of the universe.
> From camp to camp through the foul womb
>   of night
> The hum of either army stilly sounds,
> That the fix'd sentinels almost receive
> The secret whispers of each other's watch;
> Fire answers fire, and through their paly
>   flames
> Each battle sees the other's umber'd face;
> Steed threatens steed, in high and boastful
>   neighs
> Piercing the night's dull ear; and from the
>   tents
> The armourers, accomplishing the knights,
> With busy hammers closing rivets up,
> Give dreadful note of preparation.

But it is still description, and it is being
asked to do what description can never do—
turn spectacle into plot, tableau into tragedy.

The second sign of genius at loose ends is a
radical and indeed an astounding inflation in the
style. Passages of boasting and exhortation are
in place, but even the best of them, whether from
the French or from the English side, have a
forced, shrill, windy sound, as if their author
were pumping his muse for dear life in the hope
that mere speed and plangency might take the
place of matter. For a few lines like

Familiar in his mouth as household words

(IV, iii, 52)

The singing masons building roofs of gold

(I, ii, 198)

I see you stand like greyhounds in the
    slips,
Straining upon the start
(III, i, 31–2)

there are hundreds like

The native mightiness and fate of him

(II, iv, 64)

With ample and brim fullness of his force

(I, ii, 150)

That caves and womby vaultages of
    France

Shall chide your trespass and return your mock.

(II, iv, 124–5)

Mightiness and fate, ample and brim, caves and vaultages, trespass and mock—such couplings attest the poet's desperation, the rhetorician's extremity. They spring up everywhere, like birds from undergrowth: sweet and honey'd, open haunts and popularity, thrive and ripen, crown and seat, right and title, right and conscience, kings and monarchs, means and might, aim and butt, large and ample, taken and impounded, frank and uncurbed, success and conquest, desert and merit, weight and worthiness, duty and zeal, savage and inhuman, botch and bungle, garnish'd and deck'd, assembled and collected, sinister and awkward, culled and choice-drawn, o'erhang and jutty, waste and desolation, cool and temperate, flexure and low bending, signal and ostent, vainness and self-glorious pride. Shakespeare has perpetrated them before, as when in *Henry VI* he coupled ominous and fearful, trouble and disturb, substance and authority, and absurd and reasonless. But never has he perpetrated them with such thoughtless frequency. Nor has he at this point developed the compound epithet into that interesting mannerism—the only mannerism he ever submitted to—which is to be so noticeable in his next half-dozen plays, including *Hamlet*. The device he is to use will involve more than the pairing of adjectives or nouns; one part of speech will assume the duties of another, and a certain very sudden concentration of meaning will result. There is, to be sure, one approximation to the device in *Henry V*—"the quick forge and working-house of thought" (Prologue, v, 23) . . .

The third sign is a direct and puerile [juvenile] appeal to the patriotism of the audience, a dependence upon sentiments outside the play that can be counted on, once they are tapped, to pour in and repair the deficiencies of the action. Unable to achieve a dramatic unity out of the materials before him, Shakespeare must grow lyrical about the unity of England; politics must substitute for poetry. He cannot take England for granted as the scene of conflicts whose greatness will imply its greatness. It must be great itself, and the play says so—unconvincingly. There are no conflicts. The traitors Scroop, Cambridge, and Grey are happy to lose their heads for England (II, ii), and the battles in France, even though the enemy's host is huge and starvation takes

King Henry, Scroop, Cambridge, and Grey, Act II, scene ii (© *Shakespeare Collection, Special Collections Library, University of Michigan*)

its toll, are bound to be won by such fine English fellows as we have here. If the French have boasted beforehand, the irony of their doing so was obvious from the start. But it was patriotism, shared as a secret between the author and his audience, that made it obvious. It was not drama.

And a fourth sign is the note of gaiety that takes the place here of high passion. The treasure sent to Henry by the Dauphin is discovered at the end of the first act to be tennis-balls: an insult which the young king returns in a speech about matching rackets and playing sets—his idiom for bloody war. When the treachery of Scroop, Cambridge, and Grey is detected on the eve of his departure for France he stages their discomfiture somewhat as games are undertaken, and with a certain sporting relish watches their faces as they read their dooms. The conversation of the French leaders as they wait for the sun to rise on Agincourt is nervous as thoroughbreds are nervous, or champion athletes impatient for a tournament to commerce; their camp is a locker room, littered with attitudes no less than uniforms (III, vii). The deaths of York and Suffolk the next day are images of how young knights should die. They kiss each other's gashes, wearing their red blood like roses in the field, and spending their last breath in terms so fine that Exeter, reporting to the King, is overcome by "the pretty and sweet manner of it" (IV, vi, 28). And of course there are the scenes where Katharine makes fritters of English, waiting to be wooed (III, iv) and wooed at last (V, ii) by Henry Plantagenet, "king of good fellows." "The truth is," said Dr. Johnson, "that the poet's matter failed him in the fifth act, and he was glad to fill it up with whatever he could get; and not even Shakespeare can write well without a proper subject. It is a vain endeavour for the most skilful hand to cultivate barrenness, or to paint upon vacuity." That is harsh, but its essence cannot be ignored. The high spirits in which the scenes are written have their attraction, but they are no substitute for intensity.

Nor do they give us the king we thought we had. "I speak to thee plain soldier," boasts Henry in homespun vein. "I am glad thou canst speak no better English; for, if thou couldst, thou wouldst find me such a plain king that thou wouldst think I had sold my farm to buy my crown. I know no ways to mince it in love, but directly to say, 'I love you.' ... These fellows of infinite tongue, that can rhyme themselves into ladies' favours, they do always reason themselves out again ... By mine honour, in true English, I love thee, Kate" (V, ii) ...

Shakespeare has forgotten the glittering young god whom Vernon described in *Henry IV*—plumed like an estridge or like an eagle lately bathed, shining like an image in his golden coat, as full of spirit as the month of May, wanton as a youthful goat, a feathered Mercury, an angel dropped down from the clouds. The figure whom he has groomed to be the ideal English king, all plumes and smiles and decorated courage, collapses here into a mere good fellow, a hearty undergraduate with enormous initials on his chest. The reason must be that Shakespeare has little interest in the ideal English king. He has done what rhetoric could do to give us a young heart whole in honor, but his imagination has already sped forward to Brutus and Hamlet: to a kind of hero who is no less honorable than Henry but who

will tread on thorns as he takes the path of duty— itself unclear, and crossed by other paths of no man's making. Henry is Shakespeare's last attempt at the great man who is also simple. Henceforth he will show greatness as either perplexing or perplexed; and Hamlet will be both.

Meanwhile his imagination undermines the very eminence on which Henry struts. For the King and his nobles the war may be a handsome game, but an undercurrent of realism reminds us of the "poor souls" for whom it is no such thing. We hear of widows' tears and orphans' cries, of dead men's blood and pining maidens' groans (II, iv, 104–7). Such horrors had been touched on in earlier Histories; now they are given a scene to themselves (IV, i). While the French leaders chaff one another through the night before Agincourt the English common soldiers have their hour. Men with names as plain as John Bates and Micheal Williams walk up and down the dark field thinking of legs and arms and heads chopped off in battle, of faint cries for surgeons, of men in misery because of their children who will be rawly left. Henry, moving among them in the disguise of clothes like theirs, asks them to remember that the King's cause is just and his quarrel honorable. "That's more than we know," comes back the disturbing cool voice of Michael Williams. Henry answers with much fair prose, and the episode ends with a wager—sportsmanship again—which in turn leads to an amusing recognition scene (IV, viii). But the honest voice of Williams still has the edge on Henry's patronizing tone:

> *Williams.* Your Majesty came not like yourself. You appear'd to me but as a common man; witness the night, your garments, your lowliness; and what your Highness suffer'd under that shape, I beseech you take it for your own fault and not mine ...

> *King Henry.* Here, uncle Exeter, fill this glove with crowns,
> And give it to this fellow. Keep it, fellow;
> And wear it for an honour in thy cap
> Till I do challenge it.
> (IV, viii, 53–64)

Henry has not learned that Williams knows. He is still the plumed king, prancing on oratory and waving wagers as he goes. That he finally has no place to go is the result of Shakespeare's failure to establish any relation between a hero and his experience. Henry has not absorbed the vision either of Williams or of Shakespeare. This shrinks him in his armor, and it leaves the vision hanging.

The humor of the play, rich as it sometimes is, suffers likewise from a lack of vital function. The celebrated scene (II, iii) in which the Hostess describes Falstaff's death shuts the door forever on *Henry IV* and its gigantic comedy. Pistol and Bardolph continue in their respective styles, and continue cleverly; the first scene of the second act, which finds them still in London, may be indeed the best one ever written for them—and for Nym in his pompous brevity.

> I cannot tell. Things must be as they may. Men may sleep, and they may have their throats about them at the time; and some say knives have edges. It must be as it may.

Pistol was never excited to funnier effect.

> O hound of Crete, think'st thou my
>   spouse to get?
> No! to the spital go,
> And from the powdering-tub of infamy
> Fetch forth the lazar kite of Cressid's kind,
> Doll Tearsheet she by name, and her
>   espouse.
> I have, and I will hold, the quondam Quickly
> For the only she; and—*pauca*, there's
>   enough. Go to.

Yet this leads on to little in France beyond a series of rather mechanically arranged encounters in which the high talk of heroes is echoed by the rough cries of rascals. "To the breach, to the breach!" yells Bardolph after Henry, and that is parody. But Henry has already parodied himself; the device is not needed, any more than the rascals are. Shakespeare seems to admit as much when he permits lectures to be delivered against their moral characters, first by the boy who serves them (III, ii, 28–57) and next by the sober Gower (III, vi, 70–85), and when he arranges bad ends for them as thieves, cutpurses, and bawds.

There is a clearer function for Fluellen, the fussy Welsh pedant who is for fighting wars out of books. Always fretting and out of breath, he mourns "the disciplines of the wars," the pristine wars of the Romans, now in these latter days lost with all other learning. There was not this tiddle taddle and pibble pabble in Pompey's camp. The law of arms was once well known, and men—strong, silent men such as he fancies himself to be—observed it without prawls and prabbles. He has no shrewdness; he mistakes Pistol for a brave man because he talks bravely, and there is his classic comparison of Henry with Alexander because one lived in Monmouth and the other in Macedon and each city had a river and there were salmons in both. He has only his schoolmaster's eloquence; it breaks out on him like a rash, and is the one style here that surpasses the King's in fullness.

> *Fluellen.* It is not well done, mark you now, to take the tales out of my mouth, ere it is made and finished. I speak but in the figures and comparisons of it. As Alexander kill'd his friend Cleitus, being in his ales and his cups; so also Harry Monmouth, being in his right wits and his good judgements, turn'd away the fat knight with the great belly doublet. He was full of jests, and gipes, and knaveries, and mocks; I have forgot his name.
>
> *Gower.* Sir John Falstaff.
>
> *Fluellen.* That is he.
>
> (IV, vii, 43–55)

Fluellen reminds us of Falstaff. That is a function, but he has another. It is to let the war theme finally down. Agincourt is won not only by a tennis-player but by a school-teacher. Saint Crispin's day is to be remembered as much in the pibble pabble of a pedant as in the golden throatings of a hollow god. Fluellen is one of Shakespeare's most humorous men, and one of his best used.

Source: Mark Van Doren, "*Henry V,*" in *Shakespeare,* Henry Holt and Company, 1939, pp. 170–79.

SOURCES

Charney, Maurice, *All of Shakespeare*, Columbia University Press, 1993.

Goddard, Harold C., *The Meaning of Shakespeare*, University of Chicago Press, 1951.

McEachern, Claire, ed., "Introduction," in *The Life of King Henry the Fifth*, Penguin Books, 1999.

Schoenbaum, S., *Shakespeare: His Life, His Language, His Theater*, Penguin Group, 1990.

Shakespeare, William, *The Life of King Henry the Fifth*, Penguin Books, 1999.

FURTHER READING

Allmand, Christopher, *Yale English Monarchs—Henry V*, Yale University Press, 1992.
    This is a scholarly study of the English monarch, detailed, and well researched.

Berman, Ronald, *Twentieth-Century Interpretations of Henry V: A Collection of Critical Essays*, Prentice Hall, 1968.

> Some of the top critics of the twentieth century offer their views on Shakespeare's play.

Bishop, Morris, *The Middle Ages*, Mariner Books, 2001.

> This is the place to read about the monarchs in Europe, the power of the church, the wars, and the customs of the people during the Middle Ages.

Gies, Frances, and Joseph Gies, *Marriage and the Family in the Middle Ages*, Harper Perennial, 1989.

> Have you ever wondered what life would be like in the Middle Ages? These authors have put together a glimpse into the ordinary lives of citizens of the Middle Ages.

Hibbert, Christopher, *Agincourt*, Cooper Square Press, 2000.

> A concise history of the short battle that profoundly affected England and France.

Seward, Desmond, *The Hundred Years War: The English in France, 1337–1453*, Penguin, 2003.

> A study of the central issues of dispute and the resulting wars between France and England as the two countries fought for control of the French crown.

Shapiro, James, *A Year in the Life of William Shakespeare: 1599*, Harper Perennial, 2006.

> The author offers a different take on the biography of Shakespeare by telling the reader what was happening around Shakespeare while he was writing some of his plays, including *Henry V*.

Henry VI, Part Three

1595

Henry VI, Part Three, first published in 1595, is one of William Shakespeare's bloodiest plays, with a large portion of the dramatic action taking place either on the battlefield, off the battlefield but involving the details of several murders, or inside courts, discussing the need to go to war or the necessity of disposing of enemies. Ironically, it is a story about a gentle king who was a weak ruler, allowing others to take care of the affairs of his government. Henry VI, the real king, was known to be more interested in book learning and spiritual matters than warfare. Unfortunately, much of his legacy (the part that Shakespeare focuses on in this play) involved bloodshed.

This play is the third and last section of the Henry VI trilogy (preceded by the aptly named *Henry VI, Part One* and *Henry VI, Part Two*). The trilogy is ostensibly about the life and reign of Henry IV, the son of the great warrior Henry V, about whom Shakespeare also created a drama. Unlike Shakespeare's play *Henry V*, however, this particular play, *Henry VI, Part Three* has very little to do with the monarch himself. The reason for this might be that by the time King Henry VI had reached this part of his life, he had become a recluse. In his place stood his wife, Queen Margaret, a defiant woman who fought harder for Henry's throne than the king himself did. Other main characters in this drama include members of the Plantagenet family, the noblemen from York, who claim what they believe is their

legitimate inheritance of the throne. The main action of the play revolves around the battle for the crown between the Yorkists and the Lancastrians (Henry's clan); both families were legitimate descendants of King Edward III (1327–77). The play begins with Henry on the throne, which quickly changes when the Yorkists take the throne by force. After another battle, Henry is reinstated as king for a short period of time until the Yorkists recapture the throne.

These were terrible times for the English, as the country was involved in the conflict which history referred to as the Wars of Roses (1455–87). This was a civil war with the Yorkists (symbolized by a white rose on their badges) and their followers on one side and those allegiant to the Lancastrians (who wore badges with a red rose on them) on the other side. As the English rule switched back and forth between the two families, thousands of soldiers sacrificed their lives, noblemen were killed, as were young children of both families who might claim the throne in the future.

Although popular in Shakespeare's time, this play did not receive as warm a reception as many other Shakespearian dramas did between the seventeenth and nineteenth centuries. It was not until more modern times that scholars and audiences have taken an interest in this drama. Some critics believe that the atrocities of a civil war, with brother fighting against brother, father against son, might have been too much to stomach, at least for some English audiences in earlier centuries. But as a glimpse into English history, especially as Shakespeare demonstrates the human nature behind the scenes of war, this play offers a creatively documented portal into history.

PLOT SUMMARY

Act 1, Scene 1

Shakespeare's *Henry VI, Part Three* begins in the midst of a battle. The Duke of York enters the Parliament House with his sons, Edward and Richard, and several of his noblemen. They wonder where King Henry is and how they missed capturing him. They discuss their battles, with Warwick, one of the noblemen, claiming that he first wants Henry's head and next wants to see the duke crowned king. The duke commits to fighting for the title, and to prove his

intentions, he sits down on the throne. Shortly afterward, King Henry arrives on the scene with his lords. Henry is surprised to see the duke sitting on the throne and asks him what right he has to do so. After all, the duke's father was not a king, as was Henry's.

York reminds Henry that Henry's grandfather, King Henry IV, gained the throne through rebellion, not through legal accession. The lords on both sides bicker with one another, each claiming legal right of the throne for their leader. One of King Henry's lords, the Duke of Exeter, states that York might indeed have legal claim. This worries King Henry, who is afraid all his lords might side with York. Henry tries to work out a compromise by telling York that if York allows him to maintain the crown until Henry's death, Henry will make the Yorkists heir to the throne thereafter. York agrees. When the two men embrace, some of Henry's men leave, disgusted.

Henry reflects on having disinherited his own son, Edward, the prince of Wales. After York leaves with his sons and nobles, Queen Margaret and the prince arrive. The king tries to slip away from them, but the queen stops Henry. She has heard about Henry's agreement with York. When Henry says that York forced him to disinherit his son, Margaret asks: "Art thou King, and wilt be forced?" And thus begins the queen's battle to save the throne for her son. She vows to use her army to destroy the Yorkists.

Act 1, Scene 2

York's sons, Richard and Edward do not want to wait until King Henry dies before their family can claim the throne. They talk their father, the Duke of York, into forgetting his oath to the king. "I will be King, or die," the duke finally says, disavowing the oath he has just made with Henry, and then he sends his sons and noblemen out to fight for the throne again. A messenger arrives, warning the duke that the queen is coming to his castle with her army. The duke decides to keep his sons with him. As the queen approaches, the armies go out to meet her in the battlefield. York's men are greatly outnumbered, but they do not worry, because their enemies are led by a woman.

Act 1, Scene 3

The youngest son of York, Edmund, Earl of Rutland, appears with his tutor, when Clifford, one of Henry's men, encounters them. Clifford is determined to murder all of York's family in revenge of their having killed Clifford's father. Edmund pleads for his life, but Clifford is not affected. Clifford says, "Thy father slew my father. Therefore die." And then Clifford stabs the boy.

Act 1, Scene 4

The next scene is on the battlefield. York and his men are losing. York is captured, and Clifford wants to kill him. Queen Margaret wants Clifford to be patient, while she mocks York about having earlier taken the throne. Now, she asks York where his sons are. She calls his sons names. Where are York's men? Then she makes a paper crown and sticks it on top of his head, making the Duke of York an imaginary king. York talks back to her, saying she is nothing like a woman. Clifford stabs York; Queen Margaret stabs York, too. Then she orders her men to cut off York's head and impale it on the gate leading to the town of York.

Act 2, Scene 1

On another battlefield, York's sons, Edward and Richard, wonder where their father is, wonder if he is all right. Edward notices the sun rising, but instead of seeing one sun, he sees three that eventually merge into one. This is a sign, Edward believes, that the three remaining brothers, Edward, George, and Richard, should ban together to unite their power.

A messenger arrives announcing the death of York. When the messenger offers details about how their father died, Edward says he wants to hear no more. Richard, on the other hand, wants to hear every detail. Edward cries, but Richard cannot weep because his tears are being used to help cool down his impassioned mind. Richard can only think of vengeance. Edward then realizes that he has inherited the dukedom of his father. But Richard says that Edward has inherited the throne of England.

One of York's men, Warwick, arrives to announce that his men were defeated by the queen. He also tells them that their brother George has arrived from France. A messenger appears to tell them that the queen is coming.

Act 2, Scene 2

The queen and King Henry, with Clifford and the prince, are outside of York. Clifford tries to

Henry VI, King of England (Getty Images)

convince the king to be nice to the prince, Henry's son, to not disinherit him. Then Clifford tells the king that he should treat the Yorkists as enemies. The king defends his position, stating that sometimes sons do not like what their fathers give them. Henry wishes his own father had given him something other than a kingdom. The queen reminds her husband that he had promised to knight their son, which Henry does. Then the prince vows to fight to the death for the Crown.

A messenger tells the king and queen that the new Duke of York is marching an army of thirty thousand men toward them. Clifford asks the king to disappear, as the queen fights better when the king is not around. The king decides to stay.

The York brothers appear. They confront Clifford, who admits having killed their youngest brother and their father. Then the brothers ask if Henry is going to yield his authority to Edward. Edward tells Margaret that if she had been gentler, like her husband, the Yorkists might not have tried to seize the power. Henry tries to speak, but Margaret silences him. The Yorkists leave, saying they are tired of all the talk and will settle this dispute on the battlefield.

Act 2, Scene 3

In the midst of another battle, the brothers, with Warwick, find each other and swear their allegiance to fight until they gain their revenge of the deaths of their brother and father. Their brother George is now with them.

Act 2, Scene 4

Richard and Clifford fight. But when Warwick appears, Clifford sneaks out. Warwick wants to go after him, but Richard says he wants to be the one to kill Clifford.

Act 2, Scene 5

King Henry is sitting by himself in another part of the battlefield. He is reflecting on wars and on his life. Clifford and the queen have persuaded the king to leave the battle. Henry thinks about how happy life would be if he were a shepherd. Then a man appears, carrying a dead soldier he has just killed. He turns the dead soldier's face and sees that he has killed his father. Another soldier appears, also carrying a body. This soldier laments that he has unknowingly killed his son.

The queen, the prince, and Exeter appear, telling the king that they must flee. Warwick and the York brothers have found a new fierce energy and are winning this battle.

Act 2, Scene 6

In another part of the battlefield, Clifford is wounded, and he acknowledges that he is dying. He reflects on life, wishing that Henry had been more like his father (Henry V), stronger in his role as king, so the Yorkists would not have even thought of trying to take over the Crown. Clifford then calls out to the Yorkists and tells them to come and kill him. Then he faints. Edward and Warwick find Clifford, and they bemoan the fact that they cannot kill him because Clifford is already dead. Warwick tells the brothers to take their father's head off the gate of York and replace it with Clifford's.

Warwick tells the brothers to go to London to claim the throne. Warwick will go to France to ask King Lewis XI to help them. He will ask the king to allow the king's sister-in-law, Bona, to marry Edward, to once again bridge the gap between the two countries. Before the brothers leave, Edward names Richard the Duke of Gloucester and George the Duke of Clarence.

Act 3, Scene 1

King Henry is in hiding, north of England. Two hunters, who are hiding from their prey, see Henry, who is talking out loud to himself. In Henry's ruminations, he makes many references to being a king. He also talks about the queen having traveled to France to talk to the French king. Warwick is also in France to ask for the hand of Bona for Edward. The hunters come out from hiding and ask why Henry knows so much about being king. Henry tries to steer them off track, but in the end they realize who he is and take him captive.

Act 3, Scene 2

In London, Edward, now King Edward IV, is talking to Lady Grey, a widow who is asking to have her land restored to her. She lost the land when her husband died, fighting for Edward. Richard and George are present and are joking about how Edward will probably give the woman her land in exchange for becoming his lover. Edward attempts to woo Lady Grey into his bed, but the widow refuses. Edward then proposes marriage. Lady Grey accepts.

A messenger arrives, telling Edward that Henry has been apprehended. Edward tells the messenger to have Henry taken to the tower.

Everyone leaves but Richard, who thinks aloud, scheming about how he might gain the throne for himself. He lists all the people who stand in line before him. He thinks of alternative rewards for himself but concludes that, because his body is so misshapen, the only way he can find any joy is to rule over everyone. He concludes that he must gain the throne in any way possible.

Act 3, Scene 3

In France, Queen Margaret and the prince meet with King Lewis. Bona is also present in the room. The king tries to make Margaret feel comfortable, but she is too agitated. She finally tells the king that she needs his support to retake the throne. The king considers this, but then Warwick appears. Warwick also asks for the king's support, by giving him Bona for King Edward. King Lewis asks Warwick if King Edward truly loves his sister. Warwick swears that this is true.

A messenger arrives, bearing three letters, one for Queen Margaret, one for Warwick, one for King Lewis. The three of them learn of the marriage of King Edward to Lady Grey. Warwick is angry. He wonders how Edward could have betrayed him. Warwick tells the king and Queen Margaret that he will switch his allegiance and fight with the queen to regain the throne for Henry. The French king promises to send troops to help them.

Act 4, Scene 1
Back in London at the palace, Edward arrives with his new wife, Lady Grey, now queen. George and Richard do not like this marriage and tell Edward that he has made a mistake. Some of Edward's men agree. England needs France as an ally. Others of Edward's men believe England is strong enough to stand alone. Edward tells his brothers that he is king and does not have to listen to them. The messenger arrives and tells them about the reactions in France to Edward's marriage and of Warwick's promise to support Queen Margaret. Warwick has sealed his allegiance to the queen by offering his daughter in marriage to the prince. George says he will marry Warwick's other daughter and he leaves to serve the queen. Richard stays with Edward. He implies that he needs to keep close to Edward in order to find the right opportunity to gain the throne for himself.

Act 4, Scene 2
In Warwickshire, Warwick arrives back in England with French soldiers. He is greeted by George. Warwick tells George about his plan to capture Edward.

Act 4, Scene 3
Edward is encamped in a field, protected only by a small group of watchmen. Warwick and his men surprise the guard and capture Edward. Warwick refers to Edward as duke. Edward questions this, reminding Warwick that before he left for France, Warwick had called Edward king. Warwick says that was before Edward disgraced him when he went to France as Edward's ambassador. Warwick takes the crown from Edward and says that Henry will wear it now.

Act 4, Scene 4
Back in London, at the palace, Lady Grey talks to her brother Lord Rivers, telling him that she fears for Edward's life. She also announces that she is pregnant with Edward's child.

Act 4, Scene 5
Richard has learned where his brother Edward is being held captive. He also knows that Edward is

allowed out in the field to hunt. He takes some men with him, and when Edward appears, Richard and his men steal Edward away.

Act 4, Scene 6
Warwick and George go to the tower where Henry is imprisoned. They give him back the crown. Henry accepts the crown but tells them that he is going to retire from leading the government. He asks Warwick to take over that role. Warwick says that position should be given to George. So King Henry appoints them both to the position. Warwick and George agree and promise to make Henry's son, Edward, the rightful heir to the throne. Henry then notices a young boy in their midst. He predicts that the boy will one day bring peace to England. The boy is Henry, Earl of Richmond, the future Henry VII.

A messenger arrives with news that Edward has escaped. This worries Henry, Warwick, and George, who suspect that Edward will raise an army and come back to claim the crown.

Act 4, Scene 7
Edward, Richard, and their soldiers arrive at York, demanding that the mayor of York open the gates. Edward claims that, if not king, he is still the Duke of York. Before the mayor opens the gates, Edward also claims allegiance to King Henry.

Montgomery arrives with his troops and says he is there to help Edward reclaim the throne. Edward says that he is not ready to do so because his forces are not big enough yet. Montgomery, upon hearing this, says he will then leave. Richard counsels Edward, telling him that now is the time. Edward changes his mind and Montgomery stays.

Act 4, Scene 8
Warwick is with King Henry in London. They learn that Edward and his armies are heading to London to retake the throne. Warwick leaves, to prepare to meet Edward. King Henry talks with Exeter about his reign, evaluating things he has done, hoping that he has been fair. Edward enters and orders Henry be taken prisoner and sent to the tower.

Act 5, Scene 1
Warwick is in Coventry with his troops, waiting for others to join him. More troops come to join

him. Edward and Richard also arrive. Edward asks Warwick if he will support him. Warwick says that he now backs Henry. Edward tells him that Henry is his prisoner once again. When George arrives with his troops, Richard goes to speak to him. Richard changes George's mind, and George asks his brother Edward to forgive him for deserting him, and he rejoins forces with his brothers. Edward's men and Henry's men, the two opposing forces, agree to meet in the countryside to fight.

Act 5, Scene 2

On a battlefield near Barnet, Warwick has been mortally wounded. Edward leaves him to die. Two noblemen, Somerset and Oxford, appear telling Warwick that the French king has sent more troops with Margaret to help them. It is too late for Warwick, who dies.

Act 5, Scene 3

Edward, Richard, and George, the three York brothers, enter victoriously. They have won this battle. But Margaret approaches, and they go out to meet her.

Act 5, Scene 4

Queen Margaret arrives with her troops from France. She makes a grand speech to the troops, especially those who fought with Warwick. She encourages them not to give up. Prince Edward praises his mother, stating that even cowards, upon hearing his mother's speech, would be proud to fight. A messenger delivers the news that Edward and his soldiers are approaching. Both sides prepare for the battle.

Act 5, Scene 5

The battle is ended. Edward has won. Several of King Henry's nobles are killed. The prince and Margaret are prisoners. The prince tries to talk down to Edward, but this only riles Edward, who orders the prince killed. Margaret tells them to kill her too, but they take her prisoner instead. Richard disappears. George tells Edward that he thinks Richard has gone to the Tower of London to kill Henry.

Act 5, Scene 6

In London, in the Tower, Richard appears before Henry. Henry has heard of his son's death and suspects that his death is near. He refers to the story of Icarus, the man who flew too close to the sun on a pair of waxed wings and

MEDIA ADAPTATIONS

- *King Henry VI, Part Three* was adapted for television by the British Broadcasting Corporation in their *Complete Dramatic Works of William Shakespeare*, one of the most complete renditions of the play, using almost all of the text as Shakespeare wrote it.

fell into the sea. Henry likens his son to Icarus. Henry also predicts that many will mourn all the people that Richard has, and will, kill. Richard then stabs Henry to death. Richard next reflects on his future, stating that his brothers should beware of him.

Act 5, Scene 7

In the throne room, Edward takes his place. His queen and his brothers are with him. Edward asks to see his son, an infant named Edward. He kisses the baby and asks that his brothers do the same. When asked what to do with Margaret, Edward agrees that she should be sent to France, which has promised a ransom for her. The play ends with Edward hoping for "lasting joy."

CHARACTERS

Bona

Bona is the French King Lewis's sister-in-law. She has very little to say in this drama and plays a very minor role. She is used in an attempt to bridge the relationship between England and France. Warwick goes to France as King Edward's ambassador to gain the permission of King Lewis to have King Edward marry Bona. When King Lewis asks if King Edward loves Bona, Warwick confirms this to be true. Shortly afterward, letters arrive at the French court, announcing that King Edward has married Lady Grey, although King Edward had sent Warwick to France to ask for the hand of Bona. There is no other communications between

Bona and King Edward, and yet Bona claims that she has been spurred by her lover (Edward). She is never seen or heard from again.

Lord Clifford

Lord Clifford is an ally of Queen Margaret's. He is angered from the beginning of the play and throughout all of the action until his death. The Duke of York killed Clifford's father prior to the beginning of this play; Clifford's main motive throughout this drama is to seek revenge. He wants to kill every member of the York family. Clifford kills York's youngest son, Edmund, and then proceeds to kill York. He is the avowed enemy of King Edward, Richard, and George, but he does not face them in any of the battles. Clifford is killed while fighting; however, it is not known who has killed him. He appears with an arrow in his neck and knows that he is dying. By the time the Edward, Richard, and George find him, Clifford is already dead.

Duke of Exeter

The Duke of Exeter is King Henry VI's great uncle. Although a supporter of King Henry, Exeter is the lone voice on Henry's side that agrees with the Duke of York that he is the legitimate heir to the throne. It is Exeter's statement that makes King Henry worry that all his noblemen might agree with Exeter and therefore desert the king in favor of York. This leads Henry to make his compromise with York in the first act, when he declares that upon his death, Henry will make allowances so that York inherits the crown. Exeter remains loyal to King Henry and Queen Margaret, though, and at one point hopes to make peace between the House York and Henry's family. The last Exeter is seen is toward the end of the play. King Henry is using Exeter to reflect on some thoughts, right before King Edward seizes Henry and imprisons him.

Duke of Norfolk

The Duke of Norfolk is one of King Henry's and Queen Margaret's supporters.

Duke of Somerset

The Duke of Somerset, in the beginning of the play, supports the Yorks. However, when Edward's brother, George, goes to the side of the queen, Somerset goes with him. Somerset comforts Warwick when Warwick dies. When Edward wins the last battle, he orders that Somerset's head be chopped off.

Earl of Northumberland

The Earl of Northumberland is on Henry's side and is cousin to Lord Clifford. When Henry promises the throne to York, the Earl of Northumberland curses the king but later supports the queen in her battle to maintain the throne.

Earl of Oxford

The Earl of Oxford supports the queen and travels with her to France. When Edward wins the last battle, Oxford is sent to prison.

Earl of Warwick

Warwick was a nobleman in allegiance with the Plantagenet family, also called the House of York. He was very instrumental in pushing the Duke of York to claim the throne. Warwick was also the force behind Edward gaining the crown. As ambassador for Edward, Warwick goes to France to gain the hand of the French king's sister-in-law, Bona. While in France, however, Edward goes against Warwick's plan and humiliates him in front of the king by marrying Lady Grey after Warwick has just sworn to the French king that Edward loves Bona. In anger and frustration, Warwick tells Queen Margaret that he will leave Edward's side and join her forces. He cements this deal by giving the hand of one of his daughters to the queen's son; they will marry. Warwick sends a message to King Edward, telling him that he will no longer support him. Later, in a battle between the queen's forces and King Edward's, Warwick is killed.

Earl of Westmoreland

Westmoreland is on King Henry's side against the Yorks. However, in the first scene, when Henry promises the throne to the Yorks, Westmoreland becomes disgusted with the king and calls him weak and base. Westmoreland leaves the king and goes to offer his support to the queen.

Edmund, Earl of Rutland

Edmund is the youngest son of Richard, the Duke of York. He appears in only one scene, in which Clifford kills him. Later, Queen Margaret taunts the duke with a handkerchief that has been dipped in Edmund's blood.

Prince Edward

Edward is the son of King Henry and Queen Margaret. He is a young man, always in the company of his mother in this play, and seldom interacts with his father, who ultimately disinherits him. He is betrothed to Warwick's daughter, when Warwick wants to prove his allegiance to the queen. Edward has few lines in this play. Possibly the most notable is when he praises his mother after her speech to encourage her army toward the end of the play. Edward claims that after hearing his mother's remarks, even cowards would be inspired to fight. Edward is killed by King Edward's brother, Richard, thus eliminating another person in Richard's way to becoming a king.

King Edward IV

Edward is the eldest son of Richard, Duke of York. He has three brothers, George, Richard, and Edmund. Edmund, still a young boy, is killed early in the play. George and Richard are more prominent in this play, either staying at Edward's side or, in George's case, at one point actually fighting against him.

Edward becomes the Duke of York after the death of his father. He leads his brothers in battle against Queen Margaret. When they defeat her, Edward claims the crown.

Edward, in Shakespeare's point of view, becomes egotistic after he is crowned and is often heard defying his brothers, telling them that he is king and no longer needs to take their counsel. His brothers become increasingly disenfranchised with their brother, especially when Edward decides to marry Lady Grey. It is uncertain if Edward loves Lady Grey or merely lusts after her. His brothers see no advantage in the marriage to Lady Grey, such as the marriage with the French king's sister-in-law might have brought. More significantly, Edward also frustrates the Earl of Warwick, whose guidance placed Edward on the throne. Warwick and Edward's brother George abandon Edward and work against him after Edward's marriage. In the end, however, George returns and helps Edward defeat Queen Margaret, thus assuring Edward's reign.

At the end of the play, Edward feels no remorse for all the deaths that have been caused in his fight for the throne. He likens those of his so-called enemies that have died to corn that was in need of harvesting.

George, Duke of Clarence

George is son to Richard, Duke of York and younger brother to King Edward. He travels to France to gain support for his father's fight for the throne. Upon returning, he learns that his father has been killed. George supports his brother's fight to gain the throne but is disillusioned when Edward betrays Warwick and marries Lady Grey while Warwick is in France asking for the French king's sister-in-law as a bride for Edward. When Warwick decides to join forces with the queen against Edward, George decides to do the same. However, in the last battle, George reunites with Edward after his other brother, Richard, talks to him. Edward appoints George as Duke of Clarence. By the end of the play, Richard, his younger brother, says in an aside to the audience that George ought to beware because Richard has ambitions of gaining the throne and George is one of the people who is standing in line in front of him.

Lady Elizabeth Grey

Lady Grey comes to King Edward to plead for her husband's land. Her husband was killed fighting for King Edward's right to the throne. When King Edward suggests that he will give her the land if she goes to bed with him, Lady Grey refuses. However, when King Edward proposes marriage, Lady Grey accepts and becomes Queen Elizabeth. She gives King Edward a son at the end of the play.

Lord Hastings

Lord Hastings is one of Edward's supporters. He appears only in act four.

King Henry VI

King Henry VI is the son of King Henry V. Unlike his father, Henry VI is weak, both physically and mentally. He wants peace but is not strong enough to stop his warring nobles. He has made a lot of enemies and by the time the play opens, he must confront the Duke of York, who is sitting on Henry's throne. Henry does not completely back down but he is not forceful enough, being willing to compromise with the duke in order to find a settlement. He promises the duke the crown upon Henry's death. The queen and his noblemen are furious.

Suffering from mental illness, handed down to him from his mother's side, Henry wants to retreat from public life. He dreams about being a simple shepherd and spends most of his time by himself. He delegates the affairs of state to his noblemen and his leadership during battles to his wife and young son. He appears most content while imprisoned, which allows him the peace and the time to read and think of spiritual things.

Henry is a puppet, doing what he is told and going where he is directed. Henry wishes his father had disinherited him the same way he disinherits his son. Henry does not want the throne. He is told to leave the battlefield because his wife fights better when Henry is not around. Henry flees to Scotland when a battle is lost, but he is found and imprisoned. He regains the throne for a year, but not due to any effort on his part. It is in prison that his murderer (in this play it is Richard, the son of the Duke of York) finds him, at which time Henry resigns himself to his fate.

Henry is not a force in this play. He is merely an incident. He appears only when he is forced to, then disappears. He makes no grand speeches and the only forceful move he makes is when he asks (almost pleads) with the Duke of York to allow him to remain on the throne. The duke agrees but only temporarily, canceling out the authority that Henry meekly demonstrated.

King Lewis XI
King Lewis XI (referred to as King Louis XI in some texts) is the king France. He accepts Queen Margaret at court and hears her plea for assistance in putting down the rebellion of the House of York in their attempt to win the crown. King Lewis is also the brother-in-law of Bona and accepts the deal that Warwick proposes—having King Edward marry Bona. The French king is very disappointed, however, when he learns that King Edward has married Lady Grey. At this point, the French king turns all his support to Queen Margaret, sending French troops to England to fight against the Yorks.

Queen Margaret
The queen is wife to King Henry VI and mother of Prince Edward. As Shakespeare portrays her, Margaret is very strong-willed and is as fierce as the king is reticent. Throughout the play, Margaret's main goal is to fight for the throne—not just for her husband, but more importantly for her son. When she speaks forcefully, she is ridiculed for being more like a man than a woman. In turn, she berates her husband for being so mild and giving up the throne without a fight.

In the battle victory that she enjoys in the beginning of the play, she is as violent as any of

Margaret of Anjou *(Hulton Archive/Getty Images)*

her men, helping Clifford, for example, to kill the Duke of York. Her speeches as she attempts to raise the spirits of her exhausted army are of an equal to any of Shakespeare's monologues written for male leaders in the midst of war.

Margaret comes across as a strong, articulate woman, who has a goal in mind that she is determined to bring to fruition. She is not afraid of facing her enemies and is not ashamed that she can lead an army better than the king. Of the three women in this play, Margaret does not represent the ultimate vision of femininity, but is rather a woman who is not afraid to fight for what she believes in.

Marquess of Montague
Brother to the Duke of York, the Marquess of Montague supports the Duke of York's claims to the throne. However, when Warwick changes allegiance after Edward marries Lady Grey, Montague also appears on Queen Margaret's side in battle. Montague recognized that England needed the alliance with France. Montague is with Warwick in the last battle between Henry's forces and Edward's.

Richard, Duke of Gloucester

Richard is the third son of the Duke of York and youngest remaining brother of King Edward. Shakespeare paints Richard as having a very misshapen body, which is not completely confirmed by historical events. However, in the play, Richard refers to his body as the reason he will never do well with women or in the court. Richard therefore decides that the only way to gain power is to ascend to the throne. In order to do this, though, he realizes he must get rid of a long line of people in front of him. Richard's goal throughout the play is to stick close to Edward, not through allegiance but in order to keep an eye on Edward and be prepared for the chance to kill him.

Richard is responsible for several deaths in the play, most importantly Prince Edward, son of Henry VI, as well as Henry VI himself. Richard often mocks his brother, Edward, but he does not become as offended by Edward's mistakes as does George. Richard's higher goals keep him disinterested in Edward other than as a stepping stone to Richard's ultimate goal.

Some of Richard's significant statements include the image of the three suns in act two, scene one, through which he ironically implies that the three brothers should stand together as one. All the while Richard is scheming to kill his brothers. Richard also asks for all the gruesome details of his father's death, something that Edward cannot bear to hear. This possibly fuels Richard's own desires to kill. At the end of the play, when Richard kisses Edward's newborn baby, Richard implies that he kisses the baby boy as Judas kissed Jesus.

Richard, Duke of York

Richard is an old adversary of King Henry VI and Queen Margaret. He is related to Henry VI and claims he is the rightful heir to the throne, through the line of Richard II. The duke claims his inheritance from Richard II's eldest son; while Henry VI is related through Richard II's younger son. Richard has made this claim prior to this drama, but he takes advantage of King Henry's lessened involvement in the political affairs of his rule. Richard puts together an army, which includes his sons, Edward, George, and Richard, to fight for the crown. The play begins with Richard sitting on the throne, although he has not actually yet won it. When Henry enters the room in the first act, Richard makes a deal with the king, taking an oath that Henry can maintain possession of the crown until his death. At that time, Richard will be crowned king. However, Richard's sons do not want to wait that long. They talk Richard into breaking this oath and once again going against Henry's armies. Richard is killed by Queen Margaret and Clifford after one of the battles. His head is placed on the gate of York, the city that he once ruled.

Lord Rivers

Lord Rivers supports King Edward and is Lady Grey's brother. He appears briefly in act four. It is to Lord Rivers that Lady Grey announces that she is pregnant with Edward's child.

THEMES

Bloody Murder and War

Most of the action of Shakespeare's *King Henry VI, Part Three* takes place on the battlefield, as the two branches of one family, the Lancastrians and the Yorkists, fight for the right to the throne. Warfare is glorified throughout the dialogue, praising men who are proud enough to fight and sacrifice their lives. Little thought is given to the taking of life. Most of the murders are rationalized as merely a means to get what one wants—certain people have to be eliminated in order for one family, or the other, to claim the throne. Whoever has the bigger or the stronger army wins the right to rule. Oaths are broken, and there seem to be no laws that can settle the dispute. The only recourse is to fight to the death in wars. This play focuses on the War of Roses and the bloody results as the two families clash. There is less time given to other human developments in this play other than the desire to completely annihilate one another.

Accession to the Throne

The major question of this drama is who deserves the right to be called king. Two branches of one family, descendents from the same relative, Edward III, argue for the throne. Each has a logical, if not legal, case. Bloodlines cross, making the path of accession murky. So it comes down to which side has the most physical power, putting weaker members, especially young princes, at risk. Shakespeare points out the weaknesses in this system, especially through the character of Richard, who commits himself to eliminating all those who stand in his way to accede to the throne. He will kill anyone who is in line before him, or so Shakespeare implies. Whether in real life this actually happened was never confirmed, but Richard did eventually win the crown through the mysterious deaths of those who might have attained it before him. Whether Shakespeare was using this play to point out the horrors of such a system gone wrong is not known. But by emphasizing the battles and adding the element of Richard's scheming, one could argue that this was indeed Shakespeare's point.

Role of Women

There are three women in this drama, Queen Margaret, Lady Grey, and Bona. The most powerful of these women is Queen Margaret, whom Shakespeare endows with the role of saving the crown for her husband and therefore her son, the prince. Margaret's lines in this play are similar to what Shakespeare usually reserves for male characters. Margaret rallies her soldiers to fight and she also stands up to powerful people such as Richard, Edward, and the Duke of York. Even the old Duke of York chastises her for being too manly. Women are supposed to be soft and therefore pliant, the duke tells her. But not so Margaret, who leads her troops to war and even asks that the king leave her side because she fights better when he is not around. Margaret is portrayed to be almost like Joan of Arc, who led the French against the English in taking back the French land that England had once claimed. Margaret is strong willed, intelligent, and brave. She even fools the Yorkists into believing that they can defeat her merely because she is a woman. The way Shakespeare creates her, Margaret plays the so-called husband role to her diminutive Henry, who shies away from war and hides behind books. In the process, though, as the Duke of York points out, Margaret loses all definitions of femininity. In order to be this strong, Shakespeare implies, a woman can no longer be a woman. She, in all but fact, is a man. Even in her role with her son, she acts more like a father than a mother.

It is Lady Grey who plays out the role of femininity. Edward is enamored of Lady Grey's feminine charms and immediately wants to go to bed with her when he sees her. She is also the maker of children, having already conceived and given birth to three when Edward meets her. Edward seems to want to ensure that he has an heir and latches on to Lady's Grey's fertility.

Lady Grey is strong but soft spoken. She demands her land and refuses to go to bed with Edward. So the king relents and marries her. Lady Grey then produces a son for him. She is the epitome of the perfect wife: someone strong enough to stand up for her rights and yet willing to succumb when she gets what she wants. She supports her husband, worries about him when he is at war, and stays home, rather than joining him in battle, to take care of their son.

Bona, the French king's sister-in-law, plays a very minor, as well as docile, role. She is woman as object, used to create liaisons between one country and another. She has no will of her own; she does what she is told. She is a title, a piece of paper, a puppet. She is, in other words, not real. She merely holds a place. One of Bona's three lines in the play has her saying to Edward's messenger: "Tell him, in hope he'll prove a widower shortly, I'll wear the willow garland for his sake." This is a powerful line but it lacks any significance. Is she insinuating that she is going to kill Lady Grey? Or is she just hoping for it, a careless wish? There is no substance behind it. The willow garland is the sign of a disappointed lover. But even this is weak, as there was no love between her and Edward. Bona is the weakest woman of the three women in this play, the complete opposite of Queen Margaret. Through these three women, Shakespeare provides a full glimpse of womanhood of his time—at least, that which is seen in the noble classes.

Allegiance

The subject of allegiance sways back and forth through this drama. Starting at the top, King Henry has no allegiance to his son, disinheriting him in hopes that Henry will finally find peace in his life. Margaret and her son, however, have sworn themselves to the recapturing of the throne, a promise from which they do not distract themselves. As wishy-washy as Henry is, Margaret and the prince are completely committed. Shortly thereafter, the Duke of York, who had sworn to accept Henry's decree, goes back on his word and thus negates any allegiance he had shared with the king.

On the side of the Yorkists, Richard is the most committed, although his allegiance is not to his country or to his brothers. Richard's only allegiance is to himself. It is a strong commitment, one he will keep until he has won the throne, no matter what he has to do to get it.

TOPICS FOR FURTHER STUDY

- Compare the Wars of the Roses in England with the Civil War in the United States. Were there any similarities in the weaponry? Were the military strategies different? How did the casualties compare? What were the various sizes of the armies? How much land did each of the civil wars cover? Were the battles continuous or were there intervals in between? How long did each war last? Record your statistics on a chart and present your findings to your class.

- One commentator compared Queen Margaret to Britain's prime minister Margaret Thatcher. Research each woman and the roles they played in the history of England. Did you find any similarities? Write a short summary of each woman's life, challenges, and accomplishments; then present your findings to your class.

- Imagine that you are King Edward IV, and you have fallen in love with Lady Grey. She refuses to have anything to do with you because she thinks all you want is to take her to bed. Write a love poem (in any style, either modern or in an Elizabethan tone) to Lady Grey, convincing her that your love is true and that you want to marry her.

- One of the most poignant scenes in *Henry VI, Part Three* occurs in act two, scene five, in which the king thinks about the effects of war. Find two classmates who will present a portion of this scene to your class. Begin with line 55, where a son appears on the scene, dragging with him a dead body, only to find out it is his father. Continue the scene until line 124. Each person should memorize his or her lines and deliver them with as much passion as possible, imagining that each has killed someone they loved. Afterwards, lead a discussion on the topic of Henry VI's effectiveness as a king. Was he too weak, or was he a man of peace surrounded by times of war? Base the discussion on the speech that Henry makes in this scene.

Richard's brother George, however, sways one way and then the other, depending on who looks like they might win the war. He stands behind his brother Edward until he believes that having the French king on Queen Margaret's side will ensure that the queen will win. Then, just before a battle against his brother, George is easily persuaded to ask Edward's forgiveness and allow him to fight on Edward's side.

Edward's allegiance is likewise shaky. He appears to want to go forward in attaining the crown, but he is always a bit reluctant to move in that direction. Usually, Richard is the one to push him, telling Edward that now is the time, not later; or reminding Edward that not only is Edward the duke (after their father dies) but also heir to the throne. Edward does not keep his word with Warwick, either, sending his ambassador to France with one goal, to win the hand of Bona, and then no sooner is Warwick gone than Edward marries Lady Grey.

Warwick's lack of commitment is warranted, to a point. He is embarrassed when he has just told the French king that Edward truly loves Bona, then has to announce that Edward has married Lady Grey. Right on the spot, Warwick, who has spent all his life up until that moment on the side of the Yorkists, turns to his enemy, Queen Margaret, and not only tells her that he will support her in her fight to regain the throne but also commits his daughter to marry the queen's son.

Shakespeare might have presented all these different degrees of allegiance to show the meaningless of such commitments. All of the allegiances in this play are non-binding, completely

---

reliant on a person's word. The drama demonstrates that this is not a strong enough bind.

Rivalry

The rivalry between the Lancastrians and the Yorkists, two branches of the same family, brings a whole country into war. It is a long-standing rivalry, going back one hundred and fifty years. Over the course of that time, members of one or another of the families are killed in pursuit of victory.

Rivalries are not only present in the larger scope but also on a more personal level, such as is seen in Richard, King Edward's brother. Richard, who is overlooked as an heir to the throne because he is younger than Edward, is determined to do what he must to ensure that he spends time on the throne. He is not content that his brother is finally king, having won a bloody war against the Lancastrians. Richard must win the crown for himself, even if it means the death of his brothers.

Rivalry is not inherently wrong. In other words, it does not always lead to bloodshed. Rivalry, used in a positive way, can make each side stronger. But in this play, rivalry does no such thing. The battles that are fought are to the death. There are few rules of competition. If someone sneaks up on another person and stabs that person, then the one remaining standing is declared the winner. This is the way rivalry is portrayed in this play, at least. There are no noble causes, no good over evil; there is just a fight between two factions. Whoever has the biggest army claims the prize. England is not necessarily stronger or weaker depending on who wins, thus it does not really matter who wins. The best result of this rivalry is that in the end the fighting is done, and hopefully the country can enjoy some peace.

STYLE

History Play

Henry VI, Part Three is classified as one of Shakespeare's history plays. Shakespeare wrote ten history plays in all: *King John, Richard II, Henry IV, Part One, Henry IV, Part Two, Henry V, Henry VI, Part One, Henry VI, Part Two, Henry VI, Part Three, Henry VIII,* and *Richard III.* Each of these plays covers an English king's reign between the twelfth and the sixteenth

centuries. Through Shakespeare's history plays, a sense of nationalism is expressed. Great heroic speeches are presented by kings and queens who appear bigger than life, for the most part. The source for most of Shakespeare's history plays came from the study of English history by Raphael Holinshed called the *Chronicle* (1587).

Shakespeare was particular about what he chose to put into his history plays. Not all of the information is historically accurate; and he did not include all the details that were available to him. Instead, he shaped the plays so they would tell a more dramatic story. Shakespeare was also influenced by the politics of his time. For example, Richard, the brother of King Edward IV, is clearly depicted as a malformed villain, which some historians find a very distorted description. Literary scholars argue that the form of the history plays was based on propaganda, to show the evils of civil war, for example, and to celebrate the end of the rivalry between Lancaster and York. Shakespeare's last play in this series is *Henry VIII,* which marks the beginning of the Tudor monarchy, of which Queen Elizabeth I was a part. In other words, Shakespeare's reason behind creating these plays, as well as the form of his stories, may well have been dictated by his allegiance to the queen of his own time.

The history plays are broken into different cycles. The first tetralogy includes the three parts of *Henry VI* and *Richard III.* The second tetralogy includes *Richard II,* the two parts of *Henry IV,* and *Henry V.* When the whole series of history plays is performed in historic order (with the second tetralogy presented before the first tetralogy), the series is called *The War of the Roses.*

Use of Rhetoric to Inspire

Whether Shakespeare was writing *Julius Caesar, Henry V,* or any of his other plays that focus on a leader who is trying to persuade a crowd of citizens or group of soldiers, Shakespeare demonstrates his powerful use of rhetoric. *Henry VI* is no exception. The only difference might be that in *Henry VI,* most of that rhetoric is spoken by a woman.

In act one, scene one, Margaret rails against her husband after he has disinherited their son. The rhetoric is spoken in free verse, a series (usually lengthy) of phrases written in iambic pentameter with no ending rhyme. Margaret's first speech begins, "Enforced thee? Art thou King, and / wilt be forced? / I shame to hear thee speak. Ah, timorous wretch!" Here, Margaret is trying to persuade her husband to change his mind about giving the throne to the Yorkists. She is unsuccessful in encouraging her husband, who has no will to fight, but she does inspire her son and many of the nobles who remain faithful to her.

Shortly afterward in the same act and scene, Richard uses rhetoric to persuade his father, the Duke of York, to forget about his oath that he made to King Henry. The oath, Richard tells his father, is not binding because it was not taken in front of a magistrate. "Your oath, my lord, is vain and frivolous. / Therefore, to arms! And, father, do but think / How sweet a thing it is to wear a crown." Unlike Margaret's power to influence her husband, Richard is quite effective in persuading his father to forget about the oath and fight against Margaret to win the crown.

Another example of how Shakespeare uses rhetorical speeches is in act one, scene four, after Margaret has captured the Duke of York and mocks him before putting him to death. She uses her speech to encourage her troops to continue the fight until they regain the throne completely.

In this play, it seems that more rhetoric is used against the king than he himself uses it. In act two, scene two, it is Lord Clifford's turn to persuade Henry, who is disgusted at the sight of the Duke of York's head impaled on the gate to the city. But Clifford has not yet seen enough blood. The battles have just begun. Clifford knows he must persuade the king to allow the army to continue the fight. So Clifford begins: "My gracious liege, this too much lenity / And harmful pity must be laid aside." Clifford continues by describing how lions look upon beasts that might destroy them, an effective way to get the king motivated to leave and let them fight.

Throughout the play, this use of rhetoric, with its more lofty and poetic language than the ordinary prose, lifts the spirits of the characters, moving them in a specific direction through the power of Shakespeare's words.

Shakespearian Language: Viewing versus Reading

Shakespeare's plays were meant to be seen, not read. This is even truer today than in Shakespeare's time. Because the language is antiquated, with vocabulary that no longer is in use and contains word play whose references are no longer common to the modern audience, it is difficult to understand and appreciate the play just by reading it silently to oneself. When reading, it is hard to flow over the words without understanding each and every one of them. Words are the only clues that a reader has in trying to make sense of what is going on. However, when the play is dramatized with real actors and actresses, settings and atmosphere, the play comes alive. Actors use body language and phrasing that can help the audience interpret what is going on. Voice inflection also helps. The action of the play gives the audience more clues, playing out the meaning of words that are unfamiliar. While observing the play being performed, audiences do not get stuck on single words of dialogue but rather let the words flow through them, matching them with the reactions of the actors, even if the specific words do not make sense. Also, after hearing the words for a while, the audience becomes accustomed to their use and begins to make definitions for themselves, making the play so much more enjoyable than a solitary reading of what can seem like dry text. The text can be used to enhance the experience after viewing the performance.

HISTORICAL CONTEXT

Henry VI (1421–71)

The English King Henry VI was born at Windsor castle, the only child of Henry V and Catherine. His father had been a valiant and brilliant military leader, having regained ownership of lands in France as well as a legitimate claim to the French throne. Henry VI was only nine months old when his father died, thus becoming, in name, England's next king.

Henry was expected to follow in his father's footsteps. Unfortunately for England, Henry was inclined in a different direction. He was also stricken with a mental illness, inherited from his maternal grandfather, King Charles VI of France, which caused him to often disappear from view during the latter part of his reign.

Because his mother was French and only twenty years old at the time of her husband's death, she did not play a strong role in the upbringing of her son. The nobles around her were suspicious both of her heritage and her age. Henry was given a tutor, the Earl of Warwick; Cardinal Beufort and the Duke of Gloucester, uncles of Henry's, also closely guided his upbringing.

A council was formed to rule the country until Henry was of age.

In 1429, right before his eighteenth birthday, Henry was officially crowned king of England. Two years later, due to his father's previous victories in the Hundred Years' War with France, Henry was also crowned king of France. Although this coronation in France was legal, Henry did not pursue the reign, preferring peace over battle. In the meantime, the son of French King Charles VI claimed a right to the throne. With the help of Joan of Arc, Charles reclaimed most of the land the English held in France and was crowned Charles VII, so that technically England's rule of the land became a moot point.

From the beginning, Henry showed little interest in governing his country. Instead, he turned over that job to his noblemen. Instead of fighting France, Henry was advised to pursue peace through his marriage to French King Charles VII's niece, Margaret of Anjou. They were married in 1445. Henry was twenty-four, Margaret was sixteen. With Margaret's strong personality and Henry's reticence, the new queen quickly took over the reign of England. In 1453, Henry and Margaret had a son, Prince Edward. In the same year as his son's birth, Henry VI had a mental breakdown. Richard, Duke of York, was assigned as regent, protector of the realm, until Henry's recovery. Headstrong Queen Margaret alienated Richard, and he attacked her troops in 1455 at St. Albans, beginning the War of the Roses. Five years later, Richard captured Henry and forced him to recognize Richard as legal heir to the crown. Henry escaped and, in 1461, started a counter attack against Richard but lost. Richard's son, Edward IV, was crowned king and Margaret and Henry fled to Scotland. In 1465, Queen Margaret and King Henry were captured and held in the Tower of London for five years. Power was restored to Henry for one year, from 1470 until 1471. When Edward IV regained the throne, Henry and the prince, his son, were killed and Margaret was sent back to France.

Queen Margaret (1430–1482)

Margaret was the fifth child of the Count of Anjou (an accomplished artist and author) and his wife, Isabella of Lorraine. Margaret's father eventually became the king of Naples and Sicily. Margaret was much sought after, so when she was given to King Henry VI, her father got away without offering a dowry. In fact, England's ambassadors, headed by the Earl of Suffolk, as accounted by some historians, approved a deal with the French king to actually give back French lands held by England at that time in order to gain Margaret as a wife for Henry VI.

Margaret allied herself with Suffolk and two successive Dukes of Somerset, against the Duke of York. She tried in vain to gain the title of regent when her husband suffered his first mental breakdown, but this title was given to the Duke of York.

After her army was defeated and Edward IV took the throne, Margaret first retreated to Scotland and later to her homeland in Lorraine in 1463, where she set up a court in exile with her son. In 1468, the Earl of Warwick combined forces with her, and Margaret returned to England in an attempt to reclaim the throne. Unfortunately, Warwick was killed in battle the day she returned in 1471. Unwilling to give up, Margaret marched her army toward Wales to gather reinforcements. King Edward learned of this and cut off her passage to the bridge across the Severn River. Margaret had to take an alternate route, which further exhausted her already tired troops. She planned to cross the river at Tewkesbury, but Edward was right behind her. She turned her army to face Edward's on May 4, 1471. Margaret's forces were defeated. The Duke of Somerset, who had supported Margaret, was tried for treason and killed. Margaret's son died in the battle. Margaret was taken prisoner and later ransomed in 1478. Margaret spent her remaining years in Anjou and died four years later.

Wars of the Roses, 1455–1487

The Wars of the Roses were a series of battles fought in a civil war in England between two opposing houses, the House of Lancaster (symbolized by a red rose) and the House of York (symbolized by a white rose). The term Wars of the Roses was actually instigated by Shakespeare. At the time of the civil war, no such term was used.

This civil war, mostly because of such a high death toll on the nobles of the country, caused many changes in England. It marked the beginning of the end of the feudal system in England and the strong emergence of a merchant class that was accumulating wealth, land, and therefore, power. It also marked the end of Medieval England and the beginning of the country's Renaissance. Another ending was the line of

David Oyelowo as King Henry VI, at the Swan Theatre, Stratford-upon-Avon, England, 2000

(© Donald Cooper/Photostage. Reproduced by permission)

the Plantagenet monarchy and the beginning of the Tudor reign, begun with Henry VII and continued, in Shakespeare's time, with Henry's daughter, Elizabeth I.

The civil war had its roots in the overthrow of King Richard II (1367–1400) in 1399. Henry Bolingbroke (who would become King Henry IV) brought an army to England from France to reclaim an enormous amount of land that King Richard had taken away from Henry upon Henry's father's death. King Richard had a legal right to do so, seeing as Henry's land and the power it gave him was viewed as a threat to the kingdom. However, Henry was willing to fight for his land, which he did. While King Richard was putting down a rebellion in Ireland, Henry took advantage of the king's absence, fought with local nobles and gained enough power to declare himself king. Richard, who was not a very popular king, was put into prison, where he died, mysteriously, a year later.

Henry IV's reign was not an easy one. Having taken the throne by force, he had made many enemies, especially those whose legitimate claim to the throne he had ignored. Henry's oldest son (who would become Henry V) was a brilliant and courageous warrior and was responsible, on many occasions, for putting down major rebellions against his father—rebellions that came from the other side of the family who wanted the throne. Beginning in 1405, Henry IV suffered from a recurring illness that finally took his life in 1413.

Henry V (1387–1422) would go on to secure English-held lands in France and strengthen the bond between the two countries by winning the right to the French, as well as to the English, Crown. Henry V died at a young age in battle in France, leaving a nine-month-old son—King Henry VI. While Henry V was busy fighting wars in France and accumulating wealth for his country, the feud between the York and Lancaster Houses was subdued. Only one rebellion occurred, and the leader of that rebellion was tried for treason and killed. However, with Henry V's death—and only a baby for king, and Henry V's wife, who was not only young but of French blood—members of both Houses began maneuvering again for power.

Henry VI was a weak man, surrounded by poorly managed counselors. Not only did Henry suffer from mental illnesses, he lost most of the land that his father had won in France. Although Henry VI technically was king of France, he lost all authority in that country. Many English nobles, each with his own powerful army, grew discontent with Henry VI's rule. They saw a chance to overtake what they perceived to be an illegitimate monarch and replace him with one from the House of York. The Duke of York was appointed as regent when Henry had his first serious bout of mental illness in 1453. Two years later, wary of the duke's rise in power, Queen Margaret made sure the duke was booted out of the court. Then she built a powerful army, ready to face the duke's anticipated attack, which came in 1455 in St. Albans. The queen's army lost, and the duke was restored to power as a regent of the court.

After several more battles and jockeying for military power, the two armies met in Northampton for a battle that would once again see the defeat of the king's army. King Henry, as a result,

COMPARE
&
CONTRAST

- **1400s:** England is involved in a long civil war as rival members of the Plantagenet family claim their right to the throne.

  Today: England is involved in a war against terrorism, supporting the U.S. effort in Iraq. British involvement is causing dissention at home among the populace and members of Parliament.

- **1400s:** Queen Margaret forms an army and leads her men into battle to fight for the throne.

  Today: Queen Elizabeth II tries to keep her family's secrets out of the tabloids, which expose clandestine love affairs of her children, among other things.

- **1400s:** The Tower of London is used to house imprisoned royalty, including Henry VI and Lady Grey. The Tower also houses a set of ravens, kept there due to superstitions that if they are released, England will fail.

  Today: The Tower of London is a historic site that tourists often visit. There are souvenir shops and restaurants inside. The Tower also houses a set of ravens, kept there due to long historic traditions.

- **1400s:** London's population ranges between 60,000 and 100,000 people.

  Today: The population of London is approximately 7.3 million.

---

in 1460, was taken prisoner. This gave the Duke of York a surge of power; and he made a claim for the throne. The nobles in parliament were stunned. Even the men who supported York thought this was too bold a move. They had not meant to remove Henry from the throne. The parliament then worked out a compromise, which stated that the duke would inherit the throne upon Henry's death. The queen and her son were told to leave London, and the duke retained his position as regent, thus he was able to govern England when Henry was incapacitated by his disease. The queen rebelled at these actions, gathered an army around her, and positioned herself outside of York. When the duke learned of this, he went after her, although the queen's troops were double the size of the duke's. The duke's army was easily defeated.

The Duke of York was beheaded, as was his seventeen-year-old son. His head, as it was in Shakespeare's play, was placed on the gate to the city of York. Edward, eldest son of the duke and who was just eighteen at the time, led an army into London. The town favored the House of York and cheered Edward on. Parliament unofficially named Edward king.

In 1461, the Battle of Towton, one of the bloodiest battles ever fought on English soil at the time, was fought with an estimated 25,000 people dying. Edward's army greatly defeated the queen's army, forcing the queen and king, with their son, to flee to Scotland. That same year, Edward was officially crowned king of England, becoming Edward IV.

Edward enjoy a few years of peace, but when he married Elizabeth Woodville in secret, he embarrassed Richard Neville, Earl of Warwick, a long-time friend, who was working to arrange a marriage for Edward with the French king. Edward also disallowed his brothers, Richard and George, to marry Neville's daughters. Neville, no longer enjoying privileges at court as he once had, formed an allegiance with Edward's brother George, who was jealous of his brother's power. In 1469, they fought against Edward. Neville and George won a decisive battle, held Edward hostage, killed Edward's father-in-law, and forced Edward to have parliament recognize Edward as an illegitimate king and to give the crown to George. Edward's younger brother, Richard, rescued the king, and Neville and George had to flee to France.

In France, it was King Louis XI who suggested the alliance of Queen Margaret and Neville. The two agreed, Neville promised his daughter as wife to the queen's son, and returned to England with a powerful army. Edward was defeated and had to flee to Holland and then to Burgundy. Edward, supported by the king of Burgundy, returned to England. Shortly after Neville had paraded Henry VI all over London as the restored king, he was defeated by Edward's new army in 1471. Henry as well as his son were then killed, strengthening Edward's claim to the throne.

Edward died young, in 1483, leaving his twelve-year-old son heir to the throne. Edward V's reign lasted only a couple of months. Richard, the uncle to the young king, claimed that his brother (Edward IV) had married Elizabeth illegally and therefore his heirs could not be crowned king. Parliament agreed, and crowned King Richard III in 1483. Edward V was placed in the Tower of London, along with his younger brother, and was never again seen.

Two years later, in 1485, Richard would meet his death in a battle against Henry Tudor of the House of Lancaster; he would become King Henry VII. Henry married Elizabeth of York, the strongest claimant for the throne from the York house, thus securing his position and ending the long Wars of the Roses.

CRITICAL OVERVIEW

King Henry VI, Part Three was a popular drama when it first appeared. As Norrie Epstein, in the book *The Friendly Shakespeare*, writes, "The *Henry VI* trilogy was a box-office smash that turned an unremarkable actor named William Shakespeare into the most successful playwright of the day." Epstein continues that the Elizabethan audiences enjoyed watching dramas that depicted their past. In Shakespeare's time, "the Wars of the Roses were still vivid in the minds of Shakespeare's audience." The stories of the members of the House of Lancaster and the House of York were as familiar to the English audiences in the sixteenth and seventeenth centuries as stories about the Kennedys were to twentieth-century citizens of the United States. Knowing the outcome of all the historic events gave the audiences of Shakespeare's time a "double perspective," which "allowed them to observe the past while knowing its outcome—both in history and on stage. Thus the characters' words were given an extra level of meaning that is lost to us today."

Epstein then expounds on the merit of Shakespeare's history plays by stating: "Shakespeare domesticates history. Kings and queens are mothers and fathers. When not conducting state business, rulers eat, drink, make love, sleep, and gossip." In spite of this, Epstein writes, "Even many Shakespeare enthusiasts don't bother to read *Henry VI*, and it's rarely performed in its entirety" (all three parts). Although "the plot is a sweeping panorama," Epstein writes, "there's no hero, just a succession of characters who temporarily hold center stage and then quickly depart." Epstein adds, "Even Henry seems almost incidental at times."

Despite the lack of production and the length of this play (when all three parts are considered), Milton Crane, a professor at the George Washington University, who wrote an introduction to the text of Shakespeare's play *Henry VI, Part Three*, states that in the twentieth century "more persons have seen the three parts of *Henry VI* than had ever seen any one of the plays in all the centuries of their existence." Crane credits the explosion of interest to the exciting details of the play. "Though the framework of *Henry VI* is serious, moral, and didactic—a history, on the one hand, of France's efforts to free herself from English domination and, on the other, of the hideous social and political convulsions that we call the Wars of the Roses—these annals of an age of anarchy are full of thrilling and gruesome details calculated to delight the heart of a groundling." Crane then adds that this play, with its bloody feud between the Houses of Lancaster and York, is "Shakespeare's inspired anticipation of the Western movie."

Maurice Charney, writing in *All of Shakespeare*, refers to *Henry VI, Part Three* as "undoubtedly Shakespeare's most military play." Then Charney adds that from the very first scene in the play, Shakespeare "sets the tone for this murderous, savage, and chaotic play." But for all the blood, there is a scene that Charney focuses on in act two, scene five, the famous Father and Son scene, in which a son realizes that he has killed his father; and a father discovers that he has killed his own son. This scene, Charney writes, "powerfully enacts a symbolic tableau.... This is a choral scene intended to represent what the savagery of the Wars of the Roses is all about."

In John Julius Norwich's *Shakespeare's Kings*, the author writes, "Nowhere is Shakespeare's extraordinary ability to turn a chronicle into a drama more impressively demonstrated than in the third part of *King Henry VI*." It was only in part three of this play, Norwich states, that Shakespeare "is called upon to encapsulate in little more than two hours what is virtually the entire course of the Wars of the Roses," a process that, in reality, took sixteen years. "Now at last, with all the inevitability of Greek tragedy, the House of Lancaster suffers retribution for the atrocity committed at the end of the previous century: the deposition and murder of Richard II and the usurpation of his crown by Henry IV are finally avenged." Norwich then goes on to surmise that in the last scene of the play, Shakespeare makes clear the true purpose of this play, the "villainy and duplicity" of Richard, who would go on (in Shakespeare's next play as well as in history) to become Richard III. "It was this, above all else, that the Elizabethan audiences would carry home with them; it was to emphasize this that Shakespeare had been deliberately building up the character of Richard; and this that he was to make the theme of the last and greatest play of his series [the tetralogy of *Henry V, Henry VI*, and *Richard III*]."

CRITICISM

Joyce Hart

Hart, a freelance writer and published author, digs into the text of this play to find the nature of the king as Shakespeare presents him.

There are many descriptions of the historic King Henry VI, the English ruler of the fifteenth century. He was known for having inherited a mental illness from his mother's side of the family and, therefore, for being an ill and weak monarch. Others refer to King Henry VI as being a bit of a philosopher, who was a voracious reader, and an attempted peacemaker. But Henry was also a descendant of King Edward III, of the Plantagenet family, a line of kings that was not well liked, especially by the Tudors, of whom Shakespeare's Queen Elizabeth I was a member. Since Queen Elizabeth held a tight rein on the material that was presented on stage

during her time, audiences might never know for sure how Shakespeare truly felt about King Henry. Shakespeare's depiction of the king in *Henry VI, Part Three* may merely reflect what Shakespeare thought Queen Elizabeth might want to see. So the question is not what did Shakespeare like or dislike about King Henry but rather, how he presented him on the stage. What kind of ruler was Henry as presented by his actions and his speeches in this drama? What kind of a father was he? What were some of the thoughts that Shakespeare attributed to him? And how does King Henry compare with some of the other major characters in this play?

King Henry's first appearance in *Henry VI, Part Three* is in the first scene of the first act. The king enters and sees the Duke of York sitting on King Henry's throne. King Henry's tone is mild and timid, first turning to his men, specifically the Earl of Northumberland and Lord Clifford. Instead of Henry directly confronting the Duke of York and stating his outrage (if it is outrage), Henry reminds Northumberland and Clifford that the duke was responsible for their fathers' deaths. "You both have vowed revenge," the king tells them, just in case they might have forgotten. Strangely, after trying to rile Northumberland and Clifford by reminding them of the deaths of their fathers, the king then tells them to be patient, as if he has had second thoughts, which is exactly what Shakespeare implies. For the king then mentions that the citizens of London favor the duke and his noblemen, and more importantly, the king knows that the duke's army is prepared to fight. Although the king's own noblemen are ready to kill the duke for what they see as an act of treason on the part of the duke, the king informs them that he too wants a war, but it will be a war of words, not of swords. The king's reason for not wanting bloodshed (other than not having a prepared army to back him) is that the fighting would disrupt the Parliament. The king says: "Far be the thought of this [killing the Duke] from Henry's heart, / To make a shambles of the Parliament House!"

A lot could be read into these words of the king. At first seeing the duke sitting in the throne, Henry was obviously surprised. He must have felt anger or fear to have turned to his men and invited them to act out their revenge. But a bigger fear, that of being unsuccessful in removing the duke or worse that—of being defeated—also existed in Henry's mind.

Then there is a third fear, one that he hides more cleverly. It is a fear that if his men realize that their king is afraid, they might also desert him. Henry then summons up as much courage as he can, confronting the duke and telling him to remove himself from Henry's throne and kneel before him to exhibit the duke's submission. Of course, the duke refuses and a battle of words ensues.

The duke and his sons, as well as his noblemen, make the king rethink his stance. It is true that Henry's grandfather and father were both kings before him, but the duke has pointed out that they attained the crown through rebellion against Edward III, which is pretty much the same thing the duke is planning on doing against Henry. In an aside to the audience, the king acknowledges that his own argument for a legitimate title to the crown is weak; and at that moment Henry begins to think about compromise. It is at this point that the audience sees that King Henry is not willing to fight for the throne. The king wants to maintain it, and he partially believes that he is entitled to it, but his argument is standing on shaky ground. The way the king looks at it, a compromise is better than completely losing the throne, even if it comes with the high cost of sacrificing his son's inherited right to be crowned. The king sighs over this thought, pondering what consequences will result, especially in reference to his son; but the king does not change his mind. Instead, he asks the Duke of York to make an oath. In his speech to the duke, Henry sounds regal. He suggests that he is making this compromise, giving the crown to the duke upon his own death, in order to stop the civil war that the country would have to suffer through. Whereas before, Henry's avoidance of war sounded more fearful, here it sounds passionate. Henry sounds more like a king wanting to spare his people further bloodshed.

As York and his men depart, each mentioning where they are going, either to their castle, to their soldiers, or to their followers, the king states that he will be returning to his court "with grief and sorrow." Since it looks like, at this juncture in the play, Henry has ended the civil war, you would think he would be happy. But he is not. The only thing that could be troubling him is that he has taken the throne away from his son. This proves to be true when Henry hears that the queen is coming and Henry tries to sneak away. It is probably not his son that

saddens Henry. He is reluctant to confront his wife, just as he was disinclined to confront York, who was sitting in Henry's throne. The audience can feel the fear rising in Henry once again.

There is reason for Henry to be concerned. The queen enters the room in a storm, cursing her husband for the mess he has created. Henry tries to calm her, as he had Northumberland and Clifford. But the queen is not quieted as easily as the king's men. "Ah, wretched man! Would I had died a maid / And never seen thee, never borne thee son." How could Henry have disinherited his son, the queen and the prince want to know? Here, Henry appears to be at his weakest in the entire play. He tries to rationalize his actions. He tries to make an excuse for himself. He tells the queen that he had no choice, that the duke made him do it. This is, of course, a rather pathetic statement, one that a child might make when he is caught doing something wrong and is about to be punished. Henry could have told the queen that he wanted to avoid bloodshed, that he wanted to prevent a civil war. He could also have told her that he believed his claim to the throne was illegitimate. These were, after all, the thoughts that he had had before he made the compromise with the duke. The queen sees through Henry's lame excuses and begins her diatribe against him. She insinuates that Henry is a lamb in the midst of wolves. Had she, a silly woman, confronted the duke, they would have had to kill her before she gave them the throne, she tells Henry. Unlike Henry, the queen has an army prepared and leaves to fight York until she has won back her son's right to the throne. And thus, the queen takes over the role that will work its way through this play: she will be the warrior, while Henry passes his time reading.

In act two, the king turns up in York, after the queen has slain the duke. It is in the second scene that Henry's wisdom begins to shine through his fear. The queen and Clifford are proud in their accomplishments, but the king has no such feelings and even warns Clifford that "things ill got had ever bad success." Henry also mentions the battles that his own father fought. His father thought that he had left a legacy that Henry would be proud of. But the king denies this. "I'll leave my son my virtuous deeds behind; / And would my father had left me no more!" Henry says. In other words, what the queen and Clifford have done, Henry likens to actions far less than righteous. Instead, Henry is grieved to see York's head on the post, just as he grieved for the murders that his own father committed in the name of winning land and thrones. The queen, on the other hand, is embarrassed by her husband, saying that his "soft courage" is a poor example to set for her troops. They will become disenchanted if they see the king feeling sorry for the duke. So in this scene, Shakespeare displays Henry as a soft-hearted humanitarian who cannot stand the mutilation and death that comes in war. Shortly after this, the queen and king are confronted by York's sons and noblemen. The king tries to speak, but his wife and son tell Henry to pick up his sword and fight, and Clifford tells the king to be quiet. This is the last time that Henry will be this close to battle. He will depart, and the queen will do all the rest of the fighting.

By scene five in act two, Henry is in a remote field, away from the actual fighting. It is here that Shakespeare has Henry be his most reflective. Henry thinks about war and compares it to storms at sea, swaying first one way and then the other. Ironically, Shakespeare, in the first act, had the queen insinuate that Henry was like a lamb. Here, in this scene, Shakespeare has Henry ruminating on how much sweeter life would be if he were a shepherd of sheep. If he were so, Henry would sit all day and do nothing more than count the minutes. "How sweet! how lovely!" Henry says to spend the day watching his sheep rather than to spend it fearing his "subjects' treachery." To be a king, Henry states, is not what it appears to be. Some think that being a king means one sleeps in comfort and eats the best fruits of the land. Henry does not see it that way. Rather, for him, everything in his life is touched by mistrust and treason. In this scene, it is not fear that fills Henry, but compassion. He cries with the son who has just killed his father and with the father who has just killed his son. Shakespeare, through Henry, decries the consequences and suffering of a civil war, a war unlike others because no matter who wins the battles, the country suffers great losses in the war.

Removed from battle, politics, and his throne, while hiding in northern England, Shakespeare has Henry admit that he has come to a place in his life where he feels most satisfied. Henry is found out by two hunters who ask him why he talks so much about kings. When Henry admits that he is a king, the hunters ask, if that is so, where is his crown. Henry answers: "My crown is in my heart, not on my head; / Not decked with diamonds and Indian stones, / Nor to be seen. My crown is called content: / A crown it is that seldom kings enjoy." Here Henry is at his strongest psychologically. He realizes that what he thinks of himself, what definitions he holds, cannot be taken away from him. If he thinks he is king, then that is so, no matter that Edward is sitting on the throne. Henry was crowned king and king he will be to his death. He does not need outward images to prove who he is. He is content with himself. His kingdom is not out in the world but in his heart and soul. Even after Henry temporarily regains the throne, he has no further use of it. He gives Warwick and Clarence the job of ruling the country. Henry has retired from the world.

In act four, scene eight, Henry evaluates his kingship. He talks with Exeter about the possibilities of Edward gaining the throne again. Henry has been reinstated to the throne and believes he will maintain it. He is wrong, of course, but he does not yet know this. Even minutes before Edward returns to take the crown once again, Henry mistakenly forgets that he is but a lamb and for a few minutes sees himself as a mighty lion. However, the image that Henry has as a powerful beast is not a brutal one, but rather one that has led his people with pity, mildness, mercy, and moderation. He has listened to his people's needs and tried to soothe their ailments. He has consoled them when they weep and forgiven them when they did wrong. He sees no reason why the people would choose Edward over him as their king. "And when the lion fawns upon the lamb, / The lamb will never cease to follow him." This is how Henry quietly and all but passively takes upon himself the image of the lion. However, Shakespeare has set Henry up to fail. As soon as Henry utters these words, he hears Edward and his men approaching. Edward's men take Henry into custody and imprison him in the tower. Henry had the image backward; he was out of touch with reality. The people do not support him, they do not follow him. Henry is not the gentle lion. He is still the meek lamb.

And finally, just before he dies, Henry refers to the shepherd metaphor again. Henry is locked in the tower when Richard enters with the tower guard. When Richard orders that the guard leave, Henry says: "So flies the reckless shepherd from the wolf; / So first the harmless sheep doth yield his fleece, / And next his throat unto the

WHAT
DO I READ
NEXT?

- *Rose Rage* is Edward Hall and Roger Warren's adaptation of Shakespeare's three parts of *Henry VI*, first performed in 2002, which tells the story that led to the Wars of the Roses. These screenwriters set the plays in a slaughter-house and provide a musical background and choreography when staged. A script can be bought from Theatre Communications Group, also published in 2002.

- To fully gain a picture of Henry VI's reign, seeing, or reading, all three parts of Shakespeare's *Henry VI* is highly recommended. Part One of *Henry VI* begins with the death of King Henry V, Henry VI's father, and ends with Henry's marriage to Margaret. Part Two follows the development of Henry VI as king and the underpinnings of the contested right of the throne that will lead to the Wars of the Roses in Part Three.

- Shakespeare's play *Henry V* provides a glimpse into the valor of this warrior king,

the father of Henry VI. Reading this play will give you the contrast between the father and son who would succeed him. Also, Shakespeare's play *Richard III* will provide you with a more complete view of the monarchs from the House of Lancaster, as Richard takes the throne; he was the last Lancaster member to do so.

- To help you better understand the political background and fuller historical context of Shakespeare's *Henry VI* read Allison Weir's *Wars of the Roses* (1996). Weir explains the relationships between the Yorkists and the Lancastrians, showing how their counter-claims to the throne led to the bloody civil war in England. Weir also wrote *The Princes in the Tower* (1995), an account of the last part of the Wars of the Roses, with a focus on the disappearance of Edward IV's two sons, whom Weir speculates were killed by Richard III in his bid to win the crown.

---

butcher's knife." Henry, once again, sees himself as a lamb, one marked for death this time. Henry knows it is his time to die, and he faces it more bravely than any other confrontation in the play. "Ah, kill me with thy weapon, not with words!/ My breast can better brook thy dagger's point / Than can my ears that tragic history."

So Henry dies maybe with more courage than he lived, at least more courage than he fought for his throne. Shakespeare portrays Henry as a soft-hearted king, who cried more for his people than for himself. Henry was a king who did not want to be king if it meant that he had to fight in wars. But he was not strong enough to keep the peace. He was sur-rounded by warmongers who thought more of themselves and their power than of the people they led. As Shakespeare creates him, Henry was a man out of step with his court and with his times. He was fearful when forced to confront

his wife, his men, and his enemies. He might have been incapable of becoming what it took to be a king, powerless of averting a civil war, but in the end, Shakespeare has Henry appear as a self-actualized man, who knew what he wanted and, although he could not attain what he wanted, was content with himself at his death.

Source: Joyce Hart, Critical Essay on *King Henry VI, Part Three*, in *Shakespeare For Students*, Second Edition, Thomson Gale, 2007

John D. Cox and Eric Rasmussen

Cox and Rasmussen provide a general overview of King Henry VI, Part 3. Examining the historical sources of the play, the critics focus on the "magical thinking" that Shakespeare offers in the work.

Rather than ask whether *3 Henry VI* illustrates or embodies a moral principle, it is possible to ask what kind of moral thinking the play exhibits. This question draws on the insights of

SHAKESPEARE RESERVES THE MAGICAL POWER

OF CURSES FOR *RICHARD III*, BUT HE TREATS OATHS

MAGICALLY IN *3 HENRY VI*.

social anthropology (as many postmodern critics have done) by recognizing a category of 'magical' thinking. Examples include belief in the ability of language to affect the material world directly, as in spells, incantations, curses and blessings. Magical thinking also includes prophecies, omens, 'prodigies', oaths and swearing, whose power goes beyond mere words, evoking a mysterious influence that operates in spite of human knowledge or intent. In the late sixteenth century, magical thinking was still deeply bound up with moral thinking.

It is evident that many of these examples of magical thinking are present in *3 Henry VI*, and they are inspired by a variety of sources, not merely the chronicle histories of Hall and Holinshed. The Bible is certainly one source, but so is the epic tradition—newly domesticated for English writers in Spenser's first instalment of *The Faerie Queene* in 1590, just before the first records of the *Henry VI* plays on stage—and so is Senecan tragedy, the most impressive model for serious drama in late Elizabethan England. Indeed, so powerful are the cultural models for magical thinking in the *Henry VI* plays and *Richard III* that the burden of proof is on those who would deny its presence and influence.

Shakespeare reserves the magical power of curses for *Richard III*, but he treats oaths magically in *3 Henry VI*. Faye Kelly has analysed the way that 'the entire structure of *3 Henry VI*' is permeated by 'broken oaths, broken vows, and perjury' (F. Kelly, 366). An omen appears in *3 Henry VI*, when the York brothers see three suns in the sky ... Richard recognizes that 'In this, the heaven figures some event' (2.1.32), and Edward believes that it refers to the brothers' unity, determining to change his heraldic device accordingly: 'Whate'er it bodes, henceforward will I bear / Upon my target three fair-shining suns' (2.1.39–40). One remarkable example of a 'prodigy' is noticed by Margaret, in referring to York's son, Richard, when she is mocking York:

And where's that valiant crookback prodigy,
Dickie, your boy, that with his grumbling voice
Was wont to cheer his dad in mutinies?

She is referring not to Richard's precocious talent but to his deformity (hence 'crookback'), also noted by young Clifford when he calls Richard 'foul stigmatic' (*2H6* 5.1.215), and admitted by Richard later in soliloquy (*3H6* 3.2.153–71). As for prophecies, Henry utters one about the young Earl of Richmond, calling him 'England's hope' and 'our country's bliss' (4.6.68, 70) thus providing the reason for Richmond's sole appearance in the play, albeit in a non-speaking role.

The question, then, is not whether magical thinking exists in *3 Henry VI* but how it affects moral thinking. Oaths have been recognized and variously interpreted. Thus Kelly refers her analysis to 'an ordered society ordained by God, ideally upheld by king and supported by subject' (F. Kelly, 357)—in short, she refers it to [EMW] Tillyard. French, on the other hand, refers his analysis of oaths to anti-Tillyardian scepticism (A. French, 'Mills', 318–21). The celestial omen seen by the York brothers is ironized by Richard himself, in the opening soliloquy of *Richard III* (1.1.1–27), and his sardonic reading effectively undercuts his brother's brave interpretation of the omen in *3 Henry VI*, though on close examination even Edward's affirmation seems half-hearted ('Whate'er it bodes ...'). Henry's prophecy of Richmond's future success is a transparent affirmation of the Tudor regime—an indubitable trace of the Tudor myth in *3 Henry VI* ... This instance of magical thinking has not been addressed by most critics who are sceptical of providential readings, though by itself it is inadequate to resolve the many questions they have raised.

The on-again, off-again quality of magical thinking in *3 Henry VI* reveals a deep ambivalence in the sixteenth and seventeenth centuries about the way the world worked. The 'oppositional thinking' identified by Stuart Clark was in an early state of terminal crisis but was still the only way of thinking about the natural world, human history, religion and politics, because it had not yet been superseded by scientific thinking—that would not happen until the eighteenth century (Clark, *passim*). Though challenged by scepticism, oppositional thinking remained essentially intact

Death of Richard Neville, Earl of Warwick, in the battle of Barnet (Hulton Archive/Getty Images)

masques for the first two Stuart kings. Ideas of monarchical divine right are thus explicable manifestations of oppositional and magical thinking.

In the late Elizabethan regime, when Shakespeare's history plays were staged, oppositional thinking was in the early stages of a crisis occasioned less by scepticism *per se* than by developments in the Protestant Reformation. Protestants offered a way of looking at the world that appropriated the familiar lineaments of binary thinking, but what they identified as evil and demonic was not paganism or disbelief but a rival system of Christian belief. The English Church under Elizabeth was Protestant, and it distinguished itself from the papacy by identifying features of traditional belief that it rejected, such as transubstantiation and exorcism, which were regarded as violations of the Protestant belief that 'miracles are ceased', as the Archbishop of Canterbury puts it in *Henry V* 1.1.67—that is, that after the apostolic age God no longer permitted miracles to occur. How 'miracles' could have ceased when magical thinking was still in full flower is a question the English Church could not answer in the sixteenth century, because it could not get outside of itself, so to speak, to recognize that traditional oppositional thinking still lay at the heart of its identity. Scepticism about miracles and rejection of 'papist superstition' thus coincided ambiguously with open credulity about a magical world.

This ambiguity helps to explain the odd combination of magical thinking and scepticism in the history plays and in *3 Henry VI* in particular. Besides Henry's prophecy concerning Richmond, the most impressive manifestation of oppositional thinking in *3 Henry VI* is Richard of Gloucester. Margaret's remark that he is a 'prodigy' (1.4.75) is complemented by Henry's greeting when Richard arrives to kill him:

> Ay, my good lord. 'My lord' I should
> say, rather.
> 'Tis sin to flatter; 'good' was little better.
> 'Good Gloucester' and 'good devil' were
> alike,
> And both preposterous. Therefore, not
> 'good lord'.
> (5.6.2–5)

Henry refuses to associate 'good' with Gloucester, because he views his visitor oppositionally, as if Gloucester were the devil. That is why he says calling either of them 'good' would be 'preposterous', using the word in its literal Latin

because it was buttressed by the lack of a credible alternative and indeed seemed to become stronger with rationalized responses to each doubt expressed about some aspect of it.

The most fundamental opposition was cosmic—the opposition of God and the devil—but it was closely related to the moral opposition of good and evil, and these complementary oppositions were the basis of other contrarieties which seemed to make sense of things. Here, then, is where magical and moral thinking merged indistinguishably. Magical thinking was not a violation of common sense or rationality; it was a confirmation of both, an instance of good and evil manifesting themselves mysteriously but comprehensibly in the world of human experience. These oppositions were pressed into the service of particular political interests, as H. Kelly has shown in the case of providential stories about York, Lancaster and Tudor, and indeed no regime could command respect without an account of itself that made sense according to fundamental cosmic and moral oppositions—the kind of oppositions that organize Jonson's sense of 'back-to-front', in parallel with common iconography of the devil with a face in his rear end. Richard stabs Henry just as Henry seems about to describe a preposterous detail about Richard that Richard himself describes later: 'I came into the world with my legs forward' (5.6.71). Preposterousness was characteristic of the demonic, as Nicholas Rémy points out in his description of witches' gestures:

> they love to do everything in a ridiculous and unseemly manner. For they turn their backs toward the Demons when they go to worship them, and approach them sideways like a crab; when they hold out their hands in supplication they turn them downwards; when they converse they bend their eyes toward the ground; and in other such ways they behave in a manner opposite to that of other men.

(quoted in Clark, 14)

Richard of Gloucester is accurately described by saying that he behaves 'in a manner opposite to that of other men', and his implicit invocation is both preposterous and demonic: 'Then, since the heavens have shaped my body so, / Let hell make crook'd my mind to answer it' (5.6.78–9).

The emergence of a demonic, prodigious and preposterous character near the apex of Yorkist power is an effective way to orient *3 Henry VI* in the sequence of events from the death of Henry V to the accession of Henry VII. Tillyard called the play 'the culminating expression of the horrors and wickedness of civil war' (Tillyard, *History Plays*, 189), and he recognized Richard as 'a diabolic character' (195), but he did not see the apocalyptic suggestions of Richard's rise to power as a quasi-Antichrist who represents an oppositional threat to a godly ruler (see Clark, 382–4). Richard's demonism and Henry's prophecy of Richmond's 'hope' and 'bliss' for England are complementary examples of magical thinking in *3 Henry VI*, and they help to elucidate the plan of the play and of its place among the first four history plays.

At the same time, however, the moral and providential clarity suggested by magical and oppositional thinking is complicated by ambiguities. Henry himself is a poor excuse for a king, even though he is a good man; his gullibility, timidity, arbitrariness, poor judgment and inability to lead are specifically political failures that have no obvious relation to the oppositional scheme suggested by Richard's demonism (see below, pp. 75–81). Moreover, both sides are equally tainted by vengeance and wanton cruelty,

which undermines the simple opposition of a saintly Lancastrian king and a demonic Yorkist aspirant. A providential moral pattern undoubtedly operates in *3 Henry VI*, but it operates only in broad outline amid the play's crowd of secondary causes, which bear no discernible relation to it—such causes as human weakness, miscalculation, marital incompatibility, aristocratic rivalry, treachery, anger and chance. As J.P. Brockbank pointed out:

> the plays of *Henry VI* are not, as it were, haunted by the ghost of Richard II, and the catastrophes of the civil wars are not laid to Bolingbroke's charge; the catastrophic virtue of Henry and the catastrophic evil of Richard are not an inescapable inheritance from the distant past but are generated by the happenings we are made to witness.

(Brockbank, 'Frame', 98)

The principal moral concern in these events seems to involve the evil that human beings do to each other in civil wars, and the prophecy that Richmond will deliver the nation from such evil is not the essence of this story but a rare example of providential clarity in the chaos of the Wars of the Roses.

Source: John D. Cox and Eric Rasmussen, "Introduction," in *King Henry VI, Part 3*, edited by John D. Cox and Eric Rasmussen, Arden Shakespeare, 2001, pp. 57–64.

John Julius Norwich

Norwich provides a historical analysis of King Henry VI, Part 3, *comparing the action in the play with the actual historical events. In particular, the critic highlights the various places in the work where Shakespeare telescopes historical time for the sake of literary expedience. Norwich concludes with comments on the character of Richard, the Duke of Gloucester, later King Richard III.*

Nowhere is Shakespeare's extraordinary ability to turn a chronicle into a drama more impressively demonstrated than in the third part of *King Henry VI*. Its two predecessors both contain scenes of battle—in *Part I*, indeed, the fighting in France is portrayed with vigour and considerable brio—but it is only in the last play of the trilogy that the author is called upon to encapsulate in little more than two hours what is virtually the entire course of the Wars of the Roses, from the aftermath of the first battle of St. Albans in 1455 to the defeat of Queen Margaret at Tewkesbury sixteen years later. Now at last, with all the inevitability of Greek tragedy, the House of Lancaster suffers retribution for the atrocity committed at

> THE ONE GLARING HISTORICAL INACCURACY IN SHAKESPEARE'S VERSION OF THE BATTLE OF TOWTON IS THE CONTINUED PRESENCE OF EDWARD'S BROTHERS GEORGE AND RICHARD, WHO WERE ACTUALLY BROUGHT BACK FROM HOLLAND ONLY IN TIME FOR HIS CORONATION THE FOLLOWING JUNE."

the end of the previous century: the deposition and murder of Richard II and the usurpation of his crown by Henry IV are finally avenged. And the consequences of the outrage are visited not just on Henry and his successors but on the country as a whole: England loses France, is burdened with a detested French queen, and rapidly descends into anarchy. After Tewkesbury, however, it seems that Henry's crimes have been finally expiated. It will be another fourteen years before the sun of York suffers its final eclipse, but already the last of the Lancastrians, John of Gaunt's great-great-grandson Henry of Richmond, has made his appearance on the stage. He is described in the *dramatis personae* quite simply as 'a youth'; but it was he, as Shakespeare's audiences well knew, who was to inaugurate the great dynasty of the Tudors and, with it, well over a century of prosperity and peace.

Whatever those audiences might have felt, however, the opening of the play is not such as to fill the historian with confidence. 'I wonder how the King escap'd our hands!' says Warwick, after the first battle of St Albans. The short answer is that he did not escape: as we have seen, he and the Queen remained in the town for the night, and Warwick himself, with Salisbury and Gloucester, most deferentially escorted them back to London the following day. Within the first ten lines, too, Shakespeare has changed his own story: he allows York to report that his old enemy Clifford was 'by the swords of common soldiers slain', whereas at the end of *Part II* Clifford is killed by York himself. Finally, he perpetuates the solecism of the earlier play in the matter of Prince Richard's age—to have 'best deserv'd of all [York's] sons' is a remarkable tribute to a two-year-old—but this is of

course deliberate: now more than ever, historical time must be telescoped if it is to fit the two-hour traffic of the Shakespearean stage.

So drastic is this telescoping that, the play having begun in May 1455, by line 35 of the first scene we find ourselves already in October 1460 when York, having recently returned from Ireland, makes his first open claim to the crown, laying his hand on the cushion of the throne in Westminster Hall. It need hardly be said that the appearance of King Henry at this point is an invention. (Even had it not been, the King is unlikely to have said that he was crowned at the age of nine months; although this was indeed his age at his accession he received his first coronation, in London, shortly before his eighth birthday.) His presence, however—together with that of Queen Margaret, who enters a few minutes later with the seven-year-old Prince of Wales—allows a brilliant dramatization of the Act of Accord and the Queen's furious protest at her son's disinheritance.

Two months pass. Scene ii is set at York's castle of Sandal in Yorkshire, where he, with his eldest and youngest sons Edward and Richard, are about to engage Northumberland and the Lancastrians of the north. With them is John Nevill, Marquis of Montagu, who had in fact remained in London and who is unaccountably addressed by York throughout the scene as his brother—although he was in fact only his nephew by marriage. The likeliest explanation here is that Shakespeare substituted Montagu at the last moment for his father the Earl of Salisbury, who was certainly at Sandal but whom—since he was to be executed immediately after the coming battle—he had decided to leave out of the play altogether. The scene begins with a chilling conversation in which Richard (who in 1460 was still only eight years old) reveals his precociously Machiavellian nature by encouraging his father to seize the throne, on the grounds that the oath he has recently sworn to allow King Henry to reign in peace is technically invalid. A messenger then arrives to announce that Queen Margaret has arrived, with the northern lords and an army of 20,000, and is about to besiege the castle.

The last two scenes of Act I are given over to the battle of Wakefield. Like all Shakespeare's battles it is inevitably impressionistic, consisting as it does of two main episodes: first, the vengeful killing by young Clifford of York's second son, the seventeen-year-old Earl of Rutland

('Thy father slew my father; therefore die'); second, the capture and death of York himself, stabbed first by Clifford and then by the Queen in person. Shakespeare, of course, knew as well as we do that Margaret was not at Wakefield at all; at the time of the encounter she was still in Scotland, whence she was to join the triumphant Lancastrians at York only some three weeks later. Once again, however, her sudden appearance, her savage mockery of her captive (made to stand on a molehill with the paper crown on his head) and, worst of all, that terrible moment when she herself drives her dagger into York's heart—all this adds immeasurably to the drama, as well as casting a new and hideous light on her character.

The first scene of Act II—the opening line of which is curiously similar to that of Act I—is a masterpiece of concision, covering as it does two major battles, both fought within two weeks of each other in February 1461. The victory of York's son Edward—formerly Earl of March, now himself Duke of York—at Mortimer's Cross is briefly represented by the miraculous appearance, to him and his brother Richard (who with his other surviving brother George was actually in the Low Countries at the time) of three suns simultaneously in the sky; while the second battle of St Albans, in which the Lancastrians had their revenge, is reported by Warwick—who had joined the two princes after this last encounter—in a single speech (II.i.120ff). At this point, as we know, Edward and Warwick marched on London, where Edward claimed the throne before heading northwards to meet the Lancastrians, returning to the capital in May for his coronation the following month; but Shakespeare very sensibly streamlines the action by sending him off immediately after St Albans, telescoping the two London visits into one and bringing Edward to London only after the victory of Towton. This allows him to build up an impressive—if entirely unhistorical—confrontation scene at York between Edward, his two brothers (who were in fact still in Holland) and Warwick on the one hand and King Henry, Queen Margaret and the Lancastrians on the other. It is followed by the battle itself, which he somewhat uncharacteristically spreads over all four of the remaining scenes of the act.

The one glaring historical inaccuracy in Shakespeare's version of the battle of Towton is the continued presence of Edward's brothers George and Richard, who were actually brought back from Holland only in time for his coronation the following June. The first scene of the fight—in fact scene iii—opens with Warwick exhausted, Edward and George in despair. Then Richard arrives to report the death of Warwick's 'brother'—in fact his illegitimate half-brother, designated by Hall 'the bastard of Salisbury'. The news rouses Warwick to fury, filling him with a desire for revenge which enables him to breathe new spirit into the rest. Next, in the extremely short (and obviously invented) scene iv, we see Richard attacking Clifford as the man who has killed both his brother Rutland and his father Richard of York; Clifford, initially fearless, flees with the arrival of Warwick.

Scene v—which is equally imaginary and which, it has been pointed out, might have been taken from a medieval morality play—now introduces a completely different mood. Here we are at the still centre of the hurricane with King Henry, seated on a molehill—ironically enough, identical to that on which York had been mocked at Wakefield—reflecting first on the ever-changing fortunes of war and then on the miserable lives of monarchs when compared to those of the meanest of their subjects. He is joined by two symbolic figures, both illustrative of the horrors of civil war: 'a Son that hath kill'd his Father' and 'a Father that hath kill'd his Son'. He gives them his sympathy but insists—with rare insensitivity in the circumstances—that he is ten times unhappier than either of them. He is finally roused out of his self-pity by the arrival of his wife and son with the Duke of Exeter, who urge him to flee with them—for 'Warwick rages like a chafed bull'.

The last scene of the act introduces the dying Clifford, seen for the first time in the play as noble rather than vindictive, lamenting the overthrow of his beloved House of Lancaster more than his own imminent death. The three young princes come upon him as he expires, and agree that his head must now replace their father's on the battlements of York. (Hall records that the replacement heads were those of 'the erle of Devonshyre and iii. other'.) The scene ends with the victorious princes leaving for London and Edward's coronation, after which Warwick announces his intention of going to France to seek the hand of Bona of Savoy on behalf of the new King. Edward promises to give his brothers the dukedoms of Clarence and Gloucester, rejecting Richard's claim that 'Gloucester's dukedom is too ominous'—a reference, presumably, to the fate of his predecessor Duke Humphrey—and his request for that of Clarence instead.

And so to Act III, which opens with another imaginary scene in which Henry VI, wandering the countryside in disguise after the battle of Hexham, is finally recognized and arrested. For Shakespeare, this occurs not at Waddington Hall but in 'a chase in the north of England'. It hardly matters: his purpose is simply to provide another of those scenes of quietness—one might almost say religious quietism—during which the deposed King can reflect upon his fate. After just a hundred lines we are transported to London. Edward, now crowned and a dramatically different character from his predecessor on the throne, is obsessed by Elizabeth Grey (née Woodville) whom he is determined to take to his bed. She for her part holds out for marriage—Shakespeare has clearly read his Mancini—to which he eventually agrees. The stage is then left empty but for Richard of Gloucester, who in a long and magnificent soliloquy makes his first clear declaration of his ambitions:

> I'll play the orator as well as Nestor,
> Deceive more slily than Ulysses could,
> And, like a Sinon, take another Troy.
> I can add colours to the chameleon,
> Change shapes with Proteus for advantages,
> And set the murderous Machiavel to school.
> Can I do this, and cannot get a crown?
> Tut! Were it further off, I'll pluck it down.

Scene iii brings us to the French court. Queen Margaret, still determined on revenge, has taken refuge with Louis XI, from whom she is seeking military assistance. Warwick, all unaware of recent developments, arrives to negotiate on behalf of his master for Princess Bona, whose hand Louis immediately grants—though not without another outburst of anger from Margaret, who bitterly accuses them both of disloyalty to her husband. At this point a messenger arrives from London with letters informing all three of them of Edward's marriage to Elizabeth Grey; and in a moment the entire situation is changed. Warwick instantly transfers his loyalties to Henry VI; the Queen is triumphant at this new proof of Edward's duplicity; and Louis hesitates no longer in promising her the aid she seeks. To seal the new alliance, Warwick and Margaret agree that his daughter shall forthwith be married to her son, Edward Prince of Wales.

Once again, history has been drastically compressed: the events related in this single scene cover

some nine years. Warwick did indeed go to France to sue on Edward's behalf for the hand of Bona; but that was in 1461, three years before the King's marriage. The visit from which he returned in rebellion was in 1470, five years after it. It was in the later year, too, that Warwick's younger daughter, Anne (not the 'eldest', as the play has it), as betrothed to the young Prince—his elder, Isabel, having already been given to Clarence in 1469. In spite of everything, however, the diplomatic consequences of Edward's ill-advised marriage are admirably illustrated. Once again one is left with the conviction that, whatever liberties Shakespeare might take with strict historical truth, in the essentials he was almost invariably right. For the non-scholar, seeking merely an overall view of Plantagenet history, there are many worse guides to follow.

One of the inevitable consequences of Shakespeare's telescoping of time is that we are occasionally obliged to put back the clock; the opening of Act IV, in which King Edward asks his brothers their opinion of his 'new marriage', can be dated no later than 1464. Basically, its purpose is to emphasize the almost universal unpopularity of Edward's action. First the brothers themselves leave him in no doubt of their own feelings: they complain, in particular, about the heedless way in which he is marrying off all his new Woodville relations. Then, most conveniently, a messenger arrives from France to report the fury of King Louis, of the wronged and humiliated Bona and, as always, of Queen Margaret, who is 'ready to put armour on'. She has also, he continues, made up her differences with Warwick, whose daughter is to marry the young Prince of Wales. (Shakespeare's confusion between the Earl's two daughters is once again in evidence, expressed this time by Clarence.) At the end of the scene, as a result of the quarrel, Clarence and Somerset leave to join Warwick; Richard of Gloucester, Hastings and Montagu assure the King of their support.

The next scene brings us forward again to 1469. Warwick has landed in Kent with his 'articles of petition' and has hurried north-westwards in the hopes of meeting up with the rebel Robin of Redesdale in the north. (The stage directions tell us that he is accompanied by French soldiers, but this is incorrect: King Louis's men did not in fact appear on the field until the battle of Tewkesbury, still two years in the future.) In Warwickshire he is joined by

Clarence and Somerset and suspiciously inquires whose side they are on; reassured, he reiterates his promise that Clarence shall have his daughter to wife. Here again, however, Shakespeare errs: both enquiry and promise would have been unnecessary, since Clarence had already married Isabel Nevill a week or so before. Scene iii then follows straight on its predecessor, with what is presumably the field of Edgecote in which, contrary to what we see on the stage, neither King Edward nor Warwick took part. Edward was indeed captured soon after the battle, but by the king-maker's brother, the Archbishop of York.

At this point we realize that Shakespeare has been telescoping again, and that King Edward's two successive defeats—the first his captivity after Edgecote, the second his flight to Holland fifteen months later—have been deliberately run into one. In scene iv Queen Elizabeth first tells Lord Rivers that her husband has been captured and is in the hands of the Archbishop; immediately afterwards, she tells him of her pregnancy and her determination to seek sanctuary. We can thus date the first half of this extremely short scene to July 1469, the second half to October 1470. This contrivance certainly streamlines the action, but it also raises new problems for the author: if Edward is a prisoner in England, how can he land from abroad with an army? Shakespeare's solution is to invent a totally fictitious rescue of the King by Richard of Gloucester and others, after which he takes refuge in Flanders. This enables Warwick to release Henry VI from the Tower and reinstate him on the throne—which did indeed occur when Edward was away in the Low Countries— and Edward to disembark at Ravenscar for the last triumphant chapter of his long battle against the Lancastrians.

And so, in scene vii, we find him with his small army before the walls of York. At first he demands his dukedom only; but when Sir John Montgomery threatens to leave him unless he proclaims himself King, he agrees to do so. (Historically, he delayed this proclamation until he reached Nottingham.) He then heads south, and the last scene of the act finds him entering the Bishop's palace in London. Before his arrival Warwick, Clarence and other lords are discussing their resistance with King Henry: each will go to his own particular territory to rally what troops he can, and they will all meet Warwick at Coventry. Edward then appears, with Richard

of Gloucester, and summarily returns Henry to the Tower. Then he and his men themselves set off for Coventry, for what they hope and believe will be the final reckoning.

There was, as it turned out, no fighting at Coventry, and the confrontation in V.i at the walls of the city, in the course of which Edward challenges Warwick to come out and fight and Warwick refuses ('Alas, I am not coop'd here for defence!'), in fact occurred on 29 March, a fortnight before Edward's arrival in London. Shakespeare is right, on the other hand, in making Coventry the scene of Clarence's second betrayal—of Warwick this time—and of his return to his brother's allegiance; we learn from Polydore Vergil that he had first prevented Warwick from fighting by urging him to await his coming, and then on his arrival ordered the 4,000 men whom he had levied in the cause of Henry VI to espouse the Yorkist cause instead. When he and Edward met, the two brothers had 'right kind and loving language', swearing 'perfect accord for ever hereafter'. They were to fight side by side both at Barnet and at Tewkesbury.

The story of Barnet is quickly told. We hear nothing of the fighting, nor of the fog that shrouded the field and was as much a feature of the battle as the cold had been at Towton, almost exactly ten years before. For Shakespeare—and perhaps for us too—all that really matters is the death of Warwick, who lives just long enough to hear of the fate of his brother Montagu, and whose last words suggest a certainty of his own salvation that cannot have been shared by many of his hearers. A brief scene iii establishes that victory has been won, announces the landing of Margaret and her son and prepares us for Tewkesbury. Hall's account of the three weeks that followed stresses the Queen's despondency; and indeed she had good reason for gloom. But for the bad weather that had delayed her for three weeks in Normandy she would have been able to join Warwick before Barnet, and the result of that battle might have been very different. The news that her most powerful ally was dead had very nearly sent her straight back to France. Only the assurances of Somerset that Edward too had sustained heavy losses and that feeling in England was still overwhelmingly Lancastrian had persuaded her to stay, but they had not improved her spirits.

Shakespeare, on the other hand, stresses her courage. Addressing her son, Somerset, Oxford and her soldiers on 'the plains near Tewkesbury', she makes no attempt to conceal the gravity of the situation, but bids them take heart none the less; there can be no going back now:

> Great lords, wise men ne'er sit and wail
>   their loss,
> But cheerly seek how to redress their harms.
>
> What though the mast be now blown
>   overboard,
> The cable broke, the holding anchor lost,
> And half our sailors swallow'd in the flood;
> Yet lives our pilot still ...

The young Prince of Wales follows in similar vein, inviting—like his grandfather before Agincourt—all those who have no stomach for the coming fight to depart,

> Lest in our need he might infect another
> And make him of like spirit to himself.

So begins the penultimate battle of the long and tragic civil war. Scene v represents its end: Margaret, Somerset and Oxford have all been captured. The two last are sentenced to execution and go bravely to their fate; Margaret's life is of course spared, but she is obliged to stand by while her son is murdered before her eyes, stabbed by Edward, Clarence and Gloucester in turn. At this point the dramatist in Shakespeare has once again taken over from the historian. He has chosen, quite legitimately, the alternative—and far more dramatic—version of the Prince's death as reported by Hall, and has then subtly improved it. In Hall's account the King does no more than strike the boy with his gauntlet, while Dorset and Hastings use their daggers. Nor is it anywhere suggested that Queen Margaret was present, either during the battle or afterwards—still less that Gloucester was about to kill her too, but was restrained at the last moment by the King.

Edward was now supreme. The House of Lancaster was effectively destroyed, and would never again imperil his throne. True, one or two Lancastrian lords, Oxford in particular and his friend Lord Beaumont, would continue to amuse themselves with isolated raids and short bursts of irregular warfare—in September 1473 the two of them would actually seize St Michael's Mount in Cornwall and hold it for several months—but they scarcely affected the security of the realm. A more serious danger in the long term might be the fourteen-year-old Henry of Richmond, who soon after Tewkesbury would sail with his uncle

Jasper Tudor to France. But heavy storms in the Channel would oblige them to put in one of the Breton ports; and Duke Francis of Brittany, fully aware of Henry's potential importance, would keep him under close watch.

There remained the sad, defeated Henry VI—by now more an inconvenience than a threat, but still theoretically a rival to the throne. Whether the King himself would ever have ordered his elimination is arguable: Henry was widely seen to be a saint, and to Edward his murder would certainly have had overtones of sacrilege. His brother Richard, however, had no such qualms. We may perhaps doubt whether he left Tewkesbury quite as precipitately as Shakespeare suggests, 'to make a bloody supper in the Tower'; but the events represented in scene vi are, so far as we can tell, substantially true. One would love to think that the doomed King showed as much spirit at his end as his last great vituperative speech suggests; alas, it seems unlikely.

It remains only for Shakespeare to draw the various threads together and to provide a suitable closing scene. Edward refers in generous terms to the slaughtered enemies through whose blood he has 'repurchas'd' the throne, discreetly refraining to mention that several of them were not killed in battle but executed by the Yorkists afterwards; he then turns affectionately to his son—the future Edward V:

> Young Ned, for thee thine uncles and
>   myself
> Have in our armours watch'd the winter's
>   night,
> Went all afoot in summer's scalding heat,
> That thou might'st repossess the crown in
>   peace;
> And of our labours thou shalt reap the gain.

The irony would not have been lost on Shakespeare's audiences, even without Richard's two asides—in the second of which he cheerfully compares himself with Judas Iscariot. One tends to forget that at the time of King Henry's death the Duke of Gloucester was just eighteen years old.

A few lines before the end of this short scene we learn of the ransoming of Queen Margaret by her father and her return to France. This, as we have seen, did not actually occur until four years later, in 1475—but where otherwise could it be reported? It forms, in any case, little more than a parenthesis. The true subject of the scene—even though it is covered in only nine lines—is Richard's villainy and duplicity:

> And, that I love the tree from whence thou sprang'st,
> Witness the loving kiss I give the fruit.
> [*Aside*] To say the truth, so Judas kiss'd his master
> And cried 'All hail!' when as he meant all harm.

It was this, above all else, that the Elizabethan audiences would carry home with them; it was to emphasize this that Shakespeare had been deliberately building up the character of Richard; and this that he was to make the theme of the last and greatest play of his series.

But to what extent was it justified historically? Was Richard really the ogre that we see before us on the stage? These questions have been asked for over four centuries, and are still being discussed today. The next two chapters of this book will attempt to answer them.

Source: John Julius Norwich, "*King Henry VI Part III*," in *Shakespeare's Kings: The Great Plays and the History of England in the Middle Ages: 1337–1485*, Scribner, 1999, pp. 307–18.

Michael Hattaway

In his introduction to the play, Hattaway examines the themes of death and battle. The critic compares and contrasts the play with Henry VI, Part 1 *and* Henry VI, Part 2, *noting that by Part 3, "the political community of England is no more," having been destroyed by violence and treachery.*

Part 3 will always be remembered for its scenes of death: those of the children Rutland and Prince Edward, that of York, those of the arch-enemies Clifford and Warwick the kingmaker, and that, finally, of King Henry. It may be that Shakespeare had in mind the chronicles of the falls of great men recorded in *The Mirror for Magistrates*—figures from the period of the Wars of the Roses count for about half the *exempla* found in the 1559 edition—but Shakespeare's treatment of their 'tragedies' is generally more complicated than that of William Baldwin and his collaborators. As he has done throughout the sequence, Shakespeare explores not just the moral but the political dimensions of these noble lives. For despite the way that many die with a quotation or rhetorical figure on their lips, thus turning event into occasion, image into moral emblem, they may be simply cheering themselves

> JUST AS IN PUBLIC LIFE HONOUR HAS DECLINED INTO VALOUR, VIRTUE INTO *VIRTÙ*, SO IN PRIVATE LIFE, LOVE AND CHASTITY HAVE BEEN SUPPLANTED BY LUST AND LECHERY."

up, dramatising themselves *in extremis* in a way that is not categorically different from the way their political antagonists had disguised their true motives under rhetorical shows of honour or compassion. A political theme is announced in the second line of the play's second scene when Edward claims to be best at 'playing the orator': the proverbial phrase will be repeated on two other occasions. Rhetoric was traditionally distrusted: in this play eloquence, like prowess in battle, is always seen as a means to power and, as we have hinted, a way of giving understanding at least to an audience exposed, through spectacle, to what is almost intolerable.

Part 2 of the sequence was much concerned with trials: significantly the word 'trial' does not appear in *Part 3* which is largely a succession of battles that stem from feuds. Ethical systems have been suppressed by political mechanisms of the crudest variety. In 2.4 and 2.6, for example, where we see the last fight and the death of Clifford, Shakespeare departs from the chroniclers who report that Warwick 'remitted the vengeance and punishment [for his brother's death] to God'. A few lines thereafter we read of the death of Clifford, shot through the neck by 'an arrow without a head': it is at least implied by Holinshed that his death is no accident but an act of divine retribution. Shakespeare, however, has Clifford confront his Yorkist adversary Richard of Gloucester, and thereby suggests that his death depends not on a divine pattern but on the fortunes of war. Even pious King Henry, who acts as a chorus to one of the central scenes of the play, that which offers a perspective upon the battle of Towton, and who views the world in idealised pastoral terms, does not, as we might expect in a pastoral, see the battle as a trial by combat, but rather as an incursion of violence from a hostile 'natural' world into the world of art inhabited by his imagination:

This battle fares like to the morning's war
When dying clouds contend with growing
    light,
What time the shepherd, blowing of his
    nails,
Can neither call it perfect day nor night.
Now sways it this way, like a mighty sea
Forced by the tide to combat with the wind;
Now sways it that way, like the selfsame sea,
Forced to retire by fury of the wind.
Sometime the flood prevails and then the
    wind;
Now one the better, then another best,
Both tugging to be victors, breast to breast
Yet neither conqueror, nor conquerèd:
So is the equal poise of this fell war.
(2.5.1–13)

Warwick charges Edward IV with being a traitor, an action that, in a chivalric world, would draw an immediate challenge and a fight to the death. In this play, however, the battle between Edward and Warwick occurs, significantly, off-stage, and Edward comes from it to dump his dying adversary on the ground with as much ceremony as would be accorded a slaughtered wolf. Family loyalties may have been the initial cause of the feuds, but an audience watching *3 Henry VI* is likely to feel that individual ambition rather than family honour is what fuels the vendettas that inform the play. Both Henry and York seem to have forgotten that the quarrel between their families originally was a dynastic one: their claims to legitimacy and authority in this play are now validated only by the forces they can muster. Shakespeare suppresses the role of the great Council of lords spiritual and temporal which, upon consideration of both Edward's claim and Henry's abilities, and after consulting the Commons, decided that Edward ought to be king: in the play the forces of the rival claimants simply slug it out.

Few characters in *3 Henry VI* seem possessed of the conscience exhibited by the antagonists in the later plays concerning the reign of Henry IV: Clifford, descendant of the Harry Percy (Hotspur) who appears in *Henry IV*, possesses none of his forebear's brio—he backs Henry, careless of whether his title is 'right or wrong.' Edward IV, praised by Sir Thomas More as a good and politic king and beloved of the people, appears here only as an ambitious and lascivious warrior. Only Gloucester, the avatar of cruelty on the Yorkist side, a monster whose deformity is an index (and

possible cause) of his sadism and perverted will to power, does offer hints of the psychological ruin that comes from dreaming upon the crown. As in *Richard III* we find in his soliloquies (especially that of 3.2.124-95) some material from which we might impute a connection between his appearance and his personality (as opposed to his motives). His sense of self is validated by no honour system based on ethics or status, so that his proud proclamation at the end of the play might be regarded ambivalently, as a kind of apotheosis, or as a register of the terrible toll his ambition has wrought in him:

I had no father, I am like no father;
I have no brother, I am like no brother;
And this word 'love', which greybeards call
    divine,
Be resident in men like one another
And not in me: I am myself alone.
(5.6.80–4)

'A mind courageously vicious may happily furnish itself with security, but she cannot be fraught with this self-joying delight and satisfaction', wrote Montaigne in his essay 'Of Repenting' ('Du repentir')—this seems to catch the tone of the speech which may move as much towards wistfulness as well as 'Stoic self-reliance'. Richard's soliloquy, in fact, is one of the first examples in the canon of a soliloquy which serves as a developed interior monologue and not just a device for conveying information. He is moving from sense of his own malice to a sense of his own vice, defined thus by Montaigne: 'Malice sucks up the greatest part of her own venom, and therewith empoisoneth herself. Vice leaveth, as an ulcer in the flesh, a repentance in the soul which still scratcheth and bloodieth itself.' However, only in *Richard III* in his 'I am I' soliloquy does Richard exhibit that full conscience or repentance.

Deformity may give Richard a psychic energy, but it is his self-fashioning Protean quality that gives him political power, what he terms 'advantages.' (3.2.192). In this play he addresses the audience directly after he has murdered Henry (5.6.72 ff.), laying the ground plans for the schemes he will bring to fruition in *Richard III*. Ancient and Renaissance writers often addressed themselves to the problem of tyrants and the politics of resistance against them. Having demonstrated throughout this trilogy that 'the elementary disease in rule results ... not from excess of authority in king or tribune, but from a loss of hierarchical identity, or rank, in the ruler', Shakespeare begins to plot the emergence of a tyrant. The play ends with the birth of a new prince, seeming to portend future happiness but, after what we have seen of Richard, that ending and that happiness can only be provisional.

The play, like its predecessors, begins with ceremony, two linked ceremonies in fact: Gloucester's violation of the head of Somerset, cut off in battle, and Henry's entailing of the crown to York. These both have to do with rituals of honour; the former to do with the removal of honour, the latter to do with the bestowing of it. Gloucester's act of desecration signifies the extinguishing of the residual chivalric code of conspicuous virtue, the eclipsing of honour by main force. It is a prologue to a play in which many more heads will roll, including, before long, that of Gloucester's own father York. The second, political, ritual, the entailing of the crown, registers an analogous cultural shift. York provokes the sequence by the ambiguous affront, at once a threat and a theatricalised taunt, of sitting in Henry's chair of state, and the climax of this part of the scene comes with Warwick's line 'Resolve thee, Richard: claim the English crown' (1.1.49)—which acts as the cue for King Henry's entrance.

Now the word 'crown' occurs sixty times in this text, more than in any other play in the canon. In Elizabethan English, the word 'ceremony' could mean both a ceremonial occasion and a talismanic object used therein. The process of entailing the crown (1.1.196–7) takes away from any mystery or sanctity the object might have. It is desacralised, reified, no longer a metonym (here the adjunct of power) but merely a synecdoche (a part for the whole), a badge representing the material forces that sustain the king, an index of power rather than authority. The scene in fact is yet another index of a change in a whole style of political thought, change from a sacred to secular concept of monarchy. The king becomes not a man apart, but simply *primus inter pares*, and, as we see in the penultimate scene of the play when Gloucester stabs King Henry, this act of killing a king is stripped of the scene of sacrilege that we find in *Macbeth* or even *Richard II*. Shakespeare's vision of late medieval England owes little to romance, nostalgia, or any desire to evoke an idealised concept of order. It is a sketch of a political world that is very little different from the anatomy of ancient Rome that he was to

return to later—as was Ben Jonson. 'Rome is but a wilderness of tigers', proclaims Titus Andronicus: so, in this play, is England. (It was from ancient Rome that Bacon took most of his *exempla* for his essay 'Of Faction'.)

Just as in public life honour has declined into valour, virtue into *virtù*, so in private life, love and chastity have been supplanted by lust and lechery. As in *Titus Andronicus* and *King Lear* images of political chaos are infused by images of animality and sexual licentiousness. Edward who, according to certain modern historians, married the Lady Grey in order to build up an alliance that would check the power of Warwick and the Nevilles, is presented by the chroniclers and by Shakespeare as merely promiscuous and licentious. Edward here plays the role of the dauphin who starts to seduce Joan La Pucelle shortly after their first encounter. Likewise Margaret of Anjou (who, in *Part I*, seemingly stepped into Joan's role after the latter was led off to be burned as a witch) is scarcely a paragon of femininity but rather a virago, 'a manly woman, using to rule and not to be ruled', one who empowers the vendetta, mocks York's grief for the murder of his son Rutland and, as 'the better captain [than the king]', is to be found at the centre of those 'foughten fields' that brought such chaos to the commonwealth. Joan had been hailed as 'Astraea's daughter' (*I Henry VI* 1.6.4): Margaret too is associated with 'justice', but despite the lapidary weight of her rhetoric at Tewkesbury, a playhouse audience, having seen her cruelty in action, knows that this is indeed but rhetoric and comprehends the chilling truth that 'justice' can mean without the firm politic control her husband was unable to impose:

> Lords, knights, and gentleman, what I
>   should say
> My tears gainsay: for every word I speak
> Ye see I drink the water of my eye.
> Therefore, no more but this: Henry, your
>   sovereign,
> Is prisoner to the foe, his state usurped,
> His realm a slaughter-house, his subjects
>   slain,
> His statutes cancelled, and his treasure
>   spent:
> And yonder is the wolf that makes this spoil.
> You fight in justice: then, in God's name,
>   lords,
> Be valiant, and give signal to the fight.

A third recollection of *I Henry VI* is provided by Clarence who, at Coventry, seeing perhaps that the sands of Henry are running out, justifies his defection to Edward on the grounds of kinship. It is significant that an act of 'perjury' begins the act in which Edward will triumph, and we remember Joan la Pucelle's twitting of Burgundy ('Done like a Frenchman: turn and turn again.')

The extinction of justice in England, as we have seen, was one of the major themes of *Part 2*: 'Set justice aside then, and what are kingdoms but fair thievish purchases [pursuits]? For what are thieves' purchases but little kingdoms, for in thefts the hands of the underlings are directed by the commander, the confederacy of them is sworn together, and the *pillage* is shared by the law amongst them'—so St Augustine in *The City of God*, laying down a tradition of Christian political realism which, according to John D. Cox, has been neglected by literary and cultural critics who have sought to generate simple oppositional and 'radical' readings of Shakespeare. Whether Shakespeare was drawing upon the historiography of St Augustine or reacting against idealising forms of political thought from his own age, he was offering a suggestion that an examination of the relationship between *feudal* ideals and opportunistic political behaviour might tell us more about an age than, say Spenser's romanticising evocation of *chivalric* ideals. The sequence had begun with an invocation of Henry V, later to be celebrated as 'this star of England'. Talbot was introduced in *Part I* as an old-fashioned idealised chivalric warrior, a champion of the nation rather than a champion simply of the monarch, the role adopted by Sir John Montgomery in 4.7 of this play. By *Part 3*, as we have seen, this kind of honour has declined into mere valour, and courtesy has been replaced by militarism. Edward laments that in killing York, his father, Clifford has 'slain/The flower of Europe for his chivalry.' However, the act provokes no justice in the form of trial by combat but the cold-blooded pursuit of revenge—the nobles become like Pyrrhus in Seneca's *Troades*. Now Hamlet considers the figures of Pyrrhus only to reject it as a model: Clifford, Gloucester, and Edward have no such compunction. Their virtues are 'reckless courage, personal pride and self-respect ... and on the other hand savage ferocity, deliberate cruelty, anger indulged in almost to the point of madness ... the virtues and vices of Homeric heroes, not of Christian paladins as imagined in the ideal pictures of Tasso and Spenser'. Warwick names Henry as a man 'In whose cold blood no spark of honour bides', but the play gives the lie to the fancy that the honour of the war-lord has anything to offer the commonweal.

The play's second scene to offer out Gloucester's sophistical arguments which cause York to forget the oath he had sworn to Henry in the scene before: this scene is the obverse of 2.2 where Clifford tries to get Henry to forget his oath and restore his son as his heir. Principle gives way to politics, and chivalry, in the context of this play, fosters the shedding rather than the saving of blood—it serves only to sustain a fiction of feudalism. Honour deriving from virtue has given way completely to honour as status: the king is he who wears the crown. It is significant in this context that Edward is denied a coronation scene: that would have raised, legitimated, and resanctified his authority. As Julian Pitt-Rivers writes:

> thanks to its duality, honour does something which the philosophers say they cannot do: derive an *ought* from an *is*; whatever *is* becomes *right*, the *de facto* is made *de jure*, the victor is crowned with laurels, the war-profiteer is knighted, the tyrant becomes the monarch, the bully, a chief. The reconciliation between the social order as we find it and the social honour which we revere is accomplished thanks to the confusion which hinges upon the duality of honour and its associated concepts. It is a confusion which fulfils the function of social integration by ensuring the legitimation of established power.

In *Part 2*, moreover, the effects of vendettas between the war-lords included the popular uprising which was taken over by Cade. *Part 2* gave us a rebellion which contained some elements of revolution. In *Part 3*, however, the 'people' scarcely appear: constitutional change can take only one form, that of a *coup d'etat*. York wants a coup: the moment when Warwick stamps his foot to summon the Yorkist forces is a Brechtian *Gestus* that demonstrates, by its theatricality, the paltriness of the moral and political issues at play. Chivalry is dead, justice extinct, and, as under the tyrant Ninus of Assyria, 'the people [have] no law but the king's will'. The political community of England is no more.

Source: Michael Hattaway, "Introduction," in *The Third Part of King Henry VI*, edited by Mihael Hattaway, Cambridge University Press, 1993, pp. 9–19.

SOURCES

Charney, Maurice, *All of Shakespeare*, Columbia University Press, 1993, pp. 132–33.

Crane, Milton, "Introduction," in *Henry VI, Part One, Henry VI, Part Two, Henry VI, Part Three*, Scribner, 1999, pp. xxiii–xxxiv.

Epstein, Norrie, *The Friendly Shakespeare*, Penguin Books, 1993, pp. 161–63, 191.

Norwich, John Julius, *Shakespeare's Kings*, Scribner, 1999, pp. 307, 318.

Shakespeare, William, *Henry VI, Part One, Henry VI, Part Two, Henry VI, Part Three*, Signet, 1989.

FURTHER READING

Abbott, Jacob, *History of Margaret of Anjou, Queen of Henry VI of England*, Kessinger Publishing, 2004.
Abbott covers all aspects of this fascinating queen, from her time spent in France with her parents, to her wedding and hardships as a queen, a new wife of a troubled king, the loss of her child and her widowhood.

Ackroyd, Peter, *Shakespeare: The Biography*, Nan A. Talese, 2005.
Ackroyd focuses on Shakespeare's life as seen in reference to the development of the Elizabethan theatre.

Amt, Emilie, *Medieval England, 1000–1500*, Broadview Press, 2000.
Written to help students understand not only medieval times but to question the documents that bring the details of that era to modern readers, Amt's book provides an understanding of life and politics of the period of, and the ages before, the rule of Henry VI.

Baldwin, David, *Elizabeth Woodville, Mother of the Princes in the Tower*, Sutton Publishing, 2005.
Elizabeth Woodville was the wife of King Edward IV and mother of two sons who were imprisoned in the Tower of London by King Richard III. Baldwin presents her story in a more graceful light than many other historical accounts in which she was often referred to as a witch who put a spell on Edward.

Griffiths, R. A., *The Reign of King Henry VI*, Sutton Publishing, 2005.
Griffiths has written a very readable and comprehensive biography of King Henry VI, covering details of his private life, his court, and the politics that surrounded the Wars of the Roses.

Pendleton, Tom, ed., *Henry VI: Critical Essays*, Garland, 2001.
Pendleton has put together a comprehensive collection of essays covering critical interpretations of the play, customs and reception of the play in various time frames, and interviews with actors who have performed in this play for a well-rounded look at and understanding of Shakespeare's *Henry VI*.

Glossary

Note to the reader: This glossary includes terms commonly encountered in the study of Shakespeare's work. It is not intended to be comprehensive.

A

allegory: an extended metaphor or analogy in which characters in a drama or story and the characters' actions are equated with religious, historical, moral, political, or satiric meanings outside of the drama or story being told.

aside: a dramatic device by which an actor directly addresses the audience but is not heard by the other actors on the stage.

B

burlesque: a form of comedy characterized by mockery or exaggeration.

C

comedy: a form of drama in which the primary purpose is to amuse and which ends happily.

D

denouement: the final explanation or outcome of the plot.

dramatic irony: achieved when the audience understands the real significance of a character's words or actions but the character or those around him or her do not.

E

early modern literature: in England, literature from the late sixteenth and early seventeenth centuries.

F

farce: a humorous play marked by broad satirical comedy and an improbable plot.

foil: in literature, a character who, through contrast with another character, highlights or enhances the second character's distinctive qualities.

folio: a piece of paper folded in half or a volume made up of folio sheets. In 1623, Shakespeare's plays were assembled into a folio edition. The term folio is also used to designate any early collection of Shakespeare's works.

G

gender role: behavior that a society expects or accepts from a man or a woman because of his or her sex.

H

history play: a drama in which the time setting is in a period earlier than that during which the play was written.

I

induction: introductory scene or scenes that precede the main action of a play.

M

Machiavellianism: the theory, based on the work and beliefs of Italian political philosopher Niccolo Machiavelli (1469-1527), that the attainment of political power is justified by any means.

masque: in medieval England and Europe, a game or party in which participants wore masks.

morality play: a medieval drama in which abstract vices and virtues are presented in human form.

mystery play: a medieval drama depicting a story from the Bible.

P

parody: a composition or work which imitates another, usually a serious, work.

pun: a play on words.

S

satire: a piece of literature that presents human vices or foolishness in a way that invites ridicule or scorn.

soliloquy: a character's speech within a play delivered while the character is alone. The speech is intended to inform the audience of the character's thoughts or feelings or to provide information about other characters in the play.

stock character: a conventional character type that belongs to a particular form of literature.

subplot: a plot that is secondary to the main plot of the drama.

T

theme: a central idea in a work of literature.

tragedy: a drama that recounts the significant events or actions, which, taken together, bring about catastrophe.

U

unities: a term referring to the dramatic structures of action, time, and place. Each unity is defined by several characteristics. The unity of action requires that the action of the play have a beginning, a middle, and an end. The unity of time requires that the action of a play take place in one day. The unity of place limits the action of the play to one place. Many plays violate all three unities. In *The Tempest*, Shakespeare observes all three unities.

V

vice or vice figure: a stock character in the morality play, who, as a tempter, possesses both evil and comic qualities.

Cumulative Index to Major Themes and Characters

Cumulative Index to Major Themes and Characters